PREJUDICE, WAR, AND THE CONSTITUTION

Come, let us deal wisely with them, lest they multiply, and it come to pass, that, when there befalleth us any war, they also join themselves unto our enemies, and fight against us, and so get them up out of the land.

—Exodus 1:10

Prejudice, War and the Constitution

Jacobus tenBroek
Edward N. Barnhart
Floyd W. Matson

UNIVERSITY OF CALIFORNIA PRESS
BERKELEY AND LOS ANGELES
1970

UNIVERSITY OF CALIFORNIA PRESS
BERKELEY AND LOS ANGELES
CALIFORNIA

UNIVERSITY OF CALIFORNIA PRESS, LTD.
LONDON, ENGLAND

Preface To The Third Printing

"Viewed in the perspective of a decade, with all the advantages of hindsight and subsequent disclosure, the Japanese American episode of World War II looms as a great and evil blotch upon our national history." Such was the judgment of the present authors in 1954, at the conclusion of our study of the historical origins, political characteristics and constitutional consequences of the Japanese American evacuation of 1942-1945.

The perspective of a decade has now lengthened into the retrospection of a quarter-century. But with all the additional advantages of deliberation, distance, and detachment, we see no reason to modify that original judgment. The wartime episode of the Japanese Americans remains today, as it was yesterday and as it will surely be tomorrow, one of the darkest chapters in the nation's history.

That fact alone—the unique importance of the event as history—would seem to provide reason enough to reissue this book and so to make it available to scholars and students who seek an understanding of the complex course of events that culminated in the mass evacuation and detention of more than 110,000 United States citizens and resident aliens.

But there are additional, and more compelling, reasons to take another look at the episode. Of greatest moment is the "prophetic parallel" which many have claimed to see in the sweeping denial of rights to a "suspect" minority group in time of emergency. The warning was first sounded by Justice Robert M. Jackson of the Supreme Court in his dissent in the Korematsu case: "A military order, however unconstitutional, is not apt to last longer than the military emergency. . . . But once a judicial opinion rationalizes such an order to show that it conforms to the Constitution, . . . the Court for all time has validated the principle of racial discrimination in criminal procedure and of transplanting American citizens. The principle then lies about like a loaded weapon ready for the hand of any authority that can bring forward a plausible claim of an urgent need."[1]

---

[1]Mr. Justice Jackson dissenting in *Korematsu v. United States*, 323 U. S. 214 at 245-246; 65 S. Ct. 193 at 207.

In 1966 a columnist writing in the *Saturday Review* reported a curious "unconfirmed rumor" to the effect that, by way of preparation for
a possible war with Red China, "detention camps have been secretly
prepared in which will be 'relocated' all the Chinese in the United
States so that they may be screened, and prevented from sabotaging the
war effort and from signalling Peking with short-wave radios."[2] However flimsy or fanciful may have been the basis for that rumor, it is no
more fantastic than the historic precedent of the Japanese American
episode from which it has clearly derived. In actuality, there were significant stirrings of agitation against Chinese Americans in the early
1950s, following the appearance of Chinese Communist troops in the
Korean conflict: on the east coast roundups of alien Chinese, and on
the opposite coast "a variety of brawls, insults and acts of violence
against Chinese."[3] In 1951 the San Francisco Council for Civic Unity
considered the atmosphere threatening enough to secure a pledge from
its membership "to attack the sources of fear and insecurity which now
disturb Americans of Chinese ancestry."[4] A decade and a half later,
Roger Baldwin, the long-time director of the American Civil Liberties
Union, maintained that the oppressive action taken against the Japanese Americans could easily be repeated: "The laws and the machinery are ready for another day, another war, another emergency, another
minority. . . ."[5]

A somewhat different point of connection between the World War
II incident and the present day arises from the greatly vitalized interest
of the nation at large, and of social scientists in particular, with the
general issues of civil rights and racial prejudice. It is noteworthy that
the present volume—which might be viewed as a comprehensive case
history in the politics of prejudice and the withholding of civil rights—
was published in the same year as the landmark decision of the U. S.
Supreme Court in *Brown* v. *Board of Education of Topeka*. That decision, an extraordinary departure from the behavior of the Court in
the Japanese American cases of the decade before, marked the real
beginning of the civil rights movement in its twentieth-century phase.

---

[2]Jerome Beatty, Jr., "Trade Winds," *Saturday Review*, May 7, 1966. Quoted in
Allan R. Bosworth, *America's Concentration Camps* (New York: W. W. Norton &
Company, 1967) , p. 251.

[3]Floyd W. Matson, "The Outcry Against Chinese-Americans," *The Progressive*
(September 1955) , p. 25.

[4]*Ibid.*

[5]Roger Baldwin, "Introduction" to Bosworth, *op. cit.*, p. 8.

In turn, the continuing struggle for the civil rights of the Negro has nourished a wider concern with the effects of hostility and discrimination toward other target groups outside or beyond the melting pot; and the attention of a new generation of students has turned with fruitful results to such hyphenated and scapegoated Americans as the Indians, Mexicans, Puerto Ricans, Chinese, Jews, Catholics—and Japanese.[6]

This book is not, however, a sociological study of the Japanese in America. That is the subject matter of the two companion volumes published under the auspices of the University of California Evacuation and Resettlement Study: *The Spoilage,* by Dorothy Swaine Thomas and Richard Nishimoto (1946), and *The Salvage,* by Professor Thomas with the assistance of Charles Kikuchi and James Sakoda (1952). Our own study is concerned not so much with Japanese Americans as with *anti*-Japanese Americans—less with the spoilage than with the "spoilers." Its narrative, at once historical and analytic, falls naturally into the three distinct dimensions suggested by the title—*Prejudice, War, and the Constitution.* First is the dark background of prejudice: the century-long history of anti-Orientalism on the west coast of the United States, from '49 to '42, with its deadly legacy of suspicion and superstition. Second is the wartime episode itself: the story of the Japanese American evacuation from exclusion through interment to ultimate liberation. Third is the constitutional dimension: the role of the courts throughout the episode, and the fundamental issues of citizen rights and war powers, of order and freedom, which have been raised by this singular event of our recent history.

Those constitutional and political issues are not only unresolved as yet; they are newly and ominously revived by the course of events in our decade. In times of crisis and emergency, born either of foreign war or domestic riot, the tendency to rely unquestioningly on the power of the police and the authority of the military—indeed to surrender to these guardians every conflicting or discordant claim—is all but irresistible. If the present book, with its detailed documentation of one such historic surrender (by the chief executive and his cabinet, by

---

[6]Notable recent works on specific minorities within the American cultural context include Nathan Glazer and Daniel Patrick Moynihan, *Beyond the Melting Pot: The Negroes, Puerto Ricans, Jews, Italians, and Irish of New York City* (M.I.T. Press, 1963); Oscar Lewis, *La Vida* (New York, 1967); Dale Van Every, *Disinherited: The Lost Birthright of the American Indian* (New York: William Morrow & Company. 1966).

the Congress, by the Supreme Court, and by the American people),
should in any small degree help to strengthen the capacity for reason
under pressure, it will have earned its way.

Jacobus tenBroek
Edward N. Barnhart
Floyd W. Matson

March 1968

*As this is going to press, Jacobus tenBroek, at age 56, has died. We
regret that he did not live to see the book's re-emergence, for we know
that in his last days the prospect of the new printing was a source of
great satisfaction to him.*

E. N. B.
F. W. M.

March 29, 1968

PREFACE

The present volume is a part of a long-range project which began in the first months of World War II. Early in 1942, when it became apparent that the Japanese American minority on the Pacific Coast was to be uprooted and moved eastward, a group of social scientists at the University of California initiated a study of the developing episode and its effects upon the resident Japanese. Charles Aikin, Professor of Political Science, and Dorothy S. Thomas, Professor of Rural Sociology, were the originators of the project and guided its early planning. Professor Robert H. Lowie joined the group shortly after it was formed and Professors Milton Chernin and Frank Kidner participated for a number of weeks. Professors Aikin, Chernin, Kidner, and Lowie took leave from the university for governmental service shortly afterwards, but Professor Aikin became associated with the project again following his return to the campus. The organization of the study would not have been possible had it not been for the encouragement and enthusiastic support of University President Robert Gordon Sproul and the late Dean of the Graduate Division, Charles Lipman.

The project was formalized as the University of California Japanese American Evacuation and Resettlement Study, with Professor Thomas as director. Beginning its work in February, 1942, the study continued to make field observations through December, 1945, and did not formally disband until July, 1948. During this time the study received financial support of over $100,000: To assist in conducting the study the University of California contributed $29,554, the Rockefeller Foundation supplied $32,500, and the Columbia Foundation $30,000. In addition, the Rockefeller Foundation provided $6,250 to help meet the costs of publishing the study's findings and this sum was matched by the University of California. Since 1948 the university has made available additional small amounts for microfilming and travel.

The broadly conceived program drawn up at the inauguration of the study, although subject to slight modifications, was followed throughout the war and for several years thereafter. The study took as its province all phases of the evacuation. Sociologically, it was concerned with the composition of the Japanese population and the social characteristics of the response made by the minority group to the events of forced migration, detention, segregation, and resettlement. Psychologically, it studied the changes in attitude and outlook of the evacuees in response to governmental policies, to events in the centers and on the war fronts, and was concerned as well with the nature of their wartime adjustment to the artificial life in the centers and to postwar America. The study also provided data for political scientists interested not only in the formation and development of governmental policies and administrative procedures, but also in the character and operation of the forms of self-government in the centers. Economically, the study sought to discover the effect of the evacuation upon the Japanese Americans themselves and the occupations in which they had been engaged, as well as to determine the character and consequences of the governmental program designed to protect their property and interests.

Two intensive studies of the sociological aspects of the episode have been published. *The Spoilage*, by Dorothy S. Thomas and Richard S. Nishimoto (Berkeley and Los Angeles: University of California Press, 1946) concentrates primarily upon the experience of the Japanese Americans in the relocation centers, with particular emphasis on Tule Lake, analyzing the reactions of the evacuees to administrative policies, to center experience, and to the war. *The Salvage*, by Dorothy S. Thomas (Berkeley and Los Angeles: University of California Press, 1952) follows the fortunes of those who left the relocation centers to resettle in American communities before the Army released the majority of the evacuees in December, 1944.

Before leaving the University of California and the directorship of the Evacuation and Resettlement Study in 1948, Professor Thomas, together with Professor Aikin, prevailed upon Professor tenBroek to undertake the preparation of the present volume. The latter invited Professor Barnhart to participate in the enterprise, and subsequently Floyd Matson was asked to join as collaborator.

The present work is concerned with the evacuation in terms of its historical origins, its political characteristics, the responsibility for it, and the legal implications arising from it. Thus it is less a study of the Japanese Americans in particular than of Americans in general.

The three collaborators planned and completed the project as an integrated, joint enterprise. All have contributed writing, analysis, and ideas not only to the work as a whole but to each of its major parts.

However, primary responsibility for each section was taken by a different author: Matson has had primary responsibility for Part I; Barnhart for Part II; and tenBroek for Part III, the Introduction, and the Conclusion.

The Japanese American Evacuation and Resettlement Study, during the six years of its formal existence, collected a vast amount of material which has been deposited in the University of California library and, together with material collected by the present authors, is now available to scholars and interested persons. The material of the original study includes: (1) Regulations, orders, press releases, bulletins and correspondence of the government agencies involved in the evacuation. (2) War Relocation Authority material on the relocation centers: reports, histories, memoranda to staff, studies of evacuee opinion and attitudes. (3) Socio-economic studies of the pre-evacuation Japanese population, reports on activities of their groups and organizations. (4) Diaries, journals, and correspondence of internees and WRA employees; reports on life in the centers pertaining to such matters as attitudes of evacuees, self-government, education, religious and recreational activities; histories of centers, life histories of individual evacuees, statistical studies of Japanese population. (5) Diaries, journals, and correspondence of relocating Japanese, case histories of resettlers, and statistical analyses of the process of resettlement. For access to these materials, scholars should consult Professor Charles Aikin, Department of Political Science, University of California, Berkeley. Professor Aikin is chairman of the Committee on the Evacuation and Resettlement Study. (In the notes to this book the collection is cited as Study files.)

To this mass of data the present authors have added since 1948: (1) Interviews with former officials of the War and Justice departments and the War Relocation Authority. (2) Microfilm records of nonclassified files of the Western Defense Command, the War Department, and the War Relocation Authority, including internal and external correspondence, memoranda, reports, histories of units, description of operating procedures and practices, forms, regulations, orders, and proclamations. (3) Records, reports, and recommendations of special tribunals and boards established in the agencies involved.

A great deal of material bearing on the political and historical aspects of the episode had been collected by the staff of the original study. It was at first anticipated that this material would prove adequate for the preparation of the present volume; however, it soon became apparent that the file material would have to be supplemented by additional research. This eventually included studies of the development of attitudes toward Orientals and other non-Caucasians on the West Coast over the past one hundred years, the history and activities of organizations carrying on anti-Oriental agitation in this period, the changing position of the Chinese and Japanese minorities in West Coast society, and the discriminatory legislation directed against them. Further, original material was accumulated on the activities of politicians and so-called "pressure groups" agitating for anti-Japanese measures in the early days of the war and on the stages through which the evacuation and internment programs passed. The study files contained practically no data on the postrescission phases of the evacuation or on the role of the courts in the episode. This information had to be supplied by a fresh investigation.

Some of the original file material bearing on the political aspects of the evacuation had been collected by Morton Grodzins in his position as research assistant for the study. Utilizing this as well as other study materials, he prepared and published a book on the subject, *Americans Betrayed: Politics and the Japanese Evacuation* (Chicago: University of Chicago Press, 1949). Although Dr. Grodzins and the authors of the present work have all drawn upon the file material of the study, the present authors differ substantially from him in their assessment of the reliability, relevance, and significance of much of the data, and have supplemented these resources with much additional material. Accordingly, their ultimate conclusions are different from his, and sometimes flatly contradict them.

The authors are deeply indebted to Professor Charles Aikin of the University of California Political Science Department. Not only did he originally inspire and continually counsel this project, but he patiently examined various drafts and contributed valuable ideas and suggestions which have greatly improved the final product. The authors are also deeply indebted to Professor Dorothy S. Thomas, now of the Department of Sociology, Wharton School of Commerce and Finance, University of Pennsylvania. Professor Thomas arranged for and set up this study before resigning from her position as director of the University of California Evacuation and Resettlement Project. Her vast knowledge of the field, the sources, and investigative and sociological techniques, and her over-all comments on our work, have been of inestimable value to us. We have, of course, drawn freely on *The Spoilage, The Salvage*, and her article, "Some Social Aspects of Japanese American Demography," which appeared in the *Proceedings of the American Philosophical Society* (Vol. 94, 1950, p. 475).

Richard S. Nishimoto, who is as informed about the Japanese in

America as any living person, has meticulously read the manuscript; he has corrected many errors, supplied many facts, and suggested many interpretive hypotheses.

Professor Harold Lasswell, Yale Law School, read the entire manuscript and from his abundant stock of original and helpful ideas has contributed generously. Our colleagues, Professors Joseph Tussman and Richard B. Wilson, have carefully examined the chapters of constitutional analysis with their usual display of critical acumen. Professor Paul Taylor, of the Economics Department of the University of California, has been kind enough to peruse chapter iv, "Two Theories of Responsibility." His vigorous disagreement with the conclusions there expressed does not diminish but rather increases his contribution to this book.

Various persons who played official or semiofficial roles in the Japanese American evacuation have given generously of their time and their documents and other materials. Of special value has been the cooperation of Victor W. Nielsen, Chief of the Research Branch of the Civil Affairs Division, Western Defense Command, during the years 1942–1946, who subsequently prepared a voluminous study: *Supplemental Report on Civilian Controls Exercised by the Western Defense Command* (Unpublished MS). Mr. Nielsen and his report have proved invaluable sources of factual data. Other persons whose contributions have been of assistance include: Philip M. Glick, former Solicitor, War Relocation Authority; Charles Rothstein, Department of Justice; John L. Burling, Edward J. Ennis, and James H. Rowe, Jr., formerly of the Department of Justice; Karl R. Bendetsen, A. H. Moffitt, Jr., Lyle Cook, Herbert J. Wenig, and C. K. Curtright, formerly of the Western Defense Command; Ernest Besig and Wayne Collins of the American Civil Liberties Union of Northern California; James C. Purcell, counsel for Mitsuye Endo; Captain K. D. Ringle, U.S. Navy; and Colonel William P. Scobey, U.S. Army. The authors regret that General John L. DeWitt, Commanding General of the Western Defense Command, 1941–1943, declined to grant them an interview.

The thanks of the authors are also due Sherrod East and T. E. Blades, Departmental Records Branch, Office of the Adjutant General, Department of the Army, and to Paul P. O'Brien, clerk of the Ninth Circuit Court of Appeals, for assistance in locating government material.

1954

CONTENTS

Introduction   1

PART I

Genesis

CHAPTER I. THE ANTI-JAPANESE HERITAGE   11

Race Pride and Prejudice 11
The Japanese Stereotype 22
The Workers 32
The Patriots 43
The Farmers 50
The Businessmen: A House Divided 57
The State of Mind: Summary and Estimate 62

CHAPTER II. THE ACTIVATION OF THE STEREOTYPE   68

December: War and Rumors of War 69
January: The Gathering Storm 73
February: The Time of Decision 81
Conclusion: The Faces of the Stereotype 91

PART II

Exodus

CHAPTER III. THE HISTORY OF THE EVACUATION   99

Exclusion 99
Internment 120
Restraint and Conditioned Release 140
Freedom 170

[xv]

CHAPTER IV. TWO THEORIES OF RESPONSIBILITY   185

    The Pressure Group Theory 185
    Pressure Groups and Coastal Exclusion 189
    Pressure Groups and Inland Exclusion 197
    The Politician Theory 198
    Politicians and Coastal Exclusion 199
    Politicians and Inland Exclusion 206
    Conclusion 207

PART III

Leviticus

CHAPTER V. THE EPISODE IN THE COURTS   211

CHAPTER VI. THE WAR POWERS   225

    The Problem 225
    The Milligan Case and the Alternatives 227
    The Answers of the Japanese Cases 233
    The Alternative Answers Evaluated 241
    Milligan, Endo, and Detention 248
    Conclusion 259

CHAPTER VII. THE EQUAL PROTECTION OF THE LAWS   261

    Discriminatory Purpose 262
    Overinclusive Classification 265
    Emergency Justification 289
    An Alternative 294
    Underinclusive Classification 302
    The Oyama and Takahashi Cases 304
    Conclusion 308

CHAPTER VIII. CITIZENSHIP   311

Conclusion   325

NOTES 337

INDEX 399

INTRODUCTION

The Japanese bombs which cascaded upon Pearl Harbor on December 7, 1941, plunging the United States into a global struggle for existence, also plunged the nation into a critical test of its constitutional democracy. If America was to survive, could its Constitution survive with it? Under the conditions of total war, could the constitutional balance be maintained between military and civilian authority, between the executive and the legislative, between all of these and the courts? Could civil liberties, the rights of individuals and of minorities, be tolerated—let alone protected? Could limited government and unlimited war-waging power coexist?

Nowhere were these questions more clearly defined than in the closely knit series of events which might be called the Japanese American episode of World War II.

The events that constituted the episode may be briefly summarized. They began the day after Pearl Harbor with the selective apprehension and imprisonment of several hundred enemy aliens—Japanese, German, and Italian. To this precaution were soon added travel restrictions and contraband orders applying to all enemy aliens. Then came curfew, evacuation, and finally detention—the last two applied on a strict racial basis to Japanese Americans only and regardless of citizenship. Accompanying and following these events were incessant demands for the permanent exclusion of the Japanese minority from the West Coast, for a flat prohibition of their entry into agriculture or business, and for their deportation to Japan after the war. Ways and means of stripping American citizens of Japanese ancestry of their citizenship were widely discussed. State legislatures considered memorials urging Congress to propose a constitutional amendment to that end. The Native Sons of the Golden West, flanked by the American Legion, filed suits in federal courts for the same purpose. Congress amended the Nationality Act especially to facilitate the renunciation of American citizenship by Japanese Americans. The attorney general of California directed much more vigorous prosecution of Alien Land Law violations than ever before. The legislature of California passed in 1943, repassed in 1945, a law prohibiting first "alien Japanese," then (fearing that this was too specific to be constitutional) "aliens ineligible to citizenship," from commercial fishing in coastal waters.

That this was a radical departure from American ideals and principles can hardly be challenged. One hundred and twelve thousand persons, two-thirds of whom were American citizens, were uprooted from their businesses, their farms, their homes; they were banished and interned for two and one-half years under guard and behind barbed wire, "under conditions," in Judge Denman's words, "in major respects as degrading as those of a penitentiary and in important respects worse than in any federal penitentiary."[1] Justice Murphy, in a dissenting opinion in the *Korematsu* case, characterized the action as "one of the most sweeping and complete deprivations of constitutional rights in the history of this nation in the absence of martial law."[2] The truth of this judgment depends, of course, upon whether the wartime power of the military over civilians within the country is a constitutional power and whether the military in this instance acted within that power; in short, it turns upon the constitutional correctness of the opinion of the United States Supreme Court to which Justice Murphy was dissenting. But certainly, on the face of it, the American citizens of Japanese ancestry—and in many respects Japanese aliens as well—were sweepingly deprived of their constitutional rights of personal security: the rights to move about freely, to live and work where one chooses, to establish and maintain a home; and the right not to be deprived of these rights except upon an individual basis and after charges, notice, hearing, fair trial, and all the procedural requirements of due process of law. More serious still was the apparently flagrant denial—flagrant because the classification was based solely on race—of the guarantee of equal and nondiscriminatory treatment implicit in the Fifth Amendment. Not that racism in other contexts has been unknown in America—far from it. But Americans have always been profoundly concerned by this disparity between creed and practice. The courts have condoned it only with the greatest reluctance. Moreover, this latest departure from the democratic ethic was more blatant than any before it. For the first time in the nation's history, race alone became a criterion for protracted mass incarceration of American citizens.

Can the Japanese American episode be reconciled with our fundamental constitutional rights and moral ideals? Can it be reconciled with

---

[1] For notes to introduction see p. 337.

the basic tenets of our democratic system? Or does the unprecedented racism of the episode fade into insignificance before the unprecedented character of the war itself? No doubt traditional views on the limits of military power needed to be reconsidered in World War II. The power to wage war successfully was, in the end, successfully exerted. Does this fact stand as the justification?

The answers to these questions depend first of all upon an understanding of the origin and character of the Japanese American episode. None of the wartime acts of discrimination and expulsion are explainable without reference to their historical context: the heritage of prejudice and suspicion surrounding the Oriental, and more particularly the Japanese, which had grown up through nearly a century along the Pacific Coast. Only against this background is it possible to understand the conditions under which an entire minority group came to be marked for exile—and, specifically, to identify the war-activated beliefs and attitudes which bore upon that policy.

Further, in order to assess responsibility for the episode, it is necessary to follow closely the successive stages of decision: from the first steps against enemy aliens on the day after Pearl Harbor, through the bold and sweeping actions of February, to the ultimate freeing of the evacuees two and one-half years later. In making this assessment it is important to take account of the explanations most frequently advanced and most widely accepted as to the reasons and responsibility for the episode. Among both participants and observers there has been a considerable diversity of opinion. Colonel Karl R. Bendetsen, a member of the staff of the Western Defense Command and administrator of the evacuation program, has described the policy as one based solely on military considerations and originating in military necessity.[3] With the nation at war, he wrote, the possibility of sabotage, espionage, and fifth-column activity made necessary a military decision to safeguard the security of the Command. The Japanese Americans were removed in order to insure that "if our enemy were coming up the beaches, they would not be able to join hands with them."[4] This is, in brief, the official explanation for the evacuation, widely accepted during the episode but since badly eroded under critical attack.

One of the first critiques of the official theory—a critique which itself advanced a number of alternative factors in explanation—was that of the Japanese American Citizens League, speaking in behalf of the evacuees: "Evacuation was not a military necessity but was due to false reports of sabotage in Hawaii, to the activities of anti-Oriental pressure groups and unscrupulous competitors; and most important of all to the admitted race prejudice of the Commanding General who issued the evacuation orders."[5] The commanding general, indeed, himself made the most extraordinary of all avowals of racism as a primary motivating factor, in the course of his application to the War Department for authority to undertake the evacuation: "In the war in which we are now engaged racial affinities are not severed by migration. The Japanese race is an enemy race and while many second and third generation Japanese born on United States soil, possessed of United States citizenship, have become 'Americanized,' the racial strains are undiluted."[6]

A number of students of liberal persuasion have attributed the principal responsibility for the evacuation to pressure groups and politicians. Thus Bradford Smith declares that "the preponderantly loyal Japanese minority were rounded up in an illegal fashion chiefly in response to pressure from a bluntly intolerant, grasping element on the Pacific Coast." Smith also observes that "this was an election year" and "anti-Orientalism was a staple product on the Pacific Coast."[7] According to Carey McWilliams "the Federal Government was pressured or perhaps more accurately, 'stampeded' " into undertaking the evacuation "by the noisy clamor of certain individuals, groups, and organizations in the three western states," by "groups that had an obvious and readily acknowledged economic interest in evacuation," by "politicians and political units" exerting pressure directly on General DeWitt as well as indirectly "through the technique of an organized campaign."[8] Morton Grodzins—though his conclusions as to responsibility for evacuation vary from chapter to chapter of *Americans Betrayed*—adheres, in the main, to the pressure group and politician theory.[9]

This stock tenet of liberalism has been accepted completely and virtually automatically by almost all writers who questioned or condemned the exclusion and detention program on constitutional grounds. Eugene V. Rostow states the point more sharply but not more insistently than the rest: "The program of excluding all persons of Japanese ancestry from the coastal area was conceived and put through by the organized minority whose business it has been for forty-five years to increase and exploit racial tensions on the West Coast."[10]

Among the constitutionalists, when writing on the constitutionality of the program, opinion also has been divided and conflicting. Charles Fairman and Frederick B. Wiener, two outstanding experts on the law of martial rule, thought the program of curfew, evacuation, and detention constitutional in the circumstances, though apparently on somewhat different grounds. Writing shortly after the evacuation had been ordered but while it was still in progress and before the Battle of Midway, Fairman concluded that "as a rough generalization" it was not "unreasonable to go on the assumption that among the Japanese communities along the coast there is enough disloyalty, potential if not active, to make it expedient to evacuate the whole."[11] Individual processing by hearing boards to separate the loyal from the disloyal presented, said Fairman, a "seemingly insuperable practical difficulty"— lack of time and absence of adequate investigative techniques.[12] It was complicated, too, by the question whether such boards would establish loyalty affirmatively, upon the presentation of evidence of positive attachment to the United States, or negatively, by the absence of evidence of disloyalty. It was complicated, further, by the fact that "fundamental differences in mores have made them [the Japanese Americans] inscrutable to us."[13] Finally, Fairman emphasized that "the exclusion orders when they were issued did not rest merely upon the General's finding of military necessity, but had behind them the full authorization of both executive and legislative branches of the Government."[14] The constitutional test to be applied to such measures was this:

If, under the circumstances as they appeared at the time and place, the control exercised by the commander was of a character appropriate to the situation, then it is the duty of the courts to concede that—paraphrasing the language of Chief Justice Hughes in *Sterling* v. *Constantin*—"such measures conceived in good faith, in the face of an emergency and directly related" to the ending or prevention of evil, fall within the discretion of the executive government.[15]

"The true test," said Wiener, was "laid down many years ago by Chief Justice Taney." It was this: "In deciding upon . . . necessity . . . the state of the facts, as they appeared to the officer at the time he acted, must govern the decision." If the officer, "with such information as he had a right to rely upon," has "reasonable ground for believing that the peril is immediate and menacing, or the necessity urgent, he is justified in acting upon it; and the discovery afterwards that it was false or erroneous will not make him a trespasser."[16]

A third defender of the constitutionality of the curfew, evacuation, and detention programs is Maurice Alexandre. He thought them "reasonable wartime measures necessary for the protection of the national safety." Like Wiener, Alexandre identifies the military as "the proper persons to determine" finally the military danger and the measures required to meet it. Alexandre makes explicit the basis for his judgment that the Japanese Americans, both alien and citizens, were "potentially dangerous persons" who had to be "rendered harmless." They were segregated and unassimilated; the alien enemy parents, with "powerful" ties to the homeland, exerted undue influence over the American born;

"detection of traitorous individuals is virtually impossible," because they live in separate communities and speak a different language. It would be unreasonable, moreover, "to expect the military to wait for the determination of individual loyalty before taking precautionary measures."[17]

Alexandre admits that detention was most difficult to justify. He thinks it possible to do so, however. "Granting that no presumption of loyalty to this country is attached to citizenship where the Japanese are concerned," the right of free movement in the United States "would enable the disloyal individuals to commit acts inimical to the successful prosecution of the war."[18]

Other writers on the constitutionality of the wartime treatment of the Japanese Americans have taken a strongly contradictory stand. Among these are Nanette Dembitz, Edward S. Corwin, Harrop A. Freeman, Milton R. Konvitz, and Eugene V. Rostow.[19] With varying emphasis and detail, these authors have argued: that the existence of war and the supporting approval of the executive and legislative branches of the government do not relieve the military of the necessity of meeting the requirements of the Constitution, including the limitations of the amendments, when taking action concerning civilians within the country; that a discriminatory curfew, evacuation, and imprisonment, carried out on racial and ancestral lines and regardless of citizenship, must be justified, if at all, in terms of its relationship to an existing and urgent military peril, and in terms of the absence of militarily adequate alternatives which were less violative of constitutional limitations and individual rights; that the evidence that the wartime treatment of the Japanese Americans was prompted by economic, political, and racist pressures and considerations was strong and the evidence that it was prompted by military considerations was weak; that within the time limits the loyal could have been separated from the disloyal; that all of these issues were properly subjects for judicial review and investigation; and that all the measures, especially detention, should have been nullified by the courts as unconstitutional.

These fundamental constitutional-political issues, and the underlying historical facts which shed light upon them, are the subjects of investigation in this book.

Part I—Genesis—is an analysis of the origins of the evacuation, a systematic relation of the episode to its historical context. As such it deals primarily with the body of myths and attitudes surrounding the Oriental—the Oriental stereotype—which had accumulated on the West Coast over the preceding century and came to exert a critical influence upon events and decisions leading to the evacuation. Although the Japanese in America have been extensively studied by social scientists, there has been no equivalent scholarly appraisal of the anti-Japanese movement. Interpretations and conclusions often widely at variance with those of earlier writers have been made possible by the use of primary sources not before examined in this connection. Part I deals, secondly, with the activation of the stereotype by World War II, which was itself less a cause than a catalyst, bringing to a climax already existing forces and attitudes. Thus, in an important sense, the evacuation resulted from the impact of the war on the Oriental stereotype.

Part II—Exodus—encompasses the story of the evacuation itself: the stages through which it developed, its ultimate scope and character, the persons and places involved in the making of the critical decisions, and the timing of those decisions. A systematic analysis is made of the evidence advanced to support the most commonly accepted explanation of the initiation of the program—namely, that it was undertaken by the army as a direct result of the activities of pressure groups or politicians. Much new material is brought to bear upon these subjects.

Part III—Leviticus—deals with the role of the courts in the episode, and the degree to which judicial refusal to intervene and condemn the program resulted from acceptance by the judges of the main features of the Oriental stereotype. The principal constitutional issues raised by the evacuation are analyzed—the extent of the war powers of the national government, the requirements of due process and the equal protection of the laws, the character of United States citizenship and the rights appertaining to it, and the function of the courts in protecting constitutional rights, enforcing constitutional limitations and maintaining the constitutional distribution of powers among the branches of government. Various alternative theories are considered, and the constitutional consequences of the position adopted by the Supreme Court are pointed out.

In short, it is sought in this book: (1) to provide a systematic analysis and presentation of the origins, stages, and constitutional consequences of the Japanese American evacuation; (2) to formulate, develop, and substantiate a theory not hitherto advanced to account for the evacuation, the character of the decisions taken and the responsibility for them; (3) to present the political and constitutional aspects of a larger interdisciplinary project, the sociological aspects of which have been published in companion volumes, and thus to carry forward the over-all plan of the Japanese American Evacuation and Resettlement Study of the University of California.

Part I

GENESIS

Chapter I

THE ANTI-JAPANESE HERITAGE

RACE PRIDE AND PREJUDICE

The wave of antipathy toward Japanese Americans which engulfed the Pacific Coast in the opening months of World War II had its origin far back in the history of California and the West. It was generated in the climate of indiscriminate antiforeignism which characterized the gold-rush period, and took definite shape during half a century of anti-Chinese activity, during which a hostile image of the "Oriental" emerged that was subsequently shifted to the Japanese.

The long agitation against the Oriental in California, to be seen in proper perspective, must itself be set against a background of violence and conflict involving the dominant white majority and the dark-skinned minorities: a heritage of hatred which had its inception in the fiercely competitive environment of gold-rush mining camps, was institutionalized in local ordinance and state law, and came to constitute a primary cause of some of the worst outbreaks of criminal lawlessness in California history.[1] In all the annals of the Pacific Coast, declared the historian Hubert H. Bancroft in the eighties,

there is no fouler blot than the outrages perpetrated at various times and places upon Indians, Mexicans and Chinese. Viewed from any standpoint, the aspect is revolting ... As a progressive people we reveal a race prejudice intolerable to civilization; as Christians we are made to blush beside the heathen Asiatic; as just and humane men we slaughter the innocent and vie with red-handed savages in deeds of atrocity.[2]

Antiforeignism.—The Forty-Niners who crossed the plains and rounded the Cape in search of Sutter's gold brought with them more than their dreams of riches. They carried a mental cargo of customs and conventions, which included a well-defined conception of the social role of nonwhite groups and a pervasive distrust of "foreigners" in general. Except perhaps in Mexico, wrote Josiah Royce some years later, no-

---

[1] For notes to chapter i see pp. 337–347.

[11]

where was the American to show "so blindly and brutally as he often showed in early California, his innate intolerance for whatever is stubbornly foreignism."[3]

This innate intolerance was goaded to brutality by the weirdly assorted population, lawlessness, and obsessive greed which defined the coastal frontier during gold-rush days. A "mixed multitude," as Lord Bryce was to describe it, "bringing with it a variety of manners, customs and ideas, formed a society more mobile and unstable, less governed by fixed beliefs and principles" than anywhere else in the land.[4] But it was the Americans who predominated in California, both in numbers and outlook. On display from the beginning was the doctrine of white supremacy, which owed much to the heavy representation of Southerners among the Argonauts. The "pretentious, fire-eating chivalry" made up a third of the population and remained a dominant power in California society and politics until the Civil War.[5] The Southerners were far outnumbered, nonetheless, by migrants from the Border States who had survived the arduous trek across the plains, blasting from their path the Indians and any others who rose to challenge them. These were the class, in the chaste words of a New England divine, "who are called Border Ruffians with us and which there are called, more or less derisively, Pikes, from Pike County in Missouri ... uncultivated and rough, crude in their notions of religion, and like all such people, coarse in their prejudices."[6] It was substantially the combination of "low-grade southerners" and "border ruffians," comprising the bulk of the gold-rush population, which produced the twin tendencies identified by Josiah Royce as the principal causes of disorder in California: the first, "a general sense of irresponsibility, and the other a diseased local exaggeration of the common national feeling towards foreigners ... [which] they seldom recognize at all, charging to the foreigners themselves whatever trouble was due to our brutal ill-treatment of them."[7]

When the Forty-Niners arrived in California they were first thrown into contact with the native Indians and Mexican settlers. Within a few months the Chinese appeared, moving into the mining regions in large numbers from across the Pacific, from the south came a steady stream of Spanish Americans, and from Europe came other strange-tongued immigrants. There was strong resentment against these foreigners among the Americans in California. To the traditional attitude of superiority to dark-skinned peoples, accentuated by the vigorous prejudices of the Southerners and Pikes, were added nationalistic sentiment and more than a touch of greed. In these mid-century years Americans were deeply imbued with patriotic pride. The long-held hope of planting the flag on the shores of the Pacific was at last being realized; the nation's manifest destiny appeared fulfilled. Mexico lay defeated, and the vast stretches of Texas, New Mexico and California were rapidly being incorporated in the Union. Yet here on the last frontier were the despised and beaten "greasers" reaping the harvest of the mines and joined in the feast by other foreigners. Americans were incensed at this usurpation, claiming "our national divine right to all the gold in California."[8] Xenophobia combined with greed to produce a sustained wave of violence and inaugurate a tradition of antipathy toward the aliens.

The antiforeign agitation soon became concentrated against the darker-skinned elements in the polyglot population of the mines and cities: the native "Digger" Indians and Mexican citizens, the immigrant Spanish Americans, the "Kanakas" from the South Seas, the "ragheads" from India, and the multiplying Chinese. " 'Infernals,' 'celestials' and 'greasers,' " commented one observer, "or black men, yellow men and Mexicans—it is hard to say which are most despised by the American whites of California."[9] The immigrants from Europe—predominantly Irish, German, and Scandinavian—generally escaped the worst effects of the antiforeign hatred. The agitation was in fact warmly urged and supported by certain of the Europeans, who were themselves as foreign as those they attacked and eminently more so than the native Californians. What happened in effect was that all the whites in California, European and American, combined forces against the nonwhites; the Yankee immigrant was joined by the European who dubbed himself "American" and whose claim was for the most part accepted.[10]

The treatment accorded the Indian by the early Californians closely followed the pattern of previous frontiers. To the gold-seekers, reared from childhood on tales of savage tribes and often themselves survivors of Indian wars, the lives of the natives were of no more concern than those of animals. Indian settlements were often attacked by roaming bands of frontiersmen, and women and children were indiscriminately included in the slaughter. No respect was paid to the red men in death; their bodies were left where they fell for others of their kind to bury, and not infrequently the whites lifted their scalps for souvenirs.[11] Continuous violence, amounting almost to open warfare, existed between the Americans and the Indians in many parts of California until as late as the mid-seventies. The whites conducted themselves with uniform brutality and there were more than a few unprovoked massacres, the most infamous being an assault on Indian Island in Humboldt Bay in 1860 in which over 200 Indians, mostly women and children, were butchered in a surprise night foray.[12] Many Americans cherished a con-

viction that they were waging what came to be called a "war of exter-
mination," and they waged it with determination and hardly disguised
enjoyment.

Scarcely less abused than the Indians were the Spanish Americans in
California, of whom the most prominent were the Mexicans, Chileans,
and Peruvians. Even before they had encountered the "greasers," the
gold-seekers were prepared to despise them, for the feelings stirred up
by border war and conquest were still fresh. "Those we have injured
we hate," observed Bancroft, "and so it was with Mexicans and Americans in California."[13] The organized action against the Spanish Americans, which in its most intense phase was known as the "Chilean War,"[14]
lasted several years. Mass evictions from the mining camps met with
little resistance in the northern areas, but in the southern mines, where
their numbers were greater, the South Americans fought back vigorously. Nevertheless entire districts remorselessly ejected the intruders,
and eventually all but a few were forced to withdraw—some to their
homelands, others to remote backhill areas of the state, and a small
number to careers of banditry and revenge.[15] Spanish Americans who
had long lived in California under the Mexican flag were robbed of
their property and deprived of virtually all legal protection. "It was
considered safe by an average lynching jury," commented the philoso-
pher Royce, "to convict a 'greaser' on very moderate evidence . . . One
could see his guilt so plainly written . . . in his ugly, swarthy face before
the trial began."[16]

The American Negro as well, long accustomed to the position of a
pariah on the borders of white society, found little change in his status
through immigration to California. Although the Declaration of Rights
of the California State Constitution of 1849 declared that slavery
"should never be tolerated in this state," it was possible for a historian
to report that "in unusual instances [it] . . . seems to have persisted until
the period of national emancipation."[17] Advertisements were regularly
to be seen in newspapers of the period proclaiming the sale of slaves,[18]
and a *de facto* status was accorded slavery by a measure of April 15,
1852, which charged the state courts with enforcement of a fugitive-
slave law. Subsequent acts of 1853 and 1854 extended the period allotted
owners to claim their slaves, thus keeping slavery in effect six years after
the adoption of the state constitution. Hostility against the Negro was
fomented in the early years by the emigré Southern politicians, who
succeeded in submitting a provision to the Constitutional Convention
"prohibiting free persons of color from immigrating to and settling in
this state." Although the proposal failed of approval, efforts to exclude

the Negroes persisted, and Peter H. Burnett, the first governor of California, lent his support to similar measures in 1849 and 1851.[19]

Racial antipathy died slowly in the mining areas. The Mexicans eventually took to the bush or retreated to Mexico, the Chileans, Peruvians, and other Spanish Americans were forced from the mines, and the Chinese made themselves inconspicuous working inferior claims in out-of-the-way regions. But the effects of prejudice persisted. A stereotyped view of the role and character of the dark-skinned minorities had taken root in the consciousness of Californians and was to endure long after the veins had run dry of gold and the mining camps had closed down. Subsequent waves of newcomers from the East accepted the prevailing stereotype of the colored minorities and carried on the tradition of antipathy. Physical attacks, discriminatory legislation, denial of legal rights, refusal of social and political equality, and finally outright exclusion, were the common expressions of this race pride and prejudice. Full rights in American society had been reserved by the Forty-Niners "for whites only," and public opinion along the Coast acquiesced in the judgment.

The anti-Chinese movement.—The attitude of early Californians toward the Chinese was virtually identical with that held toward other nonwhite groups. From the moment of their appearance they were the objects of general antipathy, abuse, and violence. Although at first they were hardly distinguished in the public mind from other minorities, it was not long before "the ill-will turned greatly in a new direction with the growing influx of the yet more obnoxious Chinese, upon whom the wrath of the Americans gradually concentrated."[20]

The tradition that the Chinese possessed no rights had its beginning in the mines. The Forty-Niners almost universally limited them to working abandoned or inferior diggings, and frequently drove them bodily from the towns and seized their claims. The bewildered Chinese, speaking little or no English and ignorant of Western customs, became the victims of every variety of fraud and chicanery, abuses encouraged by the absence of an active public opinion which might have alerted the police and the courts, and by the law prohibiting the testimony of Chinese in cases involving whites. Robbery, assault, and murder of the "Celestials" were regularly reported, and almost all cases went unpunished. In 1857 The Shasta *Republican* declared that "hundreds of Chinamen have been slaughtered in cold blood during the last five years by desperadoes that infest our state. The murder of Chinamen was of almost daily occurrence yet . . . we have heard of but two or three instances where the guilty parties have been brought to justice."[21]

In the cities the situation was no better. One San Francisco witness reported that he had "seen them stoned from the time they passed out of the ship, rocks thrown at them, until they reached Kearney Street. I have seen them leaning over the sides of the wagons with their scalps cut open ... No arrests were made, no police interfered."[22] The slightest pretext was made the occasion for mob action. In Los Angeles, for example, when a white man was shot during a Chinese tong war a mob of Americans retaliated by looting the Chinese quarter and killing twenty-one persons—of whom fifteen, including women and children, were hanged on the spot from lampposts and awnings.[23] In San Francisco incidents of the same sort were common during the seventies, culminating in a sustained orgy of looting and burning in 1877.[24] In the same period the entire Chinatown of Tacoma, Washington, was burned to the ground, and similar depredations were attempted in Portland, Oregon, and in Seattle and Olympia, Washington. Chinese residents were forcibly driven from the Chinatowns of Pasadena, Santa Barbara, Santa Ana, Oakland, and a dozen more California cities; in some areas of the state they were compelled to evacuate entire counties.[25]

The California working man was early made aware of the "menace" of Chinese coolie labor, and throughout the ranks of labor, skilled and unskilled, hostility toward the Chinese was steady and strong for half a century and more. Acting through formal associations as well as spontaneous movements, the California worker employed a variety of devices to publicize his unflattering portrait of the Chinese and gain support for their exclusion. Special organizations dubbed the "anti-coolie clubs" sprang into being under labor auspices to carry on the agitation through mass meetings, publications, and boycotts of Chinese merchants.[26] By the late seventies, the support of labor had raised Dennis Kearney and his sandlot-bred Workingman's Party of California—with its campaign slogan, "The Chinese Must Go"—to a position of power throughout the state.

California politicians in the post-Civil War era were keenly responsive to the labor vote; and the adoption of a vigorous anti-Chinese stand soon became a test of political acceptability with all parties. The Democrats, since the early fifties both anti-Negro and anti-Chinese, took the lead in demands for Oriental exclusion. The Republicans, more responsive to commercial interests, were less rabid in their views, but nonetheless were forced to take a similar stand. The wide publicity given the issue by politicians of the state had the dual effect of bringing the "Chinese question" sharply to public attention and dignifying it as one of general, rather than exclusively working-class, concern. In 1876 a special committee of the state legislature inquired into the Chinese problem and published, along with detailed proceedings and a memorial to Congress, *An Address to the People of the United States on the Evils of Chinese Immigration*. Ten thousand copies were printed for nation-wide distribution to congressmen, state governors, and newspapers.[27]

In the seventies the anti-Chinese agitation reached its climax and infused all ranks of California society. The popular demand for exclusion was so vigorous that the astute Henry George was led to remark that "it is impossible to question the full endorsement of this legislation by the American people."[28] In 1879 the state legislature authorized a ballot to determine public sentiment on Chinese immigration; fewer than 900 voted in favor—more than 150,000 opposed their entrance. (However, the statement of Governor Irwin, frequently repeated by later agitators, that the vote was a true expression of California opinion was highly questionable in view of the peculiar character of the ballot. "Against Chinese Immigration" was printed in small type at the bottom. If this were not checked, it counted as a vote. To vote for continuing Chinese immigration, the balloter had to erase or cross out "Against" and write in "For.")[29] Parades and mass meetings protesting Chinese immigration were staged throughout the state during this period, with civic leaders and politicians in prominent attendance. In 1882 the state legislature went so far as to proclaim a legal holiday to encourage monster rallies urging the passage of an exclusion law; in San Francisco one such gathering drew an audience of 30,000, and attendance in other localities was almost equally impressive.[30]

The widespread animosity toward the California Chinese was translated into a broad range of discriminatory legislation designed to drive out those already here and to discourage the immigration of others. The grass-roots origin of the antipathy is shown by the fact that it first found unhampered legislative expression in the miners' councils, thence moving upward by stages through municipal, county, and state governments.[31] A wide variety of exclusionist measures was proposed in the 1879 Constitutional Convention; and the State Supreme Court, while it invalidated much local and state legislation directed against the Chinese, nevertheless for many years effectively excluded them from the protection of the law.[32] Eventually California turned to the federal government for relief from the Chinese problem. Senators and representatives from the West Coast states, warmly supported by Southern congressmen, were persistent in their pursuit of exclusion legislation, and their efforts paved the way for a series of steps which culminated in the passage of the restrictive immigration act of 1882.[33]

Thus, during a period of thirty years, law-making agencies at all levels of government, from miners' councils to the federal Congress, approved measures aimed directly at the Chinese. The movement which was begun in the diggings and went on to capture the public opinion of the Pacific Coast reached fulfillment with the signature of the President on legislation for the total exclusion of the Chinese. The prejudice of the California miner and workingman had become the policy of the nation.[34]

The Chinese stereotype.—The agitation against the Chinese built up early in the public mind a vivid picture of their character, habits, and motives. As early as 1852, in a special message on Asiatic immigration, Governor John Bigler of California charged that the Chinese were a moral evil, that as coolies they were little more than slaves, that they degraded white labor and were inherently incapable of playing the role of citizens.[35] With various elaborations these remained the stock charges of the anti-Chinese agitator for half a century, and formed the major features in the public's conception of the Oriental.

The principal charge of the unions, that Chinese labor drove white workers from employment, found wide expression in stories, poems, and plays as well as in political utterances, and by grace of dramatic license became associated with insinuations of stealth and treachery. Thus an 1880 novel, *Almond-Eyed,* portrayed the invasion of a California town by hordes of Chinese who, besides driving white workers into starvation, introduced an epidemic of smallpox.[36] The San Francisco *Chronicle* voiced a similar suggestion: "Who have built a filthy nest of iniquity and rottenness in our very midst? The Chinese. Who fill our workshops to the exclusion of white labor? The Chinese. Who drive away white labor by their stealthy but successful competition? The Chinese."[37]

In their efforts to deny all rights to the Chinese, the agitators painted a portrait of subhuman slaves unworthy of citizenship and incapable of assimilation. In a memorial to Congress the California Senate declared in 1876 that the Orientals were "not involuntary, but, by the unalterable structure of their intellectual being, voluntary slaves."[38] Some writers, such as the author of *The Chinese Invasion,* went so far as to assert that the Chinese would resist naturalization even if the laws permitted.[39] "It is well known," agreed a Jesuit priest, "that these people do not come among us as citizens, or hope to be citizens . . . low inferior pagans as they are."[40] Perhaps the most sweeping indictment leveled against the Chinese was that of a California congressman who accused them of introducing "slavery, concubinage, prostitution, the opium-vice, the disease of leprosy, the offensive and defensive organization of clans and guilds, the lowest standard of living known and a detestation of the people with whom they live and with whom they will not even leave their bones when dead."[41] An official spokesman of the city of San Francisco summarized the viewpoint of labor in testimony before a Joint Special Committee of Congress in 1876:

The burden of our accusations against them is that they come in conflict with our labor interests; that they can never assimilate with us; that they are a perpetual unchanging and unchangeable alien element that can never become homogeneous; that their civilization is demoralizing and degrading to our people; that they degrade and dishonor labor; that they never become citizens, and that an alien, degraded labor class, without desire of citizenship, without education and without interest in the country it inhabits, is an element both demoralizing and dangerous to the community within which it exists.[42]

The most significant feature of the Chinese stereotype—and the most meaningful for our study—was that which became familiar as the "yellow peril." From the beginning it was alleged that the Chinese had only hatred for American institutions, that their sole loyalty was to the homeland and the emperor. Their entrance into the states was seen as an "invasion" and their motive ultimate conquest of the country by infiltration and subversion; behind those already here were the masses of Asia, eyeing the North American continent. *The Chinese Invasion* (1873) bore on its cover the legend: "The Chinese Invasion—They Are Coming, 900,000 More." An introductory essay in the book declared that "for over twenty years the great free continent of America, and the free state of California has [sic] been troubled with an invasion which threatens to overrun it as the great plagues overran Egypt.... The Chinese in California are the advance guard of numberless legions that will, if no check is applied, one day overthrow the present Republic of the United States."[43] A variety of novels and stories in the same period elaborated luridly on the threat of invasion and conquest. *Last Days of the Republic* (1880) unfolded a plot in which Chinese immigration became military invasion, the Pacific states were conquered, Europe and South America lay prostrate, and the "Mongolians" captured Washington.[44] Robert Wolter's *Short and True History of the Taking of California and Oregon by the Chinese in the Year A. D. 1899* (1882) pictured the Chinese navy triumphant and the Pacific Coast overrun while "the Black Dragon Guards the Golden Gate."[45] *The Yellow Peril in Action* (1907), a thriller by Marsden Manson, dealt with a similar Sino-American conflict.[46] A dramatic prophecy that China's mounting population might soon surpass that of all the rest of the world, forcing

intervention by the West in collective self-defense, was expressed by
Jack London in a short story entitled "The Unparalleled Invasion,"
which found the solution to the population problem in a primitive form
of bacteriological warfare against the Chinese.[47]

At the heart of the "yellow peril" was the ascription of immorality
and treachery to the Chinese, extending into every aspect of living. Even
their eating habits were barely short of cannibalism. "The people are
not nice in what they eat. Dead puppydogs are publicly sold in the
streets for food. Rats and mice are frequently eaten."[48] Their recreations
were seen as further proof of savagery: they had brought prostitution
with them from Asia in the form of "slave girls" and encouraged its
spread; they were incurably addicted to the "soul-destroying habit" of
opium; they gambled incessantly; and apparently possessed no moral
code. If the Oriental had ever had such a code, declared a California
senator in 1869, "it has long since evaporated into unmeaning
phrases ... A pagan and an Asiatic, ... he is made up of the errors and
vices, moral, social and political which ... have tainted her children
with a leprosy of sin not fit to be named among men."[49] The *Goodrich
Universal History* described the Chinese as "great fibbers and very much
addicted to cheating," and asserted that "if parents have a greater number of children than they can conveniently afford, they are permitted to
throw them into a river."[50] Accusations of immorality were especially
concentrated upon Chinese women, "the most degraded of their sex."[51]
They were characterized as willing prostitutes and chattels in the hands
of evil masters; it was said that in California "the word 'Chinawoman' is
synonymous with what is most disgusting and vile."[52]

The individual Chinese was portrayed as intellectually and morally
inferior, though possessed of an inscrutable Oriental cunning. The
Jesuit Father Burchard described him as "of low intellect" deriving
from "an idolatrous, vicious and corrupt and pusillanimous race."[53]
Senator Casserly of California added: "His narrow brow, yellow, vacant
face, squat figure and dull eye show him the hereditary Asiatic laborer
of twenty centuries."[54] A missionary summarized the moral stereotype in
defining the Chinese as "an habitual thief" who "in intercourse with
others is reserved, shrewd and untrustworthy."[55]

In the fiction of the period the "heathen Chinee," as Bret Harte
dubbed him, was either a comic and ridiculous character or a villain.
As a domestic servant he was endlessly embroiled in skirmishes which
he always lost. As a villain he was treacherous, never standing up to his
enemies in open combat but attacking them with mysterious poisons or
with knives in dark alleys.[56]

Running through the popular characterization was the myth of un-bridgeable racial difference. Regarded sometimes as a separate race, sometimes as part of a larger "Oriental" or "yellow" race, the Chinese were everywhere considered unalterably and distinctively different from (i.e., inferior to) the white race, not only in physical appearance but in all moral and intellectual qualities. A graphic expression of this racist belief was set forth in the testimony of the Honorable Frank M. Pixley, representing San Franicsco before the joint congressional committee in-vestigating the Chinese issue in 1876:

The Chinese are inferior to any race God ever made . . . I think there are none so low . . . Their people have got the perfection of crimes of 4,000 years . . . The Divine Wisdom has said that He would divide this country and the world as a heritage of five great families: that to the Blacks He would give Africa; to the Red Man He would give America; and Asia He would give to the Yellow race . . . The White race is to have the inheritance of Europe and America and . . . the Yellow races are to be confined to what the Almighty originally gave them and as they are not a favored people, they are not to be permitted to steal from us what we have robbed the American savage of . . . I believe that the Chinese have no souls to save, and if they have, they are not worth the saving.[57]

The basic charges against the Chinese—of unscrupulous competition, moral degradation, treacherous character, and subversive intent—were elaborated over the latter half of the century with such variety and force that it is difficult not to conclude that they found wide acceptance in the public opinion of California. The hapless Orientals had fallen heir from the outset to the ingrained prejudices of white Americans against the dark-skinned minorities in their midst: a predisposition which was galvanized into violence by the patriotic sentiment of the miners and the wave of antiforeign feeling which swept the "gold-rush melting pot" in the early years. To this general hostility were soon added the specific apprehensions of the workingman and the grievances of special-interest groups; and the developing issue was seized upon and boldly exploited by politicians, journalists, and writers of fiction. Gradually the accusations of these disparate groups came together to reveal a distinctive stereotype which for large numbers of Californians became inseparable from reality.

Other factors were at work to develop the portrait and print it in-delibly on the public mind. Although foreigners from Europe might melt with relative ease into the population, the physiognomy of the Oriental rendered him unchangeably distinct. Again, the prevailing belief in racial difference offered an authoritative sanction for social barriers and acts of discrimination; acts which in turn could be held up as confirmation of the racist theories. Thus the Chinese, like other minorities before and after, were caught in the vicious circle of prejudice.[58] A conspicuous and convenient target, without the power of the vote and largely without the protection of law, the Chinese constituted an ideal scapegoat for the anxieties and hostilities of the dominant white majority of California.

With the passage of the Chinese Exclusion Act in 1882, immigration ceased abruptly. In succeeding years, under the hammer blows of social hostility and economic discrimination, numbers of Chinese retreated back across the sea and those who remained gradually withdrew behind the walls of Chinatowns in West Coast cities. However, the exclusion act had taken no notice of other Orientals. It escaped attention that the newly restored Japanese Emperor had removed the ancient bans on emigration of his people, and that former employers of the Chinese in California and Hawaii were quietly negotiating for Japanese labor to fill the gap. But the appearance of the Japanese in ever-increasing numbers in the last decade of the century soon made this information known throughout the Pacific Coast states.

Within the space of a few years the Chinese stereotype became the Japanese stereotype. The ways in which this conversion was accomplished, and by whom—together with its consequences for the Japanese and for the Americans—form the substance of the pages which follow.

THE JAPANESE STEREOTYPE

The history of the Japanese in the United States, through the half-century from their earliest arrival to the evacuation, constitutes a perennially fertile field for scholars and has been explored from nearly every social-science viewpoint. Because the ground has been so often covered, and more especially because the general facts of Japanese immigration and settlement are admirably presented in Dorothy S. Thomas, *The Salvage*,[59] no effort has been made to repeat them here except where mention is essential to the narrative. Instead, on the assumption that the problem of prejudice is to an important degree a problem of the prejudiced, the emphasis of the present study is upon the organizations, personalities, and events which made up the anti-Japanese movement on the Pacific Coast from 1890 to 1942; and the purpose is the limited one of tracing the development of those opinions and attitudes which gradually congealed in the public mind to form the Japanese stereotype—that special blend of fabrication, myth, and half-truth on the basis of which, in large part, the wartime evacuation of the Japanese Americans was authorized, executed, and approved.[60]

The Chinese legacy.—Before the first Japanese immigrant appeared in America, the psychological foundation of the Japanese stereotype had been laid: it was that of the "heathen Chinee." The legacy of prejudice inherited from the Chinese profoundly influenced the subsequent history of Japanese immigration and was never effectively erased. It would be difficult to overestimate the contribution to public opinion of what B. Schrieke has called "the already existing unfavorable stereotype of the Oriental and the slumbering anti-Oriental tradition of the Coast— the element dormant in its mores and impressed on it by the antecedent Chinese experiences."[61]

In the initial stages of Japanese immigration, popular confusion of the two nationalities was widespread. Newspapers along the coast frequently lumped the Japanese and Chinese together as "coolies" and "Asiatics," and as late as 1906 the San Francisco school authorities grouped the Chinese and Japanese together under the classification "Mongolian." "Under the general term 'Asiatics,'" wrote a Japanese scholar, "the Japanese shared at first, and later inherited, the painful experience of the Chinese."[62] Speeches, resolutions, and articles coupling the two races were so frequent that California Japanese were led in 1901 to distribute leaflets requesting that they be differentiated from the Chinese; despite a decade of mounting immigration, the Japanese were not yet distinguished in the public mind from other Orientals.

Early press references to the Japanese, moreover, came for the most part from hostile sources. In this context such descriptive terms as "Asiatic," "coolie," and "yellow," with all their connotations of the hated Chinese, took on new emotive overtones and soon regained their former prominence in the vocabulary of racial slurs. The contraction "Jap"—later accentuated by headline writers in World War II—first appeared consistently in the columns of the *Coast Seamen's Journal* during the 1890's.

The entrance of the Japanese into urban trades and agriculture closely coincided with the decline of the Chinese labor force. The politicians of prejudice, seeking to regain the prestige accumulated during "anti-coolie" days, lost no time in turning this new yellow peril to their advantage. One popular method was to attribute to the Japanese all the alleged crimes of the Chinese by emphasizing their similarities— and then to point to their differences as compounding the felony. Thus the United States Industrial Commission reported in 1901 that the Japanese "are more servile than the Chinese, but less obedient and far less desirable. They have most of the vices of the Chinese, with none of the virtues. They underbid the Chinese in everything, and are as a class tricky, unreliable and dishonest."[63] An especially lurid comparison was drawn by the San Francisco journal *Organized Labor* in a 1900 editorial:

Chinatown with its reeking filth and dirt, its gambling dens and obscene slave pens, its coolie labor and bloodthirsty tongs, is a menace to the community; but the snivelling Japanese, who swarms along the streets and cringingly offers his paltry services for a suit of clothes and a front seat in our public schools, is a far greater danger to the laboring portion of society than all the opium-soaked pigtails who have ever blotted the fair name of this beautiful city.[64]

"Since the agitators have directed their efforts against the Japanese almost exclusively," wrote John P. Irish in 1909, "it is noted that favor for the Chinese has risen. All of the arguments formerly made against them are now directed against the Japanese."[65] Where once it had been asserted that the Chinese displaced white workers and refused to remain in the menial jobs assigned them, they were acquitted of these charges as the Japanese came to assume the role of aggressor. "The Chinaman dreads competition with the white man, and avoids it," wrote one Californian who held the new opinion. "The Chinaman is willing to be a hewer of wood and a drawer of water; the Japanese has no aptitude for menial tasks nor any intention of performing them except as stepping stones to his own high ambitions."[66]

Perhaps the most damning aspect of the Chinese legacy was the transfer to the Japanese of the moral stereotypes earlier fixed upon the "Celestials." From the beginning the Japanese was tagged, like his predecessor, as "tricky, unreliable and dishonest." In flagrant contradiction of all evidence, he was accused of fomenting crime, menacing white women, and generally scoffing at Western concepts of law and morality.[67] Opposition to the Japanese, whatever its economic or psychological sources, was usually expressed in tones of moral indignation and outrage. The school-segregation episode of 1906, in which Japanese were ordered from the San Francisco schools, was presented solely as a moral issue; thus the San Francisco *Chronicle* observed that "we object to them in the familiar intercourse of common school life as we would object to any other moral poison."[68] A California congressman went so far as to maintain that "the vast majority of the Japanese people do not understand the meaning of the word 'morality,' but are given up to the practice of licentiousness more generally than in any nation in the world justly making any pretenses to civilization."[69]

Testimony to the persistence of these moral imputations, and incidentally to the degree of displacement of the Chinese stereotype, was furnished by a survey conducted in the late twenties among California high-school students and college freshmen. The great majority expressed a preference for the Chinese over the Japanese; and the most frequent charges against the latter were that they "take unfair advantage, are dishonest, tricky and treacherous." Typical of the responses was the following: "I don't know why I should have the feeling that they are tricky, self-centered and would cut a man's throat for fifty cents; unless it is their appearance as they quickstep down the street.... Close-cropped hair, grim unsmiling expressions, enough to make a saint suspicious, especially on a dark night."[70]

The propagation of this stereotype was powerfully assisted by the ambitions of a variety of special-interest groups and individuals; and it was further encouraged by the rapid rise of Japan to the status of an aggressive world power—a development which gave new meaning to the traditional West Coast legend of the "yellow peril."

The yellow peril.—"The Japanese, like the Negro," wrote Professor Robert E. Park in 1914, "is condemned to remain among us an abstraction, a symbol, and a symbol not merely of his own race but of the Orient and of that vague, ill-defined menace we sometimes refer to as the 'Yellow Peril.' "[71] This specter, which haunted Americans throughout the first quarter of the present century, was a vital part of the legacy unwittingly bequeathed by the Chinese to the later·arrivals from Japan. In its earliest formulation it conveyed American fears of an engulfing tide of "coolie" immigration, spurred by the uncontrolled birth rate and supposed famine conditions of China. "The great danger of the 'yellow peril,' " declared a California editor, "is its enormous size. With less than two million white men in California, and more than four hundred million Chinese in China, just across the way, the very smallest overflow from that limitless reservoir would swamp our Pacific Coast."[72]

The transfer of the yellow-peril stereotype to the Japanese resulted at first from popular confusion of the two nationalities, and was accelerated by the increasing Japanese immigration which revived fears of Oriental inundation. But it was not until 1905, when diplomatic relations between the United States and Japan became strained, that the concept came to acquire its most sinister connotations. Some years earlier the term had been applied to the Japanese by the German Kaiser, who helped instigate the Russo-Japanese War by impressing the Czar with the threat of Asiatic armies led by Japan. The threat soon came to concern President Theodore Roosevelt, who took steps toward Anglo-American coöperation to avert what he considered a new yellow peril.[73]

The sweeping Japanese victories in the Russo-Japanese War strongly reinforced this propaganda, inspiring rumors in the United States that resident Japanese were spies and soldiers in disguise, representing the first wave of a "peaceful invasion" which threatened to overrun the country. On the eve of the Battle of Mukden, the San Francisco *Chronicle* voiced the fear of many that "once the war with Russia is over, the brown stream of Japanese immigration is likely to become an inundating torrent";[74] while the San Francisco journal *Organized Labor* bluntly prophesied an attempt at peaceful conquest: "Drunk with victory and fired by uncontrollable ambitions, these one million Japanese Napoleons will turn their eyes around for new territory to conquer.... California in particular is an inviting field, and if they can capture it without powder and shell so much the better."[75]

The traditional friendship of Americans for Japan was swiftly dissipated as a result of the war and the peace-table demands of the Japanese, together with the effective propaganda of Russian agents.[76] Among the rumors which circulated widely after the war, according to Payson J. Treat, was an alarming prediction that "Japan would organize the wealth and manpower of China to provide and equip the armies which would revive the days of Ghengis Khan and create a real 'Yellow Peril.' "[77] Along the Pacific Coast such rumors had particular effect; and it was natural that the suspicion and hatred they aroused should become concentrated upon the local Japanese population. In an editorial headed "Yellow Peril," *Organized Labor* openly accused the resident Japanese of espionage:

A characteristic among Japanese ... is their propensity for spying.... Put a huge roof over the Japanese Empire, and you have a national Japanese detective agency, with which there is nothing to compare in the rest of the world.... Their spying has been done long ago about this country, and more particularly so, California, and the results are shown now. Japan intends to make California its Manchurian fields.[78]

For more than two decades after the Russo-Japanese War, the possibility of war with Japan was regularly kept before the American public, with many declaring it to be inevitable. The effect of this alarmism in aggravating race feeling on the West Coast was considered in 1909 by Homer Lea, who concluded that anti-Japanese sentiment may have been dormant prior to the Russo-Japanese War, but "since then it has openly manifested itself and ... permeates the entire social and political fabric of the West."[79] Yellow-peril agitation reached a peak of intensity during the war scare which accompanied the San Francisco school incident of 1906–1907, with patriotic elements in Japan and America vying in the exchange of threats and epithets.[80] Alleged exposures of the resident Japanese as a "secret army" were frequent and widely publicized, such as the warning of a Spanish-American war hero, Captain Richmond P. Hobson, that "Japan now has an army of soldiers in the Hawaiian Islands. They made the invasion quietly as coolies, and now we know that they are soldiers organized into companies, regiments, and brigades."[81] Subsequently a California congressman declared that "it would be easy to marshal an army of fifty thousand Japanese veterans at any point in California in forty-eight hours."[82]

In 1907 the fear of war with Japan was general throughout America. A number of diplomats warned openly that Japan was on the point of attack; even the cautious New York *Times* considered the conflict all but inevitable, and a *Literary Digest* survey found the belief to be widespread.[83] Popular fears were somewhat allayed the following year by the enthusiastic Japanese reception of the world-cruising United States fleet, as well as by the negotiation of the Root-Takahira Agreement. But by 1910 the war scare had been revived by a new rash of invasion rumors, which were aggravated by the Japanese annexation of Korea.[84]

Anti-Japanese activity in general abated somewhat during World War I because of the intervention of Japan on the Allied side. But a variety of incidents kept the fear of the yellow peril alive: notably Japan's presentation in 1915 of the Twenty-One Demands, which called for a virtual Japanese protectorate over parts of China. Meanwhile, as Treat has pointed out, German propaganda exploited the fear of Japanese aggression to divert American sympathy from the Allies.[85] It has been charged that German agents, writing for the Hearst newspapers, colored their contributions in an effort to embroil America with Japan.[86] But Hearst required little outside help; as early as 1906 he had led the crusade against Japan, and thereafter, in the words of a biographer, "his papers kept up a running fire against Japan, which had now taken the place of China as head and front of the 'yellow peril' always threatening the prosperity of California."[87]

The fear of Oriental inundation of the Western world had meanwhile become the basis for a growing body of pseudoscientific literature which lamented the passing of the great Nordic race before the onslaught of the "inferior" yellow peoples. Writers such as Lothrop Stoddard and Madison Grant, reviving the discredited racist theories of the French Count Gobineau, lent a veneer of scholarly sanction to the image of the yellow peril. In his introduction to Stoddard's *The Rising Tide of Color,* Grant called openly for a "race war." Stoddard himself maintained that "Japan must find lands where Japanese can breed by the tens of millions . . . even assuming that she does not suffocate or blow up from congestion before that time arrives."[88]

In the years following World War I the fear of "peaceful invasion" received wide publicity from West Coast racists such as Montaville Flowers,[80] from politicians seeking a sure-fire campaign issue, and from patriotic organizations such as the American Legion and the Native Sons. Much of the success of postwar agitation against resident Japanese was due to the fact that it coincided with aggressive actions by Japan in the Far East, which were resented throughout America. A counter-brief submitted in 1922 by the California Committee of Justice, in answer to arguments of the Japanese Exclusion League, noted that these arguments "cover events in Korea, China, Siberia, and the conduct of Japan in the World War and at the Versailles peace conference. These matters are not relevant to any discussion of what is known as the Japanese question in California."[90] Nevertheless it was clear that the Japanese in America were held responsible by many citizens for the actions of their national government.

Attempts by California groups in 1920 to enact legislation which would prevent the Japanese from holding land aroused serious opposition in Japan and led to renewed war talk in both countries. But the peak of anti-American feeling in the Far East was reached when the United States Congress passed the Oriental Exclusion Act four years later. According to Professor Arnold Toynbee, who was then in Japan, "The news of the enactment aroused the nation for several weeks to a dangerous pitch of excitement . . . [and] two persons committed suicide as a protest against the passage of the Act."[91] Other American actions in the same period sustained the hostility, notably a Supreme Court decision denying the citizenship previously granted a Japanese who had served with United States forces in the war.[92]

After the passage of the 1924 exclusion law, American agitation against Japan and the resident Japanese gradually subsided until the Japanese aggression in Manchuria in 1931—an action which effectively destroyed all efforts to restore a quota system of immigration and relax requirements of the alien land act. In subsequent years, as Japan deserted the League of Nations, abandoned her agreements on naval limitation, further invaded China, and bombed the American gunboat *Panay*, the familiar specter of the yellow peril returned to haunt Americans with a semblance of reality it had not before possessed. Although the traditionally anti-Oriental groups maintained a comparative silence during the thirties, the news headlines were sufficient to reëstablish the Japanese stereotype in the minds of numerous residents of the Pacific Coast. Discriminatory measures began to reappear in the California legislature, inflammatory statements and even mob violence against individual Japanese were once again reported, and various newspapers resurrected their old editorials on the dangers of Oriental competition.[93] The seeds of suspicion and distrust sown by pressure groups over the preceding quarter-century bore substantial fruit in the thirties; and for the first time the fruit was dropping of its own weight, without the intervention of a master hand. The spontaneous hostile acts and expressions against resident Japanese in the depression decade, sparked by the aggressive actions of Japan, gave a clear preview—albeit on a much smaller scale—of the subsequent reaction of the Pacific Coast to the Japanese attack on Pearl Harbor.

Hollywood and the Oriental.—In the early days of motion pictures, before the movement of the studios to Hollywood, movie audiences were acquainted with Orientals almost solely as villains: sinister and inscrutable figures who lurked in opium dens by day and emerged under cover of darkness on errands of vengeance and treachery. At first it was the Chinese who were caricatured, but the stereotype was soon extended to the Japanese—and in fact, with superficial changes, it became the basis for the representation of all dark-skinned minorities by the infant film industry.[94]

An average early example of this typecasting was a 1910 production entitled "Tsing Fu, the Yellow Devil," in which a Chinese magician "forces his attentions upon the pretty singer, but is always repulsed. . . . Very furious at this rough treatment, Tsing Fu swears revenge, and we see him next in one of the opium dens in the Chinese quarter, figuring out a plan."[95] A variation on this theme, which appeared in 1913 under the title "The Mong-Fu Tong," drew an enthusiastic review from the *Moving Picture World:*

> There's a hand-to-hand battle in two fast-moving automobiles resulting in the capture of five Chinese of the Mong-Fu-Tong. How "Arizona Bill" was himself taken, his tortures at the hands of Mong-Fu; the clever ruse by which Bill's wife was captured and her splendid knife duel with Mong-Fu; the thrilling escape from the den when fire burst from a dozen windows—all combine to realize the uttermost in spectacular effects, convincing acting and absorbing story.[96]

The impact upon suggestible audiences of this persistent portrait of the Oriental is suggested by the report of a movie fan some years later:

> A picture whose name I have forgotten comes back to me often, or rather just one part, that of the villain, a sleek, treacherous Chinese. He was employed to do the "dirty work." A white man had been murdered, and the picture showed the Chinese with a knife going into the man's room. Shortly after, he came out, with a villainous, bloodthirsty, satisfied look that haunts me now, ten or more years after. Then the American, stabbed, dead, was shown.[97]

The reaction of schoolchildren to such films is typified in the response of one child: "I saw a movie last night, and the Chinese are terrible people!"[98]

The yellow-peril propaganda resulting from the Russo-Japanese War and subsequent invasion rumors furnished early film-makers with an irresistible formula. The spy stereotype was firmly realized in a 1909 production, "The Japanese Invasion," in which the Japanese valet of an American army officer was seen to steal vital military secrets making possible an attack on the Pacific Coast; "The Red Light" (1911) dramatically exploited the theme of Asiatic war and espionage.[99] German producers followed with a similar venture, "The Engine of Death," exhibited in the United States in 1913, in which a Japanese secret-service operative was apprehended as the result of his attempt to purloin the formula for a high explosive.[100]

Hollywood's treatment of the Oriental, from 1914 to the advent of sound, is accurately mirrored in the career of Sessue Hayakawa, a Japanese actor who began as a villain and went on to become one of the most popular matinee idols of the silent screen. Characteristic of his early efforts was "The Cheat" (1914), in which a white woman offers to become the mistress of a Japanese in return for a needed sum of money, and later rejects the bargain. "The Oriental, furious, brands her on the shoulder. The husband is brought to trial for having attempted to kill the Japanese. The wife bares her branded shoulder in court and wins her husband's acquittal."[101] The exhibition of "The Cheat" aroused a strong protest from resident Japanese, who had been silent concerning earlier screen caricatures of their race. Their objections evidently had an effect upon Hayakawa, for he subsequently signed a contract stipulating "that he shall not be required to threaten the peace of certain international relations"; and he later complained in a magazine interview about the casting of Oriental actors in roles calculated to stimulate race hatred.[102]

The outbreak of World War I, and more especially America's entrance in 1917, marked a change for the better in movie treatment of aliens and minority groups. With Japan and China on the side of the Allies, efforts began to be directed toward a more sympathetic and even romantic depiction of the Oriental—although not without occasional reversions to stereotype such as the Hearst-sponsored serial "Patria," which featured Warner Oland as a Japanese secret-service agent. "Not only did the film accuse a friendly power [Japan] of the Black Tom Explosion and the incitement of labor violence, but in Episode 14 it showed the Japanese leading an invasion in force against America from the soil of Mexico."[103]

One of the first sympathetic film ventures was a 1914 Hayakawa picture, "Wrath of the Gods," in which "a Japanese girl and her father ... are converted to Christianity by a shipwrecked American sailor; fanatic [Japanese] religionists stone the father to death, but the girl and the sailor are saved when the wrath of the gods is visited on the mob in the form of a typhoon."[104] From this ambivalent gesture toward racial amity, Hayakawa progressed to become the only Oriental actor ever to play romantic leads in American films. Nevertheless, as Deems Taylor has noted, "because of racial prejudice ... he always had to relinquish the girl in the final reel."[105] The long list of Hayakawa films in the early twenties did little to discourage the popular confusion of Japanese with Chinese, since the actor himself appeared frequently in Chinese roles (e.g., "Li Tin Lang" and "The Tong Man"). This casting was to some degree a result of increasing popular interest in Chinese themes, spurred by such box-office successes as Griffith's 1923 classic, "Broken Blossoms," and Lon Chaney's "Shadows" (1922). In both these films the Chinese protagonist was sympathetically portrayed, but remained the stereotyped Asiatic: silent, obsequious, clinging to Oriental dress, and speaking little or no English, he was as inscrutable as ever and did nothing to persuade audiences that the Oriental might ever become Americanized.

A notable exception to the general sympathy of postwar pictures involving Japanese was a 1920 diatribe, "Shadows of the West," released by the American Legion as part of its campaign for an alien land law. Invoking all the malevolent aspects of the stereotype, the film described the Japanese in California as spies and cutthroats plotting to monopolize the vegetable market; and the climax was reached, not unpredictably, with the kidnaping of two white girls, followed by a dramatic chase and rescue on the part of Legionnaires.[106] The exhibition of this crude fantasy aroused considerable protest, but meetings called to organize a boycott were systematically broken up by Legion members.

After the introduction of sound and the subsequent trend toward movie realism, the popularity of exotic Oriental themes declined, and actors such as Warner Oland and Peter Lorre turned from inscrutable characterizations of Fu Manchu to portrayals of the semi-Americanized benevolence of Charlie Chan and Mr. Moto. Chan remained a favorite through the next decade, as the Sino-Japanese conflict turned American sympathies to the side of China; but Moto, a Japanese secret-service agent played by Lorre, was less fortunate. A wholly sympathetic character, Moto did not correspond to the image of the yellow peril which events were reviving in the public mind. In 1938, according to a close observer, "the movie industry [has decided] to abandon the Mr. Moto series of detective stories because anti-Japanese feeling is running so high in America that audiences can no longer take pleasure in the courage and astuteness of a member of that nation."[107]

The classic stereotype of the Oriental as "tricky, unreliable and dishonest" had once again become fixed upon the Japanese by the combined pressures of aggression abroad and depression at home. The contribution of Hollywood over the years to the build-up of the stereotype may perhaps be summarized in the remark of a West Coast movie fan interviewed during the twenties: "A few years ago, the Japanese in the picture show always took a villainous part. I have never been personally acquainted with any member of the race, but I have formed a dislike for them because of these little things."[108]

The contribution of the movies to the creation of an unfavorable stereotype was generally paralleled over the same period by mass-circulation magazines and popular fiction. Although no systematic content analysis of printed media has been made by the authors, a reading of popular literature dealing with the Japanese Americans has confirmed the conclusion of such analysts as Berelson and Salter, whose investigation of magazine fiction indicates "unintentional but consistent discrimination against minority groups of hyphenate Americans." Not all literary discrimination against the Japanese, however, has been unintentional. Deliberate use of the stereotype in its harshest aspects is to be seen in Wallace Irwin's *Letters of a Japanese Schoolboy*, which first appeared in *Collier's* during 1906–1907 and were subsequently published in two volumes. Griffing Bancroft's *The Interlopers* (1917) presented what a *Nation* reviewer described as "a study of the 'Yellow Peril,' as a subtle and irresistible absorption of California by the Japanese." The same theme was dramatized by two popular novels of 1921, Peter B. Kyne's *Pride of Palomar* and Wallace Irwin's *Seed of the Sun*.[109]

THE WORKERS

The drive for exclusion.—In keeping with the pattern of earlier anti-Chinese agitation, the first protests against the Japanese in America were those of the workingman. For over a quarter of a century, in fact, it was the growing trade-union movement along the Pacific slope which principally inspired and effectively dominated the anti-Japanese campaign. Again, as in the case of the Chinese, the opposition of West Coast labor had the express purpose of discouraging Japanese immigration, whether by federal action, discriminatory state laws, international agreements, or simply the reluctance of the Japanese to enter a land possessed by prejudice and pervaded by restrictive covenants.

The attention of the labor leaders was first drawn to the Japanese in 1888, following a move by the San Francisco Shipowners' Association to man several of its vessels with Japanese seamen. The action was hotly denounced by the *Coast Seamen's Journal*, "Official Paper of the International Seamen's Union of the Pacific," which in later years credited itself with having been "the first paper in the country to take up the [Japanese] question, away back in 1888, when the Jap was a mere premonitory symptom."[110] Protests against the practice of employing nonunion Japanese in coastal shipping were frequently voiced in subsequent years, both by the *Journal* and by the San Francisco Council of Federated Trades.[111]

But it was not until the turn of the century, when the labor unions obtained partial control of the San Francisco city government, that concerted action was taken against the resident Japanese. For twenty years thereafter, organized labor on the West Coast—operating chiefly from the trade-union center of San Francisco—continually protested the presence of the Japanese and pressed for their exclusion by such varied means as physical attacks, editorial invective, commercial boycotts, convention resolutions, and public memorials, as well as through the activities of specially formed anti-Japanese societies and union-supported political parties.

During the early years of agitation, direct attacks upon the persons and property of Japanese, inspired by union members, were not uncommon. The first reported incident occurred in 1890, when fifteen Japanese cobblers in San Francisco, secretly employed at less than union wages, were assaulted by members of the shoemaker's union.[112] In the following year, a Japanese restaurant in the same city was attacked by members of the local cook's and waiter's union.[113] Similar acts occurred sporadically during the next decade; but the climax was not reached until 1906, following the great earthquake which leveled parts of San Francisco and generally disrupted the forces of law and order. After an inspection tour of the devastated city, Secretary of Labor and Commerce V. C. Metcalf issued a report to the President documenting nineteen cases of assaults against Japanese residents of San Francisco.[114]

The boycott, a favorite labor weapon in the days of the Chinese, was again invoked in an attempt to drive the Japanese from urban trades. The most notable instance took place in the summer of 1906, when the Cook's and Waiter's Union of San Francisco, assisted by members of other unions, threw picket lines around Japanese restaurants in the city. According to a formal note of protest registered by the Japanese ambassador,

The boycotters linger about the restaurants and accost all customers who approach, giving them small match-boxes bearing the words "White men and women, patronize your own race." . . . On a number of occasions the windows of the restaurants have been stoned and groups of boycotters have gathered about the entrance in a threatening manner so as to frighten the customers away.[115]

Labor's most effective weapon against the Japanese, however, was the editorial pen. In 1900 Olaf A. Tveitmoe of the San Francisco Building Trades Council founded the weekly newspaper *Organized Labor,* which within a month initiated a long-term campaign against the Japanese. A front-page editorial on March 17 viewed with alarm the "heathen Chinee" and "the blabbering, pretentious half-civilized Japanese," who were said to be "fast supplanting white workmanship both in field and factory" and driving American girls "into the stifling beer joints and the gloomy streets, into the bawdy-houses and slums of the tenderloin district and the Barbary Coast." This opening salvo was followed by a series of editorials warning against the competitive danger of the Japanese and urging that the Chinese Exclusion Law be amended to include them. The *Coast Seamen's Journal* joined in the agitation on April 25 with a declaration that "the new evil confronting us—the Japanese immigration—is far more serious and far-reaching than the Chinese." During the following years these and other labor publications (notably the San Francisco *Labor Clarion*) continued to expatiate upon the evils of Japanese competition and to voice demands for restrictive legislation. The impact of the campaign upon the public mind, as early as 1905, was reflected in the wide support given to the issue by the general press. By that year, as C. N. Reynolds has summarized, "there was a continuous display of news of economic competition of one sort or another in the daily press . . . [and] the reiteration of the charge in the daily news convinced large numbers of Californians of its truth."[116]

Labor also pressed its case against the Japanese through a constant outpouring of resolutions and public memorials. In addition to steps taken by local unions and trade councils, resolutions to restrict Japanese immigration were regularly presented by West Coast delegates at the annual conventions of the American Federation of Labor. The AFL first went on record in 1892 in favor of putting "cheap Japanese laborers" in the same status as the Chinese. After 1900 anti-Japanese resolutions appeared in greater frequency and stronger language—typical was a 1905 warning that "unless Oriental immigration is checked, the

American people must surrender the right to occupy American soil in many sections"—and under the prodding of West Coast members the federation over the next twenty years allowed few conventions to pass without recording their unequivocal opposition to the Japanese.[117]

Another effective propaganda method employed by labor was the staging of public mass meetings and "monster rallies" featuring addresses by prominent politicians and civic leaders. The first of these was held in San Francisco on May 7, 1900, for the announced purpose of "seeking protection against Asiatic hordes." Presided over by Walter MacArthur of the Seamen's Union and the San Francisco Labor Council, the meeting was primarily intended for workers and the emphasis throughout was on the grievances of labor.

Among the speakers were Mayor James D. Phelan and Professor Edward A. Ross of Stanford University. Professor Ross was reported by the San Francisco Call as having said that "should the worst come to the worst, it would be better for us if we were to turn our guns upon every vessel bringing Japanese to our shore rather than permit them to land";[118] and Mayor Phelan declared that without drastic action "these Asiatic laborers will undermine our civilization and we will repeat the terrible experience of Rome."[119] The meeting produced a resolution urging that Congress extend the Chinese Exclusion Act to the Japanese, but its greatest achievement was in creating publicity and gaining adherents for the anti-Japanese cause. Through subsequent years mass protest meetings became increasingly popular; and in the large-scale agitation of 1905 and 1906, the monster rally was widely employed by labor and exclusionist groups.

In an effort to coördinate and dignify the campaign against the Japanese, the union leaders stimulated the formation of a variety of associations designed, like the "anti-coolie" clubs of earlier days, to spread the exclusion gospel and give an appearance of civic solidarity to the agitation. In the spring of 1905 Organized Labor conducted a two-month campaign which was climaxed by appeals for the formation of anti-Japanese societies. "Let every city in the state and every other state organize anti-Japanese leagues," the paper exclaimed. "Let the leagues be composed of delegates from all central labor bodies, mercantile associations, clubs and other civic bodies."[120] The appeal quickly bore fruit; on May 7 the Japanese and Korean Exclusion League (later renamed the Asiatic Exclusion League) was founded under the leadership of Tveitmoe. The first of a long succession of anti-Japanese societies, the league soon had affiliated with it more than 200 California labor organizations plus a miscellaneous following of "Fraternal, Civic, Political and Military" groups. It established offices in Stockton, Portland, Seattle, Denver, and other western cities (plus one in British Columbia, which permitted the league to dub itself "International"). In the preamble to its constitution, the JKEL asserted that "the Caucasian and Oriental races are unassimilable," and dedicated the league "to the end that the soil of North America be preserved to the American people of the present and all future generations."[121]

During the next decade the league was active on a broad front, staging mass meetings and demonstrations, organizing boycotts, and issuing propaganda. One year after its founding it was declared that the league's membership had reached 78,500 and that its program had been endorsed by organizations numbering four and a half million members.[122] An extensive report on league activities published in 1911 by the United States Immigration Commission concluded:

The League has always been dominated by organized labor and the position taken by it has always had the support of organized labor in general. . . . It has frequently emphasized that its opposition to Asiatics was not alone on industrial but on racial and political lines as well. . . . By its agitation no doubt the League has done much to increase the opposition to Japanese, especially in California.[123]

As a result of the swift development of the Asiatic Exclusion League, a variety of other anti-Japanese societies soon appeared on the Pacific Coast—in such numbers that a "coördinating" group, the Associated Anti-Japanese Leagues, was formed early in the second decade. The most important of the subsidiary societies was the Anti-Jap Laundry League, founded in March 1908 by members of the San Francisco Laundry Drivers' Union, which within a year had established locals in San Mateo County, San Rafael, Fresno, and Oakland.[124]

Throughout three-quarters of a century of anti-Oriental agitation by organized labor, the ultimate objective was the passage of exclusion legislation. The successes earlier achieved against the Chinese made this goal seem equally attainable in the case of the Japanese. In the beginning, however, agitation was primarily local, and as Japanese entered into competition with labor and business there emerged a succession of local ordinances and trade restrictions.[125] Municipal acts discriminating against the Japanese, notably in San Francisco, were frequent during the early years of the century and for the most part were inspired by labor. It was the incumbent Union Labor Party of San Francisco which was principally responsible for the school-segregation act of 1906. The next year the San Francisco Board of Police Commissioners denied licenses to six Japanese wishing to conduct employment bureaus. This

event, like the school act, produced international repercussions and
brought heavy criticism from federal officials.[126] Nevertheless, discriminatory actions by both municipalities and the state rose in number and
severity over succeeding years and dropped off only after the passage of
exclusion legislation in 1924.[127]

Owing largely to the pressure of labor and the Exclusion League,
anti-Japanese bills flooded the state legislature at Sacramento during
the first quarter of the century. In one year alone, 1909, the California
lawmakers discussed seventeen measures directed at the Japanese. Much
of the legislation was frustrated by the intervention of President Taft,
who feared complications with Japan, but a bill ordering an official
survey of Japanese labor conditions in the state was allowed to pass. The
report which followed, submitted by State Labor Commissioner John
D. MacKenzie, directly countered the claims of the exclusionists and
was quickly suppressed by the state senate, which released a resolution
bluntly censuring the commissioner and rejecting his opinion.[128]

Although the long-term goal of the unions was the prohibition of
Japanese immigration, it was recognized that the way must be prepared
through certain preliminary measures. One such was the California
Alien Land Law of 1913 (the Webb-Heney Act), which barred "aliens
ineligible to citizenship" from ownership of land in the state. Two years
later labor supplied almost the sole support for an unsuccessful attempt
to strengthen the act by removing the clause permitting leases to
Orientals.[129]

During World War I the emergence of a "German menace" drew the
attention of labor leaders temporarily away from the Japanese. But the
conclusion of the European conflict ushered in a large-scale revival of
anti-Japanese activity on the Pacific Coast, with broader group participation and greater public support than ever before. For the first time,
however, leadership of the agitation passed from labor's hands into
those of a variety of patriotic and agricultural groups. By 1920 organized
labor had, in fact, begun to reconsider its position, and although the
major union bodies and spokesmen remained committed to the cause
of exclusion, a growing disaffection was apparent in the city unions.
To some extent this was probably a result of increasing migration to
California of Americans from other regions, many of whom did not
share the inbred prejudice of old-stock Californians toward the Oriental. Among the labor leaders, many feared that the proposed new land
restrictions would throw large numbers of Japanese on the urban labor
market, and in various quarters there were signs of growing acceptance
of the Japanese and a willingness to include them in the unions.[130]

In the main, however, the forces of organized labor continued to carry the fight to the Japanese. The AFL passed resolutions urging total exclusion and expressing apprehension at the influx of "coolie labor."[181] In California, the State Federation of Labor participated in the formation of the Japanese Exclusion League, successor to the earlier leagues and forerunner of the California Joint Immigration Committee. Among the more prominent spokesmen for exclusion were James W. Mullen, editor of the *Labor Clarion,* and Paul Scharrenburg, secretary of the State Federation of Labor and its representative in the league. As editor of the *Coast Seamen's Journal,* Scharrenburg kept the newspaper in the vanguard of agitation; his journal campaigned vigorously for the Alien Land Law initiative amendment of 1920, and afterward asserted that "the people of California voted to preserve the Golden State as a heritage to the white race."[182]

The labor organizations also played an important role in securing the passage of Japanese exclusion legislation in 1924. The AFL, fearing a flood of cheap foreign labor, was on record in favor of a general restriction of immigration, and the state federation agitated both indirectly through various publications and directly through the Joint Immigration Committee, of which it was a prominent affiliate. The committee's director, Valentine S. McClatchy, was a major witness during Senate hearings on the law; and his arguments against the Japanese in America constituted a summary of the charges voiced by West Coast labor leaders over the preceding thirty years.[183]

With the enactment of exclusion legislation, organized agitation against the Japanese swiftly declined, although most unions and their members continued to practice discrimination in various forms. During the depression labor resentment of alleged economic competition again found expression, and the *Coast Seamen's Journal* was led to warn that "there is no common meeting ground for these races ... there should be no compromise and no lowering of the Asiatic barriers."[184] But for the most part the forces of organized labor turned their attention to other problems and the Japanese issue was allowed to lie dormant until the outbreak of the war.

The politics of prejudice.—"In the wild gorges of Siskiyou," wrote Homer Lea in 1909, "on moss-grown boulders, and half effaced by the lichens of two decades, can even now be deciphered this legend: 'The Chinese Must Go—Vote for O'Donnell.' "[185] The author of the legend, Dr. Charles C. O'Donnell, was one of the first Californians to realize the political profits of race prejudice. Elected to a minor office in 1879, on the crest of the wave which carried Dennis Kearney and the Workingman's Party briefly into power, O'Donnell was soon to see his campaign promise realized. Within three years of his election the tide of Chinese immigration had been rolled back, by virtue of the 1882 Exclusion Act. With the Chinese disposed of, however, O'Donnell found himself without a campaign issue. It was five years before he discovered a solution; but in 1887, once again, on boulders in the wild gorges of Siskiyou might have been seen this legend: "The Japanese Must Go—Vote for O'Donnell."[136]

When poured from the new bottle, however, the old wine of violence and race hatred failed at first to intoxicate—owing chiefly to the fact that there were then less than five hundred Japanese in California, mainly employed in domestic service and not noticeably in competition with the white population. But although the campaign slogan of Dr. O'Donnell—"who had been several times arrested for abortion"[137]—proved his most significant miscarriage, its potentialities were not lost upon another Irish-descended aspirant to civic leadership. When James Duval Phelan campaigned for the San Francisco mayoralty a decade later, conditions were more propitious; for during the last ten years of the century more than 30,000 Japanese had arrived in America, two-thirds of whom settled in California, and organized labor had already begun its strong appeal for their exclusion.

Owing at least in part to his position on the Oriental issue, Phelan was chosen mayor of San Francisco in 1896 and retained his post through two subsequent elections. Characteristic of his vigilance was an incident of 1900; when a single Chinese was found afflicted with bubonic plague, Mayor Phelan ordered a mass inoculation of all Orientals in the city, and the brutality with which the order was carried out led the Japanese to appeal to their consul for protection.[138] Shortly thereafter, Phelan appeared as chief speaker at a labor-sponsored mass meeting for Japanese exclusion—the rally which first signified the emergence of the tacit alliance of labor and the politicians which for a generation was to furnish the principal weapons in California's crusade to "keep America American."

In 1901 the anti-Japanese campaign was given wider significance by a message to the legislature from Governor Henry T. Gage urging the passage of memorials to Congress "for the protection of American labor against the immigration of Oriental laborers."[139] The same year saw the birth of two organizations dedicated to expulsion of the Japanese: the State Federation of Labor, which remained for a generation in the vanguard of agitation, and the Union Labor Party, which flourished under the political leadership of San Francisco boss Abe Ruef.[140] Fol-

lowing the great teamsters' strike of 1901, the Union Labor Party succeeded in electing its candidates to the majority of municipal offices.
One plank in the party's platform promised the segregation of Japanese
students, demanding "that all Asiatics, both Chinese and Japanese, be
educated separately from other children in schools exclusively for
themselves."[141]

The next attempt to exploit the Japanese issue for political advantage
occurred in 1905 with the outbreak of a vigorous anti-Japanese campaign on the part of the San Francisco *Chronicle*—whose owner,
Michael H. De Young, had once been a candidate for senator and was
widely thought to be preparing for a renewed political career.[142] The
Chronicle series rang a variety of changes on anti-Japanese sentiment,
but the message was chiefly addressed to workers. However, the nature
of the Japanese danger was variously defined. On one day, as C. N.
Reynolds has observed, the *Chronicle* pointed to "absolute evidence"
showing that Japanese competition had driven thousands of white
workers from their jobs; on the following day the paper stated edi-
torially that the Japanese were only filling a vacuum created by a "real
scarcity of effective unskilled labor."[143] The inconsistency of these arguments encourages the conclusion that, in the words of one historian,
"the specific charges against the Japanese have little significance in
themselves. They were merely the smoke pouring from a bonfire."[144]
That there was something more than economic reason behind the agitation was virtually conceded by the *Chronicle* in a statement that the
Building Trades Council "is leading in the work of uniting organized
labor in this state to demand passage of a Japanese Exclusion Act,"
although "there are probably no Japanese mechanics employed on any
building in this city [and] probably none are likely to be so employed."[145]

The principal motivation of the Building Trades Council was in fact
the political ambition of its two leaders: Patrick H. McCarthy, its president, who subsequently became mayor of San Francisco on the Union
Labor ticket; and Olaf Tveitmoe, secretary, who was appointed to the
board of supervisors in 1906 and for a time was talked of as a candidate
for mayor.[146]

The contribution of the politicians to the anti-Japanese movement
was especially evident during the school-segregation affair of 1906. On
October 11 of that year, one day before the indictment of Mayor
Eugene Schmitz and Boss Ruef on charges of municipal graft, the San
Francisco school board issued an order barring Japanese from the white
primary schools. Although not wholly unexpected, the move precipi-
tated a storm of protest in Japan and severely embarrassed the federal

government. After a tragi-comic Washington conference involving President Roosevelt, Mayor Schmitz, and two San Francisco school officials, the Californians agreed to withdraw the segregation order in return for the President's promise to negotiate with Japan toward the restriction of immigration (which was achieved the following year through the Gentlemen's Agreement).[147]

Behind the action of the school board, once again, was the alliance of labor and the politicians. Both the Union Labor Party and the Exclusion League had long been on record as advocating the ouster of Oriental students, as had the Coast Seamen's Union and the local Building Trades Council, and even President Roosevelt came to view the segregation order as part of labor's pressure for immigration restriction. With the workers united on the anti-Japanese question, both Republicans and Democrats of the state came out against immigration in their 1906 conventions, and local politicians were unanimous in demanding segregation. "The truth is," wrote a San Francisco correspondent of the London *Times* at the height of the agitation, "that the people have been worked up to a high pitch by politicians who believed that by raising the Japanese issue they could increase their popularity."[148]

In subsequent years the political trade in prejudice remained a crucial factor in creating and extending popular opposition to the Japanese. It has been held that the "peak years" of agitation were those of national elections—specifically 1908, 1912, 1916, and 1920.[149] While this inference appears extreme, it is likely that not a few California politicians were elected to office on the basis of anti-Japanese campaigns. In the 1910 state elections the platforms of all three California parties—Republican, Democratic, and Socialist—contained anti-Japanese declarations, and "Hiram Johnson became governor on this plank."[150] The attitude of Governor Johnson was made still plainer in 1913, during the legislative scramble which produced the state's discrimininatory Alien Land Law. The introduction of the bill led the San Francisco *Argonaut* to exclaim that "it is just a bit of cheap political buncombe, meaningless and ineffective in itself, useful only in that it may help somebody to get votes under the pretense of being a Japanese baiter."[151] When Secretary of State William Jennings Bryan appeared in Sacramento at the behest of President Wilson to speak against the measure, his address was followed by one from Governor Johnson, who rallied the wavering legislative forces and obtained overwhelming passage of the land act.[152]

The attention of West Coast politicians (and voters) was largely diverted from the Japanese during World War I. But in 1919, with the

German menace disposed of and elections approaching, the agitation was resumed on a broad front. Once again it was James D. Phelan—the former mayor of San Francisco, now United States senator—who led the attack against the Japanese. He made speeches throughout California and in the Senate; wrote articles for California magazines; introduced a bill to bar American-born Japanese from citizenship; and arranged for California hearings by the House Committee on Immigration and Naturalization, at which he was the first to testify.[153] The broad scale of Phelan's activities led California Governor William D. Stephens (of the opposition party) to declare that "the present agitation in California was inspired by candidacy for office.... Manifestly the grave concern [Phelan] now expresses awakened only when he found it necessary to create an agitation on which he might ride back into office."[154]

Senator Phelan's campaign for a new alien land act, however, had an ironic ending. Faced with the governor's refusal to call a special session of the legislature, he and his associates resorted to the initiative for a rigorous amendment to the land law. But when this had been arranged, politicians of all shades rushed to support the measure—including the once reluctant governor. The initiative proposal carried, but the candidate who had originated it—Senator Phelan—was defeated for re-election.

The climactic chapter in the politics of prejudice was written in 1924, when the federal immigration bill with its amendment for Japanese exclusion came before Congress. A coalition of Western and Southern congressmen formed in the lower house to overwhelm the meager opposition to the measure, and the approved bill was quickly sent to the Senate. Here Senator Samuel S. Shortridge of California, long a foe of the Japanese, introduced the exclusion amendment to the Senate bill; and it was that old campaigner in the race wars, Hiram Johnson, who as senior senator from California led the fight on the floor. For a time it seemed possible that the exclusion rider would be rejected by the upper chamber; the Republicans held control and the Coolidge administration was known to oppose Japanese exclusion in favor of continuing the Gentlemen's Agreement. But the Senate's action coincided with the Teapot Dome investigations which placed the Coolidge Cabinet in a bad light and made desirable some diversionary issue, and one-third of the senators faced elections within the following six months. As Rodman W. Paul has concluded, "an adverse decision on the Japanese question presented little danger and much political capital and support."[155] One final incident clinched the decision. On April 24 the Senate was apprised of a note from the Japanese ambassador warning that "grave consequences" would follow any move to exclude the Japanese. Senate resentment at this "veiled threat," as Senator Henry Cabot Lodge described it, was immediate and general; and the exclusion amendment was approved overwhelmingly along with the restrictive immigration bill. However, the possibility that political considerations, rather more than indignation at the Japanese note, constituted the chief influence behind the Senate's action was suggested by a remark of Senator Thomas G. Heflin: "Why is it that this step is taken now, just preceding a Presidential election, and Republican Senators pretending to get offended all of a sudden at something which the Japanese ambassador has suggested?"[156]

With the achievement of exclusion legislation, following closely upon the passage of the land laws, much of the political motive for agitation against the Japanese disappeared; and during the next few years the issue played a declining role in the politics of the Pacific Coast. With the outbreak of the depression, however, and more particularly with the rise of Japanese adventurism in China and Manchuria, popular feeling against the resident Japanese once again was aroused and came to be reflected in political circles. In 1935, 1937, and 1939, anti-Japanese measures once more appeared in the California legislature, as public opinion generally began to turn against Japan and the Japanese Americans.[157] But the attention of the politicians, as of the public, remained focused principally upon the domestic problems of the depression; and beyond the revival of the familiar stereotypes, no large-scale movement developed against the Japanese until the "dastardly and unprovoked attack" by Japan at Pearl Harbor on the morning of December 7, 1941.

THE PATRIOTS

Their name was Legion.—After 1920 effective control of the agitation passed from the hands of organized labor into those of a group more often in conflict than in alliance with labor, whose anti-Japanese objective was the same—absolute exclusion—but whose motives and philosophy were profoundly different from those of the unions. This was the American Legion, an organization of ex-servicemen which rose like a phoenix from the ashes of World War I.[158]

The Legion's participation in the Japanese issue was to some degree an expression of its opposition to aliens in general; and this attitude in turn was intimately related to its private war against "subversive" influences. The conspicuous antiradical coloration of the Legion, implanted by its military parentage and apparent big-business affiliation, has represented for thirty years its preëminent claim to distinction. The Legion's suspicion of the alien was largely conditioned by this fixation against the "Red"; for in Legion thinking it was invariably the alien—never the "hundred per cent American"—who carried the pest of bolshevism to our shores.[159] In addition there was a more concrete basis for antialien legislation; from its inception the Legion was suspicious of all who had not participated physically in the war, and especially of aliens who failed to become citizens and therefore escaped the fighting. The campaign against these "alien slackers" was begun in the first national convention with a resolution urging their deportation on grounds that this country was "too damned good for them to remain in."[160]

From this beginning it was a short step to agitation against all aliens. A typical editorial in the *American Legion Weekly* in 1919 called on the government to "Oust the Aliens" from all public employment.[161] Even the Legion could not hope for the deportation of all the foreign-born in America; and so a program was developed which aimed either at converting aliens to the Legion's brand of Americanism or sending them back where they came from. In its first convention the Legion established a National Americanism Commission, pledged to "combat all anti-American tendencies, activities and propaganda; [and] work for the education of immigrants, prospective American citizens and alien residents in the principles of Americanism."[162] Not all aliens, however, were considered worth saving. From the beginning the Legion regularly demanded the deportation of foreigners who advocated overthrow of the government by force and violence, and proposed various laws "to rid our country of this scum who hate our God, our country, our flag, and who prate of their privileges and refuse to perform their duties."[163] The Legion also worked consistently for the restriction of immigration, and in 1924 it was Legionnaire Albert Johnson, a congressman from Washington, who fathered the bill which sharply reduced general immigration quotas and totally excluded aliens ineligible to citizenship.

Meanwhile, in the first year of its existence, the California Department of the Legion joined with like-minded patriotic and agricultural groups in the revival of the Exclusion League (subsequently to become the California Joint Immigration Committee), which for many years operated under the chairmanship of Adjutant James K. Fisk of the state Legion. The major lines of Legion agitation against the Japanese were established in the first state convention, which recorded resolutions favoring Oriental exclusion, the prohibition of land rentals to Orientals, the dissolution of alien corporations, and a ban on the importation of Japanese "picture brides." In 1920 the same themes recurred, and the *California Legion Weekly* was filled with notices urging members to vote "yes" on the forthcoming initiative amendment to the alien land act. Perhaps the most powerful propaganda device contrived by the state Legion was the motion picture "Shadows of the West," widely exhibited in 1920, which dramatically portrayed the exposure by Legionnaires of a fictional Japanese plot to control California agriculture."[164]

In an effort to coördinate its anti-Japanese activities in the various states, the Legion in 1922 established the National Committee on Oriental Affairs, charged with the promotion of alien land laws and the removal of Japanese from competitive pursuits. In its annual report the next year, the Oriental committee noted that eleven states had enacted antialien legislation, and claimed that "in practically every instance these bills were introduced at the instance of and pressed to successful conclusion by representation of the American Legion in the respective states."[165] Beginning with the first national convention, Legionnaires from the West Coast had been successful in winning the support of the national organization for their anti-Japanese demands, and from this time on the Legion as a whole remained militantly opposed to the "immigration and naturalization of Orientals." Resolutions passed by the national body in the early twenties followed closely the pattern of those approved in conventions of the California Department, where a large part of the proceedings were given over to arguments against Orientals in particular and undesirable aliens in general.[166]

During the agitation which surrounded the passage of federal legislation, the Legion played a prominent role. In 1923 the California Department urged the national convention to "reaffirm its stand as to total exclusion of Oriental immigration and secure the most forceful presentation of this matter to the Congress of the United States to the end that effective legislation be passed."[167] The powerful Washington lobby of the Legion was called into action to persuade Congress of the need for exclusion. Legionnaire Johnson, as chairman of the House Committee on Immigration and Naturalization, engineered the immigration bill through the lower chamber; and Legion testimony was conspicuous during hearings of the Senate committee which laid the groundwork for passage of the legislation.[168]

"The American Legion's battle on the immigration question, though a great victory, is just half won," declared the Americanism Commission after passage of the "moderate" 1924 act.[169] For seven more years, while the national Legion carried on the battle against aliens generally, the California Department continued to devote major convention time to resolutions against the Japanese. With the depression, however, the Legion turned its attention from the alien to the more immediate threat of the radical. The major goals of agitation had been achieved with the passage of the exclusion act and alien land laws; and except for isolated expressions during the thirties, Legion feeling against the Japanese was allowed to become dormant until the attack on Pearl Harbor.

Native Sons of the Golden West.—With the exception of the American Legion, the most potent single force in the campaign for Japanese exclusion during the decisive years between the end of World War I and the passage of the immigration law was the fraternal order known as The Native Sons of the Golden West: an exclusive organization of the California-born, dedicated to preserving the state "as it has always been ánd God Himself intended it shall always be—the White Man's Paradise."[170]

The roots of Native Son antipathy toward the Japanese lay deep in the family background of the "Californian," who was long ago seen by Lord Bryce to possess "a consciousness of separate existence" and by Josiah Royce to exhibit "a blind nativism, ... a diseased local exaggeration of our common national feeling towards foreigners." The xenophobia of the white Californian—with its strong debts to the Southern politician and the Pike County plainsman, its frontier conditioning and recurrent activation by waves of "undesirable" immigration—was firmly rooted in the state's tradition. A Japanese observer early in the century remarked that "the native son of California regards himself, and not without reason, as the chosen Son of God, a superior being to whom all foreigners, whether Asiatic or European, should pay homage."[171]

"Official Native Son interest in the [Japanese] problem," according to its Grand Historian, "began in 1907."[172] Before that year, the Order had devoted most of its efforts since its inauguration in 1875 to celebrating the history of pioneer days—although there is evidence that the organization was active in anti-Chinese agitation. In 1907 the Native Sons started publication of a monthly journal, *The Grizzly Bear,* whose chief function over the next generation was presaged by a lead article in the first issue which deplored the fact that "the country is not with us, and the party leaders are not with us in our attitude toward Asiatic immigration." The article set forth in some detail "the dangers to which our white civilization in California is exposed," and concluded with the hope "that the Native Sons of the State may realize their danger, and that they may work together in this new crisis as their elders did when the first Asiatic wave threatened to overwhelm us thirty years ago."[173]

The peril of "peaceful invasion," thus announced, remained for thirty years the dominant theme of Native Sons agitation against the Japanese. And to this primary peril a variety of other dangers came to be appended. A resolution of the Grand Parlor in 1907 demanded prohibition of all Oriental immigration on grounds of "the inability of Orientals to adjust to American wage levels."[174] In the next year the threat of the yellow peril was invoked in its strongest form by a resolution warning that "Japanese attack is imminent."[175] Charges of immorality were brought forth as the Native Sons protested against "the moral hazards little Caucasian girls ran in being forced to recite in the same school room with Japanese boys."[176] In subsequent years—through articles, resolutions, and the political activity of prominent members—the Native Sons conducted a broad campaign of agitation which centered on the twin objectives of Japanese expulsion from the land and exclusion from the country.

As with most exclusionist groups, the activity of the Native Sons reached its peak in the years following World War I. Senator James D. Phelan, a member of Pacific Parlor No. 10, fired the first broadside in the postwar campaign. In a 1919 article in the *Grizzly Bear,* which asserted that Japanese immigration would "produce a mongrel and degenerate population," Phelan gave notice of the formation of an organized movement "to check the evil and to answer the extensive Japanese propaganda."[177] The role of the Native Sons in the planned agitation was indicated by a *Grizzly Bear* editorial a few months later, which climaxed a preparatory series of anti-Japanese articles and cartoons. Under the headline "Would Save California? Then Do Your Duty!" readers were advised that Valentine S. McClatchy, publisher of the Sacramento *Bee,* "deeming it proper that the voice of the Native Sons and Daughters be raised at once in protest to Congress, and that they devise effective means of organization within the state to meet the situation," had addressed letters to various officers of the order calling for action. The editorial concluded: "The *Bee* has put on its war-paint, and sounded the battle-cry. Are we, Native Sons and Native Daughters, going to stand idly by ... or are we going to emulate the Pioneers and save California for Americans? The Japanese menace IS HERE and the time for concerted action is NOW!"[178]

Pursuant to the spadework of McClatchy and Senator Phelan, the 1919 convention of the Native Sons established a Committee on Asiatic Matters which promptly instigated petitions to the governor urging anti-Japanese legislation. In January, 1920, the *Grizzly Bear* pridefully observed that "the latest flood of petitions to flow into the governor's office, beseeching him to call a special session, were set loose by the Order of N.S.G.W."[179] Governor Stephens' refusal to call the legislature into special session evoked the full wrath of the Order, which promptly demanded his impeachment. A *Grizzly Bear* editorial declared that a recall against the governor would be worth all the cost, "for, in addition to smoking out all the pro-Japs in California . . . it will impress upon the yellow-Japs and their white-Jap admirers and hirelings the knowledge that white voters predominate here, and that they are going to see to it that California remains what it has always been and God Himself intended it shall always be—the White Man's Paradise."[180]

Meanwhile, deprived of a special legislative session, the Native Sons reported that "the N.S.G.W. Anti-Japanese Committee of San Francisco" intended to undertake a nationwide campaign on behalf of an initiative amendment to the Alien Land Law.[181] A more significant decision was reached at a conference in San Francisco on March 13, attended by representatives of all major anti-Japanese organizations in the state. The meeting delegated to a committee of six—representing equally the Exclusion League and the Los Angeles County Anti-Asiatic Committee—the task of preparing an initiative measure which, in the words of the *Grizzly Bear,* "will save California from the yellow-Jap peaceful invaders and their white-Jap co-conspirators."[182]

The subsequent passage of the initiative measure, although it represented a personal triumph for the Native Sons, only spurred the Order to greater heights of activity. Together with other groups which had ostensibly based their campaigns on the land issue, the Native Sons next turned their attention to the drive for exclusion. In 1921, the Grand Parlor adopted "a very strong declaration of principles pledging the Order to fight for Japanese exclusion"; and the next year it voted to donate $1,000 per year to the Exclusion League.[183] The charge of peaceful invasion was regularly voiced in the *Grizzly Bear,* a typical editorial exclaiming that the Japanese government had sent women to "live with Japanese men for the sole purpose of breeding . . . children to gain control of this state . . . Unless routed now, within the next fifty years they will have control, if not possession, of California."[184] Years after the enactment of exclusion laws, in fact, the theme of peaceful invasion continued to figure prominently in Native Sons publicity. In 1928, for example, the official journal announced that Japanese in America were "doing their full duty in turning out hordes of citizens of the United States . . . whose hearts, minds and ambitions are linked to the welfare of Japan."[185]

The passage of the 1924 exclusion law, meanwhile, was hailed by the Native Sons as a triumph and a vindication. The president of the organization expressed "unbounded satisfaction" and pointed out that "for years our Order has led in the fight, and when others lost interest, with our voices and our funds we have kept the movement alive."[186] During subsequent years, while other anti-Japanese groups indeed lost interest, the Native Sons continued to keep the movement alive through vocal opposition to dual citizenship, to any relaxation of immigration restrictions, and to statehood for Hawaii (with its "unassimilated" Japanese population).[187]

The complex of motivations behind the agitation of the Native Sons clearly centered on the jealous antiforeignism of a small ingroup within a heterogeneous and rapidly growing population. From the outset the Order restricted its membership to "native-born Californians of the white race." Its references to dark-skinned minority groups were contemptuous and angry; it was even maintained that citizenship for Negroes had been a "grave mistake." Like their fellow patriots of the Legion, the Native Sons were driven in the demonstration of their Americanism to an indiscriminate hostility toward aliens which culminated in the imputation of subversive motives to virtually all the foreign-born—and especially to those who, like the Japanese, were ineligible to citizenship and ipso facto "unassimilable."[188]

Supplementing the antiforeign suspicions of the Native Sons were the political ambitions of individual members and of the Order itself. Almost from the time of the gold rush anti-Oriental sentiment was manipulated by California politicians. After 1900 the most prominent of these campaigners—from labor boss Abe Ruef to banker James Phelan—were Native Sons, and it is not unlikely that, as Carey McWilliams has claimed, "scores of legislators, judges, state officials, Congressmen, and Senators received their initial support and owed their election (or appointment) to public office in California in the years 1907–24 to the Native Sons of the Golden West."[189] The organization itself was not without political design; and in this respect it is instructive to note the parallel between its agitation and that of the California Grange. Founded only a year apart, both groups ended a thirty-year period of comparative tolerance in 1907 with concurrent campaigns for immigration restriction. By 1919 their agitation was openly coördinated through joint membership in the Exclusion League, and together they attained in the twenties a political potency and degree of influence which neither had known before or has since regained.

THE FARMERS

The background.—The first concerted action against the Japanese by organized agricultural interests came in 1920, with the inauguration of parallel campaigns by the California State Grange and the California State Farm Bureau Federation, aimed immediately at the ouster of Japanese from the farmlands of the state and ultimately at their total exclusion. Through intensive propaganda and political action—on local, state, and national levels—the farm organizations exerted pressure at a mounting tempo which was relaxed only after both objectives had been realized: the first through amendment of the alien land act and the second through passage of the Japanese exclusion law.

In order to understand the participation of the farm groups in the anti-Japanese movement, it is necessary first to understand the position of the Japanese in the rural society and economy of California.[190] When the Chinese Exclusion Act was first passed in 1882, there were less than a hundred Japanese in California; but at the turn of the century, it was officially reported that "in the State of California alone there is today a great army of Japanese coolies, numbering upwards of 20,000 . . . scattered about the state, doing work in the orchards, vineyards, gardens and hop and sugar-beet fields."[191] The heavy concentration of the Japanese in agricultural occupations was a result both of the labor needs of the state's expanding farm belt and the peasant background of the immigrants themselves. Immediately after the first federal legislation against the Chinese, efforts had been set in motion to encourage the introduction of Japanese to fill the labor gap. The first Japanese appeared on the farms in the late eighties while the Chinese were still numerous, and during the next decade the two races worked together in the fields and were the mutual victims of anti-Oriental attacks and demonstrations, largely from white farm workers whose fear of unfair competition fastened upon the Japanese a cheap-labor stereotype which was never wholly eradicated.

In the role of farm workers the Japanese incurred the hostility both of white competitors and of small farmers who performed their own labor, and later, through their wage demands and bargaining tactics, they began to alienate the larger agriculturists as well. But it was not until they began to lease land on a significant scale and to set up as independent farmers that anti-Japanese feeling became general throughout rural California. Virtually all sections of the agricultural population opposed the upward movement of the Japanese to the status of owners and entrepreneurs (with the exception of the large-scale landowners and speculators who derived a profit from the lease of marginal properties). The small farmers feared direct competition; the larger interests resented the loss of their primary labor supply.[102] The subsequent growth of anti-Japanese sentiment among the farmers was reflected in the passage of the 1913 Alien Land Law, which forbade the ownership of land by Orientals. To the farmers, many of whom still coveted the Japanese as a source of labor, the act represented a method of eliminating competition and forcing the Japanese back into wage-labor status. Neither objective was, however, attained. Instead of returning the Japanese to the farm labor force, the law had the effect of increasing their number in city trades and occupations. On the other hand, since the act allowed land leases, Japanese farmers continued to thrive as tenants. On the whole the Alien Land Law benefited none of its proponents: the large growers failed to receive the Japanese labor they had anticipated; the smaller farmers found themselves still in apparent competition with Japanese leaseholders; and organized labor, perhaps the chief antagonist, was confronted with new numbers of unemployed Japanese within the cities. The Japanese problem remained unsolved, and the next attempt at solution awaited the appearance of organized agitation in the years following World War I.

The role of the Farm Bureau.—The American Farm Bureau Federation came into being immediately after the war as an amalgamation of various local and state farm bureaus which had arisen to meet the problems of wartime food production.[103] By the time of the first national convention in November, 1919, twelve states had already formed their own federations of county bureaus. Among the most prominent of these was the California State Farm Bureau Federation, which by 1920 had attracted a membership of twenty thousand farmers—largely through its early and shrewd manipulation of the "Japanese Problem." Curiously, the role of the Farm Bureau has escaped notice in earlier studies of anti-Japanese agitation; but the bureau made no secret of its hostility and its aims, and in fact provided a major contribution toward the success of the exclusion movement.

The first step in the campaign took the form of agitation by local farm centers. As early as December, 1919, the Magnolia-Mulberry Farm Center of Imperial Valley passed resolutions calling for the total exclusion of Japanese, Hindus, and Mohammedans. In a letter to Governor Stephens, a spokesman for the group warned that "if something is not done in the way of legislation to bar these races, it will be only a comparatively short time until they have crowded out the white race from the most fertile parts of California."[104] A month later the Los Angeles

Times reported that anti-Japanese activity in the valley "has suddenly received fresh impetus and a movement for some action against the Japanese is growing rapidly in all parts of the Valley." Observing that the campaign was being conducted under the auspices of the Imperial County Farm Bureau, the paper listed a series of anti-Japanese resolutions on the part of local farm centers and concluded that the valley was "awakening to the seriousness of the situation."[105] At the same time the guiding hand of the Farm Bureau was displayed in another part of the state with the formation of the Merced County Anti-Japanese Association, organized "first to handle the situation locally; second to cooperate in the anti-Japanese campaign all over the state."[106]

The next move was a sweeping anti-Japanese resolution drawn up by the Japanese Problem Committee of the Los Angeles County Farm Bureau, seconded by six other southern county bureaus, and adopted by the State Federation on February 23, 1920. Constituting the first official statement of Farm Bureau policy toward the Japanese, the resolution enumerated a set of accusations and demands which were to be heard repeatedly over the next four years. Japanese exclusion was demanded both on grounds of racial incompatibility and of economic competition, and the initial goal of the movement was revealed in demands for removal of Japanese rights "to lease, rent or own agricultural lands, or own any lands whatsoever," as well as for a constitutional amendment disqualifying American-born Japanese from citizenship (thus preventing their acquisition of land titles). The resolution also extended its opposition to the immigration of all Orientals, but added significantly that "this statement is not to be construed as not favoring bonded labor."[107]

It is notable that the argument of the Farm Bureau was directed not at cheap labor—as was that of the unions—but at "cheap farmers." The expressed approval of bonded Oriental labor (workers imported under temporary contract) made clear that the Japanese remained desirable as wage laborers; the opposition of the Farm Bureau arose only when they entered the agricultural field as tenants and independent operators.[108] This ambivalent attitude resulted from the peculiar demands of a membership consisting for the most part of small-scale farmers who worked their own land but required extra labor at seasonal peak-load intervals. The large-scale corporation agriculturalist, interested primarily in the maintenance of a cheap and steady labor force, generally favored the Japanese as workers and had little fear of their competitive operations as independent farmers. But the majority of California farmers (and Farm Bureau members) fell into two less prosperous categories, both vigorously opposed to Japanese encroachment on the land: (1) the farmer who did all his own work and whose product came into competition with that of other farmers who could undersell him if their labor was worth less, and (2) the working farmer who was a part-time employer, and therefore interested in hiring cheap and efficient labor.[199]

The immediate goal of Farm Bureau agitation was attained in 1920 when the voters of California approved the initiative amendment to the Alien Land Law prohibiting leasing as well as ownership of land by Orientals. Credit for the victory was quickly claimed by farmers and their organizations, one spokesman declaring that "this legislation is a farmer's movement. . . . There was practically no division of opinion among country people who have to compete with the Japs."[200] Although this claim was an exaggeration, it is clear that by 1920 opposition to the Japanese had spread to most sections of the population and was especially intense among rural residents in areas of Japanese concentration.[201] The mounting hostility was reflected in outbreaks of violence in agricultural regions. In the summer of 1921, fifty-eight Japanese in the Turlock melon fields were rounded up by a group of several hundred white men and deported from the area. (Later reports set the number of Japanese ousted as high as seven hundred.)[202] In the same period, attempts were made to burn down the homes of rural Japanese, while numbers were driven from Merced, Hopland, and other agricultural communities of the state.[203]

The California Farm Bureau, however, together with other agitating groups, was not content with driving the Japanese from the land. The ultimate purpose of the bureau's campaign was, as a spokesman testified in 1920, "exclusion of Japanese—absolute exclusion."[204] In a referendum conducted the same year among local bureaus of the federation, some twenty thousand members, representing more than thirty counties, returned a vote of confidence in the program opposing Japanese immigration, ownership and lease of land by Orientals, introduction of "picture brides," and the like: "and on every one of those questions the vote was from 7 to 1 to 24 to 1 against the Japanese."[205]

The attitude of the California Farm Bureau on Japanese immigration undoubtedly played a part in the subsequent stand of the national organization in favor of general restriction of immigration, which was formulated in the 1923 convention. During the congressional hearings which led to the passage of the Japanese exclusion law, the viewpoint of the Farm Bureau was also closely reflected in the testimony of V. S. McClatchy, secretary of the California Joint Immigration Committee. Invoking the 1920 plebiscite of local farm bureaus, McClatchy reiterated

the charges publicized for four years by the state federation and concluded that "there is not any farmer who knows his business who is in
favor of Japanese immigration, or who has as a rule the opportunity to
use Japanese labor."[206]

The campaign of the Farm Bureau was virtually completed with the
achievement of Japanese exclusion. Thereafter, although the organization never abandoned its attitude, both the scope and intensity of its
propaganda steadily declined. In helping to bring about the passage of
the federal law, the bureau had fulfilled its announced purpose; and
the agitation had served another and perhaps equally important purpose, that of building membership and attracting favorable attention
to the bureau in the critical first years of its existence. The action of
the California Farm Bureau, like that of most participants in the anti-
Japanese movement, was determined by political as well as economic
considerations. "With the exception of a few groups," as Dr. John
Rademaker concluded in a limited survey, "the struggle was academic
to all factions supporting the acts. The benefits these groups derived
from the acts were not dependent upon the actual presence or absence
of the Japanese farmers, but rather upon the process of opposing
them."[207]

The Grange revival.—Like the concurrent campaign waged by the
Farm Bureau, the anti-Japanese agitation of the California State Grange
(and subsequently of the parent National Grange) was brief, intensive,
and markedly successful. Begun in 1919, it survived barely more than
a decade, reaching its peak in 1924 and falling off rapidly thereafter.
Like the Farm Bureau, the Grange was largely motivated by political
considerations; the politics of prejudice served to breathe new life into
an organization grown heavily senescent, and to bring about a temporary revival of the old-time Grange reputation as a militant champion
of the farmer. Unlike the Farm Bureau, however, the Grange in 1919
already had a considerable history of opposition to aliens and their
immigration. The anti-Japanese sentiment of California farmers was
readily incorporated within the larger framework of Grange agitation
for restricted immigration, and enjoyed the added advantage of a trained
and systematic pressure organization developed over generations.[208]

Grange opposition to alien land holdings first became active in 1907,
when a resolution was passed in the national convention stating that
"no alien shall be allowed to hold title to lands in the United States
before declaring his intention of becoming a citizen"[209]—a stipulation
which effectually barred all those who, like the Orientals, were ineligible
to citizenship. "From that day to this," said a Grange spokesman in

1924, "I think in every session of the National Grange some sort of resolution has been adopted dealing with the immigration question in its
various relations."[210] However, proceedings of the national conventions
show this to be an exaggeration; before 1920 only a few scattered resolutions appeared, all on the order of a 1914 statement resolving to "protect our present citizenship from those of other countries whose mode
of living, ideals and beliefs are inimical to those which have made us
great."[211] With the possible exception of the 1907 resolution, none of this
activity appears to have been directed at the Japanese. But in 1920,
thanks to the California chapter, the vagueness of Grange resolutions
was abruptly ended.

The actual decision involving the California Grange in the anti-
Japanese movement was first made in 1919. In that year the Grange
joined with other interested groups in establishing the Japanese Exclusion League (subsequently the California Joint Immigration Committee)—a revival of the old Asiatic Exclusion League which had become
inactive during the war. Representing the Grange in the league was its
Worthy State Master George R. Harrison, who was to become the author of the majority of immigration resolutions passed by the National
Grange.

By 1920 the Grange campaign, in close coördination with those of
the patriots and the labor leaders, was well under way. The first move
was a resolution passed by the local Elk Grove Grange of California,
making appeal, "as of a strangling man for breath, to all the State
Granges, and through them to every Pomona Grange and subordinate
Grange in the United States, to grapple with this problem, and by
State, but more particularly by National legislation to save the Pacific
Coast to Americans."[212] Coinciding with this action was a similar pronouncement by the Sonoma County Pomona Grange, which called for
"the widest publicity to the dangers to farming interests on the Pacific
Coast and to American civilization, from Japanese immigration, and to
aid in all ways possible the formation and passage of legislation restrict-
ing said immigration."[213] Both the Elk Grove and Sonoma resolutions
were immediately adopted by the state Grange, and the Sonoma wording was approved a few months later by the national convention.

The agitation of the Grange was rewarded in November of 1920 with
the passage of the initiative amendment to the Alien Land Law. But
in 1922 the campaign was renewed with greater vigor than ever. Declaring that "state laws have proved utterly inadequate in solution of
our 'Japanese Problems,'" the California State Grange pressed through
the national convention a strongly worded resolution which urged that

"the time be grasped as one most unusually opportune" to the passage of all-out exclusion legislation. The convention urged its membership to "advise every member of the U.S. Senate and the President of the United States of the intense feeling of our people of the West in this matter, so absolutely vital to Christian civilization and the white races of our country."[214]

As this wording suggests, the anti-Japanese action of the Grange was not limited to convention resolutions. After the formation of the farm bloc in 1921, the Grange was at the center of one of the most powerful pressure groups in the nation's capital. Through its Washington representative, Dr. Thomas C. Atkeson, the organization lobbied vigorously, concentrating especially on representatives of the farm belt. Meanwhile on the West Coast the operations of the Joint Immigration Committee drew wide attention to the demands and grievances of the California Grange. In the congressional hearings which preceded passage of the 1924 exclusion law, the Grange was doubly represented. The attitude of the state organization was reflected in the testimony of JIC Director McClatchy; the National Grange was directly represented by Dr. Atkeson, who told Congress that "on this particular subject [immigration] there has been no great diversity of opinion on the part of our membership, and that membership comprises approximately a million people, inhabitants of the open country."[215]

After passage of the law, Grange agitation against the Japanese gradually subsided. For a few years the national conventions continued to pass resolutions submitted by California's delegates, opposing "any reopening or changing of the 'Ineligible Alien' clause in the Federal Immigration Law";[216] but by 1928 the "Japanese Question" was merely referred to committee, and in the mid-thirties the state Grange withdrew its name from the letterhead of the Joint Immigration Committee.

At least three factors appear to have motivated the Grange in its participation in the exclusionist agitation of the twenties. First and most obvious was the competitive fear of Japanese expansion in agriculture, which was loudly proclaimed in all resolutions on the subject. Although Grange concern over the "awful facts" of Japanese penetration was seldom accompanied by documentation, the local ventures of Japanese farmers in such areas as Florin and Livingstone provided at least the spark from which apprehensions born of prejudice and propaganda could be ignited. Thus the second factor, operating in close conjunction with the fear of economic competition, was social and psychological: the hostility of the dominant white ingroup in rural communities toward a visibly "colored" and upwardly mobile minority—a resentment fanned by two decades of agitation on the part of politicians and labor leaders, further stimulated by agricultural depression following World War I, and rationalized through the advances of the Japanese in competitive farming. The third factor was the exploitation of rural sentiment by the Grange for purposes of consolidation and expansion. Between 1915 and 1920 the membership of the National Grange had decreased 100,000; but during the next five years, the period of active agitation against the Japanese, the membership increased nearly 150,000.[217] Doubtless many factors shared the responsibility for this Grange revival; but it is undeniable that the "Japanese Question" furnished the Grange (as it did the Farm Bureau and the patriots) with a convenient rallying-cry with which to arouse emotions of patriotism and prejudice for purposes of its own promotion.

The Businessmen: A House Divided

Throughout the fifty years of anti-Japanese agitation on the Pacific Coast, the attitude of business interests was sharply and consistently divided. On the one hand "big business" groups—bankers, large manufacturers and landowners, chambers of commerce, and agricultural corporations—either were active in defense of the Japanese or remained conspicuously absent from the campaigns against them. On the other hand most of the elements of "small business"—such as shopkeepers and tradesmen, local real estate agents and boards of trade—were vocal in their opposition to the Japanese wherever the latter gave the appearance of competition and conflict.[218]

Small business.—The first evidence of hostility on the part of small commercial interests arose in predominantly agricultural areas of California where Japanese settlement was heaviest, and was closely related to the mounting opposition of small-scale farmers to Japanese advances on the land. In its 1911 report, the Immigration Commission noted "an important indication of popular sentiment in regard to the Japanese . . . in the expressions of boards of trade through their officers," of whom a great majority were said to be strongly opposed to further Japanese immigration.[219] The report suggested that considerations of property value and social status were major factors in the opposition: "One almost universal objection made to the Japanese by the representatives of these organizations was that their presence, and especially the lease and ownership of the land by them, prevented the migration of desirable white families to the district." To some extent these charges were doubtless a rationalization of economic motives; at any rate in the 1920 immigration hearings the president of one California board of trade based his testimony for Japanese exclusion mainly on grounds of unfair competition. Various California realtors also were outspoken on behalf of alien land restriction, repeating the familiar claim that Japanese ownership reduced land values and caused the withdrawal of white residents.[220]

In the cities, meanwhile, the opposition of small business assumed a directly competitive aspect, as the Japanese graduated in increasing numbers from the status of wage laborers to that of entrepreneurs and independent proprietors. As early as 1907, the Exclusion League had successfully organized a boycott of Japanese concerns by the small businessmen of San Francisco.[221] By 1914, according to H. T. Millis, considerable feeling had developed against the Japanese among similar groups in Los Angeles: "One rather frequently hears the remark that 'the Japanese are all right as farmers and laborers, but they are not satisfied with that. They crowd into and compete for business.' "[222]

Commercial opposition in the cities was generally conditioned by the extent of Japanese competition and thus occurred chiefly in areas where their advances were conspicuous. One such area was Seattle, where the success of Japanese groceries resulted in organized opposition from white competitors led by the Retail Grocer's Association.[223] The campaign soon gained adherents from other fields of business. An appeal was published by the Seattle *Trade Register* for a petition to Congress and the President urging legislation "to prevent all members of colored races, except American Indians and negroes born in the United States, from becoming citizens of this country or engaging in business in any capacity in the United States in competition with a citizen of this country." The wide support anticipated for this move was indicated by the suggestion of the *Trade Register* that petitions "be placed upon the counters of all merchants in the Pacific Coast and Rocky Mountain states who are materially affected by the competition involved, and with their cooperation ... it ought not to be difficult to obtain enough signatures to secure the desired federal action."[224]

The agitation of small business interests in the West Coast states was strikingly paralleled some years later in the western provinces of Canada, where it was reported that opposition to the Japanese had arisen among small commercial interests owing principally to the fact that "the Japanese are moving out of certain industries as labour and are becoming a proprietary group for both voluntary and compulsory reasons." The organization of Canadian commercial interests against the Japanese was much the same as that of corresponding American groups: "The White Canada Association in British Columbia, the most dogged

antagonist of the Japanese, has on its Executive Committee ... members
of the Retailers' Association, the Fishermen's Protective Association, the
Cloverdale Farmers' Association, and a farm engineer and dealer in
rural real estate."[225]

This similarity in the activity of commercial interests in Canada and
the United States supports the conclusion of the authors of the report
that "White Americans and White Canadians in similar groups react
in the same manner to the Japanese in the measure in which their
economic and social status in the community is affected by them."[226] The
opposition of small business on the West Coast arose during the second
stage of what R. D. McKenzie has called the occupational cycle followed by Oriental immigrants; when, freed from the initial status of
wage labor in city and farm, the immigrants moved toward economic
independence and higher status.[227] Moreover, the competitive factor was
supplemented by the social disequilibrium involved in the upward
movement of Japanese farmers and entrepreneurs, which evoked from
the established white community a resentment compounded equally
of class and racial prejudice.

The agitation set in motion by small businessmen declined rapidly
after the passage of exclusion and alien land legislation, which largely
removed the threat of future competitive advances by the Japanese.
But the old charges of unequal competition, and the social antagonism
which accompanied them, were never wholly forgotten; and with the
advent of the depression they began to be noted with increasing frequency. Measures to ban the Japanese from agriculture appeared in
the California legislature in 1935 and 1937, and Japanese competition
was blamed by the Hearst press for "retarding economic recovery."[228]
The widespread job discrimination and restrictive rental practices directed against the Japanese during this period—which helped prevent
the social and economic integration of the Nisei—furnished additional
testimony to the continuing survival of anti-Japanese prejudice among
large numbers of the entrepreneurial middle class.

Big business.—In contrast to the hostile attitude of small commercial
interests, the organs and agencies of big business—on the Pacific Coast
as in the East—were on record from the beginning in opposition to the
anti-Japanese agitation, and consistently pressed for moderation in dealing with the immigration problem. The motives of these groups were
by no means wholly altruistic: the urban chambers of commerce, for
example, clearly reflected the opinion of industrial interests seeking
favorable trade relations with Japan, and the large-scale landowners

and agriculturists admittedly favored Japanese immigration because it provided them with cheap labor.[229]

As early as 1905 the Los Angeles Chamber of Commerce openly condemned the anti-Japanese agitation of the San Francisco press; and by the next year other commercial interests, such as the Merchants' and Manufacturers' Association of Los Angeles, were similarly on record.[230] During the San Francisco school incident, major business groups were outspoken in opposition to the segregation of Japanese students. Urban chambers of commerce especially denounced the agitation; the Los Angeles chamber, for example, sent a telegram to President Roosevelt asserting that public opinion was strongly opposed to discrimination against the Japanese in the schools.[231] Large business interests in other parts of the country also joined in the protest. Eastern financial concerns were said by the New York *Commercial* to be against the agitation, and in neighboring areas such as Colorado big-business sentiment echoed that of the Los Angeles chamber.[232]

Through the next years, as the exclusion movement grew in organized strength and anti-Japanese bills flooded the California legislature, big business held to its attitude of disapproval. During the 1909 legislative session, which followed the negotiation of the Gentlemen's Agreement, various chambers of commerce and merchants' associations opposed restrictive immigration measures on the ground that the issue had been satisfactorily solved. Direct steps were taken by some groups to offset the international ill-feeling engendered by the agitation. "The Chamber of Commerce in Seattle," wrote H. H. Gowen in 1909, "has taken an active interest in promoting good feeling between the merchants of Japan and those of the state, sending and receiving delegations with accompaniments of the highest courtesy."[233]

In the large-scale revival of anti-Japanese agitation which followed World War I, the representatives of big business were more than ever isolated in their efforts to mitigate the prejudice and prevent discriminatory legislation. Then as earlier, the primary concern of industrial and financial interests was the maintenance of satisfactory trade relations with Japan. Thus an editorial of the *Business Chronicle of the Pacific Northwest* warned in 1919:

Somewhere within Seattle—or is it from without?—an as yet unidentified influence is raising a hue and cry against the Japanese.

It is not good business practice to slap one's best customer in the face, nor is it good form to slam the door when friendly neighbors call. . . .

Seattle was chosen as the terminus of the great Japanese steamship lines, and it is the simple truth to state that Seattle has become great as a world port because the Japanese have in large measure made it such.[234]

The pro-Japanese attitude of Washington businessmen was closely paralleled in Oregon. In 1920 a special report to the Oregon governor observed that "among merchants, bankers and conservative business men, there is a strong spirit of toleration towards the Japanese."[235]

In the interest of forestalling hostile legislative action against resident Japanese a number of committees and missions, under the sponsorship of business groups, were exchanged between Japan and America in the postwar years. One of the most prominent of these was the Japanese American Relations Committee of the San Francisco Chamber of Commerce, which over a period of years maintained contact with a similar committee in Japan. As described by an official of the chamber, the underlying thesis was that "the proper solution to the [immigration] situation is an arrangement by friendly means through diplomatic exchanges, and agreement by treaty or otherwise which will effectively restrict further immigration ... [and] secure just and even generous treatment for Japanese now lawfully in this country."[236]

Big-business opposition to the movement for exclusion was especially pronounced during the congressional hearings which preceded passage of the 1924 immigration act. More than fifty industrial and manufacturing concerns throughout the country sent messages to Washington in protest against the legislation; while the California Committee of Justice (sponsored by the State Chamber of Commerce) and "a long list of prominent citizens—churchmen, editors, businessmen, bankers and farmers—sent a pro-Japanese brief to counteract the anti-Japanese agitation."[237] From a broad survey of press and public opinion, Eleanor Tupper and George E. McReynolds concluded that "business interests both in the Orient and in this country were opposed to the exclusion provision because of its injurious effect on American trade."[238]

The passage of the exclusion law called forth wide protests from groups representative of big business, and efforts were soon initiated for its repeal or modification (via the quota system). The California Council on Oriental Relations, associated with the State Chamber of Commerce, declared in 1931 that "many businessmen engaged in foreign trade believe that our trade with the Orient, and with Japan in particular, has suffered through the passage of this discriminatory law."[239] A similar sentiment was expressed in a report of the Immigration Committee of the United States Chamber of Commerce, which observed that "mutual good will has suffered and will continue to suffer from our action in placing a so-called 'exclusion clause' in our 1924 quota law."[240] The report drew wide and favorable publicity from the Eastern press, one New York paper declaring that "it is high time for repeal. Congress should heed the opinion of American business as expressed in the attitude of our national Chamber of Commerce."[241]

The efforts of the chambers of commerce and affiliated business organizations to modify the exclusion law, however, came to nothing; and upon the resurgence of Japanese militarism in the thirties, the campaign for modification was largely abandoned. In line with the general decline of interest by organized groups in the Japanese issue the organs and agencies of big business became apathetic and remained silent until the declaration of war against Japan.

THE STATE OF MIND: SUMMARY AND ESTIMATE

The first substantial signs of anti-Japanese sentiment on the Pacific Coast appeared at the turn of the century with the agitation of San Francisco labor unions, climaxed by the 1900 mass meeting protesting Japanese immigration. Prior to the rally *Organized Labor* exclaimed: "Our warning has been heeded. . . . Prominent citizens and leading merchants have sustained our contentions, and two of the great morning dailies have taken up the fight."[242] But early anti-Japanese opinion was limited largely to the working class; with major emphasis placed on economic competition, the ordinary laborer was both the target of the agitation and the primary source of its support.

The second phase of the anti-Japanese movement, however, coinciding with the close of the Russo-Japanese War, gained wider public support and reached for the first time into all classes of the population. Public opinion throughout the country was turned against Japan by cleverly constructed pro-Russian propaganda, by her unexpected victory, and by the subsequent spate of war rumors.[243] In the grip of "yellow peril" fear, the nation generally and the West Coast in particular developed an attitude of suspicion and apprehension which was effectively exploited by the agitators for exclusion.

The charges of "peaceful invasion" and cheap-labor competition remained vital factors in the agitation, and it is probable that, as Professor Reynolds has concluded, "the reiteration of the charge in the daily news convinced large numbers of Californians of its truth."[244] The growth of public prejudice over subsequent years owed much to this stereotype of the "coolie," and at least one historian has concluded that the race prejudice behind the school segregation incident of 1906 was due to "the belief that coolie labor was thwarting the work of the unions and lowering the American standard of living."[245] The existence of the prejudice was openly, and even proudly, admitted during the school controversy by San Francisco newspapers; the *Chronicle* confessed that "our race feeling has shown itself," while the *Call* announced that "we are unwilling that our children should meet Asiatics in intimate association. That is 'race prejudice' and we stand by it."[246]

Outside of San Francisco, however, public opinion in the first years of the century was less uniform. The Fresno *Republican* considered that "the majority of thoughtful people of California are not in sympathy with the agitation of the cities against the Japanese," and the Los Angeles *Times* openly defied the exclusionists by inviting Oriental immigration for farm labor.[247] According to President David Starr Jordan of Stanford, the population of the state in 1907 was "by no means a unit on the question of the immigration of Japanese laborers. . . . Outside of San Francisco and the labor unions, it is not clear that a majority of the people are opposed to the free admission of Japanese laborers or even of Chinese."[248] Besides the large-scale businessmen and agriculturists, who were outspokenly pro-Japanese, religious and educational leaders in California generally deplored the agitation. Elsewhere in the country, with the exception of the Deep South, what opinion was expressed was also strongly opposed to the anti-Japanese activity; Eastern journals in particular were bitter in their denunciation of the West Coast performance. Only in the South were political and commercial interests predominantly sympathetic toward California's racial discrimination.[249]

Public sentiment against the Japanese was quickened in California by a statement of President Roosevelt in December, 1906, which deplored the "unworthy feeling" of West Coast agitators and condemned the school board action as a "wicked absurdity."[250] This comment aroused a storm of protest throughout the state and led to new acts of discrimination against the Japanese. A month later the *Literary Digest,* in a canvass of fifty leading West Coast papers, found only three expressing pro-Japanese views. Although this finding was subsequently challenged,[251] there is little reason to question the conclusion of the *Digest* that "most of the coast papers display an uncompromising antipathy against Japanese aggression and competition, against the President, and against Secretary [of Labor and Commerce] Metcalf."[252]

The unfavorable reaction was not limited to California; in Seattle early in 1907 an anti-coolie petition reportedly drew 10,000 signatures, and there were various incidents such as the hissing of the Japanese flag in Seattle theaters. On the basis of a study of these actions and of inflammatory speeches of various congressmen, Professor Bailey concluded that "a strong movement for exclusion, to which Roosevelt's indictment had contributed powerfully, was now underway on the Pacific Coast. Whatever the views of this region had been before . . . there is no mistaking the fact that opinion, so far as it was expressed publicly, was now preponderantly anti-Japanese."[253]

The difficulty in gauging opinion through its public expressions, however, is that indifference rarely breaks into print. The groups most excited about the Japanese issue were those agitating for exclusion, and even where such groups were in the minority it was natural that their opinion should weigh heavily on the record. This seems especially to have been true in the Pacific Northwest; for despite the occasional incidents noted above, a University of Washington professor could maintain in 1909 that "whatever may be the temperature in [California] there is no hot blood, at the moment of writing, in Washington."[254] The Seattle *Post-Intelligencer* similarly declared that "so far as the vast majority of the men and women of this state are concerned, there is no hatred of the Japanese, no prejudice against the race, and no unkindly feeling for members of the race who reside in this commonwealth."[255] In Oregon as well, the public appears to have been largely indifferent to the Japanese. "At no time," wrote one observer in 1909, "has public feeling in Oregon run so strong against the Oriental as in the communities to the north and south. Except once or twice, when stirred by sympathy with what was happening among her neighbors, Oregon can hardly be said even to have had a consciousness of the problem."[256] Twenty years later, following an intensive study, Marjorie E. Stearns concluded that over the years "relations between Japanese and white residents in Oregon have been remarkably friendly."[257]

But if the claim of widespread anti-Japanese feeling could be questioned in the northwest states, in California it found ample support. In 1909 Homer Lea classified public opinion in the state as "8 percent pro-Japanese; 22 percent indifferent; 30 percent hostile; and 40 percent belligerently hostile."[258] In the same year the editor of the San Francisco *Chronicle* reported that "the opposition is very general, and there is not the slightest doubt that if a vote on exclusion were taken it would . . . be nearly as unanimous as the case against Chinese immigration in 1879."[259] Neither of these observers, however, could be considered unbiased, and the absence of impartial surveys during this period renders the assessment of public opinion necessarily speculative and impressionistic. Nevertheless it seems clear that by 1910 anti-Japanese feeling had reached a peak which was only exceeded during the agitation following World War I. The majority of newspapers in the state, led by the metropolitan journals and in particular by the Hearst press, were ranged against the Japanese; all three political parties (Socialist, Democratic, and Republican) had anti-Japanese planks in their platforms, and politicians generally were loud in deprecating the "coolie" and the "yellow peril." The device of the mass meeting had proved popular in various cities, while the Asiatic Exclusion League boasted a membership of more than 110,000 persons and 238 affiliated groups.[260]

After 1910, active feeling against the Japanese may have waned somewhat in the cities, but the decline was counterbalanced by rising opposition from farmers and other rural residents. The upward movement of the Japanese in agriculture during this period was viewed with alarm by virtually all sections of the rural population: the small farmers feared direct competition and the larger operators were antagonized by the "desertion" of their primary source of labor.[261] The influence of these interests was felt in the passage of the California Alien Land Law in 1913, although it was not until the twenties that rural antipathy came fully of age.

During World War I public opinion in California was decidedly less hostile to the Japanese. Among the factors contributing to better feeling were the Panama-Pacific Exposition of 1915, which displayed lavish Japanese exhibits, the wartime participation of Japan on the Allied side, and the general decline of immigration pursuant to the Gentlemen's Agreement. Newspapers and magazines of the period were strongly opposed to any renewal of agitation. Thus *Sunset* magazine maintained that "the number of Japanese in California is decreasing; Japan is faithfully observing its part of the Gentleman's Agreement."[262] Even anti-Japanese Governor Hiram Johnson was induced in 1915 to oppose any amendment to the land law, and he was promptly assured by the Oakland *Enquirer* that his action would "meet with the approval of all voters of California save that small element of organized agitation, which is wholly insignificant."[263] The approval of "thoughtful" voters, at least, was promised by a statement issued by the presidents and deans of several southern California colleges, which denied the existence of any "international ill-will" and affirmed that friendship for the Japanese" is firmly established among the thoughtful people of our coast."[264] In a report on Japanese-American relations made immediately after the war, Sidney Gulick pointed to "the hopeful situation" after 1914 and concluded that "hostility was distinctly ebbing during the war."[265]

The wartime ebb was, however, more than matched by the tidal wave of agitation and antipathy which commenced in 1919 and continued to rise until the passage of exclusion legislation five years later. The postwar anti-Japanese campaign, as we have seen, was conducted jointly by organized labor, agricultural groups, patriotic societies, and political organizations, and unquestionably achieved broader public support than ever before. Popular opinion was also turned against the Japanese by the aggressive military actions of Japan, notably the brutal suppression of the Korean rebellion in 1919; and it is reasonable to suppose that, as Professor Strong has suggested, "many citizens voted against Japanese interests because of antagonism from one or more such events."[206] Public attitudes were analyzed in 1920 by a number of prominent educators and businessmen interviewed by Tasuku Harada. Although some believed that hostility was still largely limited to labor and agricultural circles, the majority agreed with H. T. Millis, a long-time student of the problem, that "anti-Japanese feeling has been pretty general for some years in all classes of California other than the larger merchants, bankers, and professional men."[207] A similar conclusion was subsequently reported by a member of the Pacific Coast Race Relations Survey, which carried out an extensive field investigation in the early twenties:

It was soon apparent even to a newcomer on the Pacific Coast what groups were pro and what groups were anti-Oriental, and why this was so. The politician, legionnaire, native son, workingman, small farmer, shopkeeper were usually against the Oriental, or, at least, opposed to the Japanese. On the other hand, the president of the chamber of commerce, financier and banker, importer and exporter, absentee landowner, large rancher, mission secretary and church worker, social worker and many schoolteachers and university professors were friendly to the Asiatic.[208]

After 1924, having attained its major objectives of excluding the Japanese and removing their right to hold land, the united front of organized agitation—led by labor, farm groups, patriots, and politicians—rapidly disintegrated. During the late twenties most of the traditionally anti-Japanese organizations were content merely to pass resolutions reaffirming their hostility, and by 1930 even these had begun to disappear. Newspapers largely turned their attention elsewhere, and in the movies the Japanese, while still subservient, were no longer uniformly subversive. With the decline of active propaganda it was natural that public opinion should be less hostile, and the scarcity of anti-Japanese incidents prior to the Manchurian war suggests that this was indeed true.

But the new mood of passive toleration was not a sign of social acceptance. Studies of popular attitudes on the West Coast in the late twenties and early thirties show clearly that the stereotype established through three decades was firmly embedded in the public consciousness and no longer dependent for its existence upon the prodding of "pressure groups."[209] One group asked to describe the principal traits of the Japanese reported these most frequently as "sneakiness" and "intelligence"; in another study the great majority of respondents described the Japanese as "dishonest, tricky, treacherous," and accused them of being "ruinous, hard or unfair competitors." According to the author of the latter survey, the answers closely resembled "the stereotyped charges made . . . during the anti-Japanese agitation of the Alien Land Law campaign."[270] The response also recalled, in its emphasis on trickery and treachery, the nineteenth-century outcry against the Chinese.

The aggressive actions of Japan after 1931 revived in the minds of many West Coast citizens the oft-heard charges of the disloyalty and treachery of Japanese Americans. An additional stimulus of unmeasured strength was the great depression with its consequent insecurity and frustration. Earlier outbreaks of anti-Oriental feeling in California had also coincided with depressions: notably in the seventies when Dennis Kearney rallied his unemployed sandlotters around the Chinese issue, again in the nineties when white workers were driven from inactive industries into farm-labor competition with Orientals,[271] and once more in the early twenties when anti-Japanese agitation reached its climax. The age of the great depression was a time of troubles for various minority groups, as leagues of frightened men sought panaceas and scapegoats. With the brutalities of Japanese imperialism regularly noted in the headlines, the resident Japanese furnished a convenient and conspicuous target. As early as 1934 the California Council on Oriental Relations, formed only three years before to aid the Japanese, was compelled to disband in the face of growing opposition; and by 1938 the moving-picture industry reluctantly abandoned its once-profitable Mr. Moto series because "anti-Japanese feeling is running so high in America."

By the end of the depression decade, the Genesis of the Japanese stereotype was complete, and the stage was set for the Exodus—upon which the curtain rose on December 7, 1941.

Chapter II

THE ACTIVATION OF THE STEREOTYPE

Half a century of agitation and antipathy directed against Japanese Americans, following almost fifty years of anti-Chinese and antiforeign activity, had by 1941 diffused among the West Coast population a rigidly stereotyped set of attitudes toward Orientals which centered on suspicion and distrust. This hostility reached maturity in the early twenties with the passage of the Alien Land Law and the Oriental Exclusion Act, and although thereafter it became relatively inactive it was kept alive during the thirties by the stimuli of Japanese aggression and economic depression. In the weeks and months following the attack upon Pearl Harbor the traditional charges were widely revived and the stereotype recalled in detail; public attitudes toward the Japanese minority soon crystallized around the well-worn themes of treachery and disloyalty, and expressions of opinion came more and more to be characterized by suspicion, fear, and anger.

The Japanese stereotype was not created at Pearl Harbor; the basic ingredients had been mixed years before. But the enemy bombs of December 7 exploded the mixture on a vaster scale and with more far-reaching consequences than ever in the past. The rumors that emerged from Pearl Harbor gave new sustenance to racist belief in the yellow peril, to romantic movie-fed ideas of the treacherous and inscrutable Asiatic, to undefined feelings of hostility and distrust compounded of the xenophobia of superpatriots and the rationalizations of competitors. Once revitalized by enemy bombs, however, the Japanese stereotype had no need to depend upon the myth of sabotage at Pearl Harbor. Long after the rumors had been disproved, by repeated refutations from the highest authorities, the stereotype remained and Americans along the western slope and far inland were more suspicious, fearful, and angry than ever before. The very absence of anything resembling subversive activity by resident Japanese was seized upon as "disturbing and confirming" evidence that an "invisible deadline" of disaster was approaching. As weeks passed, the superstructure of rationalizations and defenses built upon this foundation grew more insensibly elaborate.

DECEMBER: WAR AND RUMORS OF WAR

The Japanese attack on Pearl Harbor came as a profound shock, if not a complete surprise, to residents of the Pacific Coast states. Although for many years most citizens had been aware that war was a possibility, many refused to believe the first reports from Honolulu and were convinced only by repeated broadcasts and ubiquitous black headlines. But the full import of the news soon became apparent as all service personnel was ordered to report to stations, as jeeps and convoys in war regalia appeared on the streets, and military aircraft began to roar overhead. By midafternoon of December 7, 1941, thousands of citizens were rushing to recruiting stations to enlist or offering their services in any capacity.

Before they could recover from the initial shock, West Coast residents were confronted with more bad news. Coincident with the Pearl Harbor attack enemy forces had struck with disastrous effect at Hong Kong, Manila, Thailand, Singapore, Midway, Wake, and Guam. Japanese bombers had at a single blow destroyed the air defenses of Hong Kong, and within a few days occupied Kowloon peninsula and placed the British crown colony in jeopardy. On December 10 the "impregnable" British warships *Repulse* and *Prince of Wales* were sunk by Japanese planes, thus upsetting the balance of naval power in the far Pacific. The little kingdom of Thailand had surrendered on December 8, and the enemy began a swift southward movement through the British Malay States toward Singapore. Other Japanese troops landed in the Philippines on December 10 and were converging on Manila. Guam was captured on December 11, the fate of Wake Island appeared sealed (it fell on December 23), and Midway was imperiled by an enemy task force. Meanwhile, dispatches which had filtered through censorship suggested that American losses at Pearl Harbor were far worse than at first indicated. It was freely predicted that Alaska and the Pacific Coast itself were next in line for Japanese attack and even attempted invasion.

People everywhere were frightened, and their fear was heightened by a feeling of helplessness. The threat of bombings and invasion, plus the absence of precise information as to events in Hawaii, quickly bred rumors of total disaster. It was whispered that the entire Pacific fleet had been destroyed; that every reinforcing ship sent out from the mainland had been sunk off the coast by Japanese submarines.

Almost at once rumors about the resident Japanese began. Japanese gardeners were said to be equipped with short-wave transmitters hidden in garden hose; Japanese servants and laborers who failed to appear for work on December 7 (a Sunday) were accused of prior knowledge of the Hawaii attack. Japanese farmers were charged with smuggling poison into vegetables bound for market, and cans of seafood imported from Japan were said to contain particles of ground glass. Signaling devices similar to those reported found in Hawaii were alleged to have been set up in coastal areas. A number of anxious Californians, according to one report, went so far as to plow up "a beautiful field of flowers on the property of a Japanese farmer," because "it seems the Jap was a fifth columnist and had grown his flowers in a way that when viewed from a plane formed an arrow pointing the direction to the airport."[1]

These rumors and accusations arose largely as a result of the stories of fifth-column activity at Pearl Harbor which were rapidly accumulating in the press. After an inspection of the Pacific base, Secretary of the Navy Knox was quoted as saying that sabotage at Pearl Harbor constituted "the most effective fifth-column work that's come out of this war, except in Norway." Newspaper headlines on the Knox report generally stressed this aspect: "Secretary of Navy Blames Fifth Columnists for the Raid," "Fifth Column Prepared Attack," "Fifth Column Treachery Told." Other stories told of secret signaling and faked air-raid alerts by Hawaiian Japanese at the time of the attack, of arrows cut in the cane fields to aid enemy pilots, and roadblocks improvised to tie up military traffic.[2]

In opposition to the rumors and scare stories was a succession of official assurances that all dangerous enemy aliens had been apprehended, that necessary precautions had already been taken, and that Japanese Americans as a whole were loyal to the United States. This viewpoint was, moreover, echoed in the editorials of most California newspapers during the first days of war. Despite these assurances, however, Americans became increasingly restive as the prospect of Japanese attack or invasion grew more plausible. For half a century they had heard of the treachery and deceitfulness of resident Japanese—of how the "Japs" were concentrated in strategic areas of the state; of how by "peaceful invasion" they hoped to take over first California and ultimately the nation; of how they formed a network of spies and soldiers in disguise, patiently awaiting the Imperial signal to rise against the white man.[3]

---

[1] For notes to chapter ii see pp. 347–352.

The news from the battle-fronts, recording new Allied losses almost daily, made the most alarmist forebodings seem realistic. Charges of fifth-column plots multiplied rapidly and broadened in scope, soon including the mainland as well as Hawaii, and possible future actions as well as past events. It was reported, for example, that a Los Angeles naval sentry had seen signal lights in a Japanese waterfront colony; that the suicide of a Japanese doctor had uncovered a spy ring in the same area; that members of the notorious Black Dragon Society had been planted in cities and fishing communities; that the fifth-column character of Japanese schools in America had been exposed. The halls of Congress echoed with such exposures; Senator Guy Gillette of Iowa warned that "Japanese groups in this country planned sabotage and subversive moves," and Congressman Martin Dies of Texas announced the discovery of a book revealing Japanese plans to attack the United States.[4]

Meanwhile the war was being brought steadily closer to home. On December 20 it was announced that Japanese submarines were attacking West Coast shipping; and on the same day two tankers were reportedly torpedoed off California. Two days later newspapers told of the shelling of a freighter by an enemy sub near Santa Barbara; the next day two more tankers were said to have been attacked off the California coast.[5] Residents of the coastal states began to feel that their shores were under virtual blockade by enemy submarines.

The refugees from Hawaii, arriving in late December, brought new rumors of sabotage by island Japanese on December 7. It was said that Japanese had placed obstructions on the road to Pearl Harbor to keep reinforcements from getting through; that they had sabotaged the planes on the landing fields; that one group had entered Hickam Field in a milk truck, let down the sides and turned machine guns on American pilots as they ran to their planes.[6]

Impressive "confirmation" of these rumors was contained in a sensational dispatch by a United Press correspondent, Wallace Carroll, who visited Honolulu shortly after the attack. Repeating with an air of authority most of the charges made by Honolulu refugees, the report declared that numbers of Hawaii Japanese had had advance knowledge of the bombing, and that Japanese produce merchants delivering to warships had been able to report on United States fleet movements. Carroll speculated that newspaper advertisements placed by Japanese firms may have been coded messages, and asserted that the enemy raiders had been aided by improvised roadblocks and arrows cut in the cane fields. The hands of Japanese pilots shot down during the assault were, he said, adorned with the rings of Honolulu high schools and of Oregon State University. The dispatch continued:

Japanese of American nationality infiltrated into the Police Departments and obtained jobs as road supervisors, sanitary inspectors or minor government officials. Many went to work in the postoffice and telephone service, ideal posts for spies. . . .

An American resident, who had studied Japanese methods in Manchuria and North China, told me that the Japanese fifth column and espionage organizations in the islands were similar to those which had been used to undermine the Chinese.[7]

Accounts such as this, together with reports of new Allied reverses and tales of atrocities in the Philippines, goaded some Filipino Americans into direct retaliation against their Japanese neighbors. On December 23 a Japanese American, honorably discharged from the United States Army, was found stabbed to death on a Los Angeles sidewalk; his assailants were reported to be Filipinos. On Christmas Day in Stockton, windows of numerous Japanese business houses were smashed, assertedly by gangs of Filipinos. The next day in the same city an alien Japanese garage attended was shot to death by a Filipino; newspapers prominently featured the incident, under such headlines as "Jap, Filipino District Under Guard; 1 Slain," "Stockton Jap Killed by Filipino; Riots Feared; Area Under Guard." By the end of December similar incidents were publicized almost daily. On December 29, a Japanese waiter was shot to death by a Filipino in Chicago. On December 30 an alien Japanese was shot and wounded in Sacramento; on New Year's Day a Japanese and his wife were murdered in the Imperial Valley. Other cases were reported from Gilroy and Livermore, and even from Utah.[8]

Thus, within the first three weeks of war, the familiar Japanese stereotype was again visible on the Pacific Coast, and aroused individuals and groups were militantly reacting to it. The surprise attack of December 7, occurring in the midst of peace negotiations, seemed a definite confirmation of the old remembered tales of Japanese deceitfulness. Although for a time many citzens were reluctant to blame resident Japanese for the actions of Japan, and newspaper comment frequently was on the side of tolerance, the accumulating "evidence" of sabotage and espionage gradually put an end to toleration. Popular anger and apprehension rose in proportion to the continuing successes of the enemy, and by the end of 1941 suspicion and animosity were the most frequently expressed attitudes toward the Japanese Americans.

JANUARY: THE GATHERING STORM

January was another month of disasters for the Allies and frustrations for the people at home. Manila fell to the Japanese on January 2, and an outnumbered American garrison began its struggle at Bataan and on Corregidor, with little hope of reinforcement. Japanese troops were advancing through Malay jungles to the crucial port of Singapore. Borneo was invaded and the entire East Indies came under attack. The scattered islands of the far Pacific were falling before the enemy with incredible rapidity; there were landings in New Guinea, and Australia was directly menaced. At home, reports continued of West Coast shipping attacked by enemy submarines; and off the eastern coast the Germans were rapidly intensifying their U-boat warfare and had torpedoed several Allied vessels.

In this atmosphere of frustration, fear, and anger, popular sentiment on the West Coast in the first month of 1942 was concentrated more and more against resident Japanese. Although the official restrictions on enemy-alien activity had been directed impartially at Germans, Italians, and Japanese,[9] in the popular mind the Japanese were special targets of suspicion. Their Oriental appearance marked them inescapably in an area whose greatest danger was from the Far Eastern end of the Axis. Acts of violence against Japanese Americans continued to be reported in the press from such widely separate areas as Seattle, Fresno, Sacramento, and Santa Maria. Front-page attention was given FBI raids and arrests of Japanese allegedly possessing contraband. Popular tensions were increased by the charge in the Roberts Committee report that espionage in Hawaii had centered in the Japanese consulate, and that through its intelligence service the Japanese had obtained complete information on Pearl Harbor. The principal effect of such disclosures, however they were intended, was strongly to support the rumors of disloyalty among Japanese in Hawaii and to cast further doubt upon the loyalty of Japanese along the coast.[10]

Early in January prominent voices began to call for more vigorous steps to control the resident Japanese, including their mass removal from the West Coast.[11] News commentators, editorial writers, and public officials expressed displeasure at the "indecision and inaction" of the Department of Justice and urged drastic measures. John B. Hughes, a Los Angeles commentator for the Mutual Broadcasting Company, gained prominence as the first widely heard newsman to press the subject of evacuation. In the first of a month-long series of anti-Japanese broadcasts, Hughes compared the treatment of local Japanese with that of Americans captured by Japanese armies and warned that the failure to adopt strong measures would result in "disaster to the Pacific Coast." In subsequent commentaries he lent his support to rumors of espionage and fifth-column activities, charging that United States Japanese had contributed funds to Japan's war chest and hinting that the control of California's vegetable output was a part of the over-all Japanese war plan.[12]

Hughes also entered into a correspondence with Attorney General Biddle in which he urged the internment of both aliens and citizens of Japanese ancestry. "Persons who know the Japanese on the west coast," he wrote, "will estimate that ninety percent or more of American-born Japanese are primarily loyal to Japan." The commentator's justification for this indictment was the old yellow peril thesis of race: "Their organization and patient preparation and obedience to unified control could never be possible among the nationals of any Caucasian people. The Japanese are a far greater menace in our midst than any other axis patriots. They will die joyously for the honor of Japan." As a clincher, a justification was offered which was to be frequently advanced by proponents of evacuation: "There was an old law in the West, the law of the Vigilantes. Its whole code was: Shoot first and argue later. That code will be invoked, I'm afraid, unless authorities formulate a policy, an adequate policy, and put it into effect."[13]

The calculated purpose of the Hughes campaign, like others which followed it in the press and on the air, was to persuade the public to demand a policy of action toward the local Japanese: specifically that of rounding them up and removing them from the coast. This policy of exclusion, frequently urged in conjunction with demands for internment, had a threefold appeal: first, in the light of what the public feared from the Japanese (espionage and sabotage) it seemed a perfect remedy; second, it offered an outlet for the public's antipathy toward the resident Japanese by urging forceful action against them; and finally it offered an opportunity for action, a chance to "do something," to a population fretting to strike back against Japan but so far offered no chance for direct action.

Hughes was not long in finding company among newspapermen. By the end of January a radical shift had taken place in the editorial position of California newspapers. During the first month of war these journals had for the most part been tolerant if not sympathetic toward the Japanese in America; but in the following three weeks unfavorable comment gradually increased to the point where it equalled expressions of tolerance. In the last days of January the trend suddenly accelerated and pro-Japanese utterances were lost in a barrage of denunciation—which centered on charges of Japanese disloyalty, demands for strict control measures, and growing sentiment for mass evacuation.[14]

The keynote of the evacuation demands was sounded by the San Diego *Union*, one of the first major journals to press the issue, which opened a sustained editorial campaign on January 20 with arguments drawn largely from fifth-column rumors:

In Hawaii and in the Philippines treachery by residents, who although of Japanese ancestry had been regarded as loyal, has played an important part in the success of Japanese attacks....

Every Japanese—for the protection of those who are loyal to us and for our protection against those who are not—should be moved out of the coastal area and to a point of safety far enough inland to nullify any inclinations they may have to tamper with our safety here.

In subsequent editorials the *Union* dwelt on the evils of Japanese citizenship, maintained that there was no way of determining the loyalty of "our so-called American citizens of Japanese ancestry," and exclaimed: "We are confronted on both sides by enemies who have devoted their entire careers to development of treachery, deceit, and sabotage. We can afford to be neither soft-headed nor soft-hearted in dealing with them or their agents."[15]

The Hearst newspapers on the Pacific Coast, which in earlier years had led in the agitation against resident Japanese, did not conspicuously join the editorial clamor for evacuation—although news articles frequently were slanted against the Japanese.[16] But it was in the Hearst press that the first of numerous syndicated columns condemning the Japanese minority was published. On January 29, Henry McLemore, a former sports reporter, wrote from Los Angeles:

The only Japanese apprehended have been the ones the FBI actually had something on. The rest of them, so help me, are free as birds. There isn't an airport in California that isn't flanked by Japanese farms. There is hardly an air field where the same situation doesn't exist....

I know this is the melting pot of the world and all men are created equal and there must be no such thing as race or creed hatred, but do those things go when a country is fighting for its life? Not in my book. No country has ever won a war because of courtesy and I trust and pray we won't be the first because of the lovely, gracious spirit....

I am for immediate removal of every Japanese on the West Coast to a point deep in the interior. I don't mean a nice part of the interior either. Herd 'em up, pack 'em off and give 'em the inside room in the badlands. Let 'em be pinched, hurt, hungry and dead up against it....

Personally, I hate the Japanese. And that goes for all of them.[17]

The mood of the McLemore attack was not widely evident in editorial comment prior to February. But the "Letters to the Editor" columns of many newspapers in the last weeks of January showed a rising tide of anti-Japanese feeling along the coast. In these informal communications, more graphically than elsewhere, the myths and slanders of bygone years were dusted off and put on display. The Sacramento *Bee* printed a letter from one of its readers who invoked the ancient battle-cry "America for Americans," and complained that Japanese were "forcing other races off the land, including whites from pioneer families." A letter in the Santa Rosa *Press Democrat* asked: "Biologically and economically, is the Jap fitted to mingle in American life?" and asserted that "when our trouble is over they must be returned to their rising sun." Another Sacramento reader declared that Japanese American citizens would "betray the land of their birth . . . simply because they are treacherous and barbarous by nature." A Native Daughter of the Golden West asked: "Did God make the Jap as He did the snake, did you hear the hiss before the words left his mouth? Were his eyes made slanting and the hiss put between his lips to warn us to be on our guard?" A San Francisco reader urged the authorities to "put all the Japs in camps. . . . First thing you know they will be pulling another surprise on us."[18]

The rapid increase of anti-Japanese sentiment during January had its effect in political circles. The first official body to make an issue of Japanese loyalty was the California legislature, which had earlier maintained a tolerant and even sympathetic attitude toward Japanese residents.

In December the legislature had approved a joint resolution urging federal officials "to prevent any and all racial discrimination in the National Defense Program" and declaring that "racial discrimination has no place . . . in our concept of American Democracy." But on January 14 two resolutions reflecting an altered sentiment were introduced in the state senate, one calling for an investigation of the Alien Land Law and the other creating a committee to study employment of Japanese American citizens by the state. Three days later the senate unanimously adopted a resolution to "investigate any and all possible evasions of the Alien Land Laws and to prosecute to the utmost . . . any violations that may be discovered." Resurrecting the anti-Oriental arguments of earlier generations, the resolution asserted that the land laws of 1913 and 1920 had been passed because of "the clash of two races and two civilizations, socially and economically incompatible." It was stated that the acts had been circumvented "by subterfuge" until they were "a virtual nullity"; moreover, Japanese aliens were said to be in control of large areas of land near vital installations, constituting "a menace to National defense, to the citizens of this State and Nation, and to the American grower and dealer."[19]

On January 17, the California senate also passed without dissent a measure aimed at Japanese employees of the state. Claiming that numbers of state workers appeared to "possess dual citizenship," the bill called upon the State Personnel Board to prevent the employment of anyone "who is not loyal to the United States and to . . . provide for the dismissal from the [state civil] service of such persons as may be proved to be disloyal to the United States."[20] Although Japanese were not directly named in the bill, all the lawmakers who spoke on the proposal referred openly to the need for examining the loyalty of Japanese American employees. Senators Jack Metzger and John Harold Swan, coauthors of the bill, produced a photostatic copy of a payroll sheet of the State Motor Vehicle Department which contained only Japanese names, and Senator Swan purported to see in this "a systematic plot to get Japanese on the state payroll and allow them to bore from within." Senator Metzger contributed to the fifth-column rumors by charging that "Japanese fifth columnists in milk wagons drew machine guns instead of milk bottles out of twenty-one wagons in Honolulu the morning of December 7 and turned them on Pearl Harbor barracks." Later the same senator was reported as saying: "I don't believe there is a single Japanese in the world who is not pulling for Japan. They will spy, commit sabotage, or die if necessary."[21]

In the national capital, outcries against the Japanese Americans began to be heard from West Coast congressmen late in January. As in other circles, congressional discussion during the first six weeks of war had generally shown confidence in the loyalty and integrity of resident Japanese.[22] An early harbinger of changing attitudes among West Coast congressmen was the insertion into the *Congressional Record* by Congressman Leland Ford of Los Angeles of an anti-Japanese telegram from movie actor Leo Carillo, which read in part: "Why wait until [the Japanese] pull something before we act. . . . Let's get them off the coast into the interior. . . . May I urge you in behalf of the safety of the people of California to start action at once."[23]

Ford was also the first congressman to urge the cause of evacuation from the floor. On January 20 he called attention to alleged fifth-column activities among California Japanese and asserted that "a patriotic native-born Japanese, if he wants to make his contribution, will submit himself to a concentration camp." In the following thirty

days bitter charges against the Japanese were voiced in Congress at
least ten times, the assertion of Congressman Homer Angell of Oregon
being typical: "We must wake up, and if we do not wake up and protect
ourselves from this menace something infinitely worse than Pearl
Harbor will be enacted on our very shores."[24]

During January, meanwhile, as military reverses in the Pacific intensified the fear of invasion and sabotage, as fifth-column rumors gained
an ever-widening audience and prominent public figures wavered in
their initial tolerance, those private organizations on the Pacific Coast
which had traditionally prospered on the issue of anti-Orientalism were
quick to seize the new advantage and exploit public fears. The composition of the pressure groups which became most active in the new
anti-Japanese movement was not, however, identical with that of earlier
crusades. Although most of the well-known names were again in evidence (the American Legion, the Native Sons, the Farm Bureau, the
Joint Immigration Committee), to these were added the names of other
organizations either recently formed or newly converted to the movement.[25] As in previous years, the particular motives of the wartime pressure groups were varied and complex, but they were alike in resorting
readily and monotonously to the familiar stereotypes—racial, social, and
economic—which in the past had proved so successful in enlisting public support.

The common attitude of these bodies in the first weeks after Pearl
Harbor was expressed in the words of a Joint Immigration Committee
official: "This is our time to get things done that we have been trying
to get done for a quarter of a century."[26] The JIC, still acting with the
support of the Native Sons and the California Department of the
Legion, singled out for primary emphasis the evil of Japanese American
"dual citizenship." In addition, the committee summarized twenty years
of anti-Japanese activity in a public manifesto dispatched to California
newspapers on January 2. The release observed that "reported fifth
column activities by Japanese residents of Hawaii and the Philippine
Islands . . . [have] brought to the fore California's effort over the years
to find a solution to the Japanese immigration question." The JIC, it
said, had "for years struggled to educate the American public" to its
views on the Japanese problem: "Now, the problem is not alone California's. It belongs to the nation." Repeating the familiar charge that
Japanese are "totally unassimilable," the proclamation declared that
"those born in this country are American citizens by right of birth, but
they are also Japanese citizens, liable . . . to be called to bear arms for
their Emperor, either in front of, or behind, enemy lines." Japanese-

language schools were attacked as "a blind to cover instruction similar to that received by a young student in Japan—that his is a superior race, the divinity of the Japanese Emperor, the loyalty that every Japanese, wherever born, or residing, owes his Emperor and Japan." Congress was scored for failing to take action on dual citizenship, and the committee voiced the hope that "perhaps the savage blow inflicted at Hawaii may cause us to awaken. It is time."[27]

In the first wartime meeting of the JIC, the issue of evacuation as well as that of dual citizenship was introduced, primarily on racist grounds. Former State Attorney General U. S. Webb—whose lifetime contributions to the anti-Oriental cause were rivaled only by those of Senator James D. Phelan and Valentine S. McClatchy—was present to urge the evacuation of all Japanese, maintaining that citizen Nisei might be more dangerous than their alien parents. H. J. McClatchy, son of the committee's founder, concurred with the observation that "so far as the individual Nisei is concerned, he has been educated to be a Jap and he is a Jap."[28]

The intimate relationship between the Joint Immigration Committee and the California Department of the Legion (illuminated by the dual role of James K. Fisk as State Legion Adjutant and Chairman of the JIC) was revealed in January in a resolution of the State Legion's War Council which closely followed the pattern set by the committee, notably in its demand that "all Japanese who are known to hold dual citizenship . . . be placed in concentration camps." Similar resolutions soon appeared from a number of local posts in California, Oregon, and Washington.[29]

Even more racist in character were the charges and proclamations issued by the Native Sons and Daughters of the Golden West. Violent denunciations of the Japanese, similar to those of earlier years, appeared in the first three wartime issues of the *Grizzly Bear*. In the January number, Clarence M. Hunt, Deputy Grand President and editor of the journal, recounted the long history of Native Son agitation, summarized the principal grievances and antipathies developed by the Order in thirty years of agitation, and advanced a singular explanation for the war:

Had the warnings been heeded—had the federal and state authorities been "on the alert," and rigidly enforced the Exclusion Law and the Alien Land Law; had the Jap propaganda agencies in this country been silenced; had legislation been enacted . . . denying citizenship to the offspring of an alien ineligible to citizenship; had the Japs been prohibited from colonizing in strategic locations; had not Jap-dollars been so eagerly sought by White landowners and businessmen; had a deaf ear been turned to the honeyed words of the Japs and the pro-Japs; had the yellow-Jap and the white-Jap "fifth columnists" been disposed of within the law; had Japan been denied the privilege of using California as a breeding-grounds for dual citizens (Nisei);—the treacherous Japs probably would not have attacked Pearl Harbor December 7, 1941, and this country would not today be at war with Japan.

The motives of the farming groups which joined the new anti-Japanese movement were not, on the surface at least, the same as those of the patriots who composed the Legion and the Native Sons. The Western Growers Protective Association and the Grower-Shipper Vegetable Association, for example, repeated the familiar allegations of cheap labor, unfair competition, and land "bleeding" which had been advanced against the Japanese in previous decades by the State Grange and the California Farm Bureau.[30] Other classic features of the stereotype were not ignored. According to an official of the Western Growers, it was "not far-fetched or beyond the realm of possibility that at least 25,000 Japanese, in the event of invasion, by exchanging civilian clothing for uniforms are full-fledged members of the Japanese armed forces."[31] The underlying grievances of the Grower-Shippers were plainly revealed in a magazine article a few months later, in which the managing secretary of the organization was quoted as saying:

We're charged with wanting to get rid of the Japs for selfish reasons. We might as well be honest. We do. It's a question of whether the white man lives on the Pacific Coast or the brown man. They came into this valley to work, and they stayed to take over . . . If all the Japs were removed tomorrow, we'd never miss them in two weeks, because the white farmers can take over and produce everything the Jap grows. And we don't want them back when the war ends, either.[32]

Thus, during January, the storm clouds gathered over the heads of the Japanese Americans. The voices which had been heard earlier in their defense were by the end of the month either silenced or lost in a swelling chorus of hatred and suspicion. Popular hostility mounted steadily with the continuing successes of the enemy in the Pacific, and numbers of newspaper writers and radio commentators, public officials, and spokesmen for private interests abandoned whatever hesitation they may once have felt and hastened to add their voices to the clamor for action. The charges they hurled against the resident Japanese were an echo of the grievances of years past; the caricature they drew was soon observed to be the familiar hateful figure, at once comic and threatening—the bespectacled and bowing Asiatic whose excessive politeness disguised a treacherous heart and a conspiratorial design.

February: The Time of Decision

By the end of January, 1942, the prospects for tolerant or even moderate treatment of Japanese Americans had all but disappeared. The ultimate fate of alien Japanese was foreshadowed by the announcement of the Justice Department that along with alien Germans and Italians they were to be removed from various prohibited zones, and that their freedom of movement in still other areas would be curtailed. The position of American citizens of Japanese descent, theoretically more secure, was almost equally precarious. Regarded generally as "descendants of the Japanese enemy," they found their status as citizens more and more in jeopardy. The confusion of alien ancestry with alien status was compounded in the public mind as newspapers referred indiscriminately to all Japanese—whether citizens or aliens, enemy forces or peaceful residents—as "Japs." An increasing number of organizations and prominent individuals were urging the evacuation of citizens as well as aliens, and the cry of "once a Jap always a Jap" was heard on all sides. A Nisei citizen expressed the bitterness of many:

There seems to be a movement to make this present conflict a war between races . . . and over here in our country some people are theorizing that this is a war to end the yellow menace . . . thousands of them [Japanese] live in the United States . . . and are wholeheartedly for the U. S. and democracy—yet they are or may be singled out for special attention if this "racial war" movement gathers momentum.[33]

The decision to evacuate all Japanese Americans from the West Coast, which came during February, was reached in a context of gathering fear, suspicion, and anger on the part of the American public—a mood occasioned by the unanticipated disasters in the Pacific. Had the United States fleet not been decimated at Pearl Harbor, but steamed off intact to meet and destroy the Japanese navy, as most Americans had been certain it would; had the Japanese armies been turned back at Singapore by the land and sea defenses which had been thought invincible; in short, had the Allies taken the initiative at the outset and shown promise of checking the Japanese advance, it is doubtful that American opinion—public and private, official and unofficial—could have been mobilized in support of evacuation. Assured of ultimate victory and sustained by a diet of war successes, a secure and confident America might well have fulfilled its democratic ideal of tolerance and hospitality toward the Japanese minority in its midst.

But the war did not go that way, and Americans were given no prospect of security or gleam of optimism. In mid-February, only seventy

days after the first attack on Malaya, "impregnable" Singapore surrendered unconditionally to the Japanese, in what Winston Churchill was
to call "the greatest disaster to British arms which history records." The
capitulation forced an Allied withdrawal to the Dutch East Indies, and
the way now lay open for an enemy attack upon Burma and India. The
Japanese, in fact, had entered Burma a week before to cut the Burma
Road and isolate China. The Indies were sealed off and their fate ordained by the fall of Sumatra, Borneo, and Celebes; and in a series of
sea engagements during February the Japanese first split and then
methodically destroyed American and Allied naval forces. Enemy penetration of the southwest Pacific was equally rapid and decisive. In January Japanese forces had leveled the centers of defense in the Solomons;
from·these positions they now struck west at New Guinea, bombing
Salamaua and Port Moresby and even neutralizing Port Darwin on
the Australian coast. By the end of February an invasion of Australia
seemed imminent; the final fall of the beleaguered Philippine garrison
was virtually assured; the surrender of Java and the complete conquest
of the rich Indies was only days away; and the great subcontinent of
India was threatened with assault. Nothing had occurred to indicate
that the bewildering tide of conquest might soon be stemmed, and not
a few Americans wondered when their turn would come in the Japanese
schedule of invasion.

Early in the month, meanwhile, in conjunction with its program of
alien evacuation from prohibited areas, the Justice Department began
a series of "spot raids" to uncover contraband and counter anticipated
sabotage. FBI agents, together with state and local officers, descended
without warning or warrant upon a number of localities and searched
the homes of Japanese. Large amounts of "contraband" were found,
and numbers of alien Japanese were apprehended. Each of these surprise raids received attention from California newspapers, usually be-
neath black banner headlines.[34] Particular stress was placed upon the
lists of contraband seized. One search, for example, was reported to
have uncovered "11 cameras, 14 short wave radio sets, 12 binoculars, a
telescope, nine rifles, six revolvers, many thousands of rounds of ammunition, 84 knives, a large searchlight, four floodlights, four telescope
gun sights, a box of sulphuric acid, Japanese maps and three sets of
maps and charts of the Monterey Bay area." The Japanese operator of
a sporting goods store was said to possess "70,000 rounds of rifle and
shotgun ammunition, 12 rifles and shotguns, a public address system,
cameras and film, books of Japanese propaganda and a radio operator's
handbook."[35]

The effect of these accounts in augmenting public suspicions may be glimpsed in a letter to Attorney General Biddle from a San Diego resident: "How much longer are we going to let these traitorous barbarians strut among us seeking every means of destroying us, storing arms and ammunition right under our noses and within stone's throw of our war industries, just because hasty action on our part might be impolite or offend the one out of every hundred Japs who is not conspiring against us?"[36] Editorial writers also were influenced by the apparent findings of the anti-Japanese raids. A typical comment in the Stockton *Record* declared that "in recent days FBI agents have operated in many parts of California and uncovered caches of arms and contraband.... The circumstances smack strongly of those who contributed to the tragedy of Pearl Harbor.... The Pacific Coast is in danger."[37]

The inevitable effect of the arrests and spot raids, dramatically pointed up by the press, was to confirm the traditional image of the Japanese handed down from earlier generations and revived upon the outbreak of war. The rising tide of popular feeling is shown by the frequent appeals of the Department of Justice—and especially of Attorney General Francis Biddle—asking the public to forego vigilantism and maintain tolerance toward the Japanese Americans. But such appeals did little to check the rise of anti-Japanese sentiment. In fact, the control measures adopted by the Department of Justice seemed to many only a further confirmation of their fears: the creation of prohibited and restricted zones, the establishment of a curfew, the dramatic searches and seizures—all appeared to justify the deepening public suspicions of the Japanese, both citizens and aliens, as actually or potentially disloyal and dangerous.

The aggravated state of public opinion was also reflected during February in the words and actions of prominent politicians and political bodies. The boards of supervisors of eleven California counties joined in a solemn declaration that "during the attack on Pearl Harbor ... the Japanese were aided and abetted by fifth columnists of the Japanese."[38] State Attorney General Earl Warren had first proclaimed his attitude on January 30, when a press dispatch quoted him as saying that the Japanese situation in the state "may well be the Achilles heel of the entire civilian defense effort. Unless something is done it may bring about a repetition of Pearl Harbor." On February 2, Warren revealed to a private conference of sheriffs and district attorneys his intense suspicion of resident Japanese—which was so profound that the very absence of sabotage seemed to him a sure sign of its future occurrence: "It seems to me that it is quite significant that in this great state of ours we have had no fifth column activities and no sabotage reported. It looks very much to me as though it is a studied effort not to have any until the zero hour arrives." He concluded that "every alien Japanese should be considered in the light of a potential fifth columnist," and urged that the Alien Land Law be enforced to remove all Japanese from areas near vital installations. (It should be emphasized, however, that the public report of the conference called only for removal of enemy aliens—*not* of all Japanese Americans.)[39]

In subsequent days Attorney General Warren produced a variety of arguments purporting to show that resident Japanese were not only dangerous but much more of a threat than resident Germans or Italians. His arguments constitute a resumé of anti-Japanese cliches which had been accumulating for over half a century. There was, he said, no way to determine the loyalty of Japanese Americans. It was impossible for Americans to comprehend Oriental ways; the alien culture was diffused through religion, language schools, and the practice of sending children to Japan for education. In Japan "they are indoctrinated with the idea of Japanese imperialism. They receive their religious instruction which tied up their religion with their Emperor, and they come back here imbued with the ideas and policies of Imperial Japan." Warren alleged that Japanese in America generally approved of Japan's military conquests, implying that they would also favor the conquest of America, and he declared that the Japanese government exerted a broad control over the activities of all Japanese in this country.[40]

Equally vigorous in his opposition to the Japanese, and in his contributions to the stereotype, was Mayor Fletcher Bowron of Los Angeles. In a radio address of February 5, Bowron warned of the danger of leaving the California Japanese at liberty. Among the Nisei there were "a number who are doubtless loyal to Japan, waiting probably, with full instructions as to what to do, to play their part when the time comes." The next day the mayor was quoted as denouncing the "sickly sentimentality" of Americans who feared injustices to the Japanese. The control "measures taken so far are so ineffectual as to be ridiculous." On Lincoln's birthday he again devoted his weekly radio address to the Japanese problem, arguing that if Lincoln were living he would round up "the people born on American soil who have secret loyalty to the Japanese Emperor." On still another occasion he disclaimed "any racial or other prejudice," but declared that "I know of no rule, no way to separate those who say they are patriotic and are, in fact, loyal at heart, and those who say they are patriotic and in fact at heart are loyal to Japan."[41]

The shift in public sentiment, visible in late January, from compara-tive tolerance to general hostility toward the Japanese minority, was accurately mirrored in the Pacific Coast press. The ratio of unfavorable to favorable editorials was nineteen to one in the five days between January 22 and 26; hostile letters to the editor, chiefly demands for mass evacuation, attained their peak between February 1 and 5. By February, also, news stories favorable to the Japanese Americans were reduced from a December high of 22 per cent to less than 3 per cent, and during the thirty-day period from January 12 to February 10, fifteen times more news space was given to unfriendly items than to favorable copy. News stories devoted to evacuation demands reached their peak in the five days from February 6 to 10; these stories alone occupied seven times the space taken by all favorable news copy in the month from January 12 to February 10.[42]

Editorial pressure in early February centered chiefly on the danger of a West Coast "Pearl Harbor." There was general agreement with the opinion of the Sacramento *Bee* that "the experience with the fifth col-umn in Hawaii is overwhelming evidence that . . . the authorities must take no chances with possible Jap or Axis sympathizers."[43] Newspapers pointed frequently to contraband seized by the FBI as sufficient evi-dence of Japanese disloyalty, and much attention was given to the growing number of evacuation demands by politicians, officials, and organizations. The activities of the Western congressional bloc were widely featured, often with speculation that federal action approving Japanese removal was soon to be taken.

Editorial writers voiced increasing opposition during February to the nonevacuation policy of the Department of Justice. Equally noteworthy were the exhortations of several widely syndicated columnists who added their voices to the cry for mass removal. Henry McLemore, whose personal campaign had begun late in January, continued to press his attack against the Department of Justice. Observing that aliens had been allowed weeks in which to evacuate the prohibited zones and would have "time to perfect their time bombs, complete their infernal ma-chines," McLemore charged the Attorney General with handling the Japanese threat "with all the severity of Lord Fauntleroy playing squat tag with his maiden aunt."[44]

Walter Lippmann, one of the most influential political columnists, added his name in mid-February to the list of those opposing federal policy and urging stronger measures.[45] Subsequently Westbrook Pegler, then a Scripps-Howard columnist, translated the Lippmann argument into his own idiom, declaring on February 16 that "the Japanese in

California should be under guard to the last man and woman right now and to hell with *habeas corpus* until the danger is over." Pegler went on:

Do you get what [Lippmann] says?... The enemy has been scouting our coast.... The Japs ashore are communicating with the enemy offshore and... on the basis of "what is known to be taking place" there are signs that a well-organized blow is being withheld only until it can do the most damage....

We are so dumb and considerate of the minute constitutional rights and even of the political feelings and influence of people whom we have every reason to anticipate with preventive action!

Under the prodding of public opinion and the press, members of Congress from the West Coast states intensified their efforts toward the formulation of a severe control program aimed at the Japanese. On February 10 a committee set up by the joint Pacific Coast delegation approved a resolution recommending total evacuation of all Japanese from the coastal area. The recommendation was made despite advice from Army and Navy authorities that a sustained Japanese attack on the coast was "impossible" and that even enemy raids, although possible, "would be sporadic and would have little, if any, bearing on the course of the war."[46] The reasons for disregarding this advice, as given in a letter to the President from the joint delegation, were plainly the exploded myth of sabotage at Pearl Harbor and the stereotyped belief in disloyalty and treachery among Japanese Americans. The letter pointed to "the seriousness of the Japanese menace along the entire Pacific Coast" which had evoked "insistent demands for prompt action," and asserted that "the critical nature of the situation and its latent subversive potentialities are so compelling as to justify the taking of extreme and drastic measures."[47]

Before mid-February, not much was said on the floor of the House or the Senate concerning evacuation. Except for the West Coast contingent, congressmen for the most part displayed only slight interest in the Japanese American problem. But at least three Southern members were conspicuous in their support of the California extremists and influential in their contributions to the stereotype of Japanese American disloyalty. They were Congressman John Rankin of Mississippi, Congressman Martin Dies of Texas, and Senator Tom Stewart of Tennessee.

Congressman Rankin, long famous as a champion of "White Supremacy" in his native south, was the most outspoken of the three in condemning all Japanese. As early as December he had declared: "So far as I am concerned, I am in favor of deporting every Jap who claims, or has claimed, Japanese citizenship, or sympathizes with Japan in this war." In mid-February he went still further: "Once a Jap always a Jap. You cannot change him. You cannot make a silk purse out of a sow's ear." Rankin put himself on record

for catching every Japanese in America, Alaska, and Hawaii now and putting them in concentration camps and shipping them back to Asia as soon as possible.... This is a race war, as far as the Pacific side of this conflict is concerned.... The white man's civilization has come into conflict with Japanese barbarism. ... One of them must be destroyed....

I say it is of vital importance that we get rid of every Japanese whether in Hawaii or on the mainland. They violate every sacred promise, every canon of honor and decency ... These Japs who had been [in Hawaii] for generations were making signs, if you please, guiding the Japanese planes to the objects of their iniquity in order that they might destroy our naval vessels, murder our soldiers and sailors, and blow to pieces the helpless women and children of Hawaii.

Damn them! Let's get rid of them now![48]

A few days later, on the House floor, Rankin renewed his insistence that the Japanese be placed in concentration camps. Pointing to the FBI raids along the coast, he declared that Japanese militarists were driving "the dagger in our backs ... at the same time their racial cohorts are undermining and sabotaging us up and down the Pacific Coast and throughout the Hawaiian Islands." The Mississippi congressman asserted that persons of Japanese ancestry born in this country were "not citizens of the United States and never can be." In support of this argument he read into the *Congressional Record* the dissenting opinion in the *Wong Kim Ark* case, and concluded: "There is a racial and religious difference they can never overcome. They are pagan in their philosophy, atheistic in their beliefs, alien in their allegiance, and antagonistic to everything for which we stand."[49]

Senator Tom Stewart, the author of a Senate bill to intern all Americans of Japanese descent, also was concerned with the status of the Nisei. He argued that

a Jap born on our soil is a subject of Japan under Japanese law; therefore, he owes allegiance to Japan.... The Japanese are among our worst enemies. They are cowardly and immoral. They are different from Americans in every conceivable way, and no Japanese ... should have a right to claim American citizenship. A Jap is a Jap anywhere you find him, and his taking the oath of allegiance to this country would not help, even if he should be permitted to do so. They do not believe in God and have no respect for an oath. They have been plotting for years against the Americas and their democracies.[50]

Congressman Dies, as head of the House Committee on Un-American Activities, had for years engaged in sensational "exposés" of allegedly disloyal individuals and organizations. Months before the war the Texas congressman had released press statements threatening an exposure of Japanese espionage and anti-American propaganda. On January 28 Dies delivered a speech in which he charged that "fear of displeasing foreign powers and a maudlin attitude toward fifth columnists was largely responsible for the unparalleled tragedy at Pearl Harbor," and announced that a forthcoming report would "disclose that if our committee had been permitted to reveal the facts last September the tragedy of Pearl Harbor might have been averted." Demanding that "there be an immediate end to this suicidal policy of coddling the tools and dupes of foreign powers," Dies concluded with· the warning that "unless this Government adopts an alert attitude towards this whole question there will occur on the west coast a tragedy that will make Pearl Harbor sink into insignificance compared with it."[51]

The heralded report of the Dies Committee was not forthcoming until late in February; but early in the month its contents were partly revealed, when a widely read columnist predicted that the Dies report would show how Japanese consuls had directed espionage activities through the "front" of the Central Japanese Association at Los Angeles. On February 9 the report was quoted as saying in part: "The United States has been and still is lax, tolerant and soft toward the Japanese who have violated American hospitality. Shinto Temples still operate, propaganda outlets still disseminate propaganda material and Japanese, both alien and American citizens, still spy for the Japanese government." The report was said to maintain that Japanese Americans were exploiting their civil rights "to promote systematic espionage such as prepared the way for the attack on Pearl Harbor on December 7."[52]

Meanwhile, on the West Coast, direct evidence of the hostile state of opinion was to be seen in the increasing acts of violence and threats of vigilantism against resident Japanese. Such incidents had begun to be noted shortly after the Pearl Harbor attack; and by February the argument that evacuation was necessary to insure the safety of the Japanese Americans as well as of the entire population had become a stock contention of public officials and spokesmen for private interests. At a conference of California district attorneys and sheriffs on February 2, it was announced that various civic and agricultural groups were actively fostering extra-legal action against the Japanese. Subsequently the sheriff of Merced County reported "rumblings of vigilante activity"; the chief of police of Huntington Beach described anti-Japanese feeling as "at fever heat"; the police chief of Watsonville announced that "racial hatred is mounting higher and higher" and that Filipinos were "arming themselves and going out looking for an argument with Japanese"; and

Oxnard's police chief reported that "it has been planned by local Filipinos and some so-called '200 percent Americans' to declare a local 'war' against local Japanese, during the next blackout."[53]

The mounting anger and suspicion of many citizens was expressed during February in the demands of various officials that the government act against the Japanese Americans without regard to legal or constitutional restraints. The mayor of one California city advised Congressman Tolan that "the Constitution can go overboard, if necessary"; should evacuation prove awkward in constitutional terms, "then we must win the war by dictatorship methods." A California congressman put the case more succinctly: "Let's move these Japanese out and talk about it afterwards." And the district attorney of Madera County declared that "we must forget such things as the right of *habeas corpus* and the prohibition against unreasonable searches and seizures. The right of self-defense, self-preservation . . . is higher than the Bill of Rights."[54]

This growing hostility toward the Japanese also became evident during the process of carrying out the early Department of Justice program of limited evacuation from prohibited zones. The intent of the program was to provide for the reëstablishment of alien enemies and their families; but the antipathy of residents of inland areas made it impossible for many Japanese to find either housing or employment. "Housing shortage is almost omnipresent in California," wrote the regional director of the Federal Security Agency, ". . . the evacuees seeking new homes are badly handicapped by the psychological attitude of landlords."[55] The inland population was for the most part only vaguely aware of the nature of voluntary resettlement and commonly assumed that if Japanese were a menace to security on the coast they were equally a menace elsewhere; if they could blow up ships in the harbors, they might also burn the forests of central California, wreck the irrigation system of Arizona, or sabotage the railroads running through Utah.

Many residents of interior states also suspected Californians of dumping a difficult minority problem in their laps. With the exception of Governor Ralph Carr of Colorado, the governors of the western states were unanimously opposed to the resettlement of Japanese within their borders. Thus Governor Sidney Osborn of Arizona announced: "We do not propose to be a dumping ground for enemy aliens from any other state. We not only vigorously protest but will not permit the evacuation of Japanese, German or Italian aliens to any point in Arizona."[56] Similar protests were heard in virtually all areas to which enemy aliens were permitted to move, and the beginnings of vigilantism were reported at many points. Repeated attempts to clarify the nature of the program and counteract local opposition were, as one official remarked, inadequate to penetrate "through the walls erected by public opinion, based upon natural fear of Japanese sabotage and inflamed by those who were envious of or inherently prejudiced against this race, irrespective of the war." The appearance of race prejudice, according to the same source, was especially marked in inland California, in Washington, and in neighboring states. "Unless we develop far better procedures and greater public confidence in the power of the Federal Government than now exists, I have real reason to fear that the spirit of vigilantism might spread in a way completely foreign to real Americanism. This is a carefully worded attempt at understatement."[57]

There were a number of protests from the interior California counties. Some farmers of the San Joaquin Valley protested the use of their area as a "dumping ground," and the San Joaquin County Farm Bureau demanded passage of a law to prevent the settlement of Japanese. The mayors' and councilmen's section of the League of California Cities called for evacuation beyond the borders of the state. The Fresno County Chamber of Commerce condemned the partial evacuation and urged that Japanese be excluded from the entire Pacific Coast. The Kern County Defense Council wired the Western bloc in Congress recommending the same action, on the grounds that the county contained many defense installations, "that the Japs would like very much to blow up, if they are in a blowing up mood."[58]

California's Tulare County was especially alert to the "dangers" presented by (and to) the Japanese evacuees. A mass meeting of county residents in mid-February demanded removal of Japanese from the state "for the public safety and for their own safety." It was feared that unless action were taken immediately the situation would "get out of hand," a spokesman freely predicted trouble if the Japanese remained, and a home guard was formed by Tulare citizens. Meanwhile District Attorney Walter C. Haight reported to the Tulare County Board of Supervisors that the movement of Japanese into the county presented a hazard and a danger "not only to the resources of our county, but to the interests of our national defense." He pointed to "the possibility of sabotage by means of the poisoning of our water supply, destruction of the metropolitan power lines ... grain fields and ... forests." Haight charged that Japanese growers of the area had designed a field of vegetables in the form of an arrowhead that "pointed directly to the Visalia Airport." Warning that under emergency conditions "hysterical people" might "take matters into their own hands," he urged the establishment of martial law requiring that "all enemy aliens, including all members of the Japanese race, be removed from the State of California."[59]

The opening days of March found the Japanese ordered away from the coast in the so-called "voluntary evacuation" program instituted by General DeWitt and the Western Defense Command. At the end of the month this "voluntary" program gave way to forced evacuation and internment. But public hostility remained; although newspaper columnists and editorialists turned most of their attention to other issues and policies, attacks against the Japanese continued. For the most part the trouble centered in Tulare and Fresno counties,[60] where open vigilante action continued as the weeks passed and local Japanese still remained in residence. During March an attempt was made to burn down a Japanese-owned hotel at Sultana. On April 13 at Del Ray five evacuees were involved in a brawl with the local constable—following which a crowd of white residents, some armed with shotguns, threatened violence to a nearby camp of Japanese Americans. On succeeding nights the windows of four Japanese stores were smashed, and similar incidents occurred in Fresno. In northern Tulare County, a group known as the "Bald Eagles"—described by one observer as "a guerilla army of nearly 1,000 farmers"—armed themselves for the announced purpose of "guarding" the Japanese in case of emergency. A similar organization was formed in the southeast part of the county, where a large number of evacuees were concentrated.[61]

Conclusion: The Faces of the Stereotype

The Japanese stereotype, as reconstructed in the early months of war, was a composite image reflecting a diversity of hates and fears on the part of the West Coast population. Frequently inconsistent and even mutually exclusive, the public expressions of these underlying attitudes were alike in their hostility and in the suspicion they revealed concerning the loyalty of resident Japanese. As rumor and opinion, they circulated through public resolutions and private declarations, while coastal residents in the weeks of crisis cast about for arguments to embody their growing anger and frustration. The arguments they found were with few exceptions neither logical nor original, but represented the tarnished banners of long-past campaigns—the yellow-peril charges of the unionists and politicians, the economic rationalizations of the farm groups, the racist outbursts of the patriots—the alarms and excursions of fifty years of agitation which had merged and recombined to form the popular stereotype of the Japanese character.

Sabotage.—Foremost among the traditional beliefs to be revived in the public mind was the myth of the yellow-peril invasion, the identification of America's Japanese as actual or potential spies and saboteurs. Emerging as an explanation of the shocking and calamitous events of December 7, the Pearl Harbor legend described such purported actions as the destruction of airplanes on the ground, the cutting of arrows in canefields, and the deliberate obstruction of traffic into military installations. The truth of these accounts, which circulated widely with the arrival of refugees from Hawaii, was seldom doubted. The widespread belief in the actuality of sabotage in Hawaii provided the basis for virtually all organized agitation to oust the West Coast Japanese; it stimulated the circulation of anonymous chain letters throughout California in January and February, and was shown regularly in letters to newspapers, to the United States Attorney General, and to congressmen.

The immediate significance of the Pearl Harbor legend to Pacific Coast residents was, of course, its portent of disaster for themselves. The Sacramento *Bee* voiced a common concern in pointing out that "the experience with the fifth column in Hawaii is overwhelming evidence that . . . the authorities must take no chances with possible Jap or Axis sympathizers," and many Californians shared the opinion of their attorney general that "we are just being lulled into a false sense of security. . . . Our day of reckoning is bound to come . . . we are approaching an invisible deadline."[62] This anticipation of disaster was heard with increasing frequency during February and March, as popular fears mounted despite the refusal of Japanese Americans to demonstrate their "disloyalty" through subversive acts. Local, state, and national officials voiced the conviction that the absence of sabotage in the present made it all the more certain in the future,[63] and the same viewpoint was expressed by private spokesmen and popular commentators. It was eventually incorporated into the final report of General DeWitt as a primary factor justifying evacuation: the absence of sabotage was, according to the general, "a disturbing and confirming indication that such action would be taken."[64]

Most of those who expressed fear over the threat of sabotage argued that American citizens of Japanese ancestry were as much suspect as aliens. This racist belief, summarized in the phrase "Once a Jap always a Jap," was publicized by congressmen such as Rankin and Stewart and appears to have made its way into the official reasoning of General Dewitt.[65] Various officials of the three Pacific Coast states conceded that some Japanese Americans might be loyal to the United States but deemed it impossible, because of racial factors, to distinguish between the loyal and disloyal. The governor and attorney general of California and the mayors of Los Angeles, Seattle, and Portland, among others, adopted this viewpoint; minor law-enforcement officers in California endorsed an equivalent line of reasoning in pleas for evacuation. The theory was greatly advanced by the accumulating stories of fifth-column plots on the mainland, and further encouraged by dramatic press descriptions of spot raids by the FBI.

There is no need to recapitulate here the official denials and refutations which established conclusively that there had been no sabotage or other fifth-column activity at Pearl Harbor, either during or after the Japanese attack.[66] On the other hand, it is impossible to disprove objectively the thesis of "latent sabotage," the argument that West Coast Japanese were awaiting an Imperial signal to rise in concerted fifth-column action. The "facts" on which this thesis was based were soon shown to be mythical; the various rumors of poisoned vegetables, undercover signal devices, messages and arrows in the fields, and so on, were one by one proved false. Moreover, the total inability of the FBI to uncover saboteurs among the Japanese population was frankly admitted by Attorney General Biddle in a memorandum to President Roosevelt in May, 1942.[67]

Geographical concentration.—Despite their shadowy character and the frequency of denials, both the Pearl Harbor rumors and the accounts of plans for sabotage remained in wide circulation among the West Coast population throughout the war. The general credence given these beliefs provided support for other traditional apprehensions regarding the Japanese Americans, one of the most persistent of which concerned their alleged "concentration" in strategic military and industrial areas.[68] Numerous persons complained in letters to the Attorney General of the presence of Japanese near "Oil Fields, Tank Farms, Air Ports, and other vital defense industries"; "our coast line"; "the foot of our mountains and the entrances to our canyons, which lead to the dams and water reservoirs"; "vantage places in harbor fisheries ... strange isolated promontories of our unguarded coastline, and ... our aircraft plants."[69] An extensive statement charging the Japanese with deliberate settlement in strategic areas was presented before the Tolan Committee by Attorney General Warren of California—a statement with which many California newspapers seemed to agree.[70]

Disloyalty.—Increasingly, under the stress of war, old and half-forgotten suspicions against the Japanese were dusted off and reintroduced as "evidence" of their disloyalty. Once again it was widely proclaimed that they were racially unassimilable. It was charged that their language schools were instruments of Imperial propaganda; that Nisei children educated in Japan had returned as spies or at least as indoctrinated Japanese fanatics; that the dual citizenship of the second generation was a mask for allegiance to the homeland; that community clubs and associations were manipulated from Tokyo; that Buddhism and Shinto-ism were agencies of Emperor worship; and that the occupation of farmlands by Japanese was a peaceful invasion which would end in domination of the American mainland.

This melange of legends, distortions, and half-truths subsequently played a prominent role in the official arguments advanced in defense of mass removal of the Japanese—arguments by which both evacuation and detention were initially justified by the military and ultimately confirmed by the courts. One of the most prevalent of the hostile beliefs took its departure from the apparent approval of Japan's victories in China by some resident Japanese before the outbreak of war with the United States. From this the suspicion grew that many had possessed prior knowledge of the December 7 attack, and that plans for future sabotage operations by individual members were foreknown in the Japanese community. Mayor Bowron of Los Angeles, for example, asserted that many resident Japanese "knew what was coming" and "overplayed their hand" in the year before the war by an excessive pretense of loyalty to America.[71]

Cultural lag.—The retention of old-world culture by Japanese Americans was frequently invoked as proof of their disloyalty. In language, education, religion, and family patterns, they were suspected of willfully avoiding Western ways and favoring alien customs. Letter writers declared that "any Japanese child that attends a Japanese school will . . . be . . . a potential enemy," and that "all of them have been back to Japan for certain educational periods."[72] Attorney General Warren sweepingly condemned as anti-American the language schools, religious organizations, and vernacular press of the resident Japanese, and considered the Japanese tongue itself a suspicious bond with the old country. Attendance at a language school, membership in an organization, or even passive acceptance of old-world customs was held to be sufficient cause for barring Japanese Americans from state employment. In a formal notice of discharge sent to all persons of Japanese ancestry employed by the state, the California State Personnel Board declared that "the defendant does read and write the Japanese language, and . . . subscribed to a Japanese newspaper . . . the defendant did attend a Japanese school . . . the defendant is a member and officer of certain Japanese organizations."[73]

Coolie labor.—The familiar accusations of cheap labor and unfair competition, which had long underlain the agitation of farm and labor groups, were once again heard as agriculturists and other interested groups joined the clamor against the Japanese. Despite their declarations that Japanese monopolized farmlands and vegetable production, the farmers saw no inconsistency in also maintaining that their removal would not hamper production. Officials of the California Farm Bureau, the Western Growers Protective Association, and the Grower-Shipper Vegetable Association wrote letters demonstrating that mass evacuation of the Japanese would not affect the food supply. California's Governor Culbert L. Olson conceded that some loss of "squat labor" might follow evacuation but did not consider it serious; Attorney General Warren declared that estimates of the importance of Japanese farm labor were based on "fantastic figures."[74]

Less often heard, but still in evidence, was the old yellow-peril warning against the alleged high birth rate of the Japanese. As always, the Native Sons were especially vociferous on this point, declaring that war might have been avoided had Japan been "denied the privilege of using California as a breeding ground for dual citizens." The Joint Immigration Committee likewise declared that the Japanese were "hardy of stock, militant opponents of race suicide, able to labor and thrive under living conditions impossible to an American."[75]

Race hatred.—The threat of riots and acts of violence against the Japanese, assertedly arising from "race hatred," constituted a potent argument for mass evacuation. The traditional Japanese stereotype included a belief in the existence of mutual hostility between the "white" and "yellow" races which it was thought must inevitably culminate in rioting and vigilantism—unless one or the other group should withdraw. This thesis, of course, was not without historical basis. California, and to a lesser extent Washington and Oregon, had a long history of vigilante activity, especially against the dark-skinned and Oriental minorities. Added to this tradition, in the months after Pearl Harbor, were the frustrating reports of Japanese victories and the accompanying tales of atrocities which were sufficient in themselves to stimulate public anger and the desire for revenge.

From the evidence that has accumulated it is possible to make an approximate appraisal of the extent of violence and vigilantism in the three coastal states during the months before evacuation. At least seven murders of Japanese Americans are known to have occurred, including among the victims a Los Angeles veteran of World War I and a middle-aged couple of Brawley, California. The number of physical assaults was substantially larger. Six Filipinos attacked a Japanese in Seattle; another Filipino shot and wounded a Japanese in Sacramento. Gunfire from moving automobiles wounded several persons (including a ten-year-old boy) in Gilroy. Similar events occurred at Costa Mesa, at Mount Eden, and at various points in Alameda County. Stockton Filipinos reportedly attacked Japanese with knives on three occasions. Robbery and assault were combined at least twice, in Seattle and in Rio Vista, California. Rape or attempted rape was recorded twice (in one case by men posing as FBI agents who were later identified as state prison guards). In Seattle a Negro truck driver shot a Nisei drugstore owner because he "wanted to get a Jap," and at Kingsburg, California, a Chinese American shot a Japanese American and then committed suicide in his jail cell.[76]

Pacific Coast newspapers generally gave much more prominence to these incidents than was customary in ordinary crime coverage. There can be little doubt that the appearance of vigilantism in the press was more substantial than the reality;[77] but there is no less doubt that the lurid news reports both confirmed and influenced public attitudes toward the Japanese minority. Many citizens felt strongly enough to demand that the government sweep away constitutional restraints in acting against the Japanese; to these extremists there seemed no contradiction between combating fascism abroad and embracing its methods at home. The crowning irony of their demand was that it was expressed almost invariably in terms of solicitude for the welfare of the Japanese who were to be its victims.

The vast assortment of rumors and suspicions, epithets and accusations, directed at Japanese Americans in the first months of war was almost totally fictitious in content and wholly tragic in effect. Its historical importance, however, lies less in the degree of truth or falsity of specific charges than in its revelation of the prevailing state of mind among the population of the Pacific Coast: a deeply rooted and broadly diffused attitude of suspicion and distrust toward all persons of Japanese descent, which demonstrated scant regard for distinctions of birth or citizenship, for "minute constitutional rights," for the record of political loyalty or the facts of social assimilation. The wave of anti-Japanese sentiment which was set in motion by the attack on Pearl Harbor, and subsequently given more impetus by an unbroken series of war disasters, swept all opposition before it and carried in its wake numbers of responsible public officials and organized private groups. By mid-February the tide of hostility reached its crest, and soon thereafter it broke over the heads of the Japanese Americans—engulfing more than 100,000 persons, citizens and aliens alike, in a vortex of popular anger and official acquiescence.

Part II

EXODUS

Chapter III

THE HISTORY OF THE EVACUATION

Actions are molded by beliefs. The broad acceptance of the stereotype of the Japanese character among the American people made a policy of watchfulness and suspicion toward Japanese Americans seem both reasonable and necessary after Pearl Harbor. The traditional view of the Japanese as inscrutable, treacherous, and disloyal merged in the public mind with tensions bred by the war; and inevitably demands for supervision and control arose. The Army moved quickly to institute stricter measures. Exclusion of all Japanese Americans from the Pacific Coast was followed by their incarceration in guarded camps. In these "relocation centers" the majority remained for the duration. Even those who eventually left the centers to pick up their lives again were subjected to constant scrutiny and investigation; remaining under the legal control of the Army, they were liable at any time to be recalled to the camps. For four years the Japanese Americans were thus herded and harassed—despite the total lack of any evidence whatsoever of acts of sabotage, espionage or "subversion," or even of intent to commit such acts, on their part. Such was the power of the beliefs held about this minority in the nation generally and on the West Coast in particular.

EXCLUSION

In the days immediately following Pearl Harbor, various restrictions were imposed upon the citizens of Germany, Italy, and Japan who were resident within the United States. In subsequent months these controls were applied with increasing severity to aliens from Japan, and soon to American citizens of Japanese ancestry, while they were substantially relaxed for German and Italian aliens. Within one year after the outbreak of war the 112,000 Japanese Americans on the Pacific Coast—two-thirds of whom were United States citizens—were in government camps under armed guard, and restrictions on citizens and aliens of German and Italian origin had become much lighter.

The history of the evacuation begins with the first imposition of controls upon enemy aliens by the Department of Justice. Increasingly severe restrictions—including exclusion of all enemy aliens from small coastal areas and the establishment of a curfew for those living in a larger zone—followed rapidly as demands for closer supervision arose from the War Department and the Western Defense Command (WDC). Before long, in response to what it deemed a serious threat to national security, the WDC sought and gained power to remove all enemy aliens whom it judged dangerous. The penultimate step was the forcible exclusion of all Japanese from the entire coastal area of the Pacific Coast states. The climax was the decision for their internment.

ALIEN ENEMY CONTROL PROGRAMS

The opening of the war found Lieutenant General John Lesesne De-Witt,[1] commanding officer of the WDC, charged with "the defense of the Pacific Coast . . . against attacks by land, sea, and air; and the local protection of establishments and communications vital to the National Defense for which adequate defense cannot be provided by local civilian authorities."[2] Among the millions under the protection of the general's forces were the 112,000 persons of Japanese ancestry.[3] Some forty thousand of these were aliens—men and women averaging approximately fifty-five years in age—born in Japan and debarred by American law from American citizenship.[4] Most of these had entered the United States before immigration from the Orient was prohibited in 1924. Their seventy thousand descendants, American citizens by virtue of their birth, were of an average age of about twenty. Scheduled to take minor roles in the episode were the 113,847 Italian and 97,080 German aliens in the Western states.

Of the five million aliens in the United States, the war converted 900,000 into enemy aliens. President Roosevelt signed three proclamations to protect the country against any overt acts by them. Presidential proclamations issued on December 7 and 8 declared all nationals and subjects of Japan, Germany, and Italy, who were not actually naturalized, to be "alien enemies" and prescribed their conduct.[5] They were enjoined to preserve the peace, to refrain from acts of hostility toward the United States, and not to give "information, aid and comfort" to its enemies. They might be excluded from any area, they were subject to various travel and living restrictions, and they were not to have in their possession any of a long list of contraband articles. Those "deemed dan-

---

[1] For notes to chapter iii see pp. 352–371.

gerous to the public peace or safety of the United States" were subject to "summary apprehension."

The Department of Justice, charged with the enforcement of the regulations of the presidential proclamations within the continental United States, acted quickly to put into effect its long-prepared program of alien-enemy control. Its first activity was to round up suspected alien enemies. By the evening of Pearl Harbor day, 736 Japanese nationals on the mainland had been taken into custody. Four days later 1,370 Japanese nationals were under guard.[6] By the middle of February, 2,192 Japanese aliens were under arrest in the United States, as well as numerous Germans and Italians.[7] In Hawaii, 879 aliens were picked up in December and the early months of 1942.[8] These first arrests on the mainland and in the islands took into custody Issei businessmen, religious and community leaders, officers of the Japanese associations, all Shinto and Buddhist priests and priestesses, many Japanese-language newspaper editors and owners, and most Japanese-language school teachers. At the request of the Navy all Japanese fishermen operating out of Terminal Island in Los Angeles Harbor, were interned.[9]

The arrests of suspected aliens on the outbreak of war had been planned for some time and were made on the basis of information gathered by the Department of Justice before Pearl Harbor. In 1941 a "delimitation agreement" had been reached between the Justice, War, and Navy departments according to which the Department of Justice, acting through the Federal Bureau of Investigation, was to be the only agency to conduct antiespionage and sabotage-security investigations of the civilian population, save that the Navy was given joint jurisdiction with the FBI over the Japanese population of continental United States. Apart from this responsibility the Navy was to be concerned only with its own personnel and employees; the Army would undertake investigations of only those civilians employed in its establishments. The exchange of information between the Office of Naval Intelligence and the FBI about the domestic Japanese population was provided for. Within the Department of Justice the Special Defense Unit had been established in 1940 to specify the criteria whereby the "dangerousness" of alien enemies was to be assessed and to conduct an "advance screening," using data secured by the FBI, of citizens as well as of aliens considered potentially dangerous. In December, 1941, an Alien Enemy Control Unit was established in the department under the jurisdiction of the assistant to the Attorney General; Edward J. Ennis was appointed director of the unit on December 22, 1941.[10] In addition to continuing the alien-enemy security program, the unit was to institute the Alien Enemy

Hearing Board program, and prepare regulations for the control of alien enemies and supervise their enforcement.[11] Preparatory to the outbreak of war, the unit had prepared dossiers on aliens who were suspected, for any reason, of being likely to commit espionage or sabotage. Japanese aliens holding office or taking active part in Japanese associations or organizations on the West Coast were considered likely to be loyal to Japan and were placed in the first category of suspicion. Those who played minor roles in the associations or made only small contributions were classified as less dangerous. Although the department had planned to intern only those aliens deemed most dangerous and to place others under surveillance, the nature of the attack and the quickly spreading rumors that resident Japanese had assisted the attackers at Pearl Harbor led it summarily to arrest all Japanese aliens in all classes of suspicion. There were no indiscriminate large-scale raids or mass round-ups of aliens: "Each arrest was made on the basis of information concerning the specific alien taken into custody."[12]

In the weeks following Pearl Harbor the Department of Justice acted to implement and enforce the travel and contraband provisions of the presidential proclamations. On December 19 the department stated that alien enemies were not prevented by the proclamations from carrying on their usual business activities within their communities.[13] On December 29, alien enemies in seven Western states were ordered to surrender radio transmitters, short-wave radio receivers, and certain types of cameras to local police by January 5, 1942. A second announcement applied these regulations to Arizona and the continental United States generally and on January 1, 1942, the surrender of "all firearms of any description" was ordered.[14]

Various other federal and state governmental agencies placed restrictions on the economic activities of alien enemies, some extending their restraints and prohibitions to Japanese of American citizenship. The federal Treasury Department at first clamped down hard on Japanese aliens in business but restrictions were considerably relaxed within a few weeks.[15] The California State Board of Equalization revoked the licenses of Japanese aliens to sell alcoholic beverages in December, 1941, and in February, 1942, revoked those of Japanese Americans and discharged its twenty Japanese employees.[16] On April 2, 1942, the California State Personnel Board dismissed all Japanese employed in the state's civil service—in spite of a ruling by Attorney General Earl Warren that such discrimination was unlawful.

In mid-December, DeWitt became dissatisfied with the manner in which the Department of Justice was moving to enforce the enemy-alien travel and contraband provisions of the presidential proclamations and especially with the fact that it had not established prohibited zones around strategic West Coast installations. According to the *Final Report* on the WDC's Japanese evacuation program, he had "become convinced that the military security of the coast required these measures."[17] On December 22 he wired the commanding general of the Army's field forces in Washington requesting that "the War Department urge the Attorney General to issue the necessary regulations to make proclamations of the President referring to Japanese aliens effective. FBI agencies ... [are] ready to enforce provisions of proclamations but are powerless to act until the Attorney General issues his instructions. This is urgent. Prompt action is required."[18] He requested that representatives of the War and Justice departments meet with him in San Francisco, "to crystallize a program of forthright action to deal with subversive segments of the population."[19]

Stimulated by the general's demand, the War Department approached the Department of Justice and a number of conferences were held in Washington in late December. Assistant Secretary of War John J. McCloy,[20] Major General Allen W. Gullion, the Provost Marshal General, and Major Karl R. Bendetsen,[21] represented the War Department. Attorney General Francis Biddle[22] appointed Mr. James H. Rowe, Jr.,[23] the Assistant to the Attorney General, and Mr. Edward J. Ennis, Chief of the Alien Enemy Control Unit, as delegates from the Department of Justice. At these conferences it was decided that a discussion of policies and programs to deal with alien enemies would be held with DeWitt in San Francisco from January 3 to 5, 1942. Mr. Rowe would attend as a representative of the Department of Justice. Major Bendetsen, who had been serving in the Judge Advocate General's office, was selected by McCloy to act as the representative requested by DeWitt to participate in the conference and for several weeks he was attached to McCloy's office to act as liaison between McCloy and DeWitt in matters pertaining to civil affairs.

Immediately after the Washington talks, Major Bendetsen was dispatched to the coast. In connection with the discussions, he presented a memorandum to DeWitt on January 3, 1942. "Immediate alien enemy control requirements" were stated to be the implementation of presidential proclamations over travel, registration of alien enemies, delegation by the Attorney General to FBI agents of authority to issue alien-enemy apprehension warrants, and the establishment of areas from which alien enemies should be excluded. Authority to establish these areas must be delegated to the military commander in each theatre of operations. "The enforcing authority, viz. power to evict or apprehend violators should be delegated concurrently to the Military Commander . . . as well as to the FBI special agents in charge." Bendetsen stated that "unless the Attorney General is prepared immediately to approve and initiate the foregoing program, the necessity for seeking Presidential transfer of authority from the Attorney General to the Secretary of War is manifest."[24] The points in this memorandum were emphasized by DeWitt in the conferences with the Department of Justice and foreshadowed future policy.

The conferences on the coast between Rowe and General DeWitt, with Major Bendetsen present as an aide to the general, were held from January 2 through 5, in San Francisco. The general urged that a broad control program be immediately undertaken by the Department of Justice which would include "spot raids" on every house in a specified locality, whether inhabited by enemy aliens or citizens, to search for and seize contraband, and the setting up of prohibited zones around coastal installations from which enemy aliens were to be barred. The Department of Justice set forth in a memorandum what it was prepared to do,[25] and the general subsequently agreed that the department's proposals were a step in the right direction but expressed dissatisfaction at its refusal to undertake "mass raids" in the search for contraband.[26] Agreement between the two parties was finally reached and expressed in a joint memorandum of January 6 embodying "the immediate understandings which had been developed." The Department of Justice would declare prohibited zones and provide for the exclusion of enemy aliens from them. It would designate restricted areas, entertain Army recommendations for them, and require the Army to describe exactly each restricted area. "Indications are that, should Army recommendations include areas in which there is resident a large number of alien enemies and evacuation will thereby be rendered necessary, he [the Attorney General] will also require the submission of detailed plans for evacuation and resettlement."[27] Raids would be directed against only the premises of enemy aliens and only if the names and addresses of the suspects were submitted to the department. As the Navy had also expressed its concern about the need for restricted areas, the conferees agreed that "the Army will request the Navy to submit its recommendations through the Commanding General."[28]

In the course of the conferences, DeWitt expressed the opinion that the measures he had proposed would be adequate to deal with the problem of subversives. Rowe later stated that General DeWitt had said in referring to the demand already made by a Los Angeles group, that "he 'thinks mass evacuation is damned nonsense!' and I agreed with him."[29]

The Department of Justice moved quickly to implement the program agreed upon. Before the conference was over it had directed enemy aliens to deposit with local police *all* contraband articles listed in the presidential proclamation by January 7, 1942. The Attorney General called on the White House for authority to register all alien enemies and on January 14, President Roosevelt issued a proclamation ordering registration during the week of February 2.[30] Further, the department initiated a series of widespread raids by the FBI, aided by sheriff's deputies and local police, of the residences and business premises of Japanese aliens to search for contraband or evidence of espionage and subversive activities. Beginning with a large-scale raid on the Japanese settlement on Terminal Island on February 2, when four hundred persons were rounded up and held for questioning, the raids continued through February and into March.[31] They received dramatic newspaper treatment.

Differences of opinion as to the significance of the results of the raids, as well as to the policy to be followed toward the aliens charged with possessing prohibited material, developed between the Department of Justice and the WDC. At first, at DeWitt's insistence, a very strict policy was adopted. According to John K. Burling, Assistant Chief of the Alien Enemy Control Unit,

DeWitt and [General George C.] Marshall, [Chief of Staff, United States Army] wanted everybody who was caught with contraband interned, irrespective of intent or of any linkage between the contraband and possible danger to internal security. DeWitt sold this idea to Marshall who in turn got after Roosevelt who in turn ordered the Solicitor General—Biddle was out of town—to follow Marshall's recommendation. An order was issued and chaos followed. People were detained for having flashlights, Red Cross medals, rusty pistols, etc.[32]

But Biddle quickly revised the policy and limited the definition of contraband when the absurdity of the strict policy became apparent. Despite the extensive character of the raids the results were negative: no espionage or sabotage was disclosed or evidence found that any was planned.[33] No Japanese, citizen or alien, was indicted or convicted of sabotage, espionage, or any major violation of wartime security laws.

In the January conferences between DeWitt and Rowe, agreement had been reached on the character of the zones to be established around militarily important installations. Alien enemies were to be totally excluded from "prohibited" areas. Those residing within such areas had to move out by a given date, after which no alien enemy could enter.[34] The time between the date of announcement and the deadline ranged from nine to twenty-six days for the five proclamations of the Department of Justice. Alien enemies residing in "restricted" areas had to keep a curfew and curtail unnecessary travel. Those violating regulations were liable to immediate apprehension and internment in the camps of the Department of Justice.

At the conclusion of the January conference in San Francisco, DeWitt immediately asked his four sector generals and the commandants of the three West Coast naval districts to send in their recommendations for prohibited and restricted zones, and these were received by him within a few days. Although DeWitt had agreed to send in his recommendations not later than January 9, his first requests were sent to the War Department for transmittal to the Department of Justice on January 21.[35] DeWitt's headquarters apparently altered some of the recommendations before forwarding them to Washington.[36]

DeWitt's first recommendations were received by the War Department on January 25, and forwarded by it to the Department of Justice that same day. The Department of Justice acted immediately. On January 29 it issued a press release announcing that "a number of areas on the west coast are being designated as prohibited areas from which all German, Italian and Japanese alien enemies are to be completely excluded" and which "have been recommended for selection by the War Department after weeks of careful study under the personal direction of Lieutenant General J. L. DeWitt." The two areas mentioned in this first proclamation were the waterfront of San Francisco and the immediate vicinity of the municipal airport in Los Angeles; aliens were to be out of these areas by February 24, 1942.[37] On January 31, an additional sixty-nine prohibited areas in California, from which all aliens were to be excluded after February 15, were described in a press release.[38] A third release on February 2 described an additional fifteen prohibited areas in California which aliens were to leave by February 24.[39]

Eighty-six prohibited zones were delineated in these first three Department of Justice announcements. There were seventeen areas along the coast, typically several miles in length and running inland from the shore to the nearest highway. There were thirteen areas around San Francisco Bay, including the dock areas of the bay cities, airports, terminals, industrial sections, and military and naval installations. There was one inland mountain area and fifteen small areas in various cities, chiefly Los Angeles and its suburbs, around airports, railroad stations, and the like. There were forty extremely small areas, five hundred to a thousand feet in diameter, around hydroelectric stations, gas works, pumping plants, dams, etc.

Sometime after January 21 (probably very near the end of January),[40] DeWitt sent in a second request, which asked for additional prohibited areas and some restricted areas in California, Oregon, and Washington. On February 3 the War Department forwarded the recommendations to the Department of Justice and on the next day they were proclaimed by that department. Seven areas in Washington and twenty-four in Oregon were classified as prohibited areas from which enemy aliens were to be excluded after February 15.[41] All of these were areas five hundred or a thousand feet in diameter around dams, power plants, or similar installations. A second release announced that the entire coast-line of California from the Oregon border south to a point approximately 50 miles north of Los Angeles, and extending inland for distances varying from 30 to 150 miles, had been declared a "restricted area" for all alien enemies.[42] Japanese, German, and Italian aliens living in this area were ordered to restrict their travel and conform to a curfew. Any alien enemy violating these regulations was subject to "immediate apprehension and internment." United States attorneys were authorized to grant exceptions "where a compelling reason exists and after completion of a suitable investigation." Eleven other small areas immediately surrounding various hydroelectric plants in the mountains of eastern California were classified as restricted; February 24 was the date on which the curfew and travel limitation became effective. Finally, on February 7, the department announced that eighteen small areas in Arizona were to be prohibited to aliens after February 24.[43]

Upon the initiation of this program, Attorney General Biddle appointed Tom C. Clark,[44] then serving as a special assistant to the Attorney General and chief of the West Coast office of the Antitrust Division, to be coördinator of the alien-enemy control program for the WDC and to act as liaison between the Command, the Department of Justice, and the federal agencies providing social assistance to the dislocated aliens. This program was set up at the request of Biddle by the Federal Security Agency on January 31. The West Coast office of the Federal Security Agency, under the guidance of Richard M. Neustadt, Pacific Coast regional director, provided general welfare services to the aliens. About 10,000 persons—8,000 Japanese and the rest German and Italians[45]—were forced to leave their homes and find other accomodations and, in many cases, other employment. Despite the federal program for their assistance, many suffered considerable distress and financial loss. Hostile public opinion made it difficult for the aliens, especially the Japanese, to secure housing and employment, and no provision was made for custodial care of their residential or business property.[46]

A third request, again asking for additional zones, sent by DeWitt to the Department of Justice sometime around the end of January or the beginning of February, recommended the establishment of prohibited zones in Arizona, Oregon, and Washington. In Washington, the recommended prohibited zone included virtually all of the territory lying west of the Cascades—which would have required general enemy-alien evacuation from this area.[47] This recommendation was forwarded by Stimson to the Department of Justice on February 3.[48] (The *Final Report* does not indicate what considerations led DeWitt to submit a third recommendation of such sweeping character so shortly after sending in requests for small zones in the two states, but it does state that "the acceptance by the Attorney General of the Washington and Oregon recommendations would not have provided the security which the military situation then required.")[49] About this time, the Department of Justice was unofficially informed that DeWitt was preparing to ask that Los Angeles County be declared a prohibited zone.

The Department of Justice, however, refused to accept the third recommendation. Biddle wrote to Stimson on February 9 that DeWitt's recommendations of prohibited areas for Oregon and Washington included the cities of Portland, Seattle, and Tacoma, and, therefore "contemplates mass evacuation of many thousands of alien enemies. No reasons were given for this mass evacuation." Biddle said that he had been advised

that Lieutenant General J. L. DeWitt is sending to you additional recommendations that all of Los Angeles County be designated as a prohibited zone. The evacuation of all alien enemies from this area would, of course, present a problem of very great magnitude. The Department of Justice is not physically equipped to carry out any mass evacuation. It would mean that only the War Department has the equipment and personnel to manage the task.

The proclamations directing the Department of Justice to "apprehend and, where necessary, evacuate alien enemies," continued Biddle, "do not, of course, include American citizens of Japanese race. Should they have to be evacuated, I believe that this would have to be done on the military necessity in the particular area. Such action, therefore, should, in my opinion, be taken by the War Department and not by the Department of Justice."[50]

In response to this request for justification, DeWitt submitted "a resume of the military considerations which prompted his recommendation."[51] But the Department of Justice, after examining the report, again refused to establish the zones requested.[52]

CITIZEN AND ALIEN CONTROL

The early controls were imposed only upon alien enemies, but later controls were enforced against citizens as well, and eventually came to be confined to Japanese American citizens and aliens. These steps toward controls over citizens began with DeWitt's request for extensive authority in mid-February, proceeded through its modification by the War Department in Washington, and culminated in its embodiment in Executive Order 9066 and subsequent ratification by Congress in Public Law 503.

DeWitt's "Final Recommendation."—None of DeWitt's requests for action by the Department of Justice in the December and January conferences or his formal recommendations to the department for zones had called for restrictions on American citizens or for their exclusion from coastal regions. During late January and early February, the problem of distinguishing Japanese aliens from citizens and the legal means available for removing American citizens of Japanese ancestry from "very limited areas" was discussed in conferences between Biddle, Rowe, Ennis, McCloy, and Gullion. President Roosevelt was informed of these discusions. On January 30 Biddle wrote to him that the War and Justice departments were "conferring on the question whether the military situation is acute enough to require that any action be taken against such citizens. The Department of Justice is also making a study concerning the legal problems involved in taking action against such citizens."[53]

In early February, when it was clear that DeWitt and the Department of Justice were reaching an impasse on the question of mass exclusion of alien enemies, McCloy dispatched Colonel Bendetsen[54] to the West Coast again to confer with DeWitt. After a week or so of discussions. Bendetsen, on or about February 16, carried back the recommendation of DeWitt that "some method be developed empowering the Federal Government to provide for the evacuation from sensitive areas of all persons of Japanese ancestry and any other persons individually or collectively regarded as potentially dangerous."[55] This recommendation, in the form of a memorandum to Secretary Stimson, dated February 14, and headed "Evacuation of Japanese and Other Subversive Persons from the Pacific Coast," is known as the "Final Recommendation."

The alien-enemy control program was under the control of the Department of Justice, which, with some reluctance, was putting DeWitt's wishes into effect. DeWitt now moved to break off this relationship and asked for a direct grant of power to take such measures to control aliens and citizens as he saw fit. In his "Final Recommendation" he asked that the Secretary of War "procure from the President direction and authority to designate military areas [in] the Western Theatre of Operations" from which he might "exclude all Japanese, all alien enemies, and all other persons suspected for any reason by the administering military authorities of being actual or potential saboteurs, espionage agents, or fifth columnists." All enemy aliens would "be evacuated and interned." Japanese American citizens would be "offered an opportunity to accept voluntary internment, under guard, at the place of internment" of the aliens. If they "declined to accept voluntary internment" they were to be "excluded from all military areas." He recommended that "mass internment be considered as largely a temporary expedient pending selective resettlement, to be accomplished by the various Security Agencies of the Federal and State Governments."

Evacuation was held necessary by DeWitt in the light of the protective mission of the WDC, an "estimate of the situation," and the "disposition of the Japanese" and of other "subversive persons." DeWitt's "estimate of the situation" itemized four "possible and probable enemy activities: (a) Naval attack on shipping in coastal waters; (b) Naval attack on coastal cities and vital installations; (c) Air raids on vital installations, particularly within two hundred miles of the coast; (d) Sabotage of vital installations throughout the WDC." The Japanese along the coast were held likely to commit acts of espionage and sabotage:

In the war in which we are now engaged racial affinities are not severed by migration. The Japanese race is an enemy race and while many second and third generation Japanese born on United States soil, possessed of United States citizenship, have become "Americanized," the racial strains are undiluted. . . . It therefore follows that along the vital Pacific Coast over 112,000 potential enemies of Japanese extraction are at large today.

DeWitt did not state that acts of sabotage or espionage had occurred; only that "there are indications that these [Japanese] are organized and ready for concerted action at a favorable opportunity. The very fact that no sabotage has taken place to date is a disturbing and confirming indication that such action will be taken."[56]

The third factor in his argument was the geographical disposition of the Japanese. The location of farms and residences of "alien Japanese and American citizens of Japanese ancestry" in Washington, Oregon, and California was described, their proximity to aircraft factories, port facilities, and navy yards emphasized. In addition to the Japanese, "disposed within the vital coastal strip already mentioned are large numbers of Italians and Germans, foreign and native born, among whom are many individuals who constitute an actual or potential menace to the safety of the nation."[57]

Executive Order 9066.—DeWitt's recommendation was considered by the War Department and accepted by the Army chiefs and civilian heads within a period of a few days. General George C. Marshall, Chief of Staff, reviewed and approved his recommendation.[58] The civilian heads, Secretary Stimson,[59] Undersecretary Robert S. Patterson,[60] and Assistant Secretary McCloy also reviewed and approved it. Patterson "strongly urged immediate and thorough action" and pushed evacuation harder than any other official.[61] All of the civilian heads of the department deferred to the military. According to McCloy: "the problem was posed to General DeWitt: was the evacuation of Japanese citizens and aliens necessary? General DeWitt consulted his staff and his area commanders. The military men made the decision. It was a military decision."[62] With the acceptance by the War Department of a policy of civilian control primarily directed at the Japanese minority, its difference of opinion with the Department of Justice was complete.[63] The Department of Justice's view generally had been that mass evacuation was unnecessary, mass evacuation of citizens was unconstitutional, and any mass evacuation was of too great a magnitude for the department to handle.[64]

The issue came to a head on the evening of February 17, when officials of the two departments met. The representatives of the Department of Justice—Biddle, Rowe, and Ennis—expected to confer on the matter of evacuating aliens from large areas and the discussion opened on that point, Ennis and Rowe arguing that such action was not necessary. Unexpectedly, the Army representative, Provost Marshal General Gullion, demanded power for the Army to remove both aliens and citizens, and read the draft of an executive order to that effect. Biddle accepted the Army proposal without argument.[65] As Rowe recalled it, "The Attorney General immediately wanted to get to work to polish up the order. His attitude amazed me. Ennis almost wept. I was so mad that I could not speak at all myself and the meeting soon broke up."[66]

On the following morning, February 18, the same Department of Justice officials met with McCloy and Bendetsen in Stimson's office to draft the order. Rowe secured the approval of the Bureau of the Budget by the afternoon of February 19 and in the early evening of that day the order was presented to President Roosevelt and received his signature. The President did not ask for a justification of the program nor was the subject considered by the Cabinet.[67]

Executive Order 9066 declared that "the successful prosecution of the war requires every possible protection against espionage and against sabotage to national defense material, national defense premises, and national defense utilities."[68] In pursuit of this goal, the Secretary of War, or the military commander whom he might designate, was authorized "to prescribe military areas in such places and of such extent as he . . . may determine, from which any or all persons may be excluded, and with respect to which, the right of any person to enter, remain in, or leave shall be subject to whatever restrictions the Secretary . . . or the Military Commander may impose in his discretion." The Secretary was also authorized "to provide for residents of any such areas who are excluded therefrom, such transportation, food, shelter, and other accommodations as may be necessary . . . until other arrangements are made, to accomplish the purpose of this order." The designation of such areas would supersede the designation of prohibited and restricted zones by the Department of Justice. There was no reference to internment.

With the issuance of the order, the War Department immediately instructed DeWitt on how he was to use the powers to be delegated to him, and significantly modified his recommendations. He had asked for a grant of power to intern all enemy aliens in the coastal area and to exclude Japanese American citizens. The department informed him that his program was not to be one of summary internment; he was to provide for "voluntary" and unsupervised movement of the groups proscribed, with free choice of residence in "open" areas, and was to supply food and housing where necessary. In a memorandum of February 20, McCloy suggested the designation of military areas, and within these areas "protective zones." From these zones, he told DeWitt, "you will provide for the exclusion of all persons" who are Japanese aliens, American citizens of Japanese lineage, and any person suspected of being a spy, saboteur, or fifth-columnist. "In most critical areas you may consider it necessary to bring about an almost immediate evacuation" of Japanese aliens and Japanese American citizens. Furthermore, German and Italian aliens as a group were not to be affected for the present. McCloy directed DeWitt to exclude "persons" who were German aliens "where in your judgment it is essential." Italian aliens and persons of Italian lineage, said Stimson in a February 20 letter to DeWitt, should be left undisturbed unless they were "undesirable" or "a definite danger," because "such persons [are] potentially less dangerous than other enemy nationalities," and because of the size of the group.[69]

The policy toward German and Italian enemy aliens set by these letters was confirmed in subsequent War Department directives to DeWitt. On May 22 the War Department informed DeWitt that "for the present time there is to be no collective evacuation of German and Italian enemy aliens in the WDC."[70] This was confirmed later in the year by a War Department memorandum to the same effect.[71]

Executive Order 9066 and the grant of power to DeWitt were made public on February 20. Immediately various federal officials and the press pointed out that the measure was directed against American citizens of Japanese ancestry. There was widespread speculation about the forthcoming program, but DeWitt revealed nothing of his plans.[72] The absence of official statements added greatly to the confusion and concern among the Japanese, as well as among the Germans and Italians, many of whom felt (erroneously) that the prohibited zone requirements had been cancelled. It was some time before it was made clear that the original Department of Justice program was still in force and that the deadlines for removal had to be met. The Japanese suffered not only from the official and unofficial restrictions placed on their commercial and agricultural activities, but from uncertainty as to their future.

Public Law 503.—Although Executive Order 9066 empowered the military commander designated by the Secretary of War to take "such steps as . . . he may deem advisable to enforce compliance" with the orders and restrictions he imposed on citizens, the War Department, with the approval of President Roosevelt and the concurrence of the Department of Justice, secured the passage by Congress of an act providing for enforcement in the federal courts.[73] Congressional consideration of the measure was perfunctory, many legislators apparently believing it was aimed only at aliens, and scarcely any objection was raised. Within twelve days after its introduction in the Senate on March 9 it was passed unanimously by both houses and signed by the President.

Immediately after the promulgation of Executive Order 9066, the War Department drafted a proposed statute describing the violation of an order of a military commander to a civilian, in a district proclaimed to be a "military area," as a misdemeanor punishable by a fine and imprisonment. The approval of President Roosevelt was secured and the Department of Justice was consulted on its content and phrasing.[74] On March 9, 1942, a draft of the legislation was sent by Secretary Stimson to Senator Robert R. Reynolds, chairman of the Senate Military Affairs Committee, and to Speaker Sam Rayburn of the House of Representatives. The covering letter, identical to both officials, noted that the purpose of the measure was "to provide for enforcement in the Federal criminal courts of orders issued under the authority of Executive Order . . . No. 9066."[75] The measure was introduced in the Senate and House on March 9 and 10, and referred by both chambers to their Committees on Military Affairs.[76]

The Senate Committee on Military Affairs considered the proposed measure on March 13. Colonel B. M. Bryan, chief of the Alien Division, Office of Provost Marshal General, represented the War Department. In the one-hour session, the legislation was treated as though it concerned only alien enemies. The discussion was given that direction by the opening remarks of Colonel Bryan, supported by statements of the chairman when he said that "the bill we are considering is authority over these aliens that we are proposing to move."[77] There was one reference to "American citizens of Japanese extraction"; they were held to be "dual citizens."[78] In support of the legislation Colonel Bryan stated that "last evening General DeWitt called me on the telephone from the west coast and he stated that the passage of this bill was necessary to enable him to properly carry out the provision of the Executive Order,"[79] and added the assurance of McCloy that "there can be no doubt that the legislation is sufficient to cover the violation of curfew and similar restrictions."[80] The committee unanimously approved the proposed act, and in its report stated the measure was "essential" for enforcement of DeWitt's orders.[81]

The House Committee on Military Affairs met to consider the bill on March 17, under the chairmanship of Congressman Andrew J. May. Secretary Stimson had written to May in support of the measures on March 14, requesting that Congress expedite passage of the bill because "General DeWitt indicated that he was preparing to enforce certain restrictions at once for the purpose of protecting certain vital national defense interests but did not desire to proceed until enforcement machinery had been set up."[82] Colonel Bryan, present as the War Department representative, opened the half-hour session of the committee by stating that DeWitt had informed him that the measure was needed "to enforce provisions of the Executive Order" and that McCloy "was particularly anxious that the committee be informed that General DeWitt proposed to impose curfew restrictions and wants the legislation broad enough to cover the violation of any such restrictions."[83] The committee members understood that the bill was "aimed at citizens," as the chairman remarked,[84] but there were no objections and the only suggestions offered were in favor of stiffening the measure.

On March 19 Senator Reynolds brought up the bill for Senate consideration. He stated that he was introducing the measure at the request of the Secretary of War and that the Committee on Military Affairs had approved it. He described the measure as dealing "primarily with the activities of aliens and alien enemies."[85] He noted once that the act would apply to American citizens. Observing that "one of our most important fronts is the American front and without the proper control of aliens and enemies of this Government" success could not be expected on other fronts, Senator Reynolds spoke for twenty minutes in support of the bill, describing what he asserted were fifth-column activities at Pearl Harbor and the possibility of sabotage on the West Coast against dams, oil fields, and defense facilities. "Japanese settlements are often near these vital areas. Let us not forget that these Japanese who constitute a grave peril to our nation are aided and abetted by an overwhelming mass of disloyal German and Italian sympathizers." He quoted a statement by Senator Guy M. Gillette that "although American-born Japanese are regarded as United States citizens, they are also held to be subjects of Nippon unless they specifically renounce the Emperor. Few renunciations have been made and all citizens may be conscripted into the Japanese service." Senator Reynolds claimed further: "Evidence that a tightly-knit fifth-column exists in the United States is daily being uncovered by the Federal Bureau of Investigation. . . . West Coast raids on Japanese colonies have yielded truckloads of guns, ammunition, dynamite and bombs. . . . Even Japanese army and navy uniforms have been found." The senator quoted newspaper headlines reporting arrests of Japanese, German, and other aliens. Admitting that many naturalized citizens were loyal, he insisted that the loyalty of many was questionable. The War Department had asked for this bill "which will confer broad powers on the military authorities charged with the protection of certain zones in our country. We well know that the necessities of our situation are such that these powers must even extend to the control of persons who are citizens of the United States." He ended by referring again to "the perils which confront the Nation" from aliens and trusted that "we have a concrete measure to deal with the peril."

There were no objections to the substance of the measure, although Senator Robert A. Taft of Ohio objected to its wording. He felt that it was the "sloppiest" criminal law he had seen: he did not wish to delay passage but he thought it should be redrafted "in some kind of legal form, instead of in the form of a military order."[86] The bill was read for the third time and passed by a voice vote.

On the same day, Congressman May introduced the measure in the House and briefly explained the provisions.[87] He said that the penalties "apply only if it shall appear that the party charged knew or should have known of the existence or extent of the restrictions. . . . We want to protect any citizen of the country against being caught up who is unaware of the order or of the restrictions or regulations made by the Secretary of War." Three members of the House spoke. Congressman E. A. Michener of Michigan objected to the lack of attention paid by the House to the bill.[88] Congressman John J. Sparkman of Alabama said that Dewitt had asked for the measure since he had no way of enforcing his orders to civilians; if excluded civilians returned, there was no penalty provided by law. Congressman R. F. Rich of Pennsylvania asked if the zones were marked plainly "so that citizens of this country cannot get into them without their knowledge and then be penalized." May replied that the zones were "definitely defined." However, "citizens of this country will never be questioned about them, as a matter of fact. This is intended for a particular situation about which the gentleman knows."[89] The measure passed by voice vote.

The legislation was laid before President Roosevelt on March 20, 1942, and signed by him on March 21.

Forced exclusion of coastal Japanese.—DeWitt's first official act, using the power granted him under Executive Order 9066, was to order the exclusion from the coast of all Japanese, aliens and citizens alike.[90] With this order began the second phase of the evacuation episode. In the first phase, under Department of Justice supervision, relatively small numbers of German, Italian, and Japanese enemy aliens had been required to move out of prohibited zones and large numbers of them living in restricted zones had had to restrict their travel and obey a curfew. Now all Japanese—Japanese nationals and American citizens of Japanese lineage—and only Japanese, were ordered out of an extensive district along the coast and allowed to resettle in interior communities of their own choice. German and Italian enemy aliens were not referred to by the order and remained undisturbed, subject only to the regulations of the Department of Justice announced in January and February governing residence in prohibited and restricted areas, travel, curfew, and the like.

The proclamation, drawing its authority explicitly from Executive Order 9066 and the subdelegation of authority to DeWitt from Stimson, asserted that

the Western Defense Command embraces the entire Pacific Coast of the United States, which by its geographical location is particularly subject to attack, to attempted invasion by the armed forces of nations with which the United States is now at war and . . . is subject to espionage and acts of sabotage,

thereby requiring the adoption of military measures necessary to establish safeguards against such enemy operations.[91]

Therefore "the present situation requires as a matter of military necessity"[92] the establishment of two extensive areas along the West Coast,
entitled Military Areas Nos. 1 and 2, and of a larger number of "zones"
within the areas. Military Area No. 1 was a coastal strip which included
the western halves of Washington, Oregon, and California, and the
southern half of Arizona. Military Area No. 2 comprised the eastern
portions of the three coastal states and the northern portion of Arizona.
The four other states in the WDC were also made military areas.[93] The
proclamation declared that "such persons or classes of persons as the
situation may require will by subsequent proclamation be excluded
from all of Military Area No. 1 and from such of those Zones A-2 to
A-99 as are within Military Area No. 2." It continued: "The designation
of Military Area No. 2 as such does not contemplate any prohibition or
regulation or restrictions except with respect to the zones established
therein." German, Italian, and Japanese aliens and "any person of
Japanese Ancestry"[94] were required to execute change-of-residence
notices.[95] The Department of Justice regulations governing restricted
and prohibited areas were to continue in force.

The proclamation did not specify who were to be excluded from
Military Area No. 1 and the prohibited zones in Area No. 2. But in a
press release accompanying the proclamation, DeWitt pointed to the
Japanese as those to be excluded. While "future proclamations would
affect . . . all persons suspected of espionage, sabotage, fifth-column or
other subversive activity" and German and Italian aliens, orders to be
issued in the near future would direct Japanese aliens and "American
born persons of Japanese lineage" to leave first. "Eventually orders will
be issued requiring all Japanese including those who are American-born
to vacate all of Military Area No. 1." DeWitt also stated that "immediate compulsory mass evacuation of all Japanese and other aliens . . .
is impracticable. . . . Those Japanese and other aliens who move into the
interior out of this area now will gain considerable advantage and in all
probability will not again be disturbed." He concluded by asserting that
"military necessity is the sole yardstick by which the Army has selected
the military areas from which the exclusion of certain groups will be
required."[96]

Official statements by DeWitt and Tom Clark spurred the Japanese
to move out of Area No. 1, Clark adding his denial that a mass evacuation was planned.[97] In a press release a week after the proclamation, the
WDC encouraged "Japanese living in the barred zone . . . to make and

follow their own plans for resettling inland."[98] The Command officially sponsored a "token movement" of 2,100 Japanese volunteers from Los Angeles to the Manzanar Assembly Center on March 21.[99]

To handle problems arising from the exclusion program, DeWitt established a Civil Affairs Division (G-5) as a planning agency of his staff on March 10, 1942. On the following day he created the Wartime Civil Control Administration (WCCA) "to carry out assigned missions involving civil control."[100] Bendetsen, who up to this time had been acting as liaison between DeWitt and McCloy and the War Department, was appointed head of both units, holding the positions of Assistant Chief of Staff for Civil Affairs and director of the Wartime Civil Control Administration.[101] The first directive from DeWitt ordered Bendetsen "to provide for the evacuation of all persons of Japanese ancestry from Military Area No. 1 and the California portion of Military Area No. 2 of the Pacific Coast with a minimum of economic and social dislocation, a minimum use of military personnel and maximum speed; and initially to employ all appropriate means to encourage voluntary migration."[102] Tom Clark, who had been coördinator of the Department of Justice's alien-enemy control program, served as coördinator of the federal civilian agencies assisting evacuees under the direction of the WCCA.

At the beginning of the forced exclusion program, Dillon Myer later related, the Command believed that "more than half the total Japanese population would be able to meet the evacuation deadlines for voluntary movement and would leave the prohibited area. For these people, the Army had no plans—they were to be free agents. For the other half of the west coast Japanese population, the Army had plans for two very large concentration points."[103] These two concentration points, according to the *Final Report*, were to be at Manzanar, California, and at Parker, Arizona, and were each to have a capacity of 10,000.[104] The two centers were planned to be "resting points from which the Japanese, once there, could proceed further eastward once they had secured jobs and community acceptance."[105] However, it was soon seen that centers would be needed for "virtually all evacuees," and accordingly site-selection teams were dispatched to the interior states.[106]

Three weeks after the first proclamation, DeWitt imposed a curfew on "all alien Japanese, all alien Germans, all alien Italians and all persons of Japanese ancestry" residing in Military Area No. 1 and in the prohibited zones of Military Area No. 2.[107] Further, the contraband prohibitions of the presidential proclamations of December 7, 1941, which had been directed to alien enemies, were now extended to all American-born Japanese within the WDC.

March was a period of strain and uncertainty for the 100,000 Japanese in the West Coast military area. Officially ordered to move, they daily read reports of the hostility of inland communities and statements by state governors and officials that Japanese were not welcome. There was widespread speculation and rumor about forthcoming policies, but no official statements clarified the situation or hinted what new programs might be in the making. Confusion was equally widespread over the policy in force. Congressman Tolan complained on March 19 that he "was unable to secure a clear-cut statement from anybody on the status of Japanese evacuees after they pass through the reception centers."[108]

Some Japanese did move out of the proscribed area. Between three and four thousand left Military Area No. 1 for the California portion of Area No. 2 in this period. Fresno County received 2,499, Tulare County 932, and Placer County 495.[109] In addition to these migrants, 4,899 left both military areas for points outside of California and did not return to be evacuated with their families or to join them in assembly or relocation centers.[110] Many of the inland-moving Japanese ran into trouble. Some were turned back by armed posses at the border of Nevada; others were jailed overnight; many interior communities posted "No Japs wanted" signs; and a few Japanese felt that they had been threatened with mob violence.[111]

POST-EXCLUSION ALIEN ENEMY CONTROLS

DeWitt, feeling that the regulations of the Department of Justice applying to alien enemies were inadequate, moved to increase the severity of the controls over them by his proclamations. Public Proclamation No. 1 (March 2, 1942) ordered all Japanese, German, or Italian nationals as well as Japanese citizens of the United States in Military Area No. 1 to send in change-of-residence notices. Public Proclamation No. 2 (March 16) broadened the area within which these classes had to report to the entire WDC. Public Proclamation No. 3 (March 24) ordered the curfew for these groups within Military Area No. 1 or the 933 zones in Military Areas Nos. 2, 3, 4, 5 and 6.[112] Applications could be made for travel permits for distances greater than those prescribed by the proclamations and for temporary curfew exemptions. As the Department of Justice differed with DeWitt over this program and refused to administer it, the WDC enlisted the services first of the United States Employment Service and later of the Office of Civil Defense to handle the thousands of applicants. Clearance from the military intelligence section of the WDC had to be obtained before permits or exemptions would be issued.

The winter of 1942 saw restrictions on all non-Japanese alien enemies further eased and then almost abolished. On October 12 President Roosevelt celebrated Columbus Day by declaring that Italian aliens were no longer considered alien enemies. DeWitt took official cognizance of this in Public Proclamation No. 13 (October 19) which exempted all citizens of Italy as well as aliens of enemy nationalities in the military service of the United States from curfew requirements, travel restrictions, and the provision of change-of-residence notices.[113] McCloy also recommended that the requirements for German alien enemies be relaxed, but DeWitt objected, stating that he would be inclined to tighten them if any practicable means existed to do so. However, six weeks later he issued Public Proclamation No. 15 (December 24) which abolished curfew and travel limitations for German aliens.[114]

Complete removal of restrictions and controls did not come until 1945. For alien enemies throughout the country, Presidential Proclamation 2647 (December 7, 1945) revoked the regulations forbidding the possession of contraband articles and the requirements for travel authorization laid down in the proclamations of December, 1941.[115]

INTERNMENT

The policy of the Justice and War departments immediately after December 7 had been to treat all alien enemies alike, but they came more and more to concentrate upon Japanese aliens and citizens—not without some reluctance by the Department of Justice, but with the clear approval of the civilian heads of the War Department and all duly constituted government officials.

Three months and three weeks after Pearl Harbor, the WDC changed its policy toward the Japanese from enforced exclusion to internment. In late March the Army ordered that no more Japanese should leave the coastal area and began to move them, under guard, into assembly centers. Early plans called for their resettlement at places of their own choice in the interior, but public hostility in the Rocky Mountain states blocked these proposals and led to the establishment of relocation centers, the "permanent" camps in which the Japanese were held under the guns of the Army and the supervision of the WRA. In June, 1942, the Japanese in the interior of California were also ordered into assembly and relocation centers. By November 1, some 110,000 Japanese were behind barbed wire in ten communities located in waste places in the Western, Mountain, and Plains states.

Coastal Japanese.—On March 27, 1942, General DeWitt's fourth public proclamation abruptly changed the treatment of the Japanese. Whereas under the proclamation of March 2 the Japanese in Military Area No. 1, the coastal strip extending from Canada to Mexico, had been told to move out, either to assembly centers or to communities in the interior, now, slightly more than three weeks after that command, they were instructed to remain where they were and to await further orders. These orders moved them under armed guard from their homes through assembly centers to confinement in relocation centers patrolled by military police.[116]

Public Proclamation No. 4 was short, and spoke only of prohibiting Japanese to leave the area, without mention of internment. Declaring that "it is necessary in order to provide for the welfare and to insure the orderly evacuation and resettlement of Japanese voluntarily migrating from Military Area No. 1, to restrict and regulate such migration," and drawing its authority implicitly from Executive Order 9066, the proclamation stated that "the present situation requires as a matter of military necessity" that "all alien Japanese and persons of Japanese ancestry who are within the limits of Military Area No. 1 be and they are hereby prohibited from leaving that area for any purpose until and to the extent that a future proclamation or order of this headquarters shall so permit or direct."[117] Violations by citizens of the proclamation and subsequent orders would be punished by the "criminal penalties of Public Law 503" and alien violators would be immediately apprehended and interned. The order took effect at midnight, March 29.

Press releases, containing statements by DeWitt and Bendetsen, accompanied the proclamation. DeWitt stated that the proclamation "means Japanese can evacuate only under military control. After Sunday, all movements of these persons will be regulated by the Army, for the protection of the Japanese, and to insure that proper shelter awaits them at their designated destination."[118] Bendetsen expanded on the reasons for the order: it was "to ensure an orderly evacuation and partly to protect the Japanese. Several groups planning voluntary evacuations have been fearful of starting through reports of threats in other states, should they pass through . . . The 'freezing' order prepares the way for an Army regulated program of removal."[119] He listed the assembly centers "where evacuees will go from their present homes when ordered to evacuate. They will be housed in present buildings and additional shelter until they are transferred to reception centers or other resettlement areas."

The development of the new policy comprised two steps: first, the decision was taken to stop the inland movement of the Japanese; second, the nature of their future residence in the interior states was determined. The first step—halting the movement of Japanese inland— was taken on the recommendation of Bendetsen and of the newly formed War Relocation Authority (WRA). On March 21 Bendetsen "recommended ... that evacuation be placed on the basis of complete Federal supervision and control."[120] On March 24, Milton H. Eisenhower, first director of the WRA,[121] formally recommended to DeWitt that the "voluntary" program be discontinued,[122] because of the public hostility displayed toward the Japanese in the interior states.[123]

After the issuance of Executive Order 9066 in February, James Rowe of the Department of Justice and others had been concerned with establishing a civilian agency to assume responsibility for the evacuees.[124] Eisenhower was called in for advice and assistance late in February. He visited the West Coast on March 7 to survey the situation at first hand. Returning to Washington on March 15 he participated in discussions on the character and responsibilities of the proposed agency with McCloy and officials in the Bureau of the Budget and assisted in preparing an executive order to establish it and define its powers and responsibilities. On March 18, 1942, Executive Order 9102, setting up the WRA, was signed by President Roosevelt and Eisenhower was appointed director.[125] Before leaving the West Coast he had informally recommended abandoning the exclusion program and his first act on taking office was formally to recommend its discontinuance.

It was only after the freezing order was issued that the Army and the WRA saw that the two existing reception centers would be inadequate and that it would be necessary to build both assembly and relocation centers.[126] It was then foreseen that relocation facilities would have to be developed for virtually all evacuees and plans were drawn up for the construction of ten large centers.[127]

The second step in the development of the new policy consisted of determining the character of the communities to which the Japanese would be moved and the activities of the Japanese after they got there. During March, WRA officials felt that their agency should provide: "(1) financial aid for Japanese who wanted to move but who were unable to do so for lack of funds; (2) small C.C.C. sort of work camps, hundreds of them scattered all over the country, the working population in each camp being employed in the surrounding neighborhood; (3) a group of way stations, perhaps as many as fifty, holding from 1,000 to 1,500 people." "In early March," Eisenhower explained later, "we had no conception of relocation centers as they finally evolved."[128] On April 2 Eisenhower announced a five-point program for employment of evacuees on public works (such as land development), agricultural and manufacturing production in relocation areas, private employment and private resettlement in independent and self-supporting communities.

But these plans and proposals had to be abandoned after a meeting called by WRA on April 7 in Salt Lake City, when WDC staff officers and federal officials, together with the governors and officials of ten western states—Utah, Nevada, Idaho, New Mexico, Arizona, Washington, Oregon, Montana, Wyoming, and Colorado—met with WRA officials. Eisenhower presented his proposals for the handling of the Japanese and pleaded for coöperation in instituting them. But most of the governors and attorney generals expressed bitter opposition to the program as outlined. Some suggested that the coastal states were using this as a method of getting rid of a long-standing problem by transferring it inland. Some denied that the Japanese, even though United States citizens, had any of the rights of citizenship. Some ominously hinted that the temper of their people was ready for vigilantism. "The official conception by State officers of the type of program best suited to the situation was one of concentration camps with workers being farmed out to work under armed guards. Some representatives advocated out-and-out detention camps for all Japanese."[129] In the opinions expressed, two points stood out, according to Eisenhower: First, "the governors and other state officials present demanded that no concentrations of Japanese Americans be allowed unless they were under military guard." Second, "the Army made it clear that it was unprepared to send out guards for small groups and that the minimum size groups for which it would supply guards was 5,000. Putting these two things together, it was clear that we had to abandon our ideas of small C.C.C. type camps and of way-stations and orient our thoughts toward large centers."[130] WRA plans were revised, and the operations of the agency were altered. Instead of acting primarily to assist the displaced persons to resettle in self-supporting communities and to set up self-supporting economic enterprises, the WRA was limited to developing agricultural production for evacuee use only, plus a short-lived camouflage-net project in three centers.

The conference's revelations of public opinion in the interior states toward the Japanese further affected the internment programs. It made necessary the abandonment of all immediate plans for individual relocation because of "the exceedingly hostile attitude demonstrated toward any resettlement by the people present at the meeting."[131] Eisenhower

informed President Roosevelt on June 18, 1942, that "a genuinely satisfactory relocation of the evacuees into American life" must await the
end of the war "when the prevailing attitudes of increasing bitterness
have been replaced by tolerance and understanding."[132]

WDC channeled the evacuees into temporary assembly centers or
reception centers and then to "permanent" relocation centers where
they were held under guard. The coastal strip, Military Area No. 1,
was divided by the Command into 99 "exclusion areas." Priorities were
established for the removal of the Japanese from these areas on the
basis of the Command's estimate of each area's military importance. As
arrangements were completed for the movement of the Japanese from
each area to a center, a Civilian Exclusion Order would be issued six
to seven days before the date of departure.[133] These orders, which did
not refer to internment, but stated only that "all persons of Japanese
ancestry, both alien and non-alien, be excluded," described, with the
aid of a sketch map, the area from which the Japanese were to be removed, gave the hour and day on which they were to be gone, and
ordered "a responsible member of each family and each individual living
alone" to report to the local civil-control station for registration. Within
five days following the posting of the order, all the Japanese in the area
were registered and processed at the stations to prepare them for movement to the assembly centers. After interviews with social workers and
representatives of various government agencies, and a medical examination, they were informed of the scheduled date and hour for their departure and were assigned to a specific bus or coach in the convoy. This
data was written on an identification tag which each person, adult or
child, wore prominently. Most of them were transported by bus or
train; some were allowed to drive to the assembly centers in their own
cars if the distance was not over a hundred miles.[134]

The evacuees were allowed to take only a few specified personal be-
longings. For each member of the family, "bedding and linens (no
mattresses) . . . toilet articles . . . extra clothing . . . sufficient knives, forks,
spoons, plates, bowls and cups . . . essential personal effects" were to be
taken.[135] Everything else had to be left behind. "No pets of any kind will
be permitted. No personal items and no household goods will be shipped
to the Assembly Center." Most evacuees had five days after official notice
of their removal in which to sell, rent, loan, store, or give away their
real property and possessions; many, of course, acted before the notice
for their area was posted. Household goods and cars could be stored
with the government, but only at the owner's risk and without insurance.

A federal program was initiated to care for the property and business interests of the evacuees, in which the Federal Security Agency and the Federal Reserve Board participated under the supervision of the Treasury Department.[136] With the liquidation of the WCCA and the interagency program in 1943, the Division of Evacuee Property of the WRA assumed responsibility and provided various services to evacuees.[137] As a consequence of the conditions under which they had to dispose of their property and of the character of the government's policies and programs for its care, the evacuees suffered heavy financial losses. One analyst of the Japanese economy estimated that "if one includes both income and property losses . . . the total would exceed $350,000,000."[138]

To ensure that no Japanese in Military Area No. 1 had been overlooked after all the Civilian Exclusion Orders had been issued, DeWitt issued Public Proclamation No. 7 on June 8: "Should there be any areas remaining in Military Area No. 1 from which Japanese have not been excluded, the exclusion of all Japanese from these areas is provided for in this proclamation."[139] Civilian Exclusion Orders Nos. 1 through 99 were "ratified and confirmed." Any Japanese remaining in the area and not exempt were ordered "to report in person to the nearest established Assembly Center."

Certain exemptions to Proclamation No. 4 were authorized. Nurses and doctors, students and members of faculties of Eastern universities, those who had purchased homes or businesses outside of Military Area No. 1 in preparation for moving and who were "caught" by the "freeze," those who wished to join their immediate families who had moved outside the area, and "mixed" families in which either husband or wife was Caucasian, were allowed to leave the area.[140] With regard to "race," WDC policy varied. At first the Command drew the net very tight. "Included among the evacuees were persons who were only part Japanese, some with as little as one-sixteenth Japanese blood."[141] However, this policy was changed in the late spring of 1942, to allow "mixed-blood (one-half Japanese or less) individuals, citizens of the United States or of friendly nations, whose backgrounds have been Caucasian" to return to the evacuation area if they had a "clean record" with the intelligence services.[142] Mixed-blood aliens were detained. Immediately after the internment program was announced, the policy toward the Japanese partners in mixed marriages was one of "no exemptions," but after months of fluctuation, a liberalized policy was made permanent in September. Exemptions to evacuation, in addition to those noted, were granted only to persons too ill to be moved without danger to life, children in orphanages, and individuals in insane asylums and penal institutions—and then only, for the adults, until their physical condition permitted movement or until they were released. On October 1, 1943, there were 613 mixed-blood and mixed-marriage cases in the evacuated area and 800 Japanese in hospitals, jails, and other institutions.

To receive the evacuees and house and restrain them until the more permanent relocation centers could be built and prepared for occupancy, twelve assembly centers were set up in California and one apiece in Oregon, Washington, and Arizona.[143] Race tracks, fair grounds, and livestock exhibition halls were pressed into service. The living quarters, especially at the race tracks, were exceedingly small and bore the atmosphere of their former use.[144] The assembly centers were surrounded by tall, strong wire fences and patrolled by military police. Guard towers were spotted at frequent intervals and searchlights were installed. The evacuees were warned by one of the first bulletins circulated in the centers that they must obey the commands of the sentries.

Permission to leave the centers for short trips were granted under certain conditions. No passes were issued for visits to points over fifteen miles away. A member of the Interior Police accompanied each evacuee or group authorized to leave a center. Permission was given evacuees to visit seriously ill hospitalized relatives, if these were in the immediate family and if a visit was "advisable"; to attend to urgent business matters; to answer subpoenas; to take professional examinations; and to attend funerals of immediate family members.[145]

The movement of the Japanese from their neighborhood gathering points to the sixteen assembly centers was supervised by the military police of the Fourth Army. In addition, troops were used for security purposes in civil-control stations and for external security at the assembly centers.[146] Escorting guards wore the usual military-police side arms; guards at assembly centers were also equipped with rifles and machine guns.

The evacuation and internment in assembly centers of the Japanese in Military Area No. 1 was completed by June 6, 1942. One hundred thousand persons were taken from their homes and removed, under guard, to assembly and relocation centers at an average rate of 3,750 per day. One Japanese resisted the evacuation—a retired United States Navy seaman named Kato. He was removed by force to an assembly center.

The government of the assembly centers was firmly in the hands of the WCCA, which laid down the policies to be followed in instituting educational, religious, and press activities. Considerable latitude was given the evacuees in setting up of educational and recreational facilities. Classes for children were organized, small libraries established,

Boy and Girl Scout troops organized, classes in music and folk-dancing given for adults, and other activities instituted, all under the supervision of Caucasian directors.[147] Religious services could be performed by Protestants, Catholics, and Buddhists. Japanese was not spoken in the services except when the evacuees did not understand English. Shinto ceremonies were forbidden and the center managers were directed to see that the permitted religious activities were not used as vehicles to "propagandize or incite the members of the center."[148]

WCCA gave evacuees permission to establish center newspapers and some fifteen appeared in mimeographed form at one time or another. The text was in English—Japanese was not allowed[149]—and was carefully censored.

During the late spring, WRA and WDC gave consideration to the location of the "permanent" relocation centers designed to house the evacuees for the duration. By June 6, 1942, sites had been selected. The two assembly centers on which construction had been begun in March, Manzanar and Poston, were made relocation centers. By June 30 the Army Corps of Engineers had three centers completed and in partial operation, and four others were under construction. By September 30 all but one center were operating.[150] Most of the centers were situated in arid desert country, bitterly cold in winter, hot in summer, and unprotected from winds in all seasons. Beginning with the movement of a few small groups in mid-May, the transfer of evacuees from the assembly centers to the relocation centers took place during the summer and was completed by the first of November.[151] The WDC set up a schedule for movements into the centers and maintained it despite the inadequate preparations in many of the centers, resulting in overcrowding and extreme discomfort. The movement of the evacuees from assembly to relocation centers was under the supervision of the military police, who maintained strict control.

The centers provided the necessities of life, but few of the comforts. They were alike in plan and construction. The buildings, wood frame covered with tar paper, were arranged in "blocks" separated from each other by wide "fire-breaks." Each block contained fourteen single-story barracks divided into four or six compartments. The barracks were 100 feet long and 25 feet wide and divided into four sections. Families or groups of unrelated individuals were assigned these apartments, which typically consisted of a single room, 20 by 25 feet, occasionally 20 by 16 feet, in size,

with bare boards, knotholes through the floor and into the next apartment, heaps of dust, and for each person an army cot, a blanket and a sack which could be filled with straw to make a mattress. There is nothing else. No shelves, closets, chairs, tables or screens. In this space five to seven people, in a few cases, eight, men, women and their children are to live indefinitely.[152]

No partitions were provided; if evacuees wanted them they had to do the carpentry themselves. Each block had its own community mess hall, recreation hall, men's and women's latrines, and a laundry room. The number of blocks in a center depended upon its size. Manzanar, in California, with a peak population of over 10,000, had 36 blocks. Each center had office buildings, a frame hospital and auxiliary structures, living quarters for the administrative staff (set apart from the evacuee's barracks), and utility buildings. School buildings, usually built later, generally included a combination gymnasium and auditorium and high-school classrooms. Elementary school classes were held in unused apartments. Most evacuees set to work to make their lodgings habitable and as attractive as possible under the circumstances.

With the creation of the WRA in March, responsibility for the evacuees was shared between it and the Army. The agency's basic executive order gave it authority to "formulate and effectuate" a program for the "relocation, maintenance and supervision" of the evacuees, "to provide for the relocation of such persons in appropriate places, provide for their needs in such manner as may be appropriate, and supervise their activities" and, among other responsibilities, "to provide, insofar as feasible and desirable, for the employment of such persons at useful work in industry, commerce and agriculture, or public projects, prescribe the terms and conditions of such public employment and safeguard the public interest in the private employment of such persons."[154] An agreement with the War Department, reached between Eisenhower and McCloy on April 17, 1942, specified the responsibilities and contributions of each agency with regard to the relocation, maintenance, and supervision of the evacuees. The Army agreed to be responsible for transporting the Japanese to the assembly centers, for operating these centers, and for transporting the evacuees to the relocation centers which it would construct and equip. The WRA was to assist in transportation to relocation centers and was to be responsible for center operations and the governing of the evacuees.[155]

An additional power explicitly delegated to the Army was that of ultimate control over the inmates. The agreement between Eisenhower and McCloy unambiguously asserted this power to be in the hands of the Army:

In the interest of the security of the evacuees, relocation sites will be designated by the appropriate Military Commander or by the Secretary of War ... as prohibited zones and military areas, and appropriate restrictions with respect to the rights of evacuees and others to enter, remain in, or leave such areas will be promulgated so that ingress and egress of all persons, including evacuees, will be subject to the control of the responsible Military Commander. Each relocation site will be under Military Police patrol and protection as determined by the War Department.[156]

To assert this control explicitly, Civilian Restrictive Orders were issued which required that all Japanese in the centers remain there except where leave was authorized.[157] Failure to comply subjected the individual to "penalties and liabilities provided by law" (but not specified in the order). Permits to leave assembly centers were issued only by the WCCA.

To assert further the Army's control over the evacuees in the relocation centers DeWitt issued Public Proclamation No. 8 on June 27, 1942, in which, acting under the authority of Executive Order 9066, he designated the areas around the relocation centers as War Relocation Project areas.[158] The penalties of Public Law 503 were invoked upon Japanese who left such an area without authority. This proclamation was followed by a series of Civilian Restrictive Orders issued during September and October, 1942, applying these regulations to the relocation centers within the Command and describing their boundaries.[159] As in the first order, the evacuees were warned that express written authority had to be obtained from the Secretary of War or the director of the WRA before leaving a center. Again Public Law 503 was invoked.

Four of the ten relocation centers lay outside the WDC.[160] To subject their evacuee residents to the same control, the War Department issued Public Proclamation WD:1 on August 13, 1942, declaring them to be War Relocation Project areas.[161]

On August 11, 1942, the War Department delegated to the WRA "fully the authority and responsibility to determine entry to and departure from the Center proper." The commanding general, however, "retained exclusive control to regulate and prohibit the entry or movement of any Japanese in the evacuated areas."[162] If, for example, a project director gave permission for an evacuee to leave a center which lay within the military area for travel to college, he had to request DeWitt to issue a travel permit. This stated the route that the evacuee must take through the area and ordered the responsible military police commander to provide an escort.

The relocation centers were guarded, as were the assembly centers, by military police units. Wire fences surrounded the centers and the entrances were guarded by troops who scrutinized the permits of all who would enter or leave. "In the event of a fire, riot, or disorder which passed beyond the control of the Center Management, or interior police, the Center manager or the superior officer of the interior police . . . was authorized to call upon the commanding officer of the military police for assistance. When the military police were called . . . the commanding officer assumed full charge of the entire Center until the emergency was ended."[163]

The military police guards remained at the centers in some force until December, 1944, when the evacuation orders were revoked, although there had been a gradual reduction in their strength. In April, 1944, the total force was reduced from 58 officers and 1,708 men to 46 officers and 1,020 men. Most of these were stationed at Tule Lake Center where "disloyal" Japanese were segregated. At the nine other centers before April, the contingents included from two to five officers and 65 to 135 men; after April, 1944, four centers had only one officer, and the rest two to four, and the contingents of enlisted men ranged from 13 to 64.[164] In December, 1944, the military police contingent totaled 43 officers and 763 men; centers other than Tule Lake had one or two officers and 9 to 40 men.

The evacuees never had a share in determining WDC policy but their participation in assisting the WRA to run the daily life in the centers increased as time went on. "Community government became in actuality an adjunct of administration."[165] Early discussions in WRA had contemplated self-governing, self-supporting communities but such plans were discarded. In August, 1942, the basic policy for community government was laid down in Administrative Instruction No. 34 which provided for the establishment of a permanent community council, which would become effective after the evacuees had approved a plan of government including provisions for election of the council and a judicial commission. The council would prescribe regulations, pass resolutions, receive and administer funds and property, and exercise other duties and responsibilities. The judicial commission would be empowered to hear cases and apply penalties for violations of the council's regulations. But the project director would retain ultimate control over these bodies, for he could set aside council regulations and remand to the commission decisions which he felt to be inappropriate. The policy statement clearly noted that the functions of these bodies were supplementary to and not substitutes for the functions of the project director.[166]

After friction between evacuees and administration at Poston and Manzanar Relocation centers in the fall of 1942 developed into mass demonstrations involving the majority of the residents, the WRA re-vised its policy for community government, deciding that legislative and judicial functions were beyond the abilities of the councils. In January, 1943, the sole responsibility of the community government for maintaining law and order was taken from it and Myer issued instructions governing the organization of police forces and the trial and punishment of offenders.[167] The *Handbook for Community Government* issued in November, 1943, outlined the functions of the council: it had power to make regulations governing traffic and sanitation and other minor matters of community concern,[168] and to conduct ceremonies such as memorial services for dead soldiers, induction ceremonies for departing servicemen, and the like.[169] The judicial commission, although it met infrequently, provided another opportunity for the expression of community sentiment. A few gambling, traffic-violation, theft, and assault cases were heard. Juveniles who got in trouble at one center were ordered to give up "zoot suits" and were given a haircut as punishment. Planning in the council was on a day-to-day basis and long-range planning was entirely an administration prerogative.

In 1942, the right to vote for council members had been extended to everyone eighteen or older, but only citizens of the United States who were over twenty-one were eligible to hold office. Aliens were eligible for membership, however, on appointed committees, commissions, and boards. In April, 1943, the policy was altered to make Issei eligible to hold office.

Some evacuees participated in community government through service as agents of the administration in the role of "block managers," and became powerful political forces within the community. For each residential block in a center there was an appointed block manager, who, with his assistants, was under the supervision of a nonevacuee civil service appointee. The block manager provided a means of communication with the residents and control over the distribution of supplies to them. He maintained records, conducted a census, and performed a myriad other necessary tasks. Block councils, elected by the evacuees from each block of a center, existed in all the centers in one form or other, their functions and organizations varying somewhat from center to center and block to block. The councils were formed to assist the block managers and acted as liaison between them and the residents. Each barrack elected one councilman; there were thus usually fourteen members on a council. They, too, became politically powerful.

Considerable freedom was allowed evacuees in their religious observances, but Shintoism, "the one Japanese sect which actually involves worship of the Emperor," was forbidden by the WRA.[170] All centers had Buddhist and Christian churches. Denominational groups had to compensate their own pastors, WRA ruling that no religious workers among the evacuees could be paid from government funds for the performance of religious duties at the centers. Many of the Protestant denominations received funds from national or regional religious organizations to pay their ministers. One hundred and seven ministers were so supported by July, 1943.[171]

Evacuees were permitted to publish newspapers, and during 1943 these appeared in all centers. In three centers they were printed, in others mimeographed. After some time, the use of the Japanese language in the press was permitted and six papers had Japanese-language sections. The newspapers were produced by evacuee staffs: the reporters were employed by the Reports Division of the center under a Caucasian officer.

Evacuees did not need to accept employment within the centers if they did not wish to do so. No subsistence charges were made except for evacuees who were temporarily employed in private industry at prevailing wages. Employment was open to those within the centers who wished work. Various changes in policy in regard to compensation occurred during 1942 but wages were finally settled at a rate ranging from $12 a month for jobs such as farm laborer, cook, and dishwasher, to $19 for teachers, doctors, and lawyers.[172]

Interior California Japanese.—The last phase of the evacuation was ushered in without advance notice. During the spring those Japanese living in localities outside of Military Area No. 1 had been free to live or travel where they wished, except in the small prohibited zones in Military Area No. 2 and, of course, in Military Area No. 1. They were required to send in change-of-residence notices and to abide by contraband and curfew regulations. On June 2, 1942, DeWitt ordered the 9,337 Japanese in the California portion of Military Area No. 2 to remain where they were and to await orders which would send them to join the other evacuees in relocation centers. Of these, 4,234 were the original Japanese population of the district. The rest had moved into the area in response to Proclamation No. 1 in early March; thus they were uprooted for a second time within a few months. The 228 Japanese in the Oregon portion of Military Area No. 2, the 549 in the Washington, and the 270 in the Arizona portion were undisturbed and remained unevacuated for the duration of the war.

Evacuation and detention for these California Japanese were ordered by Public Proclamation No. 6 which stated that "military necessity" required that "all alien Japanese and all persons of Japanese ancestry will be excluded from said California portion of Military Area No. 2 by future orders or proclamations."[173] A curfew was established for all Japanese within the area. Certain classes of persons would be "temporarily exempted or deferred from future exclusion and evacuation upon furnishing satisfactory proof," namely, "patients in hospitals or confined elsewhere and too ill or incapacitated to be removed therefrom without danger to life; inmates of orphanages and the totally deaf, dumb, or blind." On June 27 Civilian Exclusion Order No. 100, the first to cover a part of this area, was issued, and early in July the first Japanese began to move under guard directly to relocation centers. On July 27 the last such order, No. 108, was issued. By August 7, 1942, all Japanese in the area had entered a center. Public Proclamation No. 11, issued on August 18, 1942, "ratified and confirmed" the eight exclusion orders, noting that "the present situation requires as a matter of military necessity that all citizens of Japan and all persons of Japanese ancestry both alien and non-alien now be excluded from all of the California portion of Military Area No. 2 and be prohibited from entering Military Area No. 1."[174] Temporarily exempt or deferred were those in assembly or relocation centers in the area, those in custody in federal, state, or local institutions, and those with permits from the Command. Public Law 503 was again invoked.

The decision to intern the Japanese in the interior of California had been made in late February: "it became finally evident toward the end of February that a complete evacuation of all persons of Japanese ancestry from Military Area No. 1, and ultimately from the California portion of Military Area No. 2, would be ordered."[175] The WCCA had begun its operations in mid-March with a directive from DeWitt which stated that it was "to provide for the evacuation of all persons of Japanese ancestry from Military Area No. 1 and the California portion of Military Area No. 2 of the Pacific Coast."[176]

By October 31, 1942, the movement of evacuees from assembly centers and, in the case of those in the California portion of Military Area No. 2, from homes directly to relocation centers, was completed. By virtue of Executive Order 9066, the WDC had authority over and responsibility for 117,116 individuals of Japanese ancestry. Of these, 115,820 had been residents of the WDC and were brought under Army control by one or another Civilian Exclusion Order. Another 1,296 came from outside the Command; 151 were evacuees from Alaska, 504 were born in assembly centers, and 641 were aliens released or paroled from Department of Justice internment camps.[177]

The great majority of the Japanese remained under the control of the WDC, and were handed over to the administration of the WRA. Only 5,805 (about 5 per cent) were not handed over. These included 4,889 "voluntary migrants" who had left Military Area No. 1 before Proclamation No. 4 was issued and settled beyond Military Area No. 2; 465 parents and children of mixed-blood marriages who were released by the WDC; 114 evacuees turned over to the FBI or the Department of Justice; 135 who died in assembly centers; 203 who were released for unspecified reasons. The last group included, according to the *Final Report*, "a few persons who were deferred from evacuation and later released, and a few who were permitted to leave the Assembly Centers for interior points to join their families which had previously established themselves there."[178] Of the 111,311 remaining in the custody of the Command,[179] 110,066 were sent to assembly centers or directly to relocation centers. The remaining 1,245 (1,022 inmates of penal or correctional institutions or hospitals, and 223 evacuees released on work furlough for permanent employment in non-California sections of Military Area No. 2) did not enter assembly centers yet remained within the supervision of the Command.[180]

The WRA accepted into its custody, at one time or another, 120,313 Japanese.[181] Of these, 757 never entered centers, as they were inmates of penal or other institutions. A total of 1,862 evacuees died during their internment. Of the 117,694 remaining, 2,355 left the custody of the WRA to join the Army, 565 were sent to institutions after some period of center residence, 3,121 were turned over to the Department of Justice by the WRA, and 4,724 left the centers for Japan at the end of the war. Many of the evacuees left the centers before the end of hostilities to take up residence in communities outside the evacuation zones.

Alaskan and Hawaiian Japanese.—At the time of the attack on Pearl Harbor the Territory of Alaska was embraced by the Alaska Defense Command under the command of Lieutenant General Simon Bolivar Buckner, Jr. On December 12, 1941, it was placed under the WDC and declared to be a theatre of operations; two days later DeWitt declared the area to be a combat zone. On March 6, 1942, Secretary of War Stimson authorized Buckner to designate military areas. On April 7, 1942, Buckner issued Public Proclamation No. 1. Citing the authority given him by Executive Order 9066 and noting of Alaska that "by reason of its geographical location [it] is particularly subject to attack, to attempted invasion . . . and to espionage and acts of sabotage," he declared the territory to be a military area and ordered that "all persons of Japanese race of greater than half blood and all males of the Japanese race over 16 years of age of half blood" should be excluded from the area and "transported to the continental limits of the United States." Further, "any German or Italian aliens, or any persons of Japanese ancestry" were restricted in travel.[182] No law was cited for the punishment of violators of these regulations. Additional action to control alien enemies was taken on May 14, 1942, when Public Proclamation No. 3 ordered the registration of all alien enemies.[183]

One hundred and forty-five persons of Japanese ancestry were removed from Alaska and turned over to the authority of the WCCA in mid-1942. Of these 121 were American-born and 24 were foreign-born. Six more were added to WRA's roster in 1944, plus 42 aliens released or paroled from the Department of Justice internment camps who had been arrested shortly after Pearl Harbor.[184]

Of the 193 Alaskan Japanese, 80, along with two children born in relocation centers, returned to Alaska in 1945; 106 chose to relocate in the United States; six died in the centers; one was interned by the Department of Justice.[185]

The Japanese in the Hawaiian Islands, numbering a third more than those on the mainland,[186] were not subjected to mass evacuation or internment. Army officials declared shortly after the outbreak of war that their policy would be one of apprehending and interning suspicious individuals and that no mass evacaution was contemplated. On December 7, 1941, the Governor of Hawaii placed the territory under martial law, suspending habeas corpus; and General Order No. 5, (December 8, 1941) issued by Lieutenant General Walter Short, imposed the same restrictions on "all alien Japanese of the age of fourteen years and upward," as the presidential proclamations of that date placed on all alien enemies; contraband was defined and forbidden, travel was restricted, and aliens were enjoined to preserve the peace.[187] Suspected individuals were immediately rounded up by the Army. The first groups included the two hundred consular representatives of the Japanese government and their families, some forty Shinto priests, about a hundred Buddhist priests and priestesses, and over three hundred alien language-school principals and teachers. During 1942 other alien and American-born Japanese were apprehended, but the number was not large. According to A. W. Lind, "The total number of Japanese held on suspicion during the entire period of the war was only 1,440 and the number actually interned and sent to camps on the mainland was 981 or about one percent of the adult Japanese population of Hawaii."[188] Of this total, 878 were aliens, 534 were American citizens, including 468 Kibei, and 28 were Japanese nationals who requested repatriation.

Early in 1942, 13 American-born and 900 alien Japanese were deported to the mainland and held in Camp McCloy and in Department of Justice camps. After the American Civil Liberties Union protested, the citizens were flown back to Hawaii in May, 1942.[189] In September, 1942, a policy of transferring Japanese interned in the islands to relocation centers on the mainland was announced by Lieutenant General Delos C. Emmons. Aliens applying for repatriation and Kibei suspected of being dangerous made up most of the group. A board of three officers from the Military Intelligence Division of Emmons' staff made the selection.

The first contingent of 475 adult males and families of aliens shipped earlier left the islands on November 23, 1942, and were followed by other groups in January, February, and March, 1943, a total of 1,037 entering relocation centers by the end of 1943. Seventy-three excludees entered centers in 1944 and 1945 and 8 others entered centers to join their families. In addition, 99 other Hawaiian alien Japanese entered the centers on parole or release from Department of Justice camps.[190]

President Roosevelt terminated martial law in the islands on October 19, 1944, with the issuance of Proclamation 2627.[191] On the same day he issued Executive Order 9489 which authorized the Secretary of War, under Executive Order 9066, to designate a commanding general for the territory who could establish military areas "from which any and all persons may be excluded" and institute various controls, such as blackout, curfew, and supervision over the travel of alien enemies. "Authorization expires 30 days after cessation of hostilities with Japan." Under this authority, approximately 150 Japanese in centers were officially excluded from the islands and under an agreement with the War Department, the WRA transferred them, beginning in December, 1944, to Tule Lake Center. Sixty-seven of them were lodged in the center's segregation camp, or "stockade."[192]

Between July 3, 1945, and April 12, 1946, 1,108 Japanese left the mainland for Hawaii. This group was composed of 806 former residents of the islands, 96 children born to them in the centers, and 206 mainland residents who decided to relocate in Hawaii. One hundred and twenty-five Hawaiian residents decided to relocate in the states, 136 repatriated to Japan, and 115 were interned by the Department of Justice.[193]

DeWitt's "Final Report."—A comprehensive report on the role of the WDC in the evacuation episode, entitled *Final Report: Japanese Evacuation from the West Coast, 1942*, was written by Bendetsen and submitted over DeWitt's signature to General Marshall in June, 1943.[195] It purports to be a faithful record of the genesis of WDC policies of evacuation and internment and of the execution of these operations up to November, 1942, when administrative responsibility for the evacuees passed to the WRA. But its story of the formation of evacuation policy is essentially a presentation of the military argument justifying the measure, and constitutes an apologia. The major portion of the work is concerned with the mechanics of evacuation and internment. Twenty-five of its twenty-eight chapters, supplemented with statistical and pictorial summaries and appendices, describe in detail the steps in the evacuation and internment operations, the administrative procedures, the staff organization, and the operation of the assembly centers run by WDC. Over eighty tables present a detailed picture of the composition of the Japanese minority in terms of age, education, occupation, geographical location before exclusion, and so on. The *Report* also presents a picture of the development of policies in the WDC during 1942, but this presentation is uneven and inadequate. Although the various events and circumstances which, it claims, led to DeWitt's "Final Recommendation," Executive Order 9066, and the first program of forced exclusion, are set forth in some detail with relevant documents, the considerations leading the WDC to change the forced exclusion program to internment and, later, to intern the Japanese resident in central California, are scarcely mentioned.

The *Report*'s recital, in chapter two, "Need for Military Control and for Evacuation," of the factors leading DeWitt to argue for exclusion in his "Final Recommendation" of February 14, 1942, opens with a mention of the refusal of the Department of Justice to accept his request for extensive prohibited areas and proceeds to detail a set of circumstances which assertedly left DeWitt "no alternative but to conclude that the Japanese constituted a potentially dangerous element from the viewpoint of military security—that military necessity required their immediate evacuation to the interior." The discussion of these factors begins with reference to FBI raids on alien enemies and the discovery of ammunition, rifles, shotguns, and "maps of all kinds."

There were hundreds of reports nightly of signal lights visible from the coast and of intercepts of unidentified radio transmissions.... The situation was fraught with danger to the Japanese themselves. The combination of spot raids revealing hidden caches of contraband, the attacks on coastwise shipping, the interception of illicit radio transmissions, and nightly observation of visual signal lamps from constantly changing locations, and the success of the enemy offensive in the Pacific had so aroused the public along the west coast ... that it was ready to take matters into its own hands.

Therefore, "it had become essential to provide means which would remove the potential menace to which [the Japanese] subjected the west coast. It is pertinent now to examine the situation with which the military authorities were then confronted." This examination, detailed over nine pages, has six major points: (1) The Japanese minority "presented a tightly-knit racial group...a homogeneous unassimilated element bearing a close relationship through ties of race, religion, language, custom, and indoctrination to the enemy." (2) "Whether by design or accident, virtually always [the Japanese] communities were adjacent to very vital shore installations, war plants, etc." (3) "No ready means existed for determining the loyal and disloyal with any degree of safety...A positive determination could not have been made." (4) There were "over 124 separate Japanese organizations along the Pacific Coast engaged...in common pro-Japanese purposes," the great majority of their activities following "a line of control from the Japanese Government...to the Japanese residents in the United States." (5) Large numbers of American-born Japanese had been sent to Japan "for education and indoctrination" and their "influence on other Japanese could not be accurately calculated. But it could not be disregarded." (6) The "external situation obtaining in the Pacific theatre" was "grave"; and "the Pacific Coast had become exposed to attack by enemy successes in the Pacific."[196]

This chapter of the *Final Report* is an untrustworthy guide to WDC thinking before February 14. First, it is a pastiche of unacknowledged and extensive quotations from a number of documents which were not in existence until long after the period of deliberation which the chapter is describing. Of the ten pages of the chapter, almost eight were made up of selections from State Attorney General Earl Warren's testimony at the Tolan Committee hearing in San Francisco on February 21, 1942,[197] and from the *amici curiae* brief of the states of California, Oregon, and Washington in the case of *Hirabayashi* v. *United States* before the Supreme Court, dated May 7, 1943.[198] Many of the chapter's paragraphs are entirely composed of matter extracted without alteration from these two documents. In other places, the paragraphs are made up of sections of paragraphs or sentences taken from these sources and used verbatim or with slight alteration.[199] Despite this extensive borrowing, no acknowledgment is made of the original documents save for a reference to the sources of some material which is quoted in one footnote.[200] The original source of one paragraph, a paper prepared for the Institute of Pacific Relations, is acknowledged, but the date of publication is not given—the paper was written for a meeting held in December, 1942, and was not released to the public until early in 1943.[201] Finally, the material in the paragraphs dealing with the numbers of Kibei educated and residing in Japan and returning to the United States, based on ship manifests, was collected and compiled by the Research Section of the Civil Affairs Division of the WDC in late 1942 and early 1943.

Secondly, many of the events and circumstances which the chapter states impelled the WDC to evacuation occurred long after the decision of February 14. To demonstrate "the gravity of the external situation obtaining in the Pacific theater,"[202] it notes the attack on Pearl Harbor and various events in December, 1941, and January, 1942, and then mentions the Battle of the Java Sea (February 27), the occupation of Rangoon and Burma by Japanese forces (March 9), the surrender of Corregidor (April 9), the air attack on Dutch Harbor (June 3), and the occupation of Attu and Kiska (June 7).[203]

Thirdly, many of the assertions advanced as the basis for the decision—statements about transmittals of information to the enemy and the character and motives of the Japanese—are not corroborated by other evidence and some points have been flatly contradicted. As evidence for the "successful communication of information to the enemy," the *Report* cites various "enemy attacks" on the West Coast. But these occurred long after February 14. The *Report* mentions the submarine attack on Goleta, California, on February 23, 1942, an incendiary aerial bomb attack on Mt. Emily, near Brookings, Oregon, and a submarine shelling of the coast at Astoria, Oregon. The *Report* does not date the last two. The attack on Astoria was on June 21, 1942 and that on Mt. Emily was on September 9, 1942. By June, 1942, all Japanese on the coast were in assembly centers.

Finally, many of the factors stated by the *Report* to have animated the WDC are described differently than in DeWitt's "Recommendation." In that memorandum DeWitt anticipated naval attacks on coastal shipping and cities, air raids, and sabotage as "possible and probable"; he did not claim that espionage or signaling had occurred nor that the Japanese located themselves near defense installations with intent to sabotage. But in the *Report* these points are presented quite differently and some new ones are added. The situation on the coast is made out to be much more threatening. The "gravity of the external situation" is noted. "The situation in the Pacific had gravely deteriorated." The Japanese were now pictured as residing "adjacent to strategic points" with sabotage in mind. "Some of them doubtless resided there through mere coincidence. It seems equally beyond doubt, however, that the presence of others was not mere coincidence." The *Report* claims that signaling to enemy ships occurred. "There were hundreds of reports nightly of signal lights visible from the coast." "Illicit radio transmissions" were occurring. Two other points were adduced: the Japanese were in danger of attacks from the public, and social and cultural, as well as "racial," characteristics were given as additional evidence of the "tightly-knit" character of the group.[204]

The *Report's* treatment of the policy of interning the coastal Japanese, ordered in late March, 1942, is inconsistent, unclear, brief, and scattered. In a number of places it holds that the decision was taken to provide an "orderly evacuation" to protect the Japanese from vigilante action. In another place the motive is stated to be the fact that so few Japanese had left the coast under the "voluntary" program, although elsewhere the *Report* states that the voluntary program was successful. The time of making of the decision is variously given as February, early March, and late March.[205]

There is no treatment at all of the history or reasons for the decision to intern the Japanese who were resident in interior California, which was ordered in the first week of June. There are only three references to the event itself in the text. The date of the decision is variously given as late February or early March.[206]

RESTRAINT AND CONDITIONED RELEASE

Confinement of the more than one hundred thousand evacuees in the relocation centers came eventually to be modified by a program of conditional release. The requirements and conditions for release were the product of Army and WRA decisions, some made jointly and some independently. These two agencies determined who could leave the centers, temporarily or permanently, where they could live and what work they could undertake. Authority over the Japanese remained ultimately and firmly in the hands of the Army by virtue of Executive Order 9066. As the care of the Japanese became the responsibility of the WRA after they had entered the centers, the Army delegated the power to control their movements to the agency.

The WRA itself took the position that besides the authority granted it by the WDC, its own founding executive order gave it the power to detain evacuees and to recall those who left the relocation centers if it judged they should be returned. Detention of the majority of evacuees was regarded by the WRA as "holding as a step in relocation" and not as punitive or protective custody. In support of its position the WRA pointed to the section of its executive order directing it "to provide for the relocation of [evacuees] . . . and to supervise their activities."[207]

In addition, the WRA detained certain evacuees for the purpose of protecting the national security. Those evacuees whom the WRA adjudged potentially dangerous, on the basis of its own estimate of the situation and of those acts and attitudes which indicated that an evacuee would be likely to be subversive, were not allowed to leave the centers.[208] After establishing regulations for granting permission to leave, it allowed the "cleared" evacuees to depart but held those it felt were dangerous.

The WRA also assumed that the power to detain implied the power to "recover" those evacuees who had left to take up their lives in cities or towns in the Middle West or East but who it felt should be returned to a center. Although all evacuees who left the centers to resettle remained in the "constructive custody" of the Army, the WRA held that it might recall evacuees if their behavior or various factors beyond their control warranted it—i.e., if the community's attitude toward them changed or the agency decided that their freedom was somehow prejudicial to the war effort. In the event that a resettled evacuee refused to return to a center, the agency planned to call on the Department of Justice to enforce its command. But the occasion never arose; only three evacuees, a family group on work leave who rendered aid to some escaped German prisoners of war, were asked by the WRA to return to a center and they did so without resistance. The Department of Justice, on its part, indicated clearly that it would not take any action to return citizen evacuees to their former centers, Biddle writing to Myer on September 27, 1943, that he knew of no legal authority to do this.[209]

Although the responsibility for the evacuees and for "clearing" them was the WRA's, the WDC retained direct control over them in the evacuation zones and set up an extensive intelligence operation designed to secure information about the entire Japanese minority's pre-Pearl Harbor history. Various units of the War Department, notably the Provost Marshal General's Office (OPMG) and the Japanese American Joint Board (JAJB), played a part in determining where the Japanese could find homes and work.

As a consequence of the policy decisions of the WRA and of the Army, chiefly the WDC—and of evacuee reactions to these policies, their present situation, and their estimation of their future prospects—the evacuees were sifted into three groups during the two and one-half years from the opening of the relocation centers in mid-1942 to the termination of mass exclusion in December, 1944. Most evacuees (81 per cent) were eventually adjudged by the WRA as not dangerous to national security and were given conditional authorization to leave the centers and to take up a normal life again in sections of the country outside the evacuation zones. The WRA urged them to "relocate," and slightly more than one-third of this group (36,000) accepted the opportunity. Most of them were young men and women citizens; 47 per cent were American-born males and 36 per cent were American-born females. Nearly 70 per cent of the citizen Japanese over seventeen who were eligible to resettle did so. However, two-thirds of the total number of aliens and citizens eligible, some 62,000, elected to remain in the centers; these were chiefly the aging Issei.

The second group consisted of those who, amounting with their families to 16 per cent of the total evacuated population, were adjudged by the WRA to be fundamentally "disloyal" or potentially dangerous to national security and were separated from the other evacuees in a "segregation center" without the right to leave. Kibei—American citizens of Japanese ancestry who had spent some years in Japan—chiefly composed this group of "segregants."

The third group included the 3 per cent who entered the armed forces either as inductees or, less frequently, as volunteers.

RESETTLEMENT AND DETENTION

WRA and resettlement.—In the spring of 1942 the initial plans of the WRA for the development of economically self-dependent Japanese communities in the Mountain and Plains states were abandoned because of the hostility of the public. The agency immediately found itself faced with responsibility for the Japanese lodged in its centers and a lack of specific plans for their return to American life. Agency officials felt that relocation and not internment was the proper policy. Milton Eisenhower stated in May, 1942, that "the first specific task of the Authority is to resettle some 100,000 alien and American-born Japanese evacuated from military areas of the far Western states."[210] In the late spring, before relocation policies and procedures had been worked out, the WRA, in conjunction with the WCCA, allowed a number of evacuees to leave the assembly and relocation centers, some for temporary agricultural labor under private employment in areas outside the evacuation zones, some to take up their interrupted college education in Midwestern and Eastern institutions, some to accept industrial employment, and some to be employed by the WRA in places outside the centers. In all these cases the WDC asserted its authority over the evacuees and threatened violators of the conditions laid down with punishment under Public Law 503.

In the spring the persistent demands of sugar-beet growers for evacuee labor led, after considerable discussion, to the acceptance by the WDC of private employment of the Japanese at this work. DeWitt stipulated that arrangements would have to be reached between the growers, state and county officials, and the WRA, that no evacuee labor could be employed in the evacuated zones, and that no troops could be spared to guard evacuees at such work. At a series of conferences held on and after April 7, 1942, agreement was reached. When the WRA received the required assurances from officials and employers (prevailing wages would be paid, law and order maintained, etc.), "it recommended to the military authority that the recruiting of the desired labor in the assembly centers be permitted. All recruiting was done by the United States Employment Service . . . on a strictly voluntary basis."[211] The first group of workers left the Portland Assembly Center for temporary work in Malheur County in southeast Oregon, in mid-May,[212] and others soon followed. By the end of June, 1942, some 1,600 evacuees had been recruited from the assembly centers or sent directly to the fields to assist in the beet harvesting.[213] In the fall, long-stable-cotton growers in Arizona received permission from the WDC to use evacuee labor on much the same basis.[214] These workers, however, were guarded by military police who rode with them from their camp to the fields. The picking began in south-central Arizona in August and lasted until early November, when DeWitt brought an end to the program on the grounds that too few Japanese were employed or available for employment to justify the troops used to guard them.[215] By the end of 1942 some 9,000 evacuees had found temporary agricultural work at one time or another.[216] Despite apprehension about the public acceptance of the Japanese, the seasonal labor program went well. "Although many of [the evacuees] had occasional unpleasant experiences . . . and a few actually ran into situations which appeared momentarily ominous, none reported suffering any bodily harm or any really serious difficulties."[217]

A few evacuees were allowed to leave assembly centers for industrial employment by the week in nonevacuated areas. On September 20, 1942, a small number of railroad workers were allowed to return to their former jobs as maintenance workers on railroads in eastern Oregon.[218]

The WDC retained tight control over the evacuees on these projects. To reaffirm his authority over such evacuees, DeWitt issued a series of Civilian Restrictive Orders, similar to those describing the boundaries of the various centers and requiring the residents to remain within them unless they had his authority to depart. These orders authorized the release of stated numbers of evacuees to the custody of the WRA for movement by it to prescribed areas in the interior for private employment in agriculture. Each of the orders named the county or counties in which the group was to work and the assembly centers from which they were to be recruited; they also indicated the number of those allowed to go, and occasionally set the date or period of employment.[219] An express condition was that the group should proceed only to the specified county or counties and return to the assembly or relocation centers named by the WRA. In July, DeWitt issued an order allowing evacuees working in designated counties to proceed directly to other "WRA approved counties" for employment.[220]

The WRA sought to use evacuee labor in the operation of its centers. As the railheads serving Poston, Tule Lake, Gila River, and Manzanar centers were outside the project areas and within the evacuated zones, the WRA applied for permission from DeWitt to use evacuee labor in unloading supplies. On September 21, 1942, DeWitt granted authority for such "emergency employment," on grounds that the work was essential to the operation of the projects and met an emergency situation, but specified that military police be used "to prevent unauthorized departures of evacuee labor."[221]

In the spring of 1942 the first steps were taken to allow college-student evacuees to resume their studies in institutions outside the evacuation zones. A Student Relocation Committee was formed at the University of California early in March, 1942, under the guidance of President Robert G. Sproul, to facilitate the transfer of such students. During April and May about seventy-five students had entered colleges. On May 5, 1942, Eisenhower recommended the formation of a nation-wide nongovernmental agency to deal with the problem, and on May 29 the National Japanese American Student Relocation Council, supported by the WRA, the War Department, and a number of colleges, was formed at Chicago. Under the leave policy of July 20, 1942, it succeeded in placing 152 additional students in institutions outside the evacuation zones by September 30, 1942, and 250 students from the centers were granted leave.[222] By September, 143 colleges, universities, and junior colleges had been approved for student relocation by the War and Navy departments after showing that no secret war-related research was being conducted on their campuses. The first students leaving undertook to observe certain WRA-WCCA requirements, and when the WRA formulated its leave regulations they were expected to comply with them.

Early in the WRA's existence, its officials devised a plan to recruit a large body of trained workers who could be moved from area to area as employment opportunities arose, and made provision for the group, called the War Relocation Work Corps, in the agency's executive order. The WRA was directed to provide, "by general regulations, for the enlistment in [the] corps, for the duration of the present war," of evacuated persons, and to "prescribe the terms and conditions of the work to be performed by such corps and the compensation to be paid."[223] The regulations were promulgated on April 29, 1942.[224] Enlistment was open to males and females sixteen years old or over, aliens or citizens. Applicants were required to take an oath that they would remain in the corps for the duration of the war (no shorter enlistment was allowed), would accept whatever pay the WRA determined, and were prepared to be moved about at the discretion of the WRA. In the spring and summer of 1942, when enlistments were sought, the rate of payment was unspecified; regulations stated only that "the evacuees will be entitled to receive as compensation such wages, allowances, and other benefits as may be due, under the regulations of WRA or under the classifications which may from time to time be assigned to them." In September a policy was adopted under which, "as each evacuee who applies for work is assigned to a specific job at a relocation center, he automatically becomes a member of the Work Corps. . . . All members of the Corps will be rated periodically on the quality of their work and those who carry out their duties with special diligence, efficiency or skill will receive merit designations." Provision was also make for the election of a "Fair Practice Committee . . . to handle complaints regarding employment classifications, conditions of work and employment compensation."[225]

When evacuees arrived at the various assembly and relocation centers in the summer of 1942, they were solicited to take the oath of enlistment in the work corps. But the project was greeted with suspicion and the response was poor. At Poston, where enlistment was sought more energetically than at other centers,

There was anger at the nature of the Work Corps enlistment which seemed to require that the evacuees renounce all chance of reimbursement for losses, that they promise everything, and gain no definite assurance in return, not even as to wages. It was particularly resented that they had been asked to enlist during the first moment of arrival when they were too tired and exhausted to give proper thought.[226]

Attempts to secure enlistments at the Portland Assembly Center failed. The evacuees were "wary of the idea and full of questions for which no answers were ready . . . No workers were recruited."[227]

Evacuee resistance and charges by farmers of unfair competition by "prison inmate" labor (i.e., the Japanese) raised doubts in the minds of WRA officials as to the feasibility of the project. The decision was made to emphasize resettlement instead and to abandon the corps. Late in 1942 the corps was abolished.[228]

To put into practice a policy of allowing evacuees to leave the centers, either "permanently" or for a short period, the WRA had to make a number of decisions and to institute a procedure. Major decisions included the determination of those eligible to leave, the length of time and the purpose for which leaves would be granted, the extent of the freedom granted, and the conditions attached to it. The applicant's request for permission to leave was eventually handled within the agency in two steps: determination of "leave clearance" (the judgment by the agency whether or not an applicant should be allowed to leave his center), and granting a "leave permit" for the type of leave requested, which was contingent on the evacuee meeting certain specified conditions.

The basic consideration in the decision to grant or withhold leave clearance was the likelihood of the individual being "dangerous to national security" or to the war effort.[229] The agency made its own estimate of potential dangerousness.[230] The decision was based on data from the FBI, which also drew on the files of other intelligence agencies, and on the WRA's own records of evacuee behavior in centers. "If there was no evidence from either source that the applicant might endanger national security or interfere with the war effort, clearance was granted."[231]

In addition to such national security considerations, "the ability to support himself, community acceptance and promised notification of changes in address were the basic conditions upon which an evacuee was allowed to leave a relocation center."[232] The WRA justified the requirement that the individual have a definite employment offer on the grounds that this would make successful resettlement more likely; the community-acceptance requirement was to insure that the Japanese would not be attacked or regarded with alarm. The WRA insisted that it be kept informed of changes of address in order, so it asserted, that it might be able to communicate quickly with the evacuee.[233]

The first policy allowing for "permanent" resettlement, in distinction to temporary leave for seasonal agricultural labor, was put into effect in the summer of 1942. After discussion within the agency, Myer, having received assurances from McCloy that the Army probably would have no objections to the development of a program of private employment of qualified Nisei in districts outside the evacuation zone,[234] prepared a tentative set of leave regulations to be effective on July 20, 1942. Only American citizens who had never resided in Japan were eligible.[235] The applicant had to "show that he has a specific job opportunity with a prospective employer at a designated place outside the relocation center and outside the WDC." The project director was to investigate every applicant thoroughly before making a recommendation on the request. The final decision to grant or deny leave was to be made by the director of the WRA, and Public Law 503 was to be invoked against violators of the provisions. Applicants who were issued permits, and their accompanying dependents, were to remain in the constructive custody of the military commander. Permits were revocable at any time upon the order of the director. Conditions at the centers and the attitude of the evacuees were not favorable toward this policy and only eleven evacuees left under its procedures by October 1, 1942.

Stimulated by the national manpower shortage, by the success of the seasonal agricultural-leave program (over 10,000 workers employed), and by the realization that public opinion was such that evacuees could find jobs and homes in Rocky Mountain and Plains states communities, the WRA reconsidered its leave policy in the fall of 1942. After discussions among DeWitt, the War Department, and the Department of Justice—during which the latter agency declared its opposition to the granting of leave to any evacuees and favored the limiting of freedom of resettling to certain classes of applicants[236]—new leave regulations were announced on September 26, to be effective on October 1.[237] Eligibility was broadened; any alien or citizen was now able to apply for permission to visit or reside in communities outside the WDC. Three types of leave were defined and specified conditions were attached to each. The WRA administrative staffs in centers were instructed in the procedures for granting each type of leave, and the character of the control exerted over the evacuee was specified. The center record and pre-Pearl Harbor history of every applicant for even a short-term leave was subjected to an intensive scrutiny. For all types of leave, freedom was conditional.

"Short term" leaves, for periods not over thirty days, would be issued to allow evacuees to leave the center for short periods to attend to affairs requiring their presence, such as visits to doctors or lawyers. The applicant applied for this leave on a form (WRA 127) which comprised a long list of questions about his history, his family, visits to Japan, relatives in the Japanese armed forces, membership in Japanese organizations, facility in the Japanese language, and magazines customarily read.[238] On receipt of the application, the project director was instructed to interview the evacuee to "elicit any information that may be necessary to verify or to complete the answers" and to "make such further investigations as may be practical to verify and supplement at the project the information supplied by the applicant. This shall include a check with the Internal Security Officer of the project." If the applicant was a paroled alien, the Department of Justice set the terms and conditions to apply during the leave. If all other requirements were met, the project director issued the leave "when satisfied that the leave is for a necessary and proper purpose and that the date, duration and itinerary are appropriate, where applicant agrees to comply with any special conditions attached to his leave . . . [and] has made . . . arrangement to pay his transportation and other expenses." Appeal could be made, if an application was rejected, to the regional director. A leave could be revoked if improperly issued or if there was a violation of conditions.

"Work group" leaves would be issued to evacuees for temporary agricultural labor. A project director could issue such leaves if the director of the WRA had previously approved the site and employment and leave clearance had been granted. The same general procedures were followed as for short-term leaves, including investigation of the evacuee on the project and provision for appeal from a rejected application. The application for leave clearance asked for the same information as that for short-term leave but contained three additional questions about membership in Japanese organizations, magazines read by father, and extent of financial dependence on parents.[239]

"Indefinite leave" for "permanent resettlement" in communities outside the proscribed areas or for attendance at educational institutions could be granted only by the director after examination of the evacuee's record. The student evacuee had to execute the application for leave clearance as well as file an application for indefinite leave which asked questions about the institutions he planned to attend, status of his application to the National Student Relocation Council, arrangements for employment, financial status, and arrangements for support while at college.[240] The applicant had to agree that on arrival at his destination he would report within twenty-four hours to the director of the WRA and confirm his business, school, or residential addresses, and that he would give prompt notice of any change of these. The WRA had to be satisfied that the conditions as to community acceptance, reasonable prospect of self-support, and security clearance had been met.[241] A number of field relocation offices were set up by the WRA to facilitate contact between private employers and evacuees and to ascertain the reactions of communities to the Japanese. To supplement its information about evacuees, the WRA secured data from the FBI. Evacuees resettling under indefinite leave were given identifying documents.[242]

The resettler, even though he was a citizen and satisfied all the agency's requirements, was not unconditionally free, for he remained under the control of the WRA, which could revoke the leave for violations of conditions. Resettlers were not allowed within the Eastern or Southern Defense Commands. Lieutenant General Hugh A. Drum of the Eastern Command made it clear he would prefer not to have Japanese within easily accessible distance of the eastern coastline.

In December, 1942, additional regulations governing leaves for student evacuees desiring to enter colleges in areas outside the proscribed military areas were issued. The services provided by the National Student Relocation Council were described and the evacuee was informed that the services of the council should be requested. The application for student leave would "not be approved or disapproved until a report from the . . . Council had been received."[243]

The regulations effective October 1, 1942, speeded up only slightly the outward movement of evacuees. By December 31, 1942, applications for indefinite leave had been filed by 2,200 evacuees, 250 had received them, and 193 had left the centers for residence and employment in mountain and plains states.[244] A total of 414 student leaves had been granted and 250 students were enrolled in 75 different colleges.

Recognizing that the slowness of resettlement was in part due to the administrative handling of leave-clearance requests on an individual basis, the WRA decided to undertake a "wholesale" determination of eligibility for leave clearance, irrespective of whether the evacuee had filed an application for leave. The War Department had decided after conferences in December, 1942, and January, 1943, to accept citizens of Japanese ancestry into the armed forces and to allow "screened" evacuees to be employed in war plants and industries, and was planning to secure information from them to enable it to determine their loyalty, willingness to serve, and eligibility for war-plant employment. Now the WRA combined its operation with the Army's.[245] WRA staff members were given special instructions in the procedure. Project directors were notified that "beginning with a day in February . . . each project director shall arrange for each male United States citizen of Japanese ancestry in the relocation center who has reached his 17th birthday to execute DSS Form 304a and Form WRA 126."[246] The Selective Service questionnaire (DSS Form 304a), similar to that used for registering aliens (Form 304), and the WRA questionnaire (Form 126 Rev.), both contained two "loyalty" questions, numbers 27 and 28. On the Selective Service Form, for male citizens, number 27 read: "Are you willing to serve in the armed forces of the United States on combat duty, wherever ordered?" Number 28 read, "Will you swear unqualified allegiance to the United States of America and faithfully defend the United States from any or all attacks by foreign or domestic forces, and forswear any form of allegiance or obedience to the Japanese Emperor or any other foreign government, power or organization?"[247] On WRA Form 126 Rev., given to female citizens and aliens of *both* sexes, question 27 read: "If the opportunity presents itself and you are found qualified would you be willing to volunteer for the Army Nurse Corps or the W.A.C.?"[248] Question 28 was identical to question 28 on the Selective Service Form.[248] After the questionnaires had been printed and distributed in centers, an alternate question 28 was prepared for the aliens on February 12. It read: "Will you swear to abide by the laws of the United States and to take no action which would in any way interfere with the war effort of the United States?"[249] The registration—answering questions and signing the forms—was to be compulsory except for those evacuees who had requested repatriation. Project directors arranged for interviewers who filled out the forms for the evacuees up to the loyalty questions. These were answered by male citizen evacuees before the Army representative, and the evacuee then signed the questionnaires. Those who wished to volunteer for enlistment had to execute two additional forms, one of which was an "Application for Voluntary Induction" (DSS Form 165) to be signed in the presence of the Army officer. Aliens and female citizens were not interviewed by officers. Registration began on February 8 and, in most centers, ended the first week in April.

WRA and War Department officials had expected that registration would be accepted as a routine requirement by the evacuees and that military service and resettlement would be welcomed by them as a means of showing their loyalty to the United States. However, the attitude of the evacuees was critical and antagonistic.[250] Over 4,000 male Nisei—25 per cent of the 20,000 male American citizens of Japanese ancestry between the ages of 17 and 37—refused to swear allegiance. Thirteen per cent of the adults answered the questions with a flat "No," a qualified negative, or refused to answer or register.[251] Considerable differences in reactions were found in different centers. At Tule Lake Center, for instance, some 3,000, or 30 per cent, of the adults remained unregistered; those unregistered and answering "No" to the loyalty questions constituted 42 per cent of all persons 17 years of age and older.[252]

The leave regulations of fall, 1942, called for the handling by the WRA Washington office of applications for leave clearance and indefinite leave permits. In the spring and summer of 1943 new regulations were adopted which gave project directors power to grant leave permits and to participate in leave-clearance decisions, which defined more sharply those categories of evacuees whose cases were to be scrutinized before leave was granted, and which decentralized the procedures.[253] Indefinite leave could be granted in advance of clearance by Washington if the evacuee had answered "Yes" on question 28. But if the applicant had applied for expatriation or repatriation, had previously been denied leave clearance, was a Shinto priest or an alien on parole, or wished to relocate in the Eastern Defense Command (EDC), leave clearance had to come from Washington.[254]

In the summer of 1943, increasing attention was paid to the possible dangerousness of resettlers, stimulated by the adoption of the policy of segregating those adjudged dangerous. New regulations specified categories of evacuees whose cases were to be carefully scrutinized from that standpoint before leave clearance was granted.[255] These cases were those in which the individual gave an unqualified "No" to question 28 or did not answer it at all, or gave a qualified "Yes," "and the qualification raised a real question concerning the applicant's sympathies or loyalties," or gave a "No" or a qualified "No" and subsequently changed it; or in which the individual had applied for repatriation or expatriation "whether or not he subsequently retracted the request"; or in which there was "an adverse report by the Federal Bureau of Investigation or other federal intelligence agency"; or in which the Japanese American Joint Board did not recommend leave clearance; or in which "the application or other material discloses other information that in the director's judgment requires further explanation." The project director set up a board of three to five members and notified the applicant that a hearing of his case would be held. The director informed the applicant of the purpose of the interview and confronted him with the facts throwing "doubt upon the eligibility for indefinite leave." He secured the applicant's explanation and conducted such further investigation as seemed appropriate. Upon completion of the investigation the project director submitted the file and recommendation to the director of the WRA, who made the final decision for or against leave clearance.

In September, 1943, new regulations were prescribed for cases in which the applicant's file "contains a derogatory intelligence report."[256]

They required a particular investigation of the major factors, any one of which "is regarded by intelligence agencies as sufficient to warrant a recommendation that leave clearance be denied unless there is an adequate explanation." The nine major factors were (1) a negative answer to question 28 "whether or not subsequently changed either during or after registration"; (2) failure to answer question 28; (3) late registration during the February-March registration program; (4) request for repatriation or expatriation whether or not subsequently retracted; (5) military training in Japan (this was assumed if a male received any education in Japan after the age of 15 and returned to the United States after 1930); (6) employment on Japanese naval vessels; (7) three trips to Japan after the age of 6, except for seamen whose stays confined them to ports of call; (8) ten years residence in Japan by a male citizen after the age of 6 unless married to a citizen of the United States and with children; or (9) officer, organizer, agent, member, or contributor to any of the organizations on list "A," which "intelligence agencies consider to be organizations known to be subversive." Other factors "of lesser importance, twenty-four in number, covered not only the pre-Pearl Harbor activities of the evacuee but his center life—"bad project record" was one—and the characteristics of his close relatives, whether they were living in Japan or had investments there, or had answered question 28 in the negative.

To review the findings of the center boards investigating such cases and to make independent recommendations on questions of security in regard to leave clearance, a review committee of WRA officials was established in September, 1943. A case was passed to this committee, "whenever there were negative items in the docket or a combination of personal factors indicating some possibility of substantial pro-Japanese leanings."[257] Of particular concern to the committee was the data provided by intelligence agencies about the evacuee's relations with the many Japanese associations in the United States.[258]

Evacuees whose applications for leave clearance had been rejected could appeal to a Board of Appeals for Leave Clearance which was established in July, 1944, as advisory to the director of the WRA. It was composed of three qualified citizens not otherwise connected with the WRA, Professor Thomas S. Barclay of Stanford University, Garett McEnerney, II, and Philip H. Angell of San Francisco. Nineteen cases were reviewed by the board. "Twelve of these cases were recommended to the Director for leave clearance, four were recommended for denial, and three resulted in split decisions."[259]

During 1943 the Army played an increasing role in determining the character of the leave. After the Japanese American Joint Board began its work, the WRA made its leave permits subject to various conditions which depended on the board's findings, at the War Department's insistence. Those favorably recommended by the board were given permits for resettlement in the EDC if the commanding general approved. Only those who received a favorable recommendation after a special investigation by the board were given permits to relocate anywhere outside of the proscribed West Coast areas and cleared for war-plant employment.[260]

Under these conditions and requirements the rate of resettlement accelerated somewhat during 1943. Between January 1 and December 31, some 16,000 evacuees left the centers on indefinite leave, bringing the total to about 17,000.[261] A total of 1,138 student leaves had been granted to permit evacuees to study at 215 different institutions, and approximately 5,000 seasonal workers were released for agricultural labor in the summer and fall. Those whose applications for leave clearance were disapproved were declared ineligible for leave and were transferred to the center at Tule Lake.

During 1944, leave regulations remained unchanged in major particulars, although two changes designed to increase the numbers relocating were made. In February, 1944, it was announced that seasonal work leaves would be issued only to evacuees recruited for agricultural work through the War Food Administration in counties approved by the WRA and for periods of less than seven months. No return to a center was allowed except in cases of emergency.[262] In March, indefinite leave for a "trial period" was granted to permit evacuees to accept outside employment for a period of four months, during which time return to the center was prohibited. At the end of that period the evacuee was given two additional months within which he could return to the center "upon failure to make a permanent adjustment in new surroundings."[263]

By July 31, 1944, leave clearance had been completed for the majority of the evacuees. According to the WRA, some 83,000 evacuees had by that date filed applications for leave clearance, and 68,000 had been granted it or were eligible for indefinite leave in advance of clearance. Of the remaining 15,000: 12,680 had been segregated at Tule Lake (figure includes family members), 1,528 had been denied leave clearance on the basis of hearings, and 792 were in process of hearings and review.[264]

During 1944, up to the date of the revocation of the mass exclusion orders, some 18,500 evacuees left the centers on indefinite leave. The total so leaving was 35,509, the population remaining in the centers

79,763.[285] After revocation of the exclusion orders on December 17, 1944, the control of evacuees passed to the Army and the WRA played a very slight part in determining who could or could not leave the centers.

War Department and WDC policies.—The War Department and the WDC played a substantial role in determining who could leave the centers and in shaping the lives of those evacuees who left. The policies of War Department staff units and boards as well as those of the WDC determined who could serve in the Army and what the character of that service would be, whether evacuees could or could not settle in extensive areas of the country in the east and south, and how they could be employed. These decisions were based on administrative findings of "loyalty" or "disloyalty," or of "dangerousness to national security." A number of staff units were set up by the Army in post-Pearl Harbor years to collect intelligence about the Japanese to assist in these decisions.

War Department policy, decided on the highest level, determined the nature of military service of the Japanese. During 1942 and 1943 the investigations required for determining eligibility for service under the policies in force were handled by the Assistant Chief of Staff, G-2. On July 25, 1943, this function was transferred to the Office of the Provost Marshal General (OPMG). The Military Clearance Section of the Japanese American Branch (a unit of the Personnel Security Division) was created to carry on the security investigations. It became the largest single source of intelligence on Japanese citizens and worked in close contact with the Civil Affairs Division of the WDC. In the fall of 1943 it undertook a screening of all male Japanese Americans of military age in the United States in preparation for the restoration of their induction by Selective Service on January 1, 1944. The Japanese American Branch, working closely with the JAJB, assessed the "loyalty" of evacuees, classifying them as "acceptable" for service or "unacceptable." Of all the Japanese American males acceptable for service by Selective Service standards of mental and physical fitness, 7,900, or 38 per cent, were rejected on grounds of "disloyalty."[286]

War Department policy was also influential in determining who could leave the centers and what type of work they could secure. As a result of interagency conferences among the War Department (represented by McCloy), WRA, OPMG, Military Intelligence (G-2), the Office of Naval Intelligence, and the FBI, in December, 1942, and January, 1943, on the subject of "Loyalty Investigations of American Citizens of Japanese Ancestry in War Relocation Centers," it was agreed that the War Department would upon request of the WRA, assist in determining the loyalty of American citizens of Japanese ancestry under its jurisdiction. The purpose of this plan is to determine (a) loyalty . . . to permit of their release by the WRA from War Relocation Centers and (b) whether those so released may be inducted into the military service or may be available for employment in plants and facilities important to the war effort.[207]

Various procedures were announced to implement this plan, among which was the establishment of the Japanese American Joint Board and the sending of teams of army officers to the centers to conduct the campaign for volunteers in February, 1943. The JAJB's initial directive called on it to make recommendations to the WRA concerning the release of American citizens of Japanese ancestry from centers on indefinite leave, and to indicate whether it had any objection to the employment in war industries of those who were given leave permits pursuant to its recommendation.[208] Shortly after beginning its operations the board moved to enlarge its scope. It decided to screen all alien Japanese and to make recommendations to the WRA on the granting of indefinite leave to all classes of evacuees.

Myer immediately protested to McCloy about the increasing powers being assumed by the board and McCloy assured him that the board and the Office of the Provost Marshal would not be allowed to supersede the WRA in controlling evacuee resettlement.[209] Later in the year the board recommended that it be authorized to check on the loyalty of all Japanese Americans outside of the relocation centers. Myer again protested and the board was not given this task. However, the War Department and the WDC came to regard the board as "primarily an agency for controlling the leave clearance process and only secondarily as an agency handling war plant employment."[270]

The board did not undertake hearings or conduct any field investigations of its own. Its decisions were primarily based on the data about applicants contained in the questionnaires filled out at registration in the centers in February, 1943, and by reports from the FBI. In those cases in which the WRA wanted a board recommendation, it forwarded the evacuee's questionnaires. After May, 1943, these sources of data were supplemented by a record check by the Civil Affairs Division.

A number of procedures were tried by the board in an attempt to devise a system to arrive at judgments about the "loyalty" of evacuees. At first a numerical system was devised by which a plus or minus value would be assigned to biographical facts about the Japanese—for instance, residence in Japan or officership of a particular society—deemed significantly related to "loyalty." The judgment of "cleared" or "un-

cleared" was to be determined by the sum of these values. This, however, proved impractical, and a second procedure was devised whereby
one member of the board would examine a group of cases and report his
findings and recommendations to the entire board. But this produced
arguments among board members which arose from divergent opinions
on the relative significance of the various historical circumstances and
acts of the Japanese; one board member, for example, might feel that
ownership of large sums of money in Japan was a certain indication of
disloyalty while others would place no weight on it at all. The procedure finally adopted was one of deciding on policies toward specific
facts rather than that of conducting close studies of individual cases.
The board would decide, by vote, that a particular "characteristic,"
such as membership in a specified Japanese organization, was significant
of disloyalty. All cases showing that characteristic would then be classed
as "uncleared." The decisions about the policies toward various characteristics changed frequently.

However, certain characteristics were almost always regarded unfavorably and generally led to an adverse recommendation on leave
clearance for war-plant employment. These were a negative or qualified
answer to question 28 (unless the qualification fell in the category of a
complaint over deprivation of civil rights brought about through the
evacuation); request for repatriation; ten years' residence or schooling
in Japan after the age of six and a return to the States after 1930; five
years' residence or schooling, returning after 1935; Japanese academic
military training or attendance in Japanese schools for five years after
1930 if over twelve years of age in that year; activity in Japanese organizations or "disloyal" statements; employment by the Japanese government or active Shintoist connections; refusal to register in the
February, 1943, registration; segregation at Tule Lake after September,
1943; membership in the Heimusha Kai (Society for Men Eligible for
Military Duty), Botuku Kai (Military Virtue Society), or Kaigun Kyokai
(Navy League); substantial contributions to the Japanese war effort
after 1937, especially if not mentioned on the Selective Service questionnaire at the February, 1943, registration; ownership of substantial sums
of money in Japan; leadership of disturbance at a center; travel to
Japan but no disclosure of that fact. Those seven or eight thousand
evacuees who answered "Yes" to both questions 27 and 28 and who had
a clear record with the FBI were cleared. Wives were not cleared if
their husbands had not been recommended for clearance.

The policy of checking all cases with the WDC, the delays incident on
revising procedures, and the time required to come to decisions, resulted

in few evacuees being cleared for war work. The WRA submitted 27,425 cases to the board, seeking approval for war-plant employment and residence in the EDC. Of these, 21,167 were approved for residence in the EDC and 291 cleared for residence in the WDC as language instructors in Army schools. "During the entire fifteen month history of the Board's operations, less than 500 Nisei were given clearance for work in war plants and not all of these by any means were actually employed in such work."[271]

Despite its participation in the JAJB, the WRA did not regard itself as bound by the board's recommendations on indefinite leave or EDC residence. However, the agency "was guided by these recommendations to the extent of making further investigations in all cases where the Joint Board recommended denial of indefinite leave." Individuals disapproved by the board but cleared by the WRA for relocation were held in the centers until a reëxamination of their cases could be made.[272] Because of disagreement with the board on EDC relocations and the fact that the WRA considered that the "disloyal" had been segregated and sent to Tule Lake, it withdrew from the agreement. "Citizens who . . . met all WRA loyalty tests have been allowed to relocate to the eastern states while Joint Board action is pending."[273] If the JAJB opposed relocation in the EDC, then the WRA followed suit. However, on July 18, 1944, Fortas notified the War Department that the WRA would issue permits for relocation in the EDC regardless of the JAJB decision.[274]

After the abolition of the JAJB in May, 1944, the clearance of evacuees for war-plant work was handled by the Japanese American Branch of the Provost Marshal General's Office. Its policy on clearance was even more drastic. It called for the removal from war plants of those who had been hired before it assumed jurisdiction over such hiring. "This requirement led to vigorous protests both from evacuees working in war plants and from their employers. Because of these protests, the OPMG removed this requirement and allowed current employees to remain pending clearance."[275] After such investigations, many evacuees who had worked in war plants for months were removed from their positions and forced to find employment in nonwar-related industries. Evacuees and employers joined in complaining about the lack of uniformity in the rulings. In one district a railroad might hire Japanese without clearance; in another district a few miles away the same railroad could not.

The WDC, although temporarily relinquishing its leave-clearance authority over the Japanese to the WRA, retained a direct interest in their presence within the Command and strictly controlled and regulated their entrance and residence there. In the period immediately after the evacuation, the Command had issued permits for travel and temporary residence in the prohibited area, and in the spring of 1944 began a program of issuing Certificates of Exemption (from exclusion orders) which allowed individuals who passed a security investigation to return to the Pacific Coast to reside. Travel and temporary residence permits were issued to evacuees for business reasons if the WRA Evacuee Property Division recommended such travel, when there was a serious illness within the immediate family, for travel to and from relocation centers and public institutions within the exclusion zone on the request of the WRA, or for induction into the armed forces. Members of the immediate family of a soldier could travel in the company of the soldier and cleared evacuees could pass through an exclusion zone en route to or from Hawaii. At the request of the WRA, the commanding general of the WDC approved the establishment of seven "travel corridors" between relocation centers in the evacuation areas and various outside cities. The commanding officers of the military police units at these centers could issue permits for travel of evacuees without escort through these corridors. For travel by civilian evacuees to other places or through other routes escorts were required, the cost to be borne by the evacuee. About fifty per cent of the requests for travel or temporary residence permits were turned down by the WDC. The WRA could not issue a leave permit for the evacuated areas until such a pass was issued.[276]

When the WDC began the issuance of Certificates of Exemption, most of the requests for these by evacuees were scrutinized by the WRA before submission; unless the applicant's record was clear, the WRA discouraged the request. The evacuee filed an "Individual Application to Establish Residence within Military Area No. 1 or California Portion of Military Area No. 2, Western Defense Command," with the WDC and provided answers to a lengthy questionnaire (CAD-E-1). The Civil Affairs Division secured intelligence data on the applicant from the OPMG, FBI, Naval Intelligence, and Military Intelligence, and on the basis of this made a recommendation to the commanding general, who made the final decision. The Command issued a number of memoranda as guides for reaching a decision on these applications. For citizen evacuees, a policy statement of September, 1944, noted that the major consideration was whether there was any material evidence that the individual was "dangerous to military security," and listed a number of classes of individuals to whom exemption was not to be granted.[277] This policy statement noted that the fact that an individual was an enemy alien was not conclusive evidence of his loyalty to Japan, but that such loyalty should be assumed unless evidence to the contrary was present. As with citizens, the major consideration was whether he was potentially dangerous to military security. A number of categories of alien Japanese were specified as not eligible to return to the coastal zone.[278] During the spring of 1944 the applications came in very slowly; by April 1 there were 40, by July 1 there were 150. During the summer and fall, as word spread through the centers, they increased; by August 1 there were 235 and by September 15 there were 515. A good proportion were approved. By the end of 1944 there were 1,485 Japanese residing in the WDC by special permit: 58 in California, 492 in Oregon, and 935 in Washington. Most of these were wives and husbands of Caucasian residents of the coast.[279]

To secure the background data which it regarded as necessary to gauge the threat of the Japanese to military security and to separate the "dangerous" from the "non-dangerous," the WDC had set up a staff unit to collect and evaluate sociological and historical information about the entire minority. The attempts by the WCCA to secure such data about the Japanese when the evacuees were housed in the assembly centers had not been very successful. WDC reliance on the intelligence agencies was shaken when it became apparent not only that they possessed little information about the Japanese population—the FBI apparently had made studies of only two Japanese associations, the *Butoku Kai* and the *Heimusha Kai*—but that there were wide differences of opinion regarding the bearing of various activities, occupations, interests, travels, education, and other personal facts on the likelihood of an individual endangering military security. The WDC had decided in the early summer of 1942 to set up a Research Division in the Civil Affairs Division to carry out a broad program of study of the Japanese population in the United States. The first research was a study of the Japanese books, newspapers, phonograph records, photographs, and other material collected in the assembly centers by the security police. The FBI, ONI, and G-2 stated they had no personnel to analyze this data and suggested that the WDC do it. It was decided to undertake a systematic study of the Japanese vernacular press in the United States in the period after July, 1937, when the Sino-Japanese war broke out. After several months of fruitless attempts to obtain files from the Japanese, complete files were found in the libraries of the University of California and the University of Washington and a study was made of five papers. The Research Division also made an attempt to locate records of the Japanese organizations in order to study their purposes, activities, officers, and membership, but very few records were found. A study of the movements of Japanese between the United States and Japan and the length of residence in Japan of the Kibei was carried out, using the manifests of ships docking at Seattle, San Francisco, and Los Angeles from the year 1930 on. A survey was made of the records of Japanese banks in California and Washington taken over by the Alien Property Custodian in order to discover the names of contributors to the Japanese war effort and the extent of ownership of property and deposits in Japan by resident Japanese.

The research program, conducted by a staff of over fifty persons, resulted in the accumulation of a vast amount of data. The task of making a fairly accurate inventory of the Japanese organizations on the West Coast, and a record of their officers and activities, turned out to be a difficult and time-consuming one. Although the work was incomplete at the end of the war with Japan in August, 1945, the names of 3,600 organizations and associations, including branches and parent bodies, had been turned up and some information about each recorded. Some 500,000 separate items of information were recorded on the dossiers of 115,000 persons. The movements of 60,000 persons between Japan and the United States in the years from 1930 to 1941 were recorded.

SEGREGATION

Almost immediately upon its inception the WRA had considered the advisability of segregating the actively "disloyal" evacuees from the "loyal." Such a policy was advocated both within and without the agency. In 1942 the WDC pressed for a segregation program. Particularly did they believe that the Kibei should be isolated in separate centers, and DeWitt went so far as to suggest that they should be deprived of their United States citizenship through legal processes and repatriated to Japan at the war's end. On September 8, 1942, DeWitt urged that the more potentially dangerous elements be separated and restricted and that maximum information about the Japanese "race" be secured to be used for military and psychological-warfare purposes. On October 9 DeWitt sent a memorandum to Marshall calling for the separation of the Kibei from the Nisei. On December 17, 1942, he submitted a detailed plan to the War Department for the sudden and forcible seizure by the Army of several classes of evacuees and their incarceration in a separate center, which was to be under the control of a director of segregation, to be appointed by the Secretary of War and the director of the WRA.[280] On December 30, this plan was forwarded by the War Department to Myer for his comment. The accompanying letter from Stimson noted that a list of 5,600 "undesirables" who would form the nucleus of the segregated group had been drawn up. Myer was strongly opposed to the plan and the War Department did not press the matter.

During this period there was extensive discussion within the War Relocation Authority of the desirability of a program of segregation. Lieutenant Commander K. D. Ringle, of the Navy (who was detailed to the agency in May, 1942, for a short period), recommended that "all Kibei who had three or more years of schooling in Japan after the age of 13 and the parents of all such Kibei would be called up before the administrative boards at each of the centers and called upon to declare and demonstrate where their national sympathies lay."[281] Those Kibei in sympathy with Japan would be segregated, as would the strongly pro-Japanese aliens; the Kibei to be segregated, Ringle estimated, would number some eight or nine thousand.[282] However, believing that the Kibei as a group were not actively dissident and that branding them as such would hamper their return to American life, the WRA rejected the proposal.[283] At a WRA staff meeting in August, 1942, Myer indicated his readiness to adopt a limited segregation program and pointed to administrative difficulties as the only deterrent.[284] The WRA believed that segregation would reduce difficulties within the centers and would make it easier to secure public acceptance of a resettlement program for the "loyal" Japanese.[285] After the registration of February, 1943, increasing pressure was brought to bear on the administration of the WRA by the Army, the Japanese American Citizens League, and all project directors, to segregate those who had refused to answer the questionnaire or who had answered the "loyalty" questions in the negative. On July 6, 1943, the Senate adopted a resolution requesting the WRA to segregate "persons of Japanese ancestry in relocation centers whose loyalty to the United States is questionable or who are known to be disloyal."[286]

On July 15, 1943, the WRA announced adoption of a policy of segregating those persons who "by their acts have indicated that their loyalties lie with Japan during the present hostilities or that their loyalties do not lie with the United States."[287] The segregation program, as carried out, was much broader in scope than most of its proponents had advocated.

The July policy called for five classes of evacuees to be segregated at Tule Lake. The first group were the repatriates: aliens who had applied for repatriation to Japan and who had not withdrawn their requests by July 1, 1943; they were sent to Tule Lake without hearings. (The Department of Justice did not consider such a request sufficient grounds for internment of enemy aliens). The second group were the expatriates: American citizens who had applied for removal to Japan. The third group were those who had answered the revised loyalty question in the negative "or failed or refused to answer it, and (a) have not changed their answers prior to the date of this instruction, and (b) who are in the opinion of the project director loyal to Japan."[288] These individuals were given hearings by a special board. If those who had given negative answers (or none at all) to the loyalty question said that they did not wish to change, they were transferred to Tule Lake. Those who said they did wish to change were then extensively questioned as to their reasons.[289] If they failed to satisfy the board and the director that the change was made in good faith they were sent to Tule Lake. The fourth group were those who had been denied leave clearance by the WRA for one or another of the following reasons: a federal intelligence agency had submitted an adverse report on them; they had answered question 28 negatively or with a qualification; they had requested repatriation or expatriation and had not withdrawn such a request prior to July 1, 1943; had not been affirmatively recommended for leave clearance by the JAJB; or they were individuals about whom there was other information indicating "loyalty to Japan."[290] The fifth group were parolees: aliens from the Department of Justice internment camps who were recommended by that agency for detention.[291] Individuals denied leave clearance and transferred to Tule Lake could appeal to an appeals board staffed by persons not otherwise connected with the WRA.

In addition to these five groups of segregants, there were two other classes at Tule Lake. A number of residents, though eligible for leave clearance, refused to leave Tule Lake during the transfer and were allowed to remain,[292] and family members of segregants who wished to accompany them were allowed to do so. The number of persons falling into these classes in May, 1946, is shown in the table on page 163. Some 312 other segregants and their families were sent to Tule Lake during 1944, and by January 1, 1945, the inhabitants numbered 18,734.[293]

The segregation center was to hold only the "segregants," as they were called, and their families, while the other centers were to contain only those to whom leave clearance had been granted or who were, after segregation had begun, on a "stop list" pending final clearance. Tule Lake Relocation Center, in northern California, was picked by the

WRA to hold the segregants, as more of its inmates than of any other center appeared destined to be segregated; it was one of the largest centers and, lying in the evacuated zone, it was less suitable as a relocation center than the others, because of WDC restrictions on travel by Japanese. In preparation for the newcomers, the center's guard facilities were strengthened: "A double 'man proof' fence, eight feet high, was constructed around the whole area; the external guard was increased from a couple of hundred soldiers to full battalion strength; and a half dozen tanks, obsolete but impressive, were lined up in full view of the

TULE LAKE SEGREGANTS, MAY, 1946

Type of segregant	Foreign born	American born	Total
Repatriates	2,524		2,524
Expatriates		4,698	4,698
Non-registrants	1,511	3,274	4,785
Leave denials	166	348	514
Parolees.....................	134		134
Total	4,335	8,320	12,655
Family members of segregants....	1,535	4,080	5,615
Tuleans eligible for leave clearance remaining at Tule........	63	89	152
Grand Total	5,933	12,489	18,422

residents."[294] Stout turnstiles were installed at the only entrance. The military police numbered 31 officers and 899 men; after April, 1944, the complement was reduced to 29 officers and 736 men. During September and October, 1943, exchanges were made between Tule Lake and other centers. Each train load of segregants moving to Tule Lake was accompanied by a military detachment of fifty persons and a WRA staff member. The transfers continued during the winter and into spring of 1944.

Family members who accompanied the segregants to Tule Lake were eligible for relocation, but all other groups, including the Tuleans who had elected to remain, were not eligible for leave clearance. Those who qualified for indefinite leave and wished to relocate were sent to another center, from which they resettled.[295] As children reached the age of seventeen, they were registered and processed for leave clearance. Short-term leave under escort was permitted under rare circumstances "in the interest of the Government."[296] In February, 1944, leave-clearance hearings were instituted at Tule Lake under the same procedures as at other centers, and a number of family member residents made applications,

were heard, and allowed to resettle.[297] In October, 1943, the WRA
adopted the policy of allowing "a person segregated only because he
falls within one of the first two categories of segregants [repatriates or
expatriates; persons answering question 28 negatively or refusing to
register] or because he belongs to a segregant's family" to apply for
investigation and leave clearance if he wished to be transferred to
another center. If leave clearance was approved, such persons were
transferred.[298]

Tule Lake was run much as were the other centers, except for education and government. The WRA considered that these evacuees had
elected "the Japanese way," and allowed them to establish Japanese-
language schools and to carry on various Japanese ceremonies and cultural activities.[299] Self-government as established at other centers was
not allowed, though an advisory board of evacuees and various more-or-
less representative councils came to be recognized and dealt with by the
center administration.

LAW AND ORDER IN THE CENTERS

The responsibility for the administration of justice in the centers lay
in the hands of the WRA-appointed project directors. The agency's
regulations gave them sweeping powers to act as law-makers, prosecu-
tors, and judges.[300] They could decide what acts by evacuees were offenses, what offense an offending evacuee would be charged with, and
what court—federal, state, relocation center, or evacuee-composed judicial commission—would try the case. The graver crimes with severe
penalties were usually tried by federal or state courts but the project
director could try them in the center. He could fine the guilty parties
any sum up to $300 or sentence them to a maximum of three months in
the center jail.

Project directors were also permitted to remove from their centers
and dispatch to an "isolation center" males who were "addicted to
trouble-making and beyond the capacity of regular processes within the
relocation center to keep under control."[301] (If the "trouble-maker" was
an alien, the project director could either send him to the isolation
center or recommend his internment in an alien detention camp to the
Department of Justice if "his permanent removal from the center is
imperative to prevent serious disruption of center administration; and
that use of the project director's disciplinary authority, recurrently if
necessary, will not prevent such disruption.")[302] Isolation began as an
emergency disciplinary measure after disturbances at Poston in November, and at Manzanar in December, 1942. Operated at first without

administrative regulations, the isolation center, first situated at Moab, Utah, and later at Leupp, Arizona, at first received evacuees only on the personal approval of Myer. Later, regulations were issued defining the purpose of sending evacuees there and sketching the procedure to be followed. An investigation was to be held at the center and evidence prepared; and "the evacuee must be in fact a responsible agent in fomenting disorder or threatening the security of center residents, addicted to trouble-making and beyond the capacity of regular processes within the relocation center to keep under control."[303] Individuals sent to Leupp were held without trial, sentence, opportunity to defend themselves against charges, or right or opportunity to appeal.

In the course of a year's existence Leupp received a total of 83 evacuees. The first group was sent in December, 1942, the last in July, 1943.[304] Life in the center was marked by tension and conflict. After one disturbance in April, 1943, a number of residents were removed and lodged in the county jail. In August, 1943, a board of review, staffed by WRA Washington headquarters officials, conducted a review of the records of a large number of inmates and was highly critical of the procedures followed. It found that many were not proper cases for Leupp, that for many there were no records available, and that quite a few had been transferred without the required hearing or with only an inadequate one.[305] In September, 1943, a comprehensive review of cases was instituted, and later in the fall it was decided to abolish the center. The last inmates departed in December.

Isolation as an administrative and disciplinary control measure was also utilized at the Tule Lake Segregation Center, where a "stockade," officially called Area B, was maintained by the center. For periods ranging from several weeks to many months aliens and citizens were incarcerated in its confines without trial or without being charged with an offense.[306] It had been established by the Army when, on November 4, 1943, after a fight between internal security police and some young Japanese Americans, the military police took over the center, proclaimed marshal law and ran the center until January 15, 1944, when they returned administrative control to the WRA. During its period of control the Army removed persons suspected of anti-administration acts or designs and detained them in this closely guarded area. Over 250 were in confinement there in January, 1944. After martial law was ended the Army continued to run the stockade until May, "arresting" evacuees selected by center authorities. In April regulations were issued by the WRA setting forth the purpose of the area and the procedure to be followed in "sentencing" evacuees there. The project director would

make the final decision, assisted by a fact-finding commission which was
to carry out an investigation. "Since such . . . separation of individuals
is a purely administrative arrangement to secure the peaceful and
orderly administration of the center, only such investigation need be
made as is requisite for an administrative determination by the project
director."[307]

The number of "isolatees" in the stockade was reduced in the late
spring of 1944. In June there were 20 inmates: 2 aliens and 18 citizens.
After several hunger strikes by the inmates and representations by the
American Civil Liberties Union, they were all released by August 24,
1944. Of those who at one time or another were incarcerated in the
stockade approximately 100 were aliens and 275 were citizens.

SERVICE IN THE ARMED FORCES

War Department policy toward service in the armed forces by individuals of Japanese ancestry changed from one of suspicion and refusal
to induct in 1942 to one of acceptance of volunteers from among the
citizens in 1943, and the reinstitution of induction under Selective
Service procedures for both citizens and aliens in 1944. As for the Navy:
"During the war years American citizens of Japanese ancestry were not
enlisted in the Navy under any circumstances."[308]

During 1940 and 1941 some 5,000 Japanese American citizens from
the mainland and Hawaii were inducted into the Army or joined as
volunteers. Immediately after Pearl Harbor, the War Department decided that no person of Japanese ancestry was acceptable for service but
made no public announcement to that effect. Army units did not follow
a uniform policy toward their Japanese members. Some officers retained
them but "some discharged them with blue cards and no explanation—
the blue card signifying that the discharge was neither quite honorable
nor quite dishonorable; a few officers became hysterical on December 7
and gathered up any Nisei in their units and put them in the guard-
house."[309] By February, 1942, about 600 had been given honorable dis-
charges and sent home and others had been relieved of combat training
and assigned to other duties. General DeWitt refused to have any
Japanese in the WDC. He wired a recommendation to General Marshall
on January 1, 1942, that enlisted men of Japanese ancestry be removed
from the Command immediately, and the War Department complied.[310]
The early War Department policy that soldiers of Japanese descent not
be granted furloughs to enter the states of Washington, Oregon, California, and Arizona was subsequently modified in cases of personal
emergency, but special travel permits had to be obtained from the com-

manding general of the WDC. The induction practices of draft boards in early 1942 were inconsistent, in the absence of a formal announcement by the War Department. While all draft boards refused to accept volunteer Japanese and generally rejected inductees, giving them a 4-F classification of "physically unfit" or 4-C, "unacceptable because of nationality or ancestry," some inductees were nevertheless processed. A number of these were rejected by commanding officers when they reported for duty. On June 17, 1942, the War Department advised Selective Service that Japanese were not acceptable for service. Induction of any persons of Japanese descent was forbidden, "except as may be specifically authorized in exceptional cases," namely, bilingual individuals to be used as instructors in Army Japanese-language schools and as interpreters for military intelligence.[311] During 1942, 167 citizen volunteers were accepted by the Army as instructors in the language schools, after recruiting officers had visited the assembly and relocation centers; many volunteers were rejected because their knowledge of Japanese was inadequate.[312] On September 14, 1942, Selective Service regulations were adopted "providing for the classification in Class 4-C of any registrant of Japanese ancestry, a class reserved for those considered unsuitable for service because of race or ancestry."[313]

During the summer of 1942, the WRA urged the immediate reinstitution of the draft for the Nisei. McCloy agreed that this would be desirable and sought to secure a reversal of War Department policy. In September, 1942, the department set up a board to consider the matter and to make a policy recommendation. A number of high Army officers were called to testify; although several were in favor of drafting the Nisei, DeWitt and Drum were opposed and the board made an adverse recommendation. In January, 1943, further discussions were held within the War Department and an interchange of views took place with the WRA, which continued to urge the draft. The issue was settled with a compromise: the War Department agreed to form a combat team, one-third of a battalion, from Nisei volunteers, and to set up a board, the Japanese American Joint Board, to screen and clear evacuees for war-plant employment and army service.

On January 28, 1943, Stimson announced that an all-Nisei combat team would be made up of volunteers from the mainland and Hawaii. President Roosevelt declared, in a letter to Stimson made public on February 1, 1943, that the plan "had his full approval.... This is a natural and logical step toward the reinstitution of the Selective Service procedures which were temporarily disrupted by the evacuation from the West Coast. No loyal citizen of the United States should be denied the democratic right to exercise the responsibilities of his citizenship, regardless of his ancestry."[314]

The War Department arranged for teams of selected officers to visit the relocation centers to explain the program to the Nisei, to secure the completed Selective Service questionnaires, and to enroll the volunteers. The teams were formed in Washington where the officers were given an indoctrination course and were addressed by McCloy and E. R. Fryer, Deputy Director of the WRA. In February the officers held meetings of Nisei in the various centers and answered questions. Questionnaires were distributed and collected from those who wished to volunteer; these also signed a special form, an "Application for Voluntary Induction."[315] The collection of questionnaires and the enlistment of volunteers was completed about the first week in March. The teams remained in the centers longer than anticipated and in some centers reinterviewed those evacuees who originally gave negative answers to the "loyalty" questions. Many of the evacuees changed their answers; at Gila nearly one-half are said to have done so.

The campaign for volunteers was disappointing to the Army; only 1,181 Nisei enrolled as volunteers—6 per cent of the 19,963 male American citizens of Japanese ancestry between the ages of 17 and 37—although 3,500 had been expected to do so. Over a quarter of the Nisei refused to answer the "loyalty" questions in the affirmative, thus indicating an unwillingness to serve.[316] The names of the volunteers were sent to G-2 for a determination of eligibility. The Army accepted 805 who met both loyalty and physical fitness standards, and they became part of the all-Nisei 442nd Regimental Combat Team, which contained around 4,500 men. The unit sailed for the Italian campaign in May, 1944, joining the 100th Infantry Battalion, made up of Nisei national guardsmen from Hawaii, which had been sent to Italy in August, 1943.

During the February registration, many potential volunteers inquired whether their entering the service would rescind exclusion for them and their families. The War Department answer was in the negative. However, McCloy urged DeWitt to modify his stand and to allow soldiers of Japanese descent to enter prohibited areas without permits. DeWitt refused and in April sent a memorandum to the Chiefs of Staff justifying his position. He was, however, overruled and directed to modify the policy. On April 21, 1943, he issued Public Proclamation No. 17,[317] which suspended exclusion orders for Japanese serving in the Army. Permission for wives to travel with soldier husbands in the WDC was generally refused, unless it could be demonstrated that their presence was necessary.

After Selective Service was instituted, restrictions on travel in the WDC were eased. Wives of soldiers were usually allowed in the area on specific request. In May, 1944, all members of soldiers' families were allowed to enter on request after screening by intelligence and security agencies. In April, 1944, inductees were given permission to travel in the area for no longer than twenty-one days without escorts, and in May, all honorably discharged soldiers were exempt from travel restrictions in the Command.

On July 28, 1943, the War Department announced that a quota of 500 Japanese women with American citizenship had been established for the WAC and a recruiting officer was sent to visit the centers to enroll volunteers. Active induction began in November. Volunteers were screened by the Provost Marshal General and had to be approved by the service commander. A total of 139 applied, of whom 116 were accepted by the Provost Marshal's office. Recruits were allowed to state their choice of station. Many chose West Coast installations and the War Department did not refuse any such requests for reasons of ancestry alone.

One year after accepting volunteers, impressed by what the War Department described as the "excellent showing" of the combat team and the "outstanding record" of the 100th Infantry Battalion, Selective Service policy was revised and on January 20, 1944, the War Department announced the "involuntary induction," through Selective Service procedures, of American citizen Japanese would be instituted at all centers except Tule Lake. However, the Japanese inductees were given a Selective Service questionnaire (DSS Form 304A) similar to that used for aliens and different from that used for other American citizens, which asked detailed questions about their background, relatives in Japan or other foreign countries, knowledge of Japanese, registration of birth in Japan, and other matters. Further, they were required to forswear allegiance to the Japanese Emperor before acceptance into the Army. One form of the statement they were asked to sign stated:

Have you had in the past or do you now have any allegiance or obedience to the Japanese Emperor or any other foreign government? If yes, do you hereby forswear that allegiance or obedience? If you have had or now have such allegiance or obedience and do not forswear it, why do you not do so? Do you hereby declare your loyalty and obedience to the United States? If not, why not?[318]

Finally, announcements were made that Japanese were to be used only as replacements in the combat team, though this was changed later and the announcement made that some might be selected for other units.

They were not to be sent to the Pacific Theatre, they were to be trained in separate battalions, and they were not to be admitted to the Navy, Air Force, or special service units in the Army. All male Japanese, those who had relocated and those who were still in the centers, were given Form 304A to complete. On the basis of the information received from the questionnaire, the Japanese American Branch of the Office of the Provost Marshal General reviewed the cases individually and classified them as "acceptable" or "not acceptable" for military service. On November 18, 1944, Selective Service announced that it was prepared to accept the voluntary induction of alien Japanese.

Between November, 1940 and December, 1945, a total of 25,778 Japanese Americans were inducted, of whom 13,528 were from the mainland and 12,250 from Hawaii. Four hundred and thirty-eight served as officers and 25,340 as enlisted men.[319] In December, 1945, American citizens of Japanese ancestry were accepted for enlistment in the Navy.

Many Nisei responded unfavorably to the announcement of the restoration of induction. Between January 20 and August 26, 1944, Selective Service accepted 2,213, of whom 91 refused to report for induction and 164 refused to report for physical examinations.[320] Up to November 30, 1946, there were 315 inductees who refused to report for physical examinations, to answer the induction call, to be sworn in, or to take military training;[321] many were indicted for violation of the Selective Service Act, tried, and convicted. Recourse to the law did not help the recalcitrant inductees. On March 12, 1945, the Federal Court of Appeals of the Tenth Circuit confirmed the conviction of a resident of Heart Mountain Center for failure to report for a physical examination after a call by a draft board. Neither Japanese ancestry nor possible invasion of constitutional rights by the evacuation program were held to absolve him. The Supreme Court denied a writ of certiorari on May 28, 1945. Subsequently, pardons to almost all persons convicted of violating the Selective Service Act and restoration to them of rights and privileges of citizenship were granted by the President's Advisory Board Proclamation of December 23, 1947.[322]

FREEDOM

After the WDC turned over administrative responsibility for the Japanese evacuees to the WRA in November, 1942, the latter, acting under its own grant of power and under a delegation of authority from the WDC, exercised control over the evacuees, detaining some in centers and allowing others to relocate. In December, 1944, the Army reasserted its control over the Japanese population. The proclamations and orders instituting the mass exclusion program were revoked and a program of "individual exclusion" was substituted. Some 5,000 male Japanese adjudged to be "potentially dangerous to military security" were excluded from the West Coast, some 5,000 males were retained under detention in the centers, and all the rest were allowed to return. To secure the information considered necessary to make judgments about individual Japanese—whether to exclude, to detain, or to set at liberty—the WDC screened and classified the entire Japanese population of the United States: those in centers, those who had relocated, and those who had not been in the evacuated areas after Pearl Harbor or had not come under the WRA's jurisdiction. During the spring and summer of 1945 the individual exclusion orders were reviewed by the WDC and many cancelled. In September, 1945, two weeks after V-J Day, the exclusion orders were rescinded.

Many of the segregants at the Tule Lake Center during the winter and spring of 1944 decided to renounce their American citizenship under an amendment to the Nationality Act. After the substitution of individual exclusion for the mass exclusion program in December, 1944, these evacuees were detained in the centers. In mid-1945 the Department of Justice moved to send these renunciants to Japan, classifying them as "undesirable alien enemies." Military hostilities over, the renunciants prevented their deportation by legal action and secured their release from the internment camps. Taking to the courts again, some succeeded in having their citizenship restored on the grounds that they had been coerced into renunciation. Later, however, the government won a decision on appeal which in subsequent proceedings placed on the individual the burden of proof that his renunciation had been effected by coercion and was not the free play of his judgment.

Individual exclusion and detention.—Unconditional freedom for the majority of the Japanese to return to the evacuated areas of the Pacific Coast, announced by the WDC in December, 1944, came after several years of discussion in the agencies responsible for the displaced people.[323] During 1943 and 1944 the WRA pressed for revocation of the mass exclusion measures and for a screening program to select and control the disloyal or dangerous. One June 2, 1944, Secretary of the Interior Ickes wrote to President Roosevelt urging the revocation of exclusion. (The WRA had been administratively placed under the Department of the Interior earlier in the year). During early 1944 the WDC staff discussed the advisability of such a modification of control over the Japanese in order to avoid court decisions which would limit or annul the authority for military control over civilians which the Army pos-

sessed by virtue of Executive Order 9066. In the spring, General
Emmons, then the commanding general of the WDC, proposed to ter-
minate the exclusion of individuals found not to be actually or potentially dangerous and to reduce the size of the prohibited area. In a
memorandum to the War Department he suggested this and pointed
to the increasing possibility of action by the courts which would undermine authority for military restrictions over civilians.[324]

The War Department was receptive to a change of policy. Acting
Secretary of State Stettinius discussed Ickes' proposal with McCloy (at
the request of President Roosevelt who had forwarded Ickes' letter to
him), and also with Ickes. He wrote to Roosevelt on June 9, 1944, that
"the Army is in accord with the views set forth by Mr. Ickes. The question appears to be largely a political one, the reaction in California, on
which I am sure you will probably wish to reach your own decision."[325]
The President disapproved of the proposed changes, and expressed his
opinion in a memorandum of June 12, 1944, to Stettinius and Ickes:

The more I think of this problem of suddenly ending the orders excluding
Japanese Americans from the west coast the more I think it would be a mistake
to do anything drastic or sudden. As I said at Cabinet, I think the whole problem, for the sake of internal quiet, should be handled gradually, i.e., I am
thinking of two methods: (a) Seeing, with great discretion, how many Japanese
families would be acceptable to public opinion in definite localities on the
west coast. (b) Seeking to extend greatly the distribution of other families in
many parts of the United States. I have been talking to a number of people
from the Coast and they are all in agreement that the Coast would be willing
to receive back a portion of the Japanese who were formerly there—nothing
sudden and not in too great quantities at any one time. Also, in talking to
people from the Middle West, the East and the South, I am sure that there
would be no bitterness if they were distributed—one or two families to each
county as a start. Dissemination and distribution constitute a great method of
avoiding public outcry. Why not proceed along the above line—for a while at
least?[326]

Roosevelt expressed the same opinions in talks with McCloy on June
13 and with Major General C. H. Bonesteel at San Diego on July 21.[327]

The presidential ban on the return of large numbers of Japanese to
the West Coast junked immediate plans for the rescission of the mass
exclusion program and no alternative could be developed by the WRA
or the War Department, for those agencies differed sharply on what
steps could and should be taken to implement his wishes. The WDC,
however, was active in considering new policies and in preparing for
the day when a change from mass exclusion to some other procedure
could be made.

On November 10, 1944, with the election over, the matter of exclusion was again broached by Secretary Ickes. The President agreed to allow the unconditional release of the majority of the Japanese, giving them freedom to return to their West Coast homes. The War Department and the WDC now moved to put their plans into effect and at a series of conferences in Washington with WRA and Department of Justice officials prepared for the change.

On December 15, the WDC issued Civilian Restrictive Order No. 32 which established the new West Coast Exclusion Zone, composed of Military Area No. 1 and the California part of Military Area No. 2.[328] On Sunday, December 17, General Pratt, then commander of the WDC, issued Public Proclamation No. 21. Mass exclusion was terminated. All evacuees not designated by name for exclusion would be free from the provisions of all public proclamations and civilian-exclusion and restriction orders on January 20, 1945.[329] The WDC immediately clamped a strict control on the 60,000 evacuees still in the centers. Military police units were informed by Pratt of their responsibility to see that no evacuee leave the center until cleared by the WDC.[330] The WRA relinquished almost all control over the evacuees and became in effect a housekeeping agency.

In preparation for the new program the WDC had decided in the fall of 1944 which classes of individuals of Japanese ancestry would be detained in the centers, which excluded from the exclusion zone, and which set at liberty to return there. It refused to accept WRA's leave-clearance judgments and insisted on making its own appraisals. Those evacuees suspected of being "potentially dangerous to military security" were to be excluded. "Derogatory" characteristics—such as a "No" reply to questions 27 and 28 of the registration—which, in the opinion of the WDC staff, made this "dangerousness" probable or likely, were determined. To decide into which group each one of the 122,000 Japanese fell, an extensive intelligence program was set up. A wide range of information was compiled about every Japanese in the United States by the Research Branch of the Civil Affairs Division, which undertook its own research program and also drew on the files of other intelligence agencies.

On the basis of this information the Japanese population was divided in December, 1944, into three major groups. The great majority of them—108,545—were "cleared" to move into the formerly prohibited areas of the WDC or any other part of the United States. If a cleared person was in a center he was free to leave after January 20, 1945. Detained in the centers were 4,963 males, the great majority of them segregant citizens held at Tule Lake. To be excluded from the West Coast Exclusion Zone were an additional 4,810 males, the great majority of these being citizens who had applied for expatriation to Japan. These excludees were given individual exclusion orders which informed them that they were to remain out of that zone on pain of prosecution under Public Law 503, and that they might appeal this order if they wished. The boards which were set up to review appeals revoked approximately 500 orders before the program ended. An additional 4,000 or so evacuees were temporarily placed on a "suspense list" and detained until their cases could be examined and a decision made for detention, exclusion or freedom.

In the belief that the residents of the centers should return to normal American life as soon as possible, Myer acted to speed the outward flow. The leave system was largely abandoned.[331] Relocation assistance in the form of grants for travel and transportation of household goods was provided if the WRA approved the "relocation plan" of the center resident.[332] In December, 1944, it was announced that the centers would be closed sometime during the next year. The centers were put on a maintenance basis, the schools closed permanently at the end of the spring term, and agricultural projects terminated. On June 20 and July 13, 1945, specific closing dates were announced for all centers except Tule Lake. The end of the war on August 15, the closing of schools, and a threat of eviction by the WRA, led to the speeding up of the outward movement in the fall—by July 1 only 16,000 of the more than 60,000 residents had left—and all centers except Tule Lake closed between October 15 and December 5, 1945. The WRA came to its official end on June 30, 1946.

With the defeat of Japan officially proclaimed, the WDC and the War Department abolished the individual exclusion program. On September 4, 1945, Public Proclamation No. 24 was issued by the WDC, rescinding all outstanding individual exclusion orders,[333] and War Department Proclamation WD:3 of September 14 rescinded the provisions of Proclamation WD:1 and WD:2.[334]

All Japanese except those detained at Tule Lake were now free to go where they pleased. Military police were withdrawn from all centers and on the basis of an agreement reached with the Department of Justice early in the year, Tule Lake was turned over to that department, patrolmen of the Immigration and Naturalization Service replacing the military police on October 10, 1945.

Repatriation and expatriation.—During 1942 a number of Japanese citizens applied for repatriation to Japan and arrangements were completed for the return of a small number in that and the following year. In the spring of 1942 the Japanese government submitted a list of 539 aliens it would accept. Fifty-four of those named accepted the offer and sailed for Japan on June 16, 1942, on the *S.S. Gripsholm*.[335] A canvass of assembly and relocation centers was undertaken by the WDC and the WRA in the summer of 1942, and by late October [21, 1942,] 2,086 had signed requests for repatriation to Japan: 1,610 were aliens, 162 were American citizens over eighteen, 646 were American citizens under eighteen, and 363 were dual citizens.[336] The *Gripsholm* made its second and final trip on September 2, 1943, carrying 314 Japanese from the centers, 149 of whom were American-citizen family members of the alien repatriated.[337]

During 1943 and 1944 applications for repatriation continued to be filed with the WRA and the State Department despite the fact that no arrangements had been made for further exchanges. On January 1, 1943, there were 3,396 applications on file, on January 1, 1944, there were 9,028, and on January 1, 1945, there were 20,067.[338] Of those applying 6,900 were foreign-born; 6,626 were thirty-five or older; 13,737 were American-born of whom 7,581 were nineteen or younger.[339] After the rescission of mass exclusion the WRA announced that it would no longer assist individuals in making such applications and that interested persons should apply through the Spanish Embassy, which represented Japanese interests during the war.

Renunciation.—From the time it was made a segregation center in 1943 Tule Lake was filled with tension and violence. A militantly pro-Japanese minority sought to convince the center's 18,000 inhabitants that they should take an anti-American and pro-Japanese stand, renounce American citizenship, and seek repatriation to Japan. They adopted a variety of means to achieve this, including threats, violence, and propaganda.[340]

Events in the center received great attention in the press, and representatives in Congress from the West Coast sought measures to deprive the "disloyal" of their American citizenship. In the fall of 1943 the Department of Justice was under pressure from various quarters to strip them of their citizenship and to deport them to Japan. On December 8, 1943, Representative Martin Dies, Chairman of the House Select Committee to Investigate Un-American Activities, asked Biddle to appear before that committee. Biddle did so and recommended the enactment of legislation to permit the voluntary renunciation of American citizenship by citizens on American soil.[341] (Former methods of losing citizenship applied only to individuals living abroad). A bill was drafted by

the department and submitted to Congress on January 25, 1944, which
provided that a national of the United States might renounce his citizenship in time of war if the Attorney General should approve such a
renunciation as not contrary to the interests of national defense. The
measure passed both houses of Congress and was signed by President
Roosevelt on July 1, 1944.[342]

During the fall of 1944 the Department of Justice and the WRA held
conferences on the procedure to be used in processing the denaturaliza-
tion applications. On October 6, 1944, Attorney General Biddle announced that applications were receivable and described the procedures
to be followed.[343] An evacuee desiring to renounce his citizenship was
to make a signed request to the Attorney General on a prepared form,
which recorded some biographical data about the applicant and concluded with the statement, "I fully understand that if permitted to renounce my United States nationality I will divest myself of all rights
and privileges thereunto pertaining."[344] The department would then
schedule a hearing for each applicant after which he could, if he persisted in his wish, make a formal written renunciation and request for
the Attorney General's approval, renouncing his citizenship and all of
its rights and privileges. If the Attorney General granted approval, the
renunciant received a "Notice of Approval of Renunciation" which
informed him that he was no longer a citizen of the United States nor
entitled to any of the rights and privileges of such status.

During the late summer of 1944, as the Department of Justice prepared to receive applications for denationalization, the pro-Japanese
opposition at Tule Lake "emerged from an underground pressure
group to a highly formalized, institutionalized organization, with a
frankly nationalistic and exhibitionalistically disloyal program." In
the latter part of October they were enabled "to push their program
toward its ultimate goal—renunciation of American citizenship by the
young men as a symbol of their complete rejection of America and
identification with Japan."[345] The group sponsored a series of "educational" lectures and established several associations, among them the
Sokoku Kenkyu Seinen-Dan (Young Men's Association for the Study
of the Mother Country) and the *Sokuji Kikoku Hoshi-dan* (Organization to Return Immediately to the Homeland to Serve). A Japanese-
language school was organized, the "Greater East Asia Language
School," through which pro-Japanese views and propaganda were dis-
seminated. When the Department of Justice announced that applications for renunciation were receivable, the associations stepped up their
nationalistic activities and intensified their pressures for acceptance of

renunciation. In November, 1944, more than a hundred applications had been received; by mid-December over six hundred.[346]

Events in December brought a crisis to the center and a sharp increase in the applications for renunciation. On December 5, John L. Burling, a representative of the Department of Justice, arrived, to be joined later by other officials of the department, to open hearings for the would-be renunciants. A strenuous campaign was immediately begun by the pro-Japanese organizations to induce Kibei and Nisei to renounce. On December 17 the abandonment of mass exclusion was announced by the WDC and on December 18 the decision to close all relocation projects within a year was made public by the WRA. These announcements "transformed general reluctance to accept the pressure group program as a whole to popular support of the main issue—renunciation of American citizenship."[347] The pro-Japanese faction increased its pressure on the administration and on the general center population, and the number of applications for renunciation rose. In January, 1945, 3,400 citizens at Tule Lake applied. "This number represented 40 percent of the total citizen population over 17½ years of age and combined with approximately 1,200 whose applications had been received earlier, meant that by this time one out of every two Nisei and Kibei in the center had attempted to withdraw from American citizenship."[348] A thousand more applications were received in February and several hundred in subsequent weeks. Between December 22, 1944, and April 18, 1945, over 6,000 applications were received by the department. At the hearings held by the WDC in connection with the individual exclusion program, 460 evacuees in other centers said they wanted to renounce their citizenship, as did 125 who had relocated.

The flood of applications alarmed the Department of Justice and it moved to meet the situation by breaking up the pro-Japanese organizations through removal of their leaders, by preventing public displays and ceremonies, and by urging the WRA to withdraw its announcement of the early closing of the centers. Burling returned to Washington on December 23. On his recommendation, Biddle immediately approved the renunciations of the citizen leaders of the organizations and late in the month 70 of them were removed to the Department of Justice Internment Camp at Santa Fe as "undesirable enemy aliens." Most of them were *Sokoku* officers. On January 26, 1945, a second group of 171 men was removed; on February 11, about 650 more—all *Sokoku* or *Hoshi-dan* members—and on March 4, an additional 125. A total of 1,416 men—1,098 renunciants and 318 aliens—were sent to internment at one or another Department of Justice camps.[349] On March 16, the

WRA prohibited the social and cultural activities which it felt were promoting Japanese nationalistic attitudes—bugling, parades, public ceremonials, and drilling were no longer allowed[350]—and held to its decision to close the center. Myer, however, did announce that "those who do not wish to leave the center at this time are not required to do so and may continue to live here or at some similar center until January 1, 1946."[351]

The hearings on the renunciation applications began shortly after January 11, 1945, when Burling and the four hearing officers, Charles M. Rothstein, Joseph J. Shevlin, Ollie Collins, and Lillian C. Scott (attorneys from the Alien Enemy Control Unit and the Immigration and Naturalization Service), arrived at the center. In his instructions to the group on the trip west, Burling stressed that they were to be particularly diligent in endeavoring to detect any sign of coercion on a renunciant; if there was any such sign he should not be permitted to sign the form. The hearings were held in private; only the hearing officer, a stenographer, and, if needed, an interpreter were present.[352]

The Department of Justice received over six thousand applications for renunciation. The hearings were held at Tule Lake from January 12 to March 17, 1945. In July, Rothstein returned to hold hearings on some two hundred additional applications which had come in after March. All told, the department approved 5,589 applications. Of these 5,461 came from Tuleans and 128 from individuals in other centers.[353] The majority of approvals were announced in March, April, and May, 1945. Renunciations were accepted from minors over 17½ years of age and from at least eight who were later held to have been mental defectives.[354] When the evacuees were granted their new status the Department of Justice issued detention orders to the WRA to hold them in the centers.

During the summer of 1945 many approved renunciants wrote to the Department of Justice and asked for permission to withdraw their renunciations; some also asked to leave Tule Lake. (The department sent form letters to all such persons explaining that it was not within the power of the Attorney General to restore citizenship once lost through the procedure followed). The number of applications for cancellation of renunciation increased sharply in the fall.

Although many were seeking to cancel their renunciations, the Department of Justice was moving to send them all to Japan. On July 14, 1945, under the authority of the Alien Enemy Act of 1798, President Truman issued Proclamation 2655 which provided that all interned alien enemies deemed by the Attorney General to be dangerous to peace and safety "because they have adhered to aforesaid enemy governments or to the principles of their government shall be subject . . . to removal from the United States."[355] Regulations governing their deportation were published by the Department of Justice on September 26, 1945.[356] On October 8 the department began the registration of the renunciants, who were fingerprinted and photographed. They were informed that they were now classed as "native American aliens."[357] On October 10 the department announced that on and after November 15 "all persons whose applications to renounce citizenship have been approved by the Attorney General of the United States, will be repatriated to Japan, together with members of their families, whether citizens or aliens, who desire to accompany them."[358]

The renunciants were startled by the announcement of their imminent removal to Japan, and many who did not wish to be sent there took action to prevent it. A group who had been in contact with Wayne Collins, a San Francisco attorney and a representative of the American Civil Liberties Union, formed a small committee which began to raise funds to finance court action. On November 5, Collins entered two suits in federal courts asking that certain named renunciant plaintiffs be set at liberty, that the deportation orders be cancelled, that the applications for renunciations be declared void, and the plaintiffs declared to be nationals of the United States. At the time of filing these suits there were 987 plaintiffs. Many more were added during the following weeks and the number rose to 4,322.[359] The litigation thus initiated lasted many years.

On December 10, 1945, Department of Justice officials at Tule Lake announced that deportation, or so-called "mitigation," hearings (similar to those held in all cases of deportation of aliens to discover whether undue hardship would be occasioned by the move), would be held for all renunciants who did not wish to go to Japan, as well as for aliens who had been interned and who were now at Tule Lake under special-segregation or parole orders.[360] Aliens or renunciants who did not ask for a hearing, those who expressed a desire to be sent to Japan, and those aliens and citizens removed from Tule Lake during the winter of 1944–45, would not be given hearings and would be sent to Japan.

In the fall of 1945 a movement from Tule Lake began. With the cessation of hostilities with Japan, the WDC released all those it had been holding. After the Department of Justice took over on October 10 only renunciants and "segregated parolees" were detained, and resettlement of the eligible was speeded. The population of the center dropped from 17,341 on August 1, 1945, to 7,269 on January 1, 1946.

On January 31, 1946, the center held 5,045 persons, consisting of only detainees and their families.[361]

In January, 1946, there were approximately 3,200 renunciants at Tule Lake and a small number in the Department of Justice internment camps. After the announcements of the mitigation hearings, 3,161 at Tule Lake and 25 in the internment centers applied for a hearing; 107 at Tule Lake did not do so.

The mitigation hearings were held at Tule Lake and at the internment camps at Ft. Lincoln, North Dakota, and Santa Fe, New Mexico, between January 7 and April 1, 1946.[362] Fifteen hearing officers, secretaries, and translators arrived at Tule Lake on New Year's Day with Rothstein in charge. At the hearing the applicant could present evidence and witnesses in his behalf but was denied the right to counsel. On February 12, 1946, when 1,800 hearings had been completed at Tule Lake, the Department announced the names of 406 renunciants who had received unfavorable recommendations and against whom deportation orders were to be issued. The remainder of the applicants were unconditionally free. The 406 and their 43 family members were removed to camps at Crystal City, Texas, and Seabrook Farms, Bridgeton, New Jersey.[363] Removal orders were issued "only where a renunciant was a dual national prior to his renunciation. . . . A number of removal orders had to be revoked upon the discovery that renunciants were not Japanese citizens under the law of Japan."[364]

The second group of individuals held at Tule Lake, the segregated parolees from Department of Justice centers, were also given hearings. In January, 1946, a special alien board, composed of the Dean of the Law School of the University of California, Edwin DeWitt Dickinson, and two attorneys, was set up by the Department of Justice to hold hearings for the 47 segregated parolees at Tule Lake. After hearings and review of the board's recommendations by the Attorney General, all of the groups were released unconditionally on March 18, 1946, and informed that they could remain in the United States; two preferred Japan.[365] On March 20, 1946, the last inmate of Tule Lake departed.

During the fall of 1945 and the early months of 1946 over a thousand renunciants and many Japanese aliens sailed for Japan. Through February 23, 1946, a total of 4,406 residents of Tule Lake had also left. Of these, 1,116 were renunciants who did not apply for a mitigation hearing, 1,523 were aliens, and 1,767 were American citizens; of the citizens, all but 49 were the minor children of aliens or renunciants.[366] By July, 4,724 persons had left for Japan from Tule Lake and other centers. By September 27, 1948, there were 1,444 renunciants who had not applied for hearings and had left for Japan, and 1,480 were residing there on April 26, 1949.[367] Those leaving from Tule Lake or other WRA centers and the internment camps of the Department of Justice, were joined by over three thousand who had relocated or had been outside of the evacuation areas. All in all, some eight thousand persons of Japanese descent left for Japan between V-J Day and mid-1946.[368]

Legal attempts to recover citizenship.—The renunciants sought the restoration of their American citizenship and freedom from the threat of deportation in the courts.[369] Two suits were entered in the federal district court for northern California on November 5, 1945—a petition for a writ of habeas corpus, *Abo* v. *Williams*,[370] to free the petitioners from the deportation orders of the Department of Justice and to set them at liberty, and a plea in equity, *Abo* v. *Clark*,[371] that the renunciation applications be declared void and the plaintiffs be declared nationals of the United States. The briefs for the plaintiffs in the two suits made the same claim: that the signing of the renunciation applications was the result of duress and coercion and was not a free and voluntary act.

The renunciants won the first round in both suits in the district court. In the habeas corpus action Judge A. S. St. Sure issued a temporary injunction against the deportation in late 1945 and the case was heard during 1946.[372] On June 20, 1947, Judge Louis E. Goodman (the two cases having been transferred to him when Judge St. Sure became ill) granted the application for a writ of habeas corpus, holding that the plaintiffs were not alien enemies and hence could not be detained for deportation from the country.[373] On August 11, 1947, he issued the writ commanding the district director of the Immigration and Naturalization Service to release the plaintiffs from custody. Advised that the Department of Justice was intending to appeal the decision, on September 8, 1947 Judge Goodman placed all the renunciants held by the Department of Justice, including the 138 who were plaintiffs in the habeas corpus proceedings as well as the 164 who were not, in the custody of Wayne Collins, their attorney. The government agreed to bear the cost of transporting the group from the internment camps in New Jersey and Texas to their former homes in California.[374] The appeal from the district-court decision was finally filed by the government on February 28, 1949; the time for the filing was extended several times by the court at the request of the department.[375]

Hearings on the suit in equity, *Abo* v. *Clark*, began in 1946. More than four thousand plaintiffs petitioned to be declared nationals of the

United States and their renunciations set aside.[376] In support of its contention that the renunciations were the free expressions of the renunciants, the government submitted among other items a lengthy affidavit by Burling describing his visit to Tule Lake in 1945–1946 and the conduct of the renunciation hearings. Four shorter affidavits by the other hearing officers were also introduced.[377] On April 29, 1948, Judge Goodman issued an opinion cancelling the renunciations and declaring the plaintiffs to be United States citizens.[378] However, admitting that it might be possible for the government to present evidence that some of the plaintiffs did act freely and voluntarily despite the weight of evidence that they did not, Judge Goodman gave the government ninety days in which to "file a designation of any of the plaintiffs concerning whom they desire to present further evidence."

After many extensions of time granted by the court, the Department of Justice, on February 25, 1949, filed a "Designation of Plaintiffs" which stated that the evidence which would be introduced "against each such designated plaintiff proves or tends to prove that each... renounced United States nationality and citizenship of his or her own free will, choice, desire and agency, and shows that such renunciation was not caused by duress, menace, coercion, and intimidation, fraud and undue influence." This evidence consisted in showing that of every one of the 4,322 plaintiffs one or more of the following statements was true: that he or she was a Kibei; had been a leader of a pro-Japanese organization at Tule Lake; had applied for repatriation or expatriation either before or after renunciation; had been segregated at Tule Lake because of a negative answer to question 28 or because of a denial by the WRA of leave clearance; had gone to Tule Lake Center voluntarily to be with his or her family; was now in Japan; was under alien-enemy removal orders.[379] The court rejected the "Designation" on March 23, 1949. Judge Goodman found that it did not present evidence overcoming the presumption that the renunciations were the result of coercion and pressure. On April 12, 1949, he issued his opinion stating that the renunciations were void as they were the product of such influences.[380] The government appealed.[381]

On July 6, 1949, while the habeas corpus and equity actions were before the courts, a suit was entered by Andrew L. Wirin, a Los Angeles attorney, in behalf of three renunciants, Murakami, Sumi, and Shimizu, who had been refused passports by the State Department on the grounds that by virtue of their renunciations at Tule Lake they were no longer American citizens.[382] On August 27, 1949, Judge William C. Mathes rendered a decision for the plaintiffs.[383] The government appealed but lost. Judge William Denman of the court of appeals held that the findings of the lower court that the renunciations were the product of oppressive conditions at Tule Lake was fully supported by the evidence and that further findings by his court gave additional support to the judgment.[384] Many of these points were documented by references to Thomas and Nishimoto's *Spoilage,* which had also been introduced as documentary evidence in *Abo* v. *Clark.* The government decided not to contest the decision and not to oppose suits by renunciants to affirm their citizenship unless its files "disclose evidence of loyalty to Japan or disloyalty to the United States."[385]

However, the plaintiff Japanese lost both their habeas corpus and equity suits in the court of appeals. The judgments of the district courts were reversed and the cases sent back for further proceedings. In the habeas corpus suit, *Barber* v. *Abo,* the decision that the renunciations were void was denied except for minors who were held to be legally incapable of renouncing.[386] However, the threat of removal to Japan was dissipated when the Department of Justice cancelled the removal orders. On April 20, 1952, Acting Attorney General Philip B. Perlman cancelled the outstanding orders against the 302 renunciants in the Department of Justice camps. On May 6, 1952, Wayne Collins petitioned for a dismissal of the suit in the district court on the ground that the cancellation rendered the issues moot, and the motion was granted that day by Judge Goodman.

The renouncing Japanese no longer needed to fear deportation to Japan. However, their American citizenship was not affirmed, for the decision in the appeals court in the equity case also went against them. Judge Denman ruled that the renunciations were valid for all adult plaintiffs other than the fifty-eight who went to Tule Lake to be with family members and that in future proceedings they would have to demonstrate individually that they had been coerced into renouncing.[387] The Supreme Court denied a writ of certiorari on October 8, 1951.[388] Since the return of the case to the district court no action has yet (1954) been taken by the plaintiffs and their cases have yet to be heard.[389] They remain "native American aliens."

* * * *

Such was the history of the Japanese American evacuation, in the course of which an entire ethnic minority of over a hundred thousand persons was uprooted and imprisoned, submitted to grievous personal discomfort and severe economic loss, and deprived of both legal and human rights. The episode had been foreshadowed early in 1942 when the military commander responsible for the defense of the Pacific Coast voiced dissatisfaction with the control measures instituted against enemy aliens by the Department of Justice. The military sought power to remove from the coast all persons, citizens or aliens, who were judged to be dangerous—and it soon became clear that to the military the possession of Japanese blood was what made an individual dangerous. The recommendation of the military was accepted by the civilian heads of the War Department, agreed to by the Attorney General, and approved by the President of the United States without Cabinet discussion. Finally, it gained the sanction of Congress through the passage of Public Law 503.

By degrees exclusion was transformed into detention. The responsible general, exercising the power newly conferred upon him, ordered all Japanese Americans to move inland. (By direction of the War Department, the German and Italian alien population remained undisturbed.) But public opinion in the interior states opposed the settlement of the Japanese, and the Army proceeded to construct centers of concentration into which the exiles were herded and kept under armed guard. In these camps the majority of the Japanese Americans sat out the war.

Chapter IV

TWO THEORIES OF
RESPONSIBILITY

What prompted the responsible officials in the Army and the government to take the drastic step of uprooting the entire West Coast Japanese American population; removing them from their homes and confining them in camps?

In most discussions of the episode the official explanation of military necessity has been discounted. In its place various alternative hypotheses have been advanced, of which by far the most frequently defended and widely accepted are two that may be called the "pressure group" and "politician" theories.

The former theory holds that the evacuation was the direct result of pressure exerted on officials by various West Coast groups which sought the elimination of the Japanese Americans for economic or other self-interested reasons. Agricultural and commercial associations, generally left unspecified, are most often held responsible; but specific groups which assertedly stood to profit from the expulsion of the Japanese are sometimes named. Occasionally the accused economic interests are linked in their activity with patriotic organizations such as the American Legion and the Native Sons, whose record of agitation against the Japanese is notorious, but whose self-interested motives are less clearly defined.

The second of the two theories places the responsibility for the evacuation at the door of Pacific Coast politicians, who, always on the alert for causes through which to secure public approval, assertedly bid for the favor of an inflamed and apprehensive population in the early months of war by influencing the Army and the government to institute mass evacuation.

THE PRESSURE GROUP THEORY

The explanation that the evacuation program was due primarily to the influence of selfishly motivated pressure groups has been most frequently advanced and over the years has gained broadest acceptance in informed public opinion. Popular writers of a liberal persuasion have given it particular prominence in their studies of the Japanese in the United States. A typical statement is that of Bradford Smith, who observes in his *Americans from Japan* that "the preponderantly loyal Japanese 'minority' were rounded up in an illegal fashion, chiefly in response to pressure from a bluntly intolerant, grasping element on the Pacific Coast."[1] Declaring that "it was not even mistaken patriotism that caused evacuation but greed masking as patriotism,"[2] Smith attributes the agitation primarily to motives of economic competition. In like manner Carey McWilliams' *Prejudice,* although recognizing the background of popular hostility toward the Japanese, points to the pressure groups as having had crucial influence in forcing the evacuation decision: "The Federal Government was pressured, or perhaps more accurately 'stampeded' into the adoption of this unfortunate precedent by the noisy clamor of certain individuals, groups and organizations in the three Western States"—conspicuous among whom were "groups that had an obvious and readily acknowledged economic interest in evacuation."[3]

Morton Grodzins, in *Americans Betrayed,* presents the pressure-group theory in its most elaborate form. In addition to the Legion, the Native Sons, and the Joint Immigration Committee, he writes, "The most active proponents of mass evacuation were certain agricultural and business groups [and] chambers of commerce." Large business interests "were uniformly in favor of evacuation . . . powerful economic groups . . . had long wished to put an end to the competition of American Japanese." Agricultural groups were also prominent, according to Grodzins; and in fact, "there is almost no end to the number and variety of groups that devoted attention, in a more or less organized fashion, to the alleged necessity for Japanese evacuation." Moreover, the activity of these groups was not only widespread but greatly influential in shaping evacuation policy.[4]

A number of legal scholars as well, in analyzing the constitutionality of the litigation arising from the evacuation, have accepted the pressure-group theory of responsibility virtually without question. Eugene V. Rostow, for example, has written that "the program of excluding all persons of Japanese ancestry from the coastal areas was conceived and put through by the organized minority whose business it has been for forty-five years to increase and exploit racial tensions on the west coast."[5] Nanette Dembitz, in her penetrating analysis of the Japanese American

---

[1] For notes to chapter iv see pp. 371–382.

cases, criticizes the Supreme Court for failure to scrutinize the exclusion measures as rigorously as it should. The court, she declares, did not take into consideration the anti-Oriental prejudice of the West Coast or the fact that "mass racial exclusion was the perfect answer to the recurrent search by West Coast pressure groups for a method of eliminating economic competition from the minority of Japanese ancestry."[6] That many Japanese Americans themselves have adopted the pressure-group theory is indicated by the statement of an official of the Japanese American Citizens League, at the time of evacuation, that possibly the event "is primarily a measure whose surface urgency cloaks the desires of political or other pressure groups who want us to leave merely from motives of self-interest."[7]

So widely accepted has the pressure-group theory become among students of the episode that many, such as Dembitz and Rostow, are content to advance it wholly without evidence or support. A few writers, however, have offered data to substantiate the claim; and it is on this documentation that the pressure-group theory must depend for continued acceptance.

Examination of the evidence adduced by these writers reveals a common defect which would seem to be fatal to the theory. None of its proponents has effectively correlated the activities of pressure groups with the policy decisions of the responsible military and government officials *at the time when the decisions were made*. The dates of the principal decisions are known; any theory of why the policy-makers acted as they did must therefore show, as a preliminary step, that the alleged influence was brought to bear *before* the policy was determined.

For instance, Bradford Smith asserts categorically that DeWitt was "swayed by a skillfully maneuvered campaign of special interests" who operated through witnesses at the West Coast hearings of the Tolan Committee. "On March 12," he writes, "the Tolan Committee ended its hearings, having served unwittingly at the strategic moment as a sounding board for the special interests which desired the removal of the Japanese. On the same day General DeWitt had announced that he would evacuate all Japanese from the coastal area." Smith then inquires: "If the evacuation was, as DeWitt claimed, a military necessity, why was it necessary on March 12 but not on March 7? . . . How did it happen that DeWitt's decision corresponded with the end of the Tolan Hearings?"[8] The answer to the last question, of course, is that it did not. General DeWitt had come to his decision on—possibly even before—February 14, the date on which he forwarded his "Final Recommendation" to the War Department. The Tolan hearings could have had no influence whatever on this decision; and Smith presents no evidence to show that any of the "special interests" acted on DeWitt prior to this date.[9]

McWilliams' argument suffers from the same defect. Inquiring into the reason for DeWitt's evacuation order, he finds that "political pressure" was exerted both directly through politicians and "indirectly . . . through the technique of an organized campaign" carried out during the Tolan Committee hearings, where "definite pressure for evacuation was carefully organized (not because the Committee itself was unfair . . . but because the "pro" groups took possession of the hearings)."[10] This attribution of the military decision to pressure organized at the time of the hearings is especially puzzling in view of McWilliams' awareness that DeWitt had made his recommendation on February 14.[11]

Among students of the evacuation episode, Grodzins alone has presented appreciable data on the activities of a wide variety of groups and interests to support the claim of their influence upon official policy. However, his allegiance to the pressure-group theory wavers; in the early chapters of *Americans Betrayed* he upholds it with certainty, only to retract or seriously modify it later.[12] In his chronological account of evacuation policy he states the case obliquely, claiming merely that "in the light of the total evidence, it is not sufficiently precise to dismiss the relationship between pressures and military action by stating simply that one followed the other. Rather it is clear that the pressures were an integral ingredient of the military decision." The military authorities "may or may not have needed persuasion to adopt a view that race conditioned allegiance. But public persuasion was indispensable to the creation of a situation in which that fear could lead to the evacuation on racial lines."[13] This qualified claim seems to suggest that pressure-group activity, rather than bearing direct responsibility for evacuation policy, was merely a barometer for prejudiced Army officials, confirming the receptivity of the public to anti-Japanese measures. In the end Grodzins appears to attribute the decision to the unsound judgment of DeWitt, who "was subjected to many extreme pressures favoring evacuation. He was impressed with the possibility that Japanese Americans constituted a special danger, and he recommended evacuation in the firm conviction that it was demanded by military necessity."[14]

The pressure-group explanation of the evacuation is generally applied to the second and fourth policy decisions: namely, those to exclude the Japanese from the coastal areas and to intern the Japanese living in the interior of California. The initiation of the first program— controls on enemy aliens in the prohibited and restricted zones under

Department of Justice auspices—is generally recognized as due to DeWitt's instigation and insistence;[15] his promptings of the Department of Justice clearly occurred before the appearance of any significant public demands or discussions of evacuation. The third program—internment of the coastal Japanese, ordered by DeWitt three weeks after initiation of the so-called "voluntary evacuation"—also is generally accepted as resulting from the Army's recognition that public hostility toward the Japanese in interior communities rendered a program of extensive resettlement unworkable.[16] It is chiefly the second policy decision—to exclude all Japanese from the extensive coastal strip known as Military Area No. 1—to which writers refer when discussing the "evacuation," and the one which the pressure-group theorists attribute to influence upon DeWitt and the government. The fourth policy—exclusion of Japanese from the California sector of Military Area No. 2, promulgated in June—also is claimed by some to have been due to the influence of pressure groups.

How substantial is the evidence that pressure-group activity stimulated DeWitt prior to February 14 to recommend the second program: exclusion of all Japanese from the coast? Is there convincing proof that all or many of the pressure groups were conspicuously active in bringing their views to the attention of the general? Specifically, is it true that organized agricultural interests, the most commonly cited, insistently urged the banishment of the Japanese in the period after Pearl Harbor and before mid-February? Were their demands echoed by businessmen and patriotic societies, striving to make their opinions known to DeWitt? From what is known of the activities of these and other groups, are we led to conclude that the general must have succumbed to their pressure—or is the evidence so nebulous as to indicate that the truth does not lie here?

PRESSURE GROUPS AND COASTAL EXCLUSION

Agricultural groups.—Most frequently indicated for alleged influence upon DeWitt to remove the Japanese from the coast are the agricultural interests—specifically, the farmers, growers, and shippers—who are charged with acting from a desire either to eliminate competition or to secure the lands held by the Japanese. Thus McWilliams, for example, says that "the California shipper-grower interests were definitely in favor of mass evacuation and for admittedly selfish reasons." Again, "so-called 'white interests' in the nursery and florist businesses were actively seeking mass evacuation as a means of eliminating unwanted competition." Although some "economic pressure groups" did not favor mass evacuation, "it is nevertheless incontestably true that certain groups stood to profit (momentarily at least) by the elimination of the Japanese; and that they played a very important behind-the-scenes role in securing mass evacuation."[17] But McWilliams produces no evidence for these assertions. His only support consists of a statement by an official of the Grower-Shipper Vegetable Association who was reported in a magazine article as saying: "We're charged with wanting to get rid of the Japs for selfish reasons. We might as well be honest. We do. It's a question of whether the white man lives on the Pacific Coast or the brown man. They came into this valley to work and stayed to take over."[18] Apart from the fact that this statement is at least as suggestive of irrational prejudice as of rational self-interest, the assertion that some growers would benefit from removal of the Japanese does not constitute evidence that they sought actively to bring it about—let alone that their activity was influential. Such a statement requires direct confirmation and cannot safely be inferred.

Smith is even more inclined to hasty generalization. He declares that "greed masking as patriotism" caused evacuation, but to the question of which greedy interests were responsible and what evidence of their influence exists he gives no clear answer. By indirection he lays the charge at the door of agricultural groups, for among "the facts to be held in mind" are the anti-Japanese sentiments of two agricultural publications, and the testimony of a lawyer at the Tolan hearings that proevacuation interests included the Associated Farmers.[19] He advances no other support for the implication of widespread farmer influence.

Grodzins, in contrast, does present a variety of material on the actions of agricultural groups to confirm his assertion of their impact on policy. He states that various "agricultural and business groups" were "the most active proponents of mass evacuation," among them both farm groups and agricultural trade associations.[20] Not only the larger associations but "many smaller groups, whose membership were in competition with Japanese-Americans, were active in fostering the evacuation." Further, the "growing and marketing organizations were uniformly in favor of evacuation."[21] But Grodzins' evidence does not show that the agricultural community was uniformly or even substantially exercised over the Japanese issue. Only six of the hundreds of West Coast agricultural associations publicly expressed proevacuation opinions: i.e., four of the approximately one hundred food and agricultural trade associations in California, two of the many in Washington, and none of the one hundred and fifty or more in Oregon.[22] Nor does Grodzins offer evidence to support his charge that "many smaller groups" beyond the few he specifically mentions were active. Furthermore, the "pressure" prior to February 14 was altogether trifling and was not even directed primarily at DeWitt. It consisted of eight letters from officials of three associations to congressmen, a visit by the secretary of one organization to Washington early in December, the adoption of a resolution favoring evacuation by one association, and a telegram to a governor passed on to Attorney General Biddle.[23] The activity of the two other associations occurred after February 14.[24]

To Grodzins the rural villains of the piece were the Western Growers Protective Association and the Grower-Shipper Vegetable Association. Of the first he says that it "bent every effort to foster the evacuation"; yet its known activities before February 14 consisted of one letter by its president recommending evacuation to a congressman, and the passage by the board of directors of a resolution favoring evacuation which was not even published in the association's monthly publication.[25] On such evidence the indictment of the association for powerful early agitation seems grossly unjustified.[26] The activity of the Grower-Shipper Association, before February 14, consisted of a visit by an official to Washington early in December, and five letters from the association president to a congressman.[27] The governing board of the group failed even to pass a resolution favoring evacuation.[28] There is no evidence to show that the December visit had any effect on congressional or administration opinion or policy; and, indeed, since proevacuation sentiment did not begin to rise until late January, it would appear unlikely that the official's views found a sympathetic reception. Grodzins states that the Grower-Shipper Association swung into action early in support of anti-Japanese measures, and that it promoted illegal action toward the goal of evacuation while hypocritically advocating the maintenance of the law. But his intepretation of his alleged evidence of its proevacuation activity in December is open to serious question,[29] and his charge that it secretly fomented trouble is wholly without foundation.[30]

Finally, the same author's claim that "growing and marketing organizations were uniformly in favor of evacuation"[31] is not substantiated by the record. Agricultural and food associations did not present a united front. Two such groups are known to have gone on record *against* mass evacuation of the Japanese: the Washington Produce Shippers Association of Seattle, and the Olympia [Washington] Oyster Growers Association. The oyster growers complained that the removal of the Japanese would "practically paralyze the industry."[32] The manager of the produce shippers, testifying before the Tolan Committee, not only did "not concur in the recommendation of a mass evacuation," but declared that "wholesale evacuation would be an economic waste and a stupid error."[33]

Various farm groups are also charged by these writers with having influenced evacuation policy.[34] But the evidence again does not justify the claims either of sizable participation or of tangible influence. Not one of the major farm organizations of the three West Coast states officially expressed an opinion favoring exclusion of the Japanese in the critical period prior to February 14—or indeed after it. So far as is known, only two local units of one organization, the California Farm Bureau Federation, passed resolutions before that date;[35] its board of directors in January called only for the placement of all Japanese and their property "under Federal supervision."[36] The Associated Farmers' executive committee did not publicly favor mass evacuation; their only expressed opinion favored the use of Japanese on California farms as supervised laborers.[37] The State Grange did not adopt a resolution nor, apparently, did its executive board issue a statement. In Washington and Oregon, as in California, the large farm organizations are not found to have expressed views; the only known expressions in favor of evacuation were from two small rural groups and came late in February.[38]

The attention devoted by Grodzins to a civic group known as the Pacific League of Southern California seems disproportionate, considering its size (less than a hundred members) and the extent of its activity. In some places he describes the league as raising a "demand for evacuation,"[39] but modifies this picture elsewhere by noting that its lone resolution called only for the "drafting of the Japanese and their placement on suitable agricultural lands in safe areas."[40] Although various league representatives endeavored to impress local, federal, and Army officials, they admitted subsequently that they had had no success whatever.[41]

Business groups and service clubs.—Business interests of various sorts, particularly "big business," find themselves frequently and bitterly charged with influencing evacuation policy from selfish motives. Smith features the statement of a Tolan Committee witness that the evacuation demand "seems to come from the chambers of commerce, the Associated Farmers, and the newspapers notorious as spokesmen for reactionary interests."[42] Grodzins mentions various "employers' and businessmen's groups," as well as service clubs, as among "the most active proponents of mass evacuation."[43]

What evidence is there of the influence of business and trade associations, chambers of commerce, and service clubs? Did this section of society raise the cry for Japanese exclusion in such strong and imperative tones that the Army must have been stirred by it? The available data would seem to indicate otherwise. Of the approximately 1,150 nonagricultural trade and business associations in California, exactly one officially advocated evacuation in the period before February 14; and of the many similar organizations in Oregon and Washington none is known to have so acted.[44] Chambers of commerce were no more outstanding in their activity. The California State Chamber of Commerce and the Washington State Federation of Commerical Organizations passed no resolutions.[45] Of the more than 600 city and county chambers in the three West Coast states, only six adopted resolutions prior to the decision of February 14. Only one of California's 36 county chambers is known to have passed a proevacuation resolution before that date; and of the approximately 350 city chambers in the state, a total of three were on record as approving resolutions during the period.[46] None of the 80 Oregon city and county chambers expressed an opinion before mid-February; of the many Washington chambers only two are known to have done so.[47]

Service clubs are also accused by Grodzins, the Lions being said to have been among "the most active."[48] But the charge is not supported by the available evidence. Of the many hundreds of Lions, Rotary, and Kiwanis clubs in the three West Coast states, only two are known to have expressed sentiments for evacuation before February 14.[49] Not one of the three hundred Rotary clubs on the Pacific Coast was on record with a resolution favoring evacuation during the period of decision.[50]

Nor can the case against the businessmen be upheld. The data do not bear out the charge that "powerful economic interests" were significantly involved, let alone that "large business interests were uniformly in favor of evacuation."[51] But even had they been so, it is doubtful that this would confirm the contention that pressure groups acted from economic self-interest. Historically, the role of big business groups had been one of consistent support of the Japanese and voluble opposition to the anti-Japanese agitation—even during periods when public prejudice was highest against the Orientals. In this role big business was indeed acting from motives of self-interest, since its primary concern was with employment of Japanese labor and maintenance of favorable trade relations. It is not to be doubted that after Pearl Harbor numerous individual businessmen and some business groups became hostile to the Japanese Americans—but, far from sustaining any "devil theory," this proves only that they were private citizens and members of the general public, caught up with the rest of the populace in the mounting wave of indignation and fear that swept the Pacific Coast in the early months of war.

Labor unions.—"Labor unions from Ketchikan, Alaska, to Los Angeles, California," according to Grodzins, "joined in urging evacuation. Represented were fishermen, building-trades workers, carpenters, textile workers, cereal workers, meat-cutters and butchers, retail clerks, stage employees, hotel and restaurant workers, electric employees and general laborers." He asserts that "at least eighteen locals and councils passed resolutions, of which three were from Los Angeles and six from Montana."[52] Elsewhere he claims that "several dozen unions" called for evacuation and that most of them were affiliates of the American Federation of Labor.[53] However, the facts do not corroborate these generalized claims of vast labor agitation. Of the many thousands of labor unions and councils in the western states, only one union local and one council are known to have passed resolutions calling for evacuation before February 14—and these were both CIO.[54]

Military and patriotic societies.—Did the significant pressure for evacuation perhaps come from the military and patriotic societies, so long and strenuously active in the promotion of what they conceived to be the national interest? Was it the veterans who were responsible? Was it the various societies which delight in exalting the white and native-born over the dark-skinned and foreign? There can be no doubt about the attitude of these groups toward the Japanese; what is questionable is the extent of their agitation, and the degree of its influence, prior to the February decision for evacuation.

Various writers on the episode have attributed strong pressure for evacuation to "the traditionally anti-Oriental organizations, such as the American Legion, the California Joint Immigration Committee and similar organizations."[55] Grodzins maintains that besides the Legion "other military groups displayed interest in the problem," among them the United Spanish War Veterans, Veterans of Foreign Wars, Disabled American Veterans of the World War, and the Military Order of the Purple Heart. Further, "in urging the evacuation itself, the Native Sons took second place to no other organization in the number of resolutions passed or in the vehemence with which they were expressed."[56]

Of all these groups the American Legion was by far the most active in its campaign; but even Legion activity cannot be adjudged to have been so extensive that DeWitt must beyond doubt have been stirred by it. Of the 873 posts and 50 area and district organizations of the Legion on the West Coast,[57] 25 urged the removal either of enemy aliens in general, of Japanese nationals, or of all Japanese Americans, in the period before February 14. Eighteen of these resolutions called only for the removal from the coast of enemy aliens or Japanese nationals; seven

urged the exclusion or internment of all Japanese. Five resolutions came
from California, all limited to urging internment of enemy aliens or
dual citizens, or both.[58] In Oregon, three posts asked for the removal of
enemy aliens from the coast.[59] In Washington, seven resolutions asked
for concentration camps for all Japanese, and ten sought either internment of Japanese aliens (three), internment of all enemy aliens (five), or
exclusion from the coast of all enemy aliens (two).[60]

As for the other military societies, of the many hundreds of posts of
the VFW, the Order of the Purple Heart, the United Spanish War
Veterans, and the Disabled Veterans of the World War, only one isolated post is known to have asked before mid-February for Japanese
evacuation, although two called for removal or internment of all enemy
aliens.[61]

Long notorious along the Pacific Coast for their anti-Japanese activity
were the Native Sons of the Golden West and the California Joint
Immigration Committee (of which the NSGW was a prominent affiliate). Does it appear that their agitation after Pearl Harbor created
significant pressure upon DeWitt? The facts would seem to point to a
negative answer. It was not until February 14—the day of the DeWitt
recommendation and two months and one week after Pearl Harbor—
that the Board of Grand Officers of the Native Sons expressed an opinion
in favor of evacuation. Before that date only four of the more than one
hundred and fifty subordinate parlors and assemblies are known to have
expressed the same opinion.[62] For an organization allegedly "vehement"
in its proevacuation pressure, it is interesting to note that the official
journal, the *Grizzly Bear,* failed to express an editorial opinion in favor
of evacuation through the first six months of 1942—although it did continue to voice its traditional demands for the permanent removal of
Japanese from California, for enforcement of the Alien Land Law, and
denial of citizenship to Orientals. The California Joint Immigration
Committee was equally lethargic. Its executive committee did not meet
until February 7, two months after Pearl Harbor, and the organization
issued only one statement to the press calling for evacuation of the
Japanese (on the day prior to DeWitt's recommendation).[63]

Social clubs and fraternal societies.—Can the pressure-group hypoth-
esis be redeemed by the actions of the many social clubs and benevolent
societies along the Pacific slope? Was the world of clubland aflame with
a passion to move the Japanese—and did it move General DeWitt?
Grodzins, more definite than other critics, asserts that there was "almost
no end to the number and variety of groups that devoted attention, in

a more or less organized fashion, to the alleged necessity for Japanese evacuation." The list is impressive:

Lions and Elks passed resolutions in common with the Supreme Pyramid of Sciots and a California Townsend Club ... the Magnolia Study Club of Anaheim, California, and the University of Oregon Mothers. The resolutions of numerous civilian defense councils were echoed by a Palm Springs "Committee of the People" and the Orosi Citizens Committee, the Lindsay Women's Clubs and the North Hollywood Home Owners. American Legion activities were seconded by ... the Puenta Class in Christian Citizenship. An East Los Angeles Noon Club demanded evacuation in common with a West Los Angeles Breakfast Club.[64]

There may well have been "almost no end" to the variety of such groups; but there was a definite limit to their numbers. The impression conveyed by the above passage of hundreds of groups in frenzied activity is wholly unwarranted: the files of the Department of Justice contained the resolutions of only four West Coast social and civic clubs besides those specified by Grodzins. Moreover, only three of the thousands of such groups in the three coastal states,[65] are known to have demanded evacuation *before* February 14.[66] Of the fraternal and benevolent societies, only the Elks were on record: of the ninety Elk lodges in California and the many in Oregon, two passed resolutions favoring evacuation before mid-February.[67]

In short, the theory of pressure-group responsibility for the exclusion policy announced in February rests on precarious ground. The activity of the accused organizations—agricultural, commercial, patriotic, civic, and social—has not been shown to have been of such character and so timed as to have had an irresistible or even a sizable influence upon the commanding general. If DeWitt had received copies of all known resolutions of the groups which advocated Japanese evacuation in the days before February 14—an unlikely supposition, as most of them were directed elsewhere—his mail would have contained a total of thirty-two such recommendations: viz., one resolution from a grower-shipper organization, two from local chapters of a farmers' organization, one from a small manufacturing trade association, six from city and county chambers of commerce, two from service clubs, two from labor union locals and councils, eight from the American Legion and a post of another military society, four from parlors of the Native Sons, three from civic and social clubs, two from fraternal and benevolent societies, and a statement from the California Joint Immigration Committee. It seems unreasonable to suppose that these scattered expressions of opinion, from a handful of organizations for the most part obscure, would have been sufficient in themselves—even had the general known of them—to have commanded that decision.

PRESSURE GROUPS AND INLAND EXCLUSION

After the Department of Justice program was set up early in February, 1942, numbers of individuals and organizations in central California protested against the "flood" of Japanese Americans into their communities. Following announcement of the programs of exclusion and internment of the coastal Japanese on March 2 and 27, there was further pressure from inland communities to exclude all Japanese from these areas also.[68] But the Western Defense Command refused to extend the restricted zone and expressed its views on at least two occasions: first on April 12 when DeWitt's office advised the Associated Chambers of Commerce of Tulare County that the boundary of Military Area No. 1 would not be extended eastward to include all of Tulare County, and again on April 24 when Colonel Karl Bendetsen wrote that eastern Tulare County could not be considered a vital area.[69] Finally, however, on June 2, 1942, a program of exclusion of Japanese Americans from eastern California was announced and their evacuation begun.

Among students of the episode, Grodzins alone maintains that local pressure groups in the eastern San Joaquin Valley continued to make "widespread demands" of the military after its refusal to act in April, and that as a consequence of this pressure the Army adopted the policy of June 2.[70] But such a statement runs squarely up against the explicit declaration of the *Final Report* that "it became finally evident toward the end of February that a complete evacuation of all persons of Japanese ancestry from Military Area No. 1 *and ultimately from the California portion of Military Area No. 2 would be ordered.*"[71] If this statement is correct—and it is corroborated by other assertions in the *Final Report*—then the letters from DeWitt's office were intended to conceal a policy actually determined as early as February, and cannot be used as evidence that it had not been decided upon until May.

However, even if this February date for the decision be discounted, the pressure-group theory fails of substantiation. For in holding that pressures *after* April 24 (the date of the Bendetsen letter) were responsible, it must face the fact that there is no evidence of any sort to show that groups in central or eastern California passed resolutions or otherwise expressed themselves publicly on the issue in the days following that date. In discussing the "campaign" of the pressure groups, Grodzins cites the demands of a number of organizations for removal of the Japanese.[72] But their expressions of opinion occurred well before April

24 and must have been brought to DeWitt's attention immediately, if at all.[73] Seven additional associations are listed which assertedly were active in the campaign, but without any indication of the dates on which they were supposed to have expressed their views.[74] Two of these dates, however, are known; they were well in advance of April 24.[75]

That DeWitt and Bendetsen wrote the letters referred to indicates, of course, that some pressure had been exerted; and we have noted that various organizations sought to influence them. But before April 24 this pressure apparently had not been successful in moving them to change their policy (still assuming that the February date given by DeWitt for his decision is in error), for they gave public notice of their refusal to grant the demands for removal of the inland Japanese. Nor is there any evidence of continued pressure by any groups *after* April 24. If, therefore, it is maintained that the pressure groups were responsible for the change in policy effective on June 2, it must be held that after publicly rejecting the pressures the Army command reversed itself several weeks later and gave in to them—although in the meantime the pressure had decreased. How does one explain this strange delayed action on the part of the military? If it had stood its ground against obvious pressure once, why should it accede when there was no longer any evidence of pressure? It may be that the military had long since given in but did not wish to admit it; but in that case we need evidence, such as statements or memoranda by responsible officials, which would indicate when the actual policy was adopted and why. No such evidence has been brought forward.

THE POLITICIAN THEORY

The explanation that the evacuation was the result of interest-motivated efforts of politicians on the West Coast and in Congress is almost as frequently encountered as the pressure-group theory. The charge may be summarized briefly: In response to the growing apprehension of the public and its antagonism toward the Japanese Americans, and always alert to find ways of capitalizing on groundswells of opinion by acting with the appearance of leading them, politicians and office-holders on all levels of government raised their voices for the removal of the offending minority. So insistent was their pressure and so powerful their influence that the Army and the government were forced to capitulate.

Because this theory also advances motives of selfish interest as the source of pressure, it is often found in company with the theory of private pressure-group responsibility. Thus the writers whose views we have noted also give great weight to the proevacuation activity of politicians. Smith, for example, observes that local officials once tolerant toward the Japanese Americans were now "bent by some powerful force in the opposite direction"; and he notes that 1942 "was an election year [and] anti-Orientalism was a staple product on the Pacific Coast."[76] McWilliams is more definite. Public officials "were the first to advocate the evacuation of the Japanese"; the decision for evacuation was a result of "political pressure" exerted on DeWitt both directly through personal visits and indirectly through the medium of the Tolan Committee hearings where "definite pressure for evacuation was carefully organized." It came from many sources: "from politicians and political units. . . . The mayors of Los Angeles, San Francisco, Portland and Seattle all favored mass evacuation; various grand juries and city councils and boards of supervisors presented similar demands; and law-enforcement officials, in general, spoke in favor of the proposal."[77] Grodzins is still more explicit. The subtitle of his book, "Politics and the Japanese Evacuation," suggests his commitment; and the text spells it out in elaborate detail. "State and local political leaders played no subsidiary role in the movement to bring about Japanese evacuation," he asserts. "Every prominent west coast political leader and virtually every local law-enforcement officer made known their belief in the necessity for evacuation." The activities of the most prominent "were matched to some degree by office-holders from Seattle to San Diego." Moreover, the politicians great and small were vitally influential in their efforts, both on the coast where "state and local officials, in effect, became powerful influences upon Federal officials in fostering the evacuation," and on the national level where "the influence of [West Coast] congressmen on the officials in whom discretion actually rested was both strong and of the first importance." That influence "was one of several determining factors" in forcing the decision for evacuation.[78]

How does the record bear out these charges? Does a study of the activities of officials in the city halls and legislatures of the Pacific Coast and in the chambers of the federal Congress show that they were of such intensity and timing as to have decisively affected federal policy to the point of compelling evacuation? Once again, it is the two programs of excluding Japanese Americans from the coastal area (Military Area No. 1) and of interning those within the California portion of Military Area No. 2 which proponents of the theory claim to have been instigated by political influence.

POLITICIANS AND COASTAL EXCLUSION

In appraising the influence of public officials on evacuation policy it is necessary to consider separately the activities of those elected to city, county, and state offices and those serving in Congress. The office-holders on the West Coast were in a position to deal directly with DeWitt and the Western Defense Command; those in Washington were equipped to influence the decisions of the White House and the War and Justice Departments. From the known activities of these individuals what picture emerges of their influence on evacuation policy? At what stages in the development of that policy did they act, and with what effect?

The activities of public officials on the West Coast before February 14, 1942, were relatively, if not absolutely, insignificant. State, county, and city officials were not uniformly or even prominently outspoken for evacuation at a time when their views might have swayed the commanding general.

The state level.—At first, the governors of none of the three West Coast states were publicly on record in favor of mass evacuation.[79] Governor Culbert L. Olson of California even sought to have an alternative plan of his own adopted calling for employment of Japanese Americans under supervision on California farms.[80] In the period under discussion Olson's public statements were characterized by pleas for tolerance, concern for the safety of the Japanese and affirmations of their loyalty to the United States.[81]

The lieutenant governors of California and Washington made no statements in favor of evacuation,[82] nor did the secretaries of state.[83] None of the attorney generals for the three states was a public advocate of the move; Oregon's attorney general failed to make a statement of any sort,[84] and the attorney general of Washington (despite assertions that he "supplied [an] insistent voice in favor of evacuation") made his one and only public expression on March 2 when he *opposed* mass internment and recommended allowing loyal Japanese to remain on the coast.[85]

California's attorney general in 1942, Earl Warren, has been charged by several writers with great if not crucial influence in promoting evacuation.[86] However, an examination of the evidence fails to sustain the many allegations against him; and in particular there remains no proof that Warren ever publicly declared himself in favor of mass evacuation prior to mid-February.[87] His appearance before the Tolan Committee, of course, could not have influenced DeWitt. His utterances at a meeting of the Joint Immigration Committee were not made known to the general (and indeed the extent of the committee's pressure seems to have been a press release of February 13, issued on the very eve of

DeWitt's "Final Recommendation"). Further, there is no evidence one way or the other as to what Warren's sentiment was on February 11 when he accompanied Mayor Bowron of Los Angeles in a personal call on DeWitt.[88] The charge of one writer (Smith) that Warren "met with leading business groups and prevailed upon local officials to urge evacuation" is totally unsupported.[89] In short, the only pre-February-14 activity by Warren in relation to evacuation policy about which there is evidence was a public statement on January 30 to the effect that the Japanese situation was serious, and the DeWitt consultation on February 11 at which Mayor Bowron urged the exclusion of Japanese from coastal districts and their supervised employment in agriculture.

The state legislatures of Oregon and Washington, which met normally in the opening months of each odd-numbered year, were not called into special sessions in 1942. The legislature of California was called into special session[90] but no resolutions for evacuation were offered nor, so far as is known, was the matter broached.[91] There is no evidence that any state senator or assemblyman from the three states spoke out publicly for mass evacuation in the critical period.[92] There are no data to show that any of the heads or high officials of the many peacetime agencies of the three states made statements favoring evacuation[93]—but it is known that at least one high California official actually spoke against it.[94]

The state councils for defense, established shortly before the war and staffed by civilians, many of whom were officials of various state agencies, did not advocate or suggest evacuation. The councils in Oregon and Washington made no statements at all on the matter,[95] while the California council spoke out against evacuation of enemy aliens, passing a resolution on January 8 requesting federal authorities to establish a supervisory custodianship of Japanese farmers in lieu of evacuating them.[96]

The county level.—None of the governing boards of the many counties in Oregon or Washington passed resolutions calling for evacuation, and in California only seven boards expressed themselves on the point before February 14. One county called for the removal of all enemy aliens from the coast,[97] one urged the removal of enemy aliens from coastal sections of the county,[98] two called for the removal of Japanese aliens,[99] and three urged the evacuation of all Japanese Americans.[100] This last resolution was a product of the County Supervisors Association of California which circulated it to the counties late in January but did not itself adopt the resolution until February 20. The Association of Oregon Counties took no stand on evacuation;[101] the

Washington State Association of County Commissioners in a resolution of February 6 favored "the removal of all enemy aliens from the state . . . or at least from the west side of the Cascade Mountains."

Of the county grand juries of the three states, only two passed resolutions calling for the removal of Japanese from coastal areas.[102] Of the many county civilian defense councils along the coast, only two are known to have adopted resolutions favoring evacuation before February 14.[103] Moreover, despite Grodzins' assertion that "virtually every local law-enforcement officer made known [his] belief in the necessity of evacuation," there is no evidence on the extent to which county district attorneys and sheriffs publicly expressed their opinions for evacuation in the period preceding February 14. Some in California voiced opinions in the private conference called by Attorney General Warren on February 2, but the only public expression of the group's sentiment was a resolution urging the United States attorney general to evacuate "all *alien* Japanese . . . from all areas in the State of California to some place in the interior."[104]

The city level.—No more than two of the governing bodies of the 613 municipalities in the three states are known to have voiced opinions in favor of Japanese evacuation prior to mid-February.[105] Monrovia, California, recommended the removal of Japanese aliens only, and San Buenaventura, California, called for the removal of "all dangerous enemy aliens of any country." The directors of the League of California Cities wired President Roosevelt on January 29 that "all Japanese, alien and citizen alike, should be evacuated from the entire 'combat zone' along the west coast." On February 11 the Monterey Bay Area Regional Division of the league—alone among such divisions—adopted this resolution. The League of Oregon Cities did not take a stand on evacuation, nor did the Association of Washington Cities.[106] Of the many municipal civilian defense councils in the three states, only eight in California and one in Oregon are known to have gone on record for Japanese exclusion.[107]

There is no evidence to show that more than one of the thousands of mayors of West Coast municipalities—Fletcher Bowron of Los Angeles—expressed an opinion publicly prior to mid-February in favor of security measures against the Japanese. Grodzins claims that "local elected officials of small California communities were very active," but the only evidence cited is an instance in Ventura where residents were reportedly urged " 'to add their voices to the cry for action by telegraphing their congressional representatives.' "[108] (Examination of the newspaper story quoted by Grodzins shows that the officials were not urging mass evacuation but only seeking to have the Department of Justice declare Ventura a restricted area. This would not have excluded aliens but merely subjected them to curfew and travel controls.)[109]

Bowron, alone among West Coast mayors, advocated placement of the Japanese at agricultural labor in supervised camps and urged action of some sort upon General DeWitt before February 14. In a press release of February 6, he clarified his labor proposal: "I have not advocated the mass internment of all Japanese within the usual meaning of the term. . . . For alien Japanese residents, it would, in a sense, be a form of internment, but without the necessity of closely confined incarceration, there should be no need for breaking up families."[110] In company with Earl Warren and Tom Clark, Bowron called on DeWitt on February 11 to urge security measures against the Japanese. But, despite assertions to the contrary,[111] there is no substantial evidence that DeWitt was influenced in his policy decisions by this visit. Bowron himself did not claim it was causative; he said only that his comments "may have been the last straw."[112]

Hence, it would seem that the politician theory is the creature of glib and hasty generalization and almost totally lacks the support claimed for it. The activity of local elected officials in the three West Coast states before February 14 was of slight extent and slighter consequence. From the definite evidence at hand, what would have been the full weight of the pressure brought to bear on DeWitt if everything said or done had come to his attention during this period? There would not have been any pressure from the governors, lieutenant governors, secretaries of state, attorney generals, nor from the heads of state boards or agencies; nor statements by state defense councils, nor resolutions or memorials by state legislatures, nor declarations by state senators or assemblymen. DeWitt would have received resolutions favoring Japanese evacuation from the governing boards of seven of the counties of the three states, from two county grand juries, and two civilian-defense councils, plus the recommendation of California sheriffs and district attorneys that alien Japanese be excluded. He would have received resolutions from two cities, nine city defense councils and the directors of the League of California Cities, and had a visit from one mayor who advocated employment of the Japanese under supervision. In all, DeWitt would have received twenty-four resolutions from county and city governments—plus the visit of one mayor—and nothing at all from state officials.

WEST COAST CONGRESSIONAL DELEGATIONS

Some analysts of the episode have attributed the evacuation program at least in part to the activities of the West Coast delegations in Congress.

They state that the senators and representatives applied pressure on officials of the War and Justice departments, as well as on the White House, and that this pressure was responsible for instituting the policy.[113] Grodzins devotes an entire chapter to the activities of "the strongly knit organization" of West Coast congressmen, charging that "in February, 1942, the entire weight of this politically potent group was aimed at bringing about the mass evacuation of Japanese from the west coast." While he concedes that "it is oversimple and false to hold that congressional activity caused evacuation," nevertheless officials of the War and Justice departments "were strongly impressed with the vehemence of the views held by western senators and representatives" and "that activity was one of several determining factors" in bringing about evacuation.[114] Despite these implications of far-reaching influence, Grodzins' final summary does not ascribe to the congressmen the influence with which he had endowed them earlier. The War and Justice departments are said to have accepted the program advocated by DeWitt without question or review; and the reason for the Department of Justice's acquiescence was that it was unwilling to argue with the Army over "military necessity."[115] Thus, although Grodzins does not explicitly say so, it is implicit in his final analysis that the influence of the congressmen was slight; the War Department simply let DeWitt make the decision and the Department of Justice declined to argue.[116]

A study of the activities of the West Coast delegations justifies the judgment that although they generated considerable heat it was not transmuted into power. There were two points at which they might have exerted influence: upon DeWitt in the days before February 14, and upon Washington officialdom before the evening of February 17, when the decision was made by officials of the War and Justice departments to undertake the evacuation. But analysis of their activity shows that at neither of these two junctures of events were they influential. There is no evidence that any congressman from the West Coast called on or communicated with DeWitt before mid-February. If the general took his cue from news reports of debates in Congress, he would have heard almost nothing. "Except for Leland Ford's brief remarks on January 20 no statement was made on the floor of the House or Senate in favor of evacuation until the February 19 debate."[117] In the West Coast delegations, there were "sharp differences in attitudes toward American Japanese."[118] Senator Sheridan Downey of California and Congressmen Jerry Voorhies and John Coffee, "adherents of moderate action," vocally opposed the evacuation program—Downey even asserting in a radio address that "the great majority of our aliens are harmless people" and

expressing trust in the Department of Justice program of prohibited
and restricted zones.[119] It is certainly unlikely that this activity would
have influenced DeWitt to adopt the evacuation policy.

The earliest known instance of pressure by a congressman on administration officials was that of California's Leland Ford, who on January
23, 27, and 28, 1942, wrote letters to Attorney General Biddle, urging
concentration camps for the Japanese.[120] Biddle showed "firm opposition to mass evacuation" in his replies of January 24 and 27.[121] On the
latter date Congressmen Alfred J. Elliott and John Z. Anderson called
on Mr. Edward J. Ennis, Chief of the Alien Enemy Control Unit of the
Department of Justice, to urge evacuation. But they found the department very unwilling to accept that policy. On January 29 Senator Rufus
Holman of Oregon suggested to Senator Hiram Johnson of California
that a conference of West Coast senators be called to discuss the matter, and at a meeting of February 2, two committees were set up, one on
alien enemies and sabotage, under Senator Mon Wallgren of Washington, the other on defense, under Senator Holman. Senator Holman's
committee met frequently during the following months but worked at
matters unrelated to evacuation. Senator Wallgren's committee met
first on February 5 with representatives of the War and Justice departments, at which Colonel Bendetsen presented a "qualified endorsement
of citizen evacuation," and Department of Justice officials pointed out
that alien control was well in hand and that "if there is to be a wholesale evacuation, such a tremendous job must devolve on the Army."[122]
On February 10 the committee adopted a recommendation which advocated "the immediate evacuation of all persons, alien and citizen, from
all strategic areas and that only such persons be permitted to remain in
or return to such areas as shall have been granted special license for
that purpose."[123] This recommendation was presented to a meeting of
West Coast senators and congressmen on February 12, who adopted a
modified recommendation calling for "the immediate evacuation of
all persons of Japanese lineage and all others, alien and citizen alike,
whose presence shall be deemed dangerous or inimical to the safety or
the defense of the United States, from all strategic areas."[124] The group
also drafted a letter to President Roosevelt and appointed a committee
to call on him to urge the policy. However, the committee did not see
the President, since Executive Order 9066 had been signed on the
evening of February 19, before arrangements for the visit could be
made. Meanwhile, two evenings before, on February 17, representatives
of the War and Justice departments had agreed that the War Department would undertake mass evacuation.

The picture of the events and factors leading to these policy decisions shows little if any influence by congressmen. The War Department civilian heads simply put the matter up to DeWitt. As McCloy said, "The problem was posed to General DeWitt: Was the evacuation of Japanese citizens and aliens necessary? General DeWitt . . . consulted his staff and his area commanders. The military men made the decision. It was a military decision."[125] The War Department stood by this recommendation and presented it to the Department of Justice with the blunt demand that it be accepted.[126] The latter department felt that it could not reasonably debate a point of professional judgment with Army officers and stepped down. There seems no reason to believe that any pressure by congressmen stimulated this reaction.

POLITICIANS AND INLAND EXCLUSION

The decision to intern Japanese Americans living in central and eastern California, which was part of Military Area No. 2, was officially stated to have been made in late February or early March.[127] If this dating is correct, the decision in no way depended upon events occurring in subsequent months. Some writers, however, have questioned the truth of this official reckoning and instead have maintained that the decision came later in the spring in response to pressure which altered the Army's policy from that of freedom for the interior Japanese to that of their exclusion and internment. It is known that DeWitt and Bendetsen publicly refused in mid and late April to consider any change of policy. If the official dating is in fact inaccurate and it was pressure that caused the WDC to change its mind after this refusal, is there evidence to show that politicians on the West Coast or in Congress were influential?

On the known facts it can be said definitely that only one West Coast politician, Governor Olson of California, was publicly active in urging the removal of Japanese from inland California after April 24. On April 29 he met with DeWitt but the nature of his recommendations, if any, is not known. However, on May 25, after a meeting with farmers of the Central Valley, the governor did come out in favor of the removal of all Japanese.[128] This was the solitary demand upon the WDC from public officialdom on the West Coast during the period.

What then is the evidence that the June program might have resulted from the pressure of congressmen in Washington? In the first two weeks of May, Congressman Elliott of California, who had been active in earlier months in the interest of evacuation, held three meetings with Colonel Bendetsen of the WDC and with Director Milton S.

Eisenhower of the WRA. Subsequently Elliott expressed confidence that his efforts would lead to an extension of evacuation to interior California communities.[129] Although the possibility that the activity of this single congressman was responsible for the June decision cannot be wholly ruled out, neither does it seem highly probable. If the politician theory is to be accepted, surely much more evidence than now exists is needed concerning the activities of other congressmen or the reason for supposing this one to have been so singularly effective.

Thus the statement that the influence of politicians was responsible for the program of coastal exclusion, decided on in February, and of inland exclusion, begun in June, is not substantiated by their demonstrated activity. From what is known of their efforts the pressure by West Coast officials in the days before February 14 was slight at best. There was even less activity in the period after April 24 and before June 2—during which time, it is charged, the decision to exclude the Japanese from central California was adopted. As for the congressmen from the West Coast: their efforts in behalf of evacuation before February 14 were neither extensive nor uniform, revealing, in fact, sharp divisions of opinion. From the character of the decisions made by the War and Justice departments in response to DeWitt's "Final Recommendation," it would seem highly unlikely that congressional influence was a decisive factor. Unless further and stronger data are brought forth, therefore, the politician theory must be adjudged "not proven."

Conclusion

The pressure-group and politician theories of responsibility fall short of substantiation not only on the ground of activity, but also on that of influence. For why should General DeWitt have heeded these scattered recommendations and petitions? Although politicians might be expected to respond to a show of pressure from the public or from important groups, the general was not a politician. He was a career officer with no interest in public office; his job and the regard of his superiors were not dependent on popular opinion. He was faced with a military problem: the defense of the coast. Why should he depart from his military estimate of the situation to undertake an extensive, unprecedented, and "unmilitary" program at the behest of a handful of private organizations and some minor officials?

To assert that DeWitt contemplated the program of evacuation out of conviction that the military situation required it is not, of course, to concur in his judgment or to maintain that it was isolated from the surrounding community of opinion. It is a central contention of this book that the claim of "military necessity" was unjustified—but that the dereliction was one of folly, not of knavery. The racism exhibited by the general and his staff was blatant and unmistakable, and clearly corresponded to (if it did not surpass) that of articulate public opinion along the Pacific Coast in the early months of war. But this is additional reason for believing that the military did not need to be persuaded, rather than that it did.

The responsibility of the Army and the government for the decisions which led from curfew through evacuation to detention cannot be shifted. But it can be shared, in a lesser degree, by all who demanded, affirmed, or acquiesced in those decisions. These included politicians, Legionnaires, businessmen, laborers, farmers, Native Sons—in fact, the "public" of the Pacific Coast. It was not in the self-interest of "powerful economic groups" generally to move against the Japanese Americans; indeed, many who opposed evacuation acted in a manner more consistent with economic motives. But the anti-Japanese demands of all these constituent elements of the public were clearly in harmony with the suspicion and distrust which the West Coast had nurtured for so many generations and which the fortunes of war brought so painfully to its consciousness. No theory of backstage machinations and skillfully organized agitation on the part of reactionary interests and corrupt officials is needed to explain the course of events which culminated in the confinement of an entire minority group on racial grounds—although the temptation of liberal-minded students to pursue this familiar theme is admittedly heightened by a knowledge of the participation of pressure groups in the historical buildup of the Japanese stereotype.

The sporadic, unconnected, and ill-timed actions of private groups and public figures against the Japanese Americans in the early months of war more closely resemble the gestures of a desperate shadow-boxer than the careful connivance of organized interests. That among the clamoring voices there were some who stood to profit is undeniable; that there were also some who stood to lose is no less undeniable. Most undeniable of all is that the American people generally, and the people of the West Coast in particular, were anxious, angry, and afraid; that in this mood the familiar specter of the "yellow peril" appeared before them, and that they struck out blindly at its shadow—not knowing that by this blow they were to damage, not the enemy, but the constitutional safeguards of their own free way of life.

Part III

LEVITICUS

Chapter V

THE EPISODE IN THE COURTS

The basic constitutional and moral questions involved in the Japanese American episode were left to the United States Supreme Court to settle at its leisure. The court, in this situation, was the arena in which the struggle of the public conscience was most visible. There alone among the agencies of government, deed and word, practice and profession, had to be brought into some kind of harmony.

How did the court reconcile the episode with the Constitution? Specifically, how, if at all, have the episode and the cases arising from it affected: (1) the scope and character of judicial review, i.e., the ways in which and the extent to which the Supreme Court will review the actions and stay the hand of the military; (2) the constitutional requirement of equal and nondiscriminatory treatment; (3) the character of United States citizenship, particularly as to its sources, rights, and terminability; and, finally, (4) the wartime powers of the military over citizens of the United States who are civilians and within the continental limits of the United States.

The cases with which we have to deal can be organized under three heads: First, the curfew, evacuation, and detention series; second, the state discrimination series; third, the citizenship series.

The *Hirabayashi, Korematsu,* and *Endo* cases[1] are the judicial decisions which bear respectively upon the validity of curfew, evacuation, and detention. This in itself is not without significance in understanding or evaluating the role of the court. For it is only by virtue of the fiat of the court itself that this phase of the Japanese American episode can be said to be divided into three parts. Divide and conquer was the motto of the court, even though the process of division involved the court, as Justice Roberts said, in the substitution of an hypothetical case for the case actually before it and in dividing what was "single and indivisible."[2]

[1] For notes to chapter v see pp. 382–383.

In the *Hirabayashi* case, the court ruled upon the validity of the curfew order alone. In the *Korematsu* case, handed down approximately a year and a half later, the court ruled on the exclusion order alone. This is not to say, however, that a year and a half separated the presentation of the two questions to the court. Every issue with which the court found it necessary to deal in the *Korematsu* case was presented earlier in the *Hirabayashi* case. On the trial, Hirabayashi had been convicted of violating both curfew and exclusion orders. He was sentenced on both counts, sentences to run concurrently. When the Ninth Circuit Court of Appeals certified questions in the *Hirabayashi* case, it said, "this Court knows of no decision in which citizens residing in areas not subject to martial law" have been subjected to a curfew and exclusion by military order. It thought most difficult the question "whether this exercise of the war power can be reconciled with traditional standards of personal liberty and freedom guaranteed by the Constitution."[3] Accordingly, in addition to certifying the question of the constitutionality of curfew, the Ninth Circuit Court of Appeals certified the following question:

Was Lt. General DeWitt's Civilian Exclusion Order No. 57 of May 10, 1942, *excluding* all persons of Japanese ancestry, *including American citizens of Japanese ancestry*, from ... a particular area ... and *requiring* a responsible member of each family, and each individual living alone, affected by the order to *report* ... *to the Civil Control Station in the said area in connection with said exclusion*, a constitutional exercise of the war power of the President derived from the Constitution and statutes of the United States?[4]

Taking advantage of the concurrent sentences, the Supreme Court sustained the sentence on the curfew violation and found it unnecessary to rule on exclusion. On this basis, the court was able to present a front of rather wary unanimity to the world. If the careful language of Chief Justice Stone did not, the concurring opinions strongly suggested that unanimity was possible only on the narrow grounds of curfew and that evacuation and detention were deliberately being held open for a later day and another case.

In the *Korematsu* case, the precarious unanimity was shattered as the court faced, after a fashion, the problem of evacuation. The Ninth Circuit Court of Appeals had been able to dispose of the *Korematsu* case in an opinion of a few short paragraphs on the theory that the Supreme Court in *Hirabayashi* had taken a position which also settled the evacuation question.[5] The Supreme Court itself was to sustain this view, but not without the protest of Justice Jackson that "the Court is now saying that in Hirabayashi we did decide the very thing we there said we were not deciding."⁶ But in spite of this protest and the added dissents of Justices Murphy and Roberts, the momentum of the *Hirabayashi* decision carried the court past the problem of evacuation in the *Korematsu* case.

Just as *Hirabayashi* involved evacuation as well as curfew, so *Korematsu* involved detention as well as evacuation. Again, however, the court divided the indivisible. This feat was facilitated by the fact that the *Endo* case, purporting to deal with detention, was handed down with *Korematsu* on the same day as a sort of package. Said Justice Roberts: "the facts . . . show that the exclusion was but a part of an overall plan for forceable detention. This case cannot, therefore, be decided on any such narrow ground as the possible validity of a Temporary Exclusion Order under which the residents of an area are given an opportunity to leave and go elsewhere in their native land outside the boundaries of a military area."⁷

Divide and conquer, however, was the court's motto. Meeting this argument, Justice Black, speaking for the court, rejected the contention that "we must treat these separate orders as one and inseparable."⁸ The separate orders were that persons of Japanese ancestry "(1) depart from the area; (2) report to and temporarily remain in an assembly center; (3) go under military control to a relocation center there to remain for an indeterminate period. . . . There is no reason why violations of these orders . . . should not be treated as separate offenses."⁹ And since Korematsu had been convicted only for violation of the first of these, it was unnecessary to consider anything more than the validity of the exclusion order.

If one is led by Justice Black's statement in the *Korematsu* case that "it will be time enough to decide the serious constitutional issues which petitioner seeks to raise when an assembly or relocation order is applied"¹⁰ into expecting that the court in the *Endo* case would face those issues he will, of course, be disappointed.

A unanimous court decided that Mitsuye Endo, concededly loyal, should be released from the relocation center in which she was detained by the War Relocation Authority "unconditionally"—that is, without having to follow the indefinite leave procedure established by the authority.

"In reaching that conclusion," said the court, "we do not come to the underlying constitutional issues which have been argued."¹¹ Favoring "that interpretation of legislation which gives it the greater chance of surviving the test of constitutionality"¹² the court found nothing in the relevant acts of Congress or orders of the Executive which authorized the detention of loyal citizens or which subjected them to "conditional release."[13] The WRA had simply exceeded the authority conferred upon it. Only Justice Roberts in a concurring opinion protested against the court's avoidance of the "constitutional issues . . . necessarily involved."[14]

As a result of the method by which the court handled the *Hiraba-yashi, Korematsu,* and *Endo* cases, the entire program of the government in effecting the curfew and the evacuation of American citizens of Japanese ancestry from the Pacific Coast and their detention in concentration camps passed through the court without at any point encountering constitutional condemnation.[15]

Problems of internal maneuvre did not come to an end with the curfew, evacuation, and detention series. In *Oyama* v. *California,*[16] the first of the state discrimination cases, the court again divided the indivisible. It invalidated a statutory section creating a prima facie presumption of evasive transfer of land, though this could not be done except on grounds which also invalidated the Alien Land Law of which it was a part. The majority of the court, however, deemed it "unnecessary and therefore inappropriate to reëxamine"[17] the validity of the Alien Land Law. Justices Black and Douglas, concurring, would now overrule "the prior decisions of this Court,"[18] sustaining the Alien Land Law; and Justices Murphy and Rutledge, also concurring, thought the constitutionality of those laws "the controlling issue in this case."[19] That the court must either sustain both the presumption and the Alien Land Law or condemn both, was the ground of dissent by Justices Reed and Burton. The fate of the Alien Land Law accordingly remained to be settled at a later time.[20]

In *Takahashi* v. *Fish and Game Commission,*[21] the second of the state discrimination cases, the court no longer needed to divide in order to conquer. Though Justices Reed and Jackson dissented, a clear majority was left to face and settle the only issue presented. They struck down the state statute.

Regan v. *King* was still easier for the court to decide. The move to strip Japanese Americans of their United States citizenship, which had received short shrift by the United States District and Circuit courts, was disposed of in the Supreme Court by denial of *certiorari.*[22]

As is evident, though the Supreme Court indulged in tactics of division, delay, and evasion, it did not altogether escape dealing with the Japanese American episode. It did eventually pass on some of the constitutional issues raised. This is not to say, however, that it gave constitutional approval to the program—merely that it failed to disapprove it. The difference is significant: it points to the scope of the review the court will give constitutional issues when it agrees to handle them at all.

The normal doctrine of judicial review is that the court will exercise a great deal of self-restraint. It will stop short of requiring exact compliance by governmental agencies with its tests of constitutionality. It will not substitute its judgment for theirs or pass upon the wisdom of their actions. It will allow them latitude of judgment and discretion in deciding what evils to combat and what means to use in combatting them. It will not investigate all the facts and circumstances and then decide whether it would have taken the action. Rather it will inquire whether in all the facts and circumstances there is any substantial basis for the conclusions reached by the operating branch of government. This substantial-basis test, if not the rock upon which judicial review rests, is certainly the façade behind which it operates.

What was the degree of review accorded in the Japanese American cases? Did the court apply the substantial-basis test? Did it investigate whether there was any factual foundation for the military judgment either as to the existence of the danger or the appropriateness of the means to prevent it?

In the *Hirabayashi* case, the court announced that it would adopt the normal rule of review. The question, it said, was not whether the curfew orders were appropriate or reasonably related to the purpose (whatever that was proved or assumed to be), but whether there was a substantial basis for the military conclusion that they were. Could the military judgment be rejected as unfounded? Did the military have "ground for believing"? Are there "facts and circumstances . . . which support the judgment" of the military? The military judgment did not have to be supported by the preponderance of the evidence. The "facts and circumstances" did not have to tip the scale for the court as they did for General DeWitt and his advisers. The court would be satisfied if there was some evidence which would relieve General DeWitt's judgment of a charge of being unfounded or groundless.

Having thus acknowledged the substantial-basis rule, the court then failed to apply it. The rule requires that some facts be established. Moreover, those facts presumably must be established by a preponderance of the evidence after the weighing of an adequate amount of data on both sides. In the *Hirabayashi* case, no such facts were proved on the trial. Instead, the court was asked to take judicial notice of the basis for a belief in the existence of various circumstances tending to encourage an attachment to Japan on the part of some Japanese American citizens. This basis had to do with the legal and economic status of the group, its segregation and solidarity, its geographical location, the

influential position of Japanese aliens in it, the schooling of its youth
in Japanese-language schools and in Japan. But the court, in determining whether such a basis for the belief in disloyalty existed, did not
search for facts, let alone explore "all the facts and circumstances or
weigh the evidence." Instead, the court simply referred to facts and
circumstances of "public notoriety"; to facts which were "generally believed," or which had "been deemed" to exist, or which "may well" have
existed. On the foundation of the data adduced by the court, one could
not have concluded positively that most of the asserted influences
towards disloyalty existed, or even that a substantial case had been made
for their existence. One could only conclude that there was some basis
for the belief in disloyalty of some of the Japanese Americans, and that
that basis in turn was itself a mere belief.

Thus, in the *Hirabayashi* case, the search for a substantial basis for
the application of the discriminatory curfew to all Japanese Americans
as a means to prevent espionage and sabotage comes down to an attempt
to discover if there were some beliefs in existence which might have
been entertained by Congress, the Executive, and the military and
which, if true, would justify the action taken. This does not involve:
(a) a determination of whether the beliefs were entertained by Congress, the Executive, and the military; (b) a determination of whether
the beliefs were true; or (c) a determination of whether there were facts
or other beliefs which, had they been put in the balance, could have
outweighed the beliefs which might have been entertained.

Judicial review in the *Korematsu* case was even more perfunctory. In
it was no talk at all about a substantial basis, no concern with whether
the beliefs of the military authorities were founded or unfounded. In
fact, other than in language quoted from *Hirabayashi*, the court does
not even require a showing that the military had beliefs. "Apprehensions . . . of the gravest imminent danger to the public safety . . . [and]
the judgment that exclusion of the whole group was a military imperative"[23] were simply attributed to the military. These assumed views of
the military are then in turn held to render the evacuation constitutional. Taking for granted the major doctrine of the court's opinion
that pressing public necessity rather than the Constitution is the sole
measure of military action in time of dire emergency, the existence of
the emergency and the good faith of the military still would be proper
subjects of judicial review and the substantial-basis test. The court, by
accepting supposed reasons for the action taken, in effect allowed the
military, without check, to decide when to invoke its extraconstitutional
powers. And Justice Black sought to refute the claims of counsel and

the evidence of DeWitt's *Final Report* by a flat and authoritative assertion: "Korematsu," he said, "was not excluded from the Military Area because of hostility to him or his race." The *Hirabayshi* opinion arrived at this conclusion by the roundabout method of announcing and then failing to apply the substantial-basis test. From the standpoint of judicial review, as applied, this would seem to be the only difference between the two cases. In both the review was almost entirely delusive.[25]

In support of the court's refusal to intervene, at least to the extent required by the substantial-basis rule, it might be argued that the area of military power presents the problem of judicial enforcement of constitutional limitations in one of its sharpest forms. Judicial review is here tested at the critical extremes of power. Mistakes by the courts may not be correctable as in other areas. There may be no time for ameliorative legislative action or for the process of national adjustment. There may be no chance for the courts themselves to reconsider and reverse. An erroneous judgment of the courts sought to be imposed on the war-waging branches of government in an hour of crisis might dangerously impede necessary military action: in that event it must either be repudiated by these branches or contribute to national destruction. Aside from the costliness of judicial error, there is here at issue too, it may be argued, the competence of the courts to review the judgment of the expert in a field perhaps even more removed from the training, experience, and knowledge of the judges than the work of tax officials, the Interstate Commerce Commission, or the National Labor Relations Board.

This viewpoint was expressed most vigorously by Justice Jackson. In his dissent in the *Korematsu* case, he declared that the function of "the armed services" is to "protect a society, not merely its constitution. The very essence of the military job is to marshal physical force, to remove every obstacle to its effectiveness, to give it every strategic advantage."[26] He then continues:

In the very nature of things military decisions are not susceptible of intelligent judicial appraisal. They do not pretend to rest on evidence, but are made on information that often would not be admissible and on assumptions that could not be proved. Information in support of an order could not be disclosed to courts without danger that it would reach the enemy. Neither can courts act on communications made in confidence. Hence courts can never have any real alternative to accepting the mere declaration of the authority that issued the order that it was reasonably necessary from a military viewpoint.[27]

Justice Jackson recognized fully the peculiar dangers in unrestrained military authority. "The existence of a military power," he said, "rest-

ing on force, so vagrant, so centralized, so necessarily heedless of the individual, is an inherent threat to liberty."[28] But he thought the imposed
restraint of the judges could not be substituted for the self-restraint of
the generals. Not only was judicial review not feasible, but the courts
wielded no power equal to the task of subjugating "irresponsible and
unscrupulous" commanders.[29]

The most striking thing about the position represented by Justice
Jackson is the undifferentiated character it attributes to all military
authority. Military judgments and decisions are treated as if they were
all of a piece, a single and indivisible entity. The military does nothing
less sweeping and all-engulfing than "protect a society" or less violent
than "marshal physical force." It forms no judgments less intuitive than
those based on inadmissible information and assumptions that cannot
be proved. It takes no action so open and avowed that it could be justified without the disclosure of secret information of military value to
the enemy. By the use of such expressions, Justice Jackson does something more than lump in a single unified concept widely different kinds
of judgments covering widely variant subject matters, some involving
a high degree of technical skill and knowledge, others none at all. He
is thereby attempting to give to all decisions made by the military the
essential characteristics of a strictly military command. He is treating
the evacuation order as though it were an order deploying troops in
combat. Even if it is assumed that "the military reasonableness" of the
latter type of order "can only be determined by military superiors,"[30]
still, the execution of the evacuation decision was not, in any sense,
peculiarly or essentially a military operation; and the decision itself, if
General DeWitt's *Final Report* is to be believed, was not based on considerations peculiarly and essentially military. The danger of invasion
was the factor that came closest to involving something like military
judgment, and, oddly enough, it was that factor to which the court in
the *Hirabayashi* case applied the strictest standard of review. As revealed by that review, and later by DeWitt's Report, even with respect
to the danger of invasion the facts underlying the decision were of a
general rather than of a technical character, and were, in the main,
publicly knowable if not publicly known. The other factors underlying
the evacuation decision were racial, psychological, and sociological.
Since these matters, as Justice Murphy said, are "not ordinarily within
the realm of expert military judgment,"[31] the military decision, so far
as it was based on them, should properly have been given far less weight
than is customarily given to those determinations of administrative
agencies which are founded upon expertise.

The single-entity concept of judgments made by the military taken together with the corollary idea that all of such judgments are necessarily military, thus (1) belies the facts as peculiarly illustrated by the curfew and evacuation; (2) couples the refusal to review military judgments with a refusal to determine whether the judgment of the military was military in character—and thus leaves the self-restraint of the military as the only hindrance to this far-reaching threat to civil authority and constitutional limitations; (3) makes it impossible to separate the civil, near-civil, nonmilitary decisions of the military authorities involving controls over citizen civilians within the country from the decisions of the military authorities which are strictly military in character and to apply to the former, at least, the standards of review which would be applied to the very same decisions if made by civil authorities; and (4) extends judicial deference to an operative agency in areas in which the usual reasons for such deference—the special competence of the agency based on technical knowledge or administrative experience or skill—do not or may not exist. All of this is, of course, in addition to the question of whether the courts ought not to continue in the future, as they have in the past, to exercise some review of decisions by the military which are strictly military in character.

The fact that any particular military decision may be preponderantly or entirely nonmilitary in character—that is, may regulate civilians within the country and not turn upon factors within the technical competence or secret knowledge of the military—seriously weakens if it does not altogether invalidate the two reasons given by Justice Jackson for his conclusion that "in the very nature of things, military decisions are not susceptible of intelligent judicial appraisal"; namely, "they do not pretend to rest on evidence" and military information disclosed to courts might reach the enemy. The nature of the decision rather than the garb of the decision-maker should be determinative in both of these situations. The Atomic Energy Commission, a civilian agency, does not have any less need to act upon intuition and secret knowledge than it would have if it were a subordinate bureau of the War Department. The police power to maintain order in an area of industrial strife does not change its character or secret informational basis when the National Guard is brought in to aid the police. Limitation of oil production in time of depression and oversupply, established in the interest of the oil industry, does not cease to be an economic regulation simply because the governor declares martial law and calls out the militia to enforce it. Were this not so, said Justice Hughes in *Sterling* v. *Con-*

stantin, "the fiat of a state governor" would be an "avenue of escape from the paramount authority of the Federal Constitution."[32]

The rule of reasonableness as a standard of review does not fix upon either civil or military authority a rigid and unvarying norm of conduct. In each case, reasonableness depends upon the circumstances. In some circumstances, the very imponderables and uncertainties of the situation may justify action on intuition or judicially inadmissible evidence. Such circumstances probably occur more often in military than in civil affairs. They are not, however, confined to military affairs; and, in any event, they do not justify permitting the military, in other situations, to be more whimsical, arbitrary, capricious, or malicious than civil authorities are permitted to be when operating in those same situations. It would indeed be most remarkable and dangerous if an irrational and unfounded action could be made constitutional by the simple device of shifting it from civil to military hands.

This is not to deny that there are decisions whose secret basis could not be publicly revealed through judicial review or otherwise without grave or even possibly fatal injury to the war effort. The Atomic Energy Commission might need to remove all inhabitants from a given area in order to use it as a testing ground for secret weapons or for secret research. Even knowledge of the removal might be very helpful to the enemy. But a public explanation of the factual justification for the action would be virtually an open invitation to enemy bombers or other attack. To take another example: Suppose General DeWitt had evacuated all inhabitants from a given strip along the coast; and suppose this action was taken on a basis of knowledge about the activities of the Japanese fleet derived from the interception of Japanese code messages, the code having been secretly broken. Should General DeWitt in a public proceeding be required to announce that we had broken the Japanese code?

Whatever the complications for judicial review created by the fact that information supporting actions taken may be secret and of military importance to the enemy to whom it might become known if revealed to the courts, this cannot be a factor when—as was true of the Japanese American evacuation and detention—the action under consideration was not grounded on such secret information.

CONCLUSION

In the Japanese American cases, the Supreme Court carried judicial self-restraint to the point of judicial abdication. It there sustained a drastic act of military government over citizen civilians within the country without inquiring into its factual justification. The basic factual hypotheses underlying the whole program of curfew, uprooting, removal, and imprisonment—that, in time of war, permanent alien residents and American citizens having ethnic affiliations with the people of any enemy government, if that people is Oriental, may be a greater source of internal danger than those of other ancestry, and that, in the war conditions on the Pacific Coast in the spring and summer of 1942, such persons could not feasibly be isolated and dealt with individually—received no judicial investigation. Beyond that, in the *Korematsu* case, the court without proof or substantial evidence of any sort, simply attributed to the military (1) a "finding" that the curfew and other existing methods were inadequate protection against espionage and sabotage and (2) a conclusion that the program was militarily necessary. The court declined to review the military action for bad motives or unreasonableness; declined to investigate factually whether there was a military peril, whether the measures adopted were appropriate to cope with that peril, and, if so, whether they unnecessarily invaded constitutional rights and guarantees; declined even to inquire whether the judgment made by the military was a military estimate of a military situation. Apparently all that the court required to foreclose judicial scrutiny was that the action had been taken by the military. The military thus was allowed finally to determine the scope of its own power.

The war powers of the national government traverse a wide area, ranging from economic regulations such as were embodied in the Emergency Price Control Act of 1942 to the command of troops in battle. So far as those powers are exerted in the government of citizen civilians within the country, in a place not actually a battlefield, whether administered by the military or civilian executive, the court should exercise its constitutional and historical function of review and impose standards of public responsibility. This is not to say that the judges should not candidly appreciate their own fallibility. Nor is it to say that the rigor of judicial scrutiny will not or should not vary as the circumstances vary. The military must be allowed a reasonable latitude of military error when making strictly military decisions. Yet keeping the military within the confines of the Constitution, at least when it acts with respect to citizen civilians within the country, is a civil imperative if the Republic is to endure. The self-restraint and constitutional sensitivity of the generals cannot be relied upon as adequate sources of protection. Because of its organization, mode of selection and function, the military is less likely thus to confine itself than are other agencies of government which, despite their representative and responsible character, have traditionally been subjected to judicial surveillance. The techniques and instruments of judicial review are, on the whole, not less applicable or efficient in the case of the military. The courts are hardly the agency to subdue a rebellious general; but in most contexts, where the military touches the civilian in the country, the courts can render it less "vagrant," less "heedless of the individual," and less a "threat to liberty." The expectation of judicial review, or the mere continuing possibility of it, will make most generals more careful.

In the history of the United States rebellious generals have not been a substantial source of military danger to civil institutions. The real source of that danger is found in other quarters. This point has been well made by Louis Smith:

Militarism is more than a formal system of thought. It is a type of public opinion and as such is present to some degree in every society. As is true in regard to other such questions, public opinion relative to military doctrines constantly fluctuates in response to various psychological and environmental conditions. The chief danger to states in which militarism is currently in a minor position is that under stress of chronic anxiety over military insecurity, aggravated by a percussive train of war crises, each stopping short of actual conflict but tending ever nearer to it with inescapable indications of its inevitability, militaristic opinion may spread until it captures the minds of almost the whole people. These facts indicating how the garrison state may possibly come into existence among a hitherto free people are worth pondering. This state may come, not by willful usurpation by the military but by successive adaptations for defense having support of public opinion. It may be ushered in, not by conspiracy, but by plebiscite. It may come into power, not over the wreckage of the civil organs traditionally expected to repress it, but with their active support. It may arrive, not through violence, but by influence, an influence born of the demand of the masses that they not be exposed to annihilation from hostile attack by the omission of any security factor. . . . Thus, among peoples obsessed with deepening anxiety regarding imminent warfare and their slender chances of survival in it, by a process which in a less sinister context has been called the "inevitability of gradualism," the garrison state may come into full power.[33]

In this context, the role of the court is only in part that of maintaining the proper relationship between the military and civil authority. It is only in part that of seeing that the military does not become master where it should be servant. Beyond that, the function of the court is to determine the nature of the Constitution itself—the scope of the national war powers exerted by the military and by the civil officials who direct the military vis-a-vis the rights of civilians. Military usurpation may be less a danger to constitutional limitations established to protect the individual than an expansion of the war powers carried out by civil consent and popular insistence. It is the function of the court to see that "hyperlegality does not impair security and that the shibboleth of 'military necessity' does not justify unnecessary destruction of the rights of the people and bring about an improper impairment of democratic processes of government."[84] When the balance between safety and liberty is struck, it may be the hazardous and often immediately thankless task of the court to safeguard the people from itself. The performance of this stern task may call—doubtless does call—for statesmanlike self-restraint; it does not call for resignation.

Justice Jackson's worry that wartime review of military action will tend to distort the Constitution and find unhappy application in peacetime cases is certainly legitimate. Yet, it must be remembered that the Supreme Court is often the willing, sometimes the reluctant, but never the helpless victim of its own precedents. The court also always has the alternative of avoiding bad precedents by not making them. This danger, in any event, must be measured against the danger of constitutionally and judicially unfettered military power.

Chapter VI

THE WAR POWERS

The Problem

The evacuation of American citizens of Japanese ancestry from the Pacific Coast,[1] and their subsequent detention, carried out by the military under a plea or pretext of military necessity, raises the question of the extent of the war powers of the national government.[2] The circumstances in which this question is presented contain at least two complicating factors. The first is the discriminatory character of the action taken. Had that factor not been present—had the question simply been the validity of a universally applied curfew or of the evacuation of all persons from a limited area threatened even remotely by invasion—a basic constitutional issue of fact would still have had to be decided, but it is doubtful that there would have been so much question about the power of the military to impose the restriction. But the curfew, in addition to covering German, Italian, and Japanese aliens, reached citizens of Japanese ancestry, and mass evacuation and detention were applied exclusively to persons of that ancestry.[3]

Second, the problem is complicated by the fact that it involved military control over civilians within the country and thus opens to view the baffling lay and professional chaos surrounding martial law.[4] Had a civilian agency alone handled the evacuation, no martial-law questions would have been raised to confuse the war-powers problem.

"When an area is so beset," said Justice Jackson in his *Korematsu* dissent, "that it must be put under military control at all, the paramount consideration is that its measure be successful, rather than legal. . . . No court can require such a commander in such circumstances to act as a reasonable man"; the general issues orders, "and they may have a certain authority as military commands, although they may be very bad as constitutional law." "But if we cannot confine military expedients by the Constitution," added Justice Jackson, "neither would I distort the Constitution to approve all that the military may deem

[1] For notes to chapter vi see pp. 383–386.

expedient.''⁵ "I should hold that a civil court cannot be made to enforce an order which violates constitutional limitations even if it is a reasonable exercise of military authority.''⁶

To this, Justice Frankfurter, concurring with the majority, took vigorous exception. "To talk about a military order that expresses an allowable judgment of war needs by those entrusted with the duty of conducting war as 'an unconstitutional order' is to suffuse a part of the Constitution with an atmosphere of unconstitutionality. The Constitution," he said, explicitly granted the war power "for safeguarding the national life by prosecuting war effectively." Hence, "if a military order . . . does not transcend the means appropriate for conducting war, such action by the military is as constitutional as would be any authorized action by the Interstate Commerce Commission.''⁷

This Jackson-Frankfurter exchange highlighted and placed in modern context one of the oldest and most crucial problems of constitutional democracy, viz., how to reconcile the conflicting demands of unfettered military power necessary to preserve the state in times of crisis with the system of constitutional limitations and individual rights. Can this sort of military power be brought within the confines of the Constitution, subjected to rule and circumscribed by limitation—or is it governed only by necessity as uninhibited and elemental as national self-preservation?⁸ Must we, as Justice Jackson suggests, regard unconstitutionality as an inevitable concomitant of the exercise of military authority even when it is "reasonable"?

The Japanese American cases required the court to answer the following fundamental questions: (1) In time of war, what are the tests of the war power of the national government, vested by the Constitution in Congress and the Executive as the war-waging branches of government, especially over citizen civilians within the country? (2) How far does the power of the military extend over civilians within the country in time of war? (3) Does such power arise from necessity and exist independently of the Constitution, or is it constitutionally authorized and granted? (4) No matter what its sources, is such power subject to the limitations of the Constitution? (5) To what extent, if at all, is this power dependent upon the concepts of martial law? (6) Is the military judgment of the military necessity for controls over civilians final? Or does the responsibility rest primarily with Congress to determine the existence of the conditions justifying the establishment of partial or total military government and of establishing it? To what extent, and by what tests, if any, are such judgments, by the military or by Congress, subject to judicial review and control? (7) To what degree, if any, do the methods and character of modern warfare require that we relax our democratically indispensable doctrine of the civil control of the military and the responsibility of the latter for its acts?

THE MILLIGAN CASE AND THE ALTERNATIVES

Merely to mention these questions raises immediately the character and scope of the decision in *Ex parte Milligan*.[9] Decided in 1866 and arising out of an episode of the Civil War,[10] that case has stood in our constitutional history as a landmark of the nature and extent of the wartime power of the military over civilians within the country. It was a "brooding omnipresence" in the Japanese American cases, albeit undiscussed, unanalyzed, and all but unmentioned. Like many another historical landmark, it has been held to stand for various and often conflicting propositions. In recent years, the majority opinion in the *Milligan* case has been sharply criticized as importing into the Constitution "a mechanical test" which, though a "salutary restraint upon the tyranny of the Stuarts" is not "an appropriate limit on the powers of both executive and legislature in the highly responsible national government."[11] Just as sharply, the majority opinion has been defended as "a monument in the democratic tradition" which "should be the animating force of this branch of our law."[12]

The facts of the *Milligan* case were not exactly like those of the Japanese American cases. In October, 1864, Milligan was arrested by military order, tried, found guilty and sentenced to hang by a military commission. The offense charged was not disloyalty or suspicion of disloyalty but conspiracy to overthrow the government, a crime under the laws of Congress and therefore punishable in the civil courts, as disloyalty or suspicion of disloyalty is not. In May, 1865, Milligan petitioned the United States circuit court to be discharged from unlawful imprisonment. The two-judge circuit court divided and certified the question to the Supreme Court.

By Act of March 3, 1863, Congress had authorized the President to suspend the privilege of the writ of habeas corpus "whenever, in his judgment, the public safety may require it"; and the President had done so by proclamation. Under the statute, however, the privilege of the writ was not to be suspended if the person "was detained in custody by the order of the President, otherwise than as a prisoner of war; if he was a citizen . . . and had never been in the military or naval service, and the grand jury of the district had met, after he had been arrested, for a period of twenty days, and adjourned without taking any proceedings against him." Milligan was not a prisoner of war and had not been in the military or naval service. Moreover, a federal grand jury had convened in the district and failed to indict him. The privilege of the writ therefore had not been suspended as to him. So the Supreme Court unanimously held. The case being settled on these narrow grounds, here the court might have rested. Unlike their successors eighty years later, however, these judges were not seeking opportunities to evade the underlying grave constitutional issues.

Justice Davis, for a majority of the court, went on to enunciate the doctrine which is the principal heritage of the *Milligan* case. Trial by military commission, he maintained, violated the Third Article of the Constitution, which vests the judicial power in courts ordained and established by Congress and composed of judges appointed "during good behavior." It also violated the jury-trial guarantees in the original Constitution and in the Fifth and Sixth Amendments and the search and seizure provisions of the Fourth Amendment. The Fathers, said Justice Davis, "secured the inheritance they had fought to maintain, by incorporating in a written constitution the safeguards which *time* had proved were essential to its preservation. Not one of these safeguards can the President, or Congress, or the Judiciary disturb, except the one concerning the writ of habeas corpus."[13] The Fathers "limited the suspension to one great right, and left the rest to remain forever inviolable."[14] "No doctrine, involving more pernicious consequences, was ever invented by the wit of man than that any of its [the Constitution's] provisions can be suspended during any of the great exigencies of government."[15] It did not follow, said Justice Davis, that the nation was helpless in the face of a war crisis, barring the allowance of a theory of power by necessity; "for the government, within the Constitution, has all the powers granted to it, which are necessary to preserve its existence."[16]

This, then, was the system of the *Milligan* majority: that the power to wage war and to wage it successfully, the power to preserve the existence of the nation, is granted by the Constitution; but at no point and in no crisis will its exercise justify the suspension of the constitutional guarantees and limitations, with the single exception of the privilege of the writ of habeas corpus. Moreover, the privilege of the writ of habeas corpus could be suspended only to the extent of warranting detention of individuals, in an hour of emergency, without trial; not to the extent of supplying unconstitutional trials. This aspect of the *Milligan* majority opinion, showing the power of the military to be constitutionally derived and constitutionally limited, is often ignored in the preoccupation of courts and commentators with Justice Davis' remark about martial law.

This position of the *Milligan* majority is sustained and amplified by the claim that it rejected. That claim was that "in a time of war the commander of an armed force (if in his opinion the exigencies of the country demand it, has the power, within the lines of his military district, to suspend all civil rights and their remedies, and subject citizens as well as soldiers to the rule of his will"; and in the exercise of this authority "cannot be restrained, except by his superior officer or the President of the United States." "If this position is sound to the extent claimed," answered Justice Davis, "then when war exists," the commander of a military district can, "on the plea of necessity, with the approval of the Executive, substitute military force for and to the exclusion of the laws, and punish all persons, as he thinks right and proper, without fixed or certain rules." In that event, "republican government is a failure, and there is an end of liberty regulated by law." This kind of martial law

destroys every guarantee of the Constitution, and effectually renders the "military independent of and superior to the civil power"—the attempt to do which by the King of Great Britain was deemed by our fathers such an offence, that they assigned it to the world as one of the causes which impelled them to declare their independence.... Civil liberty and this kind of martial law cannot endure together; the antagonism is irreconcilable; and, in the conflict, one or the other must perish.[17]

The court's opinion in the *Milligan* case thus makes clear that military necessity, even when approved by the Executive, is not a self-justifying plea; that the military judgment that military necessity exists cannot be allowed to stand alone; that the commander is responsible not only to his superiors and the President but to the law and the courts; that the military must act, at least when dealing with citizens within the country, within the confines of the Constitution and subject to civil—that is, judicial—control.

All of this is true, said the *Milligan* majority, with one exception; and it is the scope of that exception upon which critics of the opinion have concentrated.

There are occasions [said Justice Davis] when martial rule can be properly applied. If, in foreign invasion or civil war, the courts are actually closed, and it is impossible to administer criminal justice according to law, then, on the theatre of active military operations, where war actually prevails, there is a necessity to furnish a substitute for the civil authority, thus overthrown, to preserve the safety of the army and society; and as no power is left but the military, it is allowed to govern by martial rule until the laws can have their free course. As necessity creates the rule, so it limits its duration; for, if this government is continued *after* the courts are reinstated, it is a gross usurpation of power. Martial rule can never exist where the courts are open, and in the proper and unobstructed exercise of their jurisdiction. It is also confined to the locality of actual war.

Martial law cannot arise from a *threatened* invasion. The necessity must be actual and present; the invasion real, such as effectually closes the courts and deposes the civil administration.[18]

Thus in these conditions, when warfare is actually raging in the community and has destroyed civil government, the military is in control by default and necessity. Its power arises from these facts and not from the Constitution which also does not limit it. But even here, the facts establishing the necessity are not finally determined by the military. The Supreme Court will have to be satisfied that the courts are actually closed and civil administration deposed.

Chief Justice Chase, joined by Justices Wayne, Swayne, and Miller, expressed basic disagreement. In their view, "there is no law for the government of the citizens, the armies or the navy of the United States, within American jurisdiction, which is not contained in or derived from the Constitution."[19] Thus, presumably even in the absence of a civil government, the military does not derive its power from extra-constitutional necessity. "The Constitution itself," said Chase, "provides for military government as well as for civil government."[20] Military government is derived from the constitutional powers to declare and wage war, to raise and support armies, and perhaps from the power to provide for the government of the national forces. Moreover, continued the Chief Justice, military government is not confined to the area and circumstances of actual military conflict. Though the courts are not closed and the civil officials deposed, military government may constitutionally be established "in time of insurrection or invasion, or of civil or foreign war, within districts or localities where ordinary law no longer adequately secures public safety and private rights."[21] The Chief Justice's description of the situation prevailing in Indiana at the time of Milligan's arrest, though historically incorrect, still supplies an example of particular circumstances included within this general formula: "the state was a military district, was the theatre of military operations, had been actually invaded, and was constantly threatened with invasion." In addition to these pressing factors "a powerful secret association, composed of citizens and others, existed within the state, under military organization, conspiring against the draft, and plotting insurrection, the liberation of prisoners of war at various depots, the seizure of the state and national arsenals, armed cooperation with the enemy, and war against the national government."[22] What branch or agency of government was authorized to establish military government and determine the circumstances warranting it? The answers can be guessed from the depository of the constitutional powers involved. "It is within the power of Congress," said the Chief Justice, "to determine in what states or districts such great and imminent public danger exists as justifies the authorization of military tribunals."[23] Again, "MARTIAL LAW PROPER . . . is called into action by Congress, or temporarily, when the action of Congress cannot be invited, and in the case of justifying or excusing peril, by the President."[24]

Finally, to military government, when operating within its proper sphere, "the civil safeguards of the Constitution"[25] have no application. Citizens may thus be tried by military commissions instead of constitutional courts and constitutionally guaranteed juries.

With respect to the questions above formulated and presented to the court in the Japanese American cases: the majority and minority in the *Milligan* case agreed that the wartime power of the military over civilians within the country, in most circumstances, is only such as is authorized by Congress and the Executive in the exercise of their constitutional powers to wage war and is subject to all limitations, guarantees, and civil controls of the Constitution. The majority and minority agreed moreover that there were circumstances in which the military could displace, alter, or substitute for civil government and could operate unrestrained by constitutional limitations. They disagreed as to the character of those circumstances, the majority finding them present only when civil government was destroyed and a governmental vacuum existed, the minority finding them present more broadly "where ordinary law no longer adequately secures public safety and private rights." The majority and minority agreed that when those circumstances were present the military is not limited by the civil rights and guarantees of the Constitution. They disagreed as to the source of the power of the military; the majority found it outside the Constitution in necessity, "usages of war," or "martial law"; the minority found it in the war powers vested by the Constitution—the term "martial law" merely describing the circumstances in which the war powers might be exercised uninhibited by the Constitution. The majority thus regarded martial law as a "generating source of power"; the minority, though its use of the term was not careful, seems to have regarded it as an explanatory rubric. The majority and minority disagreed as to the agency of government responsible for finally determining the existence of the conditions freeing the military from constitutional restraints, though they agreed the military judgment was not final. The majority thought

this a function of the judiciary and in this very case reversed the conclusion of the military on that point. The minority spoke mainly in
terms of a congressional determination or, "temporarily . . . in the case
of justifying or excusing peril," a presidential determination. The
minority did not say whether the judges would review the factual
determination of Congress or the President. But it must be remembered
both that discussion on this point was not necessary in the opinion, and
that in 1866 the methods and character of judicial review, as presently
conceived, were still in their infancy. Neither the majority nor the
minority commented on the provision of the act of 1863 authorizing the
President to suspend the privilege of the writ "whenever, in his judgment, the public safety may require it."

In brief, the difference between the majority and the minority in the
Milligan case comes down to this: The minority maintained that, short
of conditions of actual warfare and civil-government vacuum, there is
an area in which the military may operate with respect to civilians
within the country, unrestrained by the civil guarantees of the Constitution except that it must act pursuant to congressional or executive
findings and authorization. This the majority denied, holding rather
that in that area constitutional restraints as well as constitutional
powers apply.

Against the background of the *Milligan* case, the court in the Japanese American cases had a number of alternatives.

1. Strict application of the rule of the *Milligan* majority. This would
confine the constitutionally unhindered wartime powers of the military
over civilians within the country to those areas in which battle is raging
and civil government is unable to function. Since neither of these conditions was present on the West Coast, the rule would require testing
the validity of the curfew, evacuation, and detention program within
the ordinary framework of the constitutionally granted and constitutionally limited executive and legislative power to wage war.

2. Adoption of the position of the *Milligan* minority—that Congress
can declare martial law when there has been no breakdown of civil
government and in areas removed from actual combat; that accordingly
Congress can authorize military government over selected subjects or
activities in the presence of civil authority duly and regularly function-
ing in all other respects; that it is up to Congress to decide in what
"districts such great and imminent public danger exists" as to justify the
military measures authorized; and that once the military power is thus
properly invoked, constitutional safeguards of civil and individual
rights are irrelevant.

3. Accept the martial-rule doctrine of the *Milligan* majority but expand the area and liberalize the conditions of its application. This might be done under the guise of interpreting and applying the doctrine in the light of the conditions and methods of modern warfare. Such an attempt was made by Attorney General Warren of California: A total global war, he argued, is "not confined to the actual scene of hostilities but is waged swiftly and violently and at long range upon civilians, factories and fields far beyond the front line." It is "conducted by sabotage, espionage and propaganda everywhere." In such a war "the army must undertake certain precautionary and preventive measures in areas not directly under the siege guns of the enemy, the object of which is the protection of the civilian population and the successful prosecution of the war." The test justifying these preventive measures is military necessity. "The view of the majority [in the *Milligan* case] that martial law must be confined to the locality of actual war does not require a change of this phase of the test of necessity but merely a new and realistic conception of the type of warfare being waged today."[26]

Although this might be called an interpretation and application of the martial-law-rule-of-necessity dictum of the *Milligan* majority, it would be a basic repudiation of the whole spirit and tendency of the *Milligan* majority opinion which sought to restrict the area of martial law to the narrowest confines of absolute necessity. It would in effect be tantamount to an adoption of the inherent powers theory classically stated by John Quincy Adams in 1831:

Sir, in the authority given to Congress by the Constitution of the United States to declare war, all the powers incidental to war are, by necessary implication, conferred upon the government of the United States. Now, the powers incidental to war are derived, not from the internal municipal sources, but the laws and usages of nations. ... There are, then, in the authority of Congress and in the Executive, two classes of powers altogether different in their nature and often incompatible with each other—war power and peace power. The peace power is limited by regulations and restricted by provisions in the Constitution itself. The war power is only limited by the usages of nations. This power is tremendous. It is strictly constitutional, but it breaks down every barrier so anxiously erected for the protection of liberty and of life.[27]

THE ANSWERS OF THE JAPANESE CASES

The *Hirabayashi* case stands generally upon the first of these alternatives; the *Korematsu* case upon the third; and the *Endo* case, though the judges there evaded all constitutional alternatives, stands as a disparagement of the spirit and rule of *Milligan*.

In *Hirabayashi* v. *United States*,[28] a Japanese American, born in the

United States of Japanese immigrant parents, reared in the United States and never having visited Japan, a member of the Quaker faith, educated in our public schools and at the time a senior at the University of Washington, was criminally prosecuted for violation of the curfew order, tried by jury, convicted, and sentenced to three months' imprisonment. The United States Supreme Court upheld the conviction and sentence. The legal foundation for the prosecution rested on Executive Order 9066, Public Law 503, and Public Proclamation No. 3 of the Western Defense Command. In Executive Order 9066, the President, after declaring that "the successful prosecution of the war requires every possible protection against espionage and against sabotage to national defense material, . . . premises and . . . utilities" authorized and directed the Secretary of War or any military commander designated by him "to prescribe military areas . . . from which any or all persons may be excluded, and with respect to which, the right of any person to enter, remain in, or leave shall be subject to whatever restrictions the Secretary of War or appropriate military commander may impose in his discretion."[29]

Public Law 503 provided misdemeanor penalties for persons knowingly entering, remaining in, leaving, or committing any act in any military zone contrary to the regulations of military officials issued under an executive order of the President.[30]

Public Proclamation No. 3, issued by General DeWitt, proclaimed that "military necessity" required "the establishment of certain regulations pertaining to all enemy aliens and all persons of Japanese ancestry" within Military Area No. 1, prescribed by earlier proclamations. Accordingly, Public Proclamation No. 3 ordered that "all alien Japanese, all alien Germans, all alien Italians, and all persons of Japanese ancestry residing or being within the geographical limits of Military Area No. 1 . . . shall be within their place of residence between the hours of 8 P.M. and 6 A.M."[31]

Chief Justice Stone's opinion for the court is divided into three main parts. In the first, he considers the extent of the national war power and whether prevention of espionage and sabotage falls within it. In the second, he considers whether the military peril—that is, danger of "air attack and invasion"—actually existed, whether there was a likelihood of attempts to commit acts of espionage and sabotage and their bearing, if committed, on air attacks and invasion, and, finally, whether curfew was a device reasonably adapted to the prevention of these dangers. In the third, he specifically analyzes the issue of whether the curfew "unconstitutionally discriminated between citizens of Japanese ancestry and those of other ancestries in violation of the Fifth Amendment" stated at the outset of the opinion to be "the question for our decision."[32]

Thus, the court in the *Hirabayashi* case invokes for the military curfew the tests which are traditionally announced for all other constitutional powers: (1) was the end sought to be achieved within the war powers granted by the Constitution; (2) were the means employed appropriate to the achievement of that end; (3) were the means chosen selected with due recognition of the substantive and comparative guarantees of the Fifth and other amendments?

Whatever quarrel one may have with the court's actual decision on these points, there can be little doubt that the court regarded the exercise of military power as subject to these limitations.

Justices Murphy and Rutledge wrote concurring opinions. Justice Murphy especially asserted that "the mere existence of a state of war" does not "suspend the broad guarantees of the Bill of Rights and other provisions of the Constitution protecting essential liberties ... the war power like the other great substantive powers of government, is subject to the limitations of the Constitution."[33] Justices Murphy and Rutledge apparently agreed that drastic wartime invasion of constitutional rights could only be permitted if martial law were declared and in circumstances warranting martial law.

Like that of Hirabayashi, Korematsu's conviction was based on violation of orders issued by the WDC under the authority of the President and Congress granted in Executive Order 9066 and Public Law 503. At the time of his conviction, there were three such military orders outstanding and applicable to him. The first of these was Public Proclamation No. 4 (March 27, 1942),[34] which terminated the original exclusion program that had left free choice of route and destination to the evacuee and instituted a system of rigid controls on movement. It forbade persons of Japanese ancestry to leave the area except as authorized and directed by the WDC. The second outstanding military order applicable to Korematsu was Civilian Exclusion Order No. 34 (May 3, 1942).[35] It provided that after midnight on May 28, all Japanese Americans were to be excluded from a given portion of Military Area No. 1 which included San Leandro, Alameda County, California, the place of Korematsu's residence. Civilian Exclusion Order No. 34 required a responsible member of each family and each individual living alone to report to a civil-control station for instructions to go to an assembly center. By its terms, the order did not apply to Japanese Americans who were within the area and in assembly centers. The effect of these two orders, therefore, was to direct all Japanese Americans to proceed to assembly centers according to instructions to be received from a civil-control station. The third outstanding military order was Civilian Restrictive Order No. 1 (May 19, 1942).[36] It provided for the indefinite detention of persons of Japanese ancestry in assembly or relocation centers.

Korematsu was born in Oakland and educated in American schools. He was classified as 4-F because of stomach ulcers. After graduation from high school he worked in a shipyard as a welder until, after the outbreak of war, the Boilermakers Union cancelled his membership because of his race. He could not read or write Japanese, had never been outside of the United States, and was not a dual citizen. Romance rather than disloyalty was his undoing. The evacuation orders disrupted his plans to marry a Caucasian girl, so he decided to evade them and to remain behind. He hoped to escape detention by having a plastic surgical operation performed on his nose and by changing his name. The ruses failed and the FBI seized him.

Korematsu was prosecuted in the federal district court under Public Law 503 for knowingly remaining within the forbidden territory contrary to Civilian Exclusion Order No. 34, that is, for remaining within the forbidden territory but not in an assembly center.

The American Civil Liberties Union posted bail set by the court. Before releasing Korematsu, however, the jailer telephoned the military police, "who, without any warrants or writ whatever, placed Korematsu in military custody and took him to the Tanforan Assembly Center.... Judge Welch subsequently sanctioned this action and refused to release the bail despite the fact that the defendant was in the hands of the Government." Korematsu refused to sign the useless bail bond. The bail was then raised, the unsigned bond exonerated, and Korematsu was ordered into the custody of the United States Marshal and again placed in the county jail.[37] On the trial, Korematsu was found guilty but his sentence was suspended and he was placed on probation for five years.

Confronted with the situation of a Japanese American still at large in the prohibited area after the sanctions provided by the law of Congress had been applied, the Western Defense Command again resorted to its own devices. Once more Korematsu was picked up by soldiers and lodged in the assembly center. At no stage of the proceedings had his loyalty to the United States been put in issue.

The Supreme Court's opinion in the *Korematsu* case is an attempt to occupy both areas marked out ·and imperatively separated by the *Milligan* majority: the rule of necessity, and the rule of the Constitution.

It is a futile attempt to reconcile the irreconcilable. The opinion, as a result, is a muddled hodgepodge of conflicting and barely articulate doctrine. Justice Black, on the one hand, explicitly builds upon the *Hirabayashi* case and treats the evacuation decision as largely settled by the principles announced there. On the other hand, he lays such heavy stress upon the emergency character of the military action as in effect to take the position of the *Milligan* majority martial-law dictum that the existence of dire emergency results in substituting untrammeled military judgment for constitutional limitations.

> We upheld the curfew order [said Justice Black] as an exercise of the power of the government to take steps necessary to prevent espionage and sabotage in an area threatened by Japanese attack.[38] . . . Exclusion from a threatened area, no less than curfew, has a definite and close relationship to the prevention of espionage and sabotage.[39]
>
> The Hirabayashi conviction and this one thus rest on the same 1942 Congressional Act and the same basic executive and military orders . . .
>
> In the light of the principles we announced in the Hirabayashi case, we are unable to conclude that it was beyond the war power of Congress and the Executive to exclude those of Japanese ancestry from the West Coast war area at the time they did.[40]

Added to this explicit assimilation of the *Korematsu* and *Hirabayashi* cases must be the court's express denial that Korematsu was evacuated "because of hostility to him or his race."[41] This at least suggests that the military decision is subject to some judicial review, however perfunctory, in terms of the legitimacy of its purpose.

Side by side with these remarks and implications, however, are others far more reminiscent of the *Milligan* dictum than of Hirabayashi. For example: "Compulsory exclusion of large groups of citizens from their homes, except under circumstances of direst emergency and peril, is inconsistent with our basic governmental institutions. But when under conditions of modern warfare our shores are threatened by hostile forces, the power to protect must be commensurate with the threatened danger."[42] And further: Korematsu "was excluded because we are at war with the Japanese Empire, because the properly constituted military authorities feared an invasion of our West Coast and felt constrained to take proper security measures, because they decided that the military urgency of the situation demanded that all citizens of Japanese ancestry be segregated from the West Coast temporarily."[43] This emphasis on military necessity is augmented by other statements in the opinion. The courts, said Justice Black, must give "rigid scrutiny" to "legal restrictions which curtail the civil rights of a single racial group."[44] Just such restrictions were before the court. Yet nothing like "rigid scrutiny" was given, nor could it be in the presence of the latitude allowed the military. But in any event legal restrictions of this order—that is, legal restrictions abrogating constitutional rights—can be justified, said Justice Black, by "pressing public necessity."[45] No doubt they can be, but this is hardly a constitutional test.

In determining whether the stress on "pressing public necessity" as the justifying basis of the *Korematsu* decision should be regarded, on the one hand, as a mere shift in emphasis or a rhetorical deviation, or, on the other hand, as a real departure from the reasonable-relation formula of the *Hirabayashi* case, several factors must be borne in mind. It must be remembered, in the first place, that the court which had reached a unanimous holding in the *Hirabayashi* case was now bitterly and publicly divided. Not only did the dissenters feel that the hardship of evacuation was quite out of the class of that involved in curfew but they denied that it was justified by the military situation at the time, and raised serious questions about the extent to which nonmilitary considerations entered into the decision. General DeWitt's *Final Report,* which had come out prior to the *Korematsu* decision, besides casting a curious light on some of the general's beliefs, gave plausibility, if not something more, to the points of the dissenters. In these circumstances it was certainly easier for the court to sustain the evacuation as an emergency action within the allowable discretion of the military than to attempt to justify it as reasonable in detail. In the second place, if one rejects this interpretation of the *Korematsu* case and assumes that the reliance on the *Hirabayashi* case implies a basic acceptance of the formula there stated, the question must be answered whether the application of the formula was not so feeble and uncertain as to amount to no application at all and thus in effect to leave the Constitution suspended. The later day, the diminished emergency, the incomparably more drastic invasion of individual rights, the application of the evacuation order exclusively to Japanese Americans (whereas German and Italian enemy aliens had also been included in the curfew), the evidence that racism played a part in the final decision—all demanded, if not a rigid and minute scrutiny, at least a substantial reëvaluation of ends and means. If the reasonable-relation test was to mean anything in these circumstances, one would suppose that it required something more than the cursory and almost imperceptible application given it by Justice Black.

In view of these factors, it is difficult to avoid the conclusion that the *Korematsu* decision is the exact antithesis of the spirit and decision of the *Milligan* majority. In fact, a more complete rejection of the entire *Milligan* case, majority and minority, is hard to imagine.

The principal doctrine of the *Milligan* majority that the exigencies of government, even the exigencies of war—which the war-waging power is constitutionally granted to meet—do not suspend the limitations and guarantees of the Constitution, is spurned. *Korematsu* sustained far-reaching military controls over the lives and property of citizen civilians within the country on the theory that "pressing public necessity" or "dire emergency" justified them and were their sources of power and sole limitations, thus in effect suspending the Constitution. The *Milligan* majority dictum about martial law is also distorted out of its original proportions. That dictum was interpreted and applied in *Korematsu* in the same way that it had been used by the attorney general of California. It was simply given "a new and realistic conception" in the light of "the type of warfare being waged today." That conception, however, so interpreted and applied, is of such a character as to destroy the conception of the *Milligan* majority. *Korematsu* vastly enlarged the sphere in which the military is freed of the Constitution by necessity. It permitted the institution of constitutionally unrestrained military rule in an area which was not actually invaded, or even subjected to a sizable threat of invasion. In *Korematsu*, the threat of hit-and-run raids is apparently sufficient, for, after the Battle of Midway, that was all that was possible. Could an historical landmark such as the *Milligan* case, in which military authority had been boldly resisted and constitutional guarantees firmly vindicated, ever come to a more ignominious end than that the dictum there uttered about a rigidly confined area in which the military might prevail over the Constitution should now be expanded to consume the principle which made the case a landmark? When to this doctrine is added automatic acceptance by the court of the military judgment that the course of the war required mass evacuation of the Japanese Americans, without the court itself investigating the factual relationship of the course of the war to the evacuation, or requiring the military to make any showing on that point—and when, in addition, in the presence of an open avowal by the commander that he acted on and justified the program by beliefs about race, the court attributed to the military the judgment that the course of the war necessitated the program, without evidence or proof that the military held such judgment—one can see how far the *Korematsu* case relaxes judicial control of the military, how doubtful the standards of military responsibility have become, and the degree to which the *Milligan* dictum has been interpreted to the point of extinction. The *Milligan* majority was emphatic that, in the end, the courts—not the military—would have to decide whether the facts were such as to justify substitution of martial rule for the civil government and guarantees of the Constitution.

Finally, by the *Korematsu* ruling, even the *Milligan* minority is left far behind in the dust. The minority there contemplated martial rule in connection with the suspension of the privilege of the writ of habeas corpus. No such suspension was involved in *Korematsu;* but the martial rule was tolerated. Further, according to the *Milligan* minority, it was up to Congress—or "temporarily," "in the case of justifying or excusing peril" "when the action of Congress cannot be invited" up to the President—to determine whether the circumstances justifying martial law exist and to establish it. The *Korematsu* case leaves this to the military. Lastly, since under Public Law 503 the ordinary courts were to enforce the military decisions, the *Korematsu* case far outstrips the *Milligan* minority in permitting Congress "to throw over martial law the sanctifying aegis of civil authority."[46]

Justice Jackson dissented in the *Korematsu* case, but on the ground that the civil courts could not be required to enforce the military evacuation orders. As to the unconstitutional source of the power of the military and the absence of constitutional limitations, he agreed with the court's opinion. He merely stated it with the irresponsible clarity of a dissenter. It was Justice Frankfurter who, though he wrote a concurring opinion, was the real dissenter on the war-powers issue in the *Korematsu* case. He thought that the military power exercised in the evacuation was merely a part of the national government's power, constitutionally derived and constitutionally limited, as any other power granted by the Constitution. The real debate on this phase of the *Korematsu* case was between Justices Jackson and Frankfurter, not between the dissenter and the majority. And the division was not along the lines of the *Milligan* majority and minority. The Jackson and Frankfurter points of view followed and expanded tendencies in the *Milligan* majority opinion, Frankfurter invoking the rules applicable short of extraconstitutional martial rule, Jackson, the rules of constitutionally unfounded and unfettered power.[47]

Thus, as to the answers to the questions posed by the Japanese American cases, the *Hirabayashi* and *Korematsu* cases are poles apart. In the *Hirabayashi* case, at least as to the doctrine announced, the wartime power of the military over civilians within the country was treated as part of the war-waging powers of the national government. It is accordingly both constitutionally derived and constitutionally limited. It may be exercised under the authority of Congress and the President when it is directed to an end within the war powers, when it is reasonably appropriate to the achievement of that end, and when it does not violate the civil and individual guarantees of the Constitution. The techniques of warfare do not alter these constitutional rules or the need for civil control. They do, however, affect the circumstances which are determinative of appropriateness. The *Korematsu* case uses *Hirabayashi* as a justifying foundation but shunts its doctrine aside. It turns to necessity, rather than to the Constitution, as the source and sole limitation of authority of the military; and, in view of the character and conditions of modern warfare, apparently would apply this rule whenever the nation is at war. Neither case discusses martial law, although in *Korematsu* it is apparently the basic conception underlying the outcome.

THE ALTERNATIVE ANSWERS EVALUATED

As against the doctrine of necessity, time has, if anything, sustained and strengthened the wisdom of the doctrine of the *Milligan* majority. This results from nothing so much as the very reason given for abandoning or modifying that doctrine: namely, the changed conditions of modern warfare. Total war, we are told, implies a degree of military control over civilians not hitherto imaginable, as a military matter of waging war successfully.[48] The need for the increased participation of the military in the regulation and administration of wide areas of national life, however, increases rather than decreases the necessity to retain normal judicial safeguards in the management of war and preparations for war. To allow this expansion of military activity under an expanded martial-law doctrine, with its lack of constitutional bases and limitations—justified, if at all, only under a conception severely limited to facts that overwhelm—is to create a breach in the Constitution, relax the constitutionally and democratically required judicial control of the military and cut down immeasurably the operative sphere of civil rights. It is virtually to surrender the government to the military in time of war, and perhaps even in time of international stress and national preparedness. Standards that make sense when the allowable area of military absolutism is very small and confined to an extreme exigency, make little sense indeed when the scope of military authority is extended to embrace areas which are only related to the war effort by the nature of total warfare. Martial rule accepted and applied in these circumstances represents the sort of military accretion of power apprehended and reprobated by Justice Davis. It is based upon the doctrine characterized by him as the most "pernicious . . . ever invented by the wit of man." The Japanese American program itself stands as a most

convincing modern example that Justice Davis' conception and words
have not been outmoded by time.

Lying between the *Korematsu* surrender to the military and the
Milligan majority's insistence on the application of constitutional
limitations (but far nearer to the former than to the latter) is the ground
taken by the *Milligan* minority. The most effective and forceful ex-
ponent of this position in recent years is Charles Fairman. In a much-
quoted article, he has stated the case thus:

> When one considers certain characteristics of modern war—mobility on land,
> surprise from the air, sabotage and the preparation of fifth columns, . . . the
> depth and disperson [of the army],—it must be apparent that the dictum that
> "martial rule cannot arise from a threatened invasion" is not an adequate
> definition of the extent of the war power of the United States. . . . It does not
> take an actual bombing of Pearl Harbor or a shelling of Santa Barbara to
> unchain the hands of the commander on the spot. Facts of this sort prove
> the reality of the danger, but the courts should be prepared to sustain vigilant
> precautions without waiting for such proof. The commander should not be
> put in a worse position legally because he has contrived to keep disaster at
> arm's length.
> The war power, distributed between Congress and the President, compre-
> hends all that is requisite to wage war successfully.[49]

In modern dress and in apter phrase, this is the position of the
Milligan minority. Its essential feature is not that the war power is
traced to a constitutional source, for the *Milligan* majority does that.
Rather, its essential feature is the broad field in which the suspension
of constitutional guarantees is allowed. That can be the only point to
allowing martial law in cases of threatened invasion; the *Milligan*
majority thought that ample power existed to prepare against and resist
threats of invasion, but maintained that within that range, the war
power was subject to constitutional limitations.

There can be no quarrel with the proposition that the war power
"comprehends all that is requisite to wage war successfully." That is a
virtual tautology. The critical question is: does waging war successfully,
in the circumstances envisioned, necessarily involve removing from the
hands of the commander on the spot the chains of the Constitution?
Under the *Milligan* rule, is such a commander "put in a worse position
legally because he has contrived to keep disaster at arm's length"? To
what extent is such a military commander hindered in his military
function by the constitutional machinery and requirements of criminal
justice; by the due-process and equal-protection requirements of fair
dealing and reasonable classification? Certainly, such a commander is
not "put in a worse position legally" if he has "contrived to keep dis-

aster at arm's length" by the preparation of shore defenses, the maintenance of air and naval patrols, the disposition and maneuvre of the men
and machines of war. It is only if the commander seeks to protect Pearl
Harbor and Santa Barbara from the threat of air delivered bombs and
submarine delivered shells by abolishing jury trial and the civil courts,
by doing away with confrontation of witnesses, immunity from self-
incrimination, counsel for the defense, and the other guarantees of the
Bill of Rights that the commander is "put in a worse position legally";
and these are not likely contrivances to keep that sort of disaster at arm's
length. Moreover, even when the bombs and shells are actually falling
rather than merely threatened, it does not automatically follow that
closing the courts or suspending constitutional rights will be a helpful
military measure or one calculated to improve the military situation.
If the bombs that are falling are atomic, they may blast whole districts
into perdition and along with them all civilian agencies. Such facts as
these raise constitutional questions about the meaning of "invasion"
amid the new methods of producing a civil-government vacuum, much
more than they justify overruling the dictum about threatened invasions. Whatever one might say about Pearl Harbor, the shelling of
Santa Barbara and the threat of other such acts along the coast left
the courts open and in the unobstructed exercise of their jurisdiction,
and left the civilian agencies in the unhindered performance of their
duties. What in these conditions would justify military trial of citizen
civilians or patently unreasonable and discriminatory classification? Can
we not be mindful of Fairman's admonition that we ought not legally
to place at a disadvantage the commander who by his vigilant precautions has kept disaster from our shores without, at the same time,
automatically concluding that everything the military does in a period
of possibly threatened invasion must be permitted, even at the expense of personal rights and civil liberties? Would all of the proper
functions of the military be impaired by a constitutional rule of reasonableness applied in a context of constitutional limitations and rights?

What the *Milligan* minority says in effect is that when Congress estab-
lishes martial law in the broad area in which it is permitted to do so,
constitutional rights lose their special weight. They are then of the
order of all other rights and interests. Military measures are to be
judged exclusively in the light of their military appropriateness. Their
constitutional validity does not depend upon whether they result in
an invasion of the most precious and basic rights of men or some mere
statutory privilege.[50] By this view, a military order which will accomplish
an end within the war power will be sustained no matter what rights of

civilians are destroyed thereby. Different degrees of military necessity will not be required to sustain curfew, evacuation, and detention, since distinctions based on the character of the rights invaded by the military order are immaterial.

Though this position does not surrender to the military with the abandon of the decision in the *Korematsu* case, one must still ask whether it too does not grant to the military more than is necessary to win wars.

Some phases of the *Milligan* majority doctrine, it would seem, require modification. These phases, however, do not directly involve the basic proposition of the normal subjection of the military to the Constitution. Nor do they involve directly the dictum about threatened invasions, so vigorously attacked by Fairman.[51] They do not even directly involve the techniques and character of modern warfare. They turn rather upon the mechanical appearance of the test applied and the rigid conception of constitutional rights and guarantees apparently entertained. Both must be modified to adjust to the modern view of the function of the court as judgmatic rather than automatic and to the modern view of constitutional rights and guarantees as relative rather than absolute.

Whether the martial-rule test of the *Milligan* majority is "mechanical" is of course a matter of intepretation. So long as the test is to be applied by the courts, its rigidity or flexibility will depend upon the attitude of the court in each particular case rather than upon anything in the nature of the test itself. Certainly, its use as an absolute command unrelated to a specific situation could not be defended. Properly construed the test presents a matter of fact, not of fiction; of substance, not of form. The question is whether the courts are open in the sense that they are able to function substantially in their usual way and with their usual degree of efficiency, not whether the courts are formally closed. In the words of Charles Evans Hughes in his 1917 war-powers address,

Certainly, the test should not be a mere physical one, nor should substance be sacrificed to form. The majority [in the Milligan case] recognized "a necessity to furnish a substitute for the civil authority," when overthrown, in order "to preserve the safety of the army and society." If this necessity actually exists it cannot be doubted that the power of the Nation is adequate to meet it, but the rights of the citizen may not be impaired by an arbitrary legislative declaration. Outside the actual theatre of war, and if, in a true sense, the administration of justice remains unobstructed, the right of the citizen to normal judicial procedure is secure.[52]

In present-day judicial discussion, constitutional rights are seldom described as fixed and immutable. They are viewed rather as conditional guarantees, dependent on time, place, and circumstance for their meaning and substance. The rights of life, liberty, and property, for example, guaranteed by the due-process clause of the Fifth and Fourteenth Amendments, and mainly at stake in the curfew, evacuation, and detention, have meaning in our law only to the extent that they are governed by the rule of reason. In fact, the due-process clauses are held to impose upon government little more than a rule of judicially determined reasonableness. Life, liberty, and property may all be taken away, singly or collectively, if the courts find an adequate or reasonable factual justification.

The First Amendment's rights, too, are conditional and dependent upon circumstances, as anyone may see who reads the line of cases from *Schenk*[53] to *Dennis*.[54] Even the relatively fixed criminal law procedural safeguards of the Fifth and Sixth Amendments and, for that matter, the Third Article's vesture of the judicial power in constitutional courts, are not absolutely applied. Still other rights, of course, are stated in qualified terms. Only "unreasonable searches and seizures" are forbidden by the Fourth Amendment.

The civil rights and guarantees of the Constitution are treated as a flexible but weighty set of values which must be thrown into the scale of every relevant decision. They may never be ignored, though they may be outbalanced. They should not and need not be withdrawn from consideration altogether because the times are militarily troubled and many programs are administered by uniformed men.

But if the restraints are not absolute, neither is the war power plenary; and certainly it is not self-contained and self-defining. It "comprehends all that is requisite to wage war successfully." But that is all. It is not a grant of authority to do all manner of irrelevant things. Actions taken under the war power may not be so arbitrary as to violate the due-process requirement. They may not be so lacking in clear and present danger as to violate First Amendment guarantees of speech, press, and assembly. Without emergency justification, they may not be so sweeping as to treat dissimilar things alike or so uneven as to treat similar things differently without violating the constitutional guarantee of equality. They may not interfere with the processes and jurisdiction of the civil courts in the absence of battlefield conditions.

Understood thus as modified to encompass a conception of constitutional rights and guarantees governed by the rule of reason and as expressive of a test governed by substance rather than form, the *Milligan-Hirabayashi* doctrine, now, as in the past—precisely because of the nature of total war and the need for an omnipresent military, and notwithstanding modern techniques of fighting--is the only hopeful path to the adjustment of military power and constitutional guarantees; to allowing the military such freedom of action as is necessary to preserve the nation and at the same time retaining democratic controls. That doctrine would subject the wartime power of the military to the same rule as a peacetime exertion of the war powers or any other power.

The *Milligan-Hirabayashi* doctrine might be restated thus: Even in time of global and total war, when the nation is straining every sinew on world-wide battle fronts, when invasion is threatened and island outposts have fallen or been crippled, when the waters offshore are infested with enemy submarines, the coastline itself shelled and remote parts of the mainland bombed—in circumstances such as these, the military, though its authority increases as military necessity increases, still must act within the confines of the Constitution and the safeguards of individual rights, at least with respect to civilians within the country. The military may take drastic measures, it may impose dimouts, brownouts, blackouts. It may restrict travel of all persons within given areas. It may evacuate all inhabitants from prospective landing beaches. It may take precautionary steps to protect power and water supplies and other public utilities or productive facilities. But these measures must be both appropriate to meet the emergency and reasonable in the circumstances. One part of the circumstances with respect to which reasonableness must be determined consists of the rights invaded and the interests disturbed. Consequently, a measure thoroughly appropriate to meet the emergency when only the military features are considered may not be reasonable in the circumstances when the constitutional rights of citizens are thrown into the balance. The effect of applying constitutional limitations and guarantees to wartime exertions of the war power is to add a determinative factor in selecting among measures all reasonably appropriate to meet a given military danger; it is to forbid the choice of militarily appropriate measures which displace civil government or invade civil rights if less civilly drastic but militarily adequate alternatives are available. Curfew may not be imposed if dimouts, with their less drastic invasions of the liberty of the citizen civilians, will serve the same military purpose. Exclusion of an individual from an entire military district may not be ordered if terminating his employment in war plants and access to military secrets will end his threat of harm. Evacuation of a portion of the population is forbidden if curfew is adequate to meet the danger, or, given the time, if individual hearing will identify the disloyal. Evacuation will not be tolerated at all if the basis of selection is a trait unrelated to the war objectives.

Of course, all or any of these measures will not be tolerated if there is no military peril, or if there is a military peril but the measures are not appropriate to meet it. Even in the absence of the specific limitations of the Constitution, the war power is, after all, only the power to wage war. Military necessity and military fiat are not necessarily identical. If they turn out not to be, the fiat is null.

Because the war power is a grant within the framework of a constitutional system in which power not granted is not possessed, because the war power is subject to the amendments and guarantees provided elsewhere in the Constitution, and because in our system the judges have become the final enforcers of constitutional allocations and limitations—the courts will sit in judgment on the military requirements of the hour, at least to the extent of determining whether the military judgment as to the existence of the emergency, the appropriateness of the means, and the necessity to invade civil rights which makes that invasion reasonable, have a substantial basis.

The program for the curfew and the evacuation of Japanese Americans during World War II—the very program before the court in the *Hirabayashi* and *Korematsu* cases—especially reveals the urgent reasons supplied by total war for applying the *Milligan-Hirabayashi* doctrine.

For the first two and a half months after Pearl Harbor, dangers of espionage, sabotage, and fifth-column activity thought to arise out of the presence of Japanese on the West Coast were within the jurisdiction of the Department of Justice. Under a plan prepared in advance, sizable numbers of Japanese American aliens, believed on some evidence to be dangerous or disloyal, were apprehended and detained. Enemy aliens, including Japanese, were subjected to travel restrictions, were required to surrender as contraband firearms and other weapons and certain radio and camera equipment. Enemy aliens were registered. In fact, the department, on recommendation of the Western Defense Command, established the first prohibited zones from which all enemy aliens were excluded.[55] These surrounded airports and airfields, hydroelectric dams, pumping and power plants, gas and electric works, harbor areas, and military installations. Restricted zones were established along the coast within which enemy aliens were curtailed as to travel and were curfewed. Executive Order 9066, signed on February 19, 1942, turned the whole matter over to the War Department. This was done with the concurrence of the Department of Justice because, (1) the department thought that further restrictive measures were unnecessary, (2) it was unwilling to extend restrictions to citizens on a discriminatory basis, and, (3) it lacked the staff and facilities to carry out any more far-

reaching project. The first two of these reasons justify adamant resistance to the proposal rather than concurrence in it; and the mere possession of the facilities by the War Department is hardly an argument
for undertaking the plan.

On March 24, 1942, the WDC issued a curfew order covering all persons of Japanese ancestry, and German and Italian aliens.[56] On March
27 it announced, and on March 30 actually began, the compulsory uprooting and removal of all Japanese Americans, herding them first into
assembly and then relocation centers.[57] Once the removal was accomplished, custodianship was given, at least in part, to the WRA, a civilian
agency. The actual process of removal could have been carried on as
well by the Department of Justice as by the Army if the former had had
the manpower, the disposition, and the barbed-wire enclosures. There
was nothing peculiarly military about the function. In performing it,
the WDC and the War Department were acting as an extended arm of
the FBI.

Why should not the action of the military in such cases be measured
by the same "conventional tests of constitutionality" which are applied
to civil government when doing identical tasks? Why is it "impracticable and dangerous idealism" to insist that tasks appropriately performed by the military in time of war—and when it has much of the
manpower and many of the facilities—but which are not peculiarly
military in character, conform to the standards exacted of civilians?
There is certainly little justification for the view that a military commander, even in carrying out such civilian tasks, should not, in the
words of Justice Jackson, be required to act like a "reasonable man," or
at least to act as much like a reasonable man as a civilian is required to.

MILLIGAN, ENDO, AND DETENTION

Under the doctrine of the *Milligan* majority, curfew and exclusion
would stand or fall upon their individual merits as particular exertions
of the war power, to be judged in the light of all relevant circumstances.
If there was a danger of invasion by the forces of Japan, if ethnic affiliation with the Japanese people determined the loyalty of American citizens, if the circumstances were such that persons loyal to Japan could
and were likely to perform acts helpful to Japan and harmful to us, if
curfew or exclusion as the chosen method of prevention was appropriate
to achieve that end, and, if, finally, there were no available alternative
methods of prevention which would accomplish the military objectives,
and, at the same time, be more consistent with the individual and civil
guarantees of the Constitution—then curfew and exclusion were con-

stitutionally authorized exercises of the national war power. If these conditions did not obtain, curfew and exclusion were unconstitutional both as going beyond the granted war power and as transcending the guarantees and prohibitions of the Constitution.

The same test must be applied to detention. If detention was an appropriate means for meeting an existing or imminently threatening peril and could not reasonably have been replaced by some other means less destructive of individual rights and civil guarantees, it too was a constitutional exercise of the nation's war power. With respect to the existence of danger and the likelihood that Japanese Americans would assist the forces of Imperial Japan, exactly the same factual inquiry was necessary for detention as for evacuation. But, with respect to the appropriateness of the means, detention was far more difficult to justify than evacuation, just as evacuation in turn had been far more difficult to justify than curfew. Not only was the deprivation of rights far more drastic, but as a method of preventing Japanese American collaboration with submarine-landed saboteurs, hit-and-run air raids, or with invasion itself, detention added little to evacuation. If exclusion was not only constitutional but also successful in keeping the Japanese Americans out of the coastal area, detention was entirely unnecessary for that purpose.

If detention had been intended as a device to facilitate the separation of the disloyal from the loyal, or if, though not itself helpful in the sifting process, it had been instituted as an intermediate makeshift arrangement pending sorting, the case for the constitutionality of detention would be placed on its strongest grounds. In that event, however, the duration of the incarceration would be a determinative factor. Detention for a few weeks, or, considering the size of the group, for two or three months, might have been held administratively necessary; but hardly the two and a half years which was the period of confinement for most excludees. Under such conditions a determination of loyalty should have been followed immediately by unconditional release, instead of the continued detention and conditional leave procedure actually enforced. However, it is clear from the facts that the plan for detention originated with the WRA and not with the military, that so-called voluntary migration was tried before the program of detention was initiated, and that no plan for the separation of the disloyal from the loyal was undertaken until about four months after assembly-center detention had begun—it is clear from these facts that incarceration was not originally intended as a step in or an aid to a process of sorting.

The historical fact is that segregation of the disloyal from the loyal came almost as an afterthought.

Whatever may be said of the military's participation in its legal authorization and in its execution, the program for the wartime detention of the Japanese American population resulted not from a judgment of military necessity made by the military but from a judgment of social desirability made by civilians.

A clearcut statement in General DeWitt's *Final Report* bears upon the attitude of the WDC toward the introduction of detention and the nonmilitary reasons for it:

Essentially, military necessity required only that the Japanese population be removed from the coastal area and dispersed in the interior ... That the evacuation program necessarily and ultimately developed into one of complete Federal supervision, was due primarily to the fact that the interior states would not accept an uncontrolled Japanese migration.[58]

The reasoning of the WRA is plainly set forth in a remarkable pamphlet prepared by WRA lawyers, and published over the signature of the Director of the WRA and the Secretary of the Interior.

Detention was a policy which the responsible officers of WRA decided upon reluctantly, out of a conviction that no other course was administratively feasible or genuinely open to them. The agitation for mass evacuation had repeatedly asserted that west coast residents of Japanese ancestry were of uncertain loyalty. The Government's later decision to evacuate was widely interpreted as proof of the truth of that assertion. Hence, a widespread demand sprang up immediately after the evacuation that the evacuees be kept under guard, or at the very least, that they be sorted and that the dangerous ones among them be watched and kept from doing harm. In these circumstances it was almost inescapable that the program administrator should come to the conclusion that if the right of free movement throughout the United States was to be purchased for any substantial number of the evacuees, the price for such purchase would have to be the detention of all the evacuees while they were sorted and classified, and then the continued detention of those found potentially dangerous to internal security. The detention policy of WRA was born out of a decision that this price would have to be paid, that it was better to pay this price than to keep all the evacuees in indefinite detention, and that to refuse to pay this price would almost certainly mean that the prevailing fear and distrust could not be reasoned with and could not be allayed.[59]

Speaking of the leave program, the pamphlet continued:

These conditions to departure—that the evacuee shall have been found to be non-dangerous to internal security, that he shall have a job or some other means of support, that there shall be "community acceptance" at his point of destination, and that he shall keep the Authority notified of his changes of address—represented, in fact, the heart of the relocation program. They were designed to make planned and orderly what must otherwise have been helter-skelter and spasmodic. . . .

If the constitutionality of the evacuation itself be assumed, the situation that was inevitably created by the evacuation does of itself give rise to new problems which Government must undertake to solve by appropriate means.

Thus, the conditions attached to departure from the centers enabled a sifting of a possibly questionable minority from the wholesome majority whose relocation it became the principal object of WRA to achieve. These restrictions enabled WRA to prepare public opinion in the communities to which the evacuees wished to go for settlement, so as to avoid violent incidents, public furor, possible retaliation against Americans in Japanese hands, and other evil consequences. The leave regulations "stemmed the flow"; they converted what might otherwise be a dangerously disordered flood of unwanted people into unprepared communities into a steady, orderly, planned migration into communities that gave every promise of being able to amalgamate the newcomers without incidents, and to their mutual advantage. The detention, in other words, was regarded as a necessary incident to this vital social planning.[60]

Even as to the disloyal, detention was not justified as a means of preventing them from committing acts harmful to the war effort.

WRA took the position that it sought to detain those deemed ineligible to leave until after all those deemed eligible had been relocated. Such detention, it maintained, was necessary to build upon public acceptance of those found eligible to relocate. The detention was thus regarded as an essential step in the accomplishment of the relocation objective. Since the war ended before relocation of the eligibles had been completed, the Government never had to face the question of whether it could or would attempt to detain those deemed ineligible after the relocation objective had been fully achieved.[61]

The only course "genuinely open" or "administratively feasible"; the purchase price for "the right of free movement"; "a method of allaying popular fear and distrust"; "a necessary incident to . . . vital social planning"; "an essential step in the accomplishment of the relocation objective"—these are hardly the categorical imperatives of military necessity. They are the social desiderata of welfare planners.

In the *Korematsu* case the court passed upon the constitutionality of evacuation after declaring it to be separable from assembly-center detention. The court indicated, however, that if detention were not separable from evacuation, if detention was the means for executing evacuation, the detention would be constitutional. Said Justice Black for the majority: "The Assembly Center was conceived as a part of the machinery for group evacuation. The power to exclude includes the power to do it by force if necessary. And any forcible measure must necessarily entail some degree of detention or restraint whatever method of removal is selected."[62]

No doubt assembly centers might reasonably be instituted "as a part of the machinery for group evacuation." As such, they would serve as control points or check stations to make certain that the excludees were actually departing from the area. Once having the excludees in the assembly centers for this purpose, the government might reasonably convert the centers into permanent shelters for those who, whatever their reasons, did not wish to disperse in the interior; and the government might lay down appropriate rules of notice and sign-out prior to departure from the shelters. But control-point processing would have warranted compulsory confinement for a few days, or, at the most, a few weeks. Assembly-center detention lasted months and did not end in dispersal in the interior or a voluntary decision to remain in a government provided shelter. The assembly centers were in fact prisons and could never be properly compared to refuges—for, say, flood victims—for which the government might reasonably establish regulations governing entry and departure. Moreover, they were not so much "part of the machinery for group evacuation" as they were part of the machinery for further detention. Confinement in the assembly centers was simply a prelude to more confinement in the relocation centers. The court's analysis in the *Korematsu* case, although perhaps a reasonable statement of the general principle, had little relevance to the facts there presented.

The issue of relocation-center detention was squarely and unavoidably presented to the court in the *Endo* case.

Mitsuye Endo was an American citizen of Japanese ancestry, 22 years old, who prior to the evacuation was a civil service employee of the State of California. Her brother Kunio was serving in the United States Army. On May 14, 1942, she was ordered to an assembly center from which she was sent to the Tule Lake Relocation Center. On July 13, 1942, she petitioned for a writ of habeas corpus to seek freedom from Tule Lake. The United States district court signed a brief order declaring (1) that Endo was not entitled to the writ and (2) that she had not exhausted her administrative remedies because she had not sought to secure her release under WRA regulations. On February 19, 1943, she appealed from the district court's decision. Later in the same month the WRA granted leave clearance but Endo made no application for indefinite leave. The circuit court certified four questions to the Supreme Court on April 22, 1944:

1. May an American citizen be held in a concentration camp without the right to a hearing which has all the elements of due process merely because such citizen is of Japanese ancestry?

2. May a loyal citizen be so confined until she satisfies the WRA that she can support herself and receive assistance in the community where she desires to live?

3. May such issues of self-support and community acceptance be decided by the WRA without a hearing at which the citizen enjoys all the elements of due process?

4. May the WRA in addition require that she report after she has left the camp?

The Supreme Court held that Endo had to be given her liberty. The WRA, the court said, had "no authority to subject citizens who are concededly loyal to its leave procedure"[63] or to detain them or release them conditionally. Any power of detention possessed by the WRA, the court argued, would have had to be received by redelegation from General DeWitt of powers conferred on him under Executive Order 9066 and Public Law 503. Executive Order 9102, establishing the WRA, was issued only to implement the measures already authorized by Executive Order 9066. These two executive orders, the act of Congress, and the pertinent legislative history do not "use the language of detention."[64] Hence, the authority to detain, if it existed, must be implied. And "any such implied power must be entirely confined to the precise purpose of the evacuation program . . . if there is to be the greatest possible accommodation of the liberties of the citizen with this war measure."[65]

The "single aim" of Executive Orders 9066 and 9102 and Public Law 503, said Justice Douglas for the court,

was the protection of the war effort against espionage and sabotage . . . detention which has no relationship to that objective is unauthorized. . . . A citizen who is concededly loyal presents no problem of espionage and sabotage.

Nor may the power to detain an admittedly loyal citizen or to grant him a conditional release be implied as a useful or convenient step in the evacuation program, whatever authority might be implied in case of those whose loyalty was not conceded or established. . . . Community hostility even to loyal evacuees may have been (and perhaps still is) a serious problem. But if authority for their custody and supervision is to be sought on that ground, the Act of March 21, 1942, Executive Order 9066, and Executive Order 9102, offer no support. . . . To read them that broadly would be to assume that the Congress and the President intended that this discriminatory action should be taken against these people wholly on account of their ancestry even though the government conceded their loyalty to this country.[66]

Thus, in the *Endo* case, the Supreme Court invalidated relocation-center detention for persons whose loyalty was granted and who therefore were clearly held in confinement or subjected to leave procedures and conditional release for social rather than for military reasons. The ground for the action was that WRA and the WDC lacked authority to make such detentions under the pertinent executive orders and congressional legislation. The majority of the court steadfastly declined to place its holding upon a constitutional basis, though some of the reasons given for confining the executive orders and legislation to a narrow scope were equally, if not more, compulsive of a constitutional negative on the program. The court, however, was content to refer to the relevant constitutional provisions "not to stir the constitutional issues which have been argued at the bar but to indicate the approach which we think should be made to an act of Congress or an order of the Chief Executive that touches the sensitive area of rights specifically guaranteed by the Constitution."[67]

If the broad doctrine enunciated in the *Milligan* case and subsequently repeated but not followed in the *Hirabayashi* case were to be applied, it is difficult to see how the detention of a concededly loyal citizen, not charged and convicted of crime, could escape constitutional condemnation. Certainly, such detention cannot constitutionally be justified as "a necessary incident" of "vital social planning" or as the purchase price "of the right of free movement throughout the United States . . . for any substantial number of the evacuees." Rendering "planned and orderly what must otherwise [be] helter-skelter and spasmodic" is not a power conferred by the Constitution on the national government; and the purchase price of the right of free movement of citizens was paid a long time ago, when the right was embodied in the Constitution. To exact a new purchase price, in these circumstances, would ordinarily go by the name of extortion. Imprisonment of a hapless racial minority as an element in "vital social planning" for the improvement of race relations hardly seems a promising approach either to the Constitution or to the problem of race relations. Mass and racially discriminatory incarceration of well over 100,000 persons as a result of "vital social planning" to protect them against community hostility is the compulsory acceptance of an unwanted benefit which can be constitutionally justified, if at all, not in terms of the good done for the victims but in terms of the interests of society. In the words of Miss Dembitz, "the theme of benefaction which runs through the utterances of the military as well as, subsequently, of the War Relocation Authority, may have given the officials involved a feeling of satisfaction, it does not make the deprivations and restraints imposed on the donees any more constitutional."[68] Detention of the entire group while they were being sorted and classified as to loyalty, justified not on military grounds but as a means of reasoning with and allaying "prevailing popular fear and distrust"; detention of disloyals, not in order to prevent activities harmful to the war efforts, but "as necessary to build public acceptance of those found eligible to relocate," and thus "as an essential step in the accomplishment of the relocation objective"—these are merely variants of the selfsame protective custody argument that "it was all for their own good." As such, they stand upon the same constitutional footing as the detention of concededly loyal citizens pending efforts by the WRA "to prepare public opinion in the communities to which the evacuees wished to go." Detaining disloyal persons for the reasons given, however, could not even be rested on the spurious ground that it was for their own benefit since their detention was for the benefit of the members of the group who were eligible for leave.

If detention is to be sustained against a claim of unconstitutionality on any of the grounds advanced by the WDC or the WRA it must be on the ground that protective custody is a reasonable method for preventing disturbances of such a character or extent as to interfere with the prosecution of the war. Evaluated in these terms, the program would have had to hurdle a number of serious obstacles. What was the likelihood of such disturbances in the interior? General DeWitt's *Final Report* contains no assessment. The WRA produced none supported by fact. Could such threat as existed have been subdued by reasonably vigorous precautionary action on the part of local police backed up by firm statements from the War Department that the measures taken by it were adequate to prevent espionage and sabotage and that lawless acts against the migrants would be punished? Normally, of course, efforts to prevent violence center about those likely to perpetrate it rather than about its prospective victims. Also bearing upon the existence of the danger and its degree is the fact that all of the evidence tends to show that, had assembly and relocation centers been shelters rather than prisons, there would still have been no "dangerously disordered flood of unwanted people into unprepared communities." The Japanese Americans themselves would understandably not have been anxious to rush into hostile communities. Having been completely uprooted, many would prefer to sit out the war in government supplied refuges. Still others, possessed of more initiative and adjustive capacity, would lack the means to go and establish themselves in new communities. All but a very few, if they left the shelters at all, would in all likelihood have been anxious to avail themselves of government proffered assistance to assure "migration into communities that gave every promise of being able to amalgamate the newcomers without incidents and to their mutual advantage." In that event, the movement, though not proceeding out of compulsory confinement, would, because of the self-interest of the group affected, have been planned and orderly. That detention was necessary to the accomplishment of these objectives, even assuming the constitutionality of the objectives, is consequently far from established.

The narrow rule, or holding, of the *Milligan* case also stands squarely against the constitutionality of the detention imposed on the Japanese Americans.

Justice Davis' opinion, in substance, was that the judicial and jury trials prescribed by the Constitution do not unreasonably interfere with the prosecution of war and their abolition is not reasonably appropriate to its conduct, unless the area is a battlefield where, constitutionally, the military is supreme, not by the Constitution but by compelling fact. Accordingly, except on such battlefields, the military may not arrest, try, and punish citizen civilians within the country.

Suppose the military arrests and confines without trial. Suppose, further, that the military is aided in accomplishing detention by a civilian agency. Suppose, finally, that the persons so arrested and imprisoned are not guilty or even charged with being guilty of any crime at the common law, by the statutes of the country, or by the laws of war. In all three of these respects—true of the mass detention of Japanese Americans—the situation differed from that presented to the court in the *Milligan* case. Would these be grounds for a different decision or would they merely make the unconstitutionality of the action more apparent?

Remarkable as it may seem, the court in the *Endo* case relied on the absence of a military trial and the presence of civil participation and sanctions as bases for distinguishing and refusing to apply the *Milligan* rule.

We do not have here [said Justice Douglas for the court] a question such as was presented in Ex parte Milligan...or in Ex parte Quirin...where the jurisdiction of military tribunals to try persons according to the law of war was challenged in *habeas corpus* proceedings. Mitsuye Endo is detained by a civilian agency, the War Relocation Authority, not by the military. Moreover, the evacuation program was not left exclusively to the military; the Authority was given a large measure of responsibility for its execution and Congress made its enforcement subject to civil penalties by the Act of March 21, 1942. Accordingly, no questions of military law are involved.[69]

To Justice Douglas' list of the civil elements in the detention program should be added other items, in addition to the administrative role of the WRA and the civil sanctions under Public Law 503. As we have already pointed out, there was nothing peculiarly military about the operation of the whole program. That the decision to undertake the program itself was not strictly military is plain from General DeWitt's *Final Report*. Moreover, such steps as were taken in the total process by the Army were taken under the supervision and approval of the civilian heads of the War Department. They in turn acted under the authority of Executive Order 9066 and Public Law 503. The WRA itself and the detention camps were established by Executive Order 9102 and the civilian head of the WRA was appointed by the President. Finally, the WRA did not justify detention on grounds of military necessity, but on grounds of desirable social policy.

All of these civilian elements, however, though they existed and need to be given their due weight, do not warrant Justice Douglas' subordination of the part actually played by the military authorities. The original decision to evacuate was made by military authorities. They first made the decision to carry out evacuation on a voluntary basis, that is, leaving to the individual the choice of route, means, and destination. They later made the decision to change to a compulsory and controlled exodus. They issued all of the one hundred and eight civilian-exclusion orders which marked the step-by-step progress of the evacuation. These were published in the form of military commands and were widely publicized and understood as such. Transportation of the victims from gathering places to assembly centers was under armed military guard. The assembly centers were run by the military and armed military personnel were abundantly in evidence. Conveyance from assembly centers to relocation centers was also under military auspices and guard. At the relocation centers, the administration was civilian and some of the guards had different uniforms. Law and order were maintained within the camps in ordinary circumstances by WRA personnel. Military police, however, were at the gates to prevent unauthorized ingress and egress. At Camp Gila in the summer of 1943 they shot and killed a Nisei who strayed outside the barbed wire. Everybody understood that disturbances which could not be quelled by center authorities would bring the troops. At Tule Lake, that is exactly what happened. Following a riot—or near riot—the Army took over and actually ran the center from November 4, 1943 to January 15, 1944.[70] It was the military which suppressed the Manzanar riot of early December, 1942. The Army stood ready to intervene in the Poston disturbance of November 18, 1942, but the project director thought such intervention unnecessary. All of the relocation centers, including that in far-off and unindustrialized Arkansas, were declared by the military to be military areas.[71] This made the civil sanctions of Public Law 503 applicable—which could only be done, under Executive Order 9066, by the Secretary of War or by commanding generals, not by the WRA. By a series of orders issued by General DeWitt and by the War Department for the four camps outside of the WDC evacuees were forbidden to leave their relocation centers or their work sites except with written permission.[72] Evacuees granted indefinite or other leaves remained "in the constructive custody of the military commander."[73] The Joint Army-Navy Board, from January, 1943, to April, 1944, investigated individuals in the camps, held hearings and made recommendations to the civil administration concerning leave clearances.[74] The WDC alone could rescind the civilian-exclusion orders and proclamations. A word from it or the War Department could have brought the whole program, including the detention, to an end, conditionally or unconditionally. And that is what happened finally.

Thus, the total program of exclusion and detention began with a military order, continued during the pleasure of the military, and was terminable at the will of the military. It included the physical removal of the victims by the military. It proceeded with their incarceration in camps run by the military. It ended, for thousands of American citizens, in three years of imprisonment, the prisons being located in places designated as military areas in order to assure adequate military authority and controls, and being manned by administrators and jailers maintained in their positions at times by the active presence of troops and always with troops in the background. Throughout the process, the sounds and trappings of the military were to be heard and seen.

Yet, said Justice Douglas, there are here "no questions of military law" and the *Milligan* case is not in point! Military arrest and military confinement, says the *Milligan* case, cannot be tolerated while the courts are open. In the Japanese American cases, there was such military arrest. There was also militarily enforced and militarily terminable confinement. Surely the ground can not be taken that military arrest and imprisonment which flout the Constitution when connected with a military trial become constitutional when executed without such a trial. Surely, also, the ground can not be taken that such arrest and imprisonment lose their military character by having behind them the added sanction of civil imprisonment or when the jail is run by civilians.

The differences between *Milligan* and *Endo* advanced by Justice Douglas serve no purpose quite so much as that of making clearer the unconstitutionality of the Endo detention. To say otherwise is to say that in this context a military order has a constitutional significance different from the action of a military tribunal; or that imprisonment by civilians stands in a better constitutional position than imprisonment by the military, which, after all, is permissible in some circumstances.

CONCLUSION

The Japanese American cases—*Hirabayashi, Korematsu,* and *Endo*— though shrouded in great confusion of rhetoric, and despite the careful statement of doctrine by Chief Justice Stone in *Hirabayashi* (which he himself failed to apply), represent a constitutional yielding to the awe inspired in all men by total war and the new weapons of warfare. They disclose a judicial unwillingness to interfere with—or even to look upon—the actions of the military taken in time of global war, even to the extent of determining whether those actions are substantially or somehow connected with the prosecution of the war. That the actions were directed to and drastically affected citizen civilians within the country and involved decisions, policies, and administration dominantly civil rather than military, were facts that were hardly noticed, let alone assigned their proper significance. In this context, the Japanese American cases diminish and render uncertain the public responsibility of the military and relax democratic and judicial controls. In these cases, the historically established balance between the military and the civil— constitutionally sanctified in the United States by the classic majority opinion in *Ex parte Milligan*—has been shifted dangerously to the side of the military by the known and unknown terrors of total war and by a quiescent and irresolute judiciary. In them, the *Milligan* rule of subordination of the military to the Constitution except in battlefield conditions is abandoned. Instead, the national war powers, though explicitly conferred by the Constitution and not exempted from its limitations, are founded on and circumscribed by a military estimate of military necessity. Citizens, on a mass basis, were allowed to be uprooted, removed and imprisoned by the military without trial, without attribution of guilt, without the institutional or individual procedural guarantees of Article Three and Amendments Five and Six, and without regard to the individual guarantees of Amendments One, Four, Five, and others. The military action was taken upon a mere suspicion of disloyalty arising from racial affinity with the enemy, and was applied discriminatorily to one race only. During most of the period of evacuation and detention, there was not even a threat of invasion. The *Milligan* dissenters do not go nearly so far. Can circumstances short of battlefield conditions justify this kind of surrender of the Constitution

to the generals? Does the winning of total war require so much—that
the military be immune from review in its civil, sociological, and
anthropological judgment; that the military be allowed to do militarily
irrelevant things; that the military be permitted arbitrarily and unnecessarily to invade individual and civil rights? One may insist with
Charles E. Hughes that "the power to wage war is the power to wage
war successfully"[75] and that "that power, explicitly conferred and
absolutely essential to the safety of the Nation, is not destroyed or impaired by any later provision of the Constitution or by any one of the
amendments";[76] one may insist on all that and yet at the same time not
deviate from the basic proposition—equally plain if not equally explicit in the Constitution and "absolutely essential" to the perpetuation
of the republic—that the war power, when exerted in the military government of citizen civilians within the country, does not exist in the
absence of a grave military peril, does not exceed measures reasonably
appropriate to cope with that peril, and does not comprehend violations
of civil and individual guarantees of the Constitution in the presence
of a militarily adequate alternative.

Chapter VII

THE EQUAL PROTECTION
OF THE LAWS

The extent and nature of the wartime power of the military over civilians within the country are complex and difficult questions even when no problem of discrimination is involved. That private rights in time of war need not be treated with the solicitude constitutionally vouchsafed to them in time of peace—that indeed such rights may be invaded so far as necessary to wage war successfully are corollaries of the right of national self-preservation. Rights of speech, religion, assembly, private property, fair trial, unrestricted locomotion, home, residence, livelihood; all must yield to the demands of defense and the prosecution of war. But how far they must yield, in what circumstances and according to what tests present the complexity and difficulty. It is not hard to imagine war conditions which would justify the imposition of a curfew during the hours of darkness or even the establishment of prohibited zones, provided that all inhabitants are treated alike. When to such limitations of freedom and constitutional rights, however, is added an element of discrimination, and above all, when that discrimination is based upon race or ancestry, then the question of the power of the military over civilians within the country is raised in its sharpest form. This was, of course, the very element added to the West Coast curfew and evacuation.[1] It was also the very element most prominent in the other two major cases arising out of the Japanese American episode of World War II: *Oyama* v. *California*,[2] involving the stepped-up wartime enforcement of the Alien Land Laws of California; and *Takahashi* v. *Fish and Game Commission*,[3] involving the exclusion of persons ineligible to citizenship from commercial fishing privileges in coastal waters.

These four cases—*Hirabayashi, Korematsu, Oyama,* and *Takahashi*—taken as a group, present, therefore, the problem of the meaning of the due-process and equal-protection guarantees of the Fifth[4] and Four-

---

[1] For notes to chapter vii see pp. 386–393.

teenth Amendments.[5] They present that problem, moreover, outside the more familiar Negro-White context within which the separate-but-equal interpretation became established. The context is largely free of the constitutional tradition of the toleration of a policy of segregation. In this sense the court had a fresh opportunity to examine and face the implications of a racial classification.

The four cases cover two quite different situations: a conflict between military action taken under the war powers and the Fifth Amendment, and between state police-power action and the Fourteenth Amendment. The fact that the court sustained the federal war-power action and struck down the state police-power action is not based on any distinction drawn by the court between the meaning of the Fifth and the Fourteenth Amendments. The court makes it plain that it regards the due process of the Fifth Amendment as forbidding discriminatory classification in much the same way as does the equal-protection clause of the Fourteenth Amendment. It of course recognized that the Fifth Amendment contains no equal-protection clause and "restrains only such discriminatory legislation by Congress as amounts to a denial of due process."[6] But its subsequent treatment of the *Hirabayashi* and *Korematsu* cases in no way rests upon the distinction between the two clauses; in fact, the court virtually says that discriminatory action which would amount to a denial of equal protection would be a violation of due process.

Distinctions between citizens [said Chief Justice Stone in the *Hirabayashi* case] solely because of their ancestry are by their very nature odious to a free people whose institutions are founded upon the doctrine of equality. For that reason, legislative classification or discrimination based on race alone has often been held to be a denial of equal protection. ... We may assume that these considerations would be controlling here were it not for the fact that the danger of espionage and sabotage, in time of war and of threatened invasion, calls upon the military authorities to scrutinize every relevant fact bearing on the loyalty of populations in the danger areas.[7]

The problem of whether the curfew and evacuation cases violated the constitutional requirement of equal treatment revolves about these questions: (1) Was the purpose or intent itself discriminatory? (2) Was the classification overinclusive? (3) If so was it justified by emergency? (4) Did an adequate but less drastic alternative exist? (5) Was the classification underinclusive?[8]

DISCRIMINATORY PURPOSE

Did General DeWitt order the exclusion of all Americans of Japanese ancestry in response to popular clamor based upon the long-standing anti-Oriental stereotype activated by the war? Did he issue the order because economic pressure groups and politicians were able to convince him that it would be to the economic or political advantage of themselves or the West Coast? Did he do it as an expression of his own race prejudice aided or not aided by popular, group, or individual pressures? If the answer to any or all of these questions is yes, the evacuation doubtless was unconstitutional. "Our task would be simple, our duty clear," said Justice Black in the *Korematsu* case, "were this a case involving the imprisonment of a loyal citizen in a concentration camp because of racial prejudice."[9] The same would be true had this been a case in which the purpose of the action was private gain, group advantage, or other purpose irrelevant to an objective within the scope of a constitutionally granted power.

What is at stake here is a man's motive, intention, aim. As evidence about them the action taken in this case was completely ambiguous, the discriminatory curfew and evacuation being consistent both with the proper and the improper motive. The popular clamor for restriction and removal of the group did exist. That General DeWitt acted in response to these proddings or for reasons other than those believed by him in good faith to be related to public safety and military security, however, is altogether without substantiation. The most damning evidence against General DeWitt consists of his own statements. These naturally can be expected to be self-serving. Because of their unblushing candor, they are, however, also self-revealing to a surprising extent. They are in the nature of admissions against interest and should be given the credence due such. General DeWitt's request to the War Department for authority on February 14, 1942, contains this remarkable statement:

In the war in which we are now engaged racial affinities are not severed by migration. The Japanese race is an enemy race and while many second and third generation Japanese, born on United States soil, possessed of United States citizenship, have become "Americanized," the racial strains are undiluted.... It, therefore, follows that along the vital Pacific Coast over 112,000 potential enemies, of Japanese extraction, are at large today.[10]

In the face of this openly admitted and specifically avowed race prejudice, Justice Black in the *Korematsu* case unequivocally asserts: "Korematsu was not excluded from the Military Area because of hostility to him or his race."[11] "The judgment that exclusion of the whole group was ... a military imperative answers the contention that the exclusion was in the nature of group punishment based on antagonism to those of Japanese origin."[12] Earlier, and before General DeWitt's

Report had come out, Chief Justice Stone, in the *Hirabayashi* case, had somewhat less explicitly disavowed race prejudice as the motivation. Justice Douglas in his concurring opinion had found it necessary to "credit the military with as much good faith . . . as we would any other public official acting pursuant to his duties."[13] Even Justice Murphy, also in justifying his concurrence stated: "It is not to be doubted that the action taken by the military commander . . . was taken in complete good faith and in the firm conviction that it was required by considerations of public safety and military security."[14]

These statements show both that members of the court believed that to affirm good faith is to disavow prejudice and that the notion of prejudiced action is not without ambiguity.

Two senses of the term prejudice in the *Korematsu* case must be distinguished: (1) Prejudice as antipathy and (2) prejudice as belief. When Justice Murphy, for example, in his *Korematsu* dissent characterizes General DeWitt's action as based upon "erroneous assumption of racial guilt,"[15] and "questionable racial and sociological grounds" such as that all Japanese are "subversive" members of an "enemy race" and thus "potential enemies,"[16] he is not demonstrating that General DeWitt was indulging in his antipathies and thus not acting in good faith to provide for security. Justice Murphy is simply showing that General DeWitt had certain beliefs about the Japanese which are often perhaps associated with antipathy but do not essentially imply it. This is quite different from such statements as that quoted by Justice Murphy: "We're charged with wanting to get rid of the Japs for selfish reasons. We do. . . . And we don't want them back when the war ends, either."[17] The point of the distinction between prejudice as antipathy and as belief is that the court in denying that General DeWitt acted out of prejudice is denying only that he acted out of antipathy—out of hatred, vengeance, or for selfish reasons. The court is not denying that he held prejudiced or erroneous beliefs.

The equal-protection requirement, so far as it bears on discriminatory purpose, forbids or invalidates actions which are thus ill-motivated. It requires that the action be directed at a legitimate public purpose within the constitutional power granted— that it be an action taken in good faith—not that it be based on valid beliefs. On the evidence available, the worst that can be said about General DeWitt is that he entertained palpably false and untenable beliefs about race and biology. There is no evidence but that he acted with an upright motive aimed at a constitutional and public purpose. The nondiscriminatory purpose demanded by equal protection is a measure of knavery, not of folly.

OVERINCLUSIVE CLASSIFICATION

In other areas of equal protection, however, the measure is one of folly.

Granting the legitimacy of General DeWitt's purpose, the next phase of the equal-protection problem requires a judgment as to the reasonable relation between the classification adopted and the purpose. We must assume that race and ancestry are not absolutely forbidden classifying traits, that they may be relevant in some circumstances and to some purposes. As Chief Justice Stone pointed out in the *Hirabayashi* case: because racial classifications "are in most circumstances irrelevant and therefore prohibited,"[18] it does not follow that in dealing with the perils of war the appropriate authorities "are wholly precluded from taking into account those facts and circumstances which are relevant to measures for our national defense . . . and which may in fact place citizens of one ancestry in a different category from others."[19]

Taking the purpose of the curfew and evacuation programs to be defense against espionage and sabotage, the questions then become: What is the relation between the class of Americans of Japanese ancestry and the class of persons likely to commit espionage and sabotage? Is Japanese ancestry so related to the commission of, or likelihood of committing, espionage and sabotage as to justify or make reasonable the curfew and evacuation of all persons having such ancestry? On the face of it, the classification is unreasonably overinclusive. Few believe that the classes were identical—that all Americans of Japanese ancestry were likely to commit acts of espionage and sabotage. Only if there were evidence that some Japanese Americans were likely to commit such acts, and the number of such persons likely to do so was greater than in other groups of the population, and only if, in addition, the emergency were of such a character as to make up for the difference between the number likely to commit such acts and the total group, and to prevent the use of alternative but less drastic remedies—only in these circumstances could the classification be justified.

In the *Hirabayashi* case, Chief Justice Stone declared: "We cannot reject as unfounded the judgment of the military authorities and of Congress that there were disloyal members of that population."[20] In refusing to repudiate the classification as unconstitutional, he pointed to the concentration of Japanese Americans on the Pacific Coast and near Seattle, Portland, and Los Angeles with their military installations, shipyards, and aircraft factories; to their group solidarity and failure to assimiliate; to their Japanese-language schools; to their tendency to return to Japan for all or a part of their education; "to the maintenance by Japan of its system of dual citizenship";[21] to the maturity and "positions of influence in Japanese communities"[22] of the one-third of the Japanese Americans who were aliens; and to the "association of influential Japanese residents with Japanese Consulates"[23]—all as "data" "reasonably" warranting the conclusion of "continued attachment of members of this group to Japan and Japanese institutions."[24]

Have these data been established by competent scholars or other investigators who have directly studied the Japanese American population? Does the conclusion "reasonably" follow? Do the data show a correlation between Japanese ancestry and disloyalty to the United States, especially the active disloyalty required to commit acts of espionage and sabotage? Or are they, as has been said, merely "widely held suspicions such as may be possessed by every group of society with respect to every other group?"[25]

Geographical distribution.—Some of these facts or opinions are more easily challengeable than others as "data" warranting the inference of disloyalty of some of the members of the group.

Among the least tenable is the inference from geographical distribution. It is true that Chief Justice Stone does not explicitly draw that inference. He merely points to the well-established facts that there were 126,000 persons of Japanese ancestry in the United States; that of these about 112,000 lived in California, Oregon, and Washington; and that "the great majority . . . were concentrated in or near three of the large cities, Seattle, Portland and Los Angeles, all in Military Area No. 1."[26] As thus presented the argument drawn from geographical distribution is not an inference of disloyal design from location. It is simply, in effect, an assertion that if members of the group were disloyal and desired to commit acts of espionage and sabotage their location made it possible for them to do so. Of this there can be little doubt. The same of course was also true of all other persons living in or near Seattle, Portland, and Los Angeles. In this form, the argument has no bearing whatever on loyalty and cannot in the slightest degree aid in sustaining the conclusion of "continued attachment . . . to Japan and Japanese institutions."

It is significant, however, that Chief Justice Stone's remarks about geographical distribution are made immediately following statements about the fifth-column lessons taught by the German invasion of Western Europe and the effectiveness of espionage "by persons in sympathy with the Japanese Government"[27] in the surprise attack upon Pearl Harbor. General DeWitt's *Final Report* contains no such subtlety. In it, the Japanese Americans were not merely geographically distributed: they were "disposed" or "deployed."[28] Their places of settlement were not determined by normal, economic, geographic, and social forces; they were purposely selected.

The principal evidence for this position consisted of a set of maps purporting to show the location of Japanese Americans in relation to war facilities. The maps were prepared by county officials in California in conjunction with the state attorney general's office. They were submitted to the Tolan Committee with an explanation by the attorney general of California.[29] That explanation was copied practically verbatim, without credit of authorship, in General DeWitt's *Final Report.*[30]

According to the attorney general it was "more than just accident"[31] that these maps showed that many Japanese lived near strategic facilities. According to General DeWitt "it seems . . . beyond doubt" that the presence of the Japanese "was not mere coincidence."[32] They both thought it strange that "airplane manufacturing plants should be entirely surrounded by Japanese land occupancies . . . more than circumstance that after certain Government air bases were established Japanese undertook farming operations in close proximity to them."[33] Their conclusion was:

Notwithstanding the fact that the county maps showing the location of Japanese lands have omitted most coastal defenses and war industries, still it is plain from them that in our coastal counties, from Point Reyes south, virtually every feasible landing beach, airfield, railroad, highway, power house, power line, gas storage tank, gas pipe line, oil field, water reservoir or pumping plant, water conduit, telephone transmission line, radio station, and other points of strategic importance have several—and usually a considerable number—of Japanese in their immediate vicinity. The same situation prevails in all of the interior counties that have any considerable Japanese population.[34]

These maps were prepared in the early weeks of the war as part of a plan of state and county law-enforcement officials to remove Japanese Americans from the neighborhood of important installations by activating prosecutions under the California Alien Land Law. This purpose controlled the character of the maps and rendered them useless as support for the conclusion now reached. The maps show the location of only those Japanese having "land occupancies" and then only if the land occupied was near a strategic facility. The maps "omitted most coastal defenses and war industries": whether this was done because no Japanese land occupancies were near them is not revealed. Accordingly, the only conclusion that could legitimately be drawn from them is that some Japanese Americans lived near strategic facilities and some strategic facilities were located near Japanese land occupancies. Presumably, however, most of the farming population of the state lives near a "power line, . . . water conduit, telephone transmission line," or a "railroad or highway." It is the nature of such facilities to be near their users. And in California, especially in truck farming, the farmer who does not get water from a water conduit or who does not use electricity to pump it himself, or who does not use the highways and railroads to market his crops, is not likely to remain a farmer very long. Many if not most of these and other installations, especially military installations and war-production facilities, were built long after the settlement of the Japanese. In Southern California, for instance, Japanese had farmed at Signal Hill near Long Beach for years before oil was discovered there. The Los Angeles muncipal airport, the Northrup and the North American air-craft plants were built in the midst of the extensive Japanese truck farming area near Hawthorne and Inglewood. In some cases where oil and electric installations preceded the Japanese the companies concerned especially encouraged Japanese American farmers to work land on the rights of way and between the oil derricks. This the Japanese Americans were willing and able to do because of the nature of their farming operations.

The case for the proposition that the Japanese Americans were "deployed" for military and subversive purposes rather than that they settled as other immigrants did because of normal economic, social, and historical forces is completely without scientific substantiation. The truth is that no complete and systematic study of the geographical distribution of the Japanese Americans and the reasons for it has ever been made. Yet the United States Supreme Court plainly implies and General DeWitt expressly asserts that the Japanese Americans were "deployed"; were purposefully "disposed."

The Tolan Committee, basing its judgment on census reports, concluded that "the main geographic pattern of the Japanese population in California was pretty well fixed by 1910" and the main reason for concentration was economic.[85] Such studies as have been made of particular areas support this verdict.[86] And there can be no doubt that all of the new war-production facilities of World War II were located after the settlement of the Japanese Americans.

Japanese-language schools.—Equally without supporting evidence is the conclusion of disloyalty by virtue of attendance at Japanese-language schools. Chief Justice Stone in the *Hirabayashi* case referred to popular belief rather than fact in observing that "some of these schools are generally believed to be sources of Japanese nationalistic propaganda, cultivating allegiance to Japan."[87] In this context, the popular belief would only be significant if true, i.e., if some of the Japanese-language schools were "sources of Japanese nationalistic propaganda" and if such propaganda were effective. General DeWitt's *Final Report* concluded that "the widespread formation and increasing importance of the Japanese language schools in the United States" was "one extremely important obstacle in the path of Americanization of the second generation Japanese."[38] The evidence relied upon consisted of an assertion that "they employed only those text books which had been edited by the Department of Education of the Japanese Imperial Government,"[39] and a reference to the Japanese Society for Education of the Second Generation in America, organized in April, 1940, less than two years before the attack on Pearl Harbor. This society, said the *Final Report* (quoting from a Japanese newspaper) was founded to "Japanize the second and third generations in this country, for the accomplishment of establishing a greater Asia in the future."[40] However, the effectiveness of this newly organized society, and of the alleged editorial censorship of the Japanese government, in converting the schools into propaganda sources and cultivating allegiance to Japan, is left entirely to conjecture.

These statements must also be viewed in the light of the abundant evidence available as to the character of the Japanese-language schools, an institution much studied by reputable historians and social scientists.[41] The conclusions of these investigators are remarkably uniform. According to their findings, the development of the Japanese schools followed both an immigrant and a missionary pattern. Some of the language schools in the Japanese community were conducted by Catholic, Episcopalian, and Methodist churches, largely for missionary purposes; others were under Buddhist auspices; still others were conducted by secular Japanese American organizations. In urban areas most schools were secular; in rural areas most were religious. The teaching of Japanese served two primary purposes: (1) to make communication possible between parent and child, and (2) to provide a tool essential to the Nisei if they were to obtain employment within the Japanese community.[42] The language schools also operated as day nurseries and in some English was taught to pre-school children of the Japanese community. Few students of the language schools, however, ever approached mastery of the difficult tongue of the parent country—especially the complex caligraphy of the written language. Classes were held generally for an hour or an hour and a half in the late afternoon or on Saturday; attendance was sporadic and unenforced, and the quality of teaching was questionable at best. "The children themselves," according to one first-hand observer, "...in many cases would prefer not to attend....

Among the other children there is a very definite trend away from the schools."[43] In 1945 the War Relocation Authority branded as a "myth" the charge that the Japanese-language schools were maintained "to inculcate American-born Japanese with the national ideals of Imperial Government" and supplied evidence that the number of students who learned Japanese was not great. Said the War Relocation Authority: "A better proof of the falsity of the charge is the fact that the Army and Navy have recruited hundreds of graduates of the Japanese language schools to act as interpreters and teachers of the language. The relocation centers have been combed for them, and the supply has never equaled the demand."[44] That the effectiveness of the Japanese instruction was not a principal cause of the agitation against the schools is indicated by the statement of Professor Lind that "in general, the language schools had relatively little positive influence upon either the language or the sentiments of their pupils. The teaching was too dull and rigid ... but the mere existence of the schools continued to irritate and antagonize those who on other grounds were dubious of Japanese loyalty."[45]

In the early "sojourner" phase of Japanese immigration, when most Japanese expected eventually to return to the home country, the language schools, both religious and secular, were largely designed to prepare their children for life in Japan. As soon, however, as it became apparent that the majority of Japanese were in America to stay, steps were taken voluntarily to reorient the language schools. In 1914 the Japanese Education Association declared its purpose to build the schools "upon the spirit of the public institutions of America" and to delete textual materials considered incompatible with American ideals and traditions. A resolution of the Pacific Coast Section of the Japanese Association of America in 1918 provided: "that the goal to be attained in our education of the Japanese children shall be to make it supplementary to the American public instruction, and the curriculum shall consist wholly of the Japanese language." A committee on Americanization was selected and $10,000 was appropriated by the Japanese Association to finance the project.[46] In 1920 the Japanese in Hawaii proposed a bill placing the language schools under the jurisdiction of the public school system and generally regulating their operation. The bill was promptly adopted by the Territorial Legislature, and in the next year a similar measure was passed in California.[47]

Professor Reginald Bell, after an intensive investigation carried out under the auspices of the Pacific Coast Race Relations Survey, found that, although legal requirements were no longer enforceable after 1927 when the California Language School Law was invalidated,[48] most local language-school boards voluntarily retained the standards set up earlier by the State Department of Education. He found that the approved textbooks were still being used and that constant revisions to introduce materials pertinent to America were being made.[49] Svensrud also dismissed the charge that the language schools fostered anti-American ideas as "without basis," and stated that "a thorough study has been made of all the textbooks to eradicate such possibilities."[50]

Yet, said General DeWitt, the Japanese-language schools were an "extremely important obstacle in the path of Americanization of the second generation Japanese."[51]

Dual citizenship.—"Congress and the Executive, including the military commander," said Chief Justice Stone in *Hirabayashi,* "could have attributed special significance, in its bearing on the loyalties of persons of Japanese descent, to the maintenance by Japan of its system of dual citizenship."[52] In determining what "special significance in its bearing . . . on loyalties" might, with reason, be thus attributed to dual citizenship, a number of basic facts need to be kept in mind.

1. There is nothing mysterious about the way in which a dual citizen acquires that status or about the degree of his participation in it. Dual citizenship results simply from conflicting bases for the determination of citizenship. When Japan codified her nationality laws in 1899, she adopted the familiar European *jus sanguinis* rule providing that "a child is a Japanese if his or her father is a Japanese at the time of his or her birth."[53] In the United States, by contrast—since the adoption of the Fourteenth Amendment at the close of the Civil War and by the common law before that—the principle of *jus soli* has prevailed by which birth on American soil has been the test of citizenship.[54] Consequently, children born of Japanese immigrants in this country have been claimed as citizens by Japan on the basis of ancestry and by the United States on the basis of birthplace. Under international law, they have been dual citizens.

2. In view of the origin of the status, and its existence as a concept of international rather than of national law, Chief Justice Stone's remark about "the maintenance by Japan of its system of dual citizenship" is difficult indeed to understand. Japan has only one rule of citizenship, not two; and it is that rule alone that she maintains. The fact that the United States has a different rule and one which makes some citizens of Japan also citizens of the United States, plus the fact that both governments are aware of this state of affairs, does not mean that either nation maintains a system of two citizenships.

3. If the remark is taken to imply that Japan has aggressively maintained the principle of citizenship by descent, or that it has tenaciously clung to the Japanese citizenship of Japanese Americans, this is also without factual basis. On the contrary, at the instigation of Pacific Coast and Hawaiian Japanese, the rule of descent adopted by Japan in 1899 was successively relaxed in 1916 and in 1924.[55] In the latter year the Japanese law was revised to provide that children born of Japanese nationals in the United States and certain other countries would automatically lose Japanese citizenship from birth unless a parent or legal representative registered them at a Japanese consulate within fourteen days of birth and unless the intention to retain Japanese citizenship was then expressed. It was also provided that those born before December 1, 1924—and who therefore automatically became dual citizens—could renounce their Japanese citizenship.[56] By these changes, Japan facilitated the renunciation by dual citizens of their Japanese citizenship and destroyed its automatic acquisition by American-born children of Japanese nationals. Moreover, these actions were the direct results of petitions and pressures from Japanese Americans and represented an attempt on the part of the Japanese government to adjust its nationality laws and policies in favor of the American rule and the offspring of its emigrants to America.[57]

4. To the degree to which dual citizenship results from the operation of conflicting nationality laws upon factors over which the dual citizen has no control, no "significance" whatever can be "attributed" to its "bearing upon loyalties." Before 1924, such citizenship resulted from a combination of the blood in one's veins and the geography of his birth—two factors over which the individual's control could not be less. After 1924 a third factor was added, equally beyond the control of the dual citizen: a registration of birth and declaration of citizenship intention by his parents within fourteen days after his birth. Nowhere in the whole scheme, in fact, did the retention of dual citizenship depend upon the conscious effort of the Japanese American. Renunciation of Japanese citizenship, once acquired, was the only point at which the volition of the dual citizen could play a part, and that involved a positive act of divestiture.

5. If in this legalistic duality the fact of Japanese citizenship abstractly implies loyalty to Japan, why does not the fact of United States citizenship equally imply loyalty to the United States?

6. Dual citizenship among Japanese Americans began to decline immediately after the 1924 amendment to the Japanese law, and continued to decline at least until 1943.[58] Available data, though incomplete, con-

tradict such sweeping claims as the statement of California Congressman Thomas Ford that less than "one-tenth of one per cent of Japanese
Americans" owed allegiance only to America; as well as more moderate
estimates such as those of the California Joint Immigration Committee
that at least 75 per cent of the Japanese Americans owed allegiance both
to the United States and Japan. In 1930, six years after the change in
the nationality law, Strong found that 40 per cent of the American citizens of Japanese descent seven years old or older residing in California
held only American citizenship. Since all of these were born prior to
December 1, 1924, when the new expatriation procedure was inaugu-
rated, the above figure reflects only the number of those who voluntarily renounced Japanese citizenship. Of the children born after 1924,
it was found that two-thirds were American citizens only; in other
words, they had not been registered with the Japanese consulate within
the prescribed time and had thus never acquired Japanese citizenship.
It was also found that the proportion of the unregistered constantly
grew. According to a War Relocation Authority survey in 1943, between
15 and 25 per cent of all Japanese Americans were at the time dual
citizens.[59]

7. Dual citizenship was not, of course, the unique possession of
Japanese Americans but was and is common to large numbers of American citizens of foreign parentage. It is significant that both Germany
and Italy, Axis partners of the Japanese, follow the rule of *jus sanguinis*
with respect to the offspring of their nationals born abroad. So does the
United States.[60]

Yet, said Chief Justice Stone, "Congress and the Executive, including
the military commander, could have attributed special significance, in
its bearing on the loyalties of persons of Japanese descent, to the maintenance by Japan of its system of dual citizenship."

Segregation and solidarity.—In reviewing the "data" "reasonably"
warranting a conclusion of disloyalty on the part of some members of
the group, Chief Justice Stone particularly stressed the segregation and
solidarity of the Japanese American population. He pointed to the maturity and "positions of influence in Japanese communities" of one-
third of Japanese Americans who were aliens.[61] He spoke of their
"isolation" and referred to conditions which "have in large measure
prevented their assimilation as an integral part of the white population."[62] He asserted that "there has been relatively little social intercourse between them and the white population."[63] Again, this is a
cautious and restrained version of what was said in the briefs and in
General DeWitt's *Final Report*. There the Japanese were called "a

large, unassimilated, tightly knit racial group, bound to an enemy race by strong ties of race, culture, custom and religion."[64] Elsewhere it was said that "because of the ties of race, the intense feeling of filial piety and the strong bonds of common tradition, culture and customs, this population presented a tightly-knit racial group."[65] It is likely that on these points popular feeling and suspicion were much more intense and widespread than with respect to geographical distribution, language schools, and dual citizenship of the group. Yet at no point does popular belief and apprehension collide more directly with scientifically accumulated data and scientifically derived conclusions. Here, even more than in the three other areas, emerges the truth of Freeman's estimate that "when the final history of the Japanese evacuation is written it will almost certainly appear that decisions were made on misinformation, assumptions, prejudices, [and] half-truths, when excellent, scientifically accurate material was available."[66]

That the Japanese Americans were often as a group residentially segregated; that because of restrictive covenants, social and economic pressures, and to a lesser degree perhaps their own preference, they tended to dwell apart in separate sections of the cities; and that even in rural and agricultural areas there was a high degree of geographic concentration—these circumstances can not be challenged. But that within these communities the group was "tightly knit" under the control of the alien portion of the population, that it was culturally unassimilated, socially isolated, and "caked" with un-American customs of Oriental origin—these are charges and suspicions which have been flatly rejected by competent sociologists, anthropologists, and other social scientists who have directly studied the Japanese in America.[67]

According to these investigators, the Japanese Americans, like other immigrant groups, far from being "tightly knit" were split asunder by a sharp cleavage between the generations. The first generation (Issei), the immigrants themselves, tended to retain old-world culture patterns. The second and third generations (Nisei and Sansei), born in America, tended increasingly to adopt the values and folkways of the land of their birth and upbringing. This generational cleavage was accentuated by the "chronological peculiarities" of the Japanese migration to America which resulted in an abnormal age differential between the alien elders and the citizen children. Since Oriental exclusion had been in effect since 1924 and the immigrants had lived in this country from that year or earlier, nearly all were of advanced age. At the time of Pearl Harbor, the average age of the alien male was approximately 55. In 1940, more alien Japanese men fell into the 55-to-64 age group (33.4 per cent) than into any other; in the same year approximately 39 per cent of American citizens of Japanese ancestry were 15 or younger; 62 per cent of the alien males were 50 and over; 62 per cent of the American-born males were 19 and under.[68] The absence of a proportionate middle-aged group was the result not only of the cessation of immigration, but of the fact that many Japanese waited until they were fairly well established before starting families.[69]

These factors combined, in the words of Shotaro Miyamoto, to produce a gap between the generations so large that they tended "to live in two different worlds, neither understanding, literally or figuratively, the language of the other."[70]

Moreover, besides the generational and father-son conflict among the Japanese in America there was often rivalry and misunderstanding between the Nisei proper and the Kibei, who, although born in America, had received at least part of their education in Japan. "The Kibei's brothers and sisters," writes Forrest LaViolette, "who have been reared in the American schools, are adjusted to the American mode of life which is antithetical to all the Kibei knows and deems of merit. It is not uncommon, therefore, that the return of a Japan-reared child results in strained family relations, often leading to complete rupture or dislocation."[71]

These generational and sibling conflicts emerged, to be sure, principally after the second generation had reached adolescence, which for the most part was after 1930; and it might accordingly be argued that before that time, at least, the Japanese community represented a harmoniously welded and "tightly knit" social unit. Not a few unprejudiced observers, viewing the Japanese family and community from the outside, and mindful of the traditional solidarity of Japanese society, have come to this conclusion;[72] and it must be granted that in some respects it is justified. From the beginning, the Japanese immigrants grouped together closely not only because such association was customary but even more obviously as a matter of mutual aid and collective self-protection. For example, in 1900, after the first major instances of violence and discrimination, the San Francisco Japanese formed what was to become the Japanese Association of America, and as agitation against the Japanese increased over subsequent years, local branches of the association were established in every sizable community. One of the first functions of the Japanese Association was to supply bilingual intermediaries to facilitate contact with the white community.

Another form of social organization among Japanese Americans, less general in scope but with similar purposes, was the prefectural club or association which limited its membership to immigrants from particular Japanese prefectures.[73] In the disputes in Japanese communities or in Japanese-association politics, cleavage along prefectural lines was very common. Other types of organizations were formed along economic lines, the first of which was the "gang" employed in contract labor.[74] Organizations along trade lines soon appeared in the larger cities, where the Japanese were excluded from membership in white unions and associations. Typical of these were the Barbers' Union, Expressmen's Union, Restaurant Keepers' Association, and Suit Cleaning Union.[75]

The purpose of these Japanese organizations, both social and economic, was principally to present a common front against discriminatory practices, and secondarily to provide a meeting place for Japanese possessing mutual interests. Although some groups, such as the prefectural clubs, tended naturally to perpetuate old-world customs and recreations, the general effect of Issei organizations was to smooth relations with the dominant American community and to facilitate the social adjustment and integration of Japanese in this country. The later organizations of the Nisei, oriented wholly around American traditions and values, were sometimes formed specifically to counter the "Japanesy" aspect of the Issei group, and all were positive forces for assimilation and Americanization. The most influential of these has been the Japanese American Citizens' League, which held its first convention in 1930.[76] This second-generation body, which had some fifty chapters at the time of Pearl Harbor, has been primarily concerned with inculcating the general responsibilities of citizenship as well as with the peculiar problems of the Nisei. "Being one of the newest racial groups to become a component part of the American nation, the citizens of Japanese ancestry have their own special problems and missions to carry out. And to facilitate these matters this organization has been brought into existence."[77]

The dominant impression which emerges from a study of socioeconomic organization and solidarity among Japanese Americans is one of a wide variety of associations seeking to lessen their forced segregation through contacts with the American community, or at least to alleviate the intensity of social isolation and inferior standing in the larger community by intragroup organizations conferring the status and a sense of "belonging." However, the number and prominence of such associations among the Japanese, together with the close-knit appearance of Japanese traditional family and community relationships, has been to some degree responsible for the formation of a stereotype and for the suspicions fanned by the anti-Orientalists and summarized in the charge of General DeWitt that "because of the ties of race, the intense feeling of filial piety and the strong bonds of common tradition, culture and custom, this population presented a tightly knit racial group." This myth of solidarity is refuted by the conflict between the generations; what is less evident is that it is also refuted by conflicts within the first generation itself.

One divisive force in the Japanese American community, before the emergence of the "Nisei problem," was that created by the disproportionate numbers of "Eta" in the population. In traditional Japanese society, the Eta constitute a hereditary subordinate caste of virtually pariah status, roughly corresponding to the "untouchables" of Hindu India.[78] Seeking to escape their hereditary taint, Japanese of the Eta class emigrated to Hawaii and the mainland in large numbers. There were in 1926, according to Raushenbush, more Eta in proportion to the total population in Hawaii than in Japan, and still more Eta proportionately in the community of Florin, California, where they constituted a tenth of the population.[79]

Another factor tending to divide the Japanese communities in America was the religious cleavage between Christians and Buddhists.[80] The two religious groups developed an intense and often hostile rivalry which tended to divide families as well as the community. In 1926, one close observer of a typical community wrote of "the feud between the Christians and Buddhists which has torn [the Japanese community] wide open," and which at one point appeared ready to break into open violence.[81] To some degree the differences between the two faiths reflected the tension between forces working in the direction of Americanization, which were commonly identified with the Christian churches, and those tending to preserve old-world values, identified with Buddhism.[82] Thus anti-Japanese activity tended to assist the Buddhist cause and to embarrass the Christians—as when the effect of the Alien Land Law was felt in the agricultural community of Florin. "The Florin Japanese had walked the path of sullenness and frustration too long to be braced by any further bitterness, and so the Buddhist party, which favored Japanization, waxed strong, while the Christian group, who favored Americanization, grew weak."[83]

A further basis for friction within many of the supposedly tightly knit Japanese families was the fact that they had originated in the so-called "picture-bride" system, by which Japanese men in America obtained brides from the old country through an exchange of photographs and correspondence. Although the system often resulted in well-adjusted marriages, "it nevertheless did give rise to much confusion and dis-

ruption."[84] The marriages were often accompanied by domestic strain
and infidelity, all of which exerted a strong negative influence upon the
Nisei children.[85] This was frequently a result of the wide disparity in
the ages of husband and wife, the husband often being as much as 20
or 30 years older. The major obstacles in the way of those Japanese who
sought to establish families during this period have been summarized
by a member of the Pacific Coast Race Relations Survey: "(1) The exploitation of the picture-bride system and its consequent evil effects;
(2) the abuse by the young wives of their new-found freedom and unaccustomed advantages; (3) the disproportion of men to women; and
(4) ... resort to the divorce courts to end unsatisfactory marriages."[86]

In addition to intracommunity conflicts and divisions—those between
the generations, between Nisei and Kibei, between Issei husbands and
wives, between social classes, and between Christians and Buddhists—
there was frequently hostility and misunderstanding between Japanese
residents of different communities. Some indication of the variety and
scope of these conflicts and suspicions may be gathered from develop-
ments in the relocation centers during the war, when Japanese from
various areas were indiscriminately thrown together:

Regional and generational fissures, temporarily closed during the stress of evacuation, were reopened. . . . In Tule Lake, a project on the California-Oregon
border, evacuees from California blamed the more accommodated evacuees
from the Pacific Northwest. In all projects, leaders and active members of the
Japanese American Citizens' League, which had been officially accepted by
governmental agencies as a liaison group . . . were accused now of having betrayed the whole Japanese minority. They, in turn, often showed marked
readiness to denounce "hot-headed Kibei" or "Issei agitators" as the source of
all trouble. Mainland Nisei, in some instances, cast doubt upon the loyalty of
the Buddhists.[87]

It remains to examine the assertion that Japanese Americans constituted an "unassimilated" racial group. In determining the degree to
which the Japanese have been Americanized, social scientists who have
studied the question agree that there is a distinction between intermingling and assimilation. Intermingling, partial or unrestricted, they
declare, is not necessary for relatively complete assimilation, which depends only upon the acceptance of and participation in American culture, American habits of thought and action, and American ideas of
social organization. Thus it appears obvious that assimilation of the
American-born generations was fairly complete. They attended the same
American schools, saw the same movies, listened to the same radio programs, sang the same songs, spoke the same language and used the same
slang as other American boys and girls, and accepted American ideas

about government, politics, marriage, and the position of the home.[88] According to Strong: "The word 'assimilation' has two meanings—interbreeding and comprehension of political and social conditions. In the latter scheme, the young Japanese are more readily assimilated than people of several European races."[89] Park asserted even more definitely that the American of Japanese ancestry "born in America and educated in our Western schools is culturally an Occidental even though he be racially an Oriental, and this is true to an extent that no one who has not investigated the matter disinterestedly and at first hand is ever likely to imagine."[90]

Yet, said General DeWitt, the Japanese Americans are "a large unassimilated and tightly knit racial group, bound to an enemy nation by strong ties of race, culture, custom and religion."

Kibei; Influence of Japanese government.—Two sets of "data" relied upon by the court as supporting the military judgment had some evidentiary bearing on the issue of the "continued attachments" of individual Japanese Americans to Japan. These related to the "association of influential Japanese residents with Japanese Consulates"[91] and the "considerable numbers, estimated to be approximately 10,000 of American-born children of Japanese parentage" who were "sent to Japan for all or a part of their education,"[92] and who returned to the United States. The disinterested scholars who had so thoroughly studied other phases of the life of Japanese Americans had not, however, as fully explored these areas and were less explicit and less united in their conclusions. Moreover, the briefs in the *Hirabayashi* and *Korematsu* cases and General DeWitt's *Final Report*—though by no means free of extravagant statements and unsupported assertions—here at least supplied some factual foundation. General DeWitt's *Report* declares that

for more than 25 years American-born progeny of alien Japanese had been sent to Japan by their parents for education and indoctrination.

During 1941 alone more than 1,573 American-born Japanese entered West Coast ports from Japan. Over 1,147 Issei, or alien Japanese, re-entered the United States from Japan during that year.

The 557 male Japanese less than twenty-five years of age who entered West Coast ports from Japan during 1941 had an average age of 18.2 years and had spent an average of 5.2 years in Japan. Of these, 239 had spent more than three years there. This latter group had spent an average of 10.2 years in Japan.

Of the 239 males who spent three years or more abroad, 180 were in the age group 15 to 19 (with an assumed average age of 17.5 years) and had spent 10.7 years abroad. In other words, these 180 Kibei lived, on the average, 6.8 years at the beginning of their life in the United States and the next 10.7 years in Japan. Forty of the 239 who had spent three or more years abroad were in the age group 20 to 24, with an assumed average age of 22.5. These were returning to the United States after having lived here, on the average, for their first 13 years and having spent the last 9.5 years in Japan, including the one or more years when they were of compulsory (Japanese) military age.[93]

No source is given for these data but they are identical with those presented in the California-Oregon-Washington brief, where they are said to be "derived from ship's manifest file at the San Francisco, Seattle and Los Angeles port offices of the Federal Immigration and Naturalization Service, Department of Justice."[94]

"In a group," continued the *Final Report,* "with an average age of 17.5 years, who were returning to the United States after having spent an average of 7.4 years abroad continuously (in other words, from the time they were ten years of age), one-half had lived with their parents or grandparent in Japan."[95]

DeWitt's *Final Report,* to clinch the argument, quotes Professor Lind of the University of Hawaii to the effect that there was a "rather large Kibei group who are frequently more fanatically Japanese in their disposition than their own parents," many of whom had returned from Japan so recently as to be unable to speak the English language and some of whom were unquestionably disappointed by the lack of appreciation manifested for their Japanese education.[96] It is worth pointing out, however, that the article from which this quotation was excerpted first appeared in 1943; since it was not in existence at the time of the evacuation, it could scarcely be used as evidence of the data bearing on DeWitt's decision. More importantly, the quotation, like the report which embodies it, carries an implicit assumption that Nisei were sent to Japan for nationalistic "indoctrination," and that education there would so indoctrinate them. This assumption is not borne out by the reasons underlying the existence and development of the Kibei system, which have almost nothing to do with politics or loyalty. They are set forth by Thomas as follows:

... the Issei settlers' continuing ambivalence about permanent residence in America, their constant awareness of West Coast racial prejudice and its implications for their children, their lack of information about opportunities elsewhere in America, and their nostalgia, led them to transfer their "sojourner" attitudes, to some extent, to plans for their children's future, and to institute practices that would make American-born Japanese acceptable either as Japanese or as Americans. The most pervasive of the Japanizing practices were the Kibei movement and the establishment of Japanese language schools on the West Coast.

The practice of sending preschool-aged children to Japan for education and care was also motivated by economic convenience or necessity. Entrepreneurs formed a disproportionately large part of the foreign-born labor force: in

California and Washington in 1940, half of all the Issei males employed in agriculture were farmers or farm managers, and almost a third of those in non-agricultural pursuits were proprietors or managers. Most of the enterprises were small, and were operated with little capital and few, if any, paid employees. Their success—in many cases, their very existence—depended upon the active participation of the wife. Sending a child to relatives in Japan during his dependent years freed the mother for essential "unpaid" family labor, and was, in most instances, less expensive than rearing him in America.[97]

Other circumstances also should have cautioned against acceptance of General DeWitt's assumption that Nisei were sent to Japan for national-istic "indoctrination" and that their education there would make them ardent Japanese nationalists. Since, as the *Final Report* shows, the practice had been going on for twenty-five years, some at least of the Kibei must have received their education in Japan before the seizure of power by the military, at a time when liberalism was still a force. Some Kibei also, one might justifiably suppose, would react against the low standard of living and lack of freedom in Japan and become more ardent American patriots by virtue of their Japanese experience.[98] Still other Kibei might, as dual citizens, return to America specifically to avoid Japanese military service. In fact, for the great increase in the return of Kibei after 1937, and especially during 1940 and 1941, there are only two plausible explanations: a desire to escape Japanese military service in China or elsewhere against the prospective opponents of Japan, including the United States; or a desire to be in and on the side of the United States for family, economic, or patriotic reasons, once war with the United States became imminent and American consulates were advising American nationals to leave the Orient and return home. Either of these explanations refutes the thesis that the Kibei attachment to the ancestral homeland was of such a character that they were anxious or willing to commit acts of war for her.

A survey conducted by the War Relocation Authority in 1943, in fact, expressly confirmed the prevalence of these responses among the Kibei.[99] Although this survey was not available to the military at the time of evacuation, the material on which it was based was accessible and could have been assembled by any trained and impartial investi-gator; indeed, the facts had already been set forth in substantially the same manner by a number of scholars working in the field.

Following an intensive study of Japanese communities in America, La Violette concluded that "in point of outlook toward America, there appear to be three types of *Kibei:* those who recognize America as their home and are working hard to adjust themselves to American life; those who long to return to Japan and plan to do so at the first opportunity; and those who have no special inclination either way."[100]

The same Professor Lind whose views were brought in evidence by General DeWitt has pointed out, in a later publication, that the danger arising from possible disloyalty among the Kibei was slight at most; and their subsequent war record strongly suggests that most, if not all, considered themselves Americans and worked sincerely toward adjustment to American values.[101]

The numerical prominence of the Kibei within the American Japanese communities is also easy to exaggerate. For example, Lind estimates that by 1940 there were no more than 600 out of a total of more than 163,000 Japanese in Hawaii.[102] Of the Japanese on the Pacific Coast, according to Thomas, 9,892, or 8.8 per cent were Kibei.[103] The War Relocation Authority survey reveals that 72.7 per cent of all Americans of Japanese ancestry had never been in Japan, 14.4 per cent had visited Japan but had had no schooling there, and 12.2 per cent had received three or more years of education in Japan. Of this last group, 26.8 per cent were forty or older at the time of the survey in late 1943. Of American-born Japanese under twenty, 86.8 per cent had never been in Japan, and 11.1 per cent had been to Japan without schooling there. Only 1.8 per cent of those under twenty had had three or more years of schooling in the parent country. In all, only 38 per cent of Nisei over fifteen had visited or lived in Japan and no more than 20 per cent had attended school there.

These data from the War Relocation Survey were, of course, not available to General DeWitt at the time of the evacuation. But it must be conceded that the manifest figures presented by General DeWitt— whether modified by the facts of the above survey or only by the difficulties of assessing the extent and effect of education in Japan upon the Nisei (difficulties of which the general may be presumed to have been aware)—still represent a residue of hard fact of such a character as "reasonably to warrant" the conclusion that some members of the group of Kibei had or were likely to have had attachments to Japan and Japanese institutions greater than their attachment to the United States and its institutions.

In the same class was the evidence contained in the *Final Report* concerning organizations among the Japanese in America and their relationship to the consulates and to Japan; i.e., concerning the influence of the Japanese government. The evidence does not sustain the sweeping conclusions stated or implied but it does warrant more than grave concern about the loyalty of some leaders and members of certain organizations. The fact that there were numerous clubs, lodges, and associations is of no particular significance; even more than Americans, the Japanese are a group-conscious people, and it is natural that their traditional "joining" tendencies should be enhanced under the exposed and isolated conditions of minority existence. General DeWitt's *Final Report* asserts (without divulging the method by which the conclusion was derived) that there were "over 124 separate Japanese organizations along the Pacific Coast," not including "local branches of parent organizations, of which there were more than 310." These were "engaged," states the *Report*, "in varying degrees in common pro-Japanese purposes."[104] What such purposes were, however, is not stated. But from the high number given, and from the names of those listed, it would appear that many of the organizations were concerned with social, cultural, welfare, educational, and sports activities rather than with political affairs. What subversive inference, for example, can one draw from such titles as these: Japanese Sunday School, Sebastopol; Hiroshima Prefectural Society, Sebastopol; Sabura Baseball Team, Sebastopol; Suisun Fishing Club; Young Men's Buddhist Association, Auburn; Young Women's Buddhist Association, Auburn; Lindsay Women's Buddhist Association, Auburn; Lindsay Women's Association in Lindsay?[105]

The next assertion of the *Final Report,* however, if substantiated, would carry more weight.

Research and coordination of information, [it is declared] has made possible the identification of more than 100 parent fascistic or militaristic organizations in Japan which have had some relation either direct or indirect with Japanese organizations or individuals in the United States. Many of the former were parent organizations of subsidiary or branch organizations in the United States and in that capacity directed organizational and functional activities. There is definite information that the great majority of activities followed a line of control from the Japanese Government through key individuals and associations, to the Japanese residents in the United States.[106]

What was the character of the "research and coordination of information" showing the fascistic or militaristic nature of the organizations identified, or the "definite information" showing a line of control from the Japanese government? These questions are not answered. It is notable, however, that the statement alleging a "line of control" appears in exactly the same words in the California-Oregon-Washington brief in the *Hirabayashi* case,[107] except that the *Final Report* now adds the prefix that "there is definite information." The "definite information" would seem to be simply the statement of the earlier brief, which in turn was presented without any citation of evidence or authority. Again, one of the principal examples of "highly nationalistic and militaristic" organizations cited by General DeWitt was the Military Virtue Society of North America.[108] This organization was declared by the Japanese American Citizens League to be merely a sports and physical-training society, whose ancient Japanese military name is "no more related to militarism in modern Japan than the buttons on the sleeve of an American male are today connected with dueling."[109]

Many of the organizations listed by General DeWitt, however, stand in a different position. The Central Japanese Association, perhaps the most important, was established for the purpose of aiding the immigrant, and in later years served as a clearing house for numerous social, commercial, educational, and welfare groups. It has been charged, with some apparent basis, that the Japanese Association worked in close connection with the Japanese consulates and on several occasions received financial support from the Japanese Imperial Treasury.[110] It served as a certifying agency for passports and also handled conscription deferments. Other organizations bore appellations which might reasonably give cause for suspicion, if nothing more. Among these were, for example: The Navy Association Society for the Promotion of Asiatic Co-Prosperity, Japanese Imperial Army Men's Corps of Southern California, Imperial Japanese Reservists, North American Reserve Officers' Association, and Los Angeles Reserve Officers' Association.

The strongest evidence of disloyalty was presented against the *Heimusha Kai* (Military Servicemen's League). "The Intelligence Services (including the FBI, the Military Intelligence Service and the Office of Naval Intelligence) had reached the conclusion that this organization was engaged in espionage."[111] In the face of this conclusion by the three intelligence services, presumably founded on evidence subject to his evaluation, General DeWitt not only could reasonably conclude that there were disloyal Japanese Americans but that some preventive action was imperative. However, such preventive action had already been taken by the Department of Justice. Leadership, and sometimes even membership, in such an organization, was the basis for internment in alien-enemy camps.

With respect to the danger from Japanese organizations, Curtis B. Munson, a special representative of the State Department, has expressed the view held by the intelligence services in November, 1941. He wrote:

We must think also of the associations, some sinister, some emanating from Imperial Japan, some with Japanese consular contacts. It all weaves up into a sinister pattern on paper. This pattern has been set up in a secret document entitled "Japanese organizations and activities in the Eleventh Naval District" and may be scrutinized with proper authority in the Navy Department in Washington. We only suggest this to our reader in case our words have not built up the proper Hallowe'en atmosphere. It is like looking at the "punkin" itself. There is real fire in it yet in many ways it is hollow and dusty.[112]

Subsequent evidence of disloyalty.—Availing himself of the "calm perspective of hindsight" which he later declined to employ against the military judgment, Justice Black, speaking for the court in the *Korematsu* case, found one reason for not overruling the evacuation which had not been mentioned by Chief Justice Stone in the *Hirabayashi* case. It was that "approximately five thousand American citizens of Japanese ancestry refused to swear unqualified allegiance to the United States and to renounce allegiance to the Japanese Emperor, and several thousand evacuees requested repatriation to Japan."[113] This statement demonstrated the need for care in the use of hindsight, no less than in the sight that is contemporary. Even granting for the moment that the refusal to swear allegiance and the request for repatriation betokened disloyalty at the time they occurred, they still do not necessarily indicate the state of mind of the participants at some earlier period. The character of the supervening events and conditions—the principal one of which was the evacuation itself—should have cautioned Justice Black to display not hindsight but insight.

The figures referred to by Justice Black were derived from the registration program of the War Relocation Authority and the War Department, undertaken in 1943 to separate loyal from disloyal evacuees for leave clearance and the draft. Data derived from the registration questionnaire were later used as a major basis for the selection of disloyal persons to be segregated in the Tule Lake Center. This registration and the later segregation programs, were intensively studied by the staff of the University of California Evacuation and Resettlement Study, part of the results of which have been published by Thomas and Nishimoto in *The Spoilage* and by Thomas in *The Salvage*. The authors indicate the unreliability of the questionnaire data as an index of disloyalty at the time, let alone for the period prior to institution of the evacuation program.[114]

Thomas has written that registration involved

the execution of a lengthy questionnaire, including among some thirty items, two thought to bear directly on "loyalty." For male citizens, the first of these was: "Are you willing to serve in the armed forces of the United States on combat duty, wherever ordered?" and the second: "Will you swear unqualified allegiance to the United States of America and faithfully defend the United States from any or all attack by foreign or domestic forces, and forswear any form of allegiance or obedience to the Japanese emperor, or any other foreign government, power, or organization?"

The impropriety of asking aliens who were ineligible to American citizenship to forswear allegiance to the only country in which they could hold citizenship was recognized belatedly.... But American citizens, the bulk of whom were Nisei who had had no direct contact with Japan, were still required to forswear allegiance to the Japanese emperor.

Registration was postulated on the assumption that evacuees would define eligibility to serve in the armed service or to leave camps for the freedom of the "outside world" as just rewards for loyalty. Contrary to expectation, an appreciable proportion of the evacuees defined these situations as penalties rather than as rewards. A strong protest movement developed among Nisei and Kibei, who, having had so many of their rights as citizens abrogated through evacuation and detention, questioned the justice of the restoration of the single right of serving in the armed forces. Numbers of Issei, having lost most of their other possessions, used every means to hold their families intact, and to prevent the possible induction of their sons. Others, having acceded to a forced migration from home to camp, were now determined to avoid a further move to an outside world that they had many reasons to believe would continue to regard them with hostility.[115]

Thus, the major reasons why many individuals assumed a status of disloyalty to the United States—whether by their answers on the registration questionnaire, by stating a preference to become segregants, or otherwise—were: (1) Fear of being forced to leave the centers and face a hostile American public. Many thus regarded the centers, especially Tule Lake, as places of refuge where they might remain for the duration of the war. (2) Concern for the security and integrity of their families. Children loyal to the United States were allowed to accompany segregant parents; parents who were aliens loyal to the United States were allowed to accompany segregant children. (3) Fear on the part of the evacuee parents that their sons would be drafted if the sons did not become segregants. (4) Anger and disillusionment owing to the abrogation of citizenship rights. (5) Bitterness over economic losses brought about by the evacuation.[116]

However honorable or dishonorable, justified or not justified, these feelings and attitudes may have been, many of them have no bearing whatever on disloyalty; and others, though they may be relevant to disloyalty, do not necessarily prove it. Justice Black's figures must be read with these moderating factors in mind.

Data relied on by the court: Conclusion.—The data so far examined have eliminated geographical distribution, language schools, dual citizenship, and alleged solidarity and failure to assimilate into American life as factors reasonably justifying an inference of disloyalty. Taken singly or in combination, they do not add up to the conclusion, or even constitute a substantial basis for the conclusion, that some American citizens of Japanese ancestry possessed "continued attachments to Japan and Japanese institutions" superior to their attachments to America and American institutions, and of such a character as to create a likelihood that they would commit acts of espionage and sabotage against the United States in its war with Imperial Japan. They are not what Chief Justice Stone claimed they were: "Facts and circumstances with respect to the American citizens of Japanese ancestry residing on the Pacific Coast which support the judgment of the war-waging branches of the Government."[117] Moreover, the data presented to the United States Supreme Court in the briefs and contained in General DeWitt's *Final Report,* respecting the Kibei and the assertedly pro-Japanese organizations, do not necessitate or sustain the conclusion that all, most, or a substantial minor fraction of the American citizens who belonged to either or both of these groups were disloyal to the United States. They do, however, warrant the conclusion that some of the American citizens in these groups probably had greater attachments to Japan and might in some circumstances commit acts harmful to the United States. Put in other words—the words of Justice Black—"There was evidence of disloyalty on the part of some." Confirming evidence—the refusal of five thousand Tule Lake evacuees to swear unqualified allegiance to the United States— did exist; it was, however, not so sweeping or necessarily of the character referred to by Justice Black.[118]

Factors ignored.—What has been presented is the positive case for the primary loyalty of Japanese American citizens to Japan. It does not, however, stand alone. The rule of reasonableness, disentangled from the judicial substantial-basis test, requires that against the "facts and circumstances" indicating primary loyalty to Japan must be measured the "facts and circumstances" indicating disloyalty to Japan and primary loyalty to the United States. Some of the latter come close to the foundations of that "matter of the heart and mind" called loyalty and touched upon the alien part of the population as well.

Since few of them arrived after 1924, virtually all of the older Japanese Americans were long-term residents of the United States. Most of them had enjoyed a standard of living and an economic well-being in the United States that they had never possessed or expected in Japan. Thus, the United States was to them the place where they had lived for many years and where they had prospered. It was the place where they had established their homes and reared their families of citizen children. For the younger generation, the generation of citizen children, the United States was the land of their birth. It was the land whose culture had determined their habits of thought, their beliefs about government, and their modes of life—motivational factors far more important than considerations of race or "dim parental memories of a distant land."

Munson called attention to another point, which must be considered in any assessment of "active disloyalty," namely, the limited opportunity which persons of Japanese ancestry had to commit acts of sabotage and espionage and otherwise aid the enemy, except in the case of active invasion.

> Sabotage. The Japanese here is almost exclusively a farmer, a fisherman or a small business man. He has no entry to plants or intricate machinery. . . . The Japanese are hampered as saboteurs because of their easily recognized physical appearance. It will be hard for them to get near anything to blow up if it is guarded. . . .
> Espionage. The Japanese, if undisturbed and disloyal, should be well equipped for obvious physical espionage. A great part of this work was probably completed and forwarded to Tokyo years ago, such as soundings and photography of every inch of the coast. They are probably familiar with the location of every building and garage including Mike O'Flarety's out-house in the Siskiyous with all the trails leading thereto. . . . This would be fine for a fifth column in Belgium or Holland with the German army ready to march in over the border. . . . The dangerous part of their espionage is that they would be very effective as far as movement of supplies, movement of troops and movement of ships out of harbor mouths and over railroads is concerned. They occupy rarely positions where they can get to confidential papers or in plants. They are usually, when rarely so placed, a subject of perpetual watch and suspicion by their fellow workers. They would have to buy most of this type of information from white people.[119]

Moreover, what about the wartime record of the Japanese Americans? Surely, the fact of what they did and what they did not do from the day of Pearl Harbor to the time of their evacuation should weigh at least as heavily as inferences about their propensities. The irreproachable conduct of Japanese Americans in Hawaii during and after the attack on Pearl Harbor answers unequivocally many questions about the loyalty of Japanese Americans. Geography should show, if the actual attack on Pearl Harbor did not, that the danger of an invasion of Hawaii or an assault upon it was far greater than upon the mainland. There were about 160,000 persons of Japanese ancestry in Hawaii and they constituted not one-thousandth of the population as on the mainland but approximately 38 per cent. The islands being small, there can be no doubt that the Japanese Americans were concentrated in strategic areas. Not only were they near naval yards and military installations, but they actually worked in them both before and after Pearl Harbor. They have all the characteristics attributed to the group on the mainland; their language schools, dual citizenship, and Kibei, their alien seniors and their contact with the Japanese consulates. Yet despite the demonstrated greater imminence of the danger and their possession of the traits attributed to the mainland Japanese Americans, and despite the fact that they remained at liberty and at work during the entire war, not one single act of espionage or sabotage was ever traced to them.

The record of the Japanese Americans on the mainland seems to have been equally good. The government apparently admitted, in the *Korematsu* case, that "not one person of Japanese ancestry was accused or convicted of espionage or sabotage after Pearl Harbor while they were still free."[120]

General DeWitt not only made a similar admission, but in a remarkable example of the proof of guilt by the absence of evidence, he argued that: "The very fact that no sabotage has taken place to date is a disturbing and confirming indication that such action will be taken."[121]

Some indirect evidence was offered in the *Final Report* to show that the danger of sabotage was real. The items listed were the discovery of contraband articles during spot raids, "the nightly observation of visual signal lamps from constantly changing locations," and "the interception of illicit radio transmission."[122]

The results of spot raids, however, were quite differently interpreted by Attorney General Biddle whose department conducted them. He said

We have not . . . uncovered through these searches any dangerous persons that we could not otherwise know about. We have not found among all the sticks of dynamite and gun powder any evidence that any of it was to be used in bombs. We have not found a single machine gun nor have we found any gun in any circumstances indicating that it was to be used in a manner helpful to our enemies. We have not found a camera which we have reason to believe was for use in espionage.[123]

Likewise the "nightly observations of visual signal lamps from constantly changing locations," was said by the Department of Justice, after investigation, to be nothing more than the results of imperfections in the blackouts reported by excited persons.[124] Finally, the alleged interception of illicit radio transmission was flatly denied by the Federal Communications Commission which "through this period was engaged in a comprehensive 24-hour surveillance of the entire radio spectrum to guard against any unlawful radio activity."[125]

EMERGENCY JUSTIFICATION

It is plain from what has been said that the classification sustained in the *Hirabayashi* and *Korematsu* cases was overinclusive, that it embraced not only some but many who were not tainted with the mischief at which the order was aimed. General DeWitt seems to have been the only responsible person ever to have maintained that the available data justified an inference that all members of the group were disloyal. Such an inference, however, is fantastic, unless one believes, as General DeWitt appears to have, that there are racial strains, that these remain undiluted through many generations, and that they are the determinants of national loyalty; and in that event, one merely contradicts the findings of the world's biologists, psychologists, sociologists, and anthropologists. All that the abundant data *do* sustain is the conclusion that some of the members of the group of Japanese Americans were potential spies and saboteurs. Recognizing, as Professor Fairman has observed, that it takes only "one unascertainable one" to signal to a submarine,[126] yet does this constitutionally justify the restrictive and discriminatory curfew and evacuation of all Japanese Americans? If the classification is overinclusive why did it not go over "the very brink of constitutional power and . . . into the ugly abyss of racism,"[127] as Justice Murphy contended it did?

The equal-protection and due-process requirements do not automatically invalidate classifications that have these defects. Grossly overinclusive classifications such as that at hand may be saved from nullification by the existence of an emergency. The police road block, subjecting many to examination in order to catch a few who perpetrated a crime, is a common example. The emergency doctrine is not the same as the doctrine that the Constitution may be violated "if only you are in a hurry." The standards of classification to be exacted depend upon circumstances. In emergencies, delays that may put at hazard the public safety cannot be tolerated. But the emergency that will justify an overinclusive classification must be real and the restraint commensurate with it or appropriately designed to cope with it.

It is at this point that the doctrine's application to the evacuation, whatever may be said of curfew, leaves the greatest room for doubt. Was the danger of invasion so immediate and perilous as to justify what has been described as "one of the most sweeping and complete deprivations of constitutional rights in the history of this nation in the absence of martial law"?[128] In the *Hirabayashi* case, reviewing the course of the war down to March, 1942, the court found "that reasonably prudent men charged with the responsibility of our national defense had ample ground for concluding that they must face the danger of invasion."[129] The court thus gave its approval to what it supposed the military estimate of invasion to be. The character of the anticipated invasion attempt was thus indicated by Colonel Bendetson: "It is because of [the Japanese] potentiality [for danger] that we have had to exclude them from that strip of Pacific Coast frontier where, in the event of attack, if our enemy were coming up the beaches, they would not be able to join hands with them." Therefore, it was necessary to remove them from that strip.[130] This theme was repeated later when Colonel Bendetson summarized the Army's accomplishment in the evacuation program thus: The relationship of the Japanese population to espionage, sabotage and fifth column activity "became a problem of acute concern to the west coast." So a military decision had to be made "to take such steps immediately as would safeguard the security of the Western Defense Command. To set in motion countermeasures against espionage, sabotage and fifth column activities. To thwart any plans the enemy might have to get a foothold on the western rim of our continent."[131]

Foregoing the advantage of retrospect and using only the contemporary yardstick, it is hard to see how evacuation (whatever may be said of curfew) was justified by the peril then existing. The critical factor is the time element. Had evacuation and detention occurred in December, January, or February instead of April, May, June, and July, though it still would not have been the calm act of a military statesman, it would have appeared reasonable as a spur of the moment decision, taken in haste and in the light of devastation wrought at Pearl Harbor, the chance of a repeat performance, the rapid progress of Japanese arms in the Pacific, and the complete chaos and lack of defense on the Pacific Coast.[132]

Had the evacuation been undertaken while these conditions still prevailed, and had it consisted only of exclusion without incarceration, the criticism which has since been heaped upon General DeWitt would, in large measure, have been undeserved. But these conditions did not prevail to the date of the evacuation decision; and when evacuation came, it did include incarceration. The time lag, moreover, robbed the military of any justification of haste. Evacuation was a deliberate act taken after the shock of surprise attack had worn off and amid diminishing war pressures on the Pacific Coast. The sequence of events alone seriously weakens, if it does not belie, the claim of great and overwhelming urgency. Pearl Harbor occurred on December 7, 1941. It was not until February 19, 1942, ten weeks later, that the President signed Executive Order 9066. Still another four weeks elapsed before Congress passed its confirming legislation on March 21. It was almost a full four months after Pearl Harbor before General DeWitt issued his first general Civilian Exclusion Order. The evacuation went on during the summer of 1942 and actually was not completed until November 1—the date on which the last evacuee entered the relocation centers—close to eleven months after the beginning of the war. This slow march of events hardly suggests all-engulfing military urgency or acute apprehension of danger emanating from the group being evacuated. While the evacuation proceeded at this leisurely pace, the progress of Japanese arms, swiftly moving across the Pacific, reached its peak and began to decline. The deciphering of the Japanese code in the spring of 1942 was, in Churchill's rumored words, worth ten divisions on the Pacific islands and made it possible to keep closer track of the Japanese fleet. The Battle of Midway on June 6, 1942, decisively disposed of any possibility that the Japanese might marshal the naval effort necessary for an invasion of the West Coast or for sustaining the Japanese toehold on Attu and Kiska. This was the judgment of our military leaders at the time.[133]

Yet evacuation did not then come to an end. The inland removals which had begun on June 2 were relentlessly continued. The last Civilian Exclusion Order, No. 108, was dated July 22, 1942, and fixed August 11 as the deadline for incarceration of the last Pacific Coast Japanese Americans. On June 6, the Japanese Americans who had already been taken into custody were lodged in the temporary assembly centers. The permanent so-called relocation centers had not yet been constructed and manned. Could military necessity justify mass evacuation as distinguished from individual exclusion, let alone two-and-a-half years of imprisonment, after the Battle of Midway had removed all threat of invasion?

Moreover, all of this is based on the assumption that the military did conclude that invasion was threatened prior to Midway. The court generously attributes this conclusion to the military without requiring proof or substantial evidence that the military held it. Aside from the few statements by subordinate officials—mainly officials who were trying to justify the program—the evidence is that American military leaders did not expect an invasion attempt. Admiral Stark, Chief of Naval Operations, testified before a congressional committee in February, 1942, that he did not believe it would be possible for the enemy to engage in a sustained attack on the Pacific Coast at that time, although sporadic raids were not only possible but probable.[134] In his history of the war in the Pacific, based on official sources, S. E. Morison states that despite losses at Pearl Harbor the Navy did not expect any Japanese naval attacks east of the Hawaiian Islands but believed only that strikes on Puget Sound, San Francisco, or the Panama Canal were not beyond the range of possibilities.[185] There is some evidence that this was also the view of the Army.[186]

This also was apparently the view of President Roosevelt and Prime Minister Churchill and the British and American Chiefs of Staff. Referring to the eight major meetings of Roosevelt, Churchill, and Hopkins in the White House and to the twelve concurrent meetings of the Chiefs of Staff, in December 1941 and January 1942, Robert Sherwood writes:

There was serious discussion in the White House of the possibility of Japanese attacks on the West Coast of North America by naval bombardment, mine-laying in ports (Seattle or San Francisco), "attacks by human torpedoes" (such as those carried out by Italians in Alexandria)—or even carrier-borne air attacks or actual seaborne expeditions of troops. This last seemed improbable, to say the least, but the Japanese were demonstrating a will and a capacity for fantastic maneuvers. Churchill said he could see little likelihood that even the Japanese would attempt an invasion of the continent, but he did think that the West Coast might be "insulted" (that was his word) from time to time. . . . Roosevelt thought that the danger of carrier-borne bombing was great enough to warrant "dispersal" of aircraft factories on the West Coast, and Beaverbrook made available the British experience in working out this process. Far more serious than any spectacular demonstrations against Seattle, San Francisco or Los Angeles—or even Hollywood—was the possibility of a concerted attack on the Panama Canal. But even this vital point was considered as purely local and incidental. The main problem in the Japanese war was still on the other side of the Pacific.[187]

By February of 1942, though the Japanese had made phenomenal progress, top allied leaders still felt no concern about an invasion of the West Coast of the United States. The conviction was that the Japanese were moving in other directions. Continued Sherwood:

It had been assumed, when the grand strategy was laid down (Dec. 1941) that the Japanese could be contained within the line bounded by the Aleutian and Hawaiian Islands, Samoa, Fiji, the Solomon Islands, the East Indies, Singapore, Thailand, and the maritime provinces of Siberia. Now it was becoming evident that they could not be thus contained, that they might sweep southward over the East Indies to Australia and westward through Burma into India and even on to the Middle East.[188]

At the meeting of Churchill and British and American military leaders in London on April 14, "Marshall said that the Chiefs of Staff in Washington had made very careful calculations as to the measures that were necessary for holding the Alaska-Hawaii-Australia line in the Pacific and full provision for this had been made."[189]

General DeWitt himself was at least ambivalent on this point. His request for authority in February, 1942, omitted land attacks and invasion attempts from the list of "possible and probable enemy activities."[140] That list referred to: "(a) Naval attack on shipping in coastal waters; (b) Naval attack on coastal cities and vital installations; (c) Air raids on vital installations, particularly within two hundred miles of the coast; (d) Sabotage of vital installations throughout the Western Defence Command."[141] Significantly, however, when addressing the public rather than his Washington superiors, his claims were more sweeping. In his first proclamation, issued in March, 1942, he spoke of the "Pacific Coast ... which by its geographical location is particularly subject to attack, to attempted invasion by the armed forecs of nations with which the United States is now at war."[142]

Although military dangers, whether of invasion or of hit-and-run raids, might conceivably have a bearing on curfew and even on evacuation, they cannot be seen to have a reasonable—if any—relationship to detention.

If, as apparently estimated by our naval and military leaders at the time, the danger of invasion after Midway was practically nonexistent and before Midway was fairly remote, the justification for the sweepingly overinclusive classification and the whole vast, discriminatory program of uprooting, removal, and imprisonment becomes a mere "possibility or probability" of occasional air strikes, submarine shellings, and commando raids. Such sporadic attacks might of course be rendered more effective by inside help from disloyal residents. But this is a far cry from fifth-column juncture with invading enemy forces scrambling up the beaches. The drastic measure of mass evacuation on a discriminatory racial basis, even without incarceration, cannot be justified as a means necessary or reasonably adapted to cope with a danger of this diminished character in the absence of stronger and more impelling evidence of active and general disloyalty among Japanese Americans than was produced in General DeWitt's *Final Report*.

An Alternative

Many of these considerations that bear upon the war emergency as justification for the overinclusive classification, apply with equal force to the existence of an alternative method for meeting the danger of espionage and sabotage. The presence of some disloyal members of the Japanese American population, even in the context of war with Japan, certainly cannot be said to justify exclusion of the whole group if it was reasonably feasible to separate the disloyal from the loyal and subject them separately to precautionary measures—measures which might have included exclusion and detention. This critical question of the existence of an adequate but less drastic alternative, the court, in the *Korematsu* case, disposed of summarily. It relied again, on the one hand, upon the *Hirabayashi* case, and on the other hand, upon the supposed action of the military which the military apparently had not taken.

Here, as in the Hirabayashi case ... [said Justice Black] we cannot reject as unfounded the judgment of the military authorities and of Congress that there were disloyal members of that population, whose number and strength could not be precisely and quickly ascertained. We cannot say that the war-making branches of the Government did not have ground for believing that in a critical hour such persons could not readily be isolated and separately dealt with.... Like curfew, exclusion of those of Japanese origin was deemed necessary because of the presence of an unascertained number of disloyal members of the group.... It was because we could not reject the finding of the military authorities that it was impossible to bring about an immediate segregation of the disloyal from the loyal that we sustained the validity of the curfew order as applying to the whole group. In the instant case, temporary exclusion of the entire group was rested by the military on the same ground.[143]

As Miss Dembitz has pointed out, "Justice Black's reference to a 'finding' by the military authorities ... is a peculiar euphemism"; the "finding" was "mythical" and the reference "misleading."[144] There is not the slightest shred of evidence in General DeWitt's *Final Report*— which can be regarded as the military's best effort to justify the evacuation—that General DeWitt and his staff considered and eliminated the possibility of segregating "the disloyal from the loyal," let alone that they indulged in any such process of careful deliberation as is implied by a "finding." In fact, the *Final Report* justifies the evacuation upon a theory entirely ruling out an examination of the traits of individuals. "Undiluted racial strains" were the determinants of national loyalty; all individuals of Japanese ancestry "belong to an enemy race"; all were "subversive." Justice Black's reference to the *Hirabayashi* case was only somewhat more successful. The *Hirabayashi* case at least did exist. But the curfew stood upon a vastly different footing from evacuation. It was a relatively minor restriction, which, including German and Italian aliens as well as all Japanese, involved considerably larger numbers of people. It was applied simultaneously over a wide area. It entailed, consequently, neither the time element nor the administrative complexity of the evacuation. Segregating the disloyal from the loyal in connection with curfew, therefore, presented difficulties of a character and extent not involved in such segregation in connection with evacuation. Nevertheless, despite these differences between curfew and evacuation and despite the absence of evidence of anything approaching a "finding" by the military authorities, Justice Black treated the *Hira-*

bayashi opinion as a controlling precedent on the issue of whether the disloyal could have been separated from the loyal and sought to buttress this action by reference to a "finding of the military" that such separation was impossible within the time limits.

In estimating the availability of alternative methods for handling such danger from Japanese Americans as did exist, it must be noted that evidence of the breakdown, failure, or inadequacy of espionage and sabotage detection and prevention by the Federal Bureau of Investigation and the Military and Naval Intelligence services had never been produced. Proof of the commission of acts of espionage and sabotage by members of the group at the time of Pearl Harbor or between Pearl Harbor and evacuation would be the most compelling form that such evidence could take. There was no such proof. Beyond that, it cannot be ignored that the Department of Justice and the Intelligence Officer of the Eleventh Naval District (which included Los Angeles) thought that evacuation was not necessary.

The Munson report by itself makes it clear that the intelligence services and the FBI, to say nothing of immigration and other federal officials and local police, had long been "observing the Japanese American group as a whole" and compiling records on many individuals.[145] The Navy Department in particular had done this work intensively for at least ten years before Pearl Harbor. In the fall of 1941, there were "in each Naval District ... about 250 to 300 suspects under surveillance." It was "easy to get on the suspect list, merely a speech in favor of Japan at some banquet, being sufficient to land one there." "Privately," the intelligence services believed "that only 50 or 60 in each District" could "be classed as really dangerous."[146]

Naval Intelligence had in 1941 cracked the famous Tatibana case, breaking up the espionage work of a number of Japanese naval officers lawfully in the United States in a semidiplomatic status and seizing their files and lists of contacts.[147] The documents and materials taken filled at least two trucks and called for all the expert translators that the Navy, the Army, and the FBI could muster on short notice. Following the outbreak of war in Europe, a special defense unit was established in the Department of Justice to investigate suspicious persons and keep under surveillance those considered dangerous to national security. Under the program of this unit, a Japanese alien or citizen who did nothing more suspicious than make a contribution to a Japanese national cultural society was brought within the range of continuous scrutiny. Leaders of any Japanese organization and members of some were given an "A" rating of dangerousness.

In October, 1941, agents of the FBI descended on the officers of Japanese organizations, separately interrogated presidents, executive secretaries, and members of executive committees, and appropriated the books and membership lists of the Japanese Chamber of Commerce and the Central Japanese Association. Other records were also seized from other sources.[148]

In November, 1941, the district director of the Los Angeles office of the Immigration and Naturalization Service announced new immigration regulations, designed to keep an even closer check on aliens, and particularly on alien fishermen. Under these regulations any alien leaving the United States was required to have in his possession a valid passport, an alien-registration receipt, and, if of draft age, a clearance certificate from his draft board.[149]

In October and November, the State Department sent Curtis B. Munson to the West Coast to gauge the probable reaction and course of conduct of Japanese Americans in the event of war with Japan. He reported the view of the FBI, the military and naval intelligence services, and of segments of informed opinion in the area to be the same: "There is no Japanese problem on the coast. There will be no armed uprising of Japanese. There will undoubtedly be some sabotage financed by Japan, executed largely by imported agents or agents already imported. There will be the odd case of fanatical sabotage by some Japanese 'crackpot.' "[150]

For the work of classification and surveillance, the intelligence services had available, among others, the Tatibana lists, lists of officers and members of various Japanese organizations seized by the FBI and otherwise garnered, immigration office lists and data, catalogues of all important persons in the Japanese communities, the detailed information about all aliens in the country gathered in the alien registration of 1940 under the Alien Registration Act of that year, shipping manifest data which would particularly identify the Kibei, and public and semipublic statements showing pro-Japanese sentiments taken from the vernacular press and elsewhere. Their most important source, however, was the Japanese Americans themselves. The testimony on this point is conclusive. There were numbers of Nisei actively coöperating with the FBI, the Office of Naval Intelligence, and other responsible officials by communicating all suspicious data on the part of other members of the group. Most of these did their work voluntarily and without pay. On three days' notice, to use but one example, they secured and turned over to intelligence officers the books of the much suspected Black Dragon Society for the western portion of the United States.

Acting on the previously accumulated information and pursuant to proclamations of the President issued under the Alien Enemy Act of 1798, the federal government, within a matter of hours after the attack on Pearl Harbor, had picked up and incarcerated nearly 1,300 Japanese nationals. Every one of those taken into custody had been under observation for more than a year.[151] In the course of the next few weeks, almost 3,000 Japanese aliens were arrested.[152]

All such enemy aliens were held pending review of their cases by hearing boards established by the Attorney General. They were then released outright, paroled, or interned for the duration of the war.

After Pearl Harbor and while the Department of Justice was still in charge of such matters, Japanese aliens, together with all other enemy aliens, were subjected to a new registration, were directed not to change place of abode or occupation, to travel by plane or in public conveyances, were fully investigated as to property and financial interests, were forbidden to possess a long list of contraband articles, were made to comply with a curfew, were restricted as to travel, were excluded entirely from numerous prohibited zones, and were subjected to sudden search and seizure in spot raids.

In early February, 1942, the Intelligence Officer of the Eleventh Naval District reëxamined the whole problem of the espionage and sabotage potential of the Japanese Americans. He reviewed not only the product of his own extensive investigations and experience and the opinions of long time Pacific Coast neighbors of Japanese Americans, but also confidential reports of the FBI, the Navy, the State Department, and the Department of Commerce—some of the very documents undoubtedly before General DeWitt, when, a few days later, on February 14, he requested authority for the mass evacuation.[153] Noting, but not permitting himself to be affected by the rising tide of excited talk, Lieutenant Commander K. D. Ringle prepared, and submitted to the Chief of Naval Operations a comprehensive and categorical report together with a set of recommendations. Since Ringle's report expressed not only his own conclusions, but, in a fair measure, the thinking of the FBI, the Department of Justice, and the special representatives of the State Department, and since it contained an estimate of the situation at the very time General DeWitt was initiating the chain of events which ended in exclusion and detention, it possesses special weight.

The problem of the Japanese Americans, Ringle maintained, had been "magnified out of its true proportion" mainly "because of the physical characteristics of the people." Some measure of restraint should be applied, in the interest of the war effort, to the agitators in press and radio who were whipping up sentiment and encouraging action against these people on the basis of race alone. The Japanese American problem was no more serious than the German American, the Italian American, or the Communistic American problem and like them it should be handled on an individual basis, regardless of race and regardless of the distinction between citizen and alien.

Ringle thought that at least 85 per cent of the American-born were loyal to the United States, that the large majority of Japanese-born were at least passively loyal to the United States and that most of the remainder would not engage in active sabotage but "might well do surreptitious observation work" if given a convenient opportunity. The number of individuals, either deliberately placed by the Japanese government or actuated by fanatical loyalty to Japan, who would act as saboteurs, Ringle estimated at less than 3 per cent of the total Japanese American population, or about 3,500 persons in the entire United States. He thought the Kibei the most potentially dangerous element. But those most likely to commit acts of espionage and sabotage were either already in detention or belonged to such organizations as the Black Dragon Society, the Navy League, or the Military Men's Service League, the members of which were known to Naval Intelligence and the FBI.

In view of this assessment of the situation, Ringle condemned the proposal of mass exclusion and incarceration as "unwarranted" and "unwise." It would "undoubtedly alienate the loyalty of many thousands of persons who would otherwise be entirely loyal to the United States." Instead of this harsh and discriminatory program of rejection, Ringle advocated that the Nisei at least be "officially encouraged in their efforts toward loyalty and acceptance as bona fide citizens." Like other citizens, they should be given a responsible role in the national war effort.

For the small fraction who were potentially dangerous, Ringle recommended immediate custodial detention on the basis of evidence possessed against them as individuals. This might be done, he thought, through having the individual cases reviewed by boards composed of members of the Military and Naval Intelligence services and the Department of Justice.[154]

If, contradicting the judgment of the Department of Justice and Naval Intelligence, the military should conclude, as it apparently did, that the measures already taken were not adequate safeguards against the danger of sabotage and espionage coming from Japanese Americans, there were still a number of alternatives intermediate between these measures and evacuation. The most obvious of these was that proposed in part by Lieutenant Commander Ringle: a process of sifting through a system of hearing boards. An example in this respect had already been set. At the beginning of the war with Germany, Britain created 112 hearing boards which examined some 74,000 German and Austrian aliens in a period of six months. As a result of these proceedings, 2,000 persons were interned, approximately 8,000 were made subject to special restrictions and the remainder were allowed unrestricted freedom.[155]

During the spring of 1942, the use of hearing boards was repeatedly suggested as an alternative to mass evacuation. Prominent lawyers, educators, and churchmen urged General DeWitt and the President to apply this procedure—already applied to German and Italian aliens— to the whole Japanese American population, particularly to the American-born citizens of the United States. They argued that the Selective Service appeal boards were an already existing, virtually made-to-order agency for handling the task, and that it could be completed within six weeks.[156] The reply of General DeWitt's headquarters to these demands to preserve the rights of citizens was characteristic. Not only would hearing-board examinations "cause delay when speed was urgent" but "it would be practically impossible to establish the loyalty of any one of Japanese race"![157]

In determining whether individual loyalty hearings were a feasible alternative and an adequate substitute for the drastic measure of group exclusion and detention, General DeWitt's assertion that there were "over 112,000 potential enemies, of Japanese extraction . . . at large" "along the vital Pacific Coast"[158] must be considered in the light of his theory that all persons of Japanese ancestry were disloyal to the United States. Although capacity to commit espionage and sabotage is not confined to those who might be classified as military effectives, yet age, sex, and health are relevant factors in evaluating the potential danger from the group. Of the "over 112,000" Japanese Americans "along the vital Pacific Coast," 49,000 were women; about 15,000 were males over sixty-five or under fourteen; about 1,000 were physically disabled or in hospitals or institutions; and several thousand of the remainder were in the United States Army.[159] Accordingly, if aliens, women, children, and the infirm were not included in the program, hearing procedures would have had to be applied probably to fewer than 50,000 persons; certainly to less than half the figure mentioned by General DeWitt.

Assuming the inadequacy of existing methods of control, the British experience and our own in handling enemy aliens through the use of hearing boards and individual screening procedures plus an evaluation of the numbers of Japanese Americans involved leave little doubt as to the existence of a less drastic alternative than mass evacuation and imprisonment. Ironically, however, it was the War Department itself which produced the most convincing evidence that the dangerous part of the Japanese American population "could be isolated and separately dealt with" and that this could be done within a time span far shorter than that required to plan and execute evacuation. The method by which the War Department showed that this was possible was by doing it. Moreover, this feat was accomplished on a basis of very little more information about individuals in the group than was available at the time of the evacuation or than could have been secured by a device no more imposing and magical than a questionnaire.

The leave program from the relocation camps, begun early in 1943 and approved and participated in by the War Department, first revealed the degree to which the information possessed in the spring of 1942 was officially regarded as reliable. Leave clearance was granted on the basis of what the intelligence services had known about the applicant, plus information obtained from a questionnaire which had later been submitted to all evacuees. If the loyalty questions in the questionnaire had been answered affirmatively and if the applicant had not spent substantial time in Japan, was not a Shinto priest, had not belonged to an organization believed to be dangerous, or was not suspect on a number of other grounds—all data known to or easily procurable by the intelligence services in the spring of 1942—eligibility for leave clearance was established.

Precisely the same type of data constituted the basis for the War Department's reclassification program undertaken in preparation for the rescission of the exclusion orders and the termination of the evacuation. Though not begun until some time in the fall of 1944, the reclassification was completed during December of that year. Moreover, it covered not just the Japanese Americans still in the relocation centers, but also those who had resettled in the interior, as well as those who had been living continuously in areas not affected by evacuation orders.[100] The procedure employed was far simpler and, it might be added, far less searching than individual hearings, and involved only information already at hand. All adverse information known about an individual—such as membership in a dangerous organization, residence in Japan, denial of leave clearance, negative answers to loyalty questions—was assembled on an IBM punch card by use of code numbers. No allowance was made for favorable or counterbalancing factors. As a result of this process, the War Department, near the end of December,

1944, sent to the project administrator a list of 95,000 names of Japanese Americans who were free to go anywhere in the United States. By virtue of the system used, it can be seen that there had never been any ground for suspicion of these 95,000 persons. The remainder of the group was divided into: "excludees" to be issued individual exclusion orders forbidding them to enter the Western, Eastern, or Southern Defense Commands; "detainees," to be segregated and incarcerated; and those on a doubtful list to be held temporarily pending further investigation of their cases.

Thus, in the course of a few short months, the entire Japanese American population was screened for loyalty by the War Department. The loyal were separated from the disloyal and from those suspected of disloyalty. And this was done, not on the basis of new data assiduously collected while the evacuees were locked up in relocation centers, but largely on the basis of investigations completed and facts accumulated before evacuation plus information which could easily have been obtained at that time by the very methods later used to secure it. The data in the questionnaires could have been collected from the Japanese in their home communities almost as easily as it had been in the relocation centers.

UNDERINCLUSIVE CLASSIFICATION

Although the classification involved in the curfew and the evacuation of all Japanese Americans was overinclusive in that many individuals possessing the classifying trait were not tainted with the mischief to be prevented, it was at the same time underinclusive, since, if the reasoning justifying the classification had been applied to other groups, they too, should have been included. This underinclusiveness also raises serious questions. Within General DeWitt's own command, Germans and Italians, as well as Japanese, were distributed in strategic areas, tended to live in segregated groups, returned or sent their children to the homeland for visits, had their language schools, dual citizenship, and close contacts with consulates.[161]

Underinclusive classifications, when sustained, are sustained on the theory that a particular danger may be hit where it is seen or where it is most conspicuous "without providing for others which are not so evident or so urgent."[162] In the words of Justice Holmes, underinclusiveness may be tolerated if there is a "fair reason"[163] for not extending the measure to the unincluded groups. What was the "fair reason" in the case of the evacuation? Certainly, military necessity or war crisis cannot justify underinclusiveness in the way that they do overinclusiveness.

When the time is short and the peril great, doing too much by way of precaution may be forgiven. But the existence of the emergency and the need for taking precautions do not constitute a fair reason for not extending the order to other groups equally tainted by the mischief or for not bringing them "within the lines" "so far and so fast" as possible.[164]

The court could not reasonably maintain that the danger was more conspicuous in the case of the Japanese, since their sabotage-committing propensities were inferred from certain alleged group characteristics which, as listed by the court though not by General DeWitt, were equally the characteristics of the groups not included.

It now appears that the Italians, aliens and citizens, were exempted from mass evacuation at the special insistence of Secretary of War Henry L. Stimson. In his letter to General DeWitt of February 20, 1942, delegating authority under Executive Order 9066, Stimson directed:

I desire so far as military requirements permit, that you do not disturb, for the time being at least, Italian aliens and persons of Italian lineage except where they are, in your judgment, undesirable or constitute a definite danger to the performance of your mission to defend the west coast. I ask that you take this action in respect to Italians for the reason that I consider such persons to be potentially less dangerous, as a whole, than those of other enemy nationalities. Because of the size of the Italian population and the number of troops and facilities which would have to be employed to deal with them, their inclusion in the general plan would greatly overtax our strength.[165]

Secretary Stimson does not explain why he thought the Italians "potentially less dangerous, as a whole, than . . . other enemy nationalities." The tone of his remark, however, does not seem to imply either reliance on FBI or other intelligence services reports or on a studied comparison of immigrant populations. When bona fide, the argument of administrative impracticability is a "fair reason" for underinclusiveness. But that argument is often a protective refuge for decisions that cannot be justified on the merits. In this case, a shortage of troops and facilities would plausibly have suggested that the mass evacuation of no group should be undertaken, or at least that only aliens—Japanese, German and Italian—should be removed and the American citizens of all three descents be left alone.

The War Department was also responsible for eliminating German Americans from the sweeping authority granted General DeWitt, but gave no explanation of its reason for doing so.

Chief Justice Stone, in the *Hirabayashi* case, disposed of the underinclusiveness problem summarily. He did not, however, advert to the dearth of guards, camps, and barbed wire. He merely suggested that "the fact alone that attack on our shores was threatened by Japan rather

than another enemy power set these citizens apart from others who have
no particular associations with Japan."[106] This may seem to some a
rather parochial view of a war in which we were opposed to Germany
and Italy as well as Japan. It may also seem oddly in conflict with the
fact that a number of Caucasians had been convicted of espionage on
the mainland;[107] and with the fact that the only known act of espionage
in Hawaii at the time of Pearl Harbor was committed by a German
national.[108] But this is the only gesture the court makes in the direction
of justifying the underinclusive classification.

THE OYAMA AND TAKAHASHI CASES

In the *Hirabayashi* and *Korematsu* cases the court sustained actions as
compatible with the constitutional demand for equal treatment: in the
Oyama and *Takahashi* cases the equal-protection clause was held to
invalidate two California statutes which employed classifications based
on descent. In *Oyama* and *Takahashi* the measures complained of,
though their existence and vigor depended upon the war, were not in
any sense a product of the war. There could be no doubt in either case
that the measures were "spawned of the great anti-Oriental virus,"[109]
provided with rare conditions and opportunities for growth by the war
with Japan. Moreover, it may not be constitutionally irrelevant to notice that the action complained of was state action, not a federal-
government exercise of the warmaking power. Thus, the challenged
statutes—based upon the police power of the states, free of an emergency context and clearly revealing economic and racial elements—
placed the consideration of the scope of the equal-protection clause in
a different setting from *Hirabayashi* and *Korematsu*. It will appear,
however, that the very difference in circumstances serves to clarify the
position taken in the war cases.

The *Oyama* case involved California's Alien Land Law, enacted originally in 1913 and reënacted and greatly strengthened in 1920. Its enforcement by the escheat action which it authorized had not been
vigorous. World War II changed that. Of the 79 escheat proceedings
instituted by the state from the time of the adoption of the Alien Land
Law, 59 were begun subsequent to Pearl Harbor.[170] The *Oyama* case was
one of these. The heart of the Alien Land Law is its prohibition of the
ownership or leasing of agricultural land by aliens ineligible to citizenship. This, however, was not the subject of the court's constitutional
attack. Part of the Alien Land Law, aimed at evasion of the basic prohibition, created a statutory presumption against the bona fide character of a gift of land when the cost of the gift is borne by an alien

ineligible to citizenship. It was this feature of the law that the court found unconstitutional. The court did this even though assuming "for purposes of argument only" the constitutionality of the land-owning and leasing prohibition.

Perhaps the most significant feature of the *Oyama* case is the fact that the majority opinion makes no attempt to deal with California's argument that, given the validity of the major prohibition of the Alien Land Law, the presumption which was objected to was not unreasonably related to the prevention of evasion. In fact, the presumption placed the burden of proof squarely upon the only class of persons with motives for evasive transfer. The classification governing the presumption was thus clearly, California argued, reasonably related to the classification of those barred from owning or leasing land.

If one looks at the attempt of the court to strike down the presumption without invalidating the major prohibition of the Alien Land Law in terms of the equal-protection requirement of reasonable classification, it is difficult to avoid the conclusion that the court was undertaking a logical impossibility. The classifying trait for those who paid for land given to others was ineligibility to citizenship. The purpose of the classification was to enforce or prevent evasion of the Alien Land Law. Was the classification reasonably related to that purpose? The answer can only be yes. Few who possessed the classifying trait were not tainted with the mischief. None who did not possess the classifying trait were tainted with the mischief. Since the Alien Land Law forbids only ineligible aliens to own or lease agricultural land, all evasive transfer must involve ineligible aliens. Consequently none were omitted from the class who should have been included. Some few, those ineligible aliens making a bona fide gift, were improperly included. But there were undoubtedly not many of these; and the presumption in any event was only prima facie. The presumption, accordingly, was beyond constitutional reproach from the classification point of view if the legitimacy of the purpose is assumed. Yet the court both struck down the presumption and assumed the legitimacy of the purpose. Justices Reed and Burton dissented from the opinion of the court precisely on the ground that if the validity of the land-owning and leasing prohibition is granted, then the discrimination in the placing of the burden of proof stands the strict scrutiny of the reasonable-relation test.

The major part of the court's legal-protection discussion does not deal with the reasonableness or the unreasonableness of the classification. It deals only with the question of whether there had been discrimination. It is designed to show and reaches the conclusion that "California law points in one direction for minor citizens like Fred Oyama, whose parents cannot be naturalized, and in another for all other children—for minor citizens whose parents are either citizens or eligible aliens, and even for minors who are themselves aliens though eligible for naturalization."[171] "In our view of the case," said the majority, "the State has discriminated against Fred Oyama; the discrimination is based solely on his parents' country of origin."[172]

The court indeed later considers whether such discriminations, once found, are automatically unconstitutional or may be justified constitutionally by their reasonableness in the particular circumstances. In doing so it comes closer to the first alternative than the second.

There remains the question [said Chief Justice Vinson] of whether discrimination between citizens on the basis of their racial descent, as revealed in this case, is justifiable. Here we start with the proposition that only the most exceptional circumstances can excuse discrimination on that basis in the face of the equal protection clause and a federal statute giving all citizens the right to own land. In Hirabayashi v. United States, this Court sustained a war measure which involved restrictions against citizens of Japanese descent. But the Court recognized that, as a general rule, "Distinctions between citizens solely because of their ancestry are by their very nature odious to a free people whose institutions are founded upon the doctrine of equality."[173]

So discriminations between citizens on a basis of race can be "excused"; but only by "the most exceptional circumstances." What are such circumstances? War is one. No others are suggested. But we know from this case that the "circumstance" that the classification was almost perfectly adapted to the achievement of a purpose granted to be legitimate does not have the requisite "exceptional" character.

The concentration of the court on showing the existence of racial discrimination, the cursory reference and very limited application given to the doctrine that in some circumstances such discriminations are constitutionally justifiable, the allusions to the *Hirabayashi* case—all suggest that, in the absence of an emergency, a racial classification does not even get the benefit of a reasonable-relation test but is to be settled on a well-nigh conclusive presumption of unconstitutionality.

The *Takahashi* case tends to reinforce this conclusion. The court declared unconstitutional the California statute, enacted in 1943 and amended in 1945, which excluded aliens ineligible for citizenship from earning a livelihood as commercial fishermen in the coastal waters.[174] Here, as in *Oyama*, no emergency factor was present, no reasonable-classification test was applied.

Interestingly enough, the court did not regard the problem of the determination of the purpose of the law as very important or relevant to its decision. "For purposes of our decision," said Justice Black, "we may assume that the code provision was passed to conserve fish in the California coastal waters, or to protect California citizens engaged in commercial fishing from competition by Japanese aliens, or for both reasons."[175] This indifference to purpose is very revealing. For had the court been concerned with the reasonableness of the classification it would have been necessary to make some judgment as to purpose. A classification of ineligible aliens may have been unreasonably related to the purpose of conserving fish but perfectly adapted to protecting citizens against competition. On the other hand, had the court been concerned to rule on the question of the discriminatory character of the law's purpose it would have had to decide whether that purpose was conservation or the elimination of competition by aliens, the latter only being subject to constitutional doubt.

Evidently the court, confronted by a racial classification, here simply operated with a strong presumption of unconstitutionality which made unnecessary the application of the usual equal-protection tests. This view is supported by the court:

Congress, [said Justice Black] in the enactment of a comprehensive legislative plan for the nationwide control and regulation of immigration and naturalization, has broadly provided: "All persons within the jurisdiction of the United States shall have the same right in every State and Territory to make and enforce contracts, to sue, be parties, give evidence, and to the full and equal benefits of all laws and proceedings for the security of persons and property as is enjoyed by white citizens, and shall be subject to like punishment, pains, penalties, taxes, licenses, and exactions of every kind, and to no other."[176]
Consequently the section and the Fourteenth Amendment on which it rests in part protect "all persons" against state legislation bearing unequally upon them either because of alienage or color. . . . The Fourteenth Amendment and the laws adopted under its authority thus embody a general policy that all persons lawfully in this country shall abide "in any state" on an equality of legal privileges with all citizens under non-discriminatory laws.[177]

Justice Black then deals with the exceptional-status cases—those cases in which alienage classifications were permitted on the ground that the state or the citizens thereof have a "special public interest" with respect to the common resources of the state or the ownership of land in it. Once more the court did not look to see if aliens possess traits bearing a peculiar relationship to the common resources of the state which would justify a discrimination against them. No reasonable-relationship analysis was made. The court simply denied that a proprietary interest on the part of the citizens collectively, if such existed here, was an adequate basis, or that the Alien Land Law precedent, resting as it did on history and reasons peculiar to real property, would apply.

CONCLUSION

The decisions in the Japanese American cases dealing with curfew, exclusion, and detention constitute a damaging abrogation of the constitutional requirement of equal and nondiscriminatory treatment. One major basis of those decisions is a doctrine of judicial self-restraint amounting virtually to judicial abdication; another is a war-powers doctrine which holds that pressing public necessity frees the military from constitutional limitations. Singly or in combination, these bases would seem to rob the Japanese American cases of significant bearing on any other constitutional provision. If the court is there simply saying that it is not its function to apply the Constitution—or that, regardless of its function, the Constitution does not restrain the war powers—then, it might be argued, little can be concluded as to the content of the equality requirement of the Constitution. Yet the Japanese American cases did fall within the area of the equality requirement and did defy it. And the court, in the *Hirabayashi* case, announced that it was in fact applying that requirement.

As hitherto understood, the doctrine of equality compels a satisfactory showing that the purpose of the selective treatment of a particular group is not to be discriminatory but is to achieve a constitutionally authorized objective; that the trait relied upon as the basis of selective treatment is reasonably related to the achievement of the objective; that that trait is distinctive of the particular group, i.e., characterizes all or most of the members of the group and does not characterize other groups; or that departure from these standards is justified by an emergency and by the absence of a less drastic but adequate alternative. In the Japanese American cases, the court permitted the violation of all these standards.

Constitutionally, good intentions are normally to be measured by good faith, not by valid beliefs. Discriminatory purpose is thus a measure of knavery, not of folly. No one has charged General DeWitt with knavery. There is no evidence that he acted from other than the most commendable and constitutional motives of the proper discharge of his military duty and the security of the West Coast. But General DeWitt did act from false beliefs: namely, that there are racial strains, that they remain undiluted through many generations, and that they are determinants of national loyalty. These are not ordinary false beliefs, the holding of which is mere folly. They are so palpably false, so utterly untenable, as to create a constitutional presumption of bad motive and to render actions based upon them constitutionally void as being founded in discriminatory purpose.

More than that: The prejudicial racial beliefs of the people of the West Coast and of General DeWitt were accepted by the court not only as a test of motive but as a test of facts as well. They were accepted as showing that the proper relationship existed between classifying trait and constitutional objective, i.e., between Japanese ancestry and the likelihood of committing acts of espionage and sabotage against the United States. One by one the court itemized the racial suspicions, rumors, myths, and half-truths which it held "warranted a conclusion" of disloyalty to the United States and loyalty to Japan. The geographical distribution of the Japanese Americans was seen as a result of disloyal design rather than of normal economic and social factors. Japanese-language schools were not simply language schools but sources of nationalistic propaganda cultivating allegiance to the ancestral homeland. Dual citizenship, automatically received as a result of the divergent laws of two countries, created an inference of loyalty to the ancestral homeland but no inference of loyalty to the land of birth. Within their segregated communities, the Japanese Americans were "tightly knit," under the control of alien elders, culturally unassimilated, socially isolated, and "caked" with un-American customs of Oriental origin. The Kibei system had developed out of political loyalty to Japan rather than normal economic and family relationships. The numerous Japanese American organizations were thought to be "engaged in common pro-Japanese purposes" rather than the social, commercial, educational, welfare, and recreational activities which were their avowed goals. Thus the United States Supreme Court accepted the existence of the Oriental stereotype as proof of its truth, as evidence that the victim group in fact possessed the traits attributed to them. The court did so, moreover, in spite of the fact that extensive scholarly investigation and appraisal had invalidated most of the features of the stereotype. Further, the Supreme Court sustained this discriminatory racial classification although the very group characteristics which were used to justify it applied with equal truth (or untruth) to the Italian and German Americans who were neither incarcerated nor evacuated. The classification was thus underinclusive as well as overinclusive.

The emergency which will justify such flagrant violation of the equality command of the Constitution must be real; the action taken must be commensurate with it; there must be no existing alternative adequate to do the job but less drastic in its impact. None of these conditions was met. That the military believed that there was a threat of invasion of the West Coast by the forces of Imperial Japan, that the programs for the curfew, evacuation, and detention were designed by the military to cope with that threat, that the military found that it could not separate the disloyal Japanese Americans from the loyal within the time available—these views were all attributed to those who made the decisions without any showing or evidence whatever. The fact is that American military leaders at the time did not regard an invasion of the West Coast as probable or even possible. The course and character of the emergency, seen only later by the public but known at the time by the military, might have justified curfew in March but hardly evacuation in June; it might even have justified evacuation of all enemy aliens from a strip along the coast and from crucial production areas in the spring, but hardly their evacuation in the summer from the vast inland areas of the Western Defense Command. It might even, at the critical hour after Pearl Harbor, have justified the discriminatory mass removal finally undertaken—but never the accompanying coercive detention.

With respect to an adequate but less drastic alternative, the Army itself, ironically enough, presently demonstrated that there was one. It processed the whole Japanese American population individually, separating the disloyal from the loyal, within a period of time far less than that required for evacuation, and by the use of methods and sources of information that had been available while the Japanese Americans were still in their home communities.

In *Oyama* and *Takahashi* the Supreme Court, as if in penance, struck down a racial classification involving the Japanese on what was virtually a presumption of its unconstitutionality, without applying the normal and less stringent rules of the equal protection of the laws.

Chapter VIII

CITIZENSHIP

The possession of United States citizenship by approximately two-thirds of the Japanese Americans proved to be no irremovable constitutional barrier to discriminatory exclusion and detention. The Supreme Court, in fact, dealing with broad problems of the war power of the military over civilians within the country, the degree to which the courts would review exertions of that power, and questions of racial classification under the Fifth Amendment—which speaks only of "persons"—found little occasion to emphasize any constitutional distinctions between citizens and aliens.[1] Do citizen civilians stand in a different relationship to the military and to the war powers in time of war than law-abiding, lawfully domiciled, alien civilians? Prior to the *Korematsu* case, one would have thought so, assuming the constitutionality of the Alien Enemy Act of 1798, which, in time of war, renders "all natives, citizens, denizens or subjects of the hostile nation . . . within the United States . . . liable to be apprehended, restrained and removed as alien enemies." Granting that there is nothing constitutionally wrong with a classification that is based on race or ancestry and cuts across alien-citizen lines, are there rights of citizenship which cannot constitutionally be denied to the citizens in the class? The rights at stake in the evacuation—primarily those of locomotion, residence, livelihood, home, procedural due process, and other elements of personal security—are generally understood to be equally the constitutional endowment of alien and citizen. The First Amendment rights of speech and assembly are less clearly the possession of those who do not belong to the political body. These questions the court answered only indirectly by decisions which sustained treatment of persons of Japanese ancestry undifferentiated as to citizenship or alienage. In *Hirabayashi*, Chief Justice Stone did allow a special significance to Japanese citizenship in its bearing on loyalty. United States citizenship, however, was not conceded a similar inferen-

---

[1] For notes to chapter viii see pp. 393–396.

tial potency; at least it was thought less relevant to loyalty than was Japanese blood.

While the court dealt thus casually and indirectly with the problem of the United States citizenship of Japanese Americans, such citizenship was widely regarded as a very substantial constitutional obstacle to the discriminatory evacuation of the group. Attorney General Francis Biddle wrote to Congressman Leland Ford of California on January 24, 1942: "Unless the writ of *habeas corpus* is suspended, I do not know of any way in which Japanese born in this country and therefore American citizens could be interned."[2] Later, when the military requested the Department of Justice to remove all Japanese Americans from Bainbridge Island in Puget Sound, the department refused to remove the American citizens. "The only way in which American citizens could be moved from that area," wrote James Rowe, Jr., on February 10 to Undersecretary of the Navy James Forrestal, "would be to declare the area a military zone under partial military law . . . and to exclude from that area all civilians except those having passes issued at the discretion of the Commanding Officer."[3]

Eventually, even the Western Defense Command displayed some sensitivity to the implications of United States citizenship. Instead of openly commanding all Japanese Americans, aliens and citizens, to evacuate, Civilian Exclusion Order No. 1 (March 24, 1942), ordered that "all persons of Japanese ancestry, including aliens and non-aliens" be excluded.

A variety of plans and arguments were put forward by organizations and individuals seeking to deprive Japanese born in this country of their United States citizenship. Some maintained that many Japanese aliens had entered the United States in violation of the Root-Takahira agreement or the Exclusion Act and that therefore their children, though born in the United States, were not legally present at the place of their birth and hence were not citizens.[4] Others proposed, and some state legislatures considered, an amendment to the United States Constitution stripping Japanese Americans of their citizenship. Edward Ennis presented two possibilities: he thought that "American-born Japanese who returned to Japan for extended periods and who have A or B dangerous classifications might be considered to have expatriated themselves pursuant to the provisions of Section 402 of the Nationality Act of 1940." Similarly, he argued, American-born Japanese "who are members of the Shinto Cult" might be considered to have expatriated themselves since "the Shinto Cult is a form of state worship and . . . a Shinto worshipper must necessarily have sworn allegiance to the Japanese State."[5]

The two attacks upon United States citizenship of American-born Japanese which were pushed to the point of a constitutional test in the federal courts were, however, not based upon any of these lines of approach.

The first of these consisted of a suit in the United States District Court for the Northern District of California designed to elicit a judicial declaration that Orientals born in the United States were not, under the Constitution, citizens of the United States.[6] This decision could not be reached without overturning the holding of the United States Supreme Court in the *Wong Kim Ark* case,[7] never seriously challenged since its rendition in 1898, and without rejecting the assertion of the Fourteenth Amendment that "all persons born . . . in the United States . . . are citizens of the United States." Yet since the holding of the United States Supreme Court in *Wong Kim Ark* was plainly "in error" and the "amendment as construed is an abortive act of Congress," the proponents contended they could not be charged with "an excess of temerity" in bringing the action. And the district court was admonished that it is only "the duty of judges to follow . . . the decisions of the Supreme Court of the United States, if they can in good conscience and good judgment."[8]

This lawsuit was the device of that long-time leading anti-Orientalist, Ulysses S. Webb, former Attorney General of the State of California. He moved with the active collaboration and support of those long-time leading anti-Oriental societies, the Native Sons of the Golden West and the American Legion. The suit was instituted in the names of white electors who claimed that they had a federal constitutional right not to have their vote diluted or impaired by persons ineligible to exercise the franchise.[9]

Webb's argument was an incredible admixture of the elements of the Oriental stereotype, a distorted account of the history of the Fourteenth Amendment, some all-but-universally-rejected principles of constitutional law, and the white-man's-government thesis of the pre-Civil War proslavery forces and Chief Justice Taney in *Dred Scott* v. *Sandford*.[10] The argument began with the white-man's-government thesis. "This country was settled," said Webb, "by white people from European countries." Those who inhabited the thirteen colonies and those who framed and administered the government under the Articles of Confederation "were white people from European countries and their descendants." "The colonists had contact with whites only," excepting, of course, Indians and Negro slaves, and "they sought to establish in the New World a government of, for and by white people. The Declaration

of Independence was made by white people ... 'We the people of the
United States ... ourselves and our posterity' " mentioned in the Preamble to the Constitution as the authors and beneficiaries of the Constitution and the new government were "white people."[11]

Among the powers conferred on Congress by the Constitution was
that of providing a "uniform system of naturalization." Congress exercised that power "by providing that 'free white persons' might gain ...
the privilege of American citizenship. The naturalization law thus
adopted in 1790 has been amended a score of times and always Congress
has held steadfastly to the original policy."[12] In 1870, Congress, "in
effecting the purposes of the Thirteenth, Fourteenth and Fifteenth
Amendments," changed the naturalization law to admit " 'aliens of
African nativity and ... persons of African descent.' "[13]

Webb next rewrote the history of the Fourteenth Amendment, converting what was undoubtedly a minor motive of its backers into their
sole objective. "The reasonable and proper construction of the language," of the Fourteenth Amendment, Webb said, and one "in accord
with the intention of the framers ... would extend citizenship" only to
those who had hitherto been eligible to naturalization.[14] The congressional debates upon the Fourteenth Amendment show "conclusively
that not only its main purpose but its only purpose was to citizenize
the Negro because of the effect that such status might have upon the
election returns of the States which had seceded." If the amendment is
construed as granting citizenship to the Negroes and all whites born in
this country, every purpose is accomplished which Congress had in
mind and "the repellent thought" is excluded that "it was intended to
achieve the citizenship of all other peoples of color born in the United
States."[15]

The next step in Webb's argument was to elevate the Preamble of the
Constitution to an unaccustomed position of primacy and to limit the
power of amendment. "The Preamble of the Constitution expressly
prohibited a subsequent extension of citizenship to the Japanese by
constitutional amendment, if such action did not tend to achieve the
objectives" there set forth.[16] Any interpretation of the Fourteenth
Amendment which would extend citizenship to Japanese Americans
violates those objectives "by reason of the racial characteristics of the
Japanese people and the aims, purposes, and ambitions of their government. The admission of Japanese to citizenship does not tend to
insure domestic tranquillity. We have had fifty years of that experience,
showing that it established domestic disturbance."[17] Admission of Japanese Americans to United States citizenship does not "tend to provide

for the common defense." Since Pearl Harbor, "in frantic efforts to provide for the country's defense," we have spent more than two hundred million dollars "to segregate them, to prevent their active aid to a foreign foe, to prevent their aiding the enemy by activities behind the lines."[18]

Finally, the full face of the Oriental stereotype is uncovered. Webb asserted that:

Because of racial characteristics of the Japanese, assimilation with Caucasians is as impossible as it is undesirable. They believe themselves to have descended from Heaven. They believe their Emperor to be a descendant of the Sun-God. They deny the existence of the God whom Christians worship.... Dishonesty, deceit and hypocrisy are racial characteristics.... A Japanese born in the United States is still a Japanese. The presence of the Japanese in the United States has resulted and can result only in evil and this evil is intensified and multiplied by their ability to exercise the privileges of citizenship.[19]

The district court and the circuit court of appeals, on appeal, either disagreed with Webb's exalted view of their function or else "in good conscience and good judgment" could see nothing wrong with *Wong Kim Ark* and the long-standing interpretation of the Fourteenth Amendment. In any event, both preëmptorily refused Webb's plea on the ground that the Fourteenth Amendment and the Supreme Court had settled the question.[20] The Supreme Court was even more abrupt: it denied *certiorari* without comment.[21]

The second of the attacks upon the United States citizenship of Japanese Americans is a more serious augury for the future. It was not a sweeping and direct assault upon the whole constitutional basis of that citizenship. Nor was it apparently "spawned of the great anti-Oriental virus."[22] It presupposed and granted the constitutional status of the citizenship of persons born in this country and was made by the Department of Justice for the limited purpose of controlling and keeping in confinement the citizens who were leaders in the segregation and repatriation disturbances at the Tule Lake Center.[23] It consisted of a federal statute permitting the voluntary renunciation of citizenship.

Under this statute, which took the form of an amendment to the Nationality Act of 1940, resident citizens of the United States were, for the first time, permitted to renounce their citizenship in time of war. It provided that:

A person who is a national of the United States whether by birth or by naturalization, shall lose his nationality by ... making in the United States a formal written renunciation of nationality in such form as may be prescribed by law, and before such officer as may be designated by the Attorney General, whenever the United States shall be in a state of war and the Attorney General shall approve such renunciation as not contrary to the interests of national defense . . .[24]

Since renunciation of citizenship and expatriation are familiar principles of international law and of our own nationality code, this statute would not normally be thought to create any serious legal or constitutional issues. However, its chronology, its overly specific purpose, its discriminatory application, and above all the context of its use, all raise not only very serious factual and legal questions of the voluntary character of the renunciation under it, but constitutional questions of the equal protection of the laws and of the character of citizenship.

The statute was passed in 1944 and repealed in 1947.[25] Early in 1945, the attorney general, acting under it, took 5,522 renunciations from American-born Japanese. Of these, 5,371 were from persons confined at Tule Lake Segregation Center; only 151 were from persons in the eight other camps.

Some of the known reasons for renunciation were the very ones supplied earlier for becoming a Tule Lake segregant: harshly discriminatory treatment by and during evacuation; embitterment over economic losses; the abrogation of citizenship rights; desire to keep the family intact, to dodge the draft, or to remain in camp as a refuge from what was believed to be a hostile American public. To these mixed and varied motives must be added disloyalty to the United States—whether resulting from the factors listed or attachments to Japan—and finally, coercion, as that term is generally, though perhaps not legally, understood; coercion maintained by group persuasion, intimidation, and violence by those in the camps desiring repatriation to Japan; coercion permitted, facilitated, and directly engaged in by the government. In this sense, the statute was "the legal implementation of the government created hysteria and terror which induced the renunciations."[26]

In the words of Thomas and Nishimoto:

With mass renunciation of citizenship by Nisei and Kibei, the cycle which began with evacuation was complete. Their parents had lost their hard-won foothold in the economic structure of America. They, themselves, had been deprived of rights which indoctrination in American schools had led them to believe inviolable. Charged with no offense, but victims of a military misconception, they had suffered confinement behind barbed wire. They had been stigmatized as disloyal on grounds often far removed from any criterion of political allegiance. They had been at the mercy of administrative agencies working at cross-purposes. They had yielded to parental compulsion in order to hold the family intact. They had been intimidated by the ruthless tactics of pressure groups in camp. They had become terrified by reports of the continuing hostility of the American public, and they had finally renounced their irreparably depreciated American citizenship.[27]

Three of the renunciations were, for these reasons, held void by the district court of the United States in *Murakami* v. *Marshall*. They were made, the court concluded, "not as a result of their [renunciants] free and intelligent choice but rather because of mental fear, intimidation and coercion depriving them of the free exercise of their will."[28]

The Ninth Circuit Court adopted the district court's findings and affirmed the judgment.

"Underlying all the particular factors," said Judge Denman for the circuit court, ". . . leading to a condition of mind and spirit of the American citizens imprisoned at Tule Lake Center, which make the renunciations of citizenship" not their free and intelligent choice "is the unnecessarily cruel and inhuman treatment of these citizens," especially in three respects: "(*a*) in the manner of their deportation for imprisonment and (*b*) in their incarceration for over two and a half years" under conditions worse, in important respects, than those in a federal penitentiary, "(*c*) in applying to them the Nazi-like doctrine of inherited racial enmity, stated by the Commanding General ordering the deportations as the major reason for the action."[29]

In another case, *Abo* v. *Clark*,[30] the United States district court in effect revalidated the citizenship of 4,315 Nisei renunciants,[31] this time specifically on the ground that they had been victims of government duress.[32] "The renunciation . . . made by each plaintiff," said Judge Goodman, "was compelled and coerced and was caused by and was the direct and proximate result of the duress in which each plaintiff was held and subjected by the U.S. Government." Some renunciants were conceded to have acted freely and voluntarily. They, however, were not the ones now before the court seeking restoration of citizenship. They "were members of the pro-Japanese organizations at Tule Lake, who have already been repatriated to Japan in accordance with their express wishes."[33] The court expressly refrained from deciding whether the Department of Justice regulations and the renunciation statute were necessarily unconstitutional. It did conclude that "there was a complete lack of constitutional authority for the United States administrative, executive and military officers to detain and imprison the plaintiffs and other interned American Nisei citizens," to hold them in and subject them to duress, in the absence of a charge of criminal action or conditions warranting martial law. The renunciations executed by the plaintiffs were therefore void "from the time of their execution and the approval thereof by the ... Attorney General."[34] "It is shocking to the conscience," said Judge Goodman, "that an American citizen be confined without authority and then, while so under duress and restraint, for his Government to accept from him a surrender of his Constitutional heritage."[35]

On appeal, the Ninth Circuit Court of Appeals agreed that "the oppressive conditions prevailing [at Tule Lake] ... were in large part caused or made possible by the action and inaction of those government officials responsible" for the Japanese Americans during internment. "Because of the oppressiveness of this imprisonment by the government officials, a rebuttable presumption arises as to those confined at Tule Lake that their acts of renunciation were involuntary."[36]

The circuit court therefore affirmed the revalidations for the nearly twenty-five per cent of the total group who were minors, for eight mental incompetents, and for fifty-eight persons who went to Tule Lake to be with family members. Since the presumption was rebuttable, the remaining plaintiffs were sent back to the district court to give the government an opportunity to show that they were not affected by the "coercive conditions" but renounced freely and voluntarily, perhaps motivated by disloyalty.

The Attorney General had determined that under the law the renunciants were dangerous enemy aliens, subject to deportation to Japan, under the Enemy Alien Act of 1798. A number of them were therefore held in detention awaiting transportation. Simultaneously with the action in *Abo* v. *Clark* to rescind their renunciations and to declare their United States citizenship in force, these renunciants applied for writs of habeas corpus to gain their release from custody. This suit, *Ex parte Abo*,[37] presented issues beyond the validity of the renunciations. Suppose the United States citizenship of the Nisei had been terminated—what then was their status? Would they be merely stateless residents of the United States? Would they occupy the anamolous position suggested by their counsel, namely, that of "native American aliens"? Would they be citizens who had become aliens ineligible to citizenship in the land of their birth? If they had been dual citizens, how would this affect their new status?

The district court held that even if the renunciations were valid, the renunciants were not enemy aliens and could not be deported to Japan. They were therefore entitled to their freedom. In reaching this conclusion, Judge Goodman flatly rejected the concept of dual citizenship on which the government had acted.

The theory that a native born resident American, [he said] can at the selfsame time be an alien and a citizen of a foreign state, is . . . judicially wholly unsound. An American citizen as such, owes his entire allegiance to the United States and the United States is entitled to claim from him an indivisible loyalty. A naturalized citizen, at the time of naturalization renounces all allegiance to any foreign government and swears undivided fealty to the United States. No less is the allegiance of a native born citizen, for the Constitution makes no distinction between naturalized and native born citizens. It is Constitutionally impossible for a resident citizen of the United States to have at the same time any allegiance to any foreign government.

Possession of Japanese citizenship, *in Japan,* by a native born resident American citizen of Japanese ancestry, does not, upon renunciation of American citizenship in the United States, convert that person into an alien until he has voluntarily departed from this country.

All that the expatriation statute . . . purports to effect is termination of American citizenship. It in no way fixes or determines any particular alien nationality for the expatriate.

Assuming the petitioners' renunciations to be valid, they would cease to be American Citizens, but they would not thereby acquire an alien citizenship, which they could not lawfully theretofore have possessed.[38]

The Ninth Circuit Court of Appeals declined to adopt the view of Judge Goodman that Japanese law was altogether irrelevant and that the acquisition of Japanese citizenship by renunciants who remained in the United States was impossible. The court of appeals ruled that any person who divested himself of United States citizenship could acquire another citizenship wherever and however the law of another nation might provide. If, under Japanese law, the petitioners were citizens of Japan, and if, under Japanese law, they were permitted to assert that citizenship at any place, and if the petitioners "before renunciation sought Japanese citizenship or . . . afterwards . . . claimed it"[39] while they were still in the United States, they were citizens of Japan and subject to deportation under the Enemy Alien Act. Permission of Congress thus to attain another nationality in the United States was not necessary. The provisions of the Japanese law were to be determined by the trial court as matter of fact. Excluding minors, who were not permitted to renounce United States citizenship, the cause was therefore remanded to the district court for further proceedings.[40]

Judge Denman, in his opinion for the circuit court of appeals, touched upon one of the constitutional issues surrounding the renunciation statute. Petitioners' counsel had argued that, though the language of the statute mentioned neither Japanese Americans nor any other particular groups, "it was framed to procure renunciations solely for citizens of Japanese pedigree and . . . was applied only to such a discriminatory purpose." It was therefore "a special species of discriminatory

class legislation ... unconstitutional as applied."[41] Judge Denman found
that there was "no merit to this contention." "A statute fair on its face,"
he said, "is not invalid merely because Congress, in considering creating ... a general right, directs its attention to a particular group as
exemplifying the desirability of creating such a right." Moreover, since
the court was "not directed to any evidence showing that the right to
renounce was systematically or arbitrarily denied citizens of other than
Japanese ancestry," the claim of discriminatory application was not
borne out. Finally, heaviest reliance was placed upon the fact that the
operation of the statute "depends entirely upon the voluntary action of
the individual" and that "the initiative rests wholly with him."[42] Entirely absent from Judge Denman's consideration of the constitutionality of the renunciation statute was the emphasis which he had earlier
given in his *Murakami* opinion to the context of racial discrimination,
economic hardship, denial of the rights and responsibilities of citizenship, uprooting, removal, banishment, and imprisonment, and to the
renunciations as an integral element of this context.

Aside from Judge Denman's casual constitutional talk in *Barber* v.
Abo, and from some implications of Judge Goodman's opinion in *Ex
parte Abo,* the district courts and circuit court handled the renunciation
cases as if the only issue were one of the voluntary or involuntary nature
of the renunciations. In keeping with the precedent set by their Washington superiors in the *Korematsu* and *Endo* cases, they ignored and
postponed consideration of the grave constitutional issues raised, even
though these issues were elaborately presented by appellees' counsel.
He argued that the renunciation statute "authorized acts contrary to
sovereignty and destructive to the citizenship conferred by the Fourteenth Amendment" and that therefore it was "unconstitutional and
void on its face."[43] "The Constitution," he maintained, "grants citizenship absolutely and without qualification to the native-born." Thus, the
expatriation laws could only be held constitutional "on the theory that
they set up a temporary bar to the exercise of citizenship rights which
the individual can remove." The appellees, because they were members
of a race ineligible to citizenship under the naturalization laws, would
have no method of regaining citizenship rights if their renunciations
were held valid. Consequently, so far as the renunciation statute "attempts to make loss of citizenship rights irrevocable, it is unconstitutional."[44]

Finally, petitioner's counsel went beyond the Fourteenth Amendment to the nature of citizenship and the foundations of the Constitution: "... when it is considered that our national survival is dependent

upon the unimpaired maintenance of the citizenship status, [it be-comes] extremely doubtful that Congress could authorize renunciation of United States citizenship." If Congress cannot whittle away the Con-stitution, it "cannot deprive the Constitution of the citizens which con-stitute its support." Therefore Congress cannot "authorize the renun-ciation of citizenship or the exclusion of citizens of this nation" because it would "thereby destroy not only the grant of the 14th Amendment but impair the foundation of the Constitution itself."[45] Despite the sweep and challenge of these arguments, the courts brushed them aside and disposed of the cases on other and contradictory grounds.

Thus the story ended as it began. The basic issue of the character of United States citizenship and the rights appertaining thereto—always implicitly present in the circumstances but seldom articulated—no-where, least of all in the courts, received the systematic and careful consideration which they imperatively required. Not only were that citizenship and those rights not affirmed—they were not even adequately considered!

Conclusion

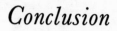

I

Viewed in the perspective of a decade, with all the advantages of hindsight and subsequent disclosure, the Japanese American episode of World War II looms as a great and evil blotch upon our national history. The whole vast, harsh, and discriminatory program of uprooting and imprisonment—initiated by the generals, advised, ordered, and supervised by the civilian heads of the War Department, authorized by the President, implemented by Congress, approved by the Supreme Court, and supported by the people—is without parallel in our past and full of ominous forebodings for our future.

The entire Japanese American program violated and degraded the basic individualism which sustains a democracy. It impaired the trial tradition of the common law. It disparaged the principle that guilt is individual. It sapped the vitality of the precept of equality. It made racism a constitutional principle. It tolerated preventive incarceration for assumed disloyal beliefs and attitudes—unaccompanied by acts—attributing them without proof, probable cause, or reasonable suspicion to an entire group on a basis of race. Recklessly and unnecessarily, it loosened judicial control of the military and produced dangerous imbalance in our government.

The episode embodied one of the most "sweeping and complete deprivations of constitutional rights in the history of this nation."[1] It destroyed basic and precious rights of personal security: the right—without arbitrary or constitutionally irrelevant interference—to move about freely, to live and work where one chooses, to establish and maintain a home; the right not to be deprived of constitutional safeguards except upon an individual basis and after charges, notice, hearing, fair trial, and all of the procedural requirements of due process. It destroyed, as well, basic and precious rights of democratic participation: the right of peaceable assembly to discuss the general welfare and problems of government; the rights of free speech and a free press; the right freely to hear, read, and learn; the rights of petition and remonstrance; the rights of franchise and election, of seeking and holding office; and, not least of all, the right and responsibility to defend one's native land, if need be with one's life.

The Japanese American episode culminated in a constitutional sanctification of these deprivations by the highest court in the land—a court

---

[1] For notes to Conclusion see p. 396.

dedicated to justice, defense of the Constitution, determination of the powers and limitations of government, and protection of the rights of men.

II

In the historical view, the wisdom of a decision is tested principally by subsequent events. Contemporary plausibility is only a minor criterion.[2] Judged by the historical test, military necessity arising out of the war emergency does not provide justification of the program of removal and imprisonment. It is true that Japanese arms, in the winter of 1941–42, advanced rapidly in southeast Asia and the southwest Pacific. Damaging blows were dealt the American navy. A foothold was gained on Attu and Kiska in the Aleutians, Dutch Harbor in Alaska was bombed. But it is also true that Japanese strength had been fully committed in the far Pacific. The mainland Pacific coastline of the United States was adequately protected even before December was out. The Battle of Midway on June 6, 1942, brought Japanese naval expansion in the Pacific to an end. Thereafter, the enemy forces on Attu and Kiska withered from lack of support.

There was no invasion of the coastal mainland. There were not even commando raids or air strikes upon it. One submarine lobbed a few shells harmlessly near an oil installation not far from Santa Barbara (February 23, 1942).[3] Another sent a midget airplane with an incendiary bomb over an Oregon forest (September 9, 1942); the bomb ignited nothing. A third submarine fired on coast defenses at Astoria, Oregon (June 21, 1942). In December, 1941, there were only three successful enemy submarine attacks on ships leaving West Coast ports. In January, 1942, there were none; in February none; in March none; in April none; in May none. No Japanese surface ship ever operated in the eastern part of the Pacific between Hawaii and the mainland.[4]

Thus, in the calm retrospect of history, it is evident that military necessity warranting the program simply did not exist. After Midway, there was no justification at all for either mass detention or mass exclusion. Even before Midway, there was no justification for mass detention or for the mass exclusion of American citizens of Japanese ancestry. There was no justification at any time for treating Japanese aliens differently from other enemy aliens.

The absence of any acts of espionage and sabotage by Japanese Americans between Pearl Harbor and evacuation—while numerous persons of other extractions were being convicted of such acts—sufficiently testifies (1) to the active or passive loyalty of the major part of the Japanese American population, and (2) to the adequacy of existing methods of control and prevention. Even were this not so, alternative methods of control were available, less drastic than evacuation and detention combined or than either of them separately, more consonant with the Constitution and wholly adequate to meet the actual danger.

All this can now be seen clearly. But even if we abandon the vantage point of history and judge the military only by what they then knew, the same conclusion must be reached. For the fact is that much of what was learned by the public only years later was, at the time, known to our military leaders. It was their judgment then that Japanese strength had been fully committed elsewhere; that, after December, the Pacific Coast was adequately protected. They knew the Japanese strength on land, sea, and in the air. They knew where it was deployed and what its capabilities were. The Navy especially believed that invasion was virtually out of the question by the spring of 1942. The significance of Midway was correctly appraised at the time. Yet it was after that battle that the inland Japanese Americans were evacuated and all Japanese Americans removed from assembly centers to relocation centers.

The weakness of the case for military necessity was spotlighted rather than concealed by General DeWitt's *Final Report,* which is a flimsy tissue of misstatements, preposterous absurdities, patently fallacious reasoning, unacknowledged quotations, and uses facts and arguments developed after the event in an obvious attempt to show that, at the time the decision for evacuation was made, it was based on facts and sound reasoning. Most remarkable of all are these two assertions, contained in a single paragraph: "The very fact that no sabotage has taken place to date is a disturbing and confirming indication that such action will be taken"; and "The Japanese race is an enemy race and while many second and third generation Japanese born on United States soil, possessed of United States citizenship, have become 'Americanized,' the racial strains are undiluted."[5]

III

The responsibility for this flagrant breach of the nation's constitutional and moral ideals may be readily assigned.

It rests first and primarily with the people: the people of the nation in general; the people of the West Coast in particular. Popular feelings and attitudes were complex, but the two major forces which contributed to their development may be identified. First, of course, was the war itself.

Germany had conquered the European continent with amazing speed and show of invincibility. She had annexed Austria, humbled England and France at Munich, overrun Czechoslovakia. She had conquered Poland in twenty-six days. She had seized Denmark and Norway; had crushed the Netherlands in four days, Belgium in seventeen, France in ten. She had taken Roumania, Bulgaria, Yugoslavia, Greece, and Crete. She had invaded Russia on a 2,000-mile front and had pushed 500 miles into that country. She had held Kharkov and Rostov, besieged Leningrad, and approached the gates of Moscow. Thus, in December, 1941, Hitler held Europe from Norway to Sicily and from the Pyrenees practically to Moscow. In the Mediterranean only Malta and Gibraltar were in British hands. The Germans were in French North Africa. Rommel was threatening Suez, which could only be reinforced by way of the Cape of Good Hope. From bases along the Atlantic Coast line, German U-boats, aircraft, and surface raiders ranged the North Sea, the Channel, and the Bay of Biscay. Shipping to Britain was under constant attack, with losses mounting to 500,000 tons a month early in 1941. Counter-measures reduced that staggering total to the still staggering figure of 180,000 tons a month in late 1941, but the British situation was still precarious. German arms, ships, and submarines terrorized shipping within 100 miles of the eastern coast of the United States.

Then came Pearl Harbor. The United States itself was suddenly in the war—a total global war, for the German declaration against us followed immediately—a war in which prior commitments and the over-all strength of the enemy oriented our principal effort first toward the Atlantic. In the light of later events, it is difficult now to believe that at the time public reaction to Pearl Harbor included the wildest kind of overconfidence in our ability to deal with Japan and underestimation of her military potential. Military experts, lay commentators, and sidewalk reporters differed only as to whether it would take one, two, or three months to wipe out the Japanese navy and bring complete and overwhelming victory. But within one month the Japanese had occupied Thailand, Guam, Wake Island, Hong Kong, and Manila; they had made landings in Malaya; they had sunk the *Prince of Wales* and the *Repulse*. In the second month Japanese conquests mounted. They invaded Burma from Thailand; they pushed British forces back in Malaya toward Singapore. From landings in Borneo and the Celebes they worked down Macassar Straits despite bombings from Flying Fortresses and attacks by American destroyers. Spreading out from Truk they landed at Rabaul, New Britain, and New Ireland on January 23 and pushed into the Solomons on January 29, having seized the Admirality Islands earlier. The sea lanes from Australia to India were now hazardous. There was a real threat that communications between Australia and the United States might be cut and shipping forced far to the east. By the end of the third month the Japanese had won a major victory in the battle of the Java Sea, established control over the Dutch East Indies, completely occupied Rangoon and Burma, and placed Bataan and Corregidor under siege. They had taken Singapore and its British army of 100,000 men. Communications between the Middle East and Australia had been rendered subject to attack. Port Darwin on the northern coast of Australia had been bombed from the air.

The reaction of the American people to these catastrophic events was not merely one of disbelief and incredulity; it was one of rising anger, fear, apprehension, and frustration. In this atmosphere few were heard to protest the removal from the western coastal area of those who had ancestral connections with Japan.

The second major force operating in the formation of popular attitudes, especially on the West Coast, was a long history of anti-Oriental and specifically anti-Japanese agitation. The Japanese attack on Pearl Harbor activated, but it did not begin, the Japanese American episode. The basis for the episode is to be found in the history of the Pacific frontier, when the first Japanese immigrants arrived to share the popular prejudice against the Chinese and eventually to inherit it. This part of the story concerns the creation, development, and widespread diffusion of an Oriental stereotype depicting first the Chinese and subsequently the Japanese as sly, tricky, inscrutable; as untrustworthy neighbors and unscrupulous competitors; and, most important of all, as spies and secret agents of the homeland government. Rising Japanese military and national strength, coupled with an aggressive policy of expansion following the Russo-Japanese War, gave seeming substance to the secret-agent element of the stereotype. The attack on Pearl Harbor provided, in the minds of the public, its complete substantiation. That Japanese immigrants and their descendants should now aid and support the ancestral government was all that was needed to bring about a total realization of the stereotype of the "yellow peril."

The primary responsibility of the people for the action taken against the Japanese Americans cannot be shifted to the shoulders of pressure groups and politicians. The activity of such organizations and individuals before the basic decision of mid-February, 1942 (and indeed after) has been greatly exaggerated both as to extent and influence.

The pressure groups of all varieties, the politicians in Congress, the state legislatures, and the executive departments, did not so much lead as follow the people. Many of them, in fact, pulled in the opposite direction; still more took no public stand at all. Some who moved against the Japanese Americans were prompted by the hope of economic gain; others acted contrary to their own self-interest. In the scattered and spasmodic, not to say desultory, actions of these varied groups along the coast in the early months of war there is little sign of systematic organization or crafty connivance; all that can be said is that if a mountainous plot existed its labors brought forth a mouse. But although the voices raised in discordant chorus against the Japanese Americans had no common organization, they did have a common heritage and a common fear. For politicians, farmers, businessmen, and exalted rulers are also people, private citizens, and members of the general public, who share the prevailing attitudes, beliefs, and habits of their communities. Not only do they respond to and exploit the prejudices of their fellows, they also possess them. In early 1942, their expression of anti-Orientalism was basically neither premonitory nor self-serving. It was an illustration and reflection of public sentiment.

Responsibility for the episode rests, secondarily, with the military, particularly with General DeWitt and the Western Defense Command. To portray General DeWitt as the sole or even the chief villain in this tragic drama, as has so often been done, is as much an injustice as to absolve him altogether. But his role, though subordinate, was important. The governmental activity which resulted in the establishment of the Japanese American program was initiatd by General DeWitt. He made the proposal to his superiors and requested authority to execute it. For having done so he must stand convicted by history of committing a military blunder—the perpetration of an outrage on citizen civilians which was not required by the emergency. The plea of military necessity cannot be sustained. Statements from General DeWitt's *Final Report* make it plain that the proposal to evacuate and imprison the Japanese Americans was not the product of a military estimate of the military situation. That the program of exclusion and incarceration resulted from a proper and commendable concern about the security of the West Coast does not mean that the decision to inaugurate it was not based on palpable race prejudice in the Western Defense Command. That General DeWitt honestly believed that race and racial strains had a decisive bearing upon the danger of espionage and sabotage from Japanese Americans does not mean that his belief was a military factor in a military judgment.

Even greater responsibility rests upon President Franklin D. Roosevelt and his civilian aides in the War Department, Secretary Henry L. Stimson and Assistant Secretary John J. McCloy, and upon the Congress of the United States. General DeWitt did not order evacuation and incarceration independently and without prior authorization from his superiors. We do not have here the imaginary problem, posed by Justice Jackson in his *Korematsu* dissent, of an "irresponsible" and "unscrupulous" commander refusing to submit to higher civil authority. What we have, on the contrary, is a commander who proceeded meticulously through duly constituted channels. He presented his plan and request for authority to the War Department, thence to the President, and eventually to Congress. In response, the President, as the President alone could, issued Executive Order 9066,[6] fully empowering the Secretary of War to put the proposed plan into operation. Thereafter, and pursuant to this delegation of authority, Secretary Henry L. Stimson, the civilian head of the War Department, and John J. McCloy, his civilian assistant, first modified the plan by exempting German and Italian American citizens and aliens, then ordered it put into effect, and, finally, continuously supervised its execution. Meanwhile, the Congress of the United States duly enacted Public Law 503,[7] encompassing and providing civilian sanctions for Executive Order 9066 and the subdelegations under it.

Thus, for these days which in their own way will live in infamy, President Roosevelt bears a large share of the responsibility. He bears it not only in the inert and formal sense that he was the chief executive of the nation and hence accountable for the acts of his subordinates whether he knew of them or not, but also in the immediate and active sense that he deliberately and knowingly authorized the program through the issuance of Executive Order 9066, thereafter supplemented it by other executive orders, and personally directed that its termination be delayed until after the presidential election of 1944. The action of Congress was also taken after due consideration. The President and the Congress of the United States were in fact, as well as in every proper constitutional and democratic sense, the agencies of ultimate decision. That their decision conformed to popular clamor and a request from the military does not and cannot relieve them of ultimate responsibility.

McCloy's apologetic statement that "the military men made the decision—it was a military decision"[8] may indicate the attitude of the Washington officials involved in the decision. It does not and it cannot, however, explain the failure of McCloy and of Secretary Stimson to perform the function implicit in the historic purpose behind the requirement that the War Department must have civilian heads.

Responsibility rests, finally, with the courts, and especially with the Supreme Court of the United States. In many ways the failure of the Supreme Court was the greatest failure of all. For the military is preoccupied with war, not with the Constitution and men's rights. The President and Congress, too, are "war-waging" branches of government. The primary action and affirmative decision was theirs; but they moved on the brink of the event when the general course and outcome of the war were altogether uncertain. In 1945 General Marshall pointed out that in "the black days of 1942 when the Japanese conquered all of Malaysia, occupied Burma, and threatened India while the German armies approached the Volga and the Suez . . . Germany and Japan came so close to complete domination of the world that we do not yet realize how thin the thread of Allied survival had been stretched."⁹

Among the branches of government, the Supreme Court occupies a unique position. It is not so much an active as a reflective body. Its decisions are made on the nether side of the event. Its job is not primary but secondary. It is the historian of events as much as it is their maker. It exerts only such constructive leadership as derives from the power to negate the policy of others. Its self-arrogated and perhaps inherent function is to strike the governmental balance between motion and stability, between new action and old doctrines, between the powers of the nation and men's rights.

If the court had struck down the program, the Japanese American episode would have lived in history as nothing worse than a military blunder. But the court approved the program as constitutional, a step with implications and consequences accurately described by Justice Jackson in his dissenting opinion on the *Korematsu* case:

Much is said of the danger to liberty from the Army program for deporting and detaining these citizens of Japanese extraction. But a judicial construction of the due process clause that will sustain this order is a far more subtle blow to liberty than the promulgation of the order itself. A military order, however unconstitutional, is not apt to last longer than the military emergency. Even during that period a succeeding commander may revoke it all. But once a judicial opinion rationalizes such an order to show that it conforms to the Constitution, or rather rationalizes the Constitution to show that the Constitution sanctions such an order, the Court for all time has validated the principle of racial discrimination in criminal procedure and of transplanting American citizens. The principle then lies about like a loaded weapon ready for the hand of any authority that can bring forward a plausible claim of an urgent need. Every repetition imbeds that principle more deeply in our law and thinking and expands it to new purposes. All who observe the work of courts are familiar with what Judge Cardozo described as "the tendency of a principle to expand itself to the limit of its logic." A military commander may overstep the bounds of constitutionality, and it is an incident. But if we review and approve, that passing incident becomes the doctrine of the Constitution. There it has a generative power of its own, and all that it creates will be in its own image.[10]

Grant that the function of the court, in reviewing war-power decisions made by the military, the President, and Congress, is not to determine whether those decisions were reasonable in the light of all the circumstances down to the date of judicial review—a very questionable concession. Grant further that the function of the court is not to substitute its judgment for that of the military, the President, and Congress on a basis of what it would have regarded as reasonable in the situation obtaining at the time of the military action—though the substantial-basis test to some degree requires just that. Grant, finally, that even with respect to military orders not strictly military in character that affect civilians within the country, the court, reviewing the military as it would a civilian agency making the same decision, must allow a fair amount of latitude to the military both in deciding whether and to what extent a danger exists and in choosing the means to cope with it. Grant all this, and the role of the court in the Japanese American episode of World War II was still one of the great failures in its history—comparable with its surrender to slavery in *Prigg* v. *Pennsylvania*[11] and in *Dred Scott* v. *Sandford*.[12]

In terms of procedure and substance—rather than of the deprivation of constitutional rights which the high judges condoned—the failure of the Supreme Court consisted in:

1. Its failure to apply the substantial-basis test to the question of whether the discriminatory curfew for Japanese American citizens was reasonably necessary and appropriate as a means of preventing espionage and sabotage in the circumstances.

2. Its refusal to pass upon and hold unconstitutional the program of detention.

3. That, with respect to evacuation, it either abandoned the Constitution to military fiat or, what amounts to the same thing, applied the subsantial-basis test in such a way as to leave the test meaningless.

4. That it attributed to the military a conclusion that the war crisis justified evacuation at the time it was ordered, without requiring (*a*) evidence that this was in fact the judgment of the military and (*b*) evidence that the conclusion was reasonably founded.

5. That it sustained the discriminatory evacuation of Japanese Americans, aliens and citizens, without requiring the military to supply substantial evidence (*a*) that there was danger of sabotage and espionage from the group, (*b*) that such danger was not already detected and controlled by existing methods, including curfew, (*c*) that the disloyal could not be separated from the loyal by other and less drastic methods than evacuation within the time limits.

6. That it apparently failed to realize and certainly failed to hold that a decision might be based on grounds so untenable and ridiculous—as that racial strains are determinants of national loyalty—that not only folly but bad motive is proved thereby, and the decision is thus constitutionally void as discriminatory in its purpose.

7. That it gave the most perfunctory scrutiny to a ruinously harsh discrimination based on race and ancestry which in moral terms deserves, and in constitutional terms requires, the most rigid scrutiny; and by this default the United States Supreme Court elevated racism to a constitutional principle.

In this way did the United States Supreme Court strike a blow at the liberties of us all.

INTRODUCTION

[1] *Acheson* v. *Murakami* (1949), 176 F. 2d. 953 at 954.

[2] *Korematsu* v. *United States* (1944), 323 U.S. 214 at 235; 65 S. Ct. 193 at 202.

[3] Karl R. Bendetsen, *An Obligation Discharged ... An Address Delivered to Personnel of the Wartime Civil Control Administration*, November 3, 1942. (U.S. Army, WDC, n.d.).

[4] *Proceedings of a Conference of State Governors and Federal Officials, Called by the War Relocation Authority, Salt Lake City, April 7, 1942.* (Processed.)

[5] Brief of Japanese American Citizens League, Amicus Curiae in *Korematsu* v. *United States* [(1944), 323 U.S. 214, 65 S. Ct. 192], p. 3.

[6] U.S. Army, Western Defense Command and Fourth Army, *Final Report: Japanese Evacuation from the West Coast, 1942.* (Washington: Government Printing Office, 1943), p. 34.

[7] *Americans from Japan* (Philadelphia: Lippincott, 1948), p. 270.

[8] *Prejudice* (Boston: Little, Brown, 1944), pp. 4, 118.

[9] *Americans Betrayed: Politics and the Japanese Evacuation* (Chicago: University of Chicago Press, 1949).

[10] "The Japanese American Cases—A Disaster," *Yale Law Journ.*, vol. 54 (1945), p. 496.

[11] "The Law of Martial Rule and the National Emergency," *Harvard Law Rev.*, vol. 55 (1942), p. 1302.

[12] *Ibid.*, p. 1301.

[13] *Ibid.*

[14] *Ibid.*, p. 1300.

[15] *Ibid.*, pp. 1288–1289.

[16] F. B. Wiener, reviewing Grodzins, in *Harvard Law Rev.*, vol. 63 (1950), p. 549, quoting Chief Justice Taney in *Mitchell* v. *Harmony* (1851), 19 U.S. (13 How.) 115 at 135.

[17] "The Nisei—A Casualty of World War II," *Cornell Law Quart.*, vol. 28 (1943), p. 403.

[18] *Ibid.*, p. 404.

[19] Nanette Dembitz, "Racial Discrimination and the Military Judgment: The Supreme Court's Korematsu and Endo Decisions," *Columbia Law Rev.*, vol. 45 (1943), p. 175; Edward S. Corwin, *Total War and the Constitution* (New York: Knopf, 1947); Harrop A. Freeman, "Genesis, Exodus and Leviticus: Genealogy, Evacuation and Law," *Cornell Law Quart.*, vol. 28 (1943), p. 414; Milton R. Konvitz, *The Alien and the Asiatic in American Law* (Ithaca, New York: Cornell Univ. Press, 1946); Eugene V. Rostow, "The Japanese American Cases—A Disaster," *Yale Law Journ.*, vol. 54 (1945), p. 496.

CHAPTER I

[1] See James Bryce, *The American Commonwealth* (New York: Macmillan, 1913), vol. 2, p. 426; Robert G. Cleland, *From Wilderness to Empire: A History of California 1542–1900* (New York: Knopf, 1944), p. 261.

[2] *California Inter Pocula*, Works, Vol. XXV (San Francisco: The History Co., 1882–1890), p. 561.

[3] *California: A Study of American Character* (Boston and New York: Houghton Mifflin, 1886), p. 276.

[4] *The American Commonwealth*, vol. 2, p. 428.

[5] See Mary E. B. Coolidge, *Chinese Immigration* (New York: Henry Holt, 1909), p. 29; Horace Bushnell, *California: Its Characteristics and Prospects* (New Haven, 1858), p. 22; Stewart Edward White, *The Forty-Niners* (New Haven: Yale University Press, 1918), pp. 179–180.

[6] Bushnell, *California*, p. 21.

[7] Royce, *California*, p. 275.

[8] *Ibid.*, p. 359. For the reaction of the California legislature, see the *Journal of the Senate of the State of California*, 1849–50, p. 493. For the penalties imposed on foreigners by General Persifer F. Smith, Pacific Military Area Commandant in 1849, see T. H. Hittell, *History of California* (San Francisco: N. J. Stone, 1897–98), vol. 3, p. 705. Cf. George D. Tinkham, *California: Men and Events* (Stockton: The Record Publishing Co., 1915), p. 127.

[9] C. W. Dilke, *Greater Britain*, quoted in W. P. Fenn, *Ah Sin and His Brethren in American Literature* (Peking: College of Chinese Studies, 1933), p. 16. See also Hittell, *History of California*, vol. 3, p. 706, n. 14.

[10] Irish, German and English immigrants in particular were blamed in varying degrees for promoting racial agitation. See Hinton R. Helper, *Land of Gold* (Baltimore: H. Taylor, 1855); Bancroft, *California Inter Pocula*, p. 561; Coolidge, *Chinese Immigration*, p. 269.

The Europeans in California, most notably the French, were not always exempt from antiforeign feelings. See F. Soulé, J. H. Gihon and J. Nisbet, *The Annals of San Francisco* (New York: Appleton, 1855), p. 463; C. S. Shinn, *Mining Camps* (New York: Scribner, 1885), p. 203; H. H. Bancroft, *History of California* (San Francisco: The History Co., 1882–1890), vol. 6, p. 407; Friedrich Gerstaecker, *California Gold Mines* (Oakland: Biobooks, 1946), p. 92.

[11] Hittell, *History of California*, vol. 3, pp. 888, 915.

[12] *Ibid.*, p. 920.

[13] Bancroft, *History of California*, vol. 6, p. 402.

[14] See the reminiscences of Colonel James J. Ayers, *Gold and Sunshine* (Boston: R. G. Badger, 1922), chap. vi: "The Chilean War in Calaveras County—A Thrilling Chapter of Unwritten History."

[15] Bancroft, *History of California*, vol. 6, p. 406.

[16] Royce, *California*, p. 363.

[17] C. A. Dunimay, "Slavery in California after 1848," in *Annual Report of the American Historical Association, 1905*, vol. 1, pp. 241–248.

[18] Ira B. Cross, *History of the Labor Movement in California* (Berkeley: University of California Press, 1935), p. 295 n.

[19] *Journal of the Senate of the State of California*, First Session, 1849–50, p. 337. Cf. Hittell, *History of California*, vol. 4, pp. 59, 244; Tinkham, *California: Men and Events*, p. 136.

[20] Bancroft, *History of California*, vol. 6, p. 408. The present account is consciously at variance with the impression conveyed by some historians that the Chinese were at first widely welcomed in California. Although there were many individuals and a few groups who championed the Chinese, these seem to have been isolated and unrepresentative of general opinion.

[21] Coolidge, *Chinese Immigration*, p. 254. See also B. S. Brooks, *A Brief Statement of Matters of Law Involved in the Inquiry upon the Chinese Question Referred to the Joint Committee of the Senate and House of Representatives* (San Francisco, 1877), p. 22.

[22] F. A. Bee, *Opening Argument of F. A. Bee before the Joint Committee of the Two Houses of Congress on Chinese Immigration* (San Francisco, 1876), p. 27 f.

[23] Coolidge, *Chinese Immigration*, p. 262. See also the accounts of attacks by hoodlums as reported in the San Francisco *Evening Bulletin* from 1855 to 1876, cited in Appendix A, "Outrages on Chinese," in B. S. Brooks, *Appendix to the Opening*

Statement and Brief of B. S. Brooks on the Chinese Question . . . Consisting of Documentary Evidence and Statistics Bearing on the Questions Involved (San Francisco, 1877).

[24] Coolidge, *Chinese Immigration*, p. 262.

[25] "In the year 1887 all Chinese residing in Del Norte County . . . were ordered by a committee of citizens to vacate Del Norte County which they did at once and since that time no Chinese have resided in this County whatsoever." (Letter, E. R. Griffin, City Clerk, Crescent City, to authors, March 18, 1949, Study files). Chinese were reportedly eliminated from Humboldt County by bombing or other violence at about the same time. (Letter, F. J. Moore, County Clerk, Humboldt County, to authors, February 3, 1948, Study files.)

[26] Lucille M. Eaves, *A History of California Labor Legislation*, Univ. Calif. Publ. Econ., Vol. 2 (Berkeley: University of California Press, 1910), pp. 26, 140.

[27] Coolidge, *Chinese Immigration*, p. 84.

[28] Eaves, *A History of California Labor Legislation*, p. 154.

[29] Coolidge, *Chinese Immigration*, p. 123.

[30] Eaves, *A History of California Labor Legislation*, pp. 141, 178.

[31] Hittell, *History of California*, p. 264; Coolidge, *Chinese Immigration*, p. 37. For typical anti-Chinese tax levies, see *Cal. Stat.* (1862), pp. 486, 462; *Lin Sing* v. *Washburn*, 20 Cal. 534.

[32] In an opinion of 1854, Chief Justice H. C. Murray ruled that "the law was intended to exclude all people of color from testifying in court against a white person." (*People* v. *Hall*, 4 Cal. 399). In effect for 18 years, this ruling was finally omitted from the California codes compiled in 1872.

[33] The "Fifteen Passenger Bill" was the first attempt, passed in 1879 but vetoed by the President. In 1880 a new treaty was concluded with China which allowed the United States to "limit, regulate or suspend" immigration of laborers. Western congressmen immediately introduced and secured the passage of bills to suspend immigration of this class for 20 years. Following a veto by President Arthur, a new bill limiting the period to 10 years was approved on May 6, 1882. (22 U.S. Stat., 58–61). The Scott Act of 1888 prohibited the return to this country of Chinese laborers who might leave it (25 U.S. Stat. 476) and the ban was made stronger by another measure the same year (25 U.S. Stat. 504). The Geary Act of 1892 extended the prohibition on immigration for another 10 years (27 U.S. Stat. 25) and subsequent acts of 1902 and 1904 further extended the ban indefinitely. (32 U.S. Stat. 176 and 33 U.S. Stat. 428).

[34] Eaves, *A History of California Labor Legislation*, p. 116.

[35] *Journal of the Senate of the State of California*, 1852. For documented refutations of the charges of Chinese labor competition, see Carl Plehn, "Labor in California," *Yale Review*, vol. 4 (1897), pp. 409–425; Coolidge, *Chinese Immigration*, chap. 18. Cf. Paul S. Taylor, *Foundations of California Rural Society* (San Francisco, 1945).

[36] Atwell Whitney, *Almond-Eyed* (San Francisco: A. L. Bancroft, 1878).

[37] Quoted in H. J. West, *The Chinese Invasion* (San Francisco: Bacon and Co., 1873), p. 105.

[38] Quoted in Coolidge, *Chinese Immigration*, p. 83.

[39] West, *The Chinese Invasion*, p. 137.

[40] Quoted in Fenn, *Ah Sin and His Brethren*, p. 27.

[41] Quoted in A. L. Sandmeyer, *The Anti-Chinese Movement in California* (Urbana: University of Illinois Press, 1939), p. 39.

[42] *Report of the Joint Special Committee to Investigate Chinese Immigration*, 44th Congress, 2d sess., Senate Report No. 689 (Washington: G.P.O., 1877).

[43] West, *The Chinese Invasion*, p. 5.

[44] Pierton W. Dooner, *Last Days of the Republic* (San Francisco: Alta California, 1880).

[45] San Francisco: A. L. Bancroft, 1882.

[46] San Francisco: Britton & Rey, 1907.

[47] Jack London, *Moon-Face and Other Stories* (New York: Macmillan, 1919), pp. 71 ff.

[48] Goodrich, *Universal History*, p. 116, quoted in Fenn, *Ah Sin and His Brethren*, p. 9.

[49] Speech by Senator Casserly, 1869, quoted in West, *The Chinese Invasion*, p. 84.

[50] Quoted in Fenn, *Ah Sin and His Brethren*, p. 9.

[51] West, *The Chinese Invasion*, p. 84.

[52] Fenn, *Ah Sin and His Brethren*, p. 110.

[53] West, *The Chinese Invasion*, p. 140.

[54] *Ibid.*, p. 83.

[55] *Ibid.*, p. 6.

[56] See Fenn, *Ah Sin and His Brethren*, pp. 68 f.

[57] Quoted in Coolidge, *Chinese Immigration*, p. 96.

[58] See Gunnar Myrdal, *An American Dilemma* (New York: Harper, 1944), pp. 75, 1065.

[59] Berkeley: University of California Press, 1952. Also regretfully omitted has been the consideration of other immigrant groups of Asian or Pacific origin—such as the Koreans, Hindus, and Filipinos—who to a greater or lesser degree came to share the stereotype of the Oriental. See Bruno Lasker, *Filipino Immigration: To Continental United States and Hawaii* (Chicago: University of Chicago Press, 1931); Eliot G. Mears, *Resident Orientals on the Pacific Coast* (Chicago: University of Chicago Press, 1927); Milton R. Konvitz, *The Alien and the Asiatic in American Law* (Ithaca: Cornell University Press, 1946); Donald R. Young, *American Minority Peoples* (New York: Harper, 1932); Carey McWilliams, *Brothers Under the Skin* (Boston: Little, Brown, 1943).

[60] On the concept of stereotypes, with reference to national and ethnic groups, see Otto Klineberg, *Tensions Affecting International Understanding: A Survey of Research* (New York: Social Science Research Council, 1950). See also the important body of work in this field by Harold D. Lasswell, especially *Psychopathology and Politics* (Chicago: University of Chicago Press, 1930) and *World Politics and Personal Insecurity* (New York: Whittlesey House, 1935). See also Walter Lippmann, *Public Opinion* (New York: Harcourt, Brace, 1922).

[61] B. Schrieke, *Alien Americans* (New York: Viking Press, 1936), p. 26.

[62] T. Iyenaga, *Japan and the California Problem* (New York and London: Putnam, 1921), p. 70.

[63] *Reports on Immigration*, United States Industrial Commission (Washington: G.P.O., 1901), vol. XV, p. 754.

[64] March 17, 1900. Cf. A. E. Yoell, "Oriental vs. American Labor," *Annals of the American Academy of Political and Social Science* (Hereinafter cited as *Annals*), vol. XXXIV, no. 2 (September, 1909), p. 32.

[65] "Reasons for Encouraging Japanese Immigration," *ibid.*, p. 74.

[66] Sidney G. P. Coryn, "The Japanese Problem in California," *ibid.*, pp. 47–48.

[67] Thus a few of the headlines displayed by the San Francisco *Chronicle* in 1905 read: Crime and Poverty Go Hand in Hand with Asiatic Labor; Japanese a Menace to American Women; Brown Men Are an Evil in the Public Schools; Japanese Bring Vile Diseases. See issues of February 5, 1905, *et seq.*

[68] Thomas A. Bailey, *Theodore Roosevelt and the Japanese-American Crises* (Stanford: Stanford University Press, 1934), p. 36.

[69] Congressman E. A. Hayes, quoted in Yamato Ichihashi, *Japanese Immigration* (San Francisco: The Marshall Press, 1915), p. 56. Cf. Walter MacArthur, "Opposition to Oriental Immigration," *Annals*, vol. XXXIV, no. 2 (September, 1909), p. 23.

[70] Charles N. Reynolds, *Oriental-White Relations in Santa Clara County, California* (Unpublished dissertation, Stanford University, 1928), p. 120.

[71] Robert E. Park, "Racial Assimilation in Secondary Groups: with Particular Reference to the Negro," *American Journal of Sociology*, vol. 19 (1914), p. 611.

[72] Chester Rowell, "Chinese and Japanese Immigrants—A Comparison," *Annals*, vol. XXXIV, no. 2 (September, 1909), p. 9.

[73] A. W. Griswold, *The Far Eastern Policy of the United States* (New York: Harcourt, Brace, 1933), p. 113.

[74] February 23, 1905.

[75] March 11, 1905.

[76] See Payson J. Treat, *Japan and the United States* (Stanford: Stanford University Press, 1928), p. 188.

[77] *Ibid.*, p. 190.

[78] March 11, 1905. The *Chronicle* exclaimed a year later: "The Japanese who come here remain Japanese . . . Every one of them, so far as his service is desired, is a Japanese spy." (November 14, 1906).

[79] *The Valor of Ignorance* (New York: Harper, 1909), p. 198.

[80] Bailey, *Theodore Roosevelt*, pp. 75, 98.

[81] Eleanor Tupper and George E. McReynolds, *Japan in American Public Opinion* (New York: Macmillan, 1931), p. 33.

[82] E. K. Strong, Jr., *The Second-Generation Japanese Problem* (Stanford: Stanford University Press, 1934), p. 139.

[83] *Literary Digest*, January 12, 1907. Cf. Bailey, *Theodore Roosevelt*, pp. 228, 256.

[84] Henry W. Taft, *Japan and America* (New York: Macmillan, 1932), pp. 111–112.

[85] Treat, *Japan and the United States*, p. 231.

[86] Ferdinand Lundberg, *Imperial Hearst* (New York: Equinox Press, 1936), p. 239.

[87] Oliver Carlson and E. S. Bates, *Hearst, Lord of San Simeon* (New York: Viking Press, 1936), p. 179.

[88] Lothrop Stoddard, *The Rising Tide of Color* (New York: Scribner, 1920), p. 49.

[89] See his *The Japanese Conquest of American Opinion* (New York: Doran, 1917).

[90] Ruth E. McKee, *California and Her Less Favored Minorities*, U. S. Department of Interior, War Relocation Authority (Washington: G.P.O., 1944), p. 25.

[91] Taft, *Japan and America*, p. 193.

[92] See R. D. McKenzie, *Oriental Exclusion* (Chicago: University of Chicago Press, 1928), p. 78.

[93] See, for example, the charge before a congressional committee in 1935 that "there are 500,000 armed Japanese in the United States." Quoted in a press release of the California Joint Immigration Committee, March 2, 1935 (Study files). See also Carey McWilliams, *Prejudice* (Boston: Little, Brown, 1944). p. 70; McKee, *California and Her Less Favored Minorities*, p. 23.

[94] See Emory S. Bogardus, *Immigration and Race Attitudes* (Boston and New York: Heath, 1928), p. 69.

[95] *Moving Picture World*, April 2, 1910, p. 532.

[96] *Ibid.*, August 9, 1913, p. 668.

[97] Bogardus, *Immigration and Race Attitudes*, p. 69.

[98] Bruno Lasker, *Race Attitudes in Children* (New York: Holt, 1929), p. 200.

[99] *Moving Picture World*, June 19, 1909; March 10, 1911.

[100] *Ibid.*, December 13, 1913.

[101] Maurice Bardeche and Robert Brasillach, *The History of Motion Pictures* (New York: W. W. Norton and the Museum of Modern Art, 1938), pp. 106–107.

[102] *Photoplay*, March, 1916, pp. 139–140; *Sunset*, July, 1916, p. 23.

[103] M. R. Mock and C. Larson, *Words that Won the War* (Princeton: Princeton University Press, 1939), p. 144.

[104] *Film Index* (New York: Museum of Modern Art, 1941), vol. 1, p. 494.

[105] *A Pictorial History of the Movies* (New York: Simon and Schuster, 1943), p. 85.

[106] R. L. Buell, *Japanese Immigration* (Boston: World Peace Foundation, 1924), p. 71.

[107] M. E. Thorp, *America at the Movies* (New Haven: Yale University Press, 1939), p. 129.

[108] Bogardus, *Immigration and Race Attitudes*, p. 69.

[109] Bernard Berelson and Patricia J. Salter, "Majority and Minority Americans: An Analysis of Magazine Fiction," *Public Opinion Quarterly*, vol. 10 (1946), pp. 168–190; *Nation*, vol. 105 (1917), p. 247. Cf. Young, *American Minority Peoples*, p. 571; McWilliams, *Prejudice*, pp. 44, 60–61.

[110] February 20, 1907.

[111] *Ibid.*, July 22, 1891. See also R. L. Buell, "The History of Japanese Agitation in the United States," *Political Science Quarterly*, vol. XXXVII (1922), p. 608.

[112] Yamato Ichihashi, *The Japanese in the United States* (Stanford: Stanford University Press, 1932), p. 229.

[113] *Ibid.*, p. 230.

[114] *Japanese in the City of San Francisco, Message from President of U.S.*, 59th Congress, 2d sess., Senate Document no. 147, 1906 (Washington: G.P.O., 1907).

[115] Bailey, *Theodore Roosevelt*, p. 23.

[116] Reynolds, *Oriental-White Relations*, p. 109.

[117] American Federation of Labor, *Reports*, 1892, p. 39; *Proceedings*, 1905, p. 193. See also Lewis L. Lorwin, *The American Federation of Labor* (Washington: Brookings Institute, 1933), pp. 7, 12, 402.

[118] San Francisco *Call*, May 8, 1900.

[119] *Organized Labor*, May 19, 1900.

[120] March 11, 1905.

[121] *Japanese and Other Immigrant Races in Pacific Coast and Rocky Mountain States*, 61st Congress, 2d sess., Senate Document no. 633, Immigration Commission Reports, vol. XXIII (Washington: G.P.O., 1911), pp. 169–170. (This document will hereinafter be cited as *Immigration Commission Report.*)

[122] Bailey, *Theodore Roosevelt*, p. 27.

[123] *Immigration Commission Report*, vol. XXIII (1911), pp. 170 ff.

[124] *Minutes of the Inaugural Meeting of the Anti-Jap Laundry League, March, 1908* (San Francisco, 1908); *Immigration Commission Report*, vol. XXIII (1911), p. 194.

[125] Strong, *The Second-Generation Japanese Problem*, p. 38; McKenzie, *Oriental Exclusion*, p. 31.

[126] Bailey, *Theodore Roosevelt*, p. 206.

[127] See Konvitz, *The Alien and the Asiatic in American Law*, p. 190.

[128] *Journal of the Senate of the State of California*, 38th Session, 1910, p. 39.

[129] Franklin E. Hichborn, *Story of the California Legislature of 1915* (San Francisco: J. H. Barry, 1916), p. 230.

[130] See the statement of Erwin B. Ault, in *Japanese Immigration*, Hearings, 66th Congress, 2d sess., House, Committee on Immigration and Naturalization (Washington: G.P.O., 1920), part IV, pp. 1417 f. See also *Survey*, vol. LVI (1926), p. 140.

[131] *Proceedings*, 1919, pp. 364, 367; 1921, pp. 129 f, 340; 1922, p. 323.

[132] November 19, 1920. See also Paul Scharrenburg, "The Attitude of Organized Labor toward the Japanese," *Annals*, vol. XCIII, no. 182 (January, 1921), pp. 34–38.

[133] *Japanese Immigration Legislation.* Hearings, 68th Congress, 1st sess., Senate, Committee on Immigration (Washington: G.P.O., 1924), pp. 23–24.

[134] December 11, 1935.

[135] *The Valor of Ignorance*, p. 182.

[136] Ichihashi, *Japanese in the United States*, p. 229.

[137] Coolidge, *Chinese Immigration*, p. 106.

[138] Ichihashi, *Japanese in the United States*, p. 231; Jean Pajus, *The Real Japanese Problem* (Berkeley: J. J. Gillick, 1937), pp. 5–6.

[139] Ichihashi, *Japanese in the United States*, p. 231.

[140] On Ruef and the Union Labor Party, see Walton E. Bean, *Boss Ruef's San Francisco* (Berkeley: University of California Press, 1952).

[141] Bailey, *Theodore Roosevelt*, p. 13.

[142] *Ibid.*, p. 10.

[143] Reynolds, *Oriental-White Relations*, p. 109.

[144] Strong, *The Second Generation Japanese Problem*, p. 125.

[145] March 11, 1905.

[146] Tveitmoe was a Norwegian immigrant who helped rule the Union Labor Party, became a henchman of AFL Leader Samuel Gompers, dominated the first Japanese exclusion league, and edited the anti-Japanese weekly *Organized Labor*. A convicted forger, he rose high in labor and political circles. In 1910 he was tried and acquitted of complicity in the dynamiting of the Los Angeles *Times;* three years later he was found guilty in a dynamite conspiracy case and sentenced to six years' imprisonment. See the San Francisco *Bulletin*, November 20, 1907; Louis Adamic, *Dynamite* (New York: Viking Press, 1935), pp. 201 f, 245 f; Lincoln Steffens, *Autobiography* (New York: Harcourt, Brace, 1931), pp. 690 ff; K. K. Kawakami, *American-Japanese Relations* (New York: Fleming H. Revell, 1912), p. 303.

[147] See the editorial of the New York *World* on this meeting, February 14, 1907.

[148] December 8, 1906.

[149] McWilliams, *Prejudice*, p. 25. See also Reynolds, *Oriental-White Relations*, on whose correlations this opinion is based. With the exception of 1920, however, the years mentioned were not "peak" periods. In 1916, for example, anti-Japanese agitation was virtually at an all-time low.

[150] McKee, *California and Her Less Favored Minorities*, p. 18.

[151] K. K. Kawakami, *Asia at the Door* (New York: Fleming H. Revell, 1914), p. 166.

[152] *Ibid.*, p. 167.

[153] *Japanese Immigration* (1920), part I, pp. 3 ff. See also *California Legion Monthly*, June, 1920, p. 3; John P. Irish, *The Anti-Japanese Pogrom* (n.p., 1920).

[154] Treat, *Japan and the United States*, p. 281.

[155] *The Abrogation of the Gentlemen's Agreement* (Cambridge: Harvard University Press, 1936), p. 75.

[156] Taft, *Japan and America*, p. 72.

[157] See McWilliams, *Prejudice*, p. 70.

[158] Critical accounts of the Legion include Marcus Duffield, *King Legion* (New York: Jonathan Cape and Harrison Smith, 1931); William Gellerman, *The American Legion as Educator* (New York: Columbia University Press, 1938); Justin Gray, *The Inside Story of the Legion* (New York: Boni and Gaer, 1948). For authorized and generally more favorable accounts, see G. S. Wheat, *Story of the American Legion* (New York and London: Putnam, 1919); Marquis James, *A History of the American Legion* (New York: W. Green, 1923); Richard S. Jones, *A History of the American Legion* (New York: Bobbs-Merrill, 1946).

[159] Arthur Warner, "The Truth about the American Legion," *Nation*, July 6, 1921; Gellerman, *The American Legion as Educator*, p. 94.

[160] American Legion, *Summary of Proceedings, First National Convention, 1919* (n.p., n.d.); Duffield, *King Legion*, p. 158.

[161] *American Legion Weekly*, October 10, 1919, p. 12.

[162] *Summary of Proceedings*, 1919.

[163] Duffield, *King Legion*, p. 158. Virtually every year until the mid-thirties the Legion urged the deportation of "undesirable aliens" and were especially opposed to permanent residence or employment of those ineligible to citizenship (i.e., Orientals). See especially *Summary of Proceedings, Second Annual Convention*, 1920 (n.p., n.d.), pp. 52, 56; *Third Annual Convention*, 1921, p. 24; *Fourth Annual Convention*, 1922, p. 30. See also Gellerman, *The American Legion as Educator*, p. 95.

[164] In 1920 the commander of the Stockton, California, Legion post testified: "We

were the first ... to agitate the question and circulate anti-Japanese-Asiatic petitions ... and we feel that we are more or less responsible for the movement in California." *Japanese Immigration* (1920), Part I, pp. 475–476. See also American Legion,
Department of California, *Proceedings of First Annual Convention, 1919* (San Francisco: Recorder Printing and Publishing Co., n.d.), pp. 49, 69, 82; *History of the
American Legion, Department of California, 1919–1928;* compiled by Fred W. Smith,
Department Historian (n.p., n.d.); *California Legion Monthly,* July, 1920, p. 3.

[165] Quoted in *Japanese Immigration Legislation* (1924), pp. 129 f.

[166] See, in addition to Legion proceedings cited above, Ruth E. Kern, *Political
Policy and Activities of the American Legion, 1919–1925* (Unpublished M. A. thesis,
University of California, 1925).

[167] American Legion, Department of California, *Summary of Proceedings, 1923*
(n.p., n.d.), p. 35.

[168] *Japanese Immigration Legislation* (1924), pp. 129 f. On the role of the Washington lobby, see Norman Hapgood, *Professional Patriots* (New York: Boni, 1928),
pp. 56 ff; Roger Burlingame, *Peace Veterans* (New York: Minton, Balch, 1932), pp.
32 ff.

[169] Duffield, *King Legion,* p. 203.

[170] *The Grizzly Bear,* March, 1920, p. 4.

[171] Kawakami, *Asia at the Door,* p. 146.

[172] Peter Conmy, *The History of California's Japanese Problem and the Part Played
by the Native Sons and Daughters of the Golden West in Its Solution* (Mimeographed;
San Francisco, 1942), p. 2.

[173] Jerome A. Hart, "The Asiatic Peril," *Grizzly Bear,* May, 1907, pp. 24–25.

[174] Conmy, *History,* p. 2.

[175] *Ibid.*

[176] McKee, *California and Her Less Favored Minorities,* p. 16.

[177] April, 1919, p. 3.

[178] October, 1919, p. 2.

[179] January, 1920, p. 1.

[180] March, 1920, p. 4.

[181] *Ibid.,* p. 7.

[182] April, 1920, **p.** 4.

[183] Conmy, *History,* p. 5.

[184] September, 1923, p. 2.

[185] Quoted in Morton Grodzins, *Americans Betrayed* (Chicago: University of Chicago
Press, 1949), p. 7.

[186] Conmy, *History,* p. 6.

[187] *Ibid.*

[188] See, for example, Lewis F. Byington, "Loyalty the Nation's Safeguard," *Grizzly
Bear,* September, 1919, p. 5.

[189] McWilliams, *Prejudice,* p. 22.

[190] The brief account given here is based primarily upon: *Immigration Commission
Report,* vol. XXIII (1911); L. Varden Fuller, *The Supply of Agricultural Labor as a
Factor in the Evolution of Farm Organization in California* (Unpublished dissertation,
University of California, 1939); Emil Bunje, *The Story of Japanese Farming in Cali-
fornia* (Unpublished dissertation, University of California, 1937); Harry T. Millis, *The
Japanese Problem in the United States* (New York: Macmillan, 1915); California
Relief Administration, *Migratory Labor in California* (Sacramento, 1936).

[191] *Reports on Immigration,* United States Industrial Commission, vol. XV (1901),
p. 754.

[192] For the view of large-scale growers, see the *Pacific Rural Press,* February 13, 1909.

[193] O. M. Kile, *The Farm Bureau Through Three Decades* (Baltimore: Waverly
Press, 1948) is an official history of the federation.

[194] Letter of T. W. G. Lyons, representative of the Magnolia-Mulberry Farm Center, in California, State Board of Control, *California and the Oriental* (Sacramento: California State Printing Office, 1920), p. 122.

[195] January 11, 1920. Similar Farm Bureau agitation in Colorado and New Mexico in early 1920 is detailed in *Japanese Immigration* (1920), Part I, p. 351.

[196] *Ibid.*, Part IV, p. 940.

[197] *Ibid.*, Part IV, p. 942.

[198] See statement by the president of the Los Angeles County Farm Bureau, *ibid.*, Part IV, p. 940.

[199] See letter by Professor R. L. Adams of the University of California, to the California State Board of Control, in *California and the Oriental*, pp. 125–127.

[200] Elwood Mead, "The Japanese Land Problem in California," *Annals*, vol. XCIII, no. 182 (January, 1921), p. 51. For contrary evidence revealing considerable division among California farmers, see John B. Wallace, *Waving the Yellow Flag in California* (Reprinted from *Dearborn Independent*, September 4, 11, 1920), p. 5.

[201] See statements of Professor H. T. Millis and Professor T. H. Reed, in Tasuku Harada, ed., *The Japanese Problem in California* (San Francisco: Privately printed, 1922), p. 23.

[202] R. L. Buell, "Again the Yellow Peril," *Foreign Affairs*, vol. 2 (1923), pp. 295 ff; McWilliams, *Prejudice*, pp. 62–63.

[203] Buell, "Again the Yellow Peril," p. 295.

[204] Statement of W. S. Rosecrans, Secretary of the Los Angeles County Farm Bureau, in *Japanese Immigration* (1920), Part IV, pp. 970 f.

[205] Statement of V. S. McClatchy, Secretary of the Joint Immigration Committee, in *Japanese Immigration Legislation* (1924), pp. 23–24.

[206] *Ibid.*, p. 24.

[207] *The Ecological Position of the Japanese Farmers in the State of Washington* (Unpublished dissertation, University of Washington, 1939).

[208] For an official account, see Thomas C. Atkeson, *Outlines of Grange History* (Washington: National Farm News, 1928).

[209] National Grange, *Journal of Proceedings, 1907* (Concord, N.Y.: Rumford Printing Co., 1907), p. 149.

[210] Statement of Thomas C. Atkeson, in *Japanese Immigration Legislation* (1924), pp. 253–254.

[211] National Grange, *Journal of Proceedings, 1914*, p. 150.

[212] California State Grange, *Proceedings, 1920* (n.p.), p. 65.

[213] National Grange, *Journal of Proceedings, 1920*, p. 158.

[214] *Ibid.*, 1922, p. 188.

[215] *Japanese Immigration Legislation* (1924), p. 254.

[216] See the *Journal of Proceedings* of the National Grange for the years 1924–1926.

[217] Atkeson, *Outlines of Grange History*, Appendix.

[218] Millis, *The Japanese Problem in the United States*, p. 77.

[219] *Immigration Commission Report*, vol. XXIII, p. 173.

[220] *Japanese Immigration* (1920), Part IV, p. 475.

[221] Bailey, *Theodore Roosevelt*, p. 16.

[222] Millis, *The Japanese Problem in the United States*, p. 77.

[223] *Ibid.*, p. 78.

[224] *Ibid.*

[225] Charles Y. Young, Helen R. Y. Reid, and W. A. Carrothers, *The Japanese-Canadians* (Toronto: University of Toronto Press, 1938), pp. 122 ff.

[226] *Ibid.*, p. 123.

[227] *Survey*, vol. LVI (1926), p. 151.

[228] McWilliams, *Prejudice*, p. 70.

[229] On the attitude of large-scale agriculturists such as the fruit growers, see Fuller, *The Supply of Agricultural Labor*, pp. 70 ff.

[230] H. B. Johnson, *Discrimination Against the Japanese in California* (Berkeley, 1907), p. 18.

[231] Bailey, *Theodore Roosevelt*, p. 77.

[232] Eleanor Tupper and George E. McReynolds, *Japan in American Public Opinion* (New York: Macmillan, 1931), pp. 29–30.

[233] "The Problem of Oriental Immigration in the State of Washington," *Annals*, vol. XXXIV, no. 2 (September, 1909), p. 116.

[234] August 23, 1919.

[235] Marjorie E. Stearns, *History of the Japanese People in Oregon* (Unpublished dissertation, University of Oregon, 1937), p. 15.

[236] Robert Newton Lynch, "The Development of the Anti-Japanese Movement," *Annals*, vol. XCIII, no. 182 (January, 1921), p. 50. See also the interview with Wallace M. Alexander, chairman of the committee, in the San Francisco *Call*, April 26, 1920. For a description of similar pro-Japanese organizations of Canadian big business, see Young, Reid, and Carrothers, *The Japanese-Canadians*, p. 124.

[237] Tupper and McReynolds, *Japan in American Public Opinion*, p. 190.

[238] *Ibid.* For the generally proimmigration attitude of big business, see testimony of James A. Emery, chief counsel of the National Association of Manufacturers; and letter of the American Bankers' Association, in *Japanese Immigration Legislation* (1924), pp. 443, 304–306.

[239] Strong, *The Second Generation Japanese Problem*, p. 61.

[240] Taft, *Japan and America*, p. 198.

[241] New York *Commercial*, quoted by Taft, *ibid.*, p. 318.

[242] April 28, 1900.

[243] See Treat, *Japan and the United States*, pp. 187–188.

[244] *Oriental-White Relations*, p. 109.

[245] Bailey, *Theodore Roosevelt*, pp. 42–43.

[246] San Francisco *Chronicle*, November 11, 1906; San Francisco *Call*, December 1, 1906.

[247] Johnson, *Discrimination Against the Japanese in California*, p. 42; Tupper and McReynolds, *Japan in American Public Opinion*, p. 29.

[248] *Out West*, March 1907. See also Manchester Boddy, *The Japanese in America* (Los Angeles: E. M. Boddy, 1921), p. 38.

[249] Johnson, *Discrimination Against the Japanese in California*, pp. 18 ff; Bailey, *Theodore Roosevelt*, pp. 67, 78; Tupper and McReynolds, *Japan in American Public Opinion*, p. 29.

[250] Bailey, *Theodore Roosevelt*, p. 106.

[251] Johnson, *Discrimination Against the Japanese in California*, pp. 18–19.

[252] January 12, 1907.

[253] *Theodore Roosevelt*, p. 107.

[254] Gowen, "The Problem of Oriental Immigration in the State of Washington," p. 111. As Jesse F. Steiner observed, "It is very easy to get an exaggerated view of the opposition to the Japanese, because stories dealing with that phase of the question make better news than facts expressive of our friendliness, and consequently get wider publicity." *The Japanese Invasion* (Chicago: McClurg, 1917), p. 70.

[255] Gowen, "The Problem of Oriental Immigration in the State of Washington," p. 112.

[256] F. G. Young, "Why Oregon Has Not Had an Oriental Problem," *Annals*, vol. XXXIV, no. 2 (September, 1909), p. 18.

[257] *History of the Japanese People in Oregon*, p. 6.

[258] *The Valor of Ignorance*, p. 225.

[259] John P. Young, "The Support of the Anti-Oriental Movement," *Annals*, Vol. XXXIV, no. 2 (September, 1909), p. 18.

[260] Ichihashi, *Japanese in the United States*, p. 239.

[261] See Fuller, *The Supply of Agricultural Labor*, p. 175.

[262] November, 1914. See also The Escondido *Advance*, January 29, 1915.

[263] January 25, 1915.

[264] Steiner, *The Japanese Invasion*, pp. 75–76.

[265] *American-Japanese Relations: 1916–1920*. Quadrennial Report, Commission on Relations with the Orient of the Federal Council of Churches of Christ in America. (New York, n.d.), p. 17.

[266] Strong, *The Second Generation Japanese Problem*, p. 47. See also Treat, *Japan and the United States*, p. 283.

[267] Harada, *The Japanese Problem in California*, pp. 23–24.

[268] Merle Davis, "We Said: Let's Find the Facts," *Survey*, vol. LVI (1926), p. 140.

[269] A study conducted by Emory Bogardus in the mid-twenties found that, among several hundred persons queried, the Japanese were described, with one exception, as the least socially desirable of 12 racial groups. See his "Social Distance: A Measuring Stick," *Survey*, vol. LVI (1926), pp. 169 ff. Elsie Monjar in 1935 interviewed 269 native white Americans in California, who declared "sneakiness" and "intelligence" to be predominant Japanese traits. See her "Racial Distance Reactions," *Sociology and Social Research*, vol. 21 (1937), pp. 559–564. A significant confirmation of the view that stereotypes toward the Japanese were largely fixed before Pearl Harbor is contained in a study conducted among women students in the South by Dorothy Seago, "Stereotypes: Before Pearl Harbor and After," *Journal of Psychology*, vol. 23 (1947), pp. 55–63. See also Ruth Fowler, *Some Aspects of Public Opinion Concerning the Japanese in Santa Clara County* (Unpublished dissertation, Stanford University, 1934); Strong, *The Second Generation Japanese Problem*, pp. 109 ff.

[270] Reynolds, *Oriental-White Relations*, chap. xiii.

[271] See L. I. Hughes, *Some Migratory Labor Problems in California's Specialized Agriculture* (Unpublished dissertation, University of California, 1945), p. 48.

CHAPTER II

[1] Los Angeles *Herald*, December 9, 1941; Sacramento *Bee*, December 17, 1941; San Francisco *Examiner*, December 29, 1941.

[2] Los Angeles *Times*, December 10, 13, 16, 1941; Los Angeles *Examiner*, December 13, 1941; San Francisco *Chronicle*, December 16, 1941; San Francisco *Examiner*, December 16, 1941. Cf. *Wartime Exile: The Exclusion of the Japanese Americans from the West Coast*, U. S. Department of Interior, War Relocation Authority (Processed; Washington, 1946), pp. 102–103.

[3] A secondary cause of apprehension among Americans was the memory of Nazi fifth-column successes in Norway and France, which made more plausible the stories of Japanese fifth-columnism at Pearl Harbor. See *Impounded People: Japanese Americans in the Relocation Centers*, U. S. Department of Interior, War Relocation Authority (Processed; Washington, 1946), p. 3.

[4] Sacramento *Bee*, December 17, 1941; Los Angeles *Times*, December 18, 19, 1941; Fresno *Bee*, December 16, 1941; Los Angeles *Examiner*, December 18, 19, 20, 1941.

[5] For the facts concerning these rumors and reports of submarine activity, see p. 326.

[6] *Wartime Exile*, pp. 102–103.

[7] New York *Times*, December 31, 1941.

[8] Oakland *Tribune*, December 23, 27, 1941; San Francisco *Examiner*, December 27, 1941, January 2, 1942; Los Angeles *News*, December 30, 1941; *Nichi Bei*, December 31, 1941; Stockton *Record*, January 3, 1942.

[9] For details, see pp. 100–120.

[10] [Report of the Roberts Commission on Pearl Harbor], New York *Times*, January 25, 1942, p. 2.

[11] At least one newspaper had openly urged evacuation early in December. The San Luis Obispo *Independent* recommended mass removal of the Japanese on December 12, but the suggestion was not then supported by other journals.

[12] "News and Views by John B. Hughes" (Transcript of broadcasts), January 5, 6, 7, 9, 19, 20, 1942 (Study files).

[13] Letter, Hughes to Biddle, January 19, 1942 (Study files).

[14] From a quantitative analysis of newspaper comment undertaken by the University of California Evacuation and Resettlement Study (Study files).

[15] January 22, 31, February 3, 1942.

[16] A few newspapers were more explicit than the Hearst chain in avoiding the anti-Japanese agitation. Among these was the San Francisco *Chronicle*, which on February 1 published a front-page editorial pleading for nondiscrimination against Japanese Americans and directly opposing the idea of mass evacuation.

[17] San Francisco *Examiner*, January 20, 1942.

[18] Sacramento *Bee*, January 20, February 2, 1942; Santa Rosa *Press Democrat*, January 18, 25, 1942; San Francisco *Examiner*, January 30, 1942.

[19] Assembly Joint Resolution 3, California Legislature, 54th (First Extraordinary) Session, 1941; *Senate Daily Journal*, pp. 133, 141, 190, *passim*.

[20] Senate Concurrent Resolution 15, California Legislature, 54th (First Extraordinary) Session, 1942.

[21] Oakland *Tribune*, February 3, 1942; *Wartime Exile*, p. 104. Following the activity of Senators Swan and Metzger, the State Personnel Board voted to bar "citizens, naturalized citizens, or native-born citizens who are descendants of nationals with whom the United States is at war" pending a loyalty investigation. See California, State Personnel Board, *Minutes of Meeting*, January 28, 1942 (Processed. Sacramento, 1942). Questionnaires were later sent to all employed or eligible personnel with names that "sounded Japanese" (San Francisco *Call-Bulletin*, February 18, 1942); dismissals were underway even before the questionnaires could be returned.

[22] See speech by Congressman John Coffee of Washington one day after Pearl Harbor, in *Congressional Record*, December 8, 1941, p. A55584. See also *ibid.*, December 10, 1941, p. 9630; December 16, 1941, p. A5706.

[23] Letter, Carillo to Ford, January 6, 1942 (Study files).

[24] Letter, Ford to Hoover and Knox, January 16, 1942 (Study files); *Congressional Record*, February 18, 1942, p. 1457.

[25] For details of the activity and degree of influence of pressure groups during this period, see pp. 185–198.

[26] California Joint Immigration Committee, *Minutes of Meeting*, February 7, 1942, p. 6.

[27] California Joint Immigration Committee, Press Release No. 544, January 2, 1942.

[28] California Joint Immigration Committee, *Minutes of Meeting*, February 7, 1942, pp. 25–30, 18–19.

[29] American Legion, Department of California, Resolution of January 5, 1942 (Mimeographed). One of the most dramatic of local actions was a circular issued in February by a Portland, Oregon, post, which declared: "Jap and Alien War Sneaks are Proving Thick in our Coast Area. It is serious. Help us Remove the Danger!!"

[30] See *Western Grower and Shipper*, vol. 13 (June, 1942), pp. 8–9.

[31] Letter to Congressman John Z. Anderson, January 22, 1942 (Study files).

[32] Frank J. Taylor, "The People Nobody Wants," *The Saturday Evening Post*, May 9, 1942, p. 66.

[33] *Nichi Bei*, February 1, 1942.

[34] A raid on Terminal Island, for example, drew a two-column article on the front page of the Los Angeles *Times*, under a banner proclaiming "Japs Evicted on

Terminal Island," and a subhead reading: "FBI, Police and Deputy Sheriffs Round up 336 of Estimated 800 Aliens in Harbor Area with Long-Planned Raids Still Continuing." (February 3, 1942). The arrest of Japanese aliens in Monterey drew scare headlines from the San Francisco *Examiner*, February 11, 1942: "Ex-Police Chief of Tokio Held by FBI in Raid on Salinas," and "Priest in Buddhist Temple Seized." The accompanying story told how a former Japanese police chief had slipped into the country a few months previously, disguised as a Buddhist priest.

[35] San Francisco *News*, February 10, 1942.

[36] Department of Justice files.

[37] February 21, 1942.

[38] Following adoption by the Los Angeles County Board of Supervisors of a resolution calling for removal of Japanese aliens (January 27), Ventura County supervisors resolved to exclude "all persons of the Japanese race" from Pacific Coast areas (February 3). Virtually identical resolutions were then passed by ten other California counties.

[39] Monterey *Press Herald*, January 30, 1942; Proceedings of a conference of sheriffs and district attorneys called by Attorney General Warren on the subject of Alien Land Law enforcement. February 2, 1942, pp. 3–7 (Typescript in Study files).

[40] *Hearings*, 77th Congress, 2d sess., House, Select Committee Investigating National Defense Migration (Washington: G.P.O., 1942), part 29, pp. 11015, 11014, 10974–10976. This committee will be cited hereinafter as Tolan Committee.

[41] *Congressional Record*, February 9, 1942, pp. A504–A505; Los Angeles *Examiner*, February 6, 1942; Los Angeles *Times*, February 13, 1942; Tolan Committee, *Hearings*, part 31, pp. 11643–11644.

[42] From quantitative-analysis charts in the Study files. Public-opinion samplings taken along the West Coast from late January through February confirmed the rising distrust of Japanese Americans and showed increasing support for stricter control measures. An exploratory survey conducted during the last week of January, based on 192 interviews in four California localities, found almost as many persons believing the Japanese "virtually all loyal" (36 per cent) as "virtually all disloyal" (38 per cent). Significantly, however, the report noted that "a substantial number among those who feel that most Japanese are loyal went on to say that since one could not tell precisely which ones are loyal and which disloyal, a certain amount of suspicion was naturally attached to all Japanese." The majority of the respondents felt that existing control measures were adequate, only about one-third calling for further action against the Japanese Americans. See U. S. Office of Facts and Figures, Bureau of Intelligence, *Exploratory Study of West Coast Reactions to Japanese*, February 4, 1942 (Processed; Washington, 1942). A subsequent study conducted in the second week of February (covering 797 citizens of California, Oregon, and Washington) found that 40 per cent of the total sample thought that there were "many disloyal aliens in their vicinity"; and practically all of these named the Japanese specifically. Three-fourths of the southern Californians interviewed believed that "only a few" or "practically none" of the Japanese aliens were loyal to the United States, and called for their segregation in camps. One-third of the southern Californians also advocated segregating citizen Japanese, but in the other three coastal areas (northern California, Oregon and Washington) only 14 per cent recommended this action. See U. S. Office of Facts and Figures, Bureau of Intelligence, *Pacific Coast Attitudes toward the Japanese Problem*, February 28, 1942 (Processed; Washington, 1942). The third opinion sampling, which covered the last three weeks of February, noted "evidence of growing tension," and observed a general rise of dissatisfaction with Department of Justice measures and of suspicion toward the Japanese Americans. Japanese loyalty to the United States was questioned by over half the respondents; and "most people who make such a judgment believe there is no limit to what a Japanese might be expected to do." Dislike and distrust of the Japanese was estimated by 77 per cent of those

interviewed as the prevailing sentiment, with racial and national antagonism as the predominant reasons for disfavor. Government measures for the solution of the Japanese problem were judged adequate by 54 per cent of those interviewed in the period before February 20, but by only 40 per cent during the last week of February. Expectation of sabotage was indicated by 60 per cent of the replies. See U.S. Office of Facts and Figures, Bureau of Intelligence, *West Coast Reactions to the Japanese Situation,* March, 1942 (Processed; Washington, 1942).

Evidence that national public opinion by the end of March, 1942, was similar to that of the Pacific Coast is given by a National Opinion Research Council nationwide poll of March 28. Some 93 per cent of those interviewed thought that "we are doing the right thing in moving Japanese aliens" away from the West Coast; only 1 per cent thought it was wrong. Fifty-nine per cent approved the evacuation of citizen Japanese, while 25 per cent disapproved. A total of 65 per cent of the respondents agreed that all Japanese evacuated should be kept "under strict guard as prisoners of war," with 28 per cent holding that "they should be allowed to go about fairly freely." See Hadley Cantril, ed., *Public Opinion 1935–1946* (Princeton: Princeton University Press, 1951), p. 380. For other polls bearing on national opinion, see *ibid.,* p. 947 ff.

[43] February 6, 1942.

[44] Los Angeles *Examiner,* February 5, 1942. See also San Francisco *Examiner,* February 9, 1942.

[45] Lippmann argued that Nisei citizens were as great a danger as aliens, and declared: "The Pacific Coast is officially a combat zone: some part of it may at any moment be a battlefield. Nobody's constitutional rights include the right to reside and do business on a battlefield.... There is plenty of room elsewhere for him to exercise his rights." (New York *Herald-Tribune,* February 12, 1942).

[46] Admiral Ernest Stark, Chief of Naval Operations, as quoted by Senator Holman of Oregon, chairman of the West Coast delegation's committee on defense, in a letter to Senator Hiram Johnson, dated February 9, 1942. The testimony of Brigadier General Mark W. Clark, representing the Army Chief of Staff, was reported by Senator Holman to be substantially similar. Further adverse testimony had been given the committees by the Department of Justice, which held evacuation to be unwise and unnecessary, and the Department of Agriculture, which warned of severe effects on coastal crop production. (Interview with Senator Sheridan Downey, October 13, 1942, notes in Study files.)

[47] The letter to President Roosevelt, dated February 13, 1942, was signed by Senators Holman and Wallgren and by Congressmen Lea Englebright, Welch, Costello and Angell.

[48] *Congressional Record,* December 15, 1941, p. 9808; February 14, 1942, pp. A691–692. Congressmen Bland of Virginia, Norrell of Arkansas, Randolph of West Virginia, and even Coffee of Washington lauded or approved sections of Rankin's address.

[49] *Congressional Record,* February 23, 1942, pp. A768–769. The majority opinion in the *Wong Kim Ark* case held that only children born in the United States of alien enemies in hostile occupation, and those of diplomatic representatives, were not "subject to the jurisdiction" of the United States.

[50] *Ibid.,* February 26, 1942, pp. 1682–1683.

[51] *Ibid.,* January 15, 1942, p. 420; January 28, 1942, pp. 828–829.

[52] Drew Pearson, "Washington Merry-go-Round" (Syndicated newspaper column), February 7, 1942; San Francisco *Chronicle,* February 9, 1942.

[53] Proceedings of a conference of sheriffs and district attorneys, pp. 52–55, 61–62; letters to Attorney General Warren from N. L. Cornell, D. M. Blossom, J. M. Graves and G. M. Pryor, all dated February 19, 1942 (Tolan Committee files).

[54] Letters: C. A. Ricks (Mayor of Martinez) to Tolan, February 20, 1942; Ward Johnson to Biddle, February 19, 1942; G. Mordecai to Earl Warren, February 19, 1942. Printed in Tolan Committee, *Hearings,* part 29, pp. 10997–10998.

[55] Richard M. Neustadt, *Report on Alien Enemy Evacuation,* [to Paul V. McNutt, Director, Federal Security Administration and Director of Defense, Health, and Welfare Services] February 18, 1942, p. 6. (Processed; n.p., n.d.)

[56] Letter, Osborn to Tolan, February 28, 1942, printed in Tolan Committee, *Preliminary Report . . . on Evacuation of Military Areas,* House Report No. 1911, March 19, 1942, p. 27.

[57] Neustadt, *Report on Alien Enemy Evacuation,* pp. 12, 15.

[58] San Francisco *Call-Bulletin,* February 17, 1942; San Francisco *Chronicle,* February 17, 1942; Fresno County Chamber of Commerce, Resolution of February 20, 1942 (Tolan Committee, *Hearings,* part 29, p. 11239); Kern County Defense Council telegram dated February 21, 1942, (Study files).

[59] San Francisco *Examiner,* February 20, 1942; Tolan Committee, *Hearings,* part 29, pp. 11061–11062; report by District Attorney Walter C. Haight before Tulare County Board of Supervisors, "Enemy Alien Situation," February 14, 1942 (Notes in Study files).

[60] Fresno *Bee,* April 21, 1942; San Francisco *Examiner,* April 21, 1942.

[61] George Dean, *Review of Anti-Japanese Incidents and Local Sentiment in Fresno and Tulare Counties* (Mimeographed; San Francisco: War Relocation Authority, April 30, 1942). Fresno *Bee,* April 23, 1942.

[62] Sacramento *Bee,* February 6, 1942; Tolan Committee, *Hearings,* part 29, pp. 11011–11012.

[63] During the hearings of his committee Congressman Tolan himself suggested, "They would be fools to tip their hand now, wouldn't they?" Seattle's Mayor Millikan maintained that "There hasn't been any sabotage, because it has been ordered withheld by Tokyo"; and Mayor Riley of Portland agreed that "the only reason the fifth columnists haven't struck so far is because their respective governments haven't given them the go-ahead." (Tolan Committee, *Hearings,* part 29, pp. 11012, 11409; San Francisco *Chronicle,* February 21, 1942.)

[64] U.S. Army, Western Defense Command and Fourth Army, *Final Report: Japanese Evacuation from the West Coast, 1942* (Washington: G.P.O., 1943), p. 34.

[65] In testimony before the House Naval Affairs Subcommittee on April 13, 1943, the general was quoted as stating: "A Jap's a Jap. They are a dangerous element, whether loyal or not. There is no way to determine their loyalty.... It makes no difference whether he is an American; theoretically he is still a Japanese and you can't change him.... You can't change him by giving him a piece of paper." (San Francisco *Chronicle,* April 14, 1943.)

[66] Perhaps the first authoritative denial of Hawaii sabotage was that of Hawaii's delegate to Congress, Samuel W. King. (San Francisco *Chronicle,* January 26, 1942.) Subsequent refutations of the Pearl Harbor stories were issued by Secretary of War Henry L. Stimson, James Rowe, Jr. (assistant to Attorney General Biddle), Honolulu Chief of Police W. A. Gabrielson, FBI Director J. Edgar Hoover, and various other local and national officials. (Tolan Committee, *Fourth Interim Report,* pp. 48 ff., *passim.* Also Tolan Committee, *House Report No. 1911,* March 19, 1942, pp. 31 f. See also Baltimore *Sun,* January 17, 1944.)

[67] The available copy of the Biddle memorandum is simply dated May, 1942. For specific corrections of fifth-column rumors, see: Los Angeles *Evening Herald,* December 9, 1941; Oakland *Tribune,* February 11, 1942; Sacramento *Bee,* February 18, 1942; San Francisco *Call-Bulletin,* February 20, 1942.

[68] For consideration of the cogency of this argument, see pp. 266–268.

[69] Letters dated January 13, January 29, March 6, and January 29, 1942.

[70] Tolan Committee, *Hearings,* part 29, pp. 11017, 10974. See San Diego *Union,* March 5, 1942.

[71] Tolan Committee, *Hearings,* part 31, p. 11644.

[72] Letters dated January 28, February 16, 1942, from Los Angeles (Department of Justice files).

[73] Tolan Committee, *Hearings,* part 29, pp. 11014–11015; California, State Personnel Board, Notice of Dismissal, April 13, 1942 (Study files).

[74] Tolan Committee, *Hearings,* part 30, pp. 11638–11639; part 29, p. 11016. Statements of a similar nature were made by the Commissioner of Agriculture for Los Angeles County; a Los Angeles County Supervisor; the agricultural coördinator of the County Defense Council, and a representative of the Los Angeles Chamber of Commerce. (*Ibid.,* part 31, pp. 11675–11691.)

[75] California Joint Immigration Committee, Press Release No. 544, January 2, 1942.

[76] *Brawley News,* January 2, 1942; *Nichi Bei,* December 31, 1941, January 3, 7, 14, 16, March 17, 1942; San Francisco *Chronicle,* January 1, 1942; Stockton *Record,* January 2, 16, 1942; *North American Times,* December 11, 1941, February 6, 1942; San Francisco *Examiner,* March 17, 1942.

[77] The motives of extralegal actions varied widely; some no doubt were within the normal incidence of crime, without anti-Japanese design. Again, the cumulative coverage of newspapers gave a misleading effect. Once duplications were eliminated, a careful check by the staff of the University of California Evacuation and Resettlement Study showed 36 cases of actual or potential vigilantism between December 8, 1941, and March 31, 1942. Of these 7 were murders (all in California), 2 were attacks on Japanese American girls, 19 were assaults with deadly weapons, and the remaining 8 consisted of robberies, extortion attempts, and property destruction. Of the assailants eighteen were tentatively identified as Filipinos, seven were white, one was a Negro, and one a Chinese; nine were unidentified. The largest incidence of anti-Japanese violence occurred between December 28 and January 1, when 8 cases were reported. In the preceding fifteen days only 5 cases had been noted. Only 6 cases were reported in February, and 4 in March.

CHAPTER III

[1] Appointed commanding general, Fourth Army, December, 1939, and Western Defense Command including Alaska, March, 1941. Awarded First Oak Leaf Cluster, Distinguished Service Medal, in 1943, for leadership in inspiring American troops to expel Japanese from Aleutian Islands and for the evacuation "of thousands of Japanese and other enemy aliens from the Pacific Coast . . . with conspicuous dispatch and efficiency."

[2] The mission of the WDC and Fourth Army as stated by DeWitt. See U.S. Army, Western Defense Command and Fourth Army, *Final Report: Japanese Evacuation from the West Coast, 1942* (Washington: G.P.O., 1943), p. 33. The WDC was established on March 17, 1941, classified as a "theatre of operations" on December 14, 1941, as a "defense command" in November, 1943, and disestablished on March 1, 1946. See U.S. Army, *The Army Almanac* (Washington: G.P.O., 1951), p. 601. The commanding generals of the WDC and Fourth Army and their dates of command: Lieut. Gen. John L. DeWitt, March, 1941–September, 1943; Lieut. Gen. Delos C. Emmons, September, 1943–June, 1944; Major Gen. Robert H. Lewis, June, 1944; Major Gen. Charles H. Bonesteel, June, 1944–November, 1944; Major Gen. Henry C. Pratt, December, 1944–November, 1945; Major Gen. Harold R. Nichols, December, 1945; General Joseph W. Stilwell, December, 1945–March, 1946.

[3] The Japanese minority in California, Arizona, Oregon, and Washington was composed as follows:

	Foreign born	American born	Total
Males	25,114	38,094	63,208
Females	15,975	33,802	49,777
Total	41,089	71,896	112,985

These figures are taken from Dorothy S. Thomas, *The Salvage* (Berkeley: University of California Press, 1952), table 4, p. 578. For the continental United States the total was 126,947. Of the American-born, 9,789 had spent some time in Japan. (*Ibid.*, table 19, p. 606). A Japanese domiciled in the United States but born in Japan is referred to as an Issei (first generation). A Japanese born in the United States of parents born in Japan is referred to as a Nisei (second generation). A Japanese born and resident in the United States but educated for some period in Japan is referred to as a Kibei (returned to America). A son or daughter of Nisei or Kibei parents is a Sansei (third generation).

⁴ The ineligibility of Orientals to acquire citizenship through naturalization stemmed from the Naturalization Act of 1790, according to which the privilege was limited to "free white persons," and from a Supreme Court decision in 1922 (*Ozawa v. United States*, 260 U.S. 178). See D. O. McGovney, "Anti-Japanese Land Laws of California and Ten Other States," *California Law Review*, Vol. 35 (1947), pp. 7–60.

⁵ Presidential Proclamations 2525 (6 *Fed. Reg.*, 6321), 2526 (6 *Fed. Reg.*, 6323), and 2527 (6 *Fed. Reg.*, 6324) respectively, issued under the authority of the Alien Enemies Act of April 16, 1918, which renders resident aliens of enemy nationality liable to apprehension, restriction, and removal from areas surrounding essential installations. (50 U.S. Code, secs. 21–24.)

⁶ Department of Justice, Press Releases, December 8 and 13, 1941. Three of the internment camps of the Department of Justice—Camp Forrest, Camp Livingston, and Camp Lordsburg—were run by the War Department, which assumed custody of male civilian internees until June, 1943, when custody was returned to the Department of Justice.

⁷ Department of Justice, Press Release, February 16, 1942.

⁸ Testimony of R. L. Shivers, FBI agent, as given in Bradford Smith, *Americans from Japan* (New York: Lippincott, 1948), p. 181.

⁹ Testimony of E. J. Ennis, as reported in unofficial minutes of meeting of West Coast congressional delegation committee on alien enemies and sabotage, February 5, 1942, pp. 1–3 (Typescript in Study files).

¹⁰ Columbia University, LL.B., 1932; admitted to New York Bar, 1933.

¹¹ Arrested alien enemies were given hearings before local Alien Enemy Hearing Boards which determined whether they should be released unconditionally, released on parole, or interned. The internees were sent to one of the sixteen camps operated by the Immigration and Naturalization Service. After August, 1942, a considerable number of interned Japanese alien enemies were paroled to WRA relocation centers.

¹² U.S. Department of Justice, *Annual Report of the Attorney General* [1941–1942] (Processed; Washington, 1943), p. 8.

¹³ Department of Justice, Press Release, December 19, 1941.

¹⁴ Department of Justice, Press Releases, December 29, 1941, and January 1, 1942. On February 5 the Attorney General published regulations governing the travel of enemy aliens, their conduct and possessions, some of which had been set forth earlier in press releases and announcements (28 U.S. Code, part 30, secs. 30.1–30.6; 7 *Fed. Reg.*, 844 and 7 *Fed Reg.*, 1476). During the early part of 1942 various groups of individuals were exempted from the class of alien enemies; first, nationals of Germany, Italy and Japan who were serving in the armed forces of the United States. (7 *Fed. Reg.*, 1474); subsequently all persons, such as anti-Nazi German refugees, whom the Attorney General, "after investigation fully establishing their loyalty, shall certify as persons loyal to the United States." (Executive Order 9106, March 20, 1942, 7 *Fed. Reg.*, 2199 and Executive Order 9372, August 27, 1943, 8 *Fed. Reg.*, 11887).

¹⁵ For pertinent executive orders, Treasury Department regulations, public circulars, etc., see U.S. Treasury Department, *Documents Pertaining to Foreign Funds Control* (Washington: G.P.O., 1942).

¹⁶ Orders No. 145A, December 21, 1941, and No. 145F, March 2, 1942.

[17] *Final Report*, p. 3. On December 19 DeWitt wrote to California's Governor Culbert L. Olson asking that he furnish the FBI with "information of suspicious aliens or other persons and of all suspicious activities whatsoever" of fifth-column sorts, and to the governors of the western states asking them to control "vice resorts" as "these places may be employed as agencies of subversive and disloyal elements in our midst." (Olson Papers, Bancroft Library, University of California.)

[18] Western Defense Command and Fourth Army records are now in custody of the Departmental Records Branch, Adjutant General's Office, Department of the Army. This collection will hereinafter be cited as AGO files.

[19] *Final Report*, p. 4.

[20] Harvard Law School, LL.B., 1921; expert consultant to Secretary of War, October, 1940; Assistant Secretary of War, April, 1941, to November, 1945.

[21] Leland Stanford University, LL.B., 1932. Special representative of the Secretary of War to General Douglas MacArthur, 1941; assigned to WDC, February, 1942, with rank of colonel, serving as Assistant Chief of Staff for Civil Affairs and Director of the WCCA. He was the major public apologist for the evacuation, explaining and defending Army policy on numerous occasions. See his addresses, *The Story of Pacific Coast Japanese Evacuation, An Address Delivered before the Commonwealth Club of San Francisco*, May 20, 1942 (U.S. Army, WDC, n.d.); *An Obligation Discharged, ... An Address Delivered to Personnel of the WCCA*, November 3, 1942 (U.S. Army, WDC, n.d.). He was awarded the Army's Distinguished Service Medal in late 1942 for, among other things, his services under DeWitt. "He organized and administered the Civil Affairs Division of the General Staff with such keen foresight, judgment and executive ability that the evacuation of persons of Japanese ancestry from the West Coast of the United States was successfully executed." He was appointed Special Assistant to the Secretary of Defense in 1948 and Assistant Secretary of the Army on January 24, 1950, resigning in October, 1952.

[22] Harvard Law School, LL.B., 1911; Solicitor General of the United States, 1940; Attorney General, September, 1941, to June 30, 1945; United States Member of the International Military Tribunal, 1945–1946.

[23] Harvard Law School, LL.B., 1934. Administrative Assistant to President Roosevelt, 1939–1941. Assistant Attorney General 1941–1943.

[24] Memo: "Immediate Alien Enemy Control Requirements," January 3, 1942 (AGO files).

[25] "Tab A: Summary of Communication, January 4, 1942" (*Final Report*, p. 23).

[26] "Memorandum from the Commanding General ... to the Assistant Attorney General, Mr. James Rowe, Jr., January 5, 1942," *ibid.*, p. 19. The memorandum concluded with a list of nine "pressing problems ... and some of the problems which remain unanswered." Among these was one on the control of civilians: "The dual citizen problem is perplexing. Self-serving declarations of an election are of little meaning, particularly where conduct is incompatible with the so-called election. What methods exist or what steps are in contemplation looking toward the control of 1. Dual citizens. 2. Disloyal, subversive citizens (where there has been no overt act detected)?" (*Final Report*, pp. 21–22.)

[27] *Final Report*, p. 5.

[28] *Ibid.*, p. 23. The War Department may have requested the Navy to adopt this procedure but the Navy did not accept it, apparently, for on January 27, 1942, Undersecretary of the Navy James K. Forrestal wrote to the Department of Justice asking that all Japanese, aliens and civilians alike, be evacuated from Bainbridge Island in Puget Sound, Washington. The Department of Justice took up the matter with the War Department, as it had previously been agreed, in the conferences on January 5 between DeWitt and Rowe, that all recommendations by the Navy Department for prohibited areas on the West Coast would be transmitted through DeWitt. On February 6 the War Department advised the Department of Justice that "the Commandant

of the Thirteenth Naval District recommends, through Lieutenant General DeWitt, that Bainbridge Island be designated as a 'military area' prohibited not only to all alien enemies but also to American citizens of the Japanese Race." (Letter, James J. Rowe, Jr., to James Forrestal, February 10, 1942, Study files.) The War Department did not express its opinion with regard to this recommendation. On February 10 Justice refused the request, on grounds it had no power to remove citizens from "military areas."

[29] Interview, October 15, 1942 (Notes in Study files).

[30] Presidential Proclamation 2537 (7 *Fed. Reg.*, 329). This was the second registration of aliens, the first having been ordered for all aliens over 14 years of age by the Alien Registration Act of 1940, passed June 18, 1940 (57 U.S. Stat. 670).

[31] An incomplete list, based on newspaper accounts, of cities where the raids took place, their dates, and the numbers of Japanese aliens taken into custody. February 2—Terminal Island (Los Angeles Harbor), 400; Bainbridge Island (Puget Sound), 15; Vallejo and Mare Island Navy Yard, 32; February 7—Los Angeles harbor area; February 10—Monterey County Peninsula, 39; February 12—San Diego; February 14—Sunnyvale; February 16—El Centro, 16; February 17—Yolo, Placer, and Yuba counties, 14; February 20—scattered raids in cities from Salinas to Redding, San Francisco Bay area to Sacramento; March 6—Alameda and Oakland; March 8—30 scattered towns and cities, 92.

[32] Interview, October 13, 1943 (Notes in Study files). Burling also stated that "even J. Edgar Hoover, on May 5, 1942, wrote a memorandum advocating extreme toughness with those caught with contraband and a broad interpretation of what contraband consisted of."

In 1942 the Department analyzed the cases of many of those picked up. "The results were ludicrous; an alien German woman being detained, for instance, because she had in her possession the sword of her husband, which she had received upon his graduation from Annapolis; a Japanese was interned because the F.B.I. man discovered that his radio had a short wave band still working, even though the man presented incontrovertible evidence to demonstrate that he had paid to have the short wave band removed. Such cases were numerous." Department of Justice Memorandum: "Possession of Prohibited Articles by Alien Enemies" (No date, prepared sometime between May 15 and June 1, 1943, typescript in Study files).

[33] "We have not . . . uncovered through these searches any dangerous persons that we could not otherwise know about. We have not found among all the sticks of dynamite and gunpowder any evidence that any of it was to be used in bombs. . . . We have not found a camera which we have reason to believe was for use in espionage." (Department of Justice Memorandum.)

[34] By announcement on February 25, 1942, exemptions were allowed for those in hospitals, those too ill to be moved when so certified by a doctor, and those over 75 years of age.

[35] *Final Report*, p. 6. This paragraph states that 99 prohibited zones were requested; however, only 86 prohibited and 11 restricted zones were established by the Department of Justice.

[36] On January 8 the Ninth Army Corps and the Thirteenth Naval District recommended that all alien enemies be evacuated from Washington and Oregon, which would be declared a prohibited zone, and all American born of Japanese racial origin who could not show actual severance of allegiance to the Japanese Imperial government be classified as alien enemies, and proposed the establishment of a large number of restricted zones. The recommendation for establishment of a prohibited zone to include the two states was revised by DeWitt; he asked only that the western half of these states be declared prohibited, and no recommendation was made by him for such a "classification" of American citizens.

Exhibit No. 3 of the *Final Report* entitled "Prohibited and Restricted Zones as Recommended to the Attorney General" (not published in that volume but deposited in the National Archives and in the Departmental Records Branch of the Adjutant General's Office) contains a description of various prohibited and restricted zones in California, Oregon, and Washington, and apparently delineates the modified sector recommendations, but the two types of zones there described differ in character from those instituted by the Department of Justice.

[37] Department of Justice, Press Release No. 6, January 29, 1942, in *Fourth Interim Report, Findings and Recommendations on Evacuation of Enemy Aliens and Others from Prohibited Military Zones*, House Report 2124, May 13, 1942, 77th Congress, 2d sess., Select Committee Investigating National Defense Migration (Washington: G.P.O. 1942), p. 302. This committee will hereinafter be cited as Tolan Committee.

[38] Department of Justice, Press Release No. 7, January 31, 1942, in Tolan Committee, *Fourth Interim Report*, p. 302. The regulations appear at 7 *Fed. Reg.*, 1084.

[39] Department of Justice, Press Release No. 8, February 2, 1942, *ibid.*, p. 306. The regulations appear at 7 *Fed. Reg.*, 1475.

[40] No date is given in the *Final Report* for this submission. Judging by the four days required for delivery of the first request, DeWitt would have dispatched it on January 29.

[41] Department of Justice, Press Release No. 9, February 4, 1942, in Tolan Committee, *Fourth Interim Report*, p. 308. The regulations appear at 7 *Fed. Reg.*, 1476.

[42] Department of Justice, Press Release No. 10, February 4, 1942, *ibid.*, p. 310.

[43] Department of Justice, Press Release No. 11, February 7, 1942, *ibid.*, p. 312. Paragraph 6 of WDC Public Proclamation No. 1 affirmed the continued existence of these prohibited and restricted zones but they and their governing regulations were "eliminated" by WDC Public Proclamation No. 9 on June 27, 1942.

[44] University of Texas, LL.B., 1922; Special Assistant to the Attorney General assigned to Antitrust Division, 1938–1940; Chief, West Coast office, 1940–1942. Assistant Attorney General, 1942–1943. Attorney General of United States, 1945–1949.

[45] *The Relocation Program*, U.S. Department of the Interior, War Relocation Authority (Processed; Washington: G.P.O., 1946), p. 2.

[46] Testimony of Richard Neustadt, Tolan Committee, *Hearings*, part 29, pp. 11024–11058.

[47] *Final Report*, p. 7. The western half of Oregon was also to be prohibited, according to the *Final Report*.

[48] Text of the letter is not given in the *Final Report* but the date of Stimson's letter is mentioned in a letter from Rowe to Forrestal of February 10, 1942 (Study files). We assume that there was a third and distinct recommendation following the second by some days because of the fact that the Department of Justice proclaimed some prohibited zones in Washington and Oregon but rejected the request for very large ones. It would seem unlikely that DeWitt would send in on the same day two conflicting recommendations—one asking for scattered small prohibited zones, the other for a very large prohibited area embracing the smaller ones. Six of the seven small prohibited zones in Washington just proclaimed by Justice were within the western half: Prohibited Areas 2, 4, 5, 6, 7, 8 (Tolan Committee, *Fourth Interim Report*, p. 308). Twenty of the twenty-four zones in Oregon were west of the Cascades.

[49] *Final Report*, p. 9.

[50] Excerpts from this letter are given in the *Final Report*, p. 7, but the reference to Los Angeles was omitted, judging by the copy in the Study files.

[51] *Final Report*, p. 8. The text of this memorandum is not given in the Report nor has it come to light in Adjutant General's Office files.

[52] The letter from the department stating its grounds for refusal is also not given in the *Final Report* and its date and contents are unknown. The *Final Report* (p. 8) states only that "The Department . . . concluded that it was not in a position to undertake any mass evacuation, and declined in any event to administer such general control measures."

[53] Study files. These matters were also discussed in letters of February 13, 1942, from Edward J. Ennis to Biddle and to J. Edgar Hoover (Study files). Ennis suggested the possibility of suspending the writ of habeas corpus and instituting a pass and permit system for aliens as well as citizens.

[54] Bendetsen had represented McCloy at a meeting of a West Coast congressional delegation committee on alien enemies and sabotage held on February 5 in the Capitol. He expressed the Army's view as one of qualified approval of citizen and alien Japanese evacuation, stated that "The Army was unable to determine whether Japs were loyal or disloyal," and pointed to the problem involved in moving and housing 130,000 Japanese (Unofficial minutes, in Study files, p. 3).

[55] *Final Report*, p. 25.

[56] In an interview on July 8, 1952, Bendetsen asserted that G-2 intelligence reports on the danger of invasion and the likelihood of disloyal acts by Japanese were partly responsible for the recommendation (Notes in Study files). The content of such reports has not been made public. Such intelligence reports from other intelligence units of the government as have come to light do not state that any subversive acts by Japanese had taken place.

[57] *Ibid.*, p. 33. The total number of Japanese, Italian, and German aliens in California, Oregon, and Washington was approximately 322,000, according to the 1940 Census.

[58] General Marshall has been criticized for giving his assent to the recommendation. For example, Major H. H. DeWeerd, author of various studies in military science and history, stated that "in the first days of the war, Marshall badly misjudged the Japanese and the real danger to our Pacific Coast. Consequently he supported DeWitt's decision to evacuate American citizens of Japanese descent from the Pacific Coast." (San Francisco *Chronicle,* January 20, 1947.)

[59] McGeorge Bundy's account of Stimson's years of Secretary of War deals only briefly with evacuation policy. He mentions War Department fears of vigilante attacks against the Japanese minority and of Japanese raids on the coast as considerations favoring the policy. Henry L. Stimson and McGeorge Bundy, *On Active Service in Peace and War* (New York: Harpers, 1947), p. 406.

[60] Harvard Law School LL.B. 1915. Assistant Secretary of War, July, 1940; Undersecretary of War, December, 1940; Secretary of War, September, 1945, to July, 1947. Died January, 1952.

[61] Interview, John J. McCloy, October 15, 1942 (Notes in Study files).

[62] *Ibid.*

[63] *Ibid.*

[64] Attorney General Biddle wrote to Congressman Leland Ford on January 24 that "unless the writ of Habeas Corpus is suspended, I do not know of any way in which Japanese born in this country and therefore American citizens could be interned." (Study files.) At a meeting of the West Coast congressional delegation committee on alien enemies and sabotage on February 5, Biddle stated among other points that "The Department of Justice had no authority to take action with respect to ... United States citizens" and that "If there is to be a wholesale evacuation, such a tremendous job must devolve on the Army as the F.B.I. has only 5,000 agents throughout the United States. The military must determine the risk and undertake the responsibility for evacuating citizens of Japanese descent." (Unofficial minutes, in Study files, p. 5.) Tom Clark stated on February 10 that he did not think "such drastic steps" as evacuation and internment were necessary. (Letter, T. C. Clark to E. J. Ennis, February 10, 1942, Study files.)

[65] Biddle's attitude has been explained by him on a number of subsequent occasions. "I never thought evacuation was necessary and I still don't think it was. Nevertheless, there was no way that I could stop it. The Army authorities were insistent, they talked in terms of military necessity and, in time of war, there is no way you

can stop the Army on such a thing. . . . At the time we were not appraised of the actual military situation. And General DeWitt may have had more grounds for fearing an attack on our shores than I thought or think he had. . . . We didn't discuss administrative feasibility—it wasn't that the Justice Department couldn't carry out the evacuation, rather it was a case where I thought the Justice Department simply should not be a party to a program in which citizens were to be deprived of their liberties. That was a military matter and the military properly had to administer it. Such a program was no program for a Department of Justice to carry out. It was a military task." (Interview, October 13, 1943, notes in Study files.) In 1945 Biddle stated that he had not been sure that evacuation was necessary "but something had to be done" and that the Army needed "undivided responsibility." (Interview, February 14, 1945, notes in Study files.)

⁶⁶ Interview, James H. Rowe, Jr., October 15, 1942 (Notes in Study files).

⁶⁷ "The President was interested in the Japanese problem but merely signed 9066 when brought to him as a joint product of War and Justice Departments on February 19. The Cabinet did not discuss the necessity of evacuation in any formal way at all." (Interview, Biddle, February 14, 1945, notes in Study files.) On February 20 Biddle sent a memorandum to the President explaining the character and purpose of the executive order. (Papers of Franklin D. Roosevelt, Franklin D. Roosevelt Library.)

⁶⁸ 7 *Fed. Reg.*, 1407.

⁶⁹ *Final Report,* p. 27.

⁷⁰ *Ibid.,* p. 25.

⁷¹ AGO files.

⁷² U.S. Army, Chief of Staff, "Memorandum of Proposed Action in the Western and Eastern Defense Command," December 1, 1942.

⁷³ "To provide a penalty for violation of restrictions or orders with respect to persons entering, remaining in, leaving or committing any act in military areas or zones." 56 U.S. Stat. 173 (1942); 18 U.S. Code, Sec. 97A (Supp. 1942); Public Law 503.

⁷⁴ *Final Report,* p. 9.

⁷⁵ *Ibid.,* p. 30.

⁷⁶ *Congressional Record,* March 9, 1942, p. 2071; March 10, 1942, p. 2230.

⁷⁷ *Proceedings,* Hearings on Senate Resolution 2352, 77th Congress, 2d Session, Senate Committee on Military Affairs, March 13, 1942 (processed), p. 24. These proceedings were never officially published. (Study files.) The Committee Report appears in *Congressional Record,* March 19, 1942, p. 2725.

⁷⁸ *Ibid.,* p. 42.

⁷⁹ *Ibid.,* p. 20.

⁸⁰ *Ibid.,* p. 21.

⁸¹ *Senate Report No. 1171* to accompany Senate Resolution 2352, March 16, 1942, 77th Congress, 2d sess., Senate Committee on Military Affairs (Washington: G.P.O. 1942).

⁸² *Final Report,* p. 30. The identical letter was sent over Undersecretary Patterson's signature to Senator Reynolds on the same day.

⁸³ *Proceedings,* Hearings on House Resolution 6758, 77th Congress, 2d sess., House Committee on Military Affairs, March 17, 1942 (processed), p. 3. These proceedings were never officially published (Study files).

⁸⁴ *Ibid.,* p. 8.

⁸⁵ *Congressional Record,* March 19, 1942, pp. 2722–2726.

⁸⁶ *Ibid.,* p. 2726.

⁸⁷ *Ibid.,* p. 2729–2730.

⁸⁸ *Ibid.,* p. 2729.

⁸⁹ *Ibid.*

[90] Despite the fact that DeWitt ordered the Japanese to leave "by virtue of the authority vested in him by the President of the United States and by the Secretary of War and his powers and prerogatives as Commanding General of the Western Defense Command" (as the first proclamation has it), the program was described by the Command as "voluntary," e.g., "voluntary exodus" (*Final Report,* p. 44), "voluntary migration" (*Ibid.,* p. 41), "voluntary evacuation" (*Ibid.,* p. 44), "voluntary emigration" (*Ibid.,* p. 43). Public Proclamation No. 4 stated that the Japanese were "voluntarily migrating." Secretary Stimson may have initiated this usage in his letter of February 20 to DeWitt.

[91] 7 *Fed. Reg.,* 2320.

[92] "Military necessity," WDC's justification for all its evacuation proclamations and orders, was never officially defined or clarified. The usage in this first proclamation, where it covers invasion as well as espionage, is broader than that in a letter from Bendetsen to a California resident in which he stated, "The term, 'military necessity,' as used in this connection must be construed and limited to relate to the tactical and logistical defense of the territory of this Command against physical attack." (Letter, Bendetsen to correspondent, April 24, 1942, Study files.)

[93] Military Area No. 1 was divided into Prohibited Zone A-1 and Restricted Zone B. Military Area No. 2 contained Prohibited Zones A-2 to A-99. These subdivisions of the areas did not play a large part in the exclusion program and were abolished by Public Proclamation No. 14, December 23, 1942, which made all of Military Area No. 1 prohibited while the other military areas were freed of prohibited zones (8 *Fed. Reg.,* 282). The boundary of Military Area No. 1 in Arizona was moved some distance to the south in Public Proclamation No. 16 of March 4, 1943 (8 *Fed. Reg.,* 3256). Public Proclamation No. 2, March 16, 1942, made the states of Idaho, Montana, Nevada, and Utah into Military Areas Nos. 3, 4, 5, and 6 respectively (7 *Fed. Reg.,* 2405).

[94] WDC's terminology, in referring to American citizens of the Japanese "race," varied from time to time, all of the expressions obscuring the fact of their American citizenship. Proclamations Nos. 3, 4, and 5 and others lumped them in with Japanese aliens as "persons of Japanese ancestry." The 108 Civilian Exclusion Orders called them "nonaliens" and also referred to "Japanese persons." The *Final Report* (p. 514) inaccurately defined Nisei as "any person of Japanese ancestry not born in Japan."

[95] Obtainable at post offices, these cards were to be filled out and mailed within five days by an individual changing his address. Public Proclamation No. 2, March 16, 1942, ordered this for all enemy aliens and all Japanese in the WDC.

[96] WDC, Press Release No. 3, March 3, 1942; San Francisco *Chronicle,* March 2, 1942.

[97] Broadcast by Clark, March 2, 1942 (Notes in Study files); WDC, Press Release No. 8, March 7, 1942.

[98] WDC, Press Release, March 9, 1942.

[99] *Final Report,* p. 48.

[100] *Ibid.,* p. 41. WCCA was abolished March 15, 1943.

[101] *Final Report,* p. 66.

[102] *Ibid.,* p. 41.

[103] Interview, Dillon S. Myer, Director, WRA, September 13, 1943 (Notes in Study files).

[104] *Final Report,* p. 44. According to Myer, Poston was originally planned to hold more than 40,000 persons.

[105] Interview, Myer.

[106] *Final Report,* p. 44.

[107] 7 *Fed. Reg.,* 2543. Public Proclamation No. 15, December 24, 1942, abolished the curfew (8 *Fed. Reg.,* 282).

[108] San Francisco *Chronicle,* March 19, 1942.

[109] *Final Report,* p. 109.

[110] *Ibid.,* table 6, p. 110.

[111] *WRA, A Story of Human Conservation,* U.S. Department of the Interior, War Relocation Authority (Processed; Washington: G.P.O., 1946), p. 26.

[112] Public Proclamation No. 5, March 30, 1942, exempted those Japanese who were hospitalized, orphans, or deaf, dumb, and blind, as well as German or Italian alien enemies over seventy years of age, who were dependent on an individual in the armed forces, or who had applied for naturalization prior to Pearl Harbor. Public Proclamation No. 9, June 27, 1942 (7 *Fed. Reg.,* 5719) abolished the areas set up by the Department of Justice in February, 1942.

[113] 7 *Fed. Reg.,* 8450.

[114] 8 *Fed. Reg.,* 282.

[115] 10 *Fed. Reg.,* 14945.

[116] The WDC variously referred to this program as "controlled evacuation" (*Final Report,* p. 51); "planned, supervised evacuation" (Bendetsen, Karl R. *The Story of Pacific Coast Japanese Evacuation,* p. 3).

[117] 7 *Fed. Reg.,* 2601.

[118] WDC, Press Release No. 33, March 27, 1942.

[119] WDC, Press Release No. 32, March 26, 1942.

[120] *Final Report,* p. 43. The WDC justification for the change of program stressed protection of the Japanese and "order." "First, it was to alleviate tension and prevent incidents involving violence between Japanese migrants and others. Second, it was to insure an orderly supervised, and thoroughly controlled evacuation with adequate provisions for the protection of the persons of evacuees as well as their property." (*Final Report,* p. 105.)

[121] Assistant Professor of Journalism, Kansas State College, 1924. Assistant to Secretary of Agriculture, 1926–28. Director of Information, Department of Agriculture, 1928–40. Land Use Coördinator, Department of Agriculture, 1937–42. Director of WRA, March 18 to June 17, 1942. Associate Director of OWI, June, 1942–43. President, Kansas State College, 1942–51. President, Pennsylvania State College, 1951—.

Dillon S. Myer succeeded Eisenhower as Director of WRA and held the position until the agency expired on June 30, 1946. He had been an administrator in the Department of Agriculture, 1934–42; Commissioner, Federal Public Housing Administration, 1946, and Commissioner, Bureau of Indian Affairs, 1950–53. On May 8, 1946, President Harry S. Truman awarded him the Medal of Merit for his WRA services.

[122] Dorothy S. Thomas and Richard S. Nishimoto, *The Spoilage* (Berkeley: University of California Press, 1946), p. 25.

[123] From a statement by Eisenhower before Congressional sub-committee, June 15, 1942, as given in *WRA First Quarterly Report March 18 to June 30, 1942* (Washington: War Relocation Authority, n.d.), p. 3: "There was widespread and bitter opposition in the inter-mountain states for a number of reasons; First, the states did not wish the evacuees to acquire real property, as some did. Evacuees moved to localities where there had previously been a small Japanese population and difficulties arose there. Second, demands arose that the Government should guarantee that evacuees would be removed from the States to which they were going as soon as the war was over. Third, the demand was made that evacuees be permitted to move only under military guard. At one location in Oregon and at another in Nevada Japanese were arrested. In Utah a stick of dynamite was set off in protest against the arrival of 25 evacuees. In Colorado and other places mass meetings were held in protest. Practically every governor of the Western states protested the dispersal of the Japanese."

[124] "WRA was formed out of disagreement between the Army and the Justice Department. Justice wanted a civilian agency to handle Japanese-American matters after the movement, itself, had taken place. Army authorities agreed but apparently didn't want Justice to do the job. I don't think Justice wanted it either. In any case, WRA

started through the efforts of James Rowe in Justice working with McCloy in the War Department and with Wayne Coy in the Bureau of the Budget. As early as March 1 or 2 Eisenhower had thought the thing out to some extent. He had been contacted by the Budget Bureau and on that date showed me a rough draft of the Executive Order. I actually wrote the Executive Order working from a draft prepared by the Budget Bureau and Eisenhower's notes. Afterwards a couple of paragraphs [including No. 10] were added at War Department suggestion." (Interview, Philip Glick, Solicitor of WRA, September 13, 1943, notes in Study files.)

[125] 7 *Fed. Reg.*, 2165.

[126] Interview, M. S. Eisenhower, September 13, 1943 (Notes in Study files).

[127] *Final Report*, p. 44.

[128] Interview, Eisenhower.

[129] *The Relocation Program*, p. 7.

[130] Interview, Eisenhower.

[131] *Ibid.*

[132] Letter, M. S. Eisenhower to President F. D. Roosevelt (Study files).

[133] These all followed the proclamation with the exception of Civilian Exclusion Order No. 1, issued on March 24, 1942, ordering the exclusion of all Japanese, 258 in number, from Bainbridge Island, Washington. (7 *Fed. Reg.*, 2581.) The Civilian Exclusion orders were published in the *Federal Register*. A specimen order is reproduced in the *Final Report*, pp. 97–100.

[134] See *Final Report*, pp. 114–126, for details of the procedure.

[135] "Civilian Exclusion Order Instructions," *ibid.*, p. 100.

[136] See *Final Report*, pp. 127–144; also pp. 89–90; 116–117, for agencies involved, responsibilities and character of operations; see also Leonard Bloom and Ruth Riemer, *Removal and Return: The Socio-Economic Effects of the War on Japanese-Americans,* Univ. Calif. Publ. Cult. and Soc., Vol. 4 (Berkeley: University of California Press, 1949), chapter v.

[137] See WRA quarterly and semi-annual reports for development and extent of services.

[138] Bloom and Riemer, *Removal and Return,* p. 203.

[139] 7 *Fed. Reg.*, 4498.

[140] Memorandum from Col. W. A. Boekel, Assistant Chief of Staff, WDC, to Col. K. R. Bendetsen, April 29, 1942 (AGO files).

[141] *Final Report,* p. 145.

[142] *Ibid.*, pp. 145–146.

[143] *Ibid.*, chapter xiii, "Assembly Center Location, Construction and Equipment," pp. 151–185.

[144] See evacuee accounts in Mine Okubo, *Citizen 13660* (New York: Columbia University Press, 1946); Alexander H. Leighton, *The Governing of Men* (Princeton: Princeton University Press, 1945); and Study files.

[145] *WCCA Operations Manual,* June 11, 1942, Section XXVI (Processed; U.S. Army, WDC), p. 21.

[146] *Final Report,* pp. 118, 125 and 215. "WDC Circular No. 19, Policies Pertaining to Use of Military Police at War Relocation Centers," September 17, 1942. (*Ibid.,* pp. 527–529.) See also DeWitt's order "Functions of Military Police Units at Centers for Japanese Evacuees." (*Ibid.,* p. 215–216.)

[147] *Ibid.*, chapter xvii, "Education, Recreation, Religion and Assembly Center Newspapers," pp. 207–214.

[148] *Ibid.*, p. 211.

[149] *WCCA Operations Manual,* sec. XXV, p. 18.

[150] *Final Report,* chapter xxi, "Construction and Equipment of Relocation Centers," pp. 248–277.

[151] *Ibid.*, chapter xxii, "Transfer of Evacuees from Assembly to Relocation Centers," pp. 278–289, and map inserts I, II and III, facing p. 290.

[152] Leighton, *The Governing of Men*, p. 65.

[153] *WRA Semi-Annual Report, July 1 to December 31, 1945.* U.S. Department of Interior, War Relocation Authority (Washington, n.d.), p. 1.

[154] Executive Order 9102 (7 *Fed. Reg.*, 2165).

[155] "Memorandum of Agreement between the War Department and War Relocation Authority" (*Final Report*, p. 239–240).

[156] *Ibid.*, p. 240.

[157] 8 *Fed. Reg.*, 982.

[158] 7 *Fed. Reg.*, 8346.

[159] Order No. 18, Gila River Center; No. 19, Colorado River; No. 20, Central Utah; No. 21, Tule Lake (modified in No. 26); No. 24, Minidoka. Two other centers used for short periods were also covered by such Civilian Restrictive Orders: No. 27, Camp Dalton Wells, Utah; No. 28, Cow Creek, California (rescinded by Order No. 29). (8 *Fed. Reg.*, 982–989.)

[160] Granada Center, Colorado; Heart Mountain Center, Wyoming; Rohwer and Jerome, Arkansas. The boundaries of Heart Mountain were amended in WRA Regulations of December 16, 1942 (7 *Fed. Reg.*, 10749) which stated that the evacuees could not leave except as authorized by Proclamation WD:1 and of May 21, 1943 (8 *Fed. Reg.*, 6913). By Public Proclamation No. 12 of the WDC (8 *Fed. Reg.*, 3256), March 2, 1943, the boundary was moved southward an average distance of sixty miles. Poston and Gila River centers, in Arizona, were thus removed from the evacuation zone.

[161] 7 *Fed. Reg.*, 6593.

[162] *Final Report*, p. 242. The WRA explicitly recognized this delegation. Administrative Instruction No. 98, July 6, 1943, read in part, "All persons of Japanese ancestry residing within one of the six War Relocation Project Areas located in the Western Defense Command are prohibited from leaving the Area without a written authorization from the Western Defense Command. The authority to issue such written authorization has been delegated to the Director (memorandum to the Director, WRA, from Capt. Hugh T. Fullerton, Asst. Adj. General, dated 11 August 1942) and redelegated by him to the Project Directors."

[163] *Final Report*, p. 215. See also WRA memo: "Understanding as to Functions of Military Police Units at Relocation Centers and Areas Administered by War Relocation Authority," July 8, 1942.

[164] *WRA Semi-Annual Report, January 1 to June 30, 1944*, U.S. Department of Interior, War Relocation Authority (Washington, n.d.), p. 52.

[165] *Community Government in War Relocation Centers*, U.S. Department of Interior, War Relocation Authority (Processed; Washington: G.P.O., 1946), p. 5.

[166] *Ibid.*, p. 12.

[167] *Ibid.*, p. 99.

[168] *Ibid.*, p. 82.

[169] For details of community government at one center, see Leighton, *The Governing of Men*, chapter 6.

[170] *WRA, A Story of Human Conservation*, p. 107.

[171] *WRA Semi-Annual Report January 1 to June 30, 1943*, U.S. War Relocation Authority (Washington, n.d.), p. 38.

[172] *WRA, A Story of Human Conservation*, pp. 75–83.

[173] 7 *Fed. Reg.*, 4436.

[174] 7 *Fed. Reg.*, 6703.

[175] *Final Report*, p. 50.

[176] *Ibid.*, p. 41.

[177] All figures in this section are taken from chapter xxviii, "Statistical Summary," of the *Final Report*.

[178] *Final Report,* p. 278.

[179] The figures in the *Final Report* and those in WRA publications show slight discrepancies, due possibly to terminological differences. According to the WRA it received from WDC 111,260 persons: direct from assembly centers, 90,491; direct from homes, 17,915; seasonal workers on furlough, 1,579; institutional inmates, 1,275. (*WRA, A Story of Human Conservation,* p. 196.)

[180] Of those in institutions, "228 had been formally inducted into an assembly center but had been placed in an institution outside of a center for health reasons and were not transferred to a relocation center with regular movements. Institutions in the evacuated area had 794 Japanese who had never been formally evacuated. This group includes many cases committed to state institutions for the insane and tubercular, as well as a few cases in penal or correctional institutions." (*Final Report,* p. 379.)

[181] *Evacuated People, A Quantitative Description,* U.S. Department of the Interior, War Relocation Authority (Processed; Washington: G.P.O., 1946), p. 10. Only 4 persons left the relocation centers without permission or without being checked out. One mentally deficient girl disappeared, a murder suspect escaped into desert country, and two old men, who were hospital patients, wandered away from camps and the WRA presumed they died from exhaustion in the desert.

[182] 7 *Fed. Reg.,* 4859.

[183] 7 *Fed. Reg.,* 5785. Public Proclamation No. 4, June 30, 1942, required any person, citizen or alien, to secure a permit from the military authorities before entering or departing from Alaska (7 *Fed. Reg.,* 5785).

[184] *Evacuated People,* p. 183. The *Final Report* states that 151 Alaskans were brought in June, 1942, to assembly centers (table 47, p. 366, and p. 356).

[185] *WRA Semi-Annual Report, January 1 to June 30, 1946,* U.S. Department of Interior, War Relocation Authority (Washington, n.d.), p. 16.

[186] Population in 1940: 157,905, or 32.5 per cent of the Island's population; 23.5 per cent, or 32,352, were aliens. In 1940 the Issei made up 22 per cent of the Island's Japanese population. See A. W. Lind, *Hawaii's Japanese* (Princeton: Princeton University Press, 1947), pp. 31 and 237.

[187] *Ibid.*

[188] *Ibid.,* p. 73, quoting figures given by Robert C. Shivers, formerly chief of the FBI in Hawaii, before a congressional committee, January 15, 1946. The figures differ from those given in a statement by Undersecretary of Interior Abe Fortas, who wrote on June 29, 1945, that "fewer than 1,100 persons of Japanese ancestry were transferred to the mainland to relocation centers. Of those transferred ... 912 were citizens, the rest aliens." Quoted in Eugene V. Rostow, "The Japanese-American Cases— a Disaster," *Yale Law Journal,* vol. 54 (1945), pp. 489–553.

[189] *American Civil Liberties Union News,* June, 1942, p. 1.

[190] *Evacuated People,* table 90, p. 191, "Hawaiians Evacuated to WRA Centers by Center and Date of Arrival."

[191] 9 *Fed. Reg.,* 12831.

[192] *WRA Semi-Annual Report, July 1 to December 31, 1944,* U.S. Department of Interior, War Relocation Authority (Washington, n.d.), p. 37.

[193] *WRA Semi-Annual Report, January 1 to June 30, 1946,* p. 16.

[194] Interview, July 23, 1952 (Notes in Study files).

[195] In September, 1943, a San Francisco printer printed ten copies which were classified confidential by WDC. In December, 1943, 2,500 copies of a slightly revised edition were printed by the Government Printing Office and placed on public sale in 1944.

[196] *Final Report,* pp. 8–17, *passim.*

[197] Tolan Committee, *Hearings,* part 29, pp. 10973–11009. Warren's material dealing with the distribution of Japanese throughout California was based on data compiled by the district attorneys of the 35 California counties with Japanese residents. Maps

prepared from this data purported to show "the location of all lands owned, operated or controlled by Japanese." This material did not come to the attention of the WDC until *after* March 12, 1942, almost three weeks after Warren had delivered his talk before the Tolan Committee. On March 4, deputy Attorney General Walter Olds of the State of California telephoned a Colonel Strohe of Army Intelligence at the Presidio in San Francisco and informed him of the existence of the maps and of the willingness of the Attorney General's office to let the Army study them. ("Memorandum for the File," Walter Olds, March 4, 1942, Study files). On March 12, Olds wrote to DeWitt summarizing the data and explaining that "several weeks ago I advised Colonel Strohe of your staff that we had in our possession maps ... showing the location of all lands owned, operated or controlled by Japanese, but as no one from the Army has yet seen them, I thought that the enclosed compilation of information from them might be of value." (Letter in Study files.)

[198] October Term, 1942, No. 870. Submitted by R. B. Kenney, I. H. VanWinkle, Smith Troy and Fred E. Lewis, attorneys for the states of California, Oregon, and Washington, respectively.

[199] In the sections of Chapter Two of the *Final Report* between paragraph 3 on page 9 and paragraph 5 on page 16, only 6 paragraphs were not directly traceable to these sources. Two of these paragraphs were one sentence in length, introducing new topics or referring to matter in a footnote. The "borrowings" in the *Final Report* from Warren's statement were noticed by the author of *Wartime Exile, the Exclusion of the Japanese Americans from the West Coast*, War Relocation Authority (Processed; Washington, G.P.O., 1946), p. 52, and by Morton Grodzins, *Americans Betrayed, Politics and the Japanese Evacuation* (Chicago: University of Chicago Press, 1949), pp. 284–285.

[200] Footnote 2, page 10, acknowledges, "All quotations in this note taken from the ... Testimony of the Attorney General of California" at the Tolan Committee hearings, but omits the date of his appearance. The footnote quotes from newspaper articles describing American Japanese contributions to Japan's war effort.

[201] Paragraph 2, p. 15, is quoted from A. W. Lind, *The Japanese in Hawaii*, American Council Paper No. 5 (New York: American Council, Institute of Pacific Relations, 1942).

[202] *Final Report*, p. 17.

[203] *Ibid.*, p. 18.

[204] *Ibid.*, pp. 8–33, *passim.* "The Chief of the Federal Communications' Radio Intelligence Division had reported a conference with General DeWitt and his staff on January 9, 1942.... The procedures of radio intelligence were explained to the general and he was informed that there had been no illegitimate radio transmission or signalling from Japanse or other coastal residents." *Wartime Exile*, p. 154, quoting from a confidential memorandum from Commissioner James L. Fly, FCC, to Attorney General Biddle on the subject "Lieut. Gen. J. L. DeWitt's Final Report on Japanese Evacuation from the West Coast," April 1, 1944.

[205] *Final Report*, pp. 41 ff., *passim.*

[206] *Ibid.*

[207] Executive Order 9102 (7 *Fed. Reg.*, 2165). According to Philip M. Glick, Solicitor of WRA, who drafted the executive order, the phrase "supervision of activities" was deliberately adopted. The agency did not want a more explicit statement for it was uncertain about the character of the evacuees, the nature of the program, and its legal position. A statement capable of various interpretations was adopted so that the agency could "jump either way." It wished to avoid a specific reference to detention so that no one could insist that it was ordered to detain the Japanese yet it wanted a phrase with an interpretation allowing for detention if WRA needed or wished to do so (Interview, May 2, 1952, notes in Study files).

[208] WRA felt less sure of its legal position in respect to detention for such a purpose than it did for detention for the sake of promoting effective resettlement. Despite the absence of an explicit authorization in its executive order for such detention, it decided to hold "dangerous" evacuees on the general grounds that such a program could be defended as reasonable in the light of the state of war and the national emergency (Interview, Philip M. Glick, May 2, 1952, notes in Study files).

[209] Study files.

[210] *Community Government*, p. 2.

[211] *Final Report*, p. 245, quoting a WRA publication.

[212] *WRA First Quarterly Report, March 18 to June 30, 1942*, U.S. War Relocation Authority (Washington, n.d.), p. 4 of "Chronology."

[213] *WRA Second Quarterly Report, July 1 to September 30, 1942*, U.S. War Relocation Authority (n.p., n.d.), p. 11.

[214] WDC, Press Release, unnumbered.

[215] WDC, Press Release, Number 11-5, November 7, 1942.

[216] *WRA [Third] Quarterly Report, October 1 to December 31, 1942*, U.S. War Relocation Authority (Washington, n.d.), p. 10.

[217] *WRA, A Story of Human Conservation*, p. 32.

[218] *WRA Second Quarterly Report, July 1 to September 30, 1942*, p. 1.

[219] Civilian Restrictive Orders Nos. 1–25 (8 *Fed. Reg.*, 982–989).

[220] Civilian Restrictive Order No. 16, July 23, 1942 (8 *Fed. Reg.*, 984).

[221] *Final Report*, p. 243.

[222] *WRA Second Quarterly Report, July 1 to September 30, 1942*, p. 18.

[223] Executive Order 9102 (7 *Fed. Reg.*, 2165).

[224] 7 *Fed. Reg.*, 3231.

[225] WRA Administrative Instruction No. 27; *WRA Second Quarterly Report, July 1 to September 30, 1942*, p. 9.

[226] Leighton, *The Governing of Men*, p. 92.

[227] *The Relocation Program*, p. 9.

[228] 7 *Fed. Reg.*, 10667.

[229] *WRA, A Story of Human Conservation*, p. 52.

[230] Interview, Philip M. Glick, May 2, 1952 (Notes in Study files).

[231] *WRA Semi-Annual Report, January 1 to June 30, 1943*, p. 15.

[232] *The Leave Program of the War Relocation Authority*, U.S. Department of Interior, War Relocation Authority (Processed; Washington, 1944), p. 12.

[233] *Ibid.*, passim.

[234] *WRA, A Story of Human Conservation*, p. 35.

[235] WRA Administrative Instruction No. 22, July 20, 1942. "Temporary Procedure for Issuance of Permits to Individuals or Single Families to Leave Relocation Centers for Employment Outside Such Centers and the WDC."

[236] *WRA, A Story of Human Conservation*, p. 39; WRA, "Letter to All Project Directors," E. M. Rowalt, Acting Director, WRA, February 1, 1943; Interview, D. S. Myer, September 29, 1943 (Notes in Study files).

[237] WRA, "Issuance of Leave for Departure from a Relocation Area," (7 *Fed Reg.*, 7656). These appeared in greater detail in WRA Administrative Instruction No. 22 (Revised), November 6, 1942.

[238] *Report of Subcommittee on Japanese War Relocation Centers*, 78th Congress, 1st sess., Senate, Military Affairs Committee, May 7, 1943 (Washington: G.P.O., 1943), p. 227.

[239] Form WRA-126, "Application for Leave Clearance." (*Ibid.*, p. 224). If leave clearance had been granted, applicant applied on Form WRA-129, "Application for Leave to Participate in a Work Group" (*Ibid.*, p. 230). If leave called for travel in a prohibited area, an escort was provided by the Army if it decided that one was necessary. All applicants had also to fill out Form WRA-26 (Rev.), "Individual Record." This

was the census form for all evacuees and called for detailed information on education, race of spouse, marital status, birthplace, languages used, residence outside the United States, military or naval service, physical description and condition, employment history, skills, and hobbies.

[240] Form WRA-130, "Application for Indefinite Leave," (*Ibid.*, p. 230).

[241] *WRA, A Story of Human Conservation*, p. 40.

[242] After February, 1943, the indefinite leave forms were printed on cards, $2\frac{1}{2} \times 4$ inches in size, containing a fingerprint of the evacuee's right index finger and a full-face photograph. (Administrative Instruction No. 22 (Rev.), Supplement 4, February 17, 1943, in *Report of Subcommittee on Japanese War Relocation Centers*, p. 251.)

[243] Administrative Instruction No. 22 (Rev.); Supplement 1 (Rev.); (*Report of Subcommittee on Japanese War Relocation Centers*, p. 241). The Council's functions were described as: "To assist students in selecting a school to attend, to examine and appraise the student's academic records, to arrange with educational institutions for the admission of students, to determine community sentiment with respect to the admission of students, to determine community sentiment with respect to the relocation of students in that community, and to determine the adequacy of the students' financial arrangements." Students might arrange for admission independently but if they did so they had to supply evidence to WRA they had been admitted; the WRA would make its own investigation of "community sentiment" if the Council was not called on.

[244] *WRA [Third] Quarterly Report, October 1 to December 31, 1942*, p. 2.

[245] "When it became known that the War Department would make this registration of draft-age Nisei men, it was decided to include in the registration all other adults, age 17 or more, as a means of speeding up our clearance procedure and with the object of providing a pool of workers, available for placement by WRA and the War Manpower Commission in private employment." ("Letter to All [WRA] Project Directors," E. M. Rowalt, January 1, 1943, in *Report of Subcommittee on Japanese War Relocation Centers*, p. 211.)

[246] WRA Administrative Instruction No. 22 (Rev.); Supplement 3, January 30, 1943, as cited in *Report of Subcommittee on Japanese War Relocation Centers*, p. 243.

[247] *Ibid.*, p. 245.

[248] *Ibid.*, p. 249.

[249] WRA Administrative Instruction No. 22 (Rev.); Supplement 6, February 26, 1943. *Ibid.*, p. 253.

[250] Thomas, *Salvage*, p. 93.

[251] *WRA Semi-Annual Report, January 1 to June 30, 1943*, p. 11.

[252] Thomas, *Salvage*, p. 93.

[253] WRA Administrative Instruction No. 22 (Rev.); Supplement 7, March 20, 1943, in *Report of Subcommittee on Japanese War Relocation Centers*, p. 253.

[254] WRA Administrative Instruction No. 22 (Rev.), Supplement 9, April 2, 1943; WRA Administrative Instruction No. 22 (Rev.), Supplement 8, March 16, 1943; WRA Administrative Instruction No. 22 (Rev.), Supplement 10 and 10 (Rev.), June 28, 1943.

[255] WRA Administrative Instruction No. 22 (Rev.), Supplement 12, June 5, 1943. These instructions were superseded by the *WRA Handbook on Issuance of Leave for Departure from a Relocation Area* (Processed; Washington, 1943), issued July 20, of which "Investigation for Leave Clearance in Doubtful Cases" was sec. 60.10.

[256] WRA Handbook Release No. 12, September 12, 1943. Sec. 60.10 superseded sec. 60.10 of July 20, 1943.

[257] *WRA, A Story of Human Conservation*, p. 68.

[258] *WRA Semi-Annual Report, July 1 to December 31, 1943*, U.S. Department of Interior, War Relocation Authority (Washington, n.d.), p. 69.

[259] *WRA, A Story of Human Conservation*, p. 69.

[260] *WRA Semi-Annual Report, July 1 to December 31, 1943*, p. 49.

[261] *Ibid.*, p. 33.

[262] WRA Handbook Release No. 82, February 16, 1944.

[263] WRA Handbook Release No. 73, March 7, 1944. A "Trial Period Agreement" (WRA Form 328) was executed which specified the dates between which permission to return would be granted. No leave assistance grants were provided.

[264] *The Leave Program of the War Relocation Authority*, p. 16.

[265] *WRA Semi-Annual Report, July 1 to December 31, 1944*, pp. 50 and 56.

[266] For material in this section we have drawn heavily on the reports of Mr. Victor W. Nielsen, former Chief, Research Division, CAD.

[267] Study files.

[268] *WRA Semi-Annual Report, July 1 to December 31, 1943*, p. 49. The Board was composed of one representative apiece from WRA, FBI, Military Intelligence (G-2), Office of the Provost Marshal General, Office of Naval Intelligence, and, in late 1943, a representative of the Air Force, as it desired then to employ Japanese on ground installations in the states. Its administrative officer was the Assistant Executive Officer in the office of McCloy; he voted only in cases of ties. The board functioned until May 25, 1944, when it was disestablished.

[269] Interview, Dillon S. Myer, September 29, 1943 (Notes in Study files).

[270] *WRA, A Story of Human Conservation*, p. 58.

[271] *Ibid.*, p. 59.

[272] *WRA Semi-Annual Report, July 1 to December 31, 1943*, p. 50.

[273] *Ibid.*

[274] Study files.

[275] *The Relocation Program*, p. 35.

[276] WRA Administrative Instruction No. 98, July 6, 1943.

[277] Leaders or members of strongly pro-Japanese societies or religious groups, such as the Imperial Military Reservists groups; those who opposed the war effort or urged others to do so (expressions of objection to exclusion of Japanese not a ground here); those who led pro-Japanese propaganda campaigns after July, 1937; those expressing a desire to renounce United States citizenship or assume Japanese; agents of the Japanese government, quasi-governmental agencies, banks, news services, etc.; those refusing to serve in American armed forces; those requesting return to Japan; agents or operatives of any enemy nation; sponsors, directors, or teachers in Japanese-language schools known to have promoted Japanese nationalism; contributors to Japanese war effort; residents in Japan for such period of time as would justify the conclusion they had received nationalistic indoctrination; those commended or decorated by any Japanese agency for aiding Japanese war effort; dual citizens over 18 who had opportunity to renounce Japanese citizenship yet did not do so; those who had served in Japanese army or navy since 1935; those whom the commanding general considered dangerous to military security in the prohibited area.

[278] Those who fell within the ineligible categories of citizens listed in the note above; those giving negative answers to question 28. Those in the following groups unless they could show strong evidence of loyalty to the United States: employees of firms, banks, or agencies controlled by the Japanese government; those whose repatriation was requested by the Japanese government; those interned by the Department of Justice after Pearl Harbor; those with children living in Japan or who registered their American-born children with the Japanese consul to secure Japanese citizenship for them or who sent their American-born children to Japan for most of their education.

[279] *WRA Semi-Annual Report, July 1 to December 31, 1944*, p. 58.

[280] *WRA, A Story of Human Conservation*, p. 59.

[281] *Ibid.*, p. 45.

[282] Ringle, K.D. *The Japanese Question in the United States: Confidential Memorandum for the WRA* (Processed; War Relocation Authority, n.d.), p. 30.

[283] *WRA, A Story of Human Conservation,* p. 46. This belief is contrary to the findings of Thomas and Nishimoto. See *Spoilage,* p. 106 and *passim.*

[284] Interview, September 29, 1943 (Notes in Study files).

[285] See statement in *WRA Semi-Annual Report, January 1 to June 30, 1943,* p. 19.

[286] Senate Resolution 166, relating to segregation of loyal and disloyal Japanese in relocation centers, 78th Congress, 1st sess., 1943.

[287] WRA Administrative Instruction No. 100, July 15, 1943. *WRA Administrative Manual,* Sec. 110.1 "Segregation Policy," October 6, 1943.

[288] WRA Administrative Instruction No. 100 and Supplement No. 1, August 25, 1943.

[289] *WRA Semi-Annual Report, July 1 to December 31, 1943,* p. 3.

[290] WRA Administrative Instruction No. 100.

[291] Some parolees from the camps were allowed to relocate. Whether this was done or whether they were segregated depended on the recommendation of the Department of Justice.

[292] It has been estimated that there were about 1,100 of these. However, as most of them applied for repatriation or took some other step "legalizing" their presence in segregant Tule Lake, the number given in the table is very small.

[293] *Evacuated People,* table 45a, p. 109; table 75, p. 168; table 76, p. 169; and table 77, p. 169.

[294] Thomas, *Salvage,* p. 94.

[295] *WRA Semi-Annual Report, July 1 to December 31, 1943,* p. 8. *WRA Administrative Manual,* sec. 110.0.2B.

[296] *WRA Administrative Manual,* sec. 110.13.1, April 26, 1944.

[297] *WRA Semi-Annual Report, January 1 to June 30, 1944,* p. 31.

[298] *WRA Administrative Manual,* sec. 110.9, October 18, 1943.

[299] *WRA Semi-Annual Report, July 1 to December 31, 1943,* p. 9.

[300] See *WRA Administrative Manual,* sec. 30, "Internal Security" as given in Manual Release No. 39, December 1, 1943, for regulations prescribing the procedures to be followed in organizing the center police force, making arrests, holding trials, sentencing offenders, etc.

[301] WRA Administrative Instruction, February 16, 1943, unnumbered. Families were not allowed to accompany offenders. Other WRA publications categorized them as "persistent trouble-makers" (*Evacuated People,* p. 180); "those who menace community living" and who "jeopardize the peace of the community." (*WRA [Third] Quarterly Report, October 1 to December 31, 1942,* p. 40).

[302] *WRA Administrative Manual,* sec. 80.2; *WRA Semi-Annual Report, January 1 to June 30, 1943,* p. 22.

[303] WRA Administrative Instruction, February 16, 1943, Sec. 1.A–C.

[304] *Evacuated People,* table 85. "Source of Original Entry and Destination of Final Departure; Leupp Center residents," p. 85.

[305] WRA Administrative Notice, September 4, 1943.

[306] See Thomas and Nishimoto, *Spoilage,* chapter xi, "Incarceration."

[307] *WRA Administrative Manual,* sec. 110.15, "Administrative Separation of Residents within a Center," April 26, 1944.

[308] Letter, Captain F.B.C. Martin, Director, Recruiting Division, Bureau of Personnel, Department of the Navy, to authors August 21, 1952 (Study files).

[309] *Wartime Exile,* p. 152.

[310] AGO files.

[311] Evacuated People, p. 125.

[312] *WRA [Third] Quarterly Report, October 1 to December 31, 1942,* p. 28.

[313] *Wartime Exile,* p. 152.

[314] *Report of Subcommittee on Japanese War Relocation Centers,* p. 297.

[315] *Ibid.,* p. 210.

[316] Discrepancies appear in figures of registration of citizen Japanese given in *WRA Semi-Annual Report, January 1 to June 30, 1943;* the *Report of Subcommittee on Japanese War Relocation Centers;* and *Report and Minority Views of Special Committee on Un-American Activities in Japanese War Relocation Centers,* 78th Congress, 1st sess., House Report No. 717, September 30, 1943 (Washington: G.P.O., 1943). The figures of the Japanese American Branch of the Office of Provost Marshall General were: total eligible male Nisei—20,679; number registered—19,014; number giving nonaffirmative answers to questions 27 and 28—5,956; proportion—28.8 per cent. Of those Japanese who had left the evacuation areas before the "freeze" in late March, 25 per cent answered question 28 in the negative.

[317] 8 *Fed. Reg.,* 5320.

[318] New York *Times,* March 17, 1945, p. 14, col. 3.

[319] War Department press releases as given in *WRA,* table 5, "Inductions into Armed Forces by Centers," p. 202.

[320] *WRA Semi-Annual Report, January 1 to June 30, 1944,* p. 20. 1,167 were rejected during this period.

[321] New York *Times,* March 23, 1947, p. 2, col. 2.

[322] New York *Times,* December 24, 1947, p. 1, col. 4.

[323] We have drawn heavily for the data in this section on material prepared by Mr. Victor M. Nielsen; see preface.

[324] WDC memorandum: "Proposed Changes in the Exclusion Program" (Study files). The argument for program revision to avoid enfeeblement of Army control over civilians was set forth in an attached memorandum, "Legal Reasons for Relaxing WDC Exclusion Program," by Col. Joel F. Watson, Staff Judge Advocate, WDC.

[325] Papers of Franklin D. Roosevelt (Franklin D. Roosevelt Library).

[326] *Ibid.*

[327] Major General Bonesteel was commanding general of the WDC from June 25 to November 1, 1944, succeeding General Emmons; Major General R. H. Lewis was acting commanding general from November 1 to December 10, 1944; Major General H. C. Pratt was commanding general from December 11, 1944 to January 3, 1946.

[328] 9 *Fed. Reg.,* 15159.

[329] *Fed. Reg.,* 53.

[330] WDC Instructions to Military Police, April 10, 1945 (AGO files); WDC Standard Operating Procedure for Military Police Detachments for the Control or Ingress at War Relocation Authority Centers, July 28, 1945 (AGO files).

[331] *WRA Manual,* sec. 120.1.2 in Manual Release No. 158, December 18, 1944.

[332] *Ibid.,* sec. 150.1.7 in Manual Release No. 187, April 28, 1945.

[333] 10 *Fed. Reg.,* 11760.

[334] 10 *Fed. Reg.,* 11848.

[335] *Final Report,* p. 319.

[336] *Ibid.,* p. 324.

[337] *WRA Semi-Annual Report, July 1 to December 31, 1943,* p. 88.

[338] *Evacuated People,* table 68, p. 157.

[339] *Ibid.,* table 71, p. 158.

[340] See Thomas and Nishimoto, *Spoilage,* chapters viii–xvi, for detailed account of events at Tule Lake up to midwinter, 1944–45.

[341] Affidavit of John L. Burling, November 8, 1946, in *Abo* v. *Clark* printed in Transcript of Record, *Clark* v. *Abo,* p. 160.

[342] Act of July 1, 1944, 58 Stat. 677; 8 U.S.C. 801 (i); Public Law 405, 78th Congress, 2d sess. Voided by Joint Resolution July 25, 1947, 61 Stat. 451, Public Law 239, 80th Congress, 1st sess.

[343] 8 C.F.R., sec. 316.1–316.9, "Renunciation of United States Citizenship"; 9 *Fed. Reg.,* 12241.

³⁴⁴ Gladys Ishida, *The Background and Effects of the Renunciation by Japanese-Americans in World War II* (Unpublished M.A. thesis, University of Chicago, 1946), p. 55.

³⁴⁵ Thomas and Nishimoto, *Spoilage*, p. 276.

³⁴⁶ *Ibid.*, p., 324.

³⁴⁷ *Ibid.*, p. 333.

³⁴⁸ *Ibid.*, p. 348.

³⁴⁹ Affidavit of John L. Burling in *Abo* v. *Clark*, p. 182.

³⁵⁰ WRA, Tule Lake Segregation Center, "Special Project Regulations," March 16, 1945.

³⁵¹ Interview, John L. Burling, January 17, 1945 (Notes in Study files).

³⁵² Affidavit of John L. Burling in *Abo* v. *Clark*, p. 174.

³⁵³ *Evacuated People*, table 80. The approvals at other centers were: Central Utah, 4; Colorado, 72; Gila, 25; Granada, 10; Heart Mountain, 1; Manzanar, 6; Minidoka, 8; Rohwer, 2.

³⁵⁴ "Analytical Classification of Plaintiffs by Groups Shown in Defendant's Offer of Proof," printed in Brief for Appellants, *McGrath* v. *Abo*, Appendix I, p. xlvii. Several renunciant plaintiffs adjudged "mental incompetents" were placed under the guardianship of another plaintiff ("Order Appointing Guardian Ad Litem," printed in Transcript of Record, *Clark* v. *Abo*, p. 138).

³⁵⁵ 10 *Fed. Reg.*, 8947.

³⁵⁶ 28 C.F.R., sec. 30.1–30.6, "Removal of Alien Enemies from the United States" (10 *Fed. Reg.*, 12189).

³⁵⁷ Brief for Appellees, *McGrath* v. *Abo*, p. 97.

³⁵⁸ Instructions to project directors as published in Newell *Star*, October 26, 1945.

³⁵⁹ "Designation of Plaintiffs," printed in Brief for Appellants, *McGrath* v. *Abo*, p. xlvi.

³⁶⁰ *WRA Semi-Annual Report, July 1 to December 31, 1945*, p. 27.

³⁶¹ *Ibid.*, table II.

³⁶² Transcript of Record, *McGrath* v. *Abo*, p. 57.

³⁶³ *WRA Semi-Annual Report, January 1 to June 30, 1946*, p. 4.

³⁶⁴ Letter, C. M. Rothstein to authors, December 24, 1952 (Study files).

³⁶⁵ *WRA Semi-Annual Report, January 1 to June 30, 1946*, p. 13.

³⁶⁶ *Evacuated People*, p. 184, table 99, p. 196.

³⁶⁷ Brief for Appellant, *McGrath* v. *Abo*, p. 30.

³⁶⁸ WRA, *A Story of Human Conservation*, p. 74. Immigration Service gives 7,686.

³⁶⁹ For the arguments in the briefs in these cases, the decisions and analysis of their implications, see chapter viii, "Citizenship," pp. 311–321.

³⁷⁰ *Tadayasu Abo et al . . . and Genshyo Ambo, et al v. Ivan Williams, as the Officer-in-Charge, United States Department of Justice, Immigration and Naturalization Service, Tule Lake Center, Newell, Modoc County, California* (U.S. Dist. Court, N. D. of Calif., Nos..25,296 and 25,297).

³⁷¹ *Tadayasu Abo et al . . . and Genshyo Ambo et al v. Tom Clark, as Attorney General of the United States, Frank J. Hennessy, as United States Attorney for the Northern District of California . . . ; James F. Byrnes, as the Secretary of State; Fred Vinson, as the Secretary of the Treasury; Ugo Carusi, as the Commissioner of the United States Immigration and Naturalization Service . . . ; James E. Markham, as the Alien Property Custodian; Harold Ickes, as Secretary of the Interior; Dillon S. Myer, as Director, War Relocation Authority; Raymond R. Best, as Project Director, Tule Lake Center; and Ivan Williams, as the Officer-in-Charge, United States Department of Justice . . . Tule Lake Center* (U.S. Dist. Court, N. D. of Calif., Nos. 25,294 and 25,295).

³⁷² The interned renunciants were held during the course of the actions. During the spring and summer of 1946 the Department of Justice released a considerable number. Left in internment were 274 at Crystal City, Texas, and on "relaxed internment"

at Seabrook Farms, Bridgeton, New Jersey, where most of them were employed at current wages in a canning plant. (Opinion in *Abo* v. *McGrath*, printed in Transcript of Record, *Clark* v. *Abo*, p. 211; 77 F. Supp. 806). Collins' Brief for Appellees, *Barber* v *Abo*, p. 14, states that 292 were released.

[373] *Ex parte Abo et al*, 76 F. Supp. 664 at 665.

[374] Transcript of Record, *Wixon* v. *Abo*, p. 195.

[375] *Wixon* v. *Abo et al* (U.S. Court of Appeals, Ninth Circuit, No. 12,195); *Wixon* v. *Mary Furuya et al* (No. 12,196), later known as *Barber* v. *Abo* and *Barber* v. *Furuya* when Barber succeeded Wixon as District Director of the Immigration and Naturalization Service.

[376] On August 16, 1948, the court refused a motion of the government to dismiss 609 plaintiffs who joined the suit after cancellation of their removal orders as a consequence of the mitigation hearings. An additional 1,947 renunciants, likewise released, were added to the suit. Many of the suing renunciants were in Japan.

[377] Transcript of Record, *Clark* v. *Abo*, pp. 147–211.

[378] 77 F. Supp. 806.

[379] Brief for Appellants, *McGrath* v. *Abo*, p. xlvi. The Designation stated that 1,444 renunciants had left for Japan without asking for mitigation hearings, 83 had not been at Tule Lake when they renounced, and 8 "admittedly lacked sufficient mental capacity to accomplish legally binding acts."

[380] 77 F. Supp. 806.

[381] *McGrath* v. *Abo* (U.S. Court of Appeals, Ninth Circuit, No. 12,251).

[382] *Murakami, Sumi, and Shimizu* v. *George C. Marshall* (U.S. Dist. Court, S. D. of Calif., No. 8,394M). The evidence presented included transcripts of the renunciation hearings in which the plaintiffs appeared and affidavits of the plaintiffs to the effect that their renunciations were influenced by conditions and events at Tule. The case became known as *Murakami* v. *Acheson* when the latter succeeded Marshall as Secretary of State.

[383] Findings of Fact and Conclusions of Law, printed in Transcript of Record, *Acheson* v. *Murakami*, p. 51.

[384] *Acheson* v. *Murakami* (U.S. Court of Appeals, Ninth Circuit, No. 12,082). 176 F. 2d 953.

[385] Assistant Attorney General H. G. Morrison to Department of State, October 25, 1949, printed in Brief for Appellants, *McGrath* v. *Abo*, Appendix E, p. xxxiii.

[386] 186 F. 2d 775.

[387] 186 F. 2d 766.

[388] 342 U.S. 832.

[389] U.S. Dist. Court, N. D. of Calif., No. 25,294. On November 26, 1952, seven defendants were dismissed, leaving only three: Attorney General McGranery, A. R. Mackey, Commissioner of the Immigration Service, and Chauncey Traumotolo, United States Attorney for Northern California.

CHAPTER IV

[1] Bradford Smith, *Americans from Japan* (Philadelphia: Lippincott, 1948), p. 10.

[2] *Ibid.*, p. 276.

[3] Carey McWilliams, *Prejudice* (Boston: Little, Brown, 1944), pp. 4, 17.

[4] Morton Grodzins, *Americans Betrayed: Politics and the Japanese Evacuation.* (Chicago: University of Chicago Press, 1949), pp. 21, 193, 88, 54, *passim.*

[5] "The Japanese-American Cases—A Disaster," *Yale Law Journal*, vol. 54 (1945), pp. 489–533.

[6] Nanette Dembitz, "Racial Discrimination and the Military Judgment: The Supreme Court's Korematsu and Endo Decisions," *Columbia Law Review*, vol. 45 (1945), pp. 196–197.

[7] *Fourth Interim Report. Findings and Recommendations on Evacuation of Enemy Aliens and Others from Prohibited Military Zones,* 77th Congress, 2d sess., House Report No. 2124, May 13, 1942, Select Committee Investigating National Defense Migration (Washington: G.P.O., 1942), p. 155. This committee will hereinafter be cited as Tolan Committee.

Some observers at the time when the policy was being determined traced the demand for evacuation to economic groups. Clarence E. Rust, an attorney, told the Tolan Committee that the clamor for evacuation "seems to come from chambers of commerce, Associated Farmers, and the newspapers, notorious as the spokesmen for reactionary interests." (*Ibid.,* p. 154.) See also testimony of Mrs. Esther S. Boyd and Floyd Oles (Tolan Committee, *Hearings,* part 30, pp. 11584 and 11432).

[8] *Americans from Japan,* pp. 274, 265, 267.

[9] The Tolan Committee held hearings on the West Coast in San Francisco, Portland, Seattle, and Los Angeles from February 21 through March 7, 1942. Smith's explanation suffers, in addition, from the defects of vagueness and inaccuracy. He has no doubts that pressure groups were responsible but admits that he does not know their identity: "Since the people who know the answers are not likely to reveal them, it is necessary to rely somewhat upon inference—but inference from a large number of facts and strange coincidences." (*Ibid.,* p. 267.) His "facts and coincidences" consist of seventeen points and six additional paragraphs which build up a picture of behind-the-scenes activity by unidentified "special interests." (*Ibid.,* pp. 268–270.) Some of the activities are at best inaccurately reported. Smith asserts, for instance, that "the [Tolan] hearing provided a field day for all the old anti-Oriental voices—the Native Sons, the Associated Farmers, the Joint Immigration Committee." (*Ibid.,* p. 264.) Only the last of the three groups sent an official representative to the hearings. Nor were the Associated Farmers among the "old anti-Oriental voices" of pre-war years.

[10] McWilliams, *Prejudice,* pp. 116–117.

[11] *Ibid.,* p. 108.

[12] *Americans Betrayed,* pp. 21, 54, 274, 297.

[13] *Ibid.,* p. 297.

[14] *Ibid.,* p. 375.

[15] See p. 102.

[16] See p. 122.

[17] *Prejudice,* pp. 126–128.

[18] Frank J. Taylor, "The People Nobody Wants," *Saturday Evening Post,* May 9, 1942, p. 24.

[19] *Americans from Japan,* pp. 265–276.

[20] *Americans Betrayed,* pp. 21, 24.

[21] *Ibid.,* p. 193.

[22] A recent list, *Directory: Trade Associations and Similar Professional and Service Clubs in California* (San Francisco: California State Chamber of Commerce, 1949), lists 102 "Commodity organizations," composed of 58 "Commodity groups" and 44 "Cooperatives." Farmer organizations are not included in these figures. List of organizations of earlier date not available, according to Chamber. The Portland Chamber of Commerce has reported: "We have in Oregon slightly over 150 cooperative farm marketing organizations ... and many commodity organizations." (Letter to authors, May 16, 1951, Study files.)

Grodzins lists seven organizations: the Southern California Floral Association, the Seattle Retail Florists Association, Eastern Washington Beet Growers, the "vegetable interests of Monterey County," the Associated Produce Dealers and Brokers of Los Angeles, the Grower-Shipper Vegetable Association, and the Western Growers Association. But there is no evidence that the Southern California Floral Association urged evacuation. It did issue a mimeographed statement giving data on Japanese activity in the cut flower business and complaining about competition but containing no suggestion of any policy toward the Japanese. (John S. White and John Brown, *Report on Japanese Activities in the Cut Flower Industry in Southern California,* February 26, 1942, mimeographed.)

[23] The letters included five from the Grower-Shipper Vegetable Association, one from the Western Grower Association, and two from the Produce Dealers and Brokers of Los Angeles. The visit was by an official of the Grower-Shipper Vegetable Association. The telegram referred to was from the Eastern Washington Beet Growers to Governor A. B. Langlie of Washington, on February 4, urging that he "use his influence with the attorney general in having enemy aliens of this valley removed from the designated war zone." (Study files.)

[24] "The vegetable interests of Monterey County" and the Seattle Retail Florists Association spoke before the Tolan Committee late in the month. (Tolan Committee, *Hearings,* part 29, p. 11087 and part 30, p. 11610.)

[25] The president of the association wrote to Congressman John Z. Anderson on January 22 commenting favorably on Congressman Ford's proposal to place all Japanese in camps and urging a six-point program involving, among other matters, registration of all Japanese, alien and native, and their movement inland at least 300 miles. Other letters of the president are discussed by Grodzins but they were either written after February 14 (e.g., those of February 17 to Congressman J. Z. Anderson and of mid-February to Congressman Leland Ford), or were to officials unconnected with evacuation policy or programs, or were not on the subject of evacuation at all (e.g., those of January 3 to L. W. Wing of the Monterey County Defense Council and of January 10 to William Cecil, then Director of the California State Department of Agriculture).

On February 8 a resolution was adopted by the Western Growers calling for the exclusion of all Japanese from points within fifty miles of the coast or a ten mile radius from munition plants or military camps and their removal "to a point where ... there may be no possibility of ... disloyal action affecting the security of the United States." (Tolan Committee, *Hearings,* part 29, p. 11005.) The resolution was not published in *Western Grower and Shipper.* However, the house organ did mention evacuation. The February issue editorialized critically with regard to "commercial interests" for interjecting themselves into the argument over evacuation for "selfish reasons" but claimed that the removals of enemy aliens under the Department of Justice's supervision were "not the result of the pressure of civilian groups."

[26] For instance, referring to a letter by the president of the Western Growers' Association answering the request of a county official for an estimate of the importance of Japanese vegetable production in California, Grodzins states that this was "one of the earliest wartime statements produced with respect to the unimportance of American Japanese in Pacific Coast Agriculture." (*Americans Betrayed,* p. 22.) Why does this private correspondence merit the characterization of a "statement"? There is no evidence that it was made public. What is its importance even if it were?

[27] The Grower-Shipper president wrote to Congressman Anderson on December 23, 1941, recommending that "all Japanese [be put] under strict and rigid governmental control and supervision." (Study files.) In mid-January he held that "all Japanese should be empounded or interned, restricted, confined, or have something done with them that will make them absolutely powerless and take them out of the reach of those who might seek to destroy them for revenge." (Study files.) On January 26 and 27 he again wrote to Anderson but the contents of these letters are not known other than that he asked for "action." A letter of February 13 suggested that after the war all Japanese be sent to Japan. (Study files; also excerpted in Grodzins, *Americans Betrayed,* pp. 28, 30.) All of his other letters were either written after February 14, as that of May 13 to Congressman Anderson, or were to individuals unconnected with evacuation policy, or were not on evacuation policy at all, as those to William Cecil on January 10 and to F. B. Sun, Secretary, Filipino Labor Supply Association.

[28] According to the association's secretary-manager who "was in Salinas during this

period" and who stated that he was "sure that the . . . Association . . . and its membership did not take any official or unofficial action in the evacuation or maneuvers to
obtain the evacuation. Any action or representations credited to the Association were
done by individuals as individuals." (Letter, Jack E. Bias to authors, July 28, 1949,
Study files.)

²⁹ Grodzins' statement that the Association was officially active in December, 1941,
in urging "mass internment" is not justified. He states that "on December 31 another
Grower-Shipper spokesman more precisely defined the organization's position. He
wrote Congressman Anderson that a joint meeting had been held of the directors of
the Vegetable Association, the Salinas Chamber of Commerce, and the Salinas Citizens
Association, and that a resolution had been passed endorsing the recommendation of
the Los Angeles Chamber of Commerce calling for the mass internment of Japanese-
Americans." (*Americans Betrayed*, p. 28.) This cannot have been the case. As Grodzins himself points out, it was not until February that the Los Angeles Chamber of
Commerce went on record (*Ibid.*, p. 34); and then its recommendation was not for
"mass internment of Japanese-Americans," but merely for the "movement of Japanese
to an area beyond fifty miles from the Pacific Coast and the Mexican border, and the
employment of Japanese thus removed to the fullest possible extent." (*Ibid.*, p. 34.)
Grodzins may have been thinking of the recommendation of the Agricultural Committee of the Chamber which recommended on December 22, 1941, that Japanese
nationals be placed "under absolute federal control" (*Ibid.*, p. 34). But this is not
"mass internment." We must conclude either that Grodzins' statement that this letter
was written on December 31, 1941, is in error and that it was written much later,
possibly in February, or that what was asserted to have been the action of the organizations which met, if they did meet, cannot have been what Grodzins says it was.

³⁰ *Ibid.*, p. 28.

³¹ *Ibid.*, p. 193.

³² Tolan Committee, *Hearings*, part 30, p. 11283.

³³ *Ibid.*, pp. 11422–11432.

³⁴ Grodzins, *Americans Betrayed*, pp. 34, 36.

³⁵ A leading official of the Kern County Farm Bureau Association, who was speaking
for the board of directors, wrote to Congressman A. J. Elliott on February 7 that "it
was the consensus of opinion that the sooner the Japanese are removed from the
Pacific Coast the better it will be for all of us." The San Bernardino County Farm
Bureau adopted a resolution on February 11 urging that "every possible step be taken
to remove all Japanese from the Pacific Coast area for the duration of the war."
(Study files.)

³⁶ *Los Angeles Farm Bureau Monthly*, March, 1942, p. 3.

³⁷ *The Associated Farmer*, January 20, 1942.

³⁸ "Various interests in the Hood River Valley, Oregon" urged the removal of all
Japanese from the valley and the Valley Protective Association of Auburn, Washington, describing itself as a "vigilante" organization, asked for the removal of the
Japanese at the Tolan Committee hearings. (Tolan Committee, *Hearings*, part 30,
pp. 11329, 11520.)

³⁹ *Americans Betrayed*, pp. 223, 276.

⁴⁰ *Ibid.*, p. 36.

⁴¹ "Mr. Woodman made a very forceful presentation of the plan and was given what
might be called a 'brush-off.' The League made other efforts to bring the matter to
the attention of Washington officials and particularly the military branch, but they
seemed to have made up their minds for a different course of action and nothing ever
came of our project." (Letter, Russell Avery to authors, December 5, 1950, Study files.)

⁴² *Americans From Japan*, p. 272.

⁴³ *Americans Betrayed*, pp. 21, 202.

⁴⁴ Figures based on the *Directory* which lists forestry, fishing, mining, construction,
manufacturing, service, and public utility organizations; wholesale and retail trade

associations; finance, insurance, and real estate associations. The lone organization on record was the Metal Trades Manufacturing Association of Southern California; on February 10, it passed a resolution calling on the Army and Navy to move "all Japanese inland at least five hundred miles from the coast-line of California." (Letter, E. T. Brown, president, to authors, December 5, 1950, Study files.)

[45] Interview with Mrs. M. T. McMahon, Research Department, California State Chamber of Commerce (Notes in Study files). There is no state chamber in Oregon, the Portland Chamber performing its duties.

[46] Figures from *Directory: Chambers of Commerce and Similar Organizations in California* (San Francisco: California State Chamber of Commerce, 1950). List of chambers of earlier date not available, according to Chamber, which estimates approximately 100 fewer than at present. On February 11, the San Benito County Chamber recommended that "the proper civil and military authorities ... take immediate action to cause the removal of all enemy alien citizens [sic] and Japanese American citizens from the entire Pacific Coast." (Tolan Committee, *Hearings*, part 29, p. 11238.) As for city chambers, on January 29 the San Luis Obispo Chamber asked that "all Japanese both alien and American-born" be removed from California. (Study files.) On February 3, the Pasadena Chamber recommended the "immediate transfer of all Japanese aliens to concentration camps established in the interior regions" and that "all members of the Japanese race living in our area be placed under careful surveillance." (Letter, J. L. Ogston, Secretary, to authors, November 28, 1950, Study files.) On February 11 the Colton Chamber asked that "all enemy aliens, all persons who acknowledge and claim dual citizenship with any enemy nation with which the United States is at war and all other persons whose sympathies with enemy nations make them a potential menace and danger to the war effort" be removed from the state (Study files). The Agricultural Committee of the Los Angeles Chamber of Commerce recommended that "all Japanese nationals and their property be immediately placed under absolute Federal control; and this be accomplished by internment of alien Japanese residents here or by such other means as will regulate their activities effectively and by direct government control of their properties and businesses." (Control of Japanese Nationals and Their Properties. Mimeographed; no date.) Grodzins says this recommendation was adopted on December 22, 1941, but the report itself is without a date. The Washington representative of the Chamber was active in promoting evacuation.

[47] The Tacoma Chamber was active in January addressing letters "to the Washington State Congressional delegation and to the FBI, urging that enemy aliens be evacuated." (Letter, E. R. Fetterolf, Secretary, to authors, November 29, 1950, Study files.) On February 2 the LeConner Chamber petitioned the Federal Government "to move all enemy aliens and citizens of Japanese descent inland from the Pacific Coast area as a security measure against sabotage, racial disturbance, etc." (Study files.)

[48] *Americans Betrayed*, p. 55.

[49] Namely, one Lions club and one Kiwanis club. On February 1 the Selma, California, Lions Club sent a telegram to Tom Clark, requesting that "measures be taken to remove enemy aliens and all persons of Japanese descent to points at least 300 miles from the Pacific Coast." (Study files.)

The Shafter, California, Kiwanis Club passed a resolution on January 23, 1942, calling for evacuation of the Japanese, and circulated letters to congressmen and government officials. This action was censured by the board of trustees of the California-Nevada District of Kiwanis International. The resolution of the board declared that the Shafter resolution has been "enacted and circularized in violation" of the bylaws of the Kiwanis International which prohibits resolutions on "state and national policies extending beyond the geographical boundaries of an individual club." (Letter, S. F. Kisteman, secretary-treasurer, to authors, July 14, 1949, Study files.)

[50] Grodzins states that "so far as the present data indicate only one West Coast Rotary Club (at Glendale, California) took similar action" (p. 55). This contradicts his later assertion that the Rotary Club of Los Angeles "raised a demand for evacuation" (p. 223). It is also contradicted by the secretary of the Glendale Club, who has stated that "Mr. Grodzins' statement that the Rotary Club demanded removal of the Japanese . . . is false as no such resolution was ever adopted by the Club." (Letter, J. W. Knight, secretary-treasurer, to authors, November 3, 1950, Study files.)

[51] See Grodzins, Americans Betrayed, pp. 88, 193, passim. See also McWilliams, Prejudice; Smith, Americans from Japan.

[52] Americans Betrayed, p. 55.

[53] Ibid., pp. 21, 56.

[54] On January 31, 1942, the United Rubber Workers, Local No. 44, Los Angeles, asked President Roosevelt to remove "all Japanese people" from the Pacific Coast to inland points. The Los Angeles Industrial Union Council requested on February 13 that "all Japanese both alien and American-born be removed from California and other western seaboard states." (Study files.) The resolution of the Textile Workers Union, Local No. 128, Portland, Oregon, passed on February 14, asking that "all enemy aliens and all aliens carrying dual citizenship of Japan, be taken from the Pacific Coast defense area," could not have reached DeWitt before his memorandum was dispatched.

[55] McWilliams, Prejudice, p. 117. See also Smith, Americans from Japan, p. 213.

[56] Americans Betrayed, pp. 21, 55, 49.

[57] "California has five areas consisting of 27 Districts, Oregon has 7 Districts and Washington 11. As of May 31, 1942, California had 581 Posts, Oregon had 122, and Washington had 170." (Letter, W. E. Sayer, Assistant National Adjutant, to authors, July 1, 1951, Study files.)

[58] Vice-Commander Tracy E. Hicks demanded in a speech on January 27 that "immediate steps be taken to see that all enemy aliens be placed in concentration camps." (Notes in Study files.) On January 5 the War Council demanded that "all . . . enemy aliens be placed in concentration camps" together with "all Japanese who are known to hold dual citizenship." (Mimeographed release.) On January 25 the First Area Group passed a resolution calling for placement in concentration camps of enemy aliens and persons with dual citizenship. The Fifth District asked for a similar policy on January 20, and on January 29 the Twenty-second District asked for the "summary arrest and internment of all aliens on the Pacific Coast." (El Centro Imperial Enterprise, January 29, 1942.)

[59] On January 20 Portland Post No. 97 adopted a resolution calling for the "removal of enemy aliens, especially Japanese, from the critical coast areas." (Tolan Committee, Hearings, part 30, p. 11389.) Clatsop Voiture No. 547, Society of 40 and 8, on January 29, recommended that "all enemy nationals" be removed to a "concentration point." (Study files.) On February 13, Seaside Post No. 99 demanded the "immediate removal of all enemy alien nationals from this area to a properly guarded concentration point sufficiently inland to eliminate the possibility of sabotage." (Study files.)

J. K. Carson, Oregon Department Commander, testified before the Tolan Committee on February 26 that he had made inquiry "of the various posts of the Legion, of which there are 125 throughout this state. . . . I believe it is practically unanimous that Japanese nationals should be interned for the duration of the emergency." He stated that the posts "expressed in resolution after resolution" that the Japanese should be moved 300 miles east. (Tolan Committee, Hearings, part 30, pp. 11325–29.) No information was given as to the dates of these resolutions or whether, as he seemed to imply, they referred to Japanese enemy aliens only.

[60] Testimony of Fred Fueker, Department Adjutant of the Washington State Legion (Ibid., part 30, p. 11433).

[61] In January the San Luis Obispo Post of the Order of the Purple Heart called for the evacuation of all Japanese from the California coast counties to inland points. Sacramento Chapter 99, on February 13, asked that "all enemy aliens be interned." (Study files.) The Albany Post, California, of the Veterans of Foreign Wars on February 2 called for the removal of enemy aliens from the Pacific Coast.

The resolution of the Disabled American Veterans of the World War, mentioned by Grodzins (p. 55), was passed on February 25. (Tolan Committee, *Hearings*, part 30, p. 11609.)

[62] Grodzins declares that the society, among others, "went on record as favoring mass evacuation in the weeks preceding General DeWitt's 'Final Recommendation.' " (*Ibid.*, p. 276.)

On January 7, Long Beach Parlor No. 278 urged the removal of "all Japs" from the coast. On January 23, the Los Angeles Ramona Parlor No. 109 and the Friday Luncheon Club took similar stands. On January 25 the Arrowhead Past Presidents' Assembly No. 14 petitioned the federal government to remove "all Japanese, both citizens and aliens, from the combat area on the Pacific Coast." It is improbable that the Board of Grand Officers' resolution of February 14 was seen by DeWitt before he sent off his memorandum the same day.

[63] Its only other press release after December 7, 1941—No. 544, January 27—was concerned primarily with the dual-citizenship question and made no reference to evacuation or internment of the Japanese (Study files).

The evacuation sentiment of the JIC was considerably modified in the Tolan Committee testimony of Robert H. Fouke, speaking as official representative of the society, who called for "the establishment of combat zones, the evacuation of all persons, aliens or citizens alike, from such zones. A one hundred mile zone would probably be far enough. And when there is no doubt as to the loyalty of the individual, be he Japanese or . . . of any other racial group . . . citizen or alien . . . that party should be permitted to remain." (Tolan Committee, *Hearings*, part 29, p. 11068.)

[64] *Americans Betrayed*, p. 21.

[65] The California Federation of Women's Clubs alone had 644 member clubs in 1941–42.

[66] On January 28 the Democratic Club of Burbank sent a telegram to President Roosevelt demanding that "all Japanese in California be interned." (Study files.) On January 29, the North Hollywood Home Owners wrote to the President "beseeching and calling" on him "to remove all Japanese—alien and citizen alike—from their vantage places in harbor fisheries, on strangely isolated promontories of our unguarded coastline, and from farms around our aircraft plants." And on February 11, the International Women's Clubs of Los Angeles petitioned the Attorney General to remove all Japanese, alien or American-born, from "the entire coastal area." (Study files.)

[67] Grodzins states that eleven Elks lodges "favored evacuation" (p. 55), but he does not give their names, dates or resolutions. He claims that the Elks Club of Los Angeles "raised a demand for evacuation" (p. 223), but this is denied by the club secretary, who writes that he "failed to find anything in our records of 1942 where a resolution was passed calling for the evacuation of the Japanese." (Letter, Frank Kryger, Lodge No. 99, to authors, December 8, 1950, Study files.) Grodzins also claims that the Supreme Pyramid of Sciots passed a pro-evacuation resolution (p. 21), but he does not give the date or the recommendation. He may have been thinking of the Fresno Sciots Lodge action which occurred in March.

[68] See Grodzins, *Americans Betrayed*, pp. 310 and 320.

[69] Visalia *Times-Delta*, April 14, 1942; Grodzins, *Americans Betrayed*, p. 312.

[70] *Ibid.*, pp. 313–315, 321.

[71] U.S. Army, Western Defense Command and Fourth Army, *Final Report, Japanese Evacuation from the West Coast, 1942* (Washington: G.P.O., 1943), p. 50. (Italics added.)

[72] *Americans Betrayed,* p. 315.

[73] Grodzins lists the Tulare County Farm Bureau, whose directors on April 16 (not April 14 as he asserts—see Fresno *Bee,* April 18, 1942) protested against making Tulare the "dumping-ground" for Japanese; plus "representatives of live-stock and cattlemen's associations of Fresno, Kern and Tulare counties, county farm bureaus, chambers of commerce, and other civic organizations" meeting in Porterville on April 20 (*Ibid.,* p. 315). He also states that "a spokesman for the Associated Chambers of Commerce of Tulare County reviewed the formal resolution of that group 'favoring the extension of the prohibited zone to include the county.' " (*Ibid.,* p. 315, citing the Fresno *Bee,* April 21, 1942.) If this is meant to indicate that the Chambers expressed their first opinion for evacuation around April 20, it is misleading. On March 16 they asked for the "inclusion of all of Tulare County in the 'Prohibited Zone' " and sent their request to DeWitt (Terra Bella *News,* March 20, 1942). On April 13 they received a letter from the WDC stating that "the boundary lines of the Japanese exclusion zone will not be extended further eastward." (Visalia *Times-Delta,* April 14, 1942.) There is no evidence from newspaper accounts of the April 20 period showing that the group reaffirmed their request or communicated their views again to DeWitt.

The same author states that "the Agricultural Committee of The Fresno County Chamber of Commerce demanded further restrictions on Japanese in the unevacuated zone." (*Ibid.,* p. 316.) This appears to be in error. The secretary of the Chamber has written: "The minutes of the meeting of our Chamber's Agricultural Committee of April 20, 1942, disclose that a suggestion was made that the movement of Japanese from the coastal areas should be restricted to the irrigated areas and the lower foothills in the eastern portion of the San Joaquin Valley. No action was taken by the Agricultural Committee to this suggestion." (Letter, C. A. Dougherty, to authors, May 2, 1951, Study files.)

[74] Grodzins, *Americans Betrayed,* p. 316.

[75] The Porterville Legion Post acted on April 1 (Terra Bella *News,* April 3, 1942). The Porterville Chamber of Commerce expressed its views on March 6. "A motion was passed to ask Congressman Elliott to make an investigation into why Japanese were left in the strategic area east of Highway 65 in Tulare County and why these Japanese, both aliens and citizens, could not be removed to a safer area." (Letter, S. J. Lloyd, to authors, May 2, 1951, Study files.)

[76] *Americans from Japan,* pp. 269–270.

[77] *Prejudice,* pp. 104, 115, 117.

[78] *Americans Betrayed,* pp. 92, 109, 90.

[79] Governor Charles Sprague of Oregon is known to have been dissatisfied with the Department of Justice program and to have wired Attorney General Biddle on February 17 recommending an internment program for enemy aliens, but there is no evidence of his stand or expressions on the matter before February 14. Governor A. B. Langlie of Washington "pursued a course of moderation," as Grodzins states (*Ibid.,* p. 109). He did not recommend either exclusion or internment in his appearance before the Tolan Committee.

[80] In a radio address on February 4, Olson outlined the plan, which he said had been "agreed upon [at a meeting with DeWitt] for the movement and placement of the entire adult Japanese population in California at useful and productive employment within the borders of our state, and under such surveillance and protection for themselves and the state and nation as shall be deemed necessary." Culbert L. Olson, *State Papers and Public Addresses* (Sacramento: California State Printing Office, 1942), pp. 345–348. See also his radio address of December 14, 1941, *ibid.,* pp. 329–333.

[81] An historian of Olson's regime has concluded that Olson "cannot be charged with any responsibility for the evacuation itself no matter what he declared after the evacuation was begun. The evacuation of the Japanese from California . . . in actuality

had little or nothing to do with that regime." Robert E. Burke, *Olson's New Deal for California* (Berkeley: University of California Press, 1953), p. 206.

[82] "As far as I know there were no public statements made." (Letter, Victor A. Meyers, Lieutenant Governor of Washington, to authors, March 19, 1951, Study files.) A search of Associated and United Press stories of the period does not disclose any statement by Ellis Patterson, then Lieutenant Governor of California. There is no position comparable to this post in Oregon.

[83] "We do not have any record of any statement by the Secretary of State of the State of California regarding the evacuation of the Japanese from the west coast." (Letter, Frank M. Jordan, Secretary of State of California, to authors, November 17, 1950, Study files.) "No public statement was issued by the Secretary of State for Oregon in 1942 regarding the desirability of evacuating Japanese enemy aliens or Japanese Americans from the State." (Letter, Earl Newbry, Secretary of State of Oregon, to authors, November 22, 1950, Study files.) "My Assistant Secretary of State ... and my Deputy, both of whom were here in the office at the time of the Japanese evacuation, can remember nothing of any official action taken by the Secretary at that time. It is our belief no official communication regarding the matter was made and a perusal of our records does not disclose any information." (Letter, Earl Coe, Secretary of State of Washington, to authors, November 21, 1951, Study files.)

[84] "There is no record of the attorney general ... having issued any statement during December, 1941, or at any time thereafter during World War II with reference to the dangers of the enemy alien population." (Letter, George Neuner, Attorney General of Oregon, to authors, October 20, 1951, Study files.)

[85] "The only time that I made any official or public statement concerning the evacuation of Japanese was before the Tolan Committee." (Letter, Smith Troy, Attorney General of Washington, to authors, August 9, 1949, Stuly files.) Troy there stated, among other things, that "evacuation of both alien and Japanese citizens, as well, is highly desirable and it should be done as quickly as possible because those things [vigilante action against the Japanese] can happen and may happen. By that, I don't mean total internment of all citizen Japanese for the duration of the war, but at least moving them out of here for their own protection. I am in favor of moving the aliens out for our protection from sabotage. Then after close scrutiny and investigation, those useful and loyal citizen Japanese could be ... brought back into the territory here where we could use them." (Tolan Committee, *Hearings*, part 30, p. 11503.) Cf. Grodzins, *Americans Betrayed*, p. 109.

[86] Grodzins, *Americans Betrayed*, pp. 6, 93–96, *passim;* Smith, *Americans from Japan*, p. 263; McWilliams, *Prejudice*, p. 118.

[87] A late January statement by Warren, quoted by Grodzins and paraphrased by McWilliams, did not advocate a course of action but merely expressed concern with the situation and was compatible with many lines of action other than mass evacuation. (See Associated Press release, Oakland *Tribune*, January 30, 1942.)

[88] There is no indication in the report of the meeting of what Warren urged the general to do. Grodzins says he presented a "similar argument" to Bowron's but he does not quote Bowron as stating this, and we have no statement by Warren himself as to his line of argument. (Interview, F. Bowron, notes in Study files. Excerpts cited in Grodzins, *Americans Betrayed*, p. 278.)

[89] Smith, *Americans from Japan*, p. 263.

[90] The First Extraordinary Session of the 54th Legislature convened on December 20, 1941, and adjourned on January 4, 1942. The legislature reconvened on January 17, 1942.

[91] Only three items of business related to the Japanese. A resolution called on federal officials "to prevent any and all racial discrimination in the national defense program"; another called on law officers to investigate evasions of the Alien Land Laws and prosecute violations; a third requested the State Personnel Board to pre-

vent disloyal individuals from securing civil service positions and to dismiss disloyal employees.

[92] Only two state assemblymen from the three states took advantage of the Tolan Committee hearings to express their opinions. State Senator Mary Farquharson of Washington spoke in defense of German refugees from Nazi Germany, protesting their classification as enemy aliens (Tolan Committee, *Hearings*, part 30, p. 11512). State Senator R. E. Jones of Oregon recommended leaving the evacuation issue to the Army: he thought that "if it was a case of invasion, I would say they should all be removed," referring to Japanese nationals, Japanese Americans, and German and Italian aliens (*ibid.*, p. 11312).

[93] The action of the California State Personnel Board, on January 28, 1942, declaring that "descendants of nationals with whom the United States is at war" would not be certified for state employment until shown to be loyal citizens, might be said to be distantly related to the evacuation issue in that an official agency threw doubts on the loyalty of Japanese Americans. The comparable bodies in Oregon and Washington did not take such action.

[94] W. J. Cecil, Director of the State Department of Agriculture, stated in a release (January 9, 1942) that if the Army carried out plans "which it has in mind of evacuating enemy aliens, the state's vegetable production would suffer."

[95] "The Oregon State Defense Council . . . did not make any public statements during January and February, 1942, with regard to the dangers in the presence of enemy aliens or the desirability of their evacuation." (Letter, Governor D. McKay, to authors, October 30, 1950, Study files.) "The record does not indicate that any public statement was made by the Defense Council regarding the evacuation of any aliens." (Letter, James A. Pryde, Chief, Washington State Patrol, to authors, November 2, 1950, Study files.)

[96] California State Council of Defense, *Minutes of Meeting, Sacramento, California, January 8, 1942* (Processed; n.p., n.d.), p. 2.

[97] Placer County, February 3. "This board goes on record as favoring the removal of such alien enemies from the coastal region, including Placer County." (Study files.)

[98] Orange County, February 3. "This board . . . requests action . . . for the removal of all enemy aliens and children of resident enemy aliens or of any enemy alien extraction from the entire coastline of Orange County." (Study files.)

[99] Los Angeles, January 27, and Alameda, January 29. The resolution requested that "Japanese aliens be transferred from coastal areas to inland points." In the Alameda action the federal government was urged to "remove from the Western Coastal area all Japanese nationals until such time as their presence may not be deemed a possible threat to the American war effort." (Study files.)

[100] Monterey, February 2; Ventura, February 3; Tulare, February 10 (Study files).

[101] "I have no recollection of any action taken at any of these meetings over the past twelve years with reference to the desirability of evacuating the Japanese residents of Oregon during the months following the attack on Pearl Harbor." (Letter, Judge F. L. Phipps, to authors, July 6, 1949, Study files.)

[102] The Orange County Grand Jury of California, on February 2, petitioned that "resident enemy aliens and children of said resident enemy aliens, as well as persons of enemy alien extraction who have entered the United States during the year 1935 or subsequent thereto and have become naturalized" "be removed from the County of Orange and all areas potentially subject to invasion." (Study files.) The Los Angeles County Grand Jury on February 5 urged the Attorney General of the United States that "all alien Japanese be forthwith evacuated from all areas in the county . . . and that serious consideration be given to the removal of Japanese other than Japanese enemy aliens from strategic locations." (Study files.) The Librarian of the State Supreme Court Library, Salem, Oregon, had no record of any county grand jury recommendation on the issue (Letter to authors, October 18, 1950, Study files). The

office of the attorney general of Washington reported that it had "no knowledge of any grand jury being called in the State ... during the period referred to which urged the evacuation of enemy aliens or Japanese." (Letter to authors, October 19, 1950, Study files.)

[103] Stanislaus County Council, February 6, called on the federal government "to remove all Japanese enemy aliens from the territory in the State of California within 200 miles of the Pacific Coast line." (Tolan Committee, *Hearings*, part 29, p. 11239.) Los Angeles County Council resolution of February 11, called for the placement of "all male citizens of enemy countries" in "working internment areas." American citizens of Japanese descent should be "invited" to enter such areas or to move to any section of the United States east of the Pacific Coast states (Testimony of Supervisor G. M. McDonough, Tolan Committee, *Hearings*, part 31, pp. 11678–82).

[104] San Francisco *Chronicle*, February 3, 1942.

[105] Based on response to letters of inquiry addressed to coastal municipalities by the University of California Evacuation and Resettlement Study. There is evidence to show that five other California cities—Gardena, Hawthorne, Lindsay, Exeter and Placerville—expressed similar opinions after February 14. Portland, Oregon, urged exclusion and internment of all Japanese on February 19. (Study files.)

[106] Letter, J. Kehrli, executive secretary of the League of Oregon Cities, to authors, June 28, 1949; letter, Chester Biesen, executive secretary of the Association of Washington Cities, to authors, June 27, 1949 (Study files). The chairman of the Executive Committee of the Washington Association testified before the Tolan Committee but did not express an opinion on the issue (Tolan Committee, *Hearings*, part 30, p. 11553).

[107] Three passed resolutions and one wired Attorney General Biddle asking that all Japanese be removed from the coast (Oceanside, February 7; Ukiah, February 10; Garden City, February 11; Altadena, wire of February 13). One resolution asked that all Japanese be removed from the county (Colfax, February 11; Lindsay wired DeWitt similarly on January 17). Two resolutions and a wire to DeWitt called for exclusion of Japanese but the specific recommendations are not known (El Monte and Atascadero, February 10); and one resolution called for the internment of all Japanese and enemy aliens (Three Rivers, Oregon, February 2). (Study files.)

[108] *Americans Betrayed*, p. 110 n.

[109] Ventura *Star-Free Press*, February 6, 1942.

[110] Los Angeles *Times*, February 7, 1942.

[111] Grodzins describes this meeting as "the high point in the application of personal pressure on the commanding general of the WDC." (*Americans Betrayed*, p. 104.) But he presents no evidence to show that any politicians other than these applied "personal pressure" for mass evacuation at this time.

[112] Interview, Mayor F. Bowron, July 22, 1943 (Notes in Study files). Excerpts in Grodzins, *ibid.*, p. 278. The general's recommendation on February 14 certainly followed the February 11 meeting in time, but Grodzins' statement implies a causal connection not clearly demonstrated by the known facts. It is true that Tom Clark informed Bowron on February 11 that DeWitt had told him the same afternoon of his decision "to move all the Japanese from coastal areas" (*ibid.*). But DeWitt had been moving in that direction for some time in his increasingly extensive recommendations forwarded to the Department of Justice (see above, chapter iii). In the absence of more definite information it is not possible to assess with any certainty the influence of the mayor's visit.

[113] See Rostow, "The Japanese American Cases"; Smith, *Americans from Japan*, pp. 263, 270.

[114] *Americans Betrayed*, pp. 62, 91.

[115] *Ibid.*, pp. 261–274, 363.

[116] Grodzins states in one place that "the regional pressures markedly influenced War Department policy," (*ibid.*, p. 362), but it is clear from the context that he is

referring to DeWitt and his officers and not to the civilian officials of the Department in Washington.

¹¹⁷ *Ibid.*, p. 83.

¹¹⁸ *Ibid.*, p. 79.

¹¹⁹ Oakland *Tribune*, February 4, 1942.

¹²⁰ Study files.

¹²¹ Study files.

¹²² Unofficial minutes of meeting of West Coast congressional delegation committee on alien enemies and sabotage, February 5, 1942, pp. 1–3 (Typescript in Study files).

¹²³ Study files.

¹²⁴ Interview, John J. McCloy, October 15, 1942 (Notes in Study files).

¹²⁵ Interview, James H. Rowe, Jr., October 15, 1942 (Notes in Study files).

¹²⁶ *Ibid.*

¹²⁷ *Final Report,* p. 50.

¹²⁸ San Francisco *Chronicle*, April 29, 1942; Oakland *Tribune*, May 26, 1942.

¹²⁹ Letter, A. J. Elliott to Tulare County farmers, May 14, 1942 (Study files).

CHAPTER V

¹ *Hirabayashi* v. *United States* (1943), 320 U.S. 81; 63 S. Ct. 1375. *Korematsu* v. *United States* (1944), 323 U.S. 215; 65 S. Ct. 193. *Ex parte Endo* v. *United States* (1944), 323 U.S. 283; 65 S. Ct. 208.

² Mr. Justice Roberts dissenting in *Korematsu* v. *United States*, 323 U.S. 215 at 226, 65 S. Ct. 193 at 198.

³ Quoted by Judge Denman in his dissent to the Hirabayashi' certification which is published in *Korematsu* v. *United States* (1943), 140 F. 2d 289 at 303, note 5.

⁴ *Ibid.*, at 292.

⁵ *Ibid.* at 289.

⁶ *Korematsu* v. *United States*, 323 U.S. 215 at 247; 65 S. Ct. 193 at 208.

⁷ Mr. Justice Roberts dissenting in *Korematsu* v. *United States*, 323 U.S. 215 at 231, 232; 65 S. Ct. 193 at 200, 201.

⁸ *Korematsu* v. *United States*, 323 U.S. 215 at 221; 65 S. Ct. 193 at 196.

⁹ *Ibid.* at 222; 65 S. Ct. at 196.

¹⁰ *Ibid.* at 222; 65 S. Ct. at 197.

¹¹ *Ex parte Endo*, 323 U.S. 283 at 297; 65 S. Ct. 208 at 216.

¹² *Ibid.* at 299; 65 S. Ct. at 217.

¹³ *Ibid.* at 302; 65 S. Ct. at 218.

¹⁴ *Ibid.* at 308; 65 S. Ct. at 221.

¹⁵ For a criticism of these tactics see Eugene V. Rostow, "The Japanese American Cases—A Disaster," *Yale Law Journal*, vol. 54 (1945), pp. 503, 504–505.

¹⁶ (1947) 322 U.S. 633; 68 S. Ct. 269.

¹⁷ *Ibid.* at 646; 68 S. Ct. at 275.

¹⁸ *Ibid.* at 672; 68 S. Ct. at 288.

¹⁹ *Ibid.* at 659; 68 S. Ct. at 277.

²⁰ *Fuji* v. *State* (Superior Court of California, 1952), 242 P. 2d 617.

²¹ (1947), 334 U.S. 410; 68 S. Ct. 1138.

²² (1943), 49 F. Supp. 222; 134 F. 2d 413; 319 U.S. 753; 63 S. Ct. 1168.

²³ *Korematsu* v. *United States*, 323 U.S. 215 at 217–219, 223–224; 65 S. Ct. 193 at 194–195, 197.

²⁴ *Ibid.* at 223; 65 S. Ct. at 197.

²⁵ While the court in the Hirabayashi and Korematsu cases did not explicitly disaffirm the judicial review doctrines of *Ex parte Milligan* (1866), 71 U.S. (4 Wall. 2) 127, *Mitchell* v. *Harmony* (1851), 19 U.S. (13 How.) 115, and *Sterling* v. *Constantin* (1932), 287 U.S. 378; 53 S. Ct. 190, it nevertheless completely repudiated them. Those

cases are emphatic in their assertion that the scope of the powers of the military and the presence of facts justifying their exercise are questions to be finally determined by the courts.

[26] 323 U.S. 215 at 244; 65 S. Ct. 193 at 206.

[27] *Ibid.* at 245; 65 S. Ct. at 207.

[28] *Ibid.* at 248; 65 S. Ct. 208.

[29] *Ibid.*

[30] *Ibid.*

[31] *Ibid.* at 236–37; 65 S. Ct. at 203.

[32] 287 U.S. 378 at 397–98; 53 S. Ct. 190 at 195.

[33] Louis Smith, *American Democracy and Military Power* (Chicago: University of Chicago Press, 1951), pp. 8–9.

[34] *Ibid.*, p. 303.

CHAPTER VI

[1] Maurice Alexandre, "The Nisei—A Casualty of World War II," *Corn. Law Quart.*, vol. 28 (1943), p. 385; Edward S. Corwin, *Total War and the Constitution* (New York: Alfred A. Knopf, 1947), pp. 91–100; Nanette Dembitz, "Racial Discrimination and the Military Judgment: The Supreme Court's Korematsu and Endo Decisions," *Columbia Law Rev.*, vol. 45 (1943), p. 175; Charles E. Fairman, "The Law of Martial Rule and the National Emergency," *Harv. Law Rev.*, vol. 55 (1942), p. 1253, and *The Law of Martial Rule* (2d ed.; Chicago: Callaghan & Co., 1943), pp. 157–167, 255–261; Harrop A. Freeman, "Genesis, Exodus, Leviticus. Geneology, Evacuation and Law," *Corn. Law Quart.*, vol. 28 (1943), p. 414; Colonel W. A. Graham, "Martial Law in California," *Calif. Law Rev.*, vol. 31 (1941), p. 6; Milton R. Konvitz, *The Alien and the Asiatic in American Law* (Ithaca, New York: Cornell Univ. Press, 1946), Chapter 11, The American of Japanese Ancestry in World War II, pp. 241–279; Eugene V. Rostow, "The Japanese American Cases—A Disaster," *Yale Law Journ.*, vol. 54 (1945), p. 489; Colonel J. Watson, "The Japanese Evacuation and Litigation Arising Therefrom," *Oregon Law Rev.*, vol. 22 (1942), p. 46; Richard F. Wolfson, "Legal Doctrine, War Power and Japanese Evacuation," *Kentucky Law Journ.*, vol. 32 (1944), p. 238.

[2] The war power of the national government is variously described as a single inherent power and as an aggregate of all the specifically delegated constitutional powers having a bearing upon the conduct of war. The most famous recent expression of the first of these theories is the statement of Justice Sutherland in *United States* v. *Curtiss-Wright Export Corporation* (1936) 299 U.S. 304; 57 S. Ct. 216: "A political society cannot endure without a supreme will somewhere. Sovereignty is never held in suspense. When, therefore, the external sovereignty of Great Britain in respect of the colonies ceased, it immediately passed to the Union." (*Ibid.* at 316–17, 57 S. Ct. at 219.) "It results that the investment of the federal government with the powers of external sovereignty did not depend upon the affirmative grants of the Constitution. The powers to declare and wage war, to conclude peace, to make treaties, to maintain diplomatic relations with other sovereignties, if they had never been mentioned in the Constitution, would have vested in the federal government as necessary concomitants of nationality." (*Ibid.* at 318; 57 S. Ct. at 220.)

A list of the specifically delegated powers having a bearing on the conduct of war might include:

"The Congress shall have power to lay and collect taxes, duties, imposts and excises, to ... provide for the common defense and general welfare of the United States." (Art. I, sec. 8, cl. 1). "To borrow money on the credit of the United States; ... To declare war ..." (cl. 2). "To raise and support armies, but no appropriation of money to that use shall be for a longer term than two years" (cl. 12). "To provide and maintain a navy" (cl. 13). "To make rules for the government and regulation of the land

and naval forces" (cl. 14). "To provide for calling forth the militia to execute the law of the Union, suppress insurrection and repel invasion" (cl 15). "To provide for organizing, arming and disciplining the militia, and for gove   y such part of them as may be employed in the service of the United States, reserving to the States respectively the appointment of the officers, and the authority of training the militia according to the discipline prescribed by Congress" (cl. 16). ". . . To make all laws which shall be necessary and proper for carrying into execution the foregoing powers, and all other powers vested by this Constitution in the government of the United States, or in any department or officer thereof" (cl. 18). ". . . The executive power shall be vested in a President of the United States of America" (Art. II, sec. 1, cl. 1). "The President shall be commander in chief of the army and navy of the United States, and of the militia of the several states, when called into the actual service of the United States . . ." (Sec. 2, cl. 1).

³ In a strict sense, the separate classification of all Japanese Americans was based on ancestry and not on race, since all Orientals belong to the same race and only the Japanese Americans were evacuated. Yet basically the classifying trait was race since those Americans having an ethnic affinity with our Asiatic enemy alone were excluded and imprisoned; those Americans having an ethnic affinity with our white European enemies were not subjected to a similar treatment.

⁴ Cf. diverse and conflicting statements of *Ex parte Milligan* (1866), 71 U.S. (4 Wall) 2 at 127; Graham, "Martial Law in California," pp. 7, 9, 14; Brief for the United States in *Yasui* v. *United States* [(1943), 320 U.S. 115; 63 S. Ct. 1393], pp. 80–81.

⁵ *Korematsu* v. *United States* (1944), 323 U.S. 214 at 244; 65 S. Ct. 193 at 206–207.

⁶ *Ibid.* at 247; 65 S. Ct. at 208.

⁷ *Ibid.* at 224–225; 65 S. Ct. at 198.

⁸ This question has been raised not only by modern total war but by the total war of years gone by. See speech of Abraham Lincoln of November 10, 1864, quoted in Corwin, *Total War and the Constitution*, p. 132.

⁹ *Ex parte Milligan*, 71 U.S. (4 Wall) 2 at 127.

¹⁰ Kenneth M. Stampp, "The Milligan Case and the Election of 1864 in Indiana," *Miss. Valley Hist. Rev.*, vol. 31 (1944), pp. 41–58, explodes the belief traditionally held by constitutional writers that the conspiracy with which Milligan was charged was a serious and substantial one.

¹¹ Fairman, "The Law of Martial Rule and the National Emergency," p. 1286.

¹² Rostow, "The Japanese American Cases—A Disaster," p. 524.

¹³ *Ex parte Milligan*, 71 U.S. (4 Wall) 2 at 125.

¹⁴ *Ibid.* at 126.

¹⁵ *Ibid.* at 121.

¹⁶ *Ibid.*

¹⁷ *Ibid.* at 124–125.

¹⁸ *Ibid.* at 127.

¹⁹ *Ibid.* at 141.

²⁰ *Ibid.* at 137.

²¹ *Ibid.* at 142.

²² *Ibid.* at 140.

²³ *Ibid.*

²⁴ *Ibid.* at 142.

²⁵ *Ibid.* at 137.

²⁶ Brief for the State of California, Amicus Curiae in *Korematsu* v. *United States*, pp. 6–7, 11.

²⁷ *Register of Debates*, vol. xii, pp. 4037–4038, quoted by Corwin, *Total War and the Constitution*, p. 78.

²⁸ *Hirabayashi* v. *United States* (1943), 320 U.S. 31; 63 S. Ct. 1375.

²⁹ 7 Fed. Reg. 1407; more fully quoted on p. 111.

[30] 56 Stat. 173, 18 U.S. Code Annotated, sec. 97a (March 21, 1942).

[31] 7 Fed Reg. 2543.

[32] *Hirabayashi* v. *United States,* 320 U.S. 31 at 83; 63 S. Ct. 1375 at 1378.

[33] *Ibid.* at 110; 63 S. Ct. at 1390.

[34] 7 *Fed. Reg.* 2601.

[35] 7 *Fed. Reg.* 3967.

[36] 8 *Fed. Reg.* 982.

[37] *American Civil Liberties Union News,* July, 1942, p. 1.

[38] *Korematsu* v. *United States,* 323 U.S. 214 at 217; 65 S. Ct. 193 at 194.

[39] *Ibid.* at 218; 65 S. Ct. at 195.

[40] *Ibid.* at 217–218; 65 S. Ct. at 194–195.

[41] *Ibid.* at 223; 65 S. Ct. at 197.

[42] *Ibid.* at 219–220; 65 S. Ct. at 195.

[43] *Ibid.* at 223; 65 S. Ct. at 197.

[44] *Ibid.* at 216; 65 S. Ct. at 194.

[45] *Ibid.*

[46] Corwin, *Total War and the Constitution,* p. 98.

[47] Justice Roberts dissented on the ground that "the indisputable facts exhibit a clear violation of constitutional rights . . . it is the case of convicting a citizen as a punishment for not submitting to imprisonment in a concentration camp, based on his ancestry, and solely because of his ancestry, without evidence or inquiry concerning his loyalty and good disposition towards the United States." (*Korematsu* v. *United States,* 323 U.S. 214 at 225–226; 65 S. Ct. 193 at 198.) "No pronouncement of the commanding officer can, in my view, preclude judicial inquiry and determination whether an emergency ever existed and whether. if so, it remained, at the date of the restraint out of which the litigation arose." (*Ibid.* at 231; 65 S. Ct. at 200–201, n. 8.)

[48] Note for example the language of the Attorney General in the case of the Nazi saboteurs in the Transcript of Oral Argument quoted by Fairman in *The Law of Martial Rule,* p. 199; *Ochikubo* v. *Bonesteel* (1945, U.S. Dist. Court, S. D. of Calif.), 69 F. Supp. 916, 932; Judge Lloyd J. Black in an oral opinion in *Ex parte Ventura* (1942, U.S. Dist. Court, W. D. of Wash.), 44 F. Supp. 520 at 522–523; Judge Denman, concurring in *Korematsu* v. *United States* (1943) 140 F. 2d 289 at 296.

[49] "The Law of Martial Rule and the National Emergency," pp. 1287–1288.

[50] Fairman does not associate himself with this phase of the *Milligan* minority position. Instead, he suggests an adaptation of the rule of appropriateness. "The nature and proximity of the danger," he argued, "must of course, have a bearing on the type of control which the military authorities may reasonably enforce. The *Milligan* case had to do with an attempt to inflict the extreme penalty, death, for an offense known to the law and triable by judges. . . . The removal of civilians, for cause and suspicion, from areas of military importance, interferes with interests of a much lower order. Measures of prevention, such as curfew, may be appropriate where no reason could be offered, for assuming the functions of the courts of law." (*Ibid.,* pp. 1287–1288.)

[51] See also Westel W. Willoughby, *Principles of the Constitutional Law of the United States* (2d ed.; New York: Baker, Voorhis & Co., 1935), III, p. 1602, and Garrard Glenn, *The Army and the Law* (New York: Columbia University Press, 1943), pp. 188–190.

[52] "War Powers Under the Constitution," *Rep. American Bar Assn.,* vol. 42 (1917), pp. 245–246.

[53] *Schenck* v. *United States* (1919), 249 U.S. 47; 39 S. Ct. 247.

[54] *Dennis* v. *United States* (1951), 341 U.S. 494; 71 S. Ct. 341.

[55] See p. 111.

[56] Curfew applied to such individuals in Military Area No. 1 and in the 1,132 small zones in the other parts of the Western Defense Command.

[57] This proclamation applied only to Military Area No. 1, of course.

[58] U.S. Army, Western Defense Command and Fourth Army, *Final Report: Japanese Evacuation from the West Coast, 1942* (Washington: G.P.O., 1943), pp. 43–44.

[59] *Legal and Constitutional Phases of the War Relocation Authority Program*, U.S. Department of the Interior, War Relocation Authority (Processed; Washington: G.P.O., 1946), p. 11.

[60] *Ibid.*, pp. 12–13. The Department of Justice made a similar justification for relocation center detention in its argument for the constitutionality of that program before the Supreme Court. (Brief for the United States in *Ex parte Endo* v. *United States*, pp. 75, 81–82.)

[61] *Ibid.*, p. 15.

[62] *Korematsu* v. *United States,* 323 U.S. 214 at 223; 65 S. Ct. 193 at 207.

[63] *Ex parte Endo* (1944), 323 U.S. 283 at 297; 65 S. Ct. 208 at 216.

[64] *Ibid.* at 300; 65 S. Ct. at 218.

[65] *Ibid.* at 302; 65 S. Ct. at 218.

[66] *Ibid.* at 302–304; 65 S. Ct. at 218–219.

[67] *Ibid.* at 309; 65 S. Ct. at 217.

[68] "Racial Discrimination and the Military Judgment," pp. 202–203.

[69] *Ex parte Endo,* 323 U.S. 283 at 297–298; 65 S. Ct. 208 at 216. In *Ex parte Quirin* (1942), 317 U.S. 1 at 37–38; 63 S. Ct. 1 at 15, the case involving the Nazi saboteurs who entered the country secretly from German submarines as embodied elements of the German armed forces, the court was at pains to point out that the military might try Haupt—the only American citizen among the saboteurs—on the ground that "citizens who associate themselves with the military arm of the enemy government . . . are enemy belligerents" under the laws of war, and to be treated as such.

[70] See Dorothy Thomas and Richard S. Nishimoto, *The Spoilage* (Berkeley: University of California Press, 1946), chapter vi.

[71] Public Proclamation No. 8 (7 *Fed. Reg.* 8346); Public Proclamation WD. 1 (7 *Fed. Reg.* 6593).

[72] WRA Administrative Instruction No. 22, June 20, 1942, paragraph 9.

[73] *Final Report,* p. 242.

[74] See p. 140.

[75] "War Powers Under the Constitution," p. 238.

[76] *Ibid.*, p. 248.

CHAPTER VII

[1] *Hirabayashi* v. *United States* (1943), 320 U.S. 81; 63 S. Ct. 1375: *Korematsu* v. *United States* (1944), 323 U.S. 214; 65 S. Ct. 193.

[2] (1947), 332 U.S. 633; 68 S. Ct. 269.

[3] (1947), 334 U.S. 410; 68 S. Ct. 1138.

[4] Amendment V. "No person shall be held to answer for a capital, or otherwise infamous crime, unless on a presentment or indictment of a Grand Jury, except in cases arising in the land or naval forces, or in the Militia, when in actual service in time of war or public danger; nor shall any person be subject for the same offense to be twice put in jeopardy of life or limb; nor shall be compelled in any criminal case to be a witness against himself, nor be deprived of life, liberty or property, without due process of law; nor shall private property be taken for public use, without just compensation."

[5] Amendment XIV: Section 1. "All persons born or naturalized in the United States, and subject to the jurisdiction thereof, are citizens of the United States and of the State wherein they reside. No State shall make or enforce any law which shall abridge the privileges or immunities of citizens of the United States; nor shall any State deprive any person of life, liberty, or property, without due process of law, nor deny to any person within its jurisdiction the equal protection of the laws."

[6] *Hirabayashi v. United States,* 320 U.S. 81 at 100; 63 S. Ct. 1375 at 1385.

[7] *Ibid.*

[8] See Joseph Tussman and Jacobus tenBroek, "The Equal Protection of the Laws," *Calif. Law Rev.,* vol. 37 (1949), p. 341.

[9] *Korematsu v. United States,* 323 U.S. 214 at 223; 65 S. Ct. 193 at 197.

[10] U.S. Army, Western Defense Command and Fourth Army, *Final Report: Japanese Evacuation from the West Coast, 1942* (Washington: G.P.O., 1943), p. 34.

[11] 323 U.S. 214 at 223; 65 S. Ct. 193 at 197.

[12] *Ibid.* at 219; 65 S. Ct. at 197.

[13] 320 U.S. 81 at 106; 63 S. Ct. 1375 at 1388.

[14] *Ibid.* at 109; 63 S. Ct. at 1389.

[15] 323 U.S. 214 at 235; 65 S. Ct. 193 at 202–203.

[16] *Ibid.* at 236; 65 S. Ct. at 202–203.

[17] Statement by Mr. Austin E. Anson, managing secretary of the Salinas Grower-Shipper Vegetable Association, *ibid.* at 239; 65 S. Ct. at 204, n. 12.

[18] 320 U.S. 81 at 100; 63 S. Ct. 1375 at 1385.

[19] *Ibid.*

[20] *Ibid.* at 99; 63 S. Ct. at 1385.

[21] *Ibid.* at 97; 63 S. Ct. at 1384.

[22] *Ibid.* at 98; 63 S. Ct. at 1384.

[23] *Ibid.*

[24] *Ibid.* at 98; 63 S. Ct. at 1385.

[25] Nanette Dembitz, "Racial Discrimination and the Military Judgment: The Supreme Court's Korematsu and Endo Decisions," *Col. Law Rev.,* vol. 45 (1945), p. 187.

[26] *Hirabayashi v. United States,* 320 U.S. 81 at 96; 63 S. Ct. 1375 at 1383.

[27] *Ibid.* at 96; 63 S. Ct. at 1383.

[28] *Final Report,* p. 35.

[29] *Hearings,* 77th Congress, 2d sess., Select House Committee Investigating National Defense Migration (Washington: G.P.O., 1942), part 29, pp. 10973 and 11011. This committee is hereinafter cited as Tolan Committee.

[30] *Final Report,* p. 9.

[31] Tolan Committee, *Hearings,* part 29, p. 11017.

[32] *Final Report,* p. 9.

[33] Tolan Committee, *Hearings,* part 29, p. 11017.

[34] *Ibid.,* p. 10974.

[35] Tolan Committee, *Fourth Interim Report: Findings and Recommendations on Evacuation of Enemy Aliens and Others from Prohibited Military Zones,* House Report 2124, p. 93.

[36] Shotaro F. Miyamoto, "Social Solidarity Among the Japanese in Seattle," *University of Washington Publications in Social Sciences,* vol. 11 (1939), p. 68; Alice M. Brown, *Japanese in Florin, California* (n.p., 1913); Marjorie R. Stearns, *History of the Japanese People in Oregon,* University of Oregon Thesis Series, no. 4 (Mimeographed; Eugene, Ore., 1939).

[37] 320 U.S. 81 at 97; 63 S. Ct. 1375 at 1384.

[38] *Final Report,* pp. 12–13.

[39] *Ibid.*

[40] *Ibid.*

[41] See especially Reginald Bell, *Public School Education of Second Generation Japanese in California* (London: Oxford University Press, 1935), pp. 23–24; Marion Svensrud, "Attitudes of the Japanese toward their Language Schools," *Sociology and Social Research,* vol. 17 (1933), pp. 259–264. A. W. Lind, *Hawaii's Japanese* (Princeton: Princeton University Press, 1946), pp. 22–24, 29–30; William C. Smith, *The Second Generation Oriental in America* (Honolulu: Institute of Pacific Relations, 1927); William C. Smith, *Americans in Process* (Ann Arbor, Mich.: Edwards Bros., 1937),

pp. 163 ff.; Yamato Ichihashi, *Japanese in the United States* (Stanford: Stanford University Press, 1932), pp. 329 ff.

[42] A joint House-Senate committee investigating statehood for Hawaii in 1937 reported concerning Hawaii's Japanese: "Much is made of the foreign-language schools and press, but it should be realized that these agencies serve a real purpose in the adjustment of an immigrant group to new conditions. Many European immigrants have turned to the same means for establishing contact between the two generations. When these transitory vehicles have served their purpose they cease to exist." (Quoted by Lind, *Hawaii's Japanese*, p. 30.)

[43] Svensrud, "Attitudes of the Japanese toward their Language Schools," p. 259. A similar study in Hawaii found most students of the language schools to be either indifferent or actively antagonistic. (W. C. Smith, *The Second Generation Oriental in America*, pp. 5 ff.)

[44] *Myths and Facts About the Japanese Americans*, U.S. Department of the Interior, War Relocation Authority (Processed; Washington: G.P.O., 1945), p. 9.

[45] *Hawaii's Japanese*, p. 24. That the language schools were not the real target of the agitation is indicated by the fact that parochial schools teaching a variety of foreign languages have existed for many years without serious objection, and that Italian schools, known to be circulating fascist propaganda, never aroused opposition on a scale comparable to the Japanese schools.

[46] Bell, *Public School Education of Second Generation Japanese in America*, pp. 23–24.

[47] The text of the bill proposed by Hawaii Japanese is contained in Lorrin A. Thurston, *The Foreign Language School Question* (Reprinted from the *Pacific Commercial Advertiser*, Nov. 10–14, 1920), pp. 29–30.

[48] In *Farrington* v. *Tokushige* (1926) 273 U.S. 284 at 298, 47 S. Ct. 406 at 409, the Supreme Court unanimously ruled against the 1920 Hawaii Law, observing that "the Japanese parent has the right to direct the education of his own child without unreasonable restrictions; the Constitution protects him as well as those who speak another tongue." See Milton R. Konvitz, *The Alien and the Asiatic in American Law* (Ithaca, N.Y.: Cornell University Press, 1946), pp. 224–225.

[49] *Public School Education of Second Generation Japanese in America*, p. 24.

[50] Svensrud, "Attitudes of the Japanese toward their Language Schools," p. 261. See also Eliot G. Mears, *Resident Orientals on the Pacific Coast* (Chicago: University of Chicago Press, 1928), p. 259.

[51] *Final Report*, p. 12.

[52] 320 U.S. 81 at 97; 63 S. Ct. 1375 at 1384. Attorney General Francis Biddle attributed "special significance" as follows. "The existence of peculiar Japanese sovereign law grants to Japanese dual nationality, that is, Japanese citizenship no matter where born even though the United States automatically grants citizenship. This fact results in the bulk of Japanese even though citizens being Japanese sympathizers." (Unofficial minutes of a West Coast congressional committee on alien enemies and sabotage, February 5, 1942, typescript in Study files.)

[53] Kiyo Sue Inui, *The Unsolved Problem of the Pacific* (Tokyo: Japan Times, 1925), p. 300.

[54] The United States, however, has added some *jus sanguinis* principles in claiming as its own all children of American citizens born on foreign soil. E. K. Strong, Jr., *The Second Generation Japanese Problem* (Stanford: Stanford University Press, 1934), p. 140; Mears, *Resident Orientals on the Pacific Coast*, p. 108.

[55] The Japanese Association of the Pacific Coast, at a general conference in 1915, resolved to encourage the *jus soli* concept and petitioned the Japanese government for a change of the nationality laws to that effect. In 1916 the Japanese law was revised to permit American-born Japanese to renounce allegiance to Japan, except for males between the ages of 17 and 28 (who were sought for military service). In 1919,

American-born Japanese in Hawaii petitioned the Japanese government for a full release of the obligations and memorialized President Wilson for assistance in pressing their claims. In 1920 the Pacific Coast Japanese Association urged its membership to drop Japanese citizenship wherever possible and asked the Japanese government for full rights of expatriation. The text of the petition by Hawaii Japanese is contained in K. K. Kawakami, *The Real Japanese Question* (New York: Macmillan, 1921), pp. 186–187. The full translation of the relevant Japanese nationality laws is in Kiyo Sue Inui, *The Unsolved Problem of the Pacific*, pp. 300–320. See also B. H. Buell, "Some Legal Aspects of the Japanese Question," *American Journ. of International Law*, vol. 17 (1923), p. 34; Mears, *Resident Orientals of the Pacific Coast*, pp. 133–136.

[56] See Kiyo Sue Inui, *The Unsolved Problem of the Pacific*, p. 319.

[57] Smith, *Americans in Process*, p. 313.

[58] Edward K. Strong, *Japanese in California* (Stanford: Stanford University Press, 1933), p. 46.

[59] War Relocation Authority, Manzanar Relocation Center, Community Analysis Section, *Report on Registration* (Processed; Manzanar, 1943). There were a variety of reasons why many Nisei born before 1924 did not expatriate. Bradford Smith observes: "Some Americans of Japanese ancestry found they could not expatriate because their parents were dead and their marriage not having been registered in Japan, the children were not registered either. Therefore they could not be released from an obligation they neither wanted nor possessed. Others did not know whether they were 'duals' or not. Some, because of the expense and red tape involved, considered it 'wastetime.' Others held that to expatriate would be to acknowledge an allegiance they had never held. A few wanted dual citizenship in order to inherit property in Japan. Some bowed to the parental belief that to erase the name from the family register was a disgrace to the ancestors." *Americans from Japan* (Philadelphia: Lippincott, 1948), p. 150. For still other causes of hesitation to expatriate see Smith, *Americans in Process*, pp. 134–136.

[60] That the American alarm over dual citizenship was largely a byproduct of hostility toward Japan and the Japanese is asserted, among others, by Mears, who points out that "Americans raise practically no objection to the dual nationality of the American Chinese," and that "the contrast can be traced, with reference to the Japanese, to their more recent immigration, the cumulative effect of anti-Japanese propaganda, ... and the imperialistic adventures on the Asiatic mainland during and immediately following the World War." (*Resident Orientals on the Pacific Coast*, p. 111.)

[61] *Hirabayashi* v. *United States*, 320 U.S. 81 at 98; 63 S. Ct. 1375 at 1384.

[62] *Ibid.* at 96; 63 S. Ct. at 1384.

[63] *Ibid.* at 98; 63 S. Ct. at 1384.

[64] *Final Report*, p. vii.

[65] *Ibid.*, p. 9.

[66] Harrop A. Freeman, "Genesis, Exodus, Leviticus: Genealogy, Evacuation and Law," *Cornell Law Quart.*, vol. 28 (1943), p. 449.

[67] See especially Forrest A. LaViolette, *Americans of Japanese Ancestry* (Toronto: Canadian Institute of International Affairs, 1946), chapters i and vii; Miyamoto, "Social Solidarity Among the Japanese in Seattle"; Lind, *Hawaii's Japanese*, chapter 2.

[68] Dorothy S. Thomas, *The Salvage* (Berkeley: University of California Press, 1952), table 4, p. 578. "In 1942 the median age of Nisei was 17 years, of Issei males 55 and of Issei females 47."

[69] U.S. Army, Western Defense Command, Wartime Civil Control Administration, *Bulletin 12* (Processed; San Francisco, 1943), p. 8.

[70] Miyamoto, "Social Solidarity Among Japanese in Seattle," p. 68. See LaViolette's overly strong statement that the attitude of the Issei toward their Americanized offspring is "actually vicious," and it is considered that "the Nisei are one focal point

toward which the hostility of the Issei is directed." *Americans of Japanese Ancestry*, p. 142.

[71] LaViolette, *Americans of Japanese Ancestry*, pp. 30–31.

[72] Jesse Frederick Steiner, *The Japanese Invasion* (Chicago: McClurg, 1917), pp. 130 ff.

[73] LaViolette, *Americans of Japanese Ancestry*, p. 42 ff.

[74] Thus the Immigration Commission reported in 1911: "This 'gang' system has greatly appealed to employers in all agricultural communities requiring large numbers of hand workers, and in some industries where the work is especially disagreeable and especially large numbers are required, as in the beet fields and vineyards, it has come to be looked upon as absolutely essential to the continuation of the industry." *Japanese and Other Immigrant Races in Pacific Coast and Rocky Mountain States*, 61st Congress, 2d sess., Senate Document no. 633, Immigration Commission Reports, Vol. XXIV (Washington: G.P.O., 1911), p. 18.

[75] Steiner, *The Japanese Invasion*, p. 135.

[76] "Third Biennial Program of the Japanese American Citizens' League" (1934), cited by LaViolette, *Americans of Japanese Ancestry*, p. 154.

[77] *Ibid.*, p. 155.

[78] Winifred Raushenbush, "Their Place in the Sun," *Survey*, vol. 56 (1926), p. 142.

[79] *Ibid.*, p. 143.

[80] In 1933 Strong found that "the first generation prefer Buddhism to Christianity (77 per cent and 18 per cent respectively) [while] the reverse is the case with the United States born, among whom 39 per cent prefer Buddhism, while 47 per cent of the males and 56 per cent of the females prefer Christianity ... Preference for Christianity instead of Buddhism is associated with better education, better use of the English language, urban life, and greater ownership of farms but not of home and businesses." *The Second Generation Japanese Problem*, p. 224.

[81] Raushenbush, "Their Place in the Sun," pp. 142–143.

[82] "When there is a Buddhist and a Christian element in a Japanese Community, it usually appears that the Christian is more Americanized than the Buddhist element," "Tentative Findings of Pacific Coast Race Relations Survey," quoted in Strong, *The Second Generation Japanese Problem*, p. 181; see also Thomas, *The Salvage*, pp. 67–70.

[83] Raushenbush, "Their Place in the Sun," p. 143.

[84] LaViolette, *Americans of Japanese Ancestry*, p. 14.

[85] *Ibid.*, p. 15.

[86] Quoted, *ibid.*, p. 16.

[87] Thomas, "Some Social Aspects of Japanese-American Demography," *Proceedings of the American Philosophical Society*, vol. 94 (1950), p. 475.

[88] See Thomas, *The Salvage*, part II.

[89] Strong, *The Second Generation Japanese Problem*, p. 26.

[90] Robert E. Park, "Behind Our Masks," *Survey*, vol. 56 (1926), p. 137.

[91] *Hirabayashi* v. *United States*, 320 U.S. 81 at 98; 63 S. Ct. 1375 at 1384.

[92] *Ibid.* at 97; 63 S. Ct. at 1384.

[93] *Final Report*, p. 14.

[94] Brief of States of California, Oregon and Washington, Amicus Curiae, May 7, 1943, *Hirabayashi* v. *United States*, U. S. Supreme Court, October term, 1942, No. 870.

[95] *Final Report*, p. 14.

[96] *Ibid.*, p. 15.

[97] Thomas, "Some Social Aspects of Japanese-American Demography," pp. 466–467.

[98] See Curtis B. Munson, "Report on Japanese on the West Coast of the United States," in *Hearings*, 79th Congress, 1st sess., Joint Committee on the Investigation of the Pearl Harbor Attack (Washington: G.P.O., 1946), pt. 6, p. 2684.

[99] *Japanese American's Education in Japan,* War Relocation Authority, Community Analysis Section, Report no. 8 (Processed; Washington, 1944), p. 1 ff.

[100] LaViolette, *Americans of Japanese Ancestry,* p. 33. Thomas, *The Salvage,* indicates higher percentage of attachment to Japan than LaViolette supposed but this may have resulted from wartime experience.

[101] Lind, *Hawaii's Japanese,* pp. 187–188.

[102] *Ibid.,* p. 183.

[103] *The Salvage,* table 5, p. 580.

[104] *Final Report,* p. 10.

[105] *Ibid.,* p. 11, n. 5.

[106] *Ibid.,* p. 10.

[107] Brief of States of California, Oregon, and Washington, *Hirabayashi* v. *United States.*

[108] *Final Report,* p. 11.

[109] Brief of Japanese American Citizens' League as Amicus Curiae in *Korematsu* v. *United States,* p. 55.

[110] Ichihashi, *Japanese in the United States,* pp. 225–256; Miyamoto, "Social Solidarity Among the Japanese in Seattle," p. 113.

[111] *Final Report,* p. 12.

[112] "Report on Japanese on the West Coast of the United States," p. 2685.

[113] 323 U.S. 214 at 219; 63 S. Ct. 193 at 195.

[114] Dorothy S. Thomas and Richard S. Nishimoto, *The Spoilage* (Berkeley: University of California Press, 1946), chapters iii and iv.

[115] Thomas, "Some Social Aspects of Japanese-American Demography," p. 476, and *The Salvage,* pp. 92–93.

[116] See finding of U. S. District Court in *Murakami* v. *Acheson* adopted by the U. S. Court of Appeals, Ninth Circuit, in *Acheson* v. *Murakami* (1949) and published along with its opinion in 176 F. 2d 953 at 960.

[117] *Hirabayashi* v. *United States,* 320 U.S. 81 at 101; 63 S. Ct. 1375 at 1386.

[118] Thomas, *The Spoilage,* chapters iii–xii.

[119] "Report on Japanese on West Coast of the United States," p. 2686.

[120] Justice Murphy dissenting in *Korematsu* v. *United States,* 323 U.S. 214 at 241; 63 S. Ct. 193 at 205.

[121] *Final Report,* p. 34.

[122] *Ibid.,* p. 8.

[123] Memorandum of Attorney General Francis Biddle to President F. D. Roosevelt, May, 1942 (Study files).

[124] Interview with Edward J. Ennis, September 25, 1942 (Notes in Study files).

[125] Letter, James Lawrence Fly, Chairman, Federal Communication Commission to Francis Biddle, April 4, 1944, as quoted in *Wartime Exile, The Exclusion of the Japanese Americans from the West Coast,* War Relocation Authority (Processed; Washington: G.P.O., 1946), pp. 154–158.

[126] Charles E. Fairman, "The Law of Martial Rule and the National Emergency," *Harv. Law Rev.,* vol. 55 (1942), p. 1301.

[127] *Korematsu* v. *United States,* 323 U.S. 214 at 233; 65 S. Ct. 193 at 202.

[128] *Ibid.* at 235; 65 S. Ct. at 202.

[129] 320 U.S. 81 at 94; 63 S. Ct. 1375 at 1383.

[130] *Proceedings of a Conference of State Governors and Federal Officials Called by the War Relocation Authority, Salt Lake City, April 7, 1942* (Processed).

[131] Karl R. Bendetsen, *An Obligation Discharged . . . An Address Delivered to Personnel of the Wartime Civil Control Administration, November 3, 1942* (U.S. Army, WDC, n.d.), p. 2.

[132] In his diary General Stillwell has given us a vivid picture of the situation as it then existed. *The Stillwell Papers,* ed. by Theo. H. White (New York: W. Sloane Associates, 1948).

[133] See following pages.

[134] Letter, Rufus Holman to Hiram Johnson, February 9, 1942 (Study files).

[135] Samuel E. Morison, *The Rising Sun in the Pacific, 1931–April 1942,* History of U. S. Naval Operations in World War II, Vol. III (Boston: Little Brown, 1948), pp. 219, 220, 257. After Pearl Harbor, the task of the Pacific Fleet was to protect Hawaii, Wake, Johnson, and Palmyra Islands, to escort supply and troop ships, and keep Japanese from Fiji and Samoa. An estimate of the situation on December 10 called for the Navy to secure communications between the Panama Canal, Samoa, Fiji and New Zealand from the West Coast to Hawaii to Fiji.

[136] K. R. Greenfield, R. R. Palmer, B. Wiley, *The Organization of Ground Combat Troops,* The U. S. Army in World War II: The Army Ground Forces, Vol. I (Washington: U.S. Army Historical Division, 1947), pp. 116, 122. Speaking of the West Coast (p. 116), "attack was unlikely except by air." Jack B. Beardwood, *History of the Fourth Army,* Study no. 18, (Processed; Washington: U.S. Army Historical Division, 1946), p. 3. "During the entire period from the outbreak of war to the occupation of Kiska Islands, the efforts of Western Defense Command were directed largely toward the defense of Alaska and expulsion of enemy Japanese from the Aleutians."

According to the *Biennial Report of the Chief of Staff of the U.S. Army, July 1, 1941 to June 30, 1943* (Washington: G.P.O., 1943), p. 8, though the attack on the Pacific Fleet had "uncovered the entire West Coast of North America . . . by December 17th the critical areas in both the Pacific and Atlantic Coasts had been provided with a reasonable degree of protection against air and sea attack."

[137] Robert E. Sherwood, *Roosevelt and Hopkins* (New York: Harper, 1948), p. 454.

[138] *Ibid.,* p. 455.

[139] *Ibid.,* p. 535.

[140] *Final Report,* p. 33.

[141] *Ibid.*

[142] Public Proclamation No. 1, March 2, 1942 (7 *Fed. Reg.* 2320).

[143] *Korematsu* v. *United States,* 323 U.S. 214 at 218–19, 65 S. Ct. 193 at 195.

[144] Dembitz, "Racial Discrimination and the Military Judgment: The Supreme Court's Korematsu and Endo Decisions" *Columbia Law Rev.* vol. 45 (1943), pp. 191, 192, 193.

[145] "Report on Japanese on the West Coast of the United States," p. 2686.

[146] *Ibid.*

[147] *Time,* June 23, 1941, p. 17; New York *Times,* June 10, 1941, p. 3.

[148] Los Angeles *Times,* November 13, 1941.

[149] *Ibid.,* November 28, 1941.

[150] "Report on Japanese on the West Coast of the United States," p. 2586.

[151] New York *Times,* December 11, 1941.

[152] John H. Oakie, "Japanese in the United States," *Far Eastern Survey,* vol. 11 (1942), p. 24.

[153] It must be noted, however, that a conference of Army and Navy Intelligence Officers, held in Seattle, on January 7, recommended that Japanese aliens be evacuated from the entire State of Oregon and Washington (Memorandum, J. Edgar Hoover to Edward Ennis, Jan. 9, 1942, Study files).

[154] Report on Japanese Question, by Lieutenant Commander K. D. Ringle, USN, to Chief of Naval Operations, Branch Intelligence Office, Eleventh Naval District, Los Angeles, California. (Undated, [*ca* February 10, 1942] typescript in Study files.) The substance of this report was published under the title of "The Japanese in America" in *Harper's Magazine,* vol. 185 (1942), pp. 489–497.

[155] Maximillian Koessler, "Enemy Alien Internment, with Special Reference to Great Britain and France" *Political Science Quart.,* vol. 57 (1942), p. 102; Robert M. W. Kemper, "The Enemy Alien Problem in the Present War" *American Journ. of International Law,* vol. 34 (1940), p. 144.

[156] Galen M. Fisher, "Japanese Evacuation from the Pacific Coast," *Far Eastern Survey*, vol. 11 (1942), p. 147. See also the "Letter to the President of the United States," signed by over 200 citizens, dated April 30, 1942, which was printed and distributed by the Post War World Council, New York City, in June 1942.

[157] Galen M. Fisher, "The Drama of the Japanese Evacuation," in *A Touchstone of Democracy*, (New York: Council for Social Action of the Congregational Christian Churches, 1942), p. 17.

[158] *Final Report*, p. 34.

[159] U. S. Army, Western Defense Command, Wartime Civil Control Administration, Statistical Division, *Bulletin 12* (March 15, 1943), pp. 4, 8–14; Thomas, *The Salvage*, table 4, p. 578.

[160] Thomas and Nishimoto, *The Spoilage*, p. 333, n. 1.

[161] The situation obtaining on the East Coast provides a comparison unfavorable to the constitutionality of the West Coast evacuation. Harrop A. Freeman, "Genesis, Exodus, Leviticus: Genealogy, Evacuation, and Law," *Cornell Law Quart.*, vol. 28 (1943), pp. 441–443, and Tolan Committee *Fourth Interim Report*, table 2, "Foreign Born Germans and Italians in the United States by Division and States, 1940," pp. 229–230.

[162] *Hirabayashi* v. *United States*, 320 U.S. 81 at 100; 63 S. Ct. 1375 at 1385.

[163] *Missouri, Kansas & Texas Ry. Co.* v. *May* (1903) 194 U.S. 267 at 269; 24 S. Ct. 638 at 639.

[164] *Buck* v. *Bell* (1927) 274 U.S. 200 at 208; 47 S. Ct. 584 at 585.

[165] *Final Report*, p. 25.

[166] *Hirabayashi* v. *United States*, 320 U.S. 81 at 101; 63 S. Ct. 1375 at 1386.

[167] Brief of Japanese American Citizens' League, Amicus Curiae in *Korematsu* v. *United States*, pp. 56–68. "William A. Schuler, Dr. Otto Willumeit, Gerhard Kunze, Rev. Kurt B. Molzahn, Nicholine Buonapane, Frederick V. Williams, David W. Ryder, Igor Stepanoff, Arthur C. Read, Mrs. Valvalee Dickinson, John Farnsworth, Harry A. Thompson, Frederick H. Wright, John C. LeClair, Joseph H. Smyth, Walker G. Matheson, Ralph Townsend, Mimo de Guzman, Bernard J. O. Kuehn."

[168] Bernard Julius Otto Kuehn, *ibid.*, at p. 64.

[169] Justice Murphy concurring in *Oyama* v. *State of California* (1948), 332 U.S. 633 at 651; 68 S.Ct. 269 at 277.

[170] *Ibid.* at 661; 68 S. Ct. at 283.

[171] *Ibid.* at 641; 68 S. Ct. at 273.

[172] *Ibid.* at 640; 68 S. Ct. at 272.

[173] *Ibid.* at 646; 68 S. Ct. at 275.

[174] *Takahashi* v. *Fish and Game Commission*, 334 U.S. 410; 68 S. Ct. 1138.

[175] *Ibid.* at 418; 68 S. Ct. at 1142.

[176] *Ibid.* at 419; 68 S. Ct. at 1142.

[177] *Ibid.* at 420; 68 S. Ct. at 1143.

CHAPTER VIII

[1] The Japanese evacuation has been characterized by E. S. Corwin as "the most drastic invasion of the rights of citizens of the United States by their government that has thus far occurred in the history of our nation." *Total War and the Constitution* (New York, Knopf, 1947), p. 91.

[2] Study files. On January 27, in another letter to Congressman Ford, Attorney General Biddle made the same point with respect to Japanese American citizens; and on January 30, he wrote to President Roosevelt: "American citizens of Japanese race present a problem which is particularly difficult if they are subject to any regulation additional to that placed upon other citizens." (Study files.)

[3] Study files.

⁴ Los Angeles *Daily Journal,* April 14 and 18, 1942.

⁵ Letter, Ennis to Attorney General Biddle, February 13, 1942 (Study files).

⁶ *Regan* v. *King* (1942, U.S. Dist. Court, N.D. of Calif.), 49 F. Supp. 222. See also *Fisk* v. *Wade,* unreported, which was begun in the Alameda County Superior Court, California, but was abandoned in favor of action in *Regan* v. *King.*

⁷ *United States* v. *Wong Kim Ark* (1898), 169 U.S. 649 at 654; 18 S. Ct. 456 at 459.

⁸ Oral argument of U. S. Webb in *Regan* v. *King,* pp. 13–14.

⁹ Among these was James K. Fisk, Legion representative and longtime chairman of the Joint Immigration Committee.

¹⁰ (1856), 22 U.S. (19 How.) 393.

¹¹ Brief for Appellant in *Regan* v. *King,* pp. 24–25.

¹² *Ibid.,* pp. 26–27. Cf. Chief Justice Taney's opinion in *Dred Scott* v. *Sandford,* 22 U.S. (19 How.) 393.

¹³ Brief for Appellant in *Regan* v. *King,* p. 27.

¹⁴ Reply Brief for Appellant in *Regan* v. *King,* pp. 23–24.

¹⁵ Brief for Appellant in *Regan* v. *King,* pp. 34–35.

¹⁶ *Ibid.,* p. 45.

¹⁷ Reply Brief for Appellant in *Regan* v. *King,* p. 23.

¹⁸ Oral argument of U. S. Webb in *Regan* v. *King,* pp. 20–21.

¹⁹ Brief for Appellant in *Regan* v. *King,* pp. 42–43.

²⁰ *Regan* v. *King,* 49 F. Supp. 222; judgment affirmed U.S. Court of Appeals, Ninth Circuit (1943), 134 F. 2d. 413.

²¹ *Regan* v. *King* (1943), 319 U.S. 753; 63 S. Ct. 1168.

²² Justice Murphy concurring in *Oyama* v. *State of California* (1948), 332 U.S. 633 at 651; 68 S. Ct. 269 at 277.

²³ John J. Burling, assistant director of the Alien Enemy Control Unit of the War Division of the Department of Justice, has stated the reasoning of the Department of Justice in his *Abo* case affidavit [*Abo* v. *Clark, Furuya* v. *Clark* (1948, U.S. Dist. Court, N.D. of Calif.), 77 F. Supp. 806], pp. 7, 8, 9, 19.

²⁴ 18 U.S. Code Annotated, sec. 801 (*i*); 58 Stat. 677 (as amended in 1944).

²⁵ 61 Stat. 454.

²⁶ Brief for Appellees, *McGrath* v. *Abo* and *McGrath* v. *Furuya* [(1951), 186 F. 2d. 766], p. 75.

²⁷ Dorothy S. Thomas and Richard S. Nishimoto *The Spoilage* (Berkeley: Univ. of California Press, 1946), p. 361. Judge Goodman's opinion in *Abo* v. *Clark* (1948), 77 F. Supp. 806; the district court findings in *Murakami* v. *Marshall* published as Exhibit No. 1 in *Acheson* v. *Murakami* (1949), 176 F. 2d. 953; Transcript of Record, *Marshall* v. *Murakami* (January, 1949), U.S. Court of Appeals, Ninth Circuit (No. 12,082), pp. 38–39; Findings of Fact and Conclusions of Law in *Clark* v. *Abo* (April, 1949), U.S. Court of Appeals, Ninth Circuit (No. 12,251), p. 466. For similar statements see Burling's Affidavit in *Abo* v. *Clark,* pp. 41, 42, 43, 44.

²⁸ Transcript of Record, *Marshall* v. *Murakami,* p. 51. For a similar holding see *Inouye* v. *Clark* (1947), 73 F. Supp. 1000, reversed on the ground that the pleadings were defective in *Clark* v. *Inouye* (1949), 175 F. 2d. 740.

²⁹ *Acheson* v. *Murakami,* 176 F. 2d. 953 at 954. The government did not seek *certiorari* in the Supreme Court.

The Department of Justice interpreted the decision by the court of appeals as applying only to those renunciants who could show by affidavit that they had renounced as a result of any or all of the coercive conditions mentioned in the court's opinion, and hence as not applying "to the cases of renunciants as to whom the government files disclosed evidence of loyalty to Japan or disloyalty to the United States." (Letter of H. G. Morison, Assistant Attorney General, to the Department of State, attention Passport Division, dated October 25, 1949, published as Appendix E in Appellant's Brief, *McGrath* v. *Abo* and *McGrath* v. *Furuya.*) The State Department also adopted this interpretation. (Letter of R. B. Shipley, Chief Passport Division, to H. G. Morison, Assistant Attorney General, Department of Justice, November 29, 1949, Appendix F in Appellant's Brief, *McGrath* v. *Abo* and *McGrath* v. *Furuya*.)

[30] *Abo* v. *Clark*, 77 F. Supp. 806.

[31] The validation was not without qualification. The Attorney General was given time in which to "present evidence that certain of the plaintiffs individually acted freely and voluntarily despite the present record facts." As to any plaintiff, not so designated by the Attorney General within the time specified, a final decree was to enter. As to any designated plaintiff, further hearings were to be held. *Abo* v. *Clark*, 77 F. Supp. 806 at 812.

[32] There was also, the court added, "incidental concurrent duress, menace, coercion, intimidation, fraud and undue influence . . . exerted upon each plaintiff by groups and individual internees likewise detained." Findings of Fact and Conclusions of Law, in Transcript of Record, *Clark* v. *Abo*, p. 462.

[33] *Abo* v. *Clark*, 77 F. Supp. 806 at 807.

[34] Findings of Fact and Conclusions of Law, in Transcript of Record, *Clark* v. *Abo*, pp. 462, 470–471. With respect to constitutional procedural requirements the court found that there was no legal requirement whatever upon the Attorney General to give the renunciation hearings but that the hearings as given "were not conducted fairly or in conformity with what otherwise would be constitutional requirements."

[35] *Abo* v. *Clark*, 77 F. Supp. 806 at 811. In view of the fact that 1,480 of the renunciants had at the time returned to Japan, District Judge Goodman on May 2, 1949, modified the final order of revalidation issued on April 12, 1949, so as not to "affect the exercise of the authority and power conferred upon [the Government of the United States] pursuant to 8 USC 903 with respect to persons abroad claiming United States nationality and citizenship." Transcript of Record in *Clark* v. *Abo*, p. 490.

[36] *McGrath* v. *Abo* and *McGrath* v. *Furuya* (1951), 186 F. 2d. 766 at 768; cert. denied, 342 U.S. 832; 72 S. Ct. 40.

[37] *Ex parte Abo* and *Ex parte Furuya* (1947), 76 F. Supp. 664.

[38] *Ibid.* at 666. For the theory on which the government acted see John J. Burling's affidavit in *McGrath* v. *Abo*, and the Minutes of the West Coast congressional delegation committee on alien enemies and sabotage, February 5, 1942 (Typescript in Study files).

[39] *Barber* v. *Abo* (1951), 186 F. 2d. 775 at 777, as amended on rehearing.

[40] Before such proceedings could take place, however, the Department of Justice canceled the deportation orders against the renunciants then remaining in custody, thus mooting the cause.

[41] Brief for Appellees in *McGrath* v. *Abo* and *McGrath* v. *Furuya*, pp. 75–76.

[42] *Barber* v. *Abo*, 186 F. 2d. 775 at 778.

[43] Cf. Judge McLaughlin's opinion in *Okimura* v. *Acheson* (1951), 99 F. Supp. 587 and *Murata* v. *Acheson* (1951) 99 F. Supp. 591: "The primary legal test by which United States citizenship is determined is place of birth. The test is a constitutional one . . . (Amendment XIV, sec. 1). It is the view of this court that while the constitution gives the Congress plenary power over citizenship by naturalization, it leaves the Congress no power whatsoever to interfere with American citizenship by birth. . . . It is wholly devoid of any power to destroy citizenship by birth." (*Okimura* v. *Acheson*, 99 F. Supp. 587 at 589–590). Accordingly, in these cases, Judge McLaughlin held unconstitutional 18 U.S. Code Annotated, sec. 801, (c) and (e), declaring: "A person who is a national of the United States whether by birth or naturalization, shall lose his nationality by: . . . (c) entering, or serving in, the armed forces of a foreign state unless expressly authorized by the laws of the United States, if he has or acquires the nationality of such foreign state; or . . . (e) voting in a political election in a foreign state or participating in an election or plebiscite to determine the sovereignty

over foreign territory. . . ." (*Ibid.*) Cf. John P. Roche, "The Loss of American Nationality—The Development of Statutory Expatriation," *Univ. of Penn. Law Rev.*, vol. 99 (1950), p. 25.

44 Brief for Appellees in *Barber* v. *Abo* and *Barber* v. *Furuya*, pp. 36–37. Cf. Corwin, *Total War and the Constitution*, p. 95: "Congress undoubtedly possesses the power to require that American citizens, of whatever ancestry, and whether native-born or naturalized, who are by the law of the ancestral country its citizens also, take an oath of loyalty to the United States or else be considered to have renounced their American citizenship."

45 Brief for Appellees in *Barber* v. *Abo* and *Barber* v. *Furuya*, p. 40.

CONCLUSION

1 Mr. Justice Murphy dissenting in *Korematsu* v. *United States* (1944), 323 U.S. 214 at 235; 65 S. Ct. 193 at 202.

2 Thus, in forming a judgment as to whether the danger of invasion justified first the curfew, later and more important the evacuation, still later and still more important the detention, the frequently expressed judicial admonition against the use of hindsight is properly ignored. The historical standard is primarily the standard of hindsight. One of the great buttresses of judicial review is that "the law's delay" and the time of judicial action enable the courts to use that standard.

3 Samuel E. Morison, *Coral Sea, Midway and Submarine Action, May 1942–August 1942*, History of Naval Operations in World War II, Vol. IV (Boston: Little, Brown, 1949), p. 165, n. 8.

4 Letter, John B. Heffernan, Rear Admiral, USN (Ret.), Director of Naval Records and History, to authors, May 15, 1951 (Study files).

5 U. S. Army, Western Defense Command and Fourth Army, *Final Report: Japanese Evacuation from the West Coast, 1942* (Washington: G.P.O., 1943), p. 34.

6 7 Fed. Reg. 1407.

7 18 U.S. Code Annotated, sec. 97a; 56 Stat. 173 (March 21, 1942).

8 Interview, October 15, 1942 (Notes in Study files).

9 *Biennial Report of Chief of Staff of the U.S. Army (1945)*, p. 1, quoted by Justice Burton in his dissent in *Duncan* v. *Kahanomuku* (1946), 327 U.S. 304 at 351; 66 S. Ct. 606 at 628.

10 Mr. Justice Jackson dissenting in *Korematsu* v. *United States*, 323 U.S. 214 at 245–246; 65 S. Ct. 193 at 207.

11 (1842), 14 U.S. (16 Pet.) 539.

12 (1856), 22 U.S. (19 How.) 393.

Index

INDEX

Abo v. *Clark*, 181–183, 317, 369 n. 341, 394 nn. 23 & 27, 395 nn. 30 & 33
Abo v. *McGrath*, 370 n. 372
Abo v. *Williams*, 181–183
Acheson v. *Murakami*, 336 n. 1, 371 n. 384, 394 nn. 27 & 29
Adamic, Louis, 343 n. 146
Adams, John Quincy, 233
Air Force, 367 n. 268
Alaska. *See* Evacuation
Alexandre, Maurice, 5, 382 n. 1
Alien enemies, 100; control measures and arrests, 82–83, 100–102, 105, 106–107, 119–120, 247–248, 289, 296–298; curfew, 107, 118, 247; exemptions of German and Italian aliens from evacuation, 112–113, 303; restrictions lifted, 120. *See also* Issei.
Alien Enemy Control Unit, 101
Alien Enemy Act, 311, 318, 319
Alien Land Law, 28, 37, 41, 44, 48, 51, 53, 55, 65, 214, 267, 304–305
American Civil Liberties Union, 136, 166, 179, 236
American Farm Bureau Federation, 51. *See also* California Farm Bureau Federation
American Federation of Labor, 34–35, 38, 194. *See also* California State Federation of Labor
American Legion, 28, 43–46, 79, 194–195, 378 n. 75
Anderson, John Z., 205, 373 nn. 25 & 27, 374 n. 29
Angell, Homer, 78
Angell, Philip H., 152
Anti-Chinese agitation, 15–17
Anti-Chinese legislation, 17–18
Anti-coolie clubs, 16
Antiforeignism, 11–15; of American Legion, 43–44; of Native Sons of Golden West, 46, 49. *See also* Race prejudice; Stereotype
Anti-Jap Laundry League, 36
Anti-Indian agitation, 13–14
Anti-Japanese agitation: popular agitation, 24–27, 62–67, 329; San Francisco School Board incident, 26, 40–41; in movies, 29–32; in fiction, 32; boycotts by labor, 32–38, 41; formation of anti-Japanese societies, 35–36; as political

issue, 38–43, 49, 54; by farm organizations, 50–57; physical assaults, 53, 72–73, 88, 91, 95–96; attitude of small business, 57–59; attitude of big business, 59–62; attitude of Canadian business, 58–59. *See also* Stereotype
Asiatic Exclusion League. *See* Japanese and Korean Exclusion League
Assembly centers, 118, 126–127
Assimilation of Japanese, 273–279
Associated Anti-Jap Leagues, 36
Associated Produce Dealers and Brokers of Los Angeles, 372 n. 22, 373 n. 23
Associated Farmers, 192
Association of Oregon Counties, 201
Association of Washington Cities, 202
Atkeson, Thomas C., 56, 345 nn. 208, 210, & 217
Ault, Erwin B., 342 n. 130
Avery, Russell, 374 n. 41
Ayers, James J., 338 n. 14

Bailey, Thomas A., 63–64, 340 n. 68, 342 nn. 115 & 126, 343 n. 141, 345 n. 221, 346 nn. 231, 245, 249, & 250
Bancroft, Griffing, 32
Bancroft, Hubert H., 11, 338 nn. 10, 13, 15, & 20
Barber v. *Abo*, 183, 319–321, 370 n. 372, 371 n. 375, 396 nn. 44 & 45
Barber v. *Furuye.* See *Barber* v. *Abo*
Barclay, Thomas S., 152
Bardeche, Maurice, 341 n. 101
Bean, Walton E., 343 n. 140
Beardwood, Jack B., 392 n. 136
Bee, F. A., 338 n. 22
Bell, Reginald, 270–271, 387 n. 41
Bendetsen, Karl R., 3, 103–104, 109, 118, 121, 122, 136, 197, 205, 206, 291, 357 n. 56, 359 n. 92
Benevolent and Protective Order of Elks, 196
Berelson, Bernard, 342, n. 109
Bias, Jack E., 373 n. 28
Bigler, John, 18
Biddle, Francis, 74, 83, 93, 103, 105, 107, 108, 109, 111, 140, 174–175, 205, 289, 312, 357 nn. 64 & 65, 358 n. 67, 388 n. 52, 393 n. 2, 394 n. 5
Black Dragon Society, 297, 298

Black, Hugo L., 213, 214, 216–217, 237
238, 251, 263, 285, 287, 295–296, 307
Black, Lloyd J., 385 n. 48
Block managers, 131
Bloom, Leonard, 361 n. 136
Boards of supervisors: proevacuation reso-
lutions, 201, 202, 380 nn. 97, 98, 99, &
100
Boddy, Manchester, 346 n. 248
Boekel, W. A., 361 n. 140
Bogardus, Emory S., 341 nn. 94 & 97, 342
n. 108, 347 n. 269
Bonesteel, Charles H., 172, 352 n. 2
Bowron, Fletcher, 84, 94, 201, 202–203
Brassillach, Robert, 341 n. 101
Brooks, B. S., 338 nn. 21 & 23
Brown, Alice M., 387 n. 36
Bryan, B. M., 114
Bryan, William J., 41
Bryce, Lord, 12, 46, 337 n. 1
Buck v. Bell, 393 n. 164
Buddhism, 127, 132, 227
Buell, B. H., 388 n. 55
Buell, R. L., 341 n. 106, 342 n. 111, 345 n.
202
Bundy, McGeorge, 357 n. 59
Bunje, Emil, 344 n. 190
Burchard, Father, 20
Burke, Robert E., 378 n. 81
Burling, John K., 105, 176–178, 369 n. 341,
370 nn. 349 & 351, 394 n. 23, 395 n. 38
Burlingame, Roger, 344 n. 168
Burnett, Peter H., 15
Burton, Harold H., 214, 305
Bushnell, Horace, 338 n. 5
Byington, Lewis F., 344 n. 186

California Committee of Justice, 28, 61
California Council on Oriental Relations,
61, 67
California County Supervisors Associa-
tion, 201
California Farm Bureau Federation, 50–
54, 90, 95, 374 n. 35, 378 n. 73. See also
American Farm Bureau Federation
California Joint Immigration Committee,
38, 44, 55, 78–79, 95, 194, 195
California State Board of Equalization,
102
California State Constitutional Conven-
tion, 17
California State Department of Agricul-
ture, 380 n. 94

California State Federation of Labor, 39.
See also American Federation of Labor
California State Grange, 49, 51, 54, 192.
See also National Grange
California State Legislature, 16–17, 18, 37,
43, 48, 51, 76–77, 201
California State Personnel Board, 102,
380 n. 93
California State Supreme Court, 17
Cantril, Hadley, 349 n. 42
Carillo, Leo, 77
Carlson, Oliver, 341 n. 87
Carr, Ralph, 89
Carroll, Wallace, 71–72
Carrothers, W. A., 345 n. 225, 346 n. 236
Carson, J. K., 376 n. 59
Casserly, Eugene, 20
Cecil, W. J., 373 n. 27, 380 n. 94
Chambers of Commerce: oppose anti-
Japanese agitation, 60; San Francisco
Chamber's Japanese American Rela-
tions Committee, 61; proevacuation
resolutions, 90, 197, 374 n. 29, 375 nn.
46 & 47, 378 n. 73
Chase, Salmon P., 230
"Chilean War," 14
Chinese Exclusion Act (1882), 22
Citizenship: voluntary renunciation stat-
ute, 175–176, 315–316; attack by Webb,
313–315; ineligibility of Japanese, 353
n. 4. See also Renunciation of citizen-
ship
Citizenship laws: jus sanguinis, 271–273;
jus soli, 271–273; dual citizenship, 271–
273, 318–319; Japanese law revised, 272
Civil Affairs Division (CAD), 118
Civil Control Stations, 124
Civilian Exclusion Orders, 124, 125, 133,
235
Civilian Restrictive Orders, 129, 143–144,
173, 236
Clark, Thomas C., 107, 117, 118, 203, 357
n. 64, 381 n. 112.
Clark v. Abo, 371 n. 377, 394 n. 27, 395 n.
32
Clark v. Inouye, 394 n. 28
Clark, Mark W., 350 n. 46
Cleland, Robert G., 337 n. 1
Coast Seaman's Journal, 23, 33, 34, 38
Coe, Earl, 379 n. 83
Coffee, John, 204, 348 n. 22
Collins, Wayne, 179, 181, 183, 219–321
Concentration camps. See Assembly cen-

ters; Internment camps; Isolation center; Relocation centers; Segregation center; "Stockade"

Conmy, Peter, 344 nn. 172, 183, & 186

Congress, United States: Joint Congressional Committee Investigating the Chinese (1876), 19, 21; Chinese Exclusion Act (1882), 22; Oriental Exclusion Act (1924), 28, 42–43; West Coast congressional delegation committees (1942), 86, 205; Public Law 503, 113–116, 121, 129, 133, 143, 174, 235; Public Law 405, 175–176, 369 n. 342; Senate Resolution 166, 368 n. 286; Public Law 239, 369 n. 342

Coolidge, Mary E. B., 338 nn. 5, 10, 21, & 23, 339 nn. 24 & 27, 342 n. 137

Coryn, Sidney, G. P., 340 n. 66

Corwin, Edward S., 6, 383 n. 1, 384 n. 27, 383 n. 1, 384 n. 8, 385 n. 46, 396 n. 44

Cross, Ira B., 338 n. 18

Curfew, 107, 118–119, 120, 248

Davis, David, 228–230, 241–242, 256

Davis, Merle, 347 n. 268

Dean, George, 351 n. 61

Defense councils: proevacuation resolutions, 90, 201, 202, 381 n. 103

Dembitz, Nanette, 6, 186, 254, 295, 371 n. 6, 383 n. 1, 387 n. 25

Democratic Club of Burbank, 377 n. 66

Dennis v. *United States*, 245

Denman, William, 2, 183, 317, 319–320, 382 n. 3, 385 n. 48

Department of Justice, 101–102, 105, 106–107, 173, 174, 177–178; rejection of DeWitt's zone recommendations, 108–109; acceptance of "mass evacuation," 111; renunciation hearings, 178; deportation of renunciants, 179, 318; mitigation hearings, 179–180. See also Federal Bureau of Investigation

Deportation of renunciants, 178–179, 318

Detention. *See* Internment

DeWitt, John L., 92, 100, 166, 168, 197, 203, 206, 207–208, 262, 264, 267, 309, 354 n. 17, 318 n. 112; criticism of alien enemy control measures, 102–105; prohibited zone recommendations, 106–107, 108; "Final Recommendation," 109–111; urges segregation, 160; race prejudice, 263. *See also* Exclusion; Internment; Western Defense Command

DeYoung, Michael H., 40

Dickinson, Edwin D., 180

Dies, Martin, 71, 86–88, 175

Dilke, C. W., 338 n. 9

Disabled American Veterans of the World War, 194, 195

Disloyalty: claims of, 93–94; segregation, 153, 160–169; registration, 149–151; analysis of evidence of claims of, 265–289; techniques for separating loyal from disloyal, 294–302. *See also* Loyalty

Dooner, Pierton W., 339 n. 44

Douglas, William O., 214, 253, 256–257, 264

Downey, Sheridan, 204–205

Dred Scott v. *Sandford,* 313, 333, 394 n. 12

Dual citizenship, 271–73; 318–319. *See also* Citizenship laws

Due process, 261–262

Duffield, Marcus, 343 nn. 158 & 163, 344 n. 169

Duncan v. *Kahanomuku,* 396 n. 9

Dunimay, C. A., 338 n. 17

Drum, Hugh A., 149, 167

Eaves, Lucille, M., 339 n. 26

Eastern Defense Command (EDC), 149

Eastern Washington Beet Growers, 372 n. 22, 373 n. 23

Eisenhower, Milton S., 122–124, 142, 206

Elliott, Alfred J., 205, 206–207, 374 n. 35, 382 n. 129

Emmons, Delos C., 172, 352 n. 2

Employment of evacuees: in centers, 132, 144; outside centers, 143. *See also* Leave regulations; Resettlement

Endo, Mitsuye, 252

Endo v. *United States,* 211, 213–214, 248–259

Enemy aliens. *See* Alien enemies

Ennis, Edward J., 101, 103, 109, 111, 205, 312, 353 n. 9, 357 n. 53, 391 n. 124, 394 n. 5

Equal protection of laws, 261–262; discriminatory purpose of evacuation, 262–264; overinclusive classification of Japanese as dangerous, 265–289; emergency justification for overinclusive classification, 290–291; underinclusive classification of Japanese as dangerous, 302–304

Espionage: rumors of, 70–72; official denials of, 93; absence of, 99, 105, 288–

289, 296, 326; DeWitt's estimate of likelihood, 111; claims in *Final Report*, 139–140; Caucasians convicted, 393 n. 167

Eta caste, 277

Evacuation: theory of pressure group responsibility, 3–4, 185 ff., 329–330; theory of politician responsibility, 3–4, 198 ff., 329–330; military and patriotic societies urging, 74, 194–195; urged by West Coast papers, 75–76, 85; from Alaska, 134–135; from Hawaii, 135–136; farmer organizations urging, 189–192; business groups urging, 192–193; service clubs urging, 193; labor unions urging, 194; social clubs urging, 195–196; activities of West Coast politicians, 199–203, 206–207; activities of congressmen, 203–206; alternative procedures, 294–302; DeWitt's responsibility for, 330; War Department responsibility for, 331–332; Roosevelt's responsibility for, 331. *See also* Exclusion; Internment

Evacuee property: protection of, 107–108, 124–125

Exclusion: of alien enemies and Japanese from prohibited zones, 106–107; forced exclusion of Japanese from Military Area No. 1, 116–117; response to order, 119; policy toward mixed-bloods, 125–126; exemptions, 158–159, 166–167; individual exclusion, 171–174; revocation of "mass evacuation," 173. *See also* Internment

Exclusion areas, 124

Exclusion orders. *See* Civilian Exclusion Orders

Executive Orders: Order 9066, 111–112, 234, 235, 247; Order 9102, 122, 141; Order 9106, 353 n. 14; Order 9372, 353 n. 14; Order 9489, 136

Ex parte Abo, 318, 371 n. 373, 395 n. 37

Ex parte Endo, 248, 253–254, 382 nn. 1 & 11, 386 nn. 60, 63 & 69

Ex parte Furuye. See *Ex parte Abo*

Ex parte Milligan, 227–228, 382 n. 25, 384 n. 4; majority opinion, 228–230, 232; Japanese cases and majority and minority opinions, 233–241; majority opinion evaluated, 241–242, 244–248; majority opinion in relation to detention, 249–259; majority opinion in relation to evacuation, 256–259; minority opinion, 230–232; minority opinion evaluated, 242–244

Ex parte Quirin, 386 n. 69

Ex parte Ventura, 385 n. 48

Fairman, Charles B., 4–5, 242, 244, 290, 383 n. 1, 384 n. 11, 385 nn. 48 & 50

Farm Bureau. *See* American Farm Bureau Federation; California Farm Bureau Federation

Farrington v. *Tokushige*, 388 n. 48

Federal Bureau of Investigation, 101, 154, 284, 296, 297, 367 n. 268; control measures and arrests of alien enemies, 82–83, 101–102, 105, 106–107, 119–120, 247–248, 289, 296–298

Federal Communications Commission, 289

Federal Reserve Board, 125

Federal Security Agency, 107, 125

Fenn, W. P., 338 n. 9, 339 n. 40, 340 nn. 52 & 56

"Final Recommendation," 109–111

Final Report: evaluation of reliability, 136–140; on justification for detention, 250; on military necessity for evacuation, 327, 330, 359 n. 92

Fisher, Galen M., 393 nn. 156 & 157

Fisk, James K., 44, 79, 394 n. 9

Fisk v. *Wade*, 394 n. 6

Flowers, Montaville, 28

Fly, James Lawrence, 364 n. 204, 391 n. 125

Ford, Leland, 77–78, 204, 205, 357 n. 64, 373 n. 25, 393 nn. 2 & 16

Forrestal, James K., 354 n. 28

Foulke, Robert H., 377 n. 63

442nd Combat Team, 168

Fowler, Ruth, 347 n. 269

Frankfurter, Felix, 226, 240

Freeman, Harrop A., 6, 274, 383 n. 1, 393 n. 161

Fueker, Fred, 376 n. 60

Fuji v. *State*, 382 n. 20

Fuller, L. Varden, 344 n. 190, 346 n. 229, 347 n. 261

Furuye v. *Clark*, 394 n. 23

Gabrielson, W. A., 351 n. 66

Gage, Henry T., 39

Gellerman, William, 343 n. 158

Geographical distribution of Japanese on West Coast, 93, 110–111, 138, 139; De-

Witt's claims of significance, 266–268; analysis of claims, 266–268; California Attorney-General's maps of, 267–268, 363 n. 197

George, Henry, 17

Gerstaecker, Friedrich, 338 n. 10

Gillette, Guy, 71

Glenn, Garrard, 385 n. 51

Glick, Philip M., 364 n. 207, 365 n. 208

Goodman, Louis E., 181–183, 317–318, 318–319

Gowen, H. H., 60, 346 n. 254

Graham, W. A., 383 n. 1, 384 n. 4

Grand juries: proevacuation resolutions, 202, 380 n. 102

Grange. See California State Grange; National Grange

Grant, Madison, 27

Gray, Justin, 343 n. 158

Greenfield, K. R., 392 n. 136

Griswold, A. W., 341 n. 73

Grodzins, Morton, 4, 186, 188, 190–191, 192, 194, 195, 197, 199, 202, 204, 364 n. 199, 371 n. 4, 372 nn. 12 & 20, 374 nn. 29, 34, & 39, 375 n. 48, 376 n. 51, 377 nn. 68 & 69, 378 nn. 72 & 73, 379 n. 86, 381 nn. 111 & 116

Grower-Shipper Vegetable Association, 80, 95, 190, 191, 372 n. 22, 373 n. 23, 387 n. 17

Gulick, Sidney, 65

Gullion, Allen W., 103, 109, 111

Haight, Walter C., 90

Hapgood, Norman, 344 n. 168

Harada, Tasuku, 345 n. 201, 347 n. 267

Harrison, George R., 55

Hart, Jerome A., 344 n. 173

Hawaii. See Espionage; Evacuation; Sabotage

Hayakawa, Sessue, 30–31

Hayes, E. A., 340 n. 69

Heffernan, John B., 396 n. 4

Heflin, Thomas G., 43

Heimusha Kai, 284

Helper, Hinton R., 338 n. 10

Hichborn, Franklin E., 342 n. 129

Hicks, Tracy E., 376 n. 58

Hirbayashi, Gordon K., 233–234

Hirabayashi v. United States, 211–213, 215–216, 233, 261–262, 264, 265, 290, 386 n. 1, 387 nn. 6 & 26, 389 n. 61, 390 n. 91, 393 n. 162; Amici curiae briefs, 138, 283, 390 n. 94, 391 n. 107

Hittell, T. H., 338 nn. 8, 11, & 19

Hobson, R. P., 27

Holman, Rufus, 205, 392 n. 134

Holmes, Oliver W., 302

Hoover, J. Edgar, 351 n. 66, 393 n. 153

Hughes, Charles Evans, 219–220, 244, 260

Hughes, John B., 73–74

Hughes, L. I., 347 n. 271

Hunt, Clarence M., 79

Ichihashi, Yamamoto, 340 n. 69, 342 nn. 112, 136, & 138, 347 n. 260, 387 n. 41, 391 n. 110

Ickes, Harold J., 171–173

Individual exclusion, 171–174

Induction, 149–150, 154, 166–170; 442nd Combat Team, 167–168; 100th Infantry Battalion, 168

Inouye v. Clark, 394 n. 28

International Seaman's Union of Pacific, 33

International Women's Clubs, 377 n. 66

Internment: of alien enemies, 101–102, 105; of Japanese in Military Area No. 1, 120–121; War Relocation Authority detention policy, 122–124, 140–141, 250–251; Army role in detention, 123, 141; movement to Assembly Centers, 124–126; exemptions, 125; military control over, 128–129; of Japanese in California section of Military Area No. 2, 132–133; revocation of "mass evacuation," 171–173. See also Leave regulations; Relocation centers

Internment camps, 133, 180, 353 nn. 6 & 11

Inui, Kiyo Sue, 388 nn. 53 & 55, 389 n. 56

Invasion of West Coast, 326; DeWitt's estimate in Final Report, 110; other estimates of likelihood, 292–294

Irish, John P., 24

Irwin, Wallace, 32

Irwin, William, 17

Ishida, Gladys, 370 n. 344

Isolation Center, 164–165

Issei, 100, 274, 287; in resettlement, 142; definition, 352 n. 3; ineligibility to citizenship, 353 n. 4

Iyenaga, T., 340 n. 62

Jackson, Robert H., 212, 214, 217–218, 219, 223, 225–226, 240, 332–333

James, Marquis, 343 n. 158

Japan: relations with United States, 25–28; Root-Takahira Agreement, 27; Oriental Exclusion Act, 28, 42–43;

Gentlemen's Agreement, 41; World War II in Pacific, 69, 73, 82, 328. *See also* Citizenship laws; Kibei

Japanese American Citizens League, 3, 161, 187, 276

Japanese American Joint Board (JAJB), 141, 153–157, 167

Japanese Association, 270, 275, 284, 297, 388 n. 55

Japanese associations and clubs, 275–277, 282–284

Japanese Education Association, 270

Japanese and Korean Exclusion League, 28, 35–36, 38, 44, 49, 55, 58. *See also* California Joint Immigration Committee

Japanese-language schools, 268–271

Japanese Society for Education of Second-Generation in America, 269

Johnson, H. B., 346 nn. 230, 247, 249, & 251

Johnson, Hiram, 41, 45, 65, 205, 392 n. 134

Jones, Richard S., 343 n. 158

Jordan, David Starr, 63

Jordan, Frank M., 379 n. 83

Judicial review: Supreme Court handling of Japanese cases, 211–215, 220–223, 332–334; substantial basis test in *Hirabayashi*, 215–216; substantial basis test in *Korematsu*, 216–217

Jus sanguinis. See Citizenship laws

Jus soli. See Citizenship laws

Kawakami, K. K., 343 nn. 146, & 151, 344 n. 171, 388 n. 55

Kearney, Dennis, 16

Kemper, R. M. W., 392 n. 155

Kern, Ruth E., 344 n. 166

Kibei, 100, 275; resettlement, 142; as segregants, 142; at Tule Lake Segregation Center, 177; influence of Japanese government on, 279–285; definition of, 352 n. 3

Kile, O. M., 344 n. 193

King, Samuel W., 351 n. 66

Kiwanis Club. *See* Service clubs

Klineburg, Otto, 340 n. 60

Koessler, M., 392 n. 155

Konvitz, Milton R., 6, 340 n. 59, 342 n. 127, 383 n. 1, 388 n. 48

Korematsu, Fred T., 236

Korematsu v. United States, 211–213, 216–218, 225, 235–240, 250, 261–262, 263,

289, 336 n. 2, 385 n. 48, 386 n. 1; *Amici curiae* briefs, 336 n. 5, 384 n. 26, 391 n. 109, 393 n. 167

Knox, Frank, 70

Kyne, Peter B., 32

Labor unions: anti-Chinese agitation, 16; anti-Japanese agitation and boycotts, 32–38; proevacuation resolutions, 194

Langlie, A. B., 378 n. 79

Larson, C., 341 n. 103

Lasker, Bruno, 340 n. 59, 341 n. 98

Lasswell, Harold D., 340 n. 60

LaViolette, Forrest, 275, 281–282, 389 n. 67, 390 nn. 71, 73, 76, & 84

Lea, Homer, 26, 64

League of California Cities, 90, 202

League of Oregon Cities, 202

Leave clearance, 146–147

Leave regulations, 146–147, 151–152, 153–154; student leave, 144–145, 149; indefinite leave, 148–149; short-term leave, 147–148; work-group leave, 148; criteria for issuance, 250–251

Leighton, Alexander H., 361 n. 144, 362 nn. 152 & 169, 365 n. 226

Leupp (WRA Isolation Center), 164–165

Lewis, Robert H., 352 n. 2, 369 n. 327

Lind, Andrew W., 270, 282, 364 n. 201, 387 n. 41, 389 n. 67

Lin Sing v. Washburn, 339 n. 31

Lions Club. *See* Service clubs

Lippmann, Walter, 85, 340 n. 60

Lodge, Henry C., 43

London, Jack, 20

Lorwin, Lewis L., 342 n. 117

Loyalty, 326–327; War Department determinations, 149, 153, 154–157; Western Defense Command determinations, 157–160, 173–174; examination of claims of disloyalty, 265–289. *See also* Disloyalty; Segregation

Lundberg, Ferdinand, 341 n. 86

Lynch, Robert N., 346 n. 236

Lyons, T. W. G., 345 n. 194

MacArthur, Walter, 35, 340 n. 69

McCarthy, Patrick H., 40

McClatchy, H. J., 79

McClatchy, Valentine A., 38, 47, 53, 56, 345 n. 205

McCloy, John J., 103, 109, 111, 112, 120, 154, 155, 167, 168, 172, 206, 331–332, 383 n. 124

McEnerney, Garrett II, 152
McGovney, D. O., 353 n. 4
McGrath v. *Abo*, 183, 370 nn. 354, 357, 359, 362 & 367, 371 nn. 379, 381, & 385, 394 nn. 26 & 29, 395 nn. 36, 38, & 41
McGrath v. *Furuye*. See *McGrath* v. *Abo*.
McKee, Ruth, 341 n. 90, 343 n. 150, 344 n. 176
MacKenzie, John D., 37
McKenzie, R. D., 59, 341 n. 92
McLaughlin, Gerald, 395 n. 43
McLemore, Henry, 75, 85
McReynolds, George E., 61, 341 n. 81, 346 nn. 232, 237, 247, & 249
McWilliams, Carey, 4, 49, 186, 189–190, 199, 340 n. 59, 341 n. 93, 342 n. 109, 343 nn. 149 & 157, 345 n. 228, 371 n. 3 372 n. 10, 372 n. 17, 376 nn. 51 & 55, 378 n. 77, 379 n. 86
Manson, Marsden, 19
Manzanar Relocation Center, 118, 130–131, 257
Maps. *See* Geographical distribution of Japanese on West Coast
Marshall, George C., 111, 332
Marshall v. *Murakami*, 394 nn. 27 & 28
Martial law, 225, 229–230, 235, 240–243; at Tule Lake Segregation Center, 257; at Manzanar, 257; at Poston, 257
Martin, F. B. C., 368 n. 308
"Mass evacuation." *See* Evacuation; Exclusion; Internment
Mathes, William C., 182
May, Andrew J., 114, 115–116
Mead, Elwood, 345 n. 200
Mears, Elliott G., 340 n. 59, 388 nn. 50, 54, & 55, 389 n. 60
Merchants and Manufacturers Association, 60
Metal Trades Manufacturing Association, 374 n. 44
Metcalf, V. C., 33
Metzger, Jack, 77
Meyers, Victor A., 379 n. 82
Michener, E. A., 116
Military Intelligence (G-2), 154, 284, 367 n. 268, 392 n. 153
Military Mens Service League, 299
Military Order of Purple Heart, 194, 195
Military Virtue Society of North America, 284
Miller, Samuel F., 230
Millis, H. T., 58, 66, 344 n. 190, 345 nn. 218 & 222

Missouri, Kansas, & Texas Ry. Co. v. *May*, 393 n. 163
"Mr. Moto," 31–32
Mitchell v. *Harmony*, 336 n. 10, 382 n. 25
Miyamoto, S. F., 275, 387 n. 36, 389 n. 67, 391 n. 110
Moab (WRA Isolation Center), 164–165
Mock, M. R., 341 n. 103
Monjar, Elsie, 347 n. 269
Morison, Samuel E., 292, 392 n. 155, 396 n. 3
Mullen, James W., 38
Munson, Curtis B., 284–285, 288, 296, 297, 390 n. 98
Murakami v. *Acheson*, 182–183, 391 n. 116
Murakami v. *Marshall*, 182–183, 317, 394 n. 27
Murata v. *Acheson*, 395 n. 43
Murphy, Frank, 2, 213, 214, 218, 235, 264, 290, 393 n. 169, 396 n. 1
Myer, Dillon S., 141, 155, 359 nn. 103 & 104; 360 n. 121
Myrdal, Gunnar, 340 n. 58

National Grange, 54–57. *See also* California State Grange
National Japanese American Student Relocation Council, 144, 148, 149
Native Sons of the Golden West, 28, 46–49, 79–80, 95, 194, 195
Nisei, 100, 274, 275, 297, 299; registration, 150; volunteers for armed services, 167–168; at Tule Lake Segregation Center, 177; definition of, 352 n. 3
Neustadt, Richard M., 89, 107, 351 nn. 55 & 57, 356 n. 46
Newbry, Earl, 379 n. 83
Nielsen, Victor M., 367 n. 266, 369 n. 323
Nichols, Harold R., 352 n. 2
Nishimoto, Richard, 285, 316, 360 n. 122, 368 nn. 283 & 306, 369 n. 340, 370 n. 345, 386 n. 70, 391 n. 118, 393 n. 160, 391 n. 114, 394 n. 27
North Hollywood Home Owners, 377 n. 66

Oakie, John N., 392 n. 152
Ochikubo v. *Bonesteel*, 385 n. 48
O'Donnell, Charles C., 38–39
Office of Civil Defense, 119
Office of Naval Intelligence, 101, 154, 284, 367 n. 268, 392 n. 153; estimate of extent of Japanese espionage, sabotage danger on West Coast, 296–298

Office of Provost Marshall General (OPMG), 141, 154–155, 157, 169–170, 367 n. 268
Okimura v. Acheson, 395 n. 43
Okubo, Mine, 361 n. 144
Olson, Culbert L., 95, 200, 206, 354 n. 17
Olympia Oyster Growers Association, 191
Organized Labor, 24, 26, 34, 35, 62
Oriental Exclusion Act, 28, 42–43
Osborn, Sidney, 89
Oyama v. California, 214, 261, 304–306, 394 n. 22

Pacific Coast Race Relations Survey, 270–271, 278
Pacific League, 192
Pajus, Jean, 342 n. 138
Palmer, R. R., 392 n. 136
Park, Robert E., 25, 279
Patterson, Ellis, 379 n. 82
Patterson, Robert S., 111
Paul, Rodman W., 42
Pegler, Westbrook, 85–86
People v. Hall, 339 n. 32
Perlman, Philip B., 183
Phelan, James D., 35, 39, 42, 47
Picture brides, 277–278
Pixley, F. M., 21
Plehn, Carl, 339 n. 35
Poston Relocation Center, 130–131
Pratt, Henry C., 173, 352 n. 2, 369 n. 327
Prefectural clubs, 275–276
Presidential Proclamations: Proclamations Nos. 2525, 2526, 2527, 100; Proclamation No. 2537, 355 n. 30; Proclamation No. 2627, 136; Proclamation No. 2647, 120; Proclamation No. 2655, 178
Pressure groups: theory of responsibility for evacuation, 185 ff. *See also* Evacuation
Prigg v. Pennsylvania, 333
Prohibited zones, 105–107, 108
Public Law 405. *See* Congress, United States
Public Law 503. *See* Congress, United States
Public Proclamations: Alaska Defense Command Proclamations, No. 1, 134–135; No. 3, 135; No. 4, 363 n. 183; War Department Proclamations, No. WD:1, 129; No. WD:3, 174; Western Defense Command Proclamations, No. 1, 116–117, 119; No. 2, 119, 359 nn. 93 & 95;

No. 3, 119, 234; No. 4, 121, 235; No. 5, 360 n. 112; No. 6, 132; No. 7, 125; No. 8, 129; No. 9, 360 n. 112; No. 11, 133; No. 12, 362 n. 160; No. 13, 120; No. 14, 359 n. 93; No. 15, 120, 359 n. 107; No. 16, 359 n. 93; No. 17, 168; No. 21, 173; No. 24, 174

Race prejudice: DeWitt, 263–264; meanings of term distinguished, 264. *See also* Anti-Chinese agitation; Antiforeignism; Anti-Indian agitation; Anti-Japanese agitation; Stereotype
Rankin, John, 86–87
Rauschenbush, Winifred, 390 nn. 78, 81, & 85
Rayburn, Sam, 113
Reception centers, 121, 124
Reed, Stanley, 214, 305
Regan v. King, 214, 313–315
Registration, 149–151, 285–286
Reid, Helen R. Y., 345 n. 225, 346 n. 236
Relocation centers, 122, 124, 127–128, 129–132; maintenance of law and order, 164–165
Renunciation of citizenship, 171, 175–181, 315–316; renunciation hearings, 178; deportation threat, 178–179; mitigation hearings, 179–180; suits to recover citizenship, 181–183; suits to prevent deportation, 181–183. *See also* Citizenship; Citizenship laws
Repatriation, 175–176
Resettlement: early War Relocation Authority policy, 122–123, 142–143; student, 144–145; extent of, 149, 153
Reynolds, Charles N., 340 n. 70, 343 n. 143, n. 149, 347 n. 270
Reynolds, Robert R., 113–114, 114–115
Rich, E. F., 116
Riemer, Ruth, 361 n. 136
Ringle, K. D., 161, 298–299, 367 n. 282
Roberts, Owen J., 211, 213, 214, 385 n. 47
Roberts Committee report, 73
Roche, John P., 395 n. 43
Roosevelt, Franklin D., 109, 111–112, 113, 116, 122, 124, 136, 167, 172, 205, 331, 358 n. 67, 393 n. 2
Ross, Edward A., 35
Rostow, Eugene V., 4, 6, 186, 371 n. 5, 381 n. 113, 382 n. 15, 383 n. 1, 384 n. 12
Rotary Clubs. *See* Service clubs

Rothstein, Charles M., 178–179, 370 n. 364

Rowalt, E. M., 365 n. 236

Rowe, James H., Jr., 103–105, 109, 111, 122, 312, 351 n. 66, 382 n. 125

Rowell, Chester, 341 n. 72

Royce, Josiah, 11–12, 46

Ruef, Abe, 39

Rutledge, Wiley, 214, 235

Sabotage: rumors of, 70–72; official denials of, 93; absence of, 99, 105, 288–289, 296, 326; DeWitt's estimate of likelihood, 111; claims in *Final Report*, 139–140

Sacramento *Bee*, 47, 85, 92

St. Sure, A. S., 181

Salinas Citizens Association, 374 n. 29

Salter, Patricia, 342 n. 109

Sandmeyer, A. L., 339 n. 41

San Francisco Board of Police Commissioners, 37

San Francisco Building Trades Council, 40

San Francisco *Chronicle*, 24, 26, 40, 62, 64

Sansei, 274; definition of, 352 n. 3

Scharrenburg, Paul, 38

Schenk v. *United States*, 245

Schrieke, B., 23

Seago, Dorothy, 347 n. 269

Seattle Retail Florists Association, 372 n. 22, 373 n. 24

Segregation, 153, 160–164

Segregation Center (Tule Lake), 130, 136, 160–164, 174–178, 257; "stockade," 165–166

Segregants, 161–164

Selective Service, 149–150, 166–170

Service clubs, 193

Sherwood, Robert E., 293

Shinn, C. S., 338 n. 10

Shintoism, 127, 131

Shivers, R. L., 353 n. 8

Shortridge, Samuel S., 42

Smith, Bradford, 4, 186, 187, 190, 192, 198–199, 201, 353 n. 8, 371 n. 1, 372 nn. 8, 9, & 17, 376 n. 51 & 55, 389 n. 59, 378 n. 76, 379 n. 86

Smith, Louis, 22, 383 n. 33

Smith, William C., 387 n. 41, 388 nn. 43 & 57

Sokoku Kenkyu Seinen-Dan, 176

Sokuji Kikoku Hoshi-dan, 176

Soulé, F., 338 n. 10

Southern California Floral Association, 372 n. 22

Southern Defense Command (SDC), 149

Spanish-Americans: attacks on, 14

Sparkman, John J., 116

Sprague, Charles, 378 n. 79

Sproul, Robert G., 144

Stampp, Kenneth M., 384 n. 10

Stark, Ernest, 292, 350 n. 46

Stearns, Marjorie E., 64, 346 n. 235, 387 n. 36

Steffens, Lincoln, 343 n. 146

Steiner, Jesse F., 346 n. 254, 347 n. 264, 390 nn. 72 & 75

Stephens, William D., 48

Stettinius, Edward R., Jr., 172

Stereotype: dark-skinned races, 15; Chinese, 18–22, 24, 29–31; Japanese, 22–24, 66–67, 68–72, 80, 91–96; revival of Japanese stereotype by Pearl Harbor attack, 68–69, 90–96; concept of, 340 n. 60. *See also* Anti-Chinese; Antiforeignism; Anti-Indian agitation; Anti-Japanese agitation

Sterling v. *Constantin*, 219–220, 382 n. 25

Stewart, Tom, 86–87

Stilwell, Joseph W., 352 n. 2, 391 n. 132

Stimson, Henry L., 108, 110, 112, 113, 303, 331–332, 351 n. 66

"Stockade," (Tule Lake Segregation Center), 165–166

Stoddard, Lothrop, 27

Stone, Harlan F., 212, 234–235, 259, 262, 264, 265–266, 268–269, 271, 273, 287, 303–304

Strong, Edward K., Jr., 66, 273, 279, 341 n. 82, 342 n. 125, 343 n. 144, 346 n. 239, 347 nn. 266 & 267, 388 n. 54, 389 n. 58, 390 nn. 80 & 82

Substantial basis test: in *Hirabayashi*, 215–216; in *Korematsu*, 216–217

Supreme Pyramid of Sciots, 377 n. 67

Svensrud, Marion, 271, 387 n. 41, 388 nn. 43 & 50

Swan, Harold, 77

Swayne, Noah H., 230

Taft, Henry W., 341 nn. 84 & 91, 343 n. 156, 346 n. 240

Taft, Robert A., 115

Takahashi v. *Fish and Game Commission*, 214, 261, 304, 306–307

Tatibana case, 296

Taylor, Frank J., 348 n. 32, 372 n. 18

Taylor, Paul S., 339 n. 35
tenBroek, Jacobus, 387 n. 8
Thomas, Dorothy S., 22, 280–281, 282, 285, 316, 352 n. 3, 360 n. 122, 366 nn. 250 & 252, 368 nn. 283, 294, & 306, 369 n. 340, 370 n. 345, 386 n. 70, 390 nn. 82, 87, & 88, 391 nn. 100, 103, 114, 115, & 118, 393 n. 160, 394 n. 27
Thorp, M. E., 342 n. 107
Thurston, Lorrin A., 388 n. 47
Tinkham, George D., 338 nn. 8 & 19
Tolan, John, 119, 351 n. 63. See also Tolan Committee
Tolan Committee, 187–188, 267, 268, 356 n. 37, 369 n. 197, 372 nn. 7 & 9, 374 nn. 32 & 38, 376 n. 59, 377 n. 61, 381 nn. 103 & 106, 387 nn. 29 & 35
Toynbee, Arnold, 28
Treasury Department, 102
Treat, Payson J., 26, 343 n. 154, 346 n. 243, 347 n. 266
Troy, Smith, 379 n. 85
Tule Lake Relocation Center. See Segregation center
Tupper, Eleanor, 61, 341 n. 81, 346 nn. 232, 237, 247, & 249
Tussman, Joseph, 387 n. 8
Tveitmoe, Olaf A., 34, 35, 40

Union Labor Party, 36, 39–40
United Spanish War Veterans, 194, 195
United States Chamber of Commerce, 61
United States Employment Service, 119
United States v. Curtiss-Wright Export Corp., 383 n. 2
United States v. Wong Kim Ark, 87, 313

Valley Protective Association, 374 n. 38
Veterans of Foreign Wars, 194, 195
Vinson, Fred M., 306
Voorhies, Jerry, 204

Wallace, John B., 345 n. 200
Wallgren, Monrad C., 205
War Department: acceptance of DeWitt's "Final Recommendation," 111–112; secures Executive Order 9066, 111–112; policy toward German and Italian aliens, 112–113. See also DeWitt; Exclusion; Induction; Internment; Japanese American Joint Board; Relocation centers; Western Defense Command
War powers, 221. See also Ex parte Milligan
War Relocation Authority (WRA): established by Executive Order 9102, 122;

abolished, 174. See also Internment; Isolation center; Leave regulations; Registration; Relocation centers; Resettlement; Segregation; Segregation Center
War Relocation Project Areas, 129, 362 n. 162
Warner, Arthur, 343 n. 159
Warren, Earl, 83–84, 93, 95, 102, 138, 200–, 201, 203, 233, 267–268
Wartime Civil Control Administration (WCCA); established, 118. See also Exclusion; Assembly centers; Western Defense Command
Washington Produce Shippers Association, 191
Washington State Association of County Commissioners, 201–202
Washington State Federation of Commercial Organizations, 193
Watson, Joel F., 369 n. 324, 383 n. 1
Wayne, James M., 230
Webb, U. S., 79, 313–315
West, H. J., 18–19
West Coast congressional delegation committees, 86, 205
West Coast Exclusion Zone, 173
Western Defense Command (WDC), 100; Civil Affairs Division, 118, 139, 154, 158–160, 173; Wartime Civil Control Administration established, 118. See also Assembly centers; DeWitt; Exclusion; Internment
Western Growers Association, 80, 95, 191, 372 n. 22, 373 n. 23
Wheat, G. S., 343 n. 158
White, Stewart E., 338 n. 5
Whitney, Atwell, 339 n. 36
Wiener, Frederick B., 4–5
Wiley, B., 392 n. 136
Willoughby, Westel W., 385 n. 51
Wirin, Andrew L., 182
Wixon v. Abo, 371 nn. 374 & 375
Wixon v. Furuye. See Wixon v. Abo
Wolfson, Richard F., 383 n. 1
Wolter, Robert, 19
Workingman's Party of California, 16
Work Corps, 145–146

Yasui v. United States, 384 n. 4
"Yellow peril," 19–21, 24–29, 30, 47, 62, 65
Yoell, A. E., 340 n. 64
Young, Charles Y., 345 n. 225, 346 n. 236
Young, Donald R., 340 n. 59, 342 n. 109
Young, F. G., 346 n. 256
Young, John P., 347 n. 259